Venturing Beyond the Classroom
Volume 2 in the Rethinking Negotiation Teaching Series

Published by DRI Press, an imprint of the
Dispute Resolution Institute at Hamline University School of Law,
with the generous financial support of the JAMS Foundation.

Dispute Resolution Institute
Hamline University School of Law
1536 Hewitt Avenue
Saint Paul, MN 55104
www.hamline.edu/law/adr

Library of Congress Control Number: 2010930064

ISBN 978-0-9827946-0-9

For bulk orders, contact the Hamline University School of Law Bookstore, 1536 Hewitt Avenue, Saint Paul, MN 55104. (651) 523-2369. For
reprint inquiries, contact the DRI program administrator, (651) 523-
2946.

Venturing Beyond the Classroom

Volume 2 in the Rethinking Negotiation Teaching Series

Christopher Honeyman
James Coben
Giuseppe De Palo

Editors

DRI PRESS
SAINT PAUL, MINNESOTA

Sacred meets secular in Istanbul: The Aya Sofia. Over 1600 years, it has served successively as a cathedral, a mosque, and a museum.

TABLE OF CONTENTS

III. Redesigning Methods

IV. Emotions and Relationships

V. Wicked Problems

VI. Epilogue

Acknowledgements

More colleagues than we can possibly name deserve our warm thanks here. First and foremost, of course, are the contributing writers in this volume. Less obviously, this book does not stand alone, but is part of a complex strategy: the contributors' work here builds on that of forty-three contributors to 2009's *Rethinking Negotiation Teaching* and to the parallel special section of eight articles in *Negotiation Journal* (April 2009), and it presages a further effort of similar proportions in 2011, which will build on this book.

Also key to this effort, and a great comfort at certain moments of doubt, have been our steering committee members: it would be impossible to imagine a more perceptive or more incisive team of advisers than Jay Folberg, Roy Lewicki, Carrie Menkel-Meadow, Sharon Press, Frank Sander, Andrea Schneider, Richard Shell, and Michael Wheeler. Special thanks also to Kitty Atkins, the Dispute Resolution Institute associate director, for her wise counsel and tireless commitment to solve any and all problems. Also essential at Hamline has been Jessica Kuchta-Miller, whose thoughtful edits and careful proofreading helped ensure a quality product, and Debra Berghoff, whose mastery of software and graphics once again has made all our lives much simpler.

Separately, this book, like its predecessor (not to mention the forthcoming editions of *Rethinking Negotiation Teaching* in Chinese, Arabic and Turkish) would have been impossible without the support of the JAMS Foundation. The Foundation's early commitment to the project was instrumental to its successful launch, and the Foundation's continued support helps to extend the project's global impact.

Finally, we offer special thanks to Istanbul's Bilgi University, the host institution for our Fall 2009 conference in Turkey, with special recognition for the unflappable Seda Peker, whose logistics skills made everything go smoothly. Last but not least, we applaud the extraordinary effort of Kenneth H. Fox and Manon A. Schonewille, who served as lead trainers for the day-long negotiation course offered at the beginning of our Istanbul conference. For accomplished teachers who are accustomed to having a certain freedom of maneuver out of the purview of their colleagues, it is no small thing to construct a course with a committee looming, and then to teach it in front of experienced peers.

To follow future developments of the project initiative, please visit http://www.hamline.edu/law/adr/negotiation2.0. There you will find the latest project updates, lists of participating scholars, and writings generated to date.

❧ 1 ❧

Introduction: Half-Way to a Second Generation

*Christopher Honeyman & James Coben**

"It is not the strongest of the species that survives, nor the most intelligent, but the one most responsive to change." (Charles Darwin)

The midpoint of a sequence is a good time to consider what has been produced, and what seems desirable to do next. In this, the second volume of the *Rethinking Negotiation Teaching* series, we present a cross-section of the new thinking that our colleagues have produced since the first volume. Below, we will briefly ruminate on the implications.

But first, a little background. This project had its formal beginning in 2008 with the realization that a huge array of knowledge, brought forth from many disciplines and published together for the first time in *The Negotiator's Fieldbook* (Schneider and Honeyman 2006),[1] was relevant in many parts to even beginning negotiation students, while almost none of it was being taught to them. The time was ripe for a comprehensive attempt to rethink what is taught and how it is taught in basic negotiation courses. The result was a collaboration between Hamline's Dispute Resolution Institute, ADR Center Foundation (Rome), the JAMS Foundation, and many of

---

* **Christopher Honeyman** is managing partner of Convenor Conflict Management, a consulting firm based in Washington, D.C. and Madison, Wisconsin. He has directed a twenty-year series of major research-and-development projects in conflict management and is coeditor of *The Negotiator's Fieldbook* (ABA 2006). His email address is honeyman@convenor.com. **James Coben** is a professor of law and senior fellow in the Dispute Resolution Institute at Hamline University School of Law. His email address is jcoben@hamline.edu.

those who had contributed to the *Fieldbook*. Our original title for the project was "Developing Second Generation Global Negotiation Education." This, however, failed to roll elegantly off the tongue, and as we described the project to more and more people we tired of the name. We have adopted the simpler "Rethinking Negotiation Teaching," the title of the project's first book, as a better name for the project as a whole as well.

The formal start was in May, 2008, at a four-day conference in Rome. The 2008 conference was intended to inspire a first set of writings that might serve as a kind of blueprint for adaptation of short courses in negotiation, to take account of recent discoveries and to confront the challenge of teaching them in cross-cultural settings. We are, of course, interested in influencing longer courses as well; but semester-length courses do not lend themselves to "benchmarking" experiments that must be begun and completed within the span of a conference. Influence on longer courses must therefore be by derivation.

Within a year, Rome conference participants had produced enough new scholarship to fill our first book in this project series, *Rethinking Negotiation Teaching* (Honeyman, Coben, and De Palo 2009a), as well as a special section of an issue of the *Negotiation Journal* published by the Program on Negotiation at Harvard Law School (Honeyman, Coben, and De Palo 2009b). In all, thirty writings emerged from that first year, many of them by cross-disciplinary and/or international teams which inherently volunteered to grapple with "difference" in one definition or another.

It is now apparent that each year's discoveries are leading to new questions and new topics. A significant critique resulting from the project's initial conference was that negotiation teachers:

1) Over-rely on "canned" material of little relevance to students; and

2) share an unsubstantiated belief that role-plays are the one best way to teach.

This led to certain key goals for our second conference, conducted in Istanbul in October, 2009. There, we sought to provide a "learning lab" to explore an adventure learning thesis derived from the first year's writings: "authenticity as priority." This suggested that all participants should:

1) Experience directly some "real" negotiations as part of the meeting, and test existing perceptions against self-reflection on that experience (including not only "cognitive/rational" responses, but also emotional responses); and

2) produce scholarship that challenges the field to think more about adventure learning opportunities (and how to implement them in typical instructional settings).

Our advisors, reviewing the panoply of scholarship offered in the project's initial products, further suggested that we try a serious bid at "adventure learning" – described below – and that in doing so, we deliberately seek to devalue the cognitive; actively encourage creativity and use of the arts; and explicitly focus on emotion.

Round Two (Istanbul)

In organizing the Istanbul conference, we took particular note of a consistent strain of criticism of the artificiality of a classroom environment, which became a running theme of many of our authors in the project's first year. It would be hard to imagine a better environment for trying something new and different outside the classroom environment than Istanbul, and in our design for the conference we tried to do honor to one of the world's greatest trading cities. In brief, we dispatched small teams of scholars into the city's famous bazaars, for one exercise in studying how negotiation might be taught more actively, and dispatched teams into the city's less touristy neighborhoods on another occasion, with instructions that required each team to negotiate internally. (For a detailed description of these exercises, see Coben, Honeyman, and Press, *Straight Off the Deep End*, in this volume.)

Perhaps not surprisingly, more than a quarter of the chapters in this book take up the challenge to examine adventure learning critically. But author teams organized around other important themes as well. We present the chapters which follow under six headings:

The Big Picture

These chapters develop a trend already visible in the 2009 book: some of our colleagues see this project as an opportunity to re-examine core assumptions of the field.

Lessons from the Field:
First Impressions from Second Generation Negotiation Teaching
Kenneth H. Fox, Manon A. Schonewille & Esra Çuhadar-Gürkaynak
The authors, invited to present a training program in one day which drew from the insights of forty-three writers in thirty book chapters and articles resulting from the first year of this project, not surprisingly concluded they would not all fit(!) Their choice of priorities and their approach to efficiency of presentation should be instructive to others who must now contemplate the "embarrassment of riches" of new ideas now on offer.

Instructors Heed the Who:
Designing Negotiation Training with the Learner in Mind
Roy J. Lewicki & Andrea Kupfer Schneider
Lewicki and Schneider argue that while our field has made great progress in determining what to teach and how to teach it in negotiation, there has been a surprising reluctance to make the move from "mass production" to "mass customization" that so many other industries have successfully adopted. "The Who" of our training has so far been addressed seriously, they surmise, by only an elite subgroup of trainers. They explain how this can and should change.

Re-Orienting the Trainer to Navigate – Not Negotiate –
Islamic Cultural Values
Phyllis E. Bernard
Business decisions based on faith? What conventional Western bargaining wisdom might deem folly, Bernard labels as mission critical as soon as Westerners step into other cultures, and perhaps increasingly at home. She makes a convincing case that the next generation of negotiation training must account for bargaining parties' "full and complex identity," including the religious values that profoundly shape perceptions and conduct even among many of those who on the surface appear thoroughly secular.

Can We Engineer Comprehensiveness
in "Negotiation" Education?
Gwen B. Grecia-de Vera
Ever since the first ripostes to Roger Fisher's magnum opus, we have known that sometimes the people *are* the problem. Or maybe it was their education. Grecia-de Vera analyzes the prevailing attitude toward negotiation in the Philippines, a nation that has not yet adopted "Negotiation 1.0," and asks – Could countries in the Philippines' situation go straight to the better stuff, maybe, and skip over all the first-generation mistakes? Or are they condemned to repeat them?

Ancient Wisdom for the Modern Negotiator:
What Chinese Characters Have to Offer Negotiation Pedagogy
Andrew Wei-Min Lee
In a project that from its inception has been devoted to second generation updates, it is instructive nonetheless to realize how much we still have to learn from the past. We believe Lee's chapter on Chinese characters and their implications for negotiation is groundbreaking. With luck, it will prove to be a harbinger of a whole variety of new ways of looking at our field that will emerge from our next round of discussion.

Beyond the Classroom

The chapters in this section discuss a radical departure for teaching negotiation: making part of the course *real* negotiations, often outside a classroom environment. This turns out to involve risks as well as benefits. But the risk of students being bored, at least, is not one of them.

Straight Off the Deep End in Adventure Learning
James Coben, Christopher Honeyman & Sharon Press

Numerous contributors to our 2009 book argued strongly for getting at least part of negotiation teaching out of the classroom and into real environments. So we tried it – in Istanbul, a famously negotiation-centric environment on many levels. In this introduction to a series of analyses of what happened and how adventure learning might be used in the future, the organizers take responsibility for a string of errors – each of which, it turned out, contributed usefully to everyone's education in the end.

Orientation and Disorientation: Two Approaches to Designing "Authentic" Negotiation Learning Activities
Melissa Manwaring, Bobbi McAdoo & Sandra Cheldelin

The authors here build on their 2009 writings for this project,[2] which were influential in setting an "adventure learning" agenda. In their new effort, they argue that adventure learning devolves into mere entertainment if it lacks *authenticity*, and they frame two contrasting approaches to achieving a sense of the real and the consequential.

Bringing Negotiation Teaching to Life: From the Classroom to the Campus to the Community
Lynn P. Cohn & Noam Ebner

Taking your students to the Grand Bazaar of Istanbul, Cohn and Ebner point out, is educational all right, but it is expensive. So they turn their attention to what might be done with adventure learning in the immediate environment of a university. A whole menu of options, it turns out, is readily available.

A Look at a Negotiation 2.0 Classroom: Using Adventure Learning Modules to Supplement Negotiation Simulations
Salvador S. Panga, Jr. & Gwen B. Grecia-de Vera

Panga and Grecia-de Vera analyze initial experiences with adventure learning from a Philippine perspective. They conclude that in a number of ways, the experimental exercises showed serious flaws – and yet demonstrated the potential of adventure learning to provide authenticity, risk, challenge, and context.

Is What's Good for the Gander Good for the Goose?
A "Semi-Student" Perspective
Adam Kamp

"Smell the fear?" Kamp forces us to consider how the shock-and-awe of adventure learning might shut down, rather than inspire, negotiation students. He offers practical tips, from his own unique "semi-student" perspective, to help ensure that activities beyond the classroom actually meet the prime objective: making students active participants in their own educational experience.

Adventure Learning: Not Everyone Gets to Play
David Allen Larson

Larson analyzes the initial experiments with adventure learning in Istanbul, a setting replete with long staircases, narrow winding alleys, and user-hostile transportation (at least to Westerners with mobility problems). He concludes that the postmodern agenda of excitement and authenticity in learning carries a serious risk of running smack into the postmodern agenda of openness to all, characterized by the Americans with Disabilities Act. The risks are not just physical; some of the "disabilities" students may encounter have an ethical or moral dimension. Larson offers a number of cautions for future applications.

A Second Dive into Adventure Learning
Sharon Press & Christopher Honeyman

Back into the potentially treacherous waters of adventure learning just weeks after Istanbul, Press and Honeyman provide a detailed account of a "next try" that was explicitly built to respond to the first critiques of the Istanbul exercises. It shows how rapidly the initial problems with adventure learning are being addressed – even while some new ones are being revealed.

Get Ripped and Cut Before Training:
Adventure Preparation for the Negotiation Trainer
Yael Efron & Noam Ebner

In this entertaining closing piece to the *Beyond the Classroom* section, Efron and Ebner argue that adventure learning cannot work unless the instructor is "up" for it. Using a metaphor from the world of professional bodybuilding to provide a useful acronym ("RIPPED & CUT"), they prescribe nine practical pre-training exercises to inspire negotiation teachers to be at their best.

Redesigning Methods

"Methods" is actually a central preoccupation among the entire group of contributors. The four chapters presented here, however, are distinguishable from the eight which focus on adventure-learning methods. They warrant having this section to themselves.

Simulation 2.0: The Resurrection
Noam Ebner & Kimberlee K. Kovach

Ebner and Kovach consider the critique of role-plays previously offered in this series (see particularly Alexander and LeBaron 2009) – and reject it. They argue that what is needed is not to move away from simulations, but to use the critique to devise more efficient, more convincing, more authentic, and more sensitive simulations. They outline a series of tactics within this strategy.

Enhancing Concept Learning: The Simulation Design Experience
Daniel Druckman & Noam Ebner

Druckman and Ebner carefully review a large number of studies which conclude that simulations (in all fields, not just negotiation) typically fail to live up to their promise. One quirk of the studies, however, drew their particular interest and inspired their own research: it seemed that students who *designed* simulations learned more than those who *participated* in them. Druckman and Ebner use this clue to develop a different kind of negotiation simulation – one in which the student plays the role of a teacher, and designs an exercise.

Using Role-Play in Online Negotiation Teaching
David Matz & Noam Ebner

Matz and Ebner consider the impending collision between teachers' strong desire to use role-play and other simulation exercises, and the rise of online teaching, in which the students may never see each other. Can the advantages of simulation teaching and the advantages of online teaching be brought together to improve both?

What Travels:
Teaching Gender in Cross-Cultural Negotiation Classrooms
Andrea Kupfer Schneider, Sandra Cheldelin & Deborah Kolb

Our cross-disciplinary team tackles the inconsistencies of gender teaching as seen from the perspectives of law, business, and peace studies negotiation courses. In the process, they reconsider gender in the context of *culture*, demanding a forthright and coherent approach to topics now too often cut up into little boxes of "content."

Emotions and Relationships

"It's bad enough that we have to have emotions," Jim's Minnesota neighbor once told him, "let alone talk about them." Such discomfort comes as no surprise to the authors of these next chapters, who argue for making emotions a center-stage priority in negotiation training, and for developing a more nuanced perspective on the complex science of relationship and trust-building.

Emotions – A Blind Spot in Negotiation Training?
Mario Patera & Ulrike Gamm

"We *must* teach about emotions," say Patera and Gamm. We see in emotions, we think in emotions, we remember in emotions. There's no way around it, and our field is increasingly irresponsible in trying to maintain the pretense that things are otherwise. Patera and Gamm offer criteria for really grappling with a topic that makes many teachers, let alone students, uncomfortable (see, e.g., the next chapter).

If I'd Wanted to Teach About Feelings,
I Wouldn't Have Become a Law Professor
Melissa Nelken, Andrea Kupfer Schneider & Jamil Mahuad

"Oh no, do we *have* to?" is these authors' mock-horrified initial reaction to the previous chapter. Their second response, however, is "Well, if we have to, we'd better get good at it." They go on to analyze how a series of exercises already widely used for other purposes could be adapted to perform double duty, to make students really *think* about their emotions.

Relationship 2.0
Noam Ebner & Adam Kamp

Ebner and Kamp examine the treatment of relationships in typical negotiation teaching, and conclude that critics of our field and its doctrines have a point: in several ways, our doctrines set students up for failure when dealing with "hard" bargainers, because of a tension that is not only unresolved but unadmitted. The authors argue that the first thing needed is for teachers to be transparent about "relationship doctrine" – because actually doing something different is going to be a daunting task. They go on to explain why.

Bazaar Dynamics: Teaching Integrative Negotiation
Within a Distributive Environment
Habib Chamoun-Nicolas, Jay Folberg & Randy Hazlett

These authors take a very different perspective from the previous chapter. Comparing Istanbul's Grand Bazaar to a pawnshop in East

St. Louis and a wedding dress shop in Mexico, they find a great deal less that is "distributive" than is typically thought of each environment, and a great deal more of relationship-building. They outline a series of recommended steps that the supposed "one-shot" customer might adopt, or be taught to adopt in a negotiation course, which would work better for the customer than typical behavior does.

Should We Trust Grand Bazaar Carpet Sellers (and vice versa)?
Jean-François Roberge & Roy J. Lewicki
Roberge and Lewicki use Lewicki's previously published model of trust and distrust to analyze transactions in the Grand Bazaar of Istanbul, and conclude that the merchants are often acting quite differently, and with different motivations, than Western customers assume. They use this insight to develop the "TRUst-rElationship" (TRUE) model, a more convenient way of defining four different kinds of relationships, each of which is based on each party's *prediction* of the trustworthiness of the other.

Wicked Problems
In this concluding section, our authors travel far beyond the classroom indeed, into the world of "wicked problems" – those ill-defined, ambiguous challenges for which even defining a solution is elusive, much less attaining it. "Negotiation 1.0" principles, the authors argue, are designed with more technical problems in mind – i.e., where the problem definition is clear (e.g., A claims B owes A money, and B denies it) and/or a range of solutions can be objectively identified and evaluated. No surprise, then, that "Negotiation 1.0" practitioners are ill-equipped to attack wicked problems. The contributors to this section call for developing a new approach, incorporating new packages of training and teaching ideas. We believe this series, of three main chapters, is groundbreaking and may itself help to jump-start that process.

Navigating Wickedness:
A New Frontier in Teaching Negotiation
Christopher Honeyman & James Coben
This short essay sets the context for the following three chapters, and introduces a remarkable group of contributors, surely one of the most extraordinary and diverse working teams we have yet seen in our field. In the chapters which follow, their collective experiences and stories are woven together for the first time. The result makes the case for enlarging our canon to include a sophisticated consideration of wicked problems.

Negotiating Wicked Problems: Five Stories
Calvin Chrustie, Jayne Seminare Docherty, Leonard Lira, Jamil Mahuad, Howard Gadlin & Christopher Honeyman

Sometimes the problem to be negotiated is itself both obscure and deeply unstable; everything you do to try to improve the situation turns out to create a new problem, and sometimes, a worse one. In these settings, the authors conclude, traditional negotiation training has often not been enough: we need something new. The contributors offer a series of personal and dramatic stories from very different settings, which together illustrate how a new set of concepts and approaches is developing. The rest of the chapters in this section set out to define what that might consist of, and how it just might – at a starting level, and with a great deal of needed development only barely under way – begin to work.

"Adaptive" Negotiation: Practice and Teaching
Jayne Seminare Docherty

Docherty argues that in addition to improved sensitivity to culture, argued in many of the writings in this series, it is time to demand that would-be negotiators and those who attempt to teach them become more sensitive to situations where the culture and norms are themselves in flux. What is needed, she says, is to re-center much of our teaching on the development of creative and critical thinking, including a critical awareness of the context, the self, the other, and the definition of the problem to be negotiated or negotiable. Docherty uses an ostensibly simple story of a negotiation in an Istanbul market to illustrate how a focus on the parties' different ways of "worldviewing" changes perception as to what is really going on, and what is possible to negotiate.

Design:
The U.S. Army's Approach to Negotiating Wicked Problems
Leonard Lira

Over twenty years of dealing with problems in post-conflict settings since the end of the Cold War, the U.S. Army has increasingly recognized that the character of the conflicts it is involved in now routinely includes pervasive, complex, and ill-structured problems – in other words, "wicked problems" – which the Army must deal with using non-violent means. The specific concept of "Design" is the foremost step yet taken by a U.S. military service toward setting forth ways of addressing wicked problems as a frequent, core need in the field. This radical departure in military doctrine is already finding its way into field manuals and training courses.

Epilogue

Two to Tango?
Ranse Howell & Lynn P. Cohn
Light of foot, light of heart? Not exactly: in an overture to a longer ballet next year, the authors contend that the appropriate way to use dance as an element in negotiation teaching starts with...fear!

The Bell Rings for Round Three (Beijing)
As noted above, the project's final conference is to be held in Beijing. As of this writing, we have reason to believe – and we are working hard to fulfill the possibility – that the 2011 Beijing conference will serve as a springboard for the entry into this field, at a sophisticated level, of Chinese and other Asian scholars whose deep experience in many related subjects has yet to be fully felt in their implications for our field.

China is an ideal venue to conclude our inquiry, not only because of its own long history with negotiation, internal and external to the country, but because it is a nation with which, tensions or no tensions, every other nation *must* negotiate in the future. We look forward to doing our part toward making that a more historically-informed, more culturally sensitive, better prepared, and less short-sighted process on all sides.

Notes

[1] Published by the American Bar Association, the *Negotiator's Fieldbook* (Schneider and Honeyman 2006) includes eighty chapters authored by social psychologists, urban planners, police and military officers, and scholars of management, law, business, genetics, and international relations, as well as judges and experienced conflict resolution practitioners whose contributions directly relate theory to practice.
[2] See Nelken (2009); McAdoo and Manwaring (2009); and Nelken, McAdoo, and Manwaring (2009).

References

Alexander, N. and M. LeBaron. 2009. Death of the role-play. In *Rethinking negotiation teaching: Innovations for context and culture*, edited by C. Honeyman, J. Coben, and G. De Palo. St. Paul, MN: DRI Press.

Honeyman, C., J. Coben, and G. De Palo (eds). 2009a. *Rethinking negotiation teaching: Innovations for context and culture*. St. Paul, MN: DRI Press.

Honeyman, C., J. Coben, and G. De Palo (guest eds). 2009b. Special section of eight articles: Second generation global negotiation education. *Negotiation Journal* 25(2): 141-266.

McAdoo, B. and M. Manwaring. 2009. Teaching for implementation: Designing negotiation curricula to maximize long-term learning. *Negotiation Journal* 25(2): 195-215.

Nelken, M. L. 2009. Negotiating classroom processes: Lessons from adult learning. *Negotiation Journal* 25(2): 181-194.

Nelken, M. L., B. McAdoo, and M. Manwaring. 2009. Negotiating learning environments. In *Rethinking negotiation teaching: Innovations for context and culture,* edited by C. Honeyman, J. Coben, and G. De Palo. St. Paul, MN: DRI Press.

Schneider, A. K. and C. Honeyman (eds). 2006. *The negotiator's fieldbook: The desk reference for the experienced negotiator.* Washington, DC: American Bar Association.

‹› 2 ‹›

Lessons from the Field: First Impressions from Second Generation Negotiation Teaching

Kenneth H. Fox, Manon A. Schonewille &
Esra Çuhadar-Gürkaynak*

Editors' Note: *The authors, invited to present a training program in one day which drew from the insights of forty-three writers in thirty book chapters and articles resulting from the first year of this project, not surprisingly concluded they would not all fit(!) Their choice of priorities and their approach to efficiency of presentation should be instructive to others who must now contemplate the "embarrassment of riches" of new ideas now on offer.*

"The only source of knowledge is experience."
(Albert Einstein)

Introduction

The Rethinking Negotiation Teaching project (NT 2.0 project) has two primary goals: to significantly advance our *understanding* of the

---

* **Kenneth Fox** is an associate professor and director of graduate and undergraduate conflict studies at Hamline University, and a senior fellow in the Dispute Resolution Institute at Hamline University School of Law. He teaches a range of conflict theory and theory-to-practice courses for students and working professionals, and focuses his research on conflict theory. His email address is kenfox@hamline.edu. **Manon Schonewille** is a mediator with Result ACB in The Netherlands. She is president of the board of the ACB Foundation, a conflict management research center, and a partner in Toolkit Company. She teaches at Utrecht University and co-chairs the International Committee of the American Bar Association's Dispute Resolution Section. Her email address is manonschonewille@home.nl. **Esra Çuhadar** is an assistant professor of political science at Bilkent University in Turkey. She teaches and conducts research in conflict resolution and political psychology. Her email address is esracg@bilkent.edu.tr.

negotiation process in all its complexity; and to improve how we *teach others* about negotiation. The first year of this four-year project focused on generating new ideas and approaches to negotiation scholarship and teaching. Some of this scholarship was published in the book *Rethinking Negotiation Teaching* (Honeyman, Coben, and De Palo 2009) and some in *Negotiation Journal.*[1] These articles call on negotiation teachers and scholars to make a paradigm shift from first generation negotiation thinking toward second generation thinking or, as has been described elsewhere, from "Negotiation 1.0" to "Negotiation 2.0" (Fox: 23).

The second year of the negotiation project challenged us to test and refine these new ideas in practice. It is one thing to have good ideas. It is quite another to translate new ideas into concrete teaching strategies and to know whether and how the strategies hold up in application. As a result, one goal of the project's second year was to deliver an actual negotiation course that would test "second generation" ideas on the ground. On October 12, 2009, we conducted a one day executive training at Bilgi University in Istanbul for that purpose.[2] This article reflects on that experience. It is divided into four sections:

1) What we mean by "second generation" negotiation teaching;
2) what second generation ideas we incorporated into the design of this pilot training;
3) what our actual experience was on the ground; and
4) what insights we can derive from the training, for ourselves and other trainers.

What We Mean by "Second Generation" Negotiation Teaching

We should explain what we mean by the term "second generation" training. The negotiation field, along with negotiation teaching, is well developed and mature. As stated elsewhere, the current (first generation) negotiation canon

- Treats negotiation as a strategic and instrumental process.
- Teaches students that the negotiator's central challenge is learning how to develop and enact rational strategies to claim and/or create maximum value that satisfy self-interest.
- Offers many diagnostic, analytic and predictive tools for negotiators, for example tools based on our understanding of individualistic factors such as brain functions (Tom et al. 2007), cognition (Birke and Fox 1999), behavioral and games theories (Bolt and Houba 2002).
- Gears negotiators' tools toward a better understanding of internal thought processes (own and counterparts); how to

"game" the process of interaction between negotiators; and how to achieve better outcomes (Fox: 13).

While "second generation" negotiation scholarship does not reject this first generation wisdom, it reflects a different focus and emphasis. Second generation negotiation thinking reorients how we examine negotiation. Instead of assuming we can plan, "game" and develop strategic roadmaps for our negotiations, "this new view shifts our focus to examining the language, interactions and meaning that emerge organically as the negotiation process unfolds" (Fox:22). Second generation thinking also calls on us to shift our focus to the deeper and more complex realm of worldview – and worldviewing. As a result, in addition to studying negotiators themselves (as is part of first generation negotiation thinking), second generation negotiation thinking challenges us to focus on the social worlds in which they operate as well as the "space between" negotiators, "where new meaning is made and remade" (Fox: 22).

At a practical level, second generation negotiation thinking calls for negotiators to develop a heightened and perhaps different awareness of themselves and others. It also calls for us to possess the tools and ability to act in the "here and now" of complex and multi-layered environments. Among other outcomes, year one of the NT 2.0 project produced articles examining a number of these "second generation" ideas including, among others: the importance of reflective practice (LeBaron and Patera 2009), curiosity (Guthrie 2009), negotiating one's own public identity (Tinsley et al. 2009), cultural difference (Nolan-Haley and Gmurzynska 2009; Bernard 2009) and worldview (Fox 2009). In designing our Istanbul training, we wanted to incorporate and test as many of these ideas as possible.

In addition to new ideas that emerged about the negotiation *process* itself, we also wanted to test new ways of engaging in the process of negotiation *teaching*. A series of articles from the project's first year also examined negotiation teaching methods, raising, among others, such questions as: Should role-plays continue to be a central part of negotiation pedagogy (Alexander and LeBaron 2009)? Can curiosity be taught (Guthrie 2009)? What lessons can we take from adult learning research (Nelken, McAdoo, and Manwaring 2009)? And what guidelines must we follow for training outside our own cultures (Abramson 2009)?

Designing a "Second Generation" Training Course

Our training was intended to test a selection of these ideas in a typical negotiation training setting. Negotiation is taught in many formats: semester-long academic courses, intensive multi-day courses tailored for a particular client or industry, short executive courses that are open to any registrant, and online and distance courses, among others. We were asked to design and test a one-day, open-enrollment executive training course (one that was not designed for any specific client or organization). The training planning group believed this would best test what many teachers and trainers face in actual practice, including the surprises and practical problems that arise on the ground.[3]

It is challenging to conduct any meaningful course in only one day, even with the most refined and proven content and methods.[4] It is much more challenging to do this while testing new content and delivery methods and while working in a new cultural setting.[5] As a result, we focused on three specific content considerations that we believed reflected the direction of the project's second-generation work:

- Increasing self-awareness;
- cultivating curiosity; and
- the over-arching importance of worldview.

At the same time, in designing the training, we did not abandon "first generation" principles. The planning team kept certain central negotiation concepts in place: positions, interests, distributive and integrative mindsets, concern for self and other, and psychological influences, among others.

We also focused on four pedagogical considerations that we believed would push the training in new directions:

- Using actual negotiation situations rather than role-plays as a primary vehicle for learning;
- approaching the course from a highly elicitive rather than didactic mind-set;
- employing multi-dimensional rather than "single purpose" exercises to examine the negotiation process; and
- considering different social worlds when addressing course design.

Each of these content and pedagogical choices is explored in detail below.

Content Design

Self-awareness

The importance of self-awareness in conflict work is not new. In the fields of psychology and mediation, a great deal of scholarship has emerged concerning mindfulness (Baer 2003; Bowling and Hoffman 2003; Riskin 2006). Even in the negotiation field, the importance of negotiator self-awareness is growing (Riskin 2006; Shapiro 2006).

Nevertheless, as the NT 2.0 project addressed emerging themes in the field, the importance of self-awareness stood out.

We wanted to test teaching concepts regarding self-awareness on two levels: First, how can we help negotiation students develop their own sense of self-awareness *as negotiators*? And second, how can we, *as teachers and trainers*, have the necessary self-awareness to approach our teaching work most effectively?

Curiosity

In his article on the subject, Chris Guthrie (2009) describes the importance of curiosity to negotiation in the following way:

> Good negotiators must understand their counterparts' perspectives, interests, and arguments to do well at the bargaining table. As Roger Fisher and his colleagues observe in *Getting to Yes*, "[t]he ability to see the situation as the other side sees it...is one of the most important skills a negotiator can possess" (Fisher, Ury, and Patton 1991: 23). To understand one's counterpart, a negotiator needs to be curious about what her counterpart has to say. In other words, a negotiator should cultivate a "stance of curiosity" (Stone, Patton, and Heen 1999: 167) or develop "relentless curiosity about what is really motivating the other side" (Shell 2006: 87). (Guthrie 2009: 63).

Curiosity can be loosely defined as "a desire to know or to explore" (Guthrie 2009: 65). This desire can be dispositional – that is, a person expresses a general trait or tendency to express interest in others, regardless of the context or setting. It can also be situational – that is, a "transitory feeling of curiosity that arises in a particular situation" (Guthrie 2009: 65). But can either form of curiosity be learned? Citing Lowenstein and other scholars in the field, Guthrie suggests that situational curiosity (and, indirectly, dispositional curiosity) can be enhanced. The question, then, is how?

Guthrie identifies several helpful factors to enhance curiosity: the importance of being in a good mood; the value of working with others; and the importance of engaging in novel or complex activities that are capable of being comprehended. He further suggests three strategies negotiators can use to enhance their own sense of curiosity: developing specific listening skills, remembering the reasons for being curious while engaging in listening and interacting at the bargaining table, and varying the forms of inquiry and eliciting information (Guthrie 2009: 67). These three strategies can also be transported into the negotiation training environment. In order to enhance curiosity, negotiation students can be asked to identify concrete listening and understanding goals prior to participating in simulations and exercises. They can also be asked to identify, ideally in writing, the purpose they believe careful listening will serve. Finally, they can be instructed to try a variety of ways to elicit information from their negotiation counterparts.

Worldview

The third concept we wanted to address in our training was "worldview" and its relation to the negotiation process. Several articles from the first year of our project pointed to the growing recognition that, as Walter Truitt Anderson has stated, "reality isn't what it used to be" (Anderson 1992). Negotiators increasingly interact across the globe and, even within the boundaries of their own communities, across different social worlds.

As has been written elsewhere, there is considerable research into culture and conflict (Faure and Rubin 1993; Menkel-Meadow 1996; Avruch 1998; Elgstrom 1999; Weiss 1999; Brett 2001; Avruch 2004). However, a great deal of this work tends to look at culture through specific national or "group" lenses, which can lead to a mechanistic understanding of how negotiators interact across social worlds. And as Michelle LeBaron has written, cultures exist within larger systems, or "worldviews" (LeBaron 2003: 11). Thus, the concept of "worldview" goes beyond "culture" as traditionally conceived. It more fully reflects the complexity and dynamic nature of how individuals and groups understand and interact with their social environment.

The *New Oxford American Dictionary* defines worldview as a "a particular philosophy of life; a concept of the world held by an individual or a group..." (New Oxford American Dictionary 2005). Pearce and Littlejohn refer to worldview as a moral order, or "the theory by which a group understands its experiences and makes judgments about proper and improper actions" (Pearce and Littlejohn 1997: 51). Worldviews are "deeply embedded in our consciousness, shaping and informing our identities and our meaning-making. They inform our big-picture ideas of the meanings of life and give us ways to learn as well as logic for ordering what we know" (LeBaron 2003: 11). As Jane Seminare Docherty states,

> In order to delineate any worldview (including our own), we need to know how the person or group under scrutiny answers the following questions[:] What is real or true (Ontology)? How is "the real" organized (Logic)? What is valuable or important (Axiology)? How do we know about what is (Epistemology)? How should I or we act (Ethics)? (Docherty 2001: 51).

This focus goes beyond what first generation negotiation scholarship generally considers. It also reflects a concept we wanted to address in our executive training.

Pedagogical Design
In addition to the three content elements discussed above, we also identified several pedagogical goals for our pilot training course. Each goal is intended either to challenge existing teaching methods or to test new approaches to learning how to negotiate.

Role-plays
As Nadja Alexander and Michelle LeBaron have written, role-plays (also referred to as simulations, practice sessions or games) have become arguably the most popular form of experiential learning in our field (Alexander and LeBaron 2009: 182). However, despite their popularity, role-plays have pitfalls. This is particularly the case when we think of teaching negotiation across very different cultural and social settings.

Role-plays are "...a learning activity in which participants are asked to assume a role, the characteristics of which are usually provided to them in written form, and to play out a negotiation or part of a negotiation with others who also have assumed roles" (Alexander and LeBaron 2009: 182). This taking on of another's role raises several concerns. First, in some cultures, "taking on others' identities may be perceived as disrespectful and nonsensical" (Alexander and LeBaron 2009: 182). Indeed, Alexander and LeBaron assert:

> When a group has a strong ethic of non-interference, then "playing" someone else may feel inappropriate and invasive. While role-playing does exist in social spaces in cultures around the world, it is generally a part of elaborately marked social rituals involving masks, music, drumming and other markers of "time outside of ordinary time" that clearly communicate the limited purposes of the role-play. Without such markers, it is an approach that – for many – may be fraught with pitfalls and potential traps. Not only does it elicit cultural stereotypes (which may be all that are available to inform the playing of an unfamiliar identity), but it literally takes people "out of their skins" into a synthetic situation that may have little relevance to their lives, and limited transferability to actual negotiations (Alexander and LeBaron 2009: 182-3).

Second, role-plays may not always be effective. Citing research from neurophysiology, Alexander and LeBaron suggest that learning is more effective when practicing and imagining oneself, rather than adopting the identity of another, fictitious character.

> People need context to interpret and understand ideas, and apply skills appropriately for a variety of real life situations. They need to be able to recognize and develop flexible strategies to deal with the emotional tension inherent in real negotiating situations where something important is at stake, and they need to understand the impact of their own attitudes to risk in negotiations. When context is artificial [as in role-plays], knowledge and skills may be similarly artificial, thus reducing the likelihood of the transfer of skills into real situations (Alexander and LeBaron 2009: 184).

Finally, even if role-play is effective in the short run, some studies have questioned the overall effectiveness of role-plays to impart skills that are later transferable into real-life settings (Movius 2008; Van Hasselt, Romano, and Vecchi 2008; Alexander and LeBaron 2009: 187, citing Lewicki 2000. See also Druckman and Ebner, *Enhancing Concept Learning*, in this volume; Ebner and Kovach, *Simulation 2.0: The Resurrection*, in this volume).

At a practical level, role-plays are written in a particular cultural context with instructions and content reflecting the assumptions, expected social norms, interaction patterns and indices of that particular culture. When simulations are used in a different cultural context (particularly without modification) there may be unexpected problems. Even small details in the written instructions of a role-play may hamper its effectiveness when used in a different setting. On previous occasions, the authors of this article experimented with role-plays written in the United States or by northern European institutions in trainings with various Turkish participants. Each time, the participants ran into problems with the role-plays themselves, distracting them from the purpose of the exercises. For example, the role-plays written in the United States assumed certain American institutional frameworks, functions, procedures and norms of conducting bank transactions that do not apply in other countries. They also assumed hourly fees for attorney services where such arrangements would not work in many communities.

These examples are easily observable and relatively simple challenges to address when transferring role-plays from one cultural context to another. However, there are also less visible differences that require an understanding of the differences in worldviews between the setting in which the original role-play was written and the community in which it is to be used. Moreover, even an understanding of differences in worldview might not address the concerns raised about the use of role-plays. Given the popularity of role-plays in first generation negotiation courses, our own previous experiences and the concerns raised about them by Alexander, LeBaron and others, we wanted to test a training that included some significant non-role-play elements. Thus, our course in Istanbul was designed to highlight experiential and "real" activities other than role-plays.

Elicitive vs. didactic teaching strategies

Negotiation courses are generally interactive. As discussed above, role-plays and subsequent de-briefings have become a central feature of negotiation training, where students and the instructor engage in regular give and take. Even class presentations often include significant discussion. At the same time, this give and take can be very directive, where students are told what to think about and how to think about it.

One of the outcomes of our first pedagogy conference in 2008 was the aspiration for "Negotiation 2.0" courses to be not only interactive but highly elicitive. By this, we mean that the instructor intentionally seeks out students' own lived experiences and views about not only topics the instructor introduces, but also topics the students introduce themselves. This elicitive philosophy honors the negotiation experience most students bring to their negotiation courses. For example, in their chapter on negotiating learning environments, Melissa Nelken, Bobbi McAdoo and Melissa Manwaring take up the idea of enlisting students in designing parts (or even all) of their negotiation course and strongly encourage this as a general teaching method (Nelken, McAdoo, and Manwaring 2009). We wanted to test this concept in our pilot training by intentionally seeking input from our students in elements of the course design and in shaping the training day as it unfolded.

At the same time that we wanted to encourage student input, we recognized from our own teaching experience that many cultures reflect traditional forms of education where formal lectures are expected. Specifically, we understood that Turkish instructional norms are different than in the United States or the Netherlands. It is challenging to adopt a purely elicitive approach to teaching in a formalistic culture with a relatively large power distance – cultural features that are commonly observed in Turkish society. In such formalistic contexts, participants may interpret a trainer's elicitive teaching approach as inadequate, if not incompetent, undermining the trainer's legitimacy, authority and effectiveness. Moreover, students may not have the experience of interacting with instructors in such informal and co-equal ways, and might not appreciate (or even understand) such a different approach to teaching and learning.

The challenge of elicitive training in formalistic cultures has received attention in the literature. For example, Mohammed Abu Nimer has reported this as a common problem in trainings conducted in Middle Eastern cultures (Abu Nimer 1998: 104). In one training, Abu Nimer notes that a participant from the Middle East advised the training team that "knowledge comes from or is delivered by the experts, otherwise, this will not be taken seriously" (Abu Nimer 1998: 104).

To complicate training design further, individuals and different sub-groups within a society may have different experiences and expectations than would be found as a general rule within a society at large. For example, seasoned businesspeople may have exposure to workshops and conferences where a variety of different teaching methods are used. They may be well traveled and adaptable to different learning environments. Moreover, they may expect a trainer to recognize and respect their professional experience. Participants like these may welcome (if not expect) a more elicitive approach to teaching, even if they are members of a formalistic society. We saw the course in Turkey as an opportunity to test out this tension between elicitive and didactic teaching and learning strategies.

Multi-dimensional activities

One common negotiation teaching method is to design an exercise or activity to highlight a single, specific, learning point. For example, students may be asked to take a written fact pattern and, working in groups, identify the various parties' positions, interests and issues or to negotiate a single-issue problem with a counterpart. In this way, students are able to try out distinct concepts through practice. Over the course of a training program, students will participate in a series of activities that, taken together, provide a conceptual frame for the negotiation process.

While single-purpose activities can offer conceptual clarity, they present a challenge for short duration courses (such as our one-day training). Each activity is time-consuming. Therefore, course designers are faced with difficult choices as to which activities (and, as a result, which discrete learning objectives) to include and which to leave out of a training agenda. In addition, a negotiator's lived experiences are typically not "single purpose." They are multi-dimensional. Their experiences are often saturated with a range of potential insights and lessons. We wanted to test ways to address this dilemma. Moreover, we wanted to try out learning activities that allowed for a richer and more sophisticated examination of negotiation and that, at the same time, could provide certain efficiencies during the training day.

There are two elements to effective experiential learning: the first is thoughtful design of the experience itself. As discussed above, we chose not to use simulations as the base for our experiential learning, but rather to look for interactions that would be real and relevant to the training participants themselves. We also chose not to use single-purpose activities. For the Istanbul training, we wanted to incorporate experiences that were more saturated with a number of potential insights.

The second element of experiential learning focuses on the debriefing process itself. Debriefing experiential learning is not a random or *ad hoc* process. It is a structured process based on its own body of research (Lederman 1992). Effective debriefing involves several distinct phases: systematic introduction to self-reflection; intensification and personalization of the debriefing process; and generalization and application of the learned principles to new situations (Lederman 1992: 151-152). Each phase helps students fully process their learning. Because we were seeking to test ideas that could work well in a "typical" short course, we wanted to explore how to design and make better use of single (real) course activities that might serve multiple learning objectives.[6]

Cultural Considerations

Our final pedagogical consideration in planning for the Istanbul training focused on culture. The Istanbul course was, purposely, to be taught by American and Dutch trainers in Turkey for Turkish professionals. This design forced the planning group and trainers to address at least some of the challenges faced when teaching in cross-national and multi-cultural contexts.

In his article *Outward Bound to Other Cultures: Seven Guidelines,* Harold Abramson identifies a set of practical considerations trainers should address before embarking on a negotiation course in a new cultural environment (Abramson 2009). These considerations emerged from observations of the negotiation training given in Rome in 2008 as part of the NT 2.0 project's first year initiative. Based on that training, and building on his own international teaching experience, Abramson identified the following seven guidelines:

1) Acquire a Culturally Educated Lens;
2) Behave Like a Guest: Be Flexible, Open-Minded, and Elicitive;
3) Be Mindful of Cultural Assumptions and Differences and Adapt Training;
4) Educate Participants about Training Techniques;

5) Adjust Presentation When English is Not the First Language of the Participants;

6) Refashion Materials and Presentation Based on Purpose(s) of Training; and

7) Plan to Evaluate the Training Program (Abramson: 294).

The planning team and trainers kept these guidelines in mind when designing the Istanbul training. Moreover, with respect to all of the design considerations addressed above, we tried to develop at least some activity that could test theory in practice. The most difficult question we faced was how to incorporate all these considerations into a one-day executive training.

Our Experience on the Ground

The one-day executive training involved approximately twenty Turkish professionals, together with a few university student participants. It was held at Istanbul Bilgi University in a lecture hall equipped and staffed for simultaneous language translation (Turkish – English; English – Turkish). As previously noted, in addition to the two primary trainers, we had the assistance of five other experienced trainers who served as coaches, representing five different cultural backgrounds.[7]

We had a total of six contact hours with the participants. Given such limited training time, we had to carefully select the activities we considered essential for an introductory training. Some elements were consistent with traditional "Negotiation 1.0" teaching and some tested "Negotiation 2.0" principles. The agenda (see Appendix One) included the following elements:

- Understanding oneself as a negotiator;
- Introduction to key negotiation concepts;
- An experiential activity related to the mid-day break;
- Addressing the tension between claiming and creating value;
- A focus on micro-skills; and
- A closing consultation.

We do not recap the entire training day here. Rather, we identify certain specific activities that tested second generation thinking. In particular, we discuss three tensions we found ourselves managing on the ground:[8]

Tension One: How to Adopt a Highly Elicitive Approach to Training While Honoring Traditional Teaching Methods of Our Host Culture

As discussed above, one key feature of second generation teaching is to approach the learning process from a highly elicitive standpoint. At the same time, as Abramson points out, it is important to adapt the training to honor the cultural assumptions and differences of our host community (Abramson 2009). From past training experience in Turkey, we understood our students to expect a certain degree of formality and to have formal lecture presentations of material. The trainers and planning team spent a great deal of time discussing how to manage this tension.

In the end, we adopted a mixed model, where some of the day was very elicitive and interactive, while some was quite traditional, particularly in formally introducing key negotiation principles. We learned the following:

1) It was very important at the beginning of the day both to acknowledge that we were guests in Istanbul and to be explicit about how we hoped to approach the training day. We began by speaking a few words of Turkish (which brought some amused smiles), acknowledged that our approach to teaching might be different than what the participants were used to, and then described the "international format" of the training we hoped to use (Abramson's guideline #4). The participants seemed comfortable with the format.

2) It was very important to observe participants' responses and interactions as the day began. As we discuss in greater detail below, we moved quickly from introductions into a highly interactive ice-breaking activity. This gave us a chance to observe and gauge how comfortable the participants were with our approach to the course.

3) Simultaneous translation interfered with our ability to interact spontaneously with participants, which had a direct impact on the degree to which we could be truly elicitive. It also tended to reinforce formal and didactic communication, where participants sat and listened through headphones rather than engaging directly with the trainers and each other. At the beginning of the training day, we did not know the English language proficiency of the participants and assumed that most participants would be listening to us through headphones. As it turned out, many of the participants understood and spoke English (although we still spoke to the group with interpreters and translation in mind). As the day went on, we worked differently with the interpreters so as to allow more natural interaction with the participants. As we discuss below, this experience led to several insights about the value of advance knowledge of participants' language proficiency and how best to work with interpreters in training.

Our experience with interpreters in Istanbul also brought to mind a previous attempt to work across language barriers. In a prior training, rather than using simultaneous translation, two of the authors organized a course where at least one trainer spoke the local language (two of the authors are English speaking and one is Turkish). We faced numerous problems related to language. First, the presence of two trainers who spoke different languages with the participants required consecutive (as opposed to simultaneous) translation. This proved to be very time consuming. In addition, in order for the non-native speaking trainer to understand everything that was happening in the training room, the native speaker had to turn her attention away from the participants, creating an added distraction.

Tension Two: How to Load Maximum Learning Into Minimum Time While Remaining Responsive and Interactive

We had a very ambitious agenda for this introductory course. Six contact hours is quite short, particularly when we wanted to remain responsive to the emergent learning moments that arose during the day.[9] Moreover, we had learned an important lesson from the NT 2.0 project's prior training experience in Rome. There, in the trainers' zeal to introduce as many important principles as possible, they somewhat lost sight of the students' ability to absorb and process the learning. We addressed this tension in two ways.

1) Keep it simple

We had to resist the temptation to introduce everything that was interesting to us, or what we thought would impress our students. Instead, we had to focus on the essentials of negotiation. During our planning process, we distilled the course down to four learning objectives: understanding oneself as a negotiator; introducing core negotiation concepts; practicing certain key "micro-skills;" and reflecting on how to carry the lessons forward. We found that even these essentials were more than enough for one training day.

2) Design multi-dimensional activities

As discussed above, negotiation courses often include single-purpose activities. While it might appear oxymoronic to have simple yet multi-dimensional activities, we wanted to make full use of each activity, not only to use our time more efficiently, but to reflect the complexity of human interaction and to test these experimental activities' effectiveness in the classroom. Two activities that we employed illustrate this concept.

Human thermometer. We opened the training by asking partici-pants to form a "human thermometer" – a single line where they organized themselves along a continuum in response to our question prompts. We encouraged the participants to talk with one another (in Turkish if they chose) as they found their proper place in the continuum. We asked that there should be no "clumping" – that is, they must locate themselves along a single line of participants rather than group around some imaginary point on the continuum. The group had to organize, and then re-organize in response to each of the following prompts:

- Line up from least to most years of professional negotiation experience.
- Re-organize based on what percentage of their work day they engage in professional negotiation.
- Re-organize based on what percentage of their negotiation work is international.
- Re-organize based on the degree to which, in their profes-sional negotiations, they care about preserving the relation-ship with their counterpart as opposed to getting the best deal for themselves that day.
- Re-organize based on how hard they work to help their coun-terpart to improve his or her own outcome at the negotiation table.
- Finally, re-organize based on how much of their negotiation activity is a regularized ritual, as opposed to specific negotia-tion choices that are unique to each negotiation situation.

Following the series of prompts and line-ups, we debriefed the activity while the participants still stood around one another in the front of the classroom. We had multiple purposes for this activity: first, to engage the participants immediately in a highly interactive (and fun) activity that set a tone for the day and that related directly to the focus of their learning; second, to provide an ice-breaker that would allow participants to talk with a large number of their col-leagues in a short amount of time about topics relevant to the day as they got to know one another; third, to elicit, from the participants' own lived experiences, key information on topics we would return to as the training day unfolded; and fourth, to give us an opportunity at the outset of the training day to check some of our assumptions regarding the experience and general approach towards negotiation of the students. We also saw this as a real, as opposed to simulated, activity since it drew directly on each participant's own life experi-ence.

Negotiating for lunch. The second example was a negotiation for the length of their lunch break. Lunch was scheduled to follow an introduction to key negotiation concepts. Shortly before the time set for the lunch break, we asked the participants to move into groups of four. Then, without further direction, we asked the participants to negotiate within their groups and decide how much time they wanted for their lunch break (we offered a range of fifteen minutes up to two hours). The group whose decision came closest to the average of all groups would win a prize. We then honored the calculated average and broke for lunch.

We wanted the participants to engage in a real (albeit simple) negotiation immediately after discussing key negotiation concepts. We also wanted not to use a role-play, but instead to engage the group in a negotiation that had some real impact (again, on a simple level). This activity served several purposes. First, participants negotiated with one another without assuming a role other than themselves, thereby supporting more natural interaction. Second, because the subject related directly to how they wanted to use their time, there was a greater possibility of investment in the outcome. Third, although we were somewhat directive (in asking the group to engage in the negotiation exercise), we were honoring participants' ability to make a training design decision for themselves – how they wanted to use their time. And fourth, it was an example of an "oblique"/"dis-orienting" exercise (see Manwaring, McAdoo, and Cheldelin, *Orientation and Disorientation*, in this volume). They were not asked to focus on their negotiation skills, although they needed to use them. This allowed us to debrief the experience after lunch on several levels: their approach (distributive vs. integrative); and the nature of their interactions with specific group members (deference to individuals because of age, experience, etc.); the relevance of the prize (strategy, competition vs. cooperation). It also set the stage for a closer look after lunch at competition vs. cooperation (we used "X-Y," a variation of the classic Prisoner's Dilemma game) and a focus on micro-skills later in the afternoon (see also Ebner and Kamp, *Relationship, Version 2.0*, in this volume).

Tension Three: How to Examine Worldview and Culture When The Trainers are the "Outsiders"

One of the central themes that emerged from the NT 2.0 project's first year was the importance of worldview and culture to negotiation. And one of the central challenges we faced was how to engage participants in a process of examining worldview during a one day executive training. A traditional way to address culture is to introduce research into cultural differences based on group membership (such as national or other identity). We did not want to do this. Instead, we wanted to explore the lived experiences of the participants. Yet, we were outsiders to their culture and views.

Rather than attempting to "teach" about culture formally, we approached the question of worldviews informally and conversationally throughout the day. We brought up our own experiences as outsiders to Turkey and asked for insights into what we observed. We asked participants to draw on their own experiences, both domestically and internationally, about what they had experienced with negotiation. We shared our own lived experiences as negotiators (and negotiation teachers) who have worked in a variety of countries, contexts and work settings. This led to a recurring conversation throughout the day about differences in how we each make sense of our interactions with others and how that "sense-making" relates to the negotiation process.

This conversational approach to examining worldview is consistent with the idea that worldview, culture and communication are deeply intertwined. (Pearce and Littlejohn 1997; LeBaron 2003; Folger, Poole, and Stutman 2009). This approach allowed us (trainers and participants alike) to practice what LeBaron calls a form of "cultural fluency," where, through conversation, we opened ourselves up to understand one another better and in a spirit of inquiry (LeBaron 2003: 53). This approach also honored several key objectives for our training: it reflected (and modeled) curiosity; it focused on achieving greater self-awareness; and it enacted an elicitive approach to teaching and learning.

Insights and Lessons from the Field
The Istanbul training offered a number of valuable lessons for future negotiation teaching, both philosophical and practical.

Philosophical Lessons
Further work is needed to develop and clarify what distinguishes first from second generation negotiation principles. While we understood these concepts in isolation from a training setting, once in the classroom, we found ourselves interacting with the students in ways quite similar to previous trainings. This reveals two insights:

First, Negotiation 2.0 is in some respects *evolutionary* in nature. That is, it involves a further refinement of what we have already learned about the negotiation process and teaching. We can use new teaching methods to better elicit long-standing negotiation principles. Our experience suggests that some of what we consider second generation thinking grows directly from first generation roots.

Second and at the same time, Negotiation 2.0 is *revolutionary*, in that some concepts require a paradigm shift in how we interact with our negotiation counterparts and our students. It requires a different "presence" at the negotiation table and in the classroom that is much more in tune with, and responsive to, those around us. As trainers in Istanbul, we had not completely made that shift. We were trying out a collection of "2.0" activities but from the standpoint of "1.0" thinking. That is not unlike a distributive negotiator believing he is being integrative simply because he is acting "nice" to his counterpart.

At least some second generation concepts require a fundamental paradigm shift, both with respect to how we understand the nature of negotiation interaction, and with respect to the nature of how negotiation teachers interact with students. The moments when we were most in tune with "2.0" thinking were the moments when we were most engaged, "present" and responsive to our participants, such as when we were talking about differences in worldviews. These moments came about, in part, because we as trainers were genuinely curious, elicitive and self-aware ourselves. And, in our own "oblique" way, by letting go of our roles as instructors, we actually enhanced what the participants were able to learn about self-awareness, curiosity and other qualities that are part of second generation negotiation thinking. This warrants further reflection and study.

Practical Lessons

There is wisdom to the proverb that "for want of a nail...the kingdom was lost." Despite months of planning with an expert consulting team, practical challenges still interfered with a smooth training. In addition to the very useful guidelines described in Harold Abramson's *Outward Bound* article (2009), we offer the following:

1) Work directly with a single local event organizer

Working from a distance with different intermediaries can complicate planning. For example, we were working with a relatively small class of twenty. However, because we requested simultaneous translation and did not have direct communication with our local organizer, we were assigned to a venue with language translation booths that did not otherwise fit our needs – a 300-seat theater-style lecture hall. Had we been able to communicate directly, we might have been able to consider different choices.[10]

2) Obtain specific information from and about trainees in advance.

Late changes in registration made it difficult for us to communicate with and learn about the course attendees in advance. As a result, we had to make final design decisions based on assumptions about our students rather than based on direct information. Working in a different cultural context complicated our ability to know our trainees. As it turned out, the students brought different backgrounds, knowledge, and language abilities than we had anticipated.

A simple advance questionnaire can provide useful planning information. This questionnaire can best be included in registration materials (as this is the moment where students have to send something back anyway) and can be either in electronic or paper form. The questionnaire could be sent either in the trainer's own language or translated into the local language. Each has its advantages. A questionnaire sent in the trainer's language does not require the assistance of a translator to write and interpret. It can also provide a rough indicator of participants' language proficiency. However, it may preclude responses from participants who are not familiar with the trainer's language. In contrast, a questionnaire that is translated into the local language will require a local language-proficient partner to assist with writing and interpreting responses, but may yield more complete information about the class. A sample questionnaire is found at Appendix 2.

3) Do your homework

Negotiation concepts, publications, and teaching are not uniquely Western and we (as negotiation teachers) are not prophets. Negotiation knowledge is ancient and widespread (Chamoun-Nicolás and Doyle 2007). As a result, it is important to learn about what the community you are working in already knows about negotiation and what has been published in the local language.[11] Consult with native speakers familiar with the negotiation literature. We had the benefit of prior experience in Turkey to know that, like elsewhere, there was a wide variation in the knowledge and sophistication about negotiation our students might bring into the classroom.

4) Meet on site in advance with coaches and translators

We worked with an international team of coaches. It was not possible to hold advance coach meetings, but we were able to communicate by voice and email. We found it valuable to provide the coaches with detailed information in advance about the training, including our underlying training philosophy and their roles. But it was not until we were all in the training room that we could work through the details of who would do what, given the realities on the ground. For example, we found it very useful when our coaches worked with small groups of participants to discuss key concepts and debrief activities. Particularly with respect to language differences, these more intimate settings allowed the coaches to help participants informally and more directly to internalize lessons from the training.

Similarly, as Abramson writes, it is important to meet with the interpreters in advance to discuss specific terms of art and to outline how the training day will unfold (Abramson 2009: 308). We gave our interpreters copies of our detailed training schedule and slides. We discussed specific terms that we would be using and made sure they agreed on the correct translations. This can be critical at a training in a different cultural context. In some cultures, multiple terms might be used to describe a particular negotiation concept. Translators may not be familiar with negotiation theory and context and, thus, may not be aware of the significance of using one term instead of another. For example, in previous training experiences in Turkey we have seen translators interpret words like "interests" to mean "financial interests" and "neutral attitude" to mean "harmless."

We also reviewed with our interpreters when we would be working with the class as a whole and when we would be working in small groups. The interpreters thus knew when they needed to work from the interpreter's booth and when to move around the room as we worked with small groups and pairings.

5) Be realistic about what can be accomplished within a set schedule

If you only have six hours to teach basic negotiation principles, accept the fact that you need to make difficult choices. You may need to discard content and group discussion that you think is "indispensable" – or a personal favorite. In the same way you work to manage participant expectations, apply the same expectation-management principles to yourself.

6) Curiosity and worldview are important to teach, but difficult to translate into specific activities

These are not discrete skills to be learned. Rather, they are qualities and insights to be understood and cultivated. We found the most valuable way to help participants appreciate these concepts was in the course of debriefing activities with apparently different learning purposes. On reflection, we also found participants best appreciating these concepts when we, as trainers, were most curious and transparent about our own worldviews. This is consistent with the concepts of "oblique" activities and multi-dimensional debriefing.

Conclusion

Albert Einstein was right to recognize the wisdom of experience. The Istanbul training taught us a great deal. It was only the first of many attempts to translate second generation negotiation thinking into practice. Moving forward, negotiation teachers would be wise to test a few concepts at a time in a familiar environment.

Notes

[1] Special Section: Second Generation Global Negotiation Education, 2009. Negotiation Journal 25(2): 141-266.

[2] The primary trainers were two of this chapter's authors, Ken Fox from the United States and Manon Schonewille from the Netherlands. Training coaches included Habib Chamoun-Nicolas from Ecuador, Noam Ebner from Israel, Idil Elveris from Turkey, Vivian Feng from China, and Bobbi McAdoo from the United States.

[3] In addition to the course trainers, the planning group included Jim Coben, Giuseppe De Palo, Chris Honeyman, Bobbi McAdoo and Sharon Press.

[4] During our first conference in 2008, a number of participants had energetic discussions on whether any negotiation teacher/trainer should *ever* agree to offer a negotiation course as short as one day. This question confronted the dilemma of trainees who insist on "quick" tips and tricks while at the same time wanting a "deeper" knowledge of the process. We do not expect the question to be resolved any time soon, but the exigencies of getting seventy professors from dozens of countries together at all have dictated using such "executive length" courses as an experimental framework. See generally Honeyman and Coben, *Introduction: Half-Way to a Second Generation*, in this volume.

[5] While this cultural setting was new for the pilot training, it was not entirely new to the training team: Manon Schonewille has worked and trained on a number of occasions in Turkey; Ken Fox has lived in Turkey.

[6] As we examined our "how to engage in multi-dimensional learning activities" concerns, we found ourselves repeatedly referring to the teaching methods of our colleague, Michael Wheeler. We came to refer to his multi-dimensional approach to debriefing as "Wheelerizing."

[7] See note two, infra.

[8] We tip our hat to Robert Mnookin and the three tensions he identifies in the negotiation process in his book *Beyond Winning*.

[9] Several participants commented in their course evaluations that they wished the course had been at least twice as long, and a number of participants said they wanted more time with each activity.

[10] We did improvise. At the last minute we organized tables and chairs on the stage portion of the theater classroom, where we invited students to do the small group work.

[11] For example, a glossary of conflict resolution terms in Turkish can be found in a dictionary (Sozlukce) in Beriker (2009).

References

Abramson, H. 2009. Outward bound to other cultures: Seven guidelines. In *Rethinking negotiation teaching: Innovations for context and culture,* edited by C. Honeyman, J. Coben, and G. De Palo. St. Paul, MN: DRI Press.

Abu-Nimer, M. 1998. Conflict resolution training in the Middle East: Lessons to be learned, *International Negotiation* 3: 99-116.

Alexander, N. and M. LeBaron. 2009. Death of the role-play. In *Rethinking negotiation teaching: Innovations for context and culture,* edited by C. Honeyman, J. Coben, and G. De Palo. St. Paul, MN: DRI Press.

Anderson, W. 1992. *Reality isn't what it used to be: Theatrical politics, ready-to-wear religion, global myths, primitive chic, and other wonders of the postmodern world.* New York: Harper Collins.

Avruch, K. 1998. *Culture and conflict resolution.* Washington, DC: USIP Press.

Avruch, K. 2004. Culture as context, culture as communication: Considerations for humanitarian negotiators. *Harvard Negotiation Law Review* 9: 391-407.

Baer, R. 2003. Mindfulness training as a clinical intervention: A conceptual and empirical review. *Psychology: Science and Practice* 10(2): 126.

Beriker, N. (ed). 2009. Uzlasmaya: Kuramlar, surecler, ve uygulamalar (From conflict to reconciliation: Theories, processes, and application). Istanbul: Bilgi Universitesi Yayinlari.

Bernard, P. 2009. Finding common ground in the soil of culture. In *Rethinking negotiation teaching: Innovations for context and culture,* edited by C. Honeyman, J. Coben, and G. De Palo. St. Paul, MN: DRI Press.

Birke, R. and C. R. Fox. 1999. Psychological principles in negotiating civil settlements. *Harvard Negotiation Law Review* 4: 1-57.

Bolt, W. and H. Houba. 2002. *Credible threats in negotiations: A game-theoretic approach.* Dordrecht: Kluwer Academic Publishers.

Bowling, D. and D. Hoffman. 2003. *Bringing peace into the room: How the personal qualities of the mediator impact the process of conflict resolution.* San Francisco: Jossey Bass.

Brett, J. 2001. *Negotiating globally: How to negotiate deals, resolve disputes, and make decisions across cultural boundaries.* San Francisco: Jossey Bass.

Chamoun-Nicolás, H. and R. Doyle. 2007. Negotiate like a Phoenician: Discover traDEAbLes. Houston: Keynegotiations.

Docherty, J. S. 2001. *Learning lessons from Waco: When the parties bring their gods to the negotiation table.* Syracuse: Syracuse University Press.

Elgstrom, O. 1999. The role of culture: A discussion and case study. In *Negotiation eclectics: Essays in memory of Jeffrey Z. Rubin,* edited by D. M. Kolb. Cambridge: PON Books.

Faure, G. and J. Rubin (eds). 1993. *Culture and negotiation: The resolution of water disputes.* Thousand Oaks: Sage.

Fisher, R., W. Ury, and B. Patton 1991. *Getting to yes. Negotiating agreement without giving in,* 2nd edn. New York: Penguin.

Folger, J., M. Poole, and R. Stutman. 2009. *Working through conflict: Strategies for relationships, groups and organizations,* 6th edn. New York: Pearson

Fox, K. 2009. Negotiation as a postmodern process. In *Rethinking negotiation teaching: Innovations for context and culture*, edited by C. Honeyman, J. Coben, and G. De Palo. St. Paul, MN: DRI Press.

Guthrie, C. 2009. I'm curious: Can we teach curiosity? In *Rethinking negotiation teaching: Innovations for context and culture*, edited by C. Honeyman, J. Coben, and G. De Palo. St. Paul, MN: DRI Press.

Honeyman, C., J. Coben, and G. De Palo (eds.) 2009. *Rethinking negotiation teaching: Innovations for context and culture.* St. Paul, MN: DRI Press.

LeBaron, M. 2003. *Bridging cultural conflicts: An approach for a changing world.* San Francisco: Jossey Bass.

LeBaron, M. and M. Patera. 2009. Reflective practice in the new millennium. In *Rethinking negotiation teaching: Innovations for context and culture*, edited by C. Honeyman, J. Coben, and G. De Palo. St. Paul, MN: DRI Press.

Lederman, L. 1992. Debriefing: Toward a systematic assessment of theory and practice. *Simulation and Gaming* 23: 145-160.

Menkel-Meadow, C. 1996. The trouble with the adversary system in a postmodern, multicultural world. *William and Mary Law Review* 38(1): 5-44.

Mnooken, R., S. Peppet, and A. Tullumello. 2000. *Beyond winning: Negotiating to create value in deals and disputes.* Cambridge, MA: Belknap Press.

Movius, H. 2008. The effectiveness of negotiation training. *Negotiation Journal* 24(4): 509-531.

Nelken, M., B. McAdoo, and M. Manwaring. 2009. Negotiating learning environments. In *Rethinking negotiation teaching: Innovations for context and culture*, edited by C. Honeyman, J. Coben, and G. De Palo. St. Paul, MN: DRI Press.

New Oxford American Dictionary. 2nd edn. 2005. New York: Oxford University Press.

Nolan Haley, J. and E. Gmurzynska. 2009. Culture – the body/soul connector in negotiation. In *Rethinking negotiation teaching: Innovations for context and culture*, edited by C. Honeyman, J. Coben, and G. De Palo. St. Paul, MN: DRI Press.

Pearce, W. B. and S. Littlejohn. 1997. *Moral conflict: When social worlds collide.* Thousand Oaks: Sage.

Riskin, L. 2006. Mindfulness: Knowing yourself. In *The negotiator's fieldbook: The desk reference for the experienced negotiator*, edited by A. K. Schneider and C. Honeyman. Washington, DC: American Bar Association.

Shapiro, D. 2006. Identity: More than meets the "I." In *The negotiator's fieldbook: The desk reference for the experienced negotiator*, edited by A. K. Schneider and C. Honeyman. Washington, DC: American Bar Association.

Shell, R. 2006. *Bargaining for advantage: Negotiation strategies for reasonable people*, 2nd edn. New York: Penguin.

Stone, D., B. Patton, and S. Heen. 1999. *Difficult conversations: How to discuss what matters most.* New York: Viking Penguin.

Tinsley, C. H., S. I. Cheldelin, A. K. Schneider, and E. T. Amanatullah. 2009. Negotiating your public identity: Women's path to power. In *Rethinking negotiation teaching: Innovations for context and culture*, edited by C. Honeyman, J. Coben, and G. De Palo. St. Paul, MN: DRI Press.

Tom, S., C. R. Fox, C. Trepel, and R. A. Poldrack. 2007. The neural basis of loss aversion in decision making under risk. *Science* 315: 515-518.

Van Hasselt, V. B., S. J. Romano, and G. M. Vecchi. 2008. Role playing: Applications in hostage and crisis negotiation skills training. *Behavior Modification 32*: 248-263.

Weiss, S. 1999. Opening a dialogue on negotiation and culture: A "believer" considers skeptics' views. In *Negotiation eclectics: Essays in memory of Jeffrey Z. Rubin*, edited by D. M. Kolb. Cambridge: PON Books.

Appendix One

Sample One-day Executive Negotiation Course Trainers' Outline

Pre-training Preparation

Generate, translate into local language and distribute the following items:

- Cover letter to participants (including request to complete and return the pre-session questionnaire and to complete in advance the Shell or Thomas-Kilmann bargaining style assessment tool)
- Course agenda
- Pre-session questionnaire
- Bargaining style assessment tool
- Interpretation of tool
- Trainer and coach biographies
- Post-training evaluation form

Hold conference call with coaches to review expectations and roles. ***Materials/Preparation Note****: Distribute overview memo, simulations and other materials.*]

Have local contact read responses to pre-session questionnaire (if translated into local language). Discuss with local contact any insights that emerge about group (cultural cues, language capabilities, prior knowledge and experience with negotiation, etc.).

Meet with language interpreters the day before training at training site. Check room set-up and translation equipment. If translation booths are used, discuss the physical flow of the training day so interpreters can identify technical issues. Discuss fallback options with interpreters in case of equipment problems. Review written materials, slides and any videos with interpreters. Discuss technical terms so as to assure correct translations. [***Materials/Preparation Note****: Provide copies of materials and videos; Make list of jargon for the translators.*]

09:30 Official Start Time

Depending on local cultural norms, assume some participants will arrive late. During the first 20 minutes or so, give participants the chance to complete the Bargaining Styles instrument (if they haven't already) and to look at and discuss the Bargaining Styles interpretive information. Invite them to sit in small groups and talk informally about the instrument. Trainers and coaches will circulate to answer questions regarding the Bargaining Style instrument and its interpretation. The small groups will likely work in their native language, therefore interpreters should circulate with coaches. [*Materials/Preparation Note: Have extra copies of Bargaining Styles instruments. Trainers and coaches will circulate, observe and note any emerging discussion themes and questions. Note them for the closing conversation.*]

10:00 Actual Start Time (or earlier, if most participants have arrived)

Welcome and Setting the Stage

- Trainers give welcome and offer special thanks to host university or organization, sponsors, etc. Introduce coaches and trainers (depending on cultural norms, have local host or "dignitary" introduce you)
- Talk explicitly about the "international" format of training (highly interactive, elicitive and participatory)

Do a very quick round of introductions (name and affiliation only). Have them write names on name tag. [*Materials/Preparation Note: Paper name tags + marker on tables or chairs.*]

10:15 Ice Breaking Exercise (which includes using bargaining styles instrument)

Have participants stand up and move to the front of the room (or along a long wall). They will be asked to line up in a single, physical, continuum in response to the question prompts, below. With each question, participants move to stand in relative position to other participants along the line (far left is least and far right is most) and they may not "cluster" around an imaginary point. They must sort themselves into a single line. [*Materials/Preparation Note: Be sure the training room has enough space for participants to move around and stand in a straight line. If not, use the corridor outside the training room. Be sure to coordinate the logistics in advance with the language interpreters.*]

During the exercise, encourage participants to talk with and ask one another questions (especially the people standing next to them as they decide where to move into line) to learn how/why they placed themselves where they did on the continuum. This provides a way to promote curiosity (which will be addressed as the day unfolds). Participants re-organize based on each new prompt.

The line-up prompts are:

- Least to most years of professional negotiation experience
- Percentage of their work-day that they engage in professional negotiation
- Percentage of their negotiation work that is international
- Degree to which they care about preserving the relationship with their counterpart as opposed to getting the best deal for themselves in a negotiation
- Degree to which they work to help their counterpart to improve his or her own outcome at the negotiation table

- Amount of negotiation activity that they see as a regularized ritual, as opposed to specific negotiation choices that are unique to each negotiation situation
- If all participants have previously completed the bargaining styles assessment, ask them to cluster around their preferred style (competing, accommodating, avoiding, compromising, collaborating).

10:45 Demonstration, Leading to Discussion of Key Concepts and Greater Self-Awareness.

This activity builds on the ice-breaker and bargaining style instrument to introduce key concepts in negotiation.

Have three coaches conduct a negotiation simulation in front of the group. Trainers will facilitate discussion. [*Materials/Preparation Note: Select a simulation that includes cultural/worldview differences between parties as well as differing needs and interests. Give interpreters advance copies of the simulation and discuss its key characteristics with them in advance. Have three coaches prepped in advance to do the demonstration. Trainers will facilitate discussion and feedback.*]

- Start with traditional positional bargaining, running the negotiation for a sufficient time period to demonstrate its underlying "mind-set." Discuss with participants what they observe happening and what negotiator style(s) they notice on the bargaining styles scale.
- Replay negotiation (or continue forward) while shifting to an integrative model. Discuss with participants what they notice that is the same/different. Discuss what is significant about these differences.
- Open up discussion to include role-players. Invite participants to talk directly with role-players about aspects of role-play that illustrate key concepts. Surface the impact of culture and worldview on the nature of negotiation interactions.

Plenary debrief: identify and discuss concepts that did not already emerge from discussion (such as positions vs. interests, partisan perceptions, psychological issus/biases, underlying cultural/worldview influences on negotiator mind-set, value of (and how to promote) curiosity, etc. These will be covered more deeply after the morning break. [*Materials/Preparation Note: Trainers will have prepared slides of key negotiation terms and concepts to complement what is illustrated in demonstration. An alternative to live demonstration is to show appropriate negotiation videos. If used, interpreters should preview them to help with translation. Interpreters move from booth to circulate among small groups.*]

Follow up the demo and plenary debrief with a more general discussion that tracks the following question prompts (in small groups with coach assistance in each group.

- From your experience, what makes an effective negotiator?
- As you think about your own negotiation experience, what are your best successes? Most difficult challenges?
- What do you need to learn more about today to help you be a more effective negotiator?
- How can you draw on your personal strengths and weaknesses to be an even more effective negotiator?

Revisit bargaining style instrument to make connections to the various threads that emerge from the discussion.

11:45 Break

12:00 Presentation of Key Concepts
Formal presentation and discussion of key negotiation concepts. Specifically, cover: Distributive and integrative mind-set (claiming and creating value); positions, interests and issues; ZOPA, BATNA, WATNA, psychological influences; perspective, culture and worldview. [*Materials/Preparation Note: Slides for each concept.*]

12:50 Negotiate for Lunch
Provide an immediate opportunity for participants to conduct a real negotiation that calls on them to use the concepts covered in the earlier session. Explore general preferences of group re: time for lunch (long lunch and move training end time beyond office hours, or short lunch and earlier finish); if sufficient spreading of preferences:

Break participants into groups of four each. Have each group negotiate how long the lunch break should be (anywhere from 15 minutes to 2 hours – the ZOPA). The afternoon session schedule will shift to an earlier or later end-time based on time allotted to lunch. The negotiation itself will be time limited (5 minutes).

At the end of the timed negotiation, each sub-group reports out the agreed upon time for lunch. All group times are then averaged. Members of the group whose own time is closest to the class average will receive a prize. [*Materials/Preparation Note: A minimum of 8 books or other valuable items to award as prizes.*]

1:00 Lunch Break
Participants go to lunch for the amount of time determined in the group negotiation. [*Materials/Preparation Note: During lunch, re-calculate afternoon schedule if needed.*]

2:00 (or as determined by negotiation)
Reconvene
Check-in regarding morning session. Debrief on lunch negotiation, reviewing key concepts (including introduction of time pressure). [*Materials/Preparation Note: Have X-Y materials translated into local language.*]

Extending Common Information Base.
Begin with X-Y exercise. Debrief exercise to pull out the following concepts (again using small groups and reporting out ideas to the whole group):
- What is, and how does one manage, the tension between competition and cooperation (claiming and creating value)? (At the end of this part of the discussion, show video clip from A Beautiful Mind or the tit-for-tat scene from the hostage film to illustrate the tension.)
- How do communication, trust, and emotion affect decision-making?

- What is the role of relationship building?
- In what ways do worldview, culture, individual perceptions, and "framing" influence one's process of choice?
- Where do concepts like "curiosity" fit in our understanding of these notions?

Have slides available to show concepts that were not drawn out in discussion. Also have questions on the slides to facilitate the small group discussions. [*Materials/Preparation Note: Have DVDs or online access to clips from "A Beautiful Mind" and other scenes to illustrate enlightened self-interest; have slides preloaded on various concepts so they can be used if necessary.*]

3:00 Micro-skills Session
Divide into groups of four, sitting at tables. Identify specific micro-skills to practice, such as:
- Listening
- Asking questions
- Addressing partisan perceptions
- Reframing
- Paraphrasing
- Engendering curiosity

Each table discusses and then enacts the micro-skill prompted by the trainers' questions. When ready, tables call out their response to the trainer prompt and other tables build on earlier responses. [*Materials/Preparation Note: Assemble "micro-skill" tools. Coaches sit with groups (including interpreters, where needed) to help small groups interpret concepts and practice activities.*]

4:00 Break

4:15 Micro-skills, continued
Continue with micro-skills activities.

5:00 Closing Consultation/Conversation
Coaches report out their observations and what learnings or recurring themes they noted during the whole day.

Trainers facilitate open-ended discussion of what participants have taken from the day, what they still want to know more about, what questions/objections/"next steps" they have. Keeping underlying principles in mind, be sure to help participants synthesize the day's elements, particularly from the micro-skills sessions. Return to over-arching themes for the day and begin pulling the threads together.

If sufficient time, end by having participants imagine they are preparing for their next negotiation situation. Discuss as a group what they will do the same, differently, and why.

Closing ritual and thank yous. [*Materials/Preparation Note: Hand out course evaluations to be completed before participants leave.*]

5:30 End

Appendix Two

[TITLE OF TRAINING]
Pre-training questionnaire

To help us plan a training that is specific to your needs, please answer this short questionnaire and return to [insert e-mail or post address] before [date]

First Name and Last Name

Company / Law Firm

Position and general areas of responsibility

1. How many years of professional experience do you have? _____

2. How long have you negotiated in a professional context? _____

3. How regularly do you negotiate professionally?
    ☐ rarely   ☐ occasionally   ☐ frequently

4. In what type(s) of negotiations are you typically involved? (business to business; business to customer; international negotiations; lawyer to lawyer (transactions or settlement); other? _____

5. Have you attended any previous training courses on negotiation?
    ☐ Yes   ☐ No
If yes, please describe the course(s): (for example, by whom was it offered, how many days, what topics were covered, and so on): _____
_____
_____

6. How is your knowledge of the English language? Indicate competence on a scale of 1 to 5 (1 – basic; 5 – very strong):
Reading ____ Speaking ____ Listening ____

7. What do you expect to learn from this course? _____
_____
_____

8. (optional) remarks: _____
_____
_____

Thank you. Please return this form with your registration materials.

❦ 3 ❧

Instructors Heed the Who:[1] Designing Negotiation Training With the Learner in Mind

Roy J. Lewicki & Andrea Kupfer Schneider[*]

Editors' Note: Lewicki and Schneider argue that while our field has made great progress in determining what to teach and how to teach it in negotiation, there has been a surprising reluctance to make the move from "mass production" to "mass customization" that so many other industries have successfully adopted. "The Who" of our training has so far been addressed seriously, they surmise, by only an elite subgroup of trainers. They explain how this can and should change.

Introduction

This book, with its forerunners (Schneider and Honeyman 2006; Honeyman, Coben, and De Palo 2009), aims to advance negotiation pedagogy into the next generation. The forward-looking progeny of the Istanbul conference and the historical overviews of the advancement of the negotiation field (see Symposium 2009) have in common their focus on particular aspects of negotiation theory – the "What" – as well as negotiation pedagogy – the "How." Unexplored up to now is a particular focus on the "Who" that we teach. This chapter addresses the important issue of whom we are teaching by first examining why we think understanding one's audience could or should matter. Next, we report the results of a non-scientific survey of some expert negotiation trainers, exploring how they assess Who is in their course or workshop, and how that impacts what and how they deliver the training. Finally, we offer several frameworks

---

[*] **Roy J. Lewicki** is the Irving Abramowitz memorial professor in the Max M. Fisher College of Business at The Ohio State University. His email address is lewicki_1@fisher.osu.edu. **Andrea Kupfer Schneider** is a professor of law at Marquette University Law School in Milwaukee, Wisconsin. Her email address is andrea.schneider@marquette.edu.

for thinking about the Who in negotiation and the implications for more effective negotiation training.

The development of the field of negotiation has been extraordinary over the last three decades. Early writing in negotiation focused on labor negotiations (McKersie and Cutcher-Gershenfeld 2009), international diplomacy (Babbitt 2009), and game theory (Dixit and Nalebuff 1991; Tsay and Bazerman 2009; Sebenius 2009). Built by economists, social psychologists, sociologists and anthropologists, negotiation had a complex body of knowledge even in the 1960s. The move from the basic social sciences into the professional schools of law and business started with a primary focus on adversarial bargaining (which at that time characterized labor relations), purchasing and contracting, but then dramatically shifted in the 1980s to teaching integrative or problem-solving negotiation (Menkel-Meadow 2009).

Within the conversations about different approaches to negotiation, classes focused on teaching about the types of negotiation, social structural factors such as power and the dynamics of agency, perception and communication, individual differences and third parties, and any cross-cultural differences (cf. Lewicki and Litterer 1985, one of the first textbooks in the field). In the 1990s negotiation pedagogy became more interdisciplinary, introducing new theory and research about perceptual and cognitive biases and emotion, and with ethics being integrated into most classes. *The Negotiator's Fieldbook* (Schneider and Honeyman 2006), updated textbooks (Lewicki, Barry, and Saunders 2010; Menkel-Meadow, Love, Schneider, and Sternlight 2004) and the books from the two Second-Generation Negotiation Teaching conferences to date continue the effort to circulate the newest interdisciplinary research – relevant research from the "hard sciences," for example – and teaching from around the world in order to keep negotiation knowledge at the cutting edge.

The How of teaching negotiation has also developed in the last three decades. Negotiation is rarely taught through lecture alone; teachers in all types of courses use case studies, role-plays, videos and other pedagogical tools to convey negotiation knowledge (Lewicki 2000). While role plays are the most ubiquitous teaching tool, others have argued for moving away from this method (Alexander and LeBaron 2009). Ongoing conversations about efforts to continue to improve pedagogy are common at academic conferences (e.g., the ABA Section on Dispute Resolution Legal Educator's Colloquium) and in journal articles (Honeyman, Hughes, and Schneider 2003; Schneider and MacFarlane 2003; Moffitt 2004).

As we have noted, much of negotiation teaching has focused on the What (content) and How (tools and technique). Variation of negotiation teaching for different audiences has so far occurred mostly by cherry-picking pieces of negotiation knowledge for different audiences. And so, despite efforts to create a single negotiation canon (Honeyman and Schneider 2004; Schneider and Honeyman 2006), textbooks and course packages for students vary depending on what field their degree will be in. Packages are designed to "cover" the body of content of the What, and the How is varied in order to make the course delivery more interesting, as well as (hopefully) to address the various ways people learn (Lewicki 1986). But to be honest, this has largely been a "shotgun" approach to education, hoping to hit all targets with a few pellets. This lack of focus on Who has largely occurred because the instructors live in the world of What and How, and assume that they can make a clear judgment of what pieces or components are suitable and acceptable to the Who.

As instructors have developed their academic courses, and as the field of negotiation has grown dramatically over the last two decades, new instructors have adopted course materials and course "packages" wholesale, with little or no attention to Who may be in the seats. Perhaps this area has remained unexplored because, for professors, the Who is often defined for us by our job titles. The Who is whoever signs up for class at the law school, business school, or other type of upper level specialty seminar (public policy, conflict management, etc.) Many of the details of the Who remain relatively homogenous in a classroom setting – the students' ages, educational background, ethnicity, even where they grew up can be relatively similar. And to be a bit more cynical about it, changes have not been made because, at a superficial level, instructors have been very successful at these courses. Negotiation courses are traditionally well rated and even oversubscribed because they create excitement, reveal students' real personalities to each other, and create an energized classroom. Success does not breed change!

At the margin, some minor adjustments have been made. Faculty have mildly "adapted" the body of knowledge to undergraduate audiences, graduate student audiences, and executive/practitioner audiences. Adaptations have also been made for different professional groups who will use and employ the knowledge in different ways and configurations, such as business, law, public policy, labor relations, finance, purchasing and sales. For teachers who take their courses overseas, the cross-cultural elements must be taken into account, but that is still a small minority of professors or trainers.

Probably the most significant adaptation of the What/How has come in the "custom" design of negotiation skills training for executive audiences. In the design and delivery of executive education for a "custom" group (e.g., travel agents, regulatory bankers, construction managers, real estate salespeople, technical sales people, attorneys), trainers have usually spent some time meeting with representatives of the Who group to learn about their regular negotiation interactions, the people they negotiate with, their own perceived strengths and weaknesses as negotiators, and the recognized needs for training to strengthen perceived deficiencies. Trainers have usually met this challenge by cherry-picking What materials from the rich negotiation knowledge bank, and by matching training activities that emphasize knowledge and skill development in these areas (e.g., a labor simulation for labor negotiators or a power simulation for community organizers). Occasionally, client groups will also commission the development of one or more unique "cases" and/or customized role-plays that do a better job of embedding the What in the unique and specific context of the Who. If the client pays for the development of these materials, they are traditionally proprietary, not shared into the wider body of accessible tools, and hence do not contribute to a broader knowledge base of materials that are unique, specific and relevant to a particular Who.

Almost anyone in the teaching/learning or training profession would argue that effective training should be grounded in the world of Who. Yet the reality is that while our knowledge base of What continues to expand (as new research is added), and while talented educators continue to expand and explore the world of How (refinement of case and simulation materials, introduction of video models and feedback, introduction of action learning techniques inside and outside the classroom, personal diaries and journals, etc.), we have done little to create a rich and coherent lexicon and organization of knowledge of the various ways we can understand Who, and how we might better customize What and How to met their needs.

Checking Our Assumptions with Experts

In order to make sure that we were not simply "out of touch" about how expert negotiation teachers diagnosed the unique learning needs of their various Who audiences, we constructed a non-scientific interview list of questions[2] and presented them to several top-notch negotiation trainers.[3] Our comments below are a summary of what we learned as well as our own thinking and experience in negotiation training.

Most trainings occur in response to a call from a specific client or group to bring in an expert for a particular training purpose. Our experts said that they attempt to understand Who will be in the audience in several ways. First, the requested training events will often be limited by either the profession or context in which the learned skills will be applied: law, business, purchasing, sales, diplomacy, finance, real estate, union-management relations, community development, etc. (It should be noted that these same clients often send small groups of professionals to open-enrollment workshops in which the What and How will either be broadly based or already customized for a particular Who profession or industry.) More specific questions in this vein might include: "What is the management level of the audience?," "Who are the ultimate decision makers?," and even "What is the audience's level of analytical competence?" (i.e., ability to understand game theory or complex analytical negotiation models). An audience can also be distinguished by some of the most visible and clear indicators: gender, culture, and national identity. But a more finely grained understanding of Who usually requires the trainer to collect more data, to get to know the Who better, and every one of our trainers asked more questions about the type of negotiations the audience engaged in:

- How and with whom do they negotiate?
- Are the negotiations internal or external?
- Are the negotiations two party or multiparty?
- How do they "think about" and approach negotiations?
- What are the major issues in a typical negotiation?
- What is their negotiation vocabulary?
- What are their most nagging challenges or problems?
- How do they typically define a successful negotiation?
- Finally, why have they brought you, the trainer, in to teach negotiation (i.e., how will training success be defined)?

Our expert trainers also differed on the amount of customization – and hence detail needed – about the audiences. For those trainers who are hired for either a specific audience or who only do general training, detail was not as necessary. For others, who might construct a customized case or want to tailor the materials more specifically, questions like the audience's level of perspective, conceptual ability, level of education and experience, language issues, or whether there are participants from different levels in the company, all became relevant. Most trainers seemed to fall in the middle range, employing a general repertoire of expertise and content matter that was incorporated into almost any training experience, while also fitting their materials and exercises into learning events that made sense for the audience.

Organizing Knowledge in the World of Who

The reader might assume that we are suggesting that to be effective, every negotiation teaching and training event should be customized to the unique and specific Who (the client or receiver of training). But clearly, such an approach would be highly inefficient, because it would require extensive and time-consuming interaction with a specific Who in order to gain access to their world, and elaborate design of training for each unique individual and each unique group. Moreover, it is not clear that the What and How require extensive tailoring to be accessible to different groups of Who. Instead, as we listened to our experts and thought about our own teaching experiences, we believe that (beyond the already-accepted customization for culture, gender, etc.) the design and delivery of negotiation education can be thought of in terms of three different levels of "sophistication" to address the needs of the Who.

The first level is when negotiation education is mass-delivered in pre-designed packages of content, and through several pre-designed methods (a combination of readings, lectures, several short role-plays or cases). Learners accept the package as delivered, and there is seldom opportunity to modify the package in any way. Pricing for the package is relatively fixed. (This is the most common model used in academia.) The next level is when negotiation education has a fixed menu of options, but there are considerably more items on the menu, and some modification of options is permissible by the learner. The highest level is when negotiation education also has a reasonably fixed menu of options, but each of the options is assembled elegantly, with great care and thought to the needs of the learner. Such a trainer is normally thoroughly versed in the wide range of What and How, so much so that if the Who has a unique and distinctive set of learning needs, the trainer is able to invent and reinvent learning experiences to meet their needs. The client (the group of learners) becomes a full interactive participant in the decision-making process at the design and delivery stages. The extreme example is probably an experience of our colleague Carrie Menkel-Meadow, who in the 1990s was once retained to design and present a short course in mediation to the Attorney General of the United States and her senior staff. Not surprisingly, the preparations to teach even a short course in this environment were extensive (and very sensitive), as the student in question attempted to mediate some major conflicts immediately thereafter!

This kind of differentiation is not unique to our field, and some comparison to other kinds of services may be helpful. Let us offer two sets of examples to illustrate these differences: one from the food industry, and a second from the world of auto repair. In each case, the metaphor may not be completely suitable, but it should suffice to explain the differences. Also be aware that while we have reduced these options to three possibilities, there are clearly a larger number of discrete possibilities that lie along a dimension from "simple and basic" to "complex and unique" in What they do and How they do it.

It is lunchtime, and I am hungry. I am deciding where to eat. I have three basic choices:

- *Fast food restaurant.* Fast food outlets have a limited menu. There are 25-30 items on the menu that the restaurant can efficiently and effectively provide, given that low price and quick turnaround in the transaction are two of the most important criteria for market success. "Packages" of options (e.g., a "value meal") are offered at discount prices. I enter the restaurant, look at the complete menu posted on the wall, and order either separate elements or a component package (burger, fries and a soft drink). While I might be able to modify the package slightly (no pickle on the burger), I cannot order what is not explicitly on the menu (e.g., an apple).

- *Family restaurant.* Family restaurants have a more expansive menu. There are 50-100 items on the menu. Again, packages may be offered (e.g., a three course dinner or each item a la carte), and the cook may be able to modify the preparation of any item on the menu. So, for example, I can order the pasta without garlic, even though the menu does not say that. Or if I want scrambled eggs and toast with jam for dinner and scrambled eggs do not appear anywhere on the menu, the chances are the cook can be convinced to prepare this for me even if it is a nontraditional request for a dinner meal.

- *Gourmet restaurant.* Gourmet restaurants are the most expensive. The menu is often less expansive than the family restaurant. The food is delicately and elegantly prepared, and many of the dishes are "unique" to the chef. Moreover, at least in the United States, the menu specializes in food of a specific type and from a specific origin or location (fish, nouvelle cuisine, steak, Italian, etc.) The uniqueness of the restaurant is grounded not only in the quality and thoroughness of food preparation, but also in the sophistication of preparation and the ability of the chef to "invent" new food combinations and preparations almost "on the spot."

A second example could be when we need to have our car repaired. Depending on what the need is, we can go to one of three basic types of mechanics.

- *Quick repair shop.* Like fast food, a quick repair shop offers a limited menu of services for a fixed price. Oil change, lubrication, tune up, muffler and exhaust system repair, tires rotation and change, brake service, etc. Prices and "packages" of services are fixed. The customer buys and accepts the package as is.

- *Full service mechanic.* Full service mechanics offer a more expansive portfolio of services. There may be a list of broad services posted in the garage (e.g., a tune-up, oil change and lube, tire rotation and balancing, etc.) and the mechanic may be able to modify the work that needs to be done on any item on the menu. So, for example, I can order the oil change with special quality oil, even though the menu does not say that. Or if I want minor repairs to scratches on the car door, the mechanic may have the capacity to do touch-up paint.

- *Specialized mechanic.* Specialized mechanics are the most expensive. The menu of service options, again, is actually less expansive than the full service garage. The repair work is done with the highest quality parts, tools and sensing equipment. Moreover, the services are usually customized and unique to certain high-end brands of cars or clusters of high quality automobiles. The uniqueness of the mechanic is grounded not only in the quality and thoroughness of repair, but also in the sophistication of preparation and the ability of the mechanic to invent new procedures for cleaning, tuning and improving the performance of the automobile almost "on the spot."

	Level One	**Level Two**	**Level Three**
Food Service	Fast Food	Family Style	Gourmet
Car Repair	Quick Repair	Full Service	Specialized

Negotiation Training	Pre-packaged content; open enrollment; collection of "basic content and skills" suitable for any audience; content, training design and applications selected to highlight expertise of the instructor.	"Semi-customized" program for audiences in a broad occupational field, profession, industry group. Broad fixed menu of What and How options; trainer works with client to "mix and match" a suitable package.	Fully customized program to suit the unique training needs of the customer, audience, needs, etc. Specific training events designed to address customer's critical needs, skills and deficiencies. Individualized coaching of key clients a likely component.

Table 1: Market Segmentation and Sophistication

As we can easily understand this rough "market segmentation" approach to selling dinners and repairing automobiles, it is also clearly applicable to the way that the negotiation training marketplace has been segmented as it has become a mature industry. Indeed, as shown in Table One, the design and delivery of negotiation education can be thought of as being delivered at three different levels of "sophistication":

Level One: Negotiation education is mass-delivered in pre-designed packages of content, and through several pre-designed methods (typically a combination of readings, lectures, and several short role-plays or cases). Learners accept the package as delivered, and there is seldom opportunity to modify the package in any way. Pricing for the package is fixed.

Level Two: Negotiation education has a fixed menu of options, but there are considerably more items on the menu, and some modification of options is permissible by the customer. Materials are usually "semi-customized" to fit a particular occupational group (agents), profession (attorneys or hospital executives), or industry (health care, industrial chemicals, etc.). The trainer understands enough about the customer group to "mix and match" a package of What and How to meet their needs.

Level Three: Negotiation education is presented as a broad menu of options, and each of the options is assembled elegantly, with great care and consideration to the needs of the learner. The trainer spends significant time studying the customer's environment from a negotiation perspective, and is so thoroughly versed in the wide range of What and How that if the Who has a unique and distinctive set of learning needs, the trainer is able to invent and reinvent learning experiences to meet their needs. The Who becomes a full interactive participant in the decision-making process at the design and delivery stages, while the trainer often maintains a long-term relationship with the Who in order to assure effective skill improvement and training implementation.

It should also be noted that different levels of instructional design and delivery skill, as well as general knowledge in the field of negotiation, are likely tied to each of these levels. Delivery of Level One programs can be accomplished by trainers with only the most rudimentary training in conflict and negotiation, and usually by working from a predesigned or "canned" curriculum. Level Two programs are more likely delivered by faculty with some formal postgraduate training in negotiation dynamics, while Level Three programs are traditionally reserved for academics and practitioners who have both an extensive academic background and significant training experience.

Given that the "World of Who" in negotiation training – at both the university, workshop and customized levels – has been informally segmented in this manner, what implications can be drawn for understanding the next generation of negotiation training?

Implications of Thinking About the Who for the Delivery of Negotiation 2.0

If this analysis is correct – i.e., that there are roughly three levels of "adaptation" or sophistication in diagnosing and understanding the needs of the Who in negotiation education – there are several major implications for the future development, design, and delivery of negotiation training. First, more precisely and completely diagnosing the Who is a necessary first step in training. Furthermore, focusing on the learner's needs will help to clarify the What that exists across disciplines. Second, teaching to the Who (uniquely adapting the content and methods to the needs of a specific learner population) will improve teaching overall (see Avruch 2009 on educating versus training and Wade 2009 on defining success in training). Third, more precise teaching to the Who will even improve teaching in larger classrooms. Finally, perhaps most interestingly, teaching to the Who has the potential to change the way we organize and access the How and What. In this remaining section, we amplify on these implications.

1) Focusing on Who Clarifies the What

We believe that making the diagnostic process explicit would have several beneficial impacts. First, it would help us all to understand how various elements of the field's knowledge base (the What) are being addressed across the levels of negotiation training and across disciplines. Among the variety of negotiation educators who practice in fields of law, business, diplomacy, community relations, etc., we should acknowledge that there is a negotiation knowledge base constructed on the specific learning needs and practice implications within each professional domain. To some degree, this understanding has already happened, as educators within each discipline talk more to each other, prepare textbooks and case materials that are most relevant to each discipline, and develop both university-based courses and practitioner-based programs for each audience (see Honeyman and Schneider 2004, outlining the overlapping areas of negotiation training versus the discipline-specific negotiation elements). But the bases and organizing principles for these aggregations are often not explicit and are based simply on the contexts/background settings of various cases and role-plays. Making the discriminating criteria explicit – not only within the discipline but to others outside the discipline – would facilitate a better understanding of the key skills, capabilities, and practice applications required *for each discipline*, and would also further the opportunity for better integration and refinement of the What and How *across disciplines*.

Second, more explicit diagnoses by all trainers may help to increase the quality and effectiveness of those diagnostic tools currently being used by educators to design unique and customized programs for Level Two and particularly for Level Three. For example, the differences in diagnostic questions asked by our small focus group of negotiation educators revealed strong differences in the type and depth of diagnosis that they performed before working with a Level Three client.

2) Teaching to the Who Will Improve Client Training

We believe that a considerable "stratification" of negotiation educators has already begun. Given the growth and demand for negotiation educators across various dimensions of Who (professional schools, university courses, community and technical colleges, training institutes, web-based seminars, etc.), no single trainer or training entity has the knowledge and capability to effectively address the needs of every Who audience, or master the broad range of What and How that can be brought to bear. Those who wish to expand their capabilities to become more sophisticated in delivering education to meet the needs of Who might consider several strategies.

First, there is a need to acquire more concepts by expanding their own repertoire of What – i.e., developing a broader understanding of the complex knowledge base of negotiation theory and dynamics. Second, the educator might acquire more tools in the scope of How; this would require learning how to deliver the concepts in new ways, such as through orchestrating more complex simulations, writing training materials, learning how to "model" key negotiating behaviors, etc. (see Schneider and MacFarlane 2003; McAdoo and Manwaring 2009; Nelken 2009). Finally, educators might become better diagnosticians of the clients, so as to learn how to adapt to clients who have unique needs and do not want to be "turned off" with an education program that they consider to be simplistic in either content or design. To do so, educators must develop sophisticated client-centered diagnostic and listening skills. They must know how to use the insights from their client interviews to draw links between their expanded knowledge of What and How, so as to become a "Level Three Educator," the unique chef who can use old tools and knowledge in new ways. We hope that surfacing these diagnostic questions will help all of us.

3) Teaching to the Who Will Improve Classroom Teaching

One of the implications of developing an increased sophistication of the learning needs and competencies of Who is that it may also be possible to enhance the application of these practices to traditional classroom populations. Most university-based classrooms simply accept all students who enroll, and present them with an undifferentiated curriculum of What and How. Occasionally, an "advanced" course might "pre-require" the associated entry-level course, but in and of itself, it again offers an undifferentiated curriculum of somewhat more esoteric and specialized What, usually combined with somewhat more complex application exercises (How). But the students in these classes are often of different ages, genders, cultural identities, specific negotiation experience, and comfort with the negotiation process. Thus, it should be possible to apply an increased sophistication of our knowledge of What and How so as to offer more specialized educational products and packages to different subgroups within the larger heterogeneous classroom. Negotiation educators should be doing a better job of assessing how much people *are* learning in these contexts, so that further fine-tuning can occur.

For example, one of the experts we interviewed noted how he tries to conduct the negotiation training more like a typical consultant. He uses the diagnostic questions not only to set up the training, but then to help set goals and implementation plans with the company. After the training, specific targets are set, software is adopted, and negotiation success is measured as part of the service to the client. Thus, as educators, we should strive to attain a more complex understanding of all these different identities in the room, and to attempt to meet them in an instructional design that meets the learners at their current level of understanding and sophistication. We should also determine whether learners who bring different levels of understanding and sophistication learn "better" or "more" when they are mixed together, or when they are grouped more homogeneously – an unanswered question at present. As educators, we need to assess better how much we can rely on the learner to extrapolate effectively "what they need" from the portfolio of What and How that we present to them, or whether we should be working hard to customize the design and delivery of this content across different levels of learner need and sophistication (cf. Alexander and LeBaron 2009).

4) Focusing on Who Might Help Develop a Better How and What

Finally, for the most part the negotiation knowledge base of What is organized around a grammar and syntax derived from fifty or more years of research on negotiation processes. So, for example, in negotiation, educators in this field teach about distributive or integrative negotiation processes. Each of these approaches has a distinct and very complex knowledge base about how we conduct such negotiation, as well as a complex set of interrelated skills that are taught as part of the "package" of a unit, for instance, on distributive negotiation. Training in distributive negotiation requires novice negotiators to learn how to conceptualize a distributive strategy, determine target points and resistance points, frame an opening offer, respond to the other's counteroffer, consider and make concessions, read and incorporate the other's negotiation verbal statements and concession behaviors, determine how many concessions to make, determine whether to use various tactics to enhance the other's concessions, etc.

Similarly, if we are training in the skills that permit more collaborative negotiations, we require negotiators to work on active listening, asking questions to find out what the other side's point of view might be, thinking creatively about possible solutions, etc. If a learner is deficient in one or more of these component elements, as teachers we seldom do more than point out that deficiency, but what we typically do *not* do is invent customized micro-training events that would "rehearse" or do remedial drills on one or more of the core elements of this complex skill set.

Imagine, instead, that in Negotiation Teaching 2.0, our training processes were categorized around a rather long but complete dictionary of simple "core skill" elements (setting a goal, setting a Resistance Point, understanding a bargaining range, making a first concession, making inferences from the other's negotiation behaviors, asking questions, listening actively, brainstorming solutions, selling your case most persuasively, etc.). Skill development might not be using a repertoire of Hows (simple or more complex negotiation scenarios), but more "micro" knowledge/skill units that are taught/drilled and practiced, and then used as building-blocks to create the talent to execute more complex negotiations. Another advantage of teaching negotiation in this way is that it may be easier to assess the effectiveness of negotiation training, because we could create assessment tools and activities to determine whether any given individual is competent in that skill area. We can even imagine the construction of specific trainings and training centers to do that work.

Conclusion

In this paper, we challenge the development of negotiation pedagogy by indicating that it has extensively attended to the growth and importance of pedagogical content (the What) and begun to develop more sophistication in the delivery of that pedagogy (the How), but has thus far generally neglected anything more than the most primitive understanding of the nature of the learner (the Who).

We point out that the "packaging" of negotiation education has roughly differentiated into a three-tier marketplace, but that even in this context, the diagnosis of the specific skills and needs of the learner has not kept pace with the field's capacity to diagnose and customize negotiation education, a state which was reasonably confirmed through interviews with several of the field's teachers and trainers. At best, almost all of design and delivery of the teaching of negotiation concepts has achieved Level Two in our three level approach. We do not blame anyone for this problem, but do believe that as negotiation educators, we may have become a bit too "comfortable" with the success of the status quo. We then pointed to several important implications of this state of affairs, and offer observations and suggestions for future development initiatives that may provide a richer understanding of learning needs and adaptation of content and pedagogy to meet those needs.

If our assessment of the current state of negotiation education is correct – that the field has reached some reasonable state of "maturity" on the What and the How – the Who may be the "next frontier." Many basic textbooks in the field of management training and development (e.g., Noe 2008) begin with a complex needs analysis of the training population. This needs analysis can include three major components:

- An assessment of the "organization" in which the skills are to be utilized and the appropriateness of the training for this organization and its key managers. In the context of negotiation, this analysis would differentiate labor negotiators from purchasing managers from diplomats from community organizers.
- An assessment of the "tasks" that are required, that is, the important knowledge, skills and behaviors that need to be emphasized for trainees (negotiators) to perform well.
- An assessment of the "persons" who will be part of the training. This would include an assessment of their current performance capabilities and deficiencies, and an assessment of the specific knowledge or skills that are required to build the desired level of capabilities.

Based on our analysis of the current state of negotiation teaching, there is work left to do. With regard to the organization level, the various disciplines that teach negotiation (law, labor relations, business, government and public policy, etc.) have broadly specified the nature of the organization context, although as recent work by Movius and Susskind (2009) has shown, considerably more work can be done at the organization level to assure that negotiators receive the kind of organizational acceptance and support they require. At the task level, as we have pointed out, the knowledge base has received considerable attention, but in fact the skill development approach may be underdeveloped. Rather than simulate and rehearse "whole" negotiations through simulations, perhaps trainers should be diagnosing and rehearsing more "micro" skills such as listening, discerning interests, inventing options, packaging trade-offs, etc. Finally, the person analysis is clearly where the most work is required. The development of assessment centers to diagnose current knowledge and skills, and the construction of training approaches based on that assessment, represent the "next frontier" in negotiation education.

Much has been done, but much remains to be done. To again paraphrase our muse in the writing of this article, Dr Seuss, "Imagine all the places we will go!"

Notes

[1] With apologies to Ted Geisel, "Dr Seuss." We also considered the title "Honeyman Hears a Who" but decided that hearing isn't his strength.
[2] The questions are listed in the attached Appendix.

[3] Thanks go to Max Bazerman, Leonard Greenhalgh, Sheila Heen, Chris Honeyman, Deborah Kolb, Marty Latz, Deepak Malhotra, and Bruce Patton for their time and willingness to share their expertise.

References

Alexander, N. and M. LeBaron. 2009. Death of the role-play. In *Rethinking negotiation teaching*, edited by C. Honeyman, J. Coben, and G. De Palo. St. Paul, MN: DRI Press.

Avruch, K. 2009. What is training all about? *Negotiation Journal* 25(2): 161-170.

Babbitt, E. F. 2009. The evolution of international conflict resolution: From Cold War to peacebuilding. *Negotiation Journal* 25(4): 539-49.

Dixit, A. and B. Nalebuff. 1991. *Thinking strategically: The competitive edge in business, politics and everyday life.* New York: W.W. Norton.

Honeyman, C., J. Coben, and G. De Palo (eds). 2009. *Rethinking negotiation teaching: Innovations for context and culture.* St. Paul, MN: DRI Press.

Honeyman, C., S. Hughes, and A. Schneider. 2003. How can we teach so it takes? *Conflict Resolution Quarterly* 20: 429-33.

Honeyman, C. and A. Schneider. 2004. Catching up with the major-general: The need for a "Canon of Negotiation." *Marquette Law Review* 87: 637-48.

International Mediation Institute. Available at http://www.imimediation.org/.

Legal Educators' Colloquium. 2003. American Bar Association Section on Dispute Resolution.

Lewicki, R. J. 1986. Challenges of teaching negotiation. *Negotiation Journal* 2(1): 15-27.

Lewicki, R. J. 2000. Teaching negotiation and dispute resolution in colleges of business: The state of the practice. In *Teaching negotiation: Ideas and innovations*, edited by M. Wheeler. Cambridge: PON Books.

Lewicki, R. J., B. Barry, and D. M. Saunders. 2010. *Negotiation*, 6th edn. Burr Ridge: McGraw Hill Higher Education.

Lewicki, R. J. and J. Litterer. 1985. *Negotiation*, 1st edn. Homewood, IL: Richard D. Irwin.

McAdoo, B. and M. Manwaring. 2009. Teaching for implementation: Designing negotiation curricula to maximize long-term learning. *Negotiation Journal* 25(2): 195-215

McKersie, R. and J. Cutcher-Gershenfeld. 2009. Labor-management relations: Understanding and practicing effective negotiations. *Negotiation Journal* 25 (4): 499-514.

Menkel-Meadow, C. 2009. Chronicling the complexification of negotiation theory and practice. *Negotiation Journal* 25(4): 415-429.

Menkel-Meadow, C., L. Love, A. Schneider, and J. Sternlight. 2004. *Dispute resolution: Beyond the adversarial model.* New York: Aspen Publishers.

Moffitt, M. L. 2004. Lights, camera, begin final exam: Testing what we teach in negotiation courses. *Journal of Legal Education* 54: 91-114.

Nelken, M. L. 2009. Negotiating classroom processes, lessons from adult learning. *Negotiation Journal* 25(2): 181-194.

Patton, B. 2009. The deceptive simplicity of teaching negotiation: Reflections on thirty years of the negotiation workshop. *Negotiation Journal* 25(4): 481-498.

Schneider, A. and C. Honeyman (eds). 2006. *The negotiator's fieldbook: The desk reference for the experienced negotiator.* Washington, DC: American Bar Association.

Schneider, A. and J. MacFarlane. 2003. Having students take responsibility for their learning. *Conflict Resolution Quarterly* 20(4): 455-462.

Sebenius, J. K. 2009. Negotiation analysis: From games to inferences to decisions to deals. *Negotiation Journal* 25(4): 449-465.

Symposium: Celebrating 25 Years. 2009. *Negotiation Journal* 25: 411-592.

Tsay, C. and M. H. Bazerman. 2009. A decision-making perspective to negotiation: A review of the past and a look to the future. *Negotiation Journal* 25(4): 467-480.

Wade, J. 2009. Defining success in negotiation and other dispute resolution training. *Negotiation Journal* 25(2): 171-180.

Appendix

Below are the questions that we sent out via email to our interviewees and then asked in phone interviews to discuss their answers:

Generally,

- when you are asked to design training or teaching for a specific audience, what characteristics of that audience are important to you that influence the way you design the training?
- do you have a specific set of questions for all customers, or are your questions unique and different for each customer?

Specifically,

- do you ask questions about the general occupational and educational backgrounds of the potential customer? What questions do you ask?
- do you ask questions about the types of negotiations that the potential customer is engaged in? What questions do you ask?
- do you ask questions about the specific negotiation training needs or deficiencies of the potential customer? What questions do you ask?
- do you ask questions do you ask questions about the organizational rank and seniority of seminar participants of the potential customer? What questions do you ask?
- what other diagnostic questions do you ask?

Finally,

- once you have learned something about the indicated "needs" of a potential customer, what processes do you use to distill this information and decide what specific training content or activities will be used?

✃ 4 ✄

Re-Orienting the Trainer to Navigate – Not Negotiate – Islamic Cultural Values

*Phyllis E. Bernard**

Editors' Note: Business decisions based on faith? What conventional Western bargaining wisdom might deem folly, Bernard labels as mission critical as soon as Westerners step into other cultures, and perhaps increasingly at home. She makes a convincing case that the next generation of negotiation training must account for bargaining parties' "full and complex identity," including the religious values that profoundly shape perceptions and conduct even among many of those who on the surface appear thoroughly secular.

Navigating the Human Geography

Skeptics may deem it naïve or nostalgic to propose that cultural values grounded in faith traditions play a role in modern business transactions. Granted, commercial transactions seeking short-term gains from episodic contractual arrangements may operate satisfactorily without focusing on deep cultural context. However, entrepreneurs seeking long-term, self-sustaining international business partners want and need more. Especially if markets involve suppliers, manufacturers, financing or labor entrenched in Islamic cultures, the business person seeking maximum satisfaction strives to understand the human geography of the operating environment and how to navigate through it.

Standard Westernized/Americanized templates for business negotiation "flatten" the human terrain, enforcing a false homogeneity. Explicit reference points to "landmarks" of Western clothing,

---

* **Phyllis E. Bernard** is a professor of law and director of the Center on Alternative Dispute Resolution at the Oklahoma City University School of Law. Her email address is phyllis_bernard@sbcglobal.net.

education, technology are taken as implicit assimilation of Western material values. Not so. Islamic values embedded in culture may shape the perceptions and conduct of persons who otherwise appear thoroughly secular.

Istanbul – straddling both Asia and Europe – offers an actual and metaphorical bridge between Eastern and Western cultures, non-Western spiritual traditions and Western modernity. The Western negotiator who can bridge intangible values across cultures will attain greater tangible results for long-term commercial ventures. However, most Western negotiation trainers feel ill-equipped to address such sensitive matters.

In an experiment for the Istanbul Rethinking Negotiation Teaching conference, two dozen conference participants met in small groups of three to five with moderate, relatively progressive Muslim businessmen in Istanbul to discuss whether and how their faith affected their commercial affairs. These dialogues were a new venue for outreach by the Institute for Interfaith Dialog for World Peace ("IID"), a Turkish-Muslim organization headquartered in Houston, Texas.

This chapter describes and contextualizes the dialogue in which this author and the co-editors of this book participated. To the extent feasible, I shall refer to experiences of other conference participants shared informally during and after the conference. Final thoughts offered include a second round of interviews addressing the primary issue that opens this chapter: namely, in a rough and tumble world of hard bargaining and sharp practices, is it misguided to assume faith-based values play a bona fide role?

Dialogues on Faith and Folly in Commerce

One must grant that among Jews, Christians and Muslims alike we find business people who profess religious principles they do not actually practice. This remains such a truism that standard negotiation training presumes party hypocrisy rather than sincerity. Impasse due to "a matter of principle" is deemed in reality impasse due to "a matter of money." Western negotiators generally assume that no one would make business decisions based upon faith, for that would be folly.

The Istanbul dialogues exposed Western negotiation trainers to a way of doing business that seeks a balance between faith and what skeptics would consider folly. Most businessmen in these dialogues were members of the Confederation of Turkish Businessmen, working with IID – all of whom are part of the sometimes controversial Gülen Movement. The movement's middle-of-the-road approach earns them few supporters. They are too devout to gain the confidence of secularists, yet too modernistic for radical Islamists. The leader of the movement, Mr. Fetullah Gülen, has embraced global peace and cooperation,[1] often placing him at odds with the views of powerful Turkish politicians and the military (Yavuz and Esposito 2003).

These businessmen fully engage in commerce with a wide array of global entities. On the surface their businesses – auto dealerships, textile manufacturing, food import and export, construction, mining, oil products – appear little different than any other highly Westernized, modern commercial undertaking. However, they operate their businesses according to values embedded in their faith and in traditional Islamic culture, which differ significantly from the core principles that typify the aggressive, commodity-oriented brand of Western business negotiation training.

Discussions with conference participants during the days after the dialogues, and this author's own follow-up interviews in Turkey, suggest that while devout, these businessmen are not "soft"; they can be demanding, yet fair.[2] They also recognize that not every prospective business partner will share their principles. As discussed later in this chapter, approaches to business negotiations may shift, depending upon orientation of the parties. When both parties seem ready to operate according to the traditional Islamic cultural values described in this chapter, negotiations may follow that path. When values diverge, the otherwise traditionally-oriented businessman shifts methods, and brings in the lawyers.

The central lesson or theme of the many dialogues and this author's follow-on interviews could probably be encapsulated through a saying attributed to the Prophet Muhammad: "Trust God, but tie your camel." Negotiate in good faith, but write a contract, especially when dealing with entities where the levels of trust and mutual understanding are not high.

For negotiation training, this represents a different orientation entirely: not idealism or pragmatism, but both. This requires more than changing a few exercises or role-plays. It asks for a change in the fundamental orientation of negotiation training.

Challenging the Standard Orientation of Negotiation Training

Stripped bare, the core principles that shape much of the most popular, interest-based, "get the most that you can" training in Western/American-style commercial negotiation can be summarized as follows:

1) Everything is negotiable.
2) Everything has a price.

3) The goal of negotiation is to identify the price both parties are willing to accept for a service or substance. It should be as low as possible for the buyer, and as high as possible for the seller.

Thus, negotiation trainers – consciously or not – fundamentally teach how to monetize the world. When something is not already overtly a commodity – to be bought, sold, traded – trainees learn how to make it so. Intangibles such as sentiment, loyalty, identity and values matter insofar as they can be manipulated to achieve the one goal that matters: the best price.

Next generation negotiation would retire the commodity-orientation, because not everything is negotiable. Not everything has a price. Sometimes a business person's values – including reputation and religion – matter more than price. Any price. The standard training orientation teaches how to negotiate – that is to say, how to lead people to compromise – personal values. We do this generally by assuming that such values have only illusory or manipulative significance. A shift in orientation would recognize that such values actually shape the business landscape. Cultural and religious values make meaning for international trading partners, whether the unstated implications of that meaning are fully appreciated, or not.

Cultural Reciprocity as a Key to Business Success

Americans and Western Europeans frequently observe that it is difficult for outsiders to enter the seemingly closed system of business relationships in Turkey and other Islamic cultures (Morris 2005). Established local commercial relationships appear insular, distrusting of outsiders. This chapter argues that these allegedly closed systems may be more permeable than they appear. For the Westerner open to learning about that "closed" system – doors can open. It begins by acknowledging and respecting the complex nature of cultural identity among persons in modern Islamic cultures.

Consider the observations of a French-Lebanese intellectual, Amin Maalouf, analyzing current discourse about identity. He notes that trust and openness increase among Middle Easterners when Westerners sincerely appreciate Islamic culture and traditions. Of course, the highest mark of appreciation occurs when Western business people speak the native tongue of the people with whom they seek to trade. A large number of Turkish business people know not only English, but several other languages (French, German, Russian, Bulgarian, Greek, and Arabic being typical). Few Americans or Western Europeans can claim the obverse.

Maalouf identifies the deeper layers of mistrust embedded in such lack of reciprocity: "If I study someone else's language, but he doesn't respect mine, to go on speaking his tongue ceases to be a token of amity and becomes an act of servitude and submission" (Maalouf 2000: 43). Most non-Western business people would not state this aloud. Yet, it remains as a silent, unacknowledged road-block to building sustainable commercial relationships.

Maalouf attempts to identify other interior, private roadblocks to successful globalization efforts; the sorts of things negotiators also seek to know. What groups does the person identify with in terms of religion, family, clan, music, literature, education, age cohorts? These factors create an internal subtext that may not be shared externally. Nevertheless, the various "belongings" a global business-person identifies with all matter and are, likely, indivisible.

Negotiation workshops cannot fully teach language, culture and history as part and parcel of a forty-hour, twenty-hour or even shorter training. However, next generation trainer-teachers can introduce the importance of respect and reciprocity with regard to cultural values embedded in faith traditions. The enlarged understanding of the trainer-teacher will manifest in how this workshop leader conducts feedback, observations, the set-up and debriefing of role-plays; it may also lead to new confidence in seeking opportunities for contextual learning. As much as anything else, the next generation teacher-trainer will lead by example.

The Negotiation Trainer as Leader, "Adapter" and Guide

Attaining these different goals asks the commercial negotiation trainer to reframe the very nature of the undertaking and his/her role. "Training" implies that negotiation consists of a mechanistic set of skills that can be learned through rote conditioning of demonstration and drill (Avruch 2009). Many workshops operate as if a single template can apply to most, if not all, transactions.

This template fails to address adequately the complexities and nuances especially of non-Western, indigenous and Islamic cultures. A capacity to recognize and accommodate the ineffable cannot be transmitted as part of a set of tactics. It is found instead in the additional insight the workshop leader can share if he or she is acquainted with the cultural landscape. The more familiar and direct the leader's exposure, the more alternative interpretations, nuanced problem-solving, and embodied, contextual learning the leader can offer in organizing exercises, debriefing role-plays, and providing feedback.

The basic sets of communication skills to be learned – stating, restating, framing and reframing to identify interests underlying stated positions – remain largely the same in first and next generation approaches. However, in the next generation they are transmitted through an enlarged understanding of issues now pigeonholed as "diversity." Abramson argues that "interests" are a culturally neutral concept, but that trainers need to be "consummate guests" – "flexible, open-minded and elicitive about local practices" (Abramson 2009: 296-297). One analogy familiar to international travelers might assist. Visualize the frequent dilemma of converting the electrical voltage common in one country to the voltage your own laptop computer or cell phone has been hardwired to accept as normal. An adapter converts the electrical power into a form that is usable.

Similarly, when considering the teachable skills for negotiating business deals, skills are skills, just as electricity is electricity – although abilities and knowledge are different. But, as with diverse international standards for electrical power, skills must be adapted to suit different environments. In negotiation workshops, the "converter" or "adapter" is the trainer; here, referred to as workshop leader. We teachers become suitable "adapters" by placing ourselves in environments where we become learners. Finding such environments may not be easy, but they exist.

Not Secular *or* Sacred, but Secular *and* Sacred

Some years ago, discussions about globalization usually accepted unquestioningly the theory that modernization (through international business deals) and secularization go hand in hand. Presumably, standardized templates of law and business practices would not only harmonize the law but eventually nullify the impact of religion. As the globalization theory went, faith would have little impact on commerce except perhaps among the less educated, less sophisticated, lower class masses.

Emerging reality has not tracked past theory. Globalization and modernity thrive in a secular world, while not requiring people to jettison cultural values rooted in religious tradition (Berger 1999). Many of the traditional patterns and rituals of commerce in modern Turkey reflect cultural norms inextricably interwoven with the tapestry of Islamic business ethics. To open doors to this lucrative international market, it is worthwhile to learn those norms; to create opportunities for both the workshop leader as adapter and workshop participants as contextual learners to give voice to the unspoken subtext of Islamic cultural values in business affairs.

Finding Suitable Forums for Dialogue

The pre-conference dialogues provided formal opportunities for informal discussions where teachers and scholars could become learners, asking questions that otherwise might seem intrusive, and allowing more revealing responses than would otherwise be considered polite. Afterwards, some participants described the dialogues as "moving," "illuminating," "one of the most powerful experiences" in memory. For most, if not all, the dialogues were a surprising, refreshing, often unsettling encounter with "the Other."

Included among the dialogue participants were self-described atheists, agnostics, lapsed and practicing Catholics, secular and observant Jews, devout and disaffected Protestants, some Zen practitioners, and many who would describe themselves as "spiritual" but not "religious." Smaller groups of three to five, accompanied by a Turkish translator from IID, traveled to one or another Istanbul business where they met members of Gülen local circles active with IID. (Most businessmen actually understood English, but felt more comfortable having a translator available.) These local circles among businessmen committed to the Gülen movement provide peer support in their social outreach. Further, the circles encourage adherence to a faith-inspired sense of business ethics that may not be shared by the general population.[3]

A key characteristic of businessmen inspired by the Gülen movement is the commitment to "quality education for the development of the human person and, simultaneously, for bringing Turkey into the modern era" (Ebaugh 2010: 52). Businessmen support these efforts through large and sustained donations that average ten percent of yearly income; with many persons contributing as much as one-third of their income to support Gülen schools, hospitals, and other activities to promote tolerance and modernization (Ebaugh 2010: 59).

At the request of this author, Dr. Orhan Osman, Director of the Raindrop Turkish House in Oklahoma City, arranged the dialogues, working long-distance through his contacts in Istanbul. The Istanbul IID dialogues were a unique extension of IID activities linking Oklahoma City and Turkey, in which this author had previously participated. While these dialogues fit the general mission of IID and the Gülen movement, nothing like this had previously been envisioned. The experiment was in many ways a mutual exercise in courage, trust and hope: courage to speak candidly in a secular state backed by a powerful military; trust that the dialogue would be heard with compassion and patience; hope that these personal engagements would have some positive impact.

Speaking Aloud the Silent Content of Business Customs

Much of the learning was contextual. Each group learned by experience the bedrock of Islamic business custom: hospitality. In Turkey, as throughout the Middle East, hospitality means far more than mere courtesy. It is an expression of sacred obligations dating to times that some believe even predated Islam. Further, in a time and place where the rule of law and even-handed law enforcement were virtually unknown, accepted norms of hospitality filled the gap. Even if parties were unsure about what external law should apply, everyone had a reasonably consistent understanding about what rituals of hospitality required – and that those norms would be enforced through the actions of clans, bonded by friendship to mutual protection.

Under Islam, however, these bonds and rituals gained enriched value. Hence, the "courtesies" of sharing tea are not merely secular, but also sacred. Embodied in the rituals of hospitality one sees fundamental principles seriously at odds with the supposedly core principles of negotiation enunciated earlier in this chapter. I would describe them as focusing on "three T's": 1) tempo; 2) tea; and 3) trust.

The tempo of negotiations is far slower than is usual in America and much of Western Europe. The pace allows time for parties to understand each other, their stated and unstated interests. The slower tempo allows time to consult with and consider the needs of others whose interests are affected by the transaction. Given time, the Western potential partner who believes they have all the answers may recognize that they have much to learn from their non-Western hosts. The slower pace creates opportunities for such learning. This mutual education will usually take place over cups of tea.

There are, of course, different ways to interpret this slower tempo and its role. For, inevitably, it places at a disadvantage the Western party who does not believe s/he has time "to waste," but instead needs to proceed on a faster schedule. Here, we gain insight into why some Westerners may feel shut out from Turkey's lucrative markets, while others find opportunities. As Maalouf pointed out in his observations on identity, the Westerner who cannot speak the local language, but at least tries to accommodate local customs, will be perceived more as a friend than as an interloper. The significance of friendship cannot be overstated.

Drinking tea is a central ritual establishing the business relationship. As described in the bestseller *Three Cups of Tea: One Man's Mission to Promote Peace...One School at a Time*, "The first time you share tea...you are a stranger. The second time you take tea, you are an honored guest. The third time you share a cup of tea, you become family, and for our family we are prepared to do anything, even die" (Mortenson and Relin 2006: 150). Drinking tea is more than imbibing a refreshment. It is a ritual filled with symbolic significance. The end-point of the ceremony is to understand whether, and to what degree, the parties can trust each other. It is a rite of negotiation.

Trust is the essential ingredient, without which no business will be conducted. The higher one's earned reputation for being reliable and trustworthy, the greater value the person's name can carry (note, however, the distinct kinds of trust discussed in Roberge and Lewicki, *Should We Trust*, in this volume.) All transactions are based upon trust, particularly since the commitment made extends far beyond the individual to that person's extended family and clan. The commitment to do business with a person steeped in these traditions extends much deeper than the understanding many Westerners bring to the table; at least some Westerners, however, operate on related principles. Consider, for example, the quiet but firm recognition among "old school" New York businessmen that "pride, reputation and good will" are important in negotiations and, "although...intangible,...are absolutely real" (Rose 2006: 714).

The Three T's in Action

The IID host of the particular small group I went with, Mr. Hossein Guzell, operates the family business Guzella, Inc., an international high fashion design and textile business. As did virtually all of the other pre-conference dialogue hosts, he taught by example, through "total immersion" – demonstrating the "three T's" in action. We observed many teaching moments, which he graciously explained.

But one key resource that I sought out was not displayed in a manner that facilitated easy access. It was a framed poster situated across from his desk, out of the line of sight for visitors, but directly in Mr. Guzell's own view. Translated from the Turkish, "I Say to Myself (The Way of Life)" articulated principles of servant leadership that many business people might recognize, including those from humanist Western, or observant Christian, or Jewish backgrounds (Beekun and Badawi 1999).

I shall discuss next how the principles articulated in this poster fit into the "three T's" of tempo, tea and trust.

Tempo

Two seemingly contrasting concepts demand equal respect: industriousness and neighborliness. "Be punctual, straightforward and just" (Osman, trans. 2010: line 4); "Work hard, be insistent, and look at the lives of those who are successful" (Osman, trans. 2010: line 11); "Don't waste your time. God doesn't like those who kill time" (Osman, trans. 2010: line 14). This suggests support for a tempo and profit-driven focus similar to the fast pace and goals of Western commerce.

Yet much more emphasis is placed on how to prioritize one's time, which also sets the pace to conduct work. The overarching guideline is to remember: "The things that you do today should serve today and tomorrow. The things that you do in this world should serve this world and hereafter" (Osman, trans. 2010: line 28). In today's world, one must take the time to serve others. It is seen not only as a duty, but as a source of happiness. "Live for the other more than yourself; happiness is a perfume that makes you more aromatic if you shower it on the ones around you" (Osman, trans. 2010: line 19).

These concepts are synthesized in the Turkish understanding of neighborliness, where persons are expected never to be in such a rush that they cannot take time to show caring and compassion for others no matter how "thin" the relationship may be. Virtually everyone acts in relationship to/with others. Acknowledging this interdependency renders business in Istanbul much more like business in rural America, where even if you do not know a person's name, you are expected to exchange greetings, engage in conversation, as a sign of respect and membership in the community (Honeyman 2007).

Tea

In a Western world that admires multi-tasking, where Tweets and text messages often constitute conversation among family members and intimate friends – the concept of taking time to give one human being undivided, face-to-face attention becomes less and less familiar. Yet, this is what the ritual of tea as part of business negotiations achieves. At the surface level, the lengthy process of drinking tea together carves out time and space for people to engage in mindful conversation. In this process people can begin to build relationships.

At a deeper level, the ritual of tea is a modern iteration of an ancient tradition, born from nomadic cultures where life depended upon mutual assistance, later reinforced and given a spiritual dimension by Islam. Groups that visited a Turkish business host were lavished with not only tea, coffee, soft drinks and pastries, but with full meals and gifts. This phenomenon is common throughout the Middle East, and was repeated with each pre-conference dialogue group. Often Westerners (including some conference participants) either take the hospitality for granted, or react skeptically, questioning whether it is merely a gimmick to lay the foundation for getting the best price.

Turkish generosity, however, springs both from sincerity and from the desire to be virtuous in the eyes of God. Hospitality is open-ended, not necessarily tied to a commercial result. That being said, generosity can work for commercial purposes (Chamoun and Hazlett

2009). Given that these particular businessmen are part of a movement marked thus far by tangible works of faith – highlighted by building and supporting schools for students of all ethnicities, clinics and promoting the education of females in developing nations around the globe – skepticism must reach a level of near-conspiracy theory. Moreover, shouldn't one at times simply accept a person and their culture on that person's own terms?

This may be difficult for some Westerners to accept, until they consider the deep roots of the modern practice of generous hospitality. Turkish oral traditions describe the underlying principle, which predates Islam: "If a stranger knocks at the door, s/he should be invited inside, given ample food and shelter for three days; and only at the end of three days should the cause of the visit be asked" (Ebaugh 2010: 68). A guest who arrives unexpectedly should be considered "a guest from God" (Ebaugh 2010: 69). The tradition is not unbounded. After three days a guest becomes family, and is expected to help with chores.

More frequent than the tradition of household hospitality that can confer family status upon guests, there is the third cup of tea, which similarly marks the crossing of a threshold. With the third cup of tea, the relationship, the trust has built to a point of mutual obligations that extend beyond merely completing the terms of a commercial contract. They mark bonds of unquestioned loyalty and integrity; levels of performance that few Western businesses contemplate in an ostensibly straightforward business deal.

How much should one rely upon these constraints, especially in regions famous not only for hospitality, but also for treachery? In a follow-up visit to Turkey, I addressed this issue directly with businessmen who were followers of Mr. Fetullah Gülen, but engaged in commerce in legendarily corrupt areas: construction and mining in Central Asia and Russia. Their answers blended idealism and pragmatism. I venture to summarize:[4]

1) You cannot do business with thieves, period. Even if a deal sounds enticing initially, over time the problems that inevitably arise will outweigh any benefits.
2) Therefore, you need to be ready to not do business at all in some areas. So be it. Short-term profits are not worth long-term regrets.
3) When dealing with persons who are merely "slippery," but not treacherous, do not take a step without good legal counsel.

Again, we see the theme: "Trust God, but tie your camel."

Trust

Trust in business deals in Turkey – and other Middle Eastern cultures – goes well beyond soft sentiment. Among other reasons, integrity is vital because traditionally transactions are handled based upon a person's word, their reputation. Cash is the preferred method for doing business. Thousands, even millions, of dollars will transfer from person to person across vast distances based solely upon a verbal request. How? Why? Because the sender knows that the receiver – and the receiver's family – will fulfill the obligation no matter what. It is difficult to imagine a Western business with the same expectations about commitments.

Trust serves as a guiding principle not only outside but inside the company. Most Western concepts of management do not contemplate trust within the corporation as a central feature of the business model. However, at Guzella it is.

The Guzella human resources model puts in action a consultative, shared notion of power in the workplace. It sounds nearly "New Age" but actually stems from a commitment to Islamic concepts of leadership. A leader, including an officer of a for-profit business, must fulfill a sacred duty of trust, whereby all decisions are made with an eye toward protecting the best interests of the entire organization, as a community. Indeed, one might go so far as to identify them as a family; albeit a family with over 700 members/employees.

The worldview shows in the vocabulary used; the value of the framing is something negotiators can appreciate. To paraphrase Mr. Guzell: "I do not call my employees 'workers' or 'employees.' I call them 'friend.' I eat what they eat. I believe in their honesty, so they believe in my honesty." He deals similarly with business colleagues, and has never been to court.

The Value of a Values-Orientation Instead of a Commodity-Orientation

The experiential learning obtained through the IID dialogues with Turkish businessmen was a rare opportunity. Still, key elements can be replicated in other settings. Because the "three T's" are so pervasive in Islamic cultures, a trainer should not have difficulty finding a Muslim professional, teacher or even graduate student willing to share their experiences: recreating the ritual of tea and hospitality during the training itself, while explaining the significance, should be possible.

Can learning how to have tea make enough difference to render it a valuable addition to commercial negotiation training? Does it matter enough to merit seeking out some of the many moderate Muslim organizations throughout North America whose mission is to promote better cross-cultural understanding? Especially when a trainer's own experiences run counter to the message of trust, should this even be attempted?

I found sufficient confirmation when participating in April 2010 at the TRADOC Culture Summit IV, supported by the Army's Training, Development & Support Directorate centered at Fort Huachuca, Arizona. This approach to building relationships in Islamic cultures – one cup of tea at a time – has become standard operating procedure for American operations in Iraq and Afghanistan. (For more on this theme, see Lira, *Design: The U.S. Army's Approach,* in this volume.) I asked several officers to help me understand why we – academics – are far more skeptical and slow to embrace these concepts. To condense the responses:[5]

> It's because for us, it's a matter of life and death. We *have to* stretch, to learn how these cultures do things, instead of just doing everything our way. In the early years of the Iraq war we lost a lot of good people – military and civilian, ours and theirs – because we didn't understand Islamic culture. We made a lot of costly mistakes. We don't intend to repeat those errors. At least, we're trying not to.

The book *Three Cups of Tea* and the principles articulated in it – largely the same principles underlying the Istanbul dialogues – are now standard reading for American troops deployed to Islamic countries, where the military negotiates much more than commercial arrangements. They use the principles to negotiate how to stay alive. Surely, if they deem this knowledge so valuable, it merits our full attention in teaching how to negotiate successful, sustainable arrangements for commercial ventures in Islamic cultures.

Conclusion

While the U.S. military may have made the shift (see Lira, *Design: The U.S. Army's Approach,* in this volume), many multinational businesses thus far seem content to continue with a status quo reliance on a standardized Western model of negotiation. Why then should a "Next Generation" model of negotiation training incorporate cultural norms that seem nearly anachronistic?

To answer this question, let me share the insights of Mr. Guzell concerning the typical approach of American multinationals, compared to the values he follows:

They have looked at the money, at financial gain as the measure of success, not giving due consideration to morals, values, people and relationships. A focus on money can only take you so far. And now such companies have maxed out. They've gone as far as a money model can take them. Now they are slipping backwards. They are having to relearn, restructure around these more lasting cultural values which have sustained other businesses for generations.

We, as teachers, must learn and then teach others how to navigate a human geography of embedded cultural values. Those values are real to the parties involved – even if we, personally, may not accept them as our own. The next generation of negotiation training will be defined, as much as anything else, by its capacity to encourage basic steps that demonstrate reciprocal respect for the other party's full and complex identity – instead of asking them to compromise what matters most.

Notes

[1] In a 2008 Foreign Policy/Prospect poll the Islamic/Sufi scholar Fetullah Gülen was voted "the world's top public intellectual," winning "in a landslide." Foreign Policy, August 2008 at 12.

[2] This became a topic of intense discussion in one workshop following the dialogues. At least one participant found a disconnect between perceptions of hospitality and relationship developed during the visits, and actual negotiations with the same business person later in the Spice Bazaar; i.e., shouldn't the prior relationship have translated into a lower price for purchases the next day? On the other hand, one could ask whether it was appropriate to apply insights offered "off the record" in the pre-conference dialogue to obtain special advantage later in the field exercise of bargaining for merchandise? This led to a valuable insight about subtle differences between "relationship" – as concerns business transactions – and "connection." One might further question, as described later in this chapter: Had the prior day's visit to the Spice Bazaar merchant's offices reached the point of "three cups of tea," or only one? Was the conference participant still a stranger – not a friend?

[3] Follow-up interviews conducted by this author sought and obtained specificity that concretized general statements in other texts about this. Business colleagues in the Gülen movement support not only the local Gülen-inspired school or college, but also support schools in particular countries overseas. They contribute money, personal time, and – it was stressed to me – prayers and friendship. One group may adopt a school in Angola, another group will choose a school in Haiti, and so on. These schools are open to all students, free of charge, so long as they and their parents are willing to set

aside traditional ethnic or religious animosities, to live and learn in a cooperative environment. They must also be willing to encourage the education of females and to take instruction from female teachers. As an example, businessmen of Kutahya (a rural city of fewer than 200,000 persons) contribute $15,000 (U.S.D.) per month to support a Gülen-inspired school in Kyrgyzstan. This school's mission is to educate a new generation of Kyrgyz, Uzbeks and Russians who will be less likely to tolerate or participate in long-standing violent conflicts. (Personal interviews with members of the Confederation of Turkish Businessmen in Kutahya: Suleyman Doğan, Husein Karakuzu, and founder of the Kyrgyzstan school, Suleyman Akkay, May 26, 2010.)

[4] Summary based on personal interviews with Süleyman Maltaş (Kutahya May 27, 2010); Metin Sağil and Eyup Kaynak (Istanbul May 25, 2010).

[5] Summary based on personal interviews with Col. Sonny Reeves, Director, Training, Development and Support Initiative; Lt. Col. M. Kevin May, Executive/Operations Officer, New Systems Training & Integration; and speech by Maj. General John M. Custer III, Commander, U.S. Army Intelligence Center at Ft. Huachuca (Tucson, Arizona, April 19-20, 2010).

References

Abramson, H. 2009. Outward bound to other cultures. In *Rethinking negotiation teaching: Innovations for context and culture*, edited by C. Honeyman, J. Coben and G. De Palo. St. Paul, MN: DRI Press.

Avruch, K. 2009. What is training all about? *Negotiation Journal* 25(2): 161-169.

Beekun, R. and J. Badawi. 1999. *Leadership: An Islamic perspective*. Beltsville, MD: Amana Publications.

Berger, P. 1999. *The desecularization of the world: Resurgent religion and world politics*. Washington, DC: Eerdmans.

Chamoun, H. and R. Hazlett. 2009. The psychology of giving and its effect on negotiation. In *Rethinking negotiation teaching: Innovations for context and culture*, edited by C. Honeyman, J. Coben and G. De Palo. St. Paul, MN: DRI Press.

Ebaugh, H. 2010. *The Gülen movement: A sociological analysis of a civic movement rooted in moderate Islam*. Dordrecht, Germany: Springer.

Honeyman, C. 2007. A sale of land in Somerset County. *Negotiation Journal* 23(2): 203-212.

Maalouf, A. 2000. *In the name of identity: Violence and the need to belong*. New York: Penguin Books.

Morris, C. 2005. *The new Turkey: The quiet revolution on the edge of Europe*. London: Granta Books.

Mortenson, G. and D. Relin. 2006. *Three cups of tea: One man's mission to promote peace...one school at a time*. New York: Penguin Books.

Osman, S. (trans). 2010. *I say to myself (The way of life)*. Author unknown.

Rose, D. 2006. Ulysses and business negotiation. In *The negotiator's fieldbook: The desk reference for the experienced negotiator*, edited by A. K. Schneider and C. Honeyman. Washington, DC: American Bar Association.

Yavuz, M. and J. Esposito (eds). 2003. *Turkish Islam and the secular state: The Gülen movement*. Syracuse, NY: Syracuse University Press.

ca 5 so

Can We Engineer Comprehensiveness in "Negotiation" Education?

Gwen B. Grecia-de Vera[*]

Editors' Note: Ever since the first ripostes to Roger Fisher's magnum opus, we have known that sometimes the people are the problem. Or maybe it was their education. Grecia-de Vera analyzes the prevailing attitude toward negotiation in the Philippines, a nation that has not yet adopted "Negotiation 1.0," and asks – Could countries in the Philippines' situation go straight to the better stuff, maybe, and skip over all the first-generation mistakes? Or are they condemned to repeat them?

Introduction

The existing state of "embedded" understanding of negotiation may vary greatly from one legal culture to another. When faced with a legal culture that has been particularly recalcitrant, this raises a question: must such a culture pass slowly through every stage of discovery of "1.0" negotiation elements, or could that process be speeded up?

An anecdotal but, I think, typical example of the current state of legal culture in one such country may be helpful. In a settlement process during the pre-trial stage of a dispute that had been in litigation before a Philippine court for over a year, the defendant, despite having a sufficient basis to resist the suit and ultimately succeed in her defense, decided to invite the plaintiff to negotiate. The defendant was aware that civil suits for money claims can remain pending in the Philippine courts for an average of eight years, and did not want to be burdened for such a period of time even if she were to be vindicated in the end. So she asked her lawyer to extend an invita-

---

[*] **Gwen B. Grecia-de Vera** is director of the Institute of International Legal Studies and an assistant professor at the University of the Philippines College of Law. Her email address is ggdevera@up.edu.ph.

tion to the plaintiff through the latter's lawyer, to meet and discuss a possible settlement over breakfast in a neutral place. With the plaintiff's consent and with the court's permission, the date, for what defendant and her lawyer thought would be one of perhaps two or three settlement meetings, was set.

Defendant and her counsel prepared for the breakfast meeting, and having had previous experience dealing with both plaintiff and her lawyer, the defendant took the initiative in letting her own lawyer know that she intended to be reasonable and to maintain her equanimity even if the plaintiff and her team proved to be difficult. On the morning of the meeting, both plaintiff and defendant arrived in good spirits and broke bread before commencing the discussion. When the negotiation began, plaintiff, through her lawyer, handed defendant a piece of paper with some figures. Plaintiff's lawyer said that they were willing to settle for less than half of the amount they were claiming provided defendant shouldered certain fees payable to the government (which the plaintiff failed to take care of while at the helm of the company they formed together). The figures on the piece of paper represented the amount in arrears and penalties imposable. Defendant and her lawyer nodded in tandem as they unfolded the piece of paper. They then asked for a few minutes to discuss privately by taking a separate table. Plaintiff immediately shot up from her seat to say,

> "Negosasyon ba 'to? 'Di ba kayo ang nagimbita? O, pumayag kami, tapos ngayon na may proposal kami kelangan pag-usapan niyo pa? Wala kayong balak makipag-ayos kung ganyan?" [Is this what you call a negotiation? Didn't you invite us to this meeting? We agreed to sit down with you. But now that we have a proposal you tell us you need to discuss it further? That tells us you don't intend to settle.]

Consistent with their plan to remain reasonable and patient, defendant's lawyer tried to explain that they were in the very thick of negotiating, having just received what they considered an offer, and needed only time to discuss whether it was acceptable or if they would like to make a counter-offer. She then dropped a few buzzwords associated with integrative or principled negotiation, hoping that plaintiff's lawyer at least would be familiar with them and react positively. She also calmly explained that never before that day had the arrears to the government been mentioned, and certainly it was only natural for defendant to want to consider their impact, to which plaintiff's lawyer responded that all defendant had to do was verify the amount. If the amount turned out to be accurate then defendant should pay, if she intended to negotiate. A further attempt by the defendant's lawyer to explain was dismissed curtly, followed by plaintiff and her lawyer's abrupt departure. The case stayed in trial for six years and was decided in favor of the defendant.[1]

Not Being Difficult, Just Not a Negotiator?

After having heard about this particular negotiation, I tried to understand the process that took place, and noted areas where defendant's lawyer could have been more effective in her role as lawyer representing a client in a negotiation of a dispute already in litigation. I thought of the steps I would take, and the tactics then available to the defendant, and the reasons why together defendant and her lawyer chose one rather than another. But, as generally happens in most legal negotiations (whether to settle a dispute or complete a transaction),[2] no actual negotiation debrief took place, even though this could have provided a wealth of information.

For the negotiation I describe, I initially assumed that plaintiff's lawyer was simply being "difficult" and had deliberately strayed from principled negotiation. Taking my own copy of *Getting to Yes* (Fisher, Ury, and Patton 1991: 17-18), I am reminded that, indeed, "negotiators are people first." And of "separating people from the problem" Roger Fisher and his colleagues said:

> If negotiators view themselves as adversaries in a personal face-to-face confrontation, it is difficult to separate their relationship from the substantive problem. In that context, anything one negotiator says about the problem seems to be directed personally at the other and is received that way. Each side tends to become defensive and reactive and to ignore the other side's legitimate interests altogether.

> A more effective way for the parties to think of themselves is as partners in a hardheaded, side-by-side search for a fair agreement advantageous to each (Fisher, Ury, and Patton 1991: 37).

But is it possible for parties in a legal negotiation[3] to think of themselves as partners (as if in a dance), if neither has ever had any exposure to negotiation theory and method?

The typology that has been developed over the last thirty years on kinds of negotiations (e.g., integrative and distributive) and types of negotiators (e.g., cooperative or competitive) makes it appear possible to neatly categorize either the process or the players, if not both, and therefore to think strategically in addressing positions or interests. But what if we are dealing with someone who does not know how to negotiate, who is engaged in the activity simply as herself, and who is acting without direction?[4] The typology does not help us here; this means what we perceive as tactics, deliberately employed under a distributive strategy, could really be merely a personal quirk, or a tantrum without any tactical objective. Worse, what if we are dealing with opposing counsel, who is not aware of negotiation principles and has agreed to negotiate (perhaps without caring to know what negotiation is or entails) as a tactic in itself (to delay proceedings, for example)? What do we do then, and is it fair to leave the process and possible settlement in her hands?

I will not attempt to answer these questions[5] in this reflection piece, but only to explore the impact they have in the narrow context of legal negotiation, both as a mode of putting an end to litigation and in the transactional setting. I will do so specifically in reference to various legal negotiations in the Philippines that have been described to me, exclusively among local counterparts,[6] and in relation to the effort of developing second generation global negotiation education. I will begin with the idea of negotiating in bad faith based on E. Allan Farnsworth's (1987) discussion, and address briefly why it has particular resonance for those in the legal profession, to highlight the importance of making negotiation part of legal education and continuing professional development. I will then turn to some initiatives that could form part of "Negotiation 2.0." In closing, I will turn to the potential role of the Rethinking Negotiation Teaching project in jurisdictions similar to the Philippines, where apart from revisiting the integrative negotiation classroom and formulating 2.0 negotiation teaching, the work ahead appears to require promoting the study of negotiation, both theory and skills, and including "Negotiation 1.0." I will argue not only for courses in negotiation to be part of every lawyer's basic training, but for knowledge of negotiation to positively inform personal and professional conduct in relation to the law.

Learning How to Negotiate: Should Lawyers Care?

In an informal survey conducted among participants to a consultative meeting conducted in late 2009 as an initial effort at exploring negotiation practice and pedagogy in the Philippines,[7] a good number replied that they engaged in negotiation daily – whether at home, in the office, or as part of what they do. Lawyer-participants, in particular, stated that they regularly took part in negotiations for their work in companies or in firms. Two law firm partners, one who heads his firm's litigation department and another who leads the banking department, confirmed the importance of having "negotia-tion skills" as lawyers, and said that they appreciated younger law-yers who possess "negotiation skills." But neither of their firms invests in in-house training or professional development costs for negotiation training.[8] When asked further about what they thought were "excellent" negotiation skills, invariably the answer was tied to "bringing home a winning deal (for litigation)" or "getting what the client wanted." Two other lawyers who were regularly engaged as in-house counsel in transacting supplier deals at least used the term "win-win." The jargon of integrative negotiation did not appear widespread, and its total absence in some of the conversations I had indicated to me that while integrative negotiation is not without adherents, formal negotiation training has not gained traction in the Philippine law community, whether as part of the law school cur-riculum or as part of professional development initiatives.[9]

In further conversations, stories emerged of lawyers walking away from a negotiation, and not necessarily towards their clients' best alternative to a negotiated agreement (BATNA), particularly in processes involving disputes in litigation. Let us take the story with which I began this reflection. The lawyer who shared it with me (without of course disclosing particulars such as the identity of the parties) felt she would have no qualms about walking away from a negotiation, even if it would appear unseemly. When I asked about the possibility of her conduct rendering her client liable for having engaged in bad faith negotiation, she shrugged it off, saying that a cause of action for the purpose cannot be made out under Philippine law. Since having that conversation, I learned that in other jurisdic-tions, the act of walking away from negotiations may lead to an as-sessment of damages against the negotiating party who breaks off the process, for having engaged in negotiation "without serious in-terest" (Farnsworth 1987: 11).[10]

As of this writing, a survey of Philippine Supreme Court cases and academic writing does not disclose support for such bad faith negotiation claims. But if the Human Relations provisions of the Philippines New Civil Code are considered (Republic Act No. 386: articles 19-21), it would seem that a cause of action for bad faith negotiation, particularly in the context of transactional negotiation, can be made.[11] To the extent then that there is potential liability on the part of the negotiating party for bad faith negotiation, with pos-sible adverse consequences upon a client and her interests, it seems irresponsible to advise on and engage in negotiations without the benefit of previous experience, basic education (delivered at the law school) or adequate training. There is also another reason for law-yers to pay close attention to their participation in negotiation.

Thinking about and training in negotiation, even for lawyers who will not be engaged in negotiations, encourages self-awareness that can inform professional conduct. As negotiation thinking progresses in different areas, including psychology (see, e.g., Birke and Fox 1999; Korobkin and Guthrie 2004), neuroscience (see, e.g., Yarn and Jones 2004; Birke 2010), and game theory (see, e.g., Sally and Jones 2006), ideas emerge that can be helpful for the legal profession. Take for example the challenge of "rigorous investigation into one's own actions, skills, and behavioral patterns" proposed by Scott Peppet and Michael Moffitt to those seeking to improve themselves as negotiators (Peppet and Moffitt 2006: 617). While my examples here are from the Philippines, I submit that similar considerations may apply in numerous countries. Thus, the need for a lawyer's better negotiation training can arise out of the law itself, rendering the typical lawyer's disinterest intellectually and professionally bankrupt.

Formulating the Negotiation Curriculum for the Law School

While there may be legal foundation for finding a negotiating party liable for, among other things, engaging in negotiation without serious intent to reach an agreement, it may not be consistent with ideas of fairness to impose such liability in jurisdictions where legal negotiation processes may not be informed by contemporary negotiation theory and education (i.e., where negotiation is absent from the law school curriculum) and where even what constitutes negotiation may not be consistently understood.[12] Considering Metro Manila alone, only one law school offers a course in negotiation.[13] A lawyer who thinks he would benefit from taking an executive training seminar on negotiation, meanwhile, would as yet have very few options.[14]

Thinking of negotiation in "2.0 terms" means, to me, taking into consideration where negotiation education has yet to be introduced as applicable (e.g., in law schools, business schools) and taking the opportunity to design appropriate curriculum models, which perhaps may require challenging current models. Moffitt (2004) noted, as part of his research, that in more than 100 American law schools' curricular offerings related to negotiation, most cited skills development as the primary focus of the course. If this focus persists today, then perhaps 2.0 thinking should also place emphasis on principles, theory, and culture, among other elements.

Training Professionals to Guide Negotiation Processes

If typical lawyers do not receive negotiation education or training, what can they do to prevent either lack of knowledge, experience or skill from impeding the process of negotiation? During a casual exchange on our negotiation experiences, a friend (also a lawyer) remarked that he learned in a two-day, executive-type seminar about how to deal with a negotiator who employs distributive bargaining. When he finished describing the prescription given to manage the distributive negotiator, we both had the same questions. What if the distributive negotiator was immune to every countermeasure already devised? What if our counterparty had never before picked up a single article or book on negotiation or attended a training course on negotiation? What if she is just being herself, and does not subscribe to any theory of negotiation? Neither of us had picked up advice on how to deal with a "non-negotiator" tasked to negotiate. Setting aside our concern on how much it might cost, is there a professional who can help those negotiating and who think they are negotiators to actually engage in a negotiation?

While in Istanbul I had occasion to bring up this question in separate conversations with conference colleagues Manon Schonewille (of the Netherlands) and Dana Potockova (Czech Republic). I shared with them that in the Philippines, mediation is considered as synonymous with "assisted negotiation" (Tabucanon 2010: 43)[15] and that one possible bit of advice to the lawyer who needs help during actual negotiations is to seek third party intervention, perhaps through mediation. But mediation has its own set of issues in the Philippine context[16] and may not be the optimal form of intervention where the basic problem is that a process that is intended to be a negotiation falls into the hands of legal professionals who have either no previous experience in negotiating that type of dispute or transaction or no previous training in negotiation at all.

This is where the possibility of auxiliary professionals in the field of negotiation becomes relevant. However, apart from mediators, I have not encountered anyone trained specifically for intervention in the Philippines. There are negotiation trainers who extend some guidance to lawyers (particularly those involved in the negotiation of public issues), but the assistance comes before the negotiation takes place. What I have in mind are auxiliary professionals who not only provide training pre-negotiation, but who can be called upon to provide assistance while the negotiations are taking place.

Bernard Mayer, author of *Beyond Neutrality: Confronting the Crisis in Conflict Resolution* (2004), provides a framework for understanding the roles that these auxiliary professionals, whom he calls conflict specialists or conflict engagement specialists, can assume in order to help parties engage in constructive conflict. As identified by Mayer, the three broad categories of roles that can be played by conflict specialists are ally roles, third-party roles and system roles. Allies assume non-neutral functions in which they assist particular parties to engage more effectively. Third party roles, such as facilitators, mediators, fact finders, evaluators or arbitrators, involve neutrals who extend assistance to conflicting parties in engaging more effectively. System roles may be potentially neutral or non-neutral; these refer to case managers, trainers, and researchers, and impact the system and culture in which a dispute takes place.

Ally Roles

Advocate[17]

Mayer further suggested that there are many ways in which one can assume an ally role. He considered four approaches. One is as advocate, whose goal is to help people engage effectively and powerfully in conflict. A distinguishing characteristic of this approach to the ally role is that the advocate provides a voice for the disputant (Mayer 2004: 224). While advocacy has been traditionally associated with legal representation, there are other types of advocates such as diplomats, union representatives, community organizers and victims' advocates. An example provided by Mayer is the community organizer. He described organizers as working on all sides of issues and in many arenas and as "key players in allowing a conflict to develop and have a lot to do with whether a conflict process unfolds in a constructive manner." They play an "essential role in articulating issues, framing the story of a dispute, defining the parties, and developing an engagement strategy" (Mayer 2004: 226).

Strategist

The strategist role assumes the specific task of helping design a strategy for how to approach a conflict. It may require substantive expertise. The role as described by Mayer is broad enough to incorporate many specific activities, but he identified the following as key (Mayer 2004: 230):

1) Conducting conflict analyses;
2) identifying the pros and cons of alternative approaches to engagement;
3) planning how to pursue a strategic approach; and
4) assessing how an engagement process is going and how to modify it.

Coach

Mayer's articulation of the coach role includes personal coaches, executive coaches, leadership coaches, among others. While the term "coaching" has different meanings, the common conception of the term involves helping individuals achieve goals, whether personal or professional. Differentiating this role from other conflict specialist roles is its "primary focus on helping people develop their competence to engage in conflict effectively" (Mayer 2004: 233).

Third Party Roles

Mayer postulates that third party neutrals, while traditionally looked upon as being engaged to resolve a conflict, may be utilized instead to contain conflict and to design processes, within which issues, differences, even animosity and anger, may be allowed to surface as part of paving the way for the parties to be engaged effectively.

System Roles

System roles, such as that assumed by a corporation's ombudsman or a project's evaluator, help promote what Mayer calls a "culture of constructive conflict" (Mayer 2004: 243). According to Mayer,

> All of the system roles have in common that they are at least in part intended to ensure that an organization, agency, or program allows for effective conflict processes. Some system roles are focused on design and creation of approaches to conflict (process design, dispute system design, and system adviser). Some are oriented toward system maintenance and operation (ombudsperson, case manager, conflict program administrator) and some to system feedback and review (research, evaluation, and system consultant) (Mayer 2004: 244).

As an example of what the auxiliary professional or conflict specialist can do, Peter S. Adler, President of the Keystone Center, has described[18] developing a "study" format, where those who ought to be negotiating an issue, but who are reluctant to participate in negotiation, are drawn to a "pre-bargaining" table by an invitation to "study" the problem or dispute.

These seem to me to be types of professional and third party intervention that might work where lawyers without adequate background are constrained to negotiate with each other. I would argue, then, that "Negotiation 2.0" should be broadly enough construed within the Philippines, and perhaps elsewhere, that it can serve also as a platform for looking at identifying those who may have experience as conflict specialists,[19] and establishing not only a community of practice, but also a program. In such a program, they could assist in providing specific training in assuming any of the roles described by Mayer; help in developing models of intervention to aid lawyers in undergoing the process of negotiation in the legal context; and perhaps, help them learn and train on the job.

Conclusion: A 2.0 Environment – Negotiation in Legal Education

In places such as the Philippines, some lawyers are surprised to learn that negotiation scholars from other parts of the world are rethinking Western models, particularly the interest-based approach – for the simple reason that not even "Negotiation 1.0" has yet been taught in the law schools. Perhaps a "2.0 initiative" should be to promote negotiation education and training in general, i.e., in a comprehensive context along with ancillary forms of practice as described above. With "2.0 thinking" stretching our minds to consider questions on both the substance of education and training and the methodology – including culture, emotions, language and adult learning models – this is a opportune time not only to design law school negotiation classes and executive-type negotiation courses to introduce the basic development of negotiation principles. Along with these, if they are to be successful in the Philippines and similar countries on a much faster pace of development than by repeating a whole generation of Western practice, we need to focus on the challenges to current models, explore the role of indigenous modes of dispute resolution, identify communities of practice in related fields (such as peace studies and conflict management), and evaluate the other new thinking that is going into the design of "Negotiation 2.0."

It is important, in other words, to consider negotiation education not only as a way of obtaining a particularized new set of skills to add to those we already possess as lawyers, but as an opportunity to see and work with the whole picture of conflict. What is needed is to make the principles of negotiation and conflict management so integrated into law education that they truly inform the practice of the legal profession.

Notes

[1] The narration is based on an actual case as described to me by a colleague. As far as I now know, the case is still on appeal before the Philippine Court of Appeals.

[2] The term legal negotiation is used here to refer to a narrow set of negotiations involving either: a) a dispute that is pending before the regular courts of the Philippines, where the parties are in negotiations principally through their respective counsels of record for the possible settlement of the case (particularly those involving collection of debt, monetary claim and/or contract breach); or b) a transaction or deal, typically a sale of goods, rendition of services, or licensing.

This is a functional definition for this reflection piece. Full exploration of the range of practices constituting legal negotiation in the Philippines merits separate articulation. In other jurisdictions, particularly the United States, specific courses on legal negotiation have been developed, and differences between negotiation in general and legal negotiation have been explored. Here the term is used also to isolate the process from related studies, such as those involving peace processes and indigenous modes of dispute settlement. Cultural aspects that can be drawn from the example provided will not be discussed here, although it is certainly a significant part of considering designs for the negotiation classroom in the Philippines.

One basic difference that has been pointed out is that legal negotiations involve "not only a relationship between two negotiating attorneys, but also relationships between each lawyer and her respective client" (Gifford 1989: 3).

[3] It is useful to note that in legal negotiation involving a dispute pending adjudication, participating lawyers become involved in negotiation as advocates and adversaries. As Michael Moffitt (2004: 101) pointed out:

> Almost all legal negotiations involve clear distributive issues (e.g., who gets how much money) and opportunities to create or destroy value (e.g., by expanding the scope of the agreement to include other terms). Many legal negotiations also involve complex ongoing relationships (e.g., joint venture agreements or parenting plans between divorcing spouses).

[4] "People rarely act randomly" (Peppet and Moffitt 2006: 619-620) and particular action may be guided by either "theories in action," or "explicit 'rules' that we hold about how the world works, and how to act within it" or "theories in use" – those implicit rules of action which in practice govern what we do, but which we do not admit to, or which sometimes we are only dimly aware of. This thinking must form part of designing the 2.0 class.

[5] There are other questions that the scenario described raises within the context of law practice in the Philippines and the role of lawyers in legal negotiation. The questions presented here are among the few that I shared with Istanbul Conference colleagues Manon Schoneville and Dana Potockova, as I explored the availability of resources to better prepare lawyers for legal negotiation. I hope to write further on the other questions such as professional responsibility in the context of conducting negotiations within the Philippine setting.

[6] I will not discuss here the unique dynamics of negotiation with foreign negotiation partner-lawyers, and negotiating public issues.

[7] In *A Look at a Negotiation 2.0 Classroom*, also in this volume, Salvador P. Panga, Jr. and I share that in preparation for our participation in the Istanbul Conference, we organized a consultative meeting for the purpose of exploring negotiation practice and pedagogy in the Philippine setting.

[8] Indeed, it is possible, as observed by Peppet and Moffitt (2006), that there is some belief that negotiation is learned through experience, by actual and constant involvement in negotiations – whether at home, in the workplace, in our personal purchases or during our representation of clients. But the same authors also observe that "simply having more experience negotiating does not necessarily make someone a better negotiator" (Peppet and Moffitt 2006: 615). Neither does reading about negotiation theories, it seems. This highlights the importance of devoting some thinking to how to improve our ability to engage in negotiation and/or to assist others to do so.

[9] This very preliminary finding gains significance when I consider the local commercial contracts I have reviewed. In not a few of these contracts, dispute resolution clauses often include "executive negotiation" as an initial step towards resolution. While intended to take the dispute away from operations where it might have started and allow cooler heads to intervene, in the person of higher company officials or executives, the contemplated negotiation is likely to take place with the help of lawyers or, in some instances, exclusively between the parties' lawyers.

[10] See, e.g., Markov v. ABS Transport & Storage Co., 457 P. 2d. 535 (Wash. 1969), which provides a framework for understanding how a claim may be made against one who walks away from the negotiation. In this case, the Supreme Court of Washington said that the lessor had fraudulently promised to renew the lease and to negotiate the amount of rentals in good faith. The lessor misrepresented to the lessee that it intended to renew the lease, while it was at the same time negotiating a sale with another party. The motive of the lessor was to have the premises occupied during negotiations with the potential purchaser, so that if the sale fell through, the lease could be renewed. Since a representation of a serious intent to reach agreement is implicit in the act of negotiating (Farnsworth 1987: 11), the rationale of Markov finds relevance even in the absence of explicit representation and supports recovery in the following scenarios: a) if a party enters into negotiations without serious intent to reach agreement; b) if a party, having lost that intent, continues in negotiations; or c) if a party, having lost that intent, fails to give prompt notice of its change of mind. Farnsworth adds that this may apply to a misrepresentation by nondisclosure, which upon being discovered caused negotiations to fail.

[11] The applicable Human Relations provisions of Republic Act No. 386 or the New Civil Code of the Philippines are as follows:

> Art. 19. Every person must, in the exercise of his rights and in the performance of his duties, act with justice, give everyone his due, and observe honesty and good faith.
> Art. 20. Every person who, contrary to law, willfully or negligently causes damage to another, shall indemnify the latter for the same.

Art. 21. Any person who willfully causes loss or injury to another in a manner that is contrary to morals, good customs or public policy shall compensate the latter for the damage.

[12] Consider our reference story at the beginning of this reflection, where plaintiff and plaintiff's lawyer understood negotiation as taking place only if the other party accepts the offer. Any resistance, no matter how slight or reasonable, immediately serves to indicate that there never was a negotiation.

[13] Based on a brief interview with the professor offering the course, there is no prescribed text. Simulations form a significant portion of the course, with case studies drawn from various sources and revised for use in the particular classroom. This information was obtained in the course of an informal survey of law and business schools in Metro Manila, made preparatory to the consultative conference organized by the Institute of International Legal Studies (see note 7). The Institute staff was informed by at least one business school representative that it is possible that negotiation, whether theory or practice, is discussed as part of substantive courses, such as sales and business transactions.

[14] A program regularly offered is a two-day course entitled "Learning the Art of Negotiation" run by the Center for Continuing Education of the Ateneo de Manila University Graduate School of Business. See www.cce.ateneo.edu (last accessed June 22, 2010). Also available is an executive type course offered by Guthrie-Jensen Consultants Inc. See www.guthriejensen.com (last accessed June 22, 2010). While the cost would be considered prohibitive by most lawyers, the fact that only two courses are available for a metro population of some 20 million is remarkable. We have not had the opportunity to conduct a similar survey for areas outside of Metro Manila.

[15] It is helpful to review here that "[a]lthough the ultimate objective of mediation is the same as arbitration – to resolve the dispute – the major difference is that mediation seeks to achieve the objective by having the parties themselves develop and endorse the agreement. In fact, mediation has been called a form of 'assisted negotiation'" (Susskind and Cruikshank 1987: 1360), an "an extension and elaboration of the negotiation process" (Moore 1996: 8), and an "informal accompanist of negotiation" (Wall and Blum 1991: 284). Mediation can help reduce or remove barriers to settlements, adding value to the negotiation process because it tends to produce or enhance much of what the parties desire and value in negotiation itself (Lewicki, Barry, and Saunders 2010: 529).

[16] Pursuant to the Philippines Supreme Court Resolution A.M. No. 01-10-5-SC-PHILJA issued in 2001, and in line with the objectives of the Action Program for Judicial Reforms (APJR) to decongest court dockets, among others, a court-referred mediation program was introduced in the Philippines. With respect to disputes pending litigation, one current consequence is that mediation is currently seen as something associated with the judicial process. This has not helped it attract voluntary support among lawyers. The typical lawyer's initial concern of a drop in revenue (seen in many countries in the initial stages of mediation development in legal settings,

until enough lawyers figure out how to derive revenue from it) also has yet to be overcome in the Philippines.

[17] Mayer uses the following to define an advocate: "An advocate is the representative of one particular interest in actual or potential conflict with others, and it is not his duty to define the collective well-being of those involved or to determine how it can be achieved. The advocate's job as most people see it, is simply to get as much as he can for his client." (Mayer 2004: 251, citing Kronman 1993: 147).

[18] Multi-Stakeholder Processes and Water Governance in Asia: Lessons and Next Steps, held January 28-29th, 2010.

[19] I have been informed that there may be Philippine scholars and/or professionals, working specifically on peace processes, who have prepared studies on intervention and third party participants whose roles may be comparable to those assumed by Mayer's conflict specialists. As of this writing, I am still trying to identify these scholars and to locate their work.

References

Birke, R. 2010. Neuroscience and settlement: An examination of scientific innovations and practical applications. *Ohio State Journal on Dispute Resolution* 25: 477-529.

Birke, R. and C. R. Fox. 1999. Psychological principles in negotiating civil settlements. *Harvard Negotiation Law Review* 4: 1-57.

Craver, C. 2005. *Effective legal negotiation and settlement,* 5th edn. Albany, NY: Matthew Bender & Company.

Craver, C. 2002. *The intelligent negotiator.* New York: Three Rivers Press.

Farnsworth, E. A. 1987. Precontractual liability and preliminary agreements: Fair dealing and failed negotiations. *Columbia Law Review* 87: 217-294.

Fisher, R., W. Ury, and B. Patton. 1991. *Getting to yes: Negotiating agreement without giving in,* 2nd edn. New York: Penguin.

Fisher, R. and D. Shapiro. 2005. *Beyond reason: Using emotions as you negotiate.* New York: Penguin Group.

Gifford, D. G. 1989. *Legal negotiation theory and applications.* St. Paul, MN: West Publishing Co.

Korobkin, R. 2008. Against integrative bargaining. *Case Western Reserve Law Review* 58: 1323-1342.

Korobkin, R. and C. Guthrie. 2004. Heuristics and biases at the bargaining table. In *The negotiator's fieldbook: The desk reference for the experienced negotiator,* edited by A. K. Schneider and C. Honeyman. Washington, DC: American Bar Association.

Kritzer, H.M. 1986. The Lawyer As Negotiator: Working in the Shadows (Working Paper # 4). University of Wisconsin – Madison Law School Institute of Legal Studies.

Lewicki, R., B. Barry and D. Saunders. 2010. *Negotiation. Intl. edn.,* 6th edn. Boston: McGraw-Hill.

Mayer, B. 2004. *Beyond neutrality: Confronting the crisis in conflict resolution*. San Francisco: Jossey-Bass.

Mayer, B. 2006. Allies in negotiation. In *The negotiator's fieldbook: The desk reference for the experienced negotiator*, edited by A. K. Schneider and C. Honeyman. Washington, DC: American Bar Association.

Menkel-Meadow, C. 1997. When dispute resolution begets disputes of its own: Conflicts among dispute professionals. *UCLA Law Review* 44: 1871-1933.

Moffitt, M. 2004. Lights, camera, begin final exam: Testing what we teach in negotiation courses. *Journal of Legal Education* 54: 91-114.

Moore, C. 1996. The mediation process, 2nd edn. San Francisco, CA: Jossey-Bass.

Palmer, M. 2000. Problem-solving negotiation – What's in it for you...and your clients. *Vermont B. Journal* 26 (Oct.): 21-26.

Peppet, S. R. and M. Moffitt. Learning how to learn to negotiate. In *The negotiator's fieldbook: The desk reference for the experienced negotiator*, edited by A. K. Schneider and C. Honeyman. Washington, DC: American Bar Association.

Republic Act No. 386 (1941), or the New Civil Code of the Philippines.

Sally, D. F. and G. T. Jones. 2006. Game theory behaves. In *The negotiator's fieldbook: The desk reference for the experienced negotiator*, edited by A. K. Schneider and C. Honeyman. Washington, DC: American Bar Association.

Schneider, A. and C. Honeyman (eds). 2006. *The negotiator's fieldbook: The desk reference for the experienced negotiator*. Washington, DC: American Bar Association.

Susskind, L. and J. Cruikshank. 1987. *Breaking the impasse: Consensual approaches to resolving public disputes*. New York: Basic Books, Inc. USA.

Tabucanon, G. 2010. *Mediation manual for Barangay and Lupon officials*. Manila: Rex Bookstore, Inc.

Thompson, L. 2008. *The truth about negotiations*. Saddle River, NJ: FT Press.

Yarn, D. H. and G. T. Jones. 2006. In our bones (or brains): Behavioral biology. In *The negotiator's fieldbook: The desk reference for the experienced negotiator*, edited by A. K. Schneider and C. Honeyman. Washington, DC: American Bar Association.

Wall, J. A. and M. W. Blum. 1991. Negotiations. *Journal of Management* 17(2): 273-303.

⚝ 6 ⚝

Ancient Wisdom for the Modern Negotiator:
What Chinese Characters Have to Offer
Negotiation Pedagogy

Andrew Wei-Min Lee[*]

Editors' Note: In a project that from its inception has been devoted to second generation updates, it is instructive nonetheless to realize how much we have to learn from the past. We believe Lee's chapter on Chinese characters and their implications for negotiation is groundbreaking. With luck, it will prove to be a harbinger of a whole variety of new ways of looking at our field that will emerge from our next round of discussion.

Introduction

To the non-Chinese speaker, Chinese characters can look like a chaotic mess of dots, lines and circles. It is said that Chinese is the most difficult language in the world to learn, and since there is no alphabet, the struggling student has no choice but to learn every single Chinese character by sheer force of memory – and there are tens of thousands!

I suggest a different perspective. While Chinese is perhaps not the easiest language to learn, there is a very definite logic and system to the formation of Chinese characters. Some of these characters date back almost eight thousand years – and embedded in their make-up is an extraordinary amount of cultural history and wisdom.

---

[*] **Andrew Wei-Min Lee** is founder and president of the Leading Negotiation Institute, whose mission is to promote negotiation pedagogy in China. He also teaches negotiation at Peking University Law School. His email address is andrewlee008@gmail.com. This article draws primarily upon the work of Feng Ying Yu, who has spent over three hundred hours poring over ancient Chinese texts to analyze and decipher the make-up of modern Chinese characters.

This chapter looks at nine Chinese characters that are related to negotiation and analyzes how they are written and why they are written that way. It proposes that a deeper understanding of the formation of Chinese characters can enrich the field of negotiation pedagogy. This article has three parts: Part A introduces some background knowledge of Chinese characters. How long ago did they evolve? How are they formed? And how have they changed and become simplified over the years? Part B looks at nine Chinese characters related to the field of negotiation: "negotiation," "co-operation," "conflict," "dispute," "compromise," "relationship," "forgive," "mediation," and "crisis." Why are these characters written in the way they are, and what does that mean? Part C considers four avenues through which understanding these characters might enrich the field of negotiation pedagogy.

Part A: Background Knowledge About Chinese Characters

Historical Evolution of Chinese Characters (6000 Years in the Blink of an Eye)

A comprehensive history of the evolution of Chinese characters is beyond the scope of this article – especially given that some historians trace Chinese characters back to before 6000 BC. However, it is illuminating to have a basic understanding of the history and amount of time that has gone into developing the Chinese character language form.

The earliest *generally accepted* set of characters was found in He'nan province, in the center east of China (Rincon 2003). Strategically located around the Yellow River, He'nan (whose name itself translates to "south of the Yellow River") is referred to as the cradle of Chinese civilization and the tortoise shell carvings found in this region date to around 6600 BC (Longwen 2009).

Chinese history texts refer to a golden age of cultural development during the Xia dynasty of around 2100 BC, during which great poetry and music were composed and literary masterpieces were written.[1] However, since no documents have survived from this period, claims are difficult to verify (Allan 1991).

The earliest *undisputed* set of characters is the set known as the "Oracle Bones" (甲骨文) of 1250 BC, which were once used by the Shang dynasty royalty to divine the future (in a broadly similar way to the "Tarot cards" of the West) (Boltz 1986: 436). Popular history tells of a government official who, in 1899, discovered strange inscriptions on animal bones used in the Chinese medicine being used to treat his cold (Xianghong 2009: 55). A scholar of ancient texts, he recognized that these inscriptions were ancient Chinese characters, and he mounted a campaign to oppose the use of these bones by doctors and instead preserve these bones for study. Today, over 100,000 bone fragments have been found and approximately 1,400 distinct ancient Chinese characters identified.

Between 1250 BC and 220 BC, different social groups began to emerge throughout different parts of China, each with its own "script" or writing style (Xianghong 2009: 60). Similar but not identical, each script was said to have its own unique cultural and geographic characteristics, e.g., the characters of the Chu were considered "vivid and flamboyant" whereas the characters of the Qin were "tidy and organized" and easily carved into a seal (earning it the title of the "seal script") (Xianghong 2009: 60).

In 221 BC, one social group, the Qin, succeeded in conquering all the others and uniting China – forming the Qin Dynasty. As part of its rulership, the Qin prescribed one unified writing style to be used throughout the whole country. From this point forward, historians generally accept that there was a formal set of "Chinese characters" (Xianghong 2009: 60).

How are Chinese Characters Formed?

Chinese characters are formed by assembling smaller elements known as "radicals." There are 214 generally accepted radicals. Some radicals are as basic as one vertical stroke or two horizontal lines. Many radicals however are more advanced and hold greater meaning.

One set of radicals, the "pictograms," are graphical representations of a "thing," e.g., the radicals for "sun," "moon" and "mountain" all are based on (quite stylized) pictures of a sun 日, a moon 月 and a mountain 山. Pictograms are radicals that often represent the most simple and basic of nouns.

Another set of radicals, the "Ideograms," are graphical representations of a "concept" e.g., the character for "up" is an arrow pointing up 上 and the character for "down" is the opposite 下. The character for "big" is a man with his arms and legs spread wide 大. The character for "small" is a man with his arms and legs held close to his body 小.

By combining radicals together, a character is given form and meaning. For example, the "water" radical of three dots arranged in a vertical line is used in the characters for lake 湖, river 河 and tears 泪. The radical for "mouth," which is similar to a square, is used in the characters for eat 吃, sing 唱 and drink 喝. The radical for "female," a stylized symbol of a pregnant woman nursing a child, is used in the characters for mother 妈, sister 姐 and peace 安 (the character for peace is made up of the radical for "ceiling" over the radical for "female" – suggesting that a female under the ceiling and in the room brings peace).

The original assembly of characters was often done with extraordinary thought and poetic consideration. For example, the character "flight" 飛 was made up of the radical for a mother bird leading a baby bird, above a bridge which crosses a river. The character "love" 愛 came from the radical for "placement" combined with "heart" over "friendship." The character "rest" 休 comes from "man" adjacent to "tree."

The Process of Simplification

While it is tempting to marvel at the deep thought behind these characters, one challenge was that many of these characters were created at a time when literacy was for the elite and often involved numerous and complicated brushstrokes: some characters could have over forty strokes. It might have been lyrical to compose poetry with such characters, but the ordinary person on the street was more likely to be interested in practicality than in poetry.

In 1956, the modern Chinese government enacted a national policy to promote literacy. Part of this policy involved adopting a new "simplified" version of Chinese characters, greatly reducing the number of strokes required to write the "correct" form of a character. Today, the "pre-1956" characters are now referred to as "traditional characters" or 繁体字 (literally translated to "numerous stroke characters"). The "post-1956" characters are now referred to as "simplified characters" or 简体字 (literally translated to "simple stroke characters"). This process has continued with further rounds of refinement and simplification occurring in 1964, 1977 and 1986. Some examples of the difference between traditional and simplified characters:

English word	Pronunciation	Traditional Chinese	Simplified Chinese
Fly (verb)	Fēi	飛	飞
Love	Aì	愛	爱
Horse	Mǎ	馬	马
Nation/ Kingdom	Gúo	國	国
Dragon	lóng	龍	龙
Book	Shū	書	书
Magnificent[2]	Weǐ	偉	伟

There remains considerable controversy as to whether simplification has been a good thing for China. Proponents of simplified characters point to the increase in literacy and the ease of use in modern day life (scribbling a note on the fridge about going to the store to buy some milk using simplified characters is much quicker than doing so using traditional characters) and suggest that concrete issues of practicality, education and literacy should trump whimsical and elitist notions of "linguistic beauty" (Gunde 2002). They also point to the long tradition of simplification over thousands of years, meaning recent simplifications are just another step in the natural evolution of the language (Norman 1988).

Proponents of traditional characters argue that the process of simplification diminishes Chinese culture by removing some of the most significant elements of the language, and contributes towards dumbing down the populace. It is argued that traditional characters are more aesthetically pleasing and are more meaningful. Using the "flight" example, the traditional character of two birds, the river and the bridge has been simplified to a squiggle with wings – from 飛 to 飞. The character for "love" has been simplified by removing the centrally placed radical for heart – from 愛 to 爱. There is also the argument that literacy in "traditional character" regions such as Taiwan and Hong Kong is better than that of "simplified character" regions such as Mainland China – so "the literacy argument" is not valid as a reason to promote simplification.[3]

In 2009, there has been much public discourse and debate in Mainland China about the next stage in Chinese character script development: Should we further simplify the language, and if so how? How should new terms such as "internet speak" be incorporated into the language, and should we perhaps consider a return of some characters back to their more "complicated but meaningful" state?[4]

In 2010, living in Beijing, I notice a blending of traditional and simplified characters in ordinary life. Newspapers, university text books and television subtitles (for the deaf) are all in simplified characters. Much "modern" pop-culture, such as comic books produced in Hong Kong, online computer games produced in Taiwan and pop tune lyrics displayed on the MTV channel regularly use traditional characters.

Finally, it should be noted that the most "everyday" characters used today to write legal documents, to send emails and to read a newspaper, are remarkably similar to the characters of the Qin dynasty dating back to 221 BC. A young primary school student with a basic command of simplified Chinese characters can make some sense of texts dating back 2000 years – something that might be difficult with other languages. (For comparison, consider how much English has changed just since Chaucer's time.) Some characters can even be recognizable against their 6600 BC counterparts – the characters for "sun" and "mountain" have changed very little over this time.

With this as background, I will turn to nine characters that are related to the field of negotiation pedagogy and trace these characters back to their ancient roots, explaining the thinking and consideration behind the original formation of these characters. I use the simplified form of Chinese characters since I am most familiar with this form.

Part B: Nine Chinese Characters Related to Negotiation[5]

Negotiation 谈判 (tán pàn)

谈(tán): This character has a "left" and a "right" part. On the left, there is the radical for "speech." On the right, there is the pictogram for "fire," repeated twice. This character came from the idea of a group of village elders "talking around a fire."

判(pàn): This character has a "left" and a "right" part. On the left there is an ideogram of an item, perhaps a goat, being carved in two (the vertical stroke being the "slash" of the knife). On the right, there is a pictogram of a blade. This character symbolizes a blade cutting something in two.

Hence, the characters for *negotiation* come from "talking around a fire" so that we can "split something into two pieces."

Co-operation 合作 *(hé zùo)*

合(hé): This is a pictogram of a box with a neatly fitting lid.

作(zùo): This character is a heavily simplified pictogram of two sticks of wood being rubbed together rapidly to make fire.

Hence, the characters for *co-operation* come from the concept of being "neatly fitting" with each other so that we can achieve something important (like making a fire).

Conflict 冲突 *(chōng tu)*

冲(chōng): This character has a "left" and a "right" part. On the left is a representation of two rivers. On the right is the character for "middle." The character therefore represents the point at which two rivers crash together.

突 (tu): This character originally came from the pictogram of an angry dog bursting out of a cage. It has been simplified almost beyond recognition now.

Hence, the characters for *conflict* come from the idea of being in a state of great agitation – like being trapped between two raging rivers or like an angry dog escaping from a cage.

Dispute 争议 *(zhēng yì)*

争(zhēng): a highly simplified and stylized picture of two hands, owned by different people, pulling a cow's head in two different directions.

议(yì): another very highly simplified character that used to have three separate parts, which are no longer identifiable in the modern simplified version. The first part was the symbol for "speech" (which is still observable as the radical on the left hand side of the modern character). The second part was the symbol for "me." The third part was the symbol for "goat." The overall character represented the act of "talking to convince you to give me the goat."

Hence the modern characters for *dispute* can be traced back to the idea of two herders arguing over the ownership of livestock.

Compromise 妥协 *(tǔo xie)*

妥(tǔo): This character has an "upper" and a "lower" part. The upper part represents a hand and is an ideogram for "placing" or "sending." The lower part is the radical for female, derived from the pictogram of a woman nursing a child. The thinking behind this character is the act of "sending one's daughter away to a rival in order to forge a bond." In ancient times, the daughter of one "tribe" would often be married to the son of another tribe, thus linking the two tribes as one.

协(xíe): This character is a heavily simplified pictogram of two dogs using a lot of strength to do something together.

Hence, the characters for *compromise* come from the idea of giving up something highly treasured, to help you and me to work strongly in the same direction.

Relationship 关系 (guān xi)

关(guān): This character is a pictogram of the vertical latch that formed the lock of old wooden doors.

系(xi): This character is an ideogram of someone tying two pieces of silken rope together.

Hence, the characters for *relationship* come from the concept of connecting and locking two people together – much in the way that a door can be locked or two pieces of rope can be attached to each other.

Forgive 谅解 (liàng jíe)

谅 (liàng): This character represents the concept of "cooling down" or "reducing temperature."

解 (jíe): This character has three parts. The left hand side represents the idea of "using." The right upper side is the radical for "knife." The right lower side is the pictogram for a horned bull. Assembled together, this character is the concept of using a knife to cut the horns off a bull.

Hence, the characters for *forgive* come from the concept of hot heads cooling down, so that we can cut away the "bad and dangerous parts" of something important.

Mediation 调解 (tíao jie)

调 (tíao): This character is made up of two parts. The left-hand side is the radical for "speech." The right-hand side is the character for "round" or "circular." (It was originally a picture of a granary, which traditionally was built in a round shape.) Together, these two radicals combine to form the idea of "sitting in a round shape to arrange the doing of things."

解 (jíe): This is the same character used in "forgive" – the concept of using a knife to cut the horns off a bull. Hence, the characters for *mediation* come from the concept of sitting around in a circle to arrange the "cutting away" of bad and dangerous things from our relationship.

Interestingly, one can observe that there is only one character's difference between "forgive" and "mediation."

Crisis 危机 (wei jī)

危 (wei): This is the character for "danger." Originally, it involved a man standing too close to a cliff face and falling off. It has been heavily simplified.

机 (jī): This is the character for "opportunity." On the left hand side is the radical for "wood." On the right hand side is the radical for "tool." The original non-simplified version involved the picture of a wooden trap that was used to hunt wild animals for food.

This oft-quoted character therefore indicates that to the ancient Chinese, a "crisis" was the conjunction of danger and opportunity.

Part C: What Does This Mean for Negotiation Pedagogy?

How can understanding the construction of Chinese characters enrich the field of negotiation pedagogy? I propose the following four avenues for further research and sharing.

1) Richer and Alternate Perspectives

Understanding the history behind these characters can offer different perspectives and illuminating insights into "accepted" ideas and concepts in the field. Consider the word "compromise" as not only "giving up something important" but doing so as a means to ensure that "you and I can work together in the same direction." Interpret the word "forgiveness" through the metaphor of cutting the "sharp dangerous parts" off an angry bull such that we can focus on the more important positive things. Look at a "relationship" as a way in which two people can be connected to each other as if tied by silk rope or latched by a wooden door-bolt.

The field of modern negotiation pedagogy has been created by extraordinarily brilliant people and we have words and concepts like "creating value," "mutual gains" and "developing options" – all of which are important to teaching negotiation. I wonder, however, whether some words and concepts have become so well taught and so entrenched that entertaining other perspectives can be challenging For example, a "compromise" is generally interpreted as a bad thing. Perhaps greater knowledge and understanding of Chinese characters, developed from a cultural and philosophical background different from that of modern Western thinking, may encourage creative thought and interesting alternative perspectives.

2) A Richer Cross-Cultural Understanding

With the world becoming increasingly smaller and interest in cross-cultural negotiation also increasing, a deeper appreciation of Chinese characters and their embedded cultural history may offer insights into traditional cultural norms and values.

There is already, I believe, much interest in Chinese culture and philosophy. I note that the Chinese character for "crisis" as a combination of "danger and opportunity" appears frequently in Western commentary. Confucius is often cited in the West. And I have more than once seen the mysterious nature of ancient Chinese culture being illustrated by the supposedly ancient curse, "May you live in interesting times."

I hope that this interest in Chinese culture might evolve into a richer understanding of China – and that this in turn may translate into more effective, and deeper, cross-cultural negotiation research. There are of course many illustrations of interesting philosophy beyond the word "crisis" and many more scholars than Confucius whose knowledge could be added to the field. There is also no such Chinese curse as, "May you live in interesting times."

Additionally, a deeper understanding of Chinese characters is not just something that should be promoted among Western scholars. In China, we are reading newspapers, checking the internet and sending off emails every day – but how much do we really consider the wisdom and history behind the characters we use, read, type and write? Chinese people, eager to learn about other cultures, could enhance our cross-cultural awareness by learning more about our own culture.

I believe that an appreciation of the Chinese language and of the make-up of our characters is a fundamental part of better cross-cultural negotiation. Studying these characters, of which there are over 50,000, is a largely untapped goldmine for research in the negotiation pedagogy field, especially as it relates to cross-cultural negotiations.

3) Understanding the Reason for and Impact of "Simplification"

Above, I have referenced the deep controversy behind the simplification of Chinese characters and outlined some of the major arguments for and against the simplification process. While debating the merits of simplification is important, I believe that for the negotiation pedagogy field, the question is not so much whether the simplification process is good or bad, but rather how and why it is happening.

How did a character of thirty strokes become a character of five? When we simplify, what do we keep and what do we throw out – and why? What was the thinking behind removing the radical for "heart" from the character "love?" It may be that one of the original justifications for simplification was to ease writing – but in today's China where we type emails and rarely lift a pen, why do we continue to simplify? [6]

I suspect that a better understanding of the simplification process may provide insights into modern Chinese social thinking, which in turn may reveal wisdom about Chinese negotiation practices.

4) Exploring Other Regions That Use Chinese Characters

Mainland China is the birthplace of Chinese characters and also the founder of "simplified characters." However, it is not the only region to use Chinese characters for writing. Of the regions that started using Chinese characters, some but not all have followed Mainland China along the simplification process. It is interesting to consider what other regions use Chinese characters and the similarities and differences between those regions and China.

In Singapore, Chinese is one of the nation's three national languages. Singapore has completely embraced simplified characters, to the point of exclusion of traditional characters.

In Malaysia, Chinese is spoken, read and written by the large Chinese community, in addition to Malaysia's primary language, Bahasa Malaysia. Malaysia uses a combination of both simplified and traditional characters.

Taiwan, Hong Kong and Macau only use traditional characters and explicitly reject the use of simplified characters. Hong Kong and Macau have retained the use of traditional characters beyond their handovers from British and Portuguese to Mainland Chinese administration.

Korea used traditional Chinese characters prior to adopting their own script in the fifteenth century.[7] Korean characters ("hangul"), as opposed to traditional Chinese characters ("hanja") became formally adopted in official documents in 1894, and today Hangul is by far the most prevalent language of both North and South Korea.[8] My understanding is that today, North Korea has phased out Chinese characters altogether and South Korea retains only a minimal use of traditional Chinese characters, and does not use simplified characters at all. To illustrate the differences between traditional, simplified and Korean Hangul characters, consider the words "Republic of Korea":

- Traditional Chinese: 大韓民國 (pronounced as dà hán mín gúo)
- Simplified Chinese: 大韩民国 (pronounced unchanged as dà hán mín gúo)
- Korean Hangul: 대한민국 (pronounced as daehan-minguk)

Japan has three completely separate scripts that are combined to form the Japanese written language. One of these scripts ("kanji") is based on the Chinese traditional characters. Japan has had its own process of simplification, similar but not always identical to that used in Mainland China. One illustration of differences between simplification is the character for "dragon":

- Traditional Chinese: 龍 (pronounced lóng)
- Simplified Chinese: 龙 (pronounced unchanged as lóng)
- Modern (simplified) Kanji Japanese: 竜 (pronounced as ryu)

Finally, simplified Chinese is one of the five official languages of the United Nations. The United Nations does not recognize traditional characters.

Interestingly, although spoken Chinese, Korean, Japanese and the dialects used in Taiwan (Taiwanese) and Hong Kong and Macau (Cantonese) are completely unintelligible to each other, the common use of Chinese characters means we are usually able to communicate in writing.

There is already considerable research on the difference between "Western" and "Asian" styles of negotiation. Just as there are differences within Western styles (I suggest a traditional "American" style is somewhat different to a traditional "German" style), I believe there are many differences between and within "Asian" styles (see generally Barnes 2006). An analysis of Chinese characters, how and whether those characters have changed over time, may give greater insight into the negotiation traits of each culture.

A Personal Note

My introduction to the world of negotiation pedagogy was through the Program on Negotiation (PON) at Harvard Law School. There, I was exposed for the first time in my life to the teaching of negotiation, to learning through role-play, to writing journals, to decision trees and concepts of "mutual gains," the "7 elements" and "Getting to Yes." I remain incredibly grateful to the PON for nurturing me and inspiring me and starting me on this journey.

When I came to teach negotiation in China, my first class was basically "what I learned from the PON, but delivered in Mandarin." It was *Sally Soprano*, the *Oil Pricing Game* and *Win As Much As You Can* – taught in Chinese. Fast forward six years, and the negotiation syllabus at Peking University has changed greatly. One of the major additions to the course has been sharing with my own Chinese-speaking students the historical development of our own characters. This article has come out of the teachings in my own class.

There is much we in China have to learn from the field of negotiation pedagogy. In the United States and some other countries, law schools, business schools, public policy and planning schools all have long-established negotiation classes, tenured faculty, journals and text-books, while we do not.

But we do have a culture and a history that is longer than any current civilization on the planet. We have been negotiating for a very long time. I deeply believe that in addition to having much to learn, we also have much to offer. Chinese people should look back on and learn from our own linguistic history. Our friends in Japan, Korea and other "Chinese character using cultures" may have their own insights and perspectives to offer. Once we better appreciate our own language, we may be able to share this knowledge more efficiently with our friends from other cultures.

I hope that through sharing this understanding of the history behind Chinese characters, we might be able to make a contribution to the exciting field of negotiation pedagogy.

Notes

[1] One of the most well known and cited texts is the 史记 or *Records of the Grand Historian* by Si Ma Qian. Considered the first authoritative history of China dating from 2600 BC onwards, it lists the Xia dynasty as the first dynasty of Ancient China. An electronic version of 史记 is available at http://www.guoxue.com/shibu/24shi/shiji/sjml.htm

[2] The inclusion of the character for "magnificent" in this list is due to that fact that this character is part of my own name. The simplification process is not some abstract practice that only affects technical words – many of our own names have been changed.

[3] There is an English language summary of some of the other contentious points of view on the topic of Chinese language simplification at http://en.wikipedia.org/wiki/Debate_on_traditional_and_simplified_Chinese_characters#cite_note-Gunde.2C_Richard_2002-6.

[4] Some preliminary reports about this process are available at 汉字，该繁还是简？ - XINHUA NEWS, April 9, 2009   http://news.xinhuanet.com/focus/2009-04/09/content_11154357.htm; *China to Regulate use of Simplified Characters.* CHINAVIEW August 12, 2009, http://news.xinhuanet.com/english/2009-08/12/content_11871748.htm

[5] See generally, "说文解字" (*An Analysis and Explanation of Charac*ters) written by Xu Shen in the Han Dynasty, in approximately 100 AD. There are many versions and printings of this text – the one I favor is the version edited by Xu Xuan of the Song Dynasty (960-1279) and published in Beijing by Zhong Hua Book Company, first printed in 1963 and reprinted in 2008.

[6] In Mainland China, we use standard western "QWERTY" keyboards to type. We follow the "Hanyu Pinyin" system which converts Chinese pronunciations into Romanized characters. If we want to write the character "wo," we type "w" then "o" and the computer automatically brings up the character 我 on our screens. If there is more than one character pronounced "wo," then the computer will generate a list of all similar-sounding characters and we select the desired character. In this way, a person typing Chinese need only be able to recognize a character, she or he need not remember how to write it. The argument against simplification is that recognizing a character with fourteen strokes is just as easy as recognizing a character with four (for example, an octagon is just as easy to recognize as a triangle even though an octagon has many more strokes). Hence, the argument goes, simplification of characters is unnecessary.

[7] See, Background of the Invention of Hangeul (2010).

[8] See, Providing Process of Hangeul (2010).

References

Allan, S. 1991. The shape of the turtle: Myth, art and cosmos in early China. New York: State University of New York Press.

Background of the invention of Hangeul. The. 2010. The National Academy of the Korean Language available at http://www.korean.go.kr/eng_hangeul/setting/002.html (last accessed Apr. 16, 2010).

Barnes, B. 2006. *Culture, conflict, and mediation in the Asian Pacific.* Lanham, MD: University Press of America.

Boltz, W. G. 1986. Early Chinese writing. *World Archaeology* 17(3): 420-436.

Gunde, R. 2002. *Culture and customs of China.* Westport, CT: Greenwood Press.

Longwen, C. 2009. Henan: The cradle of Chinese civilization. *China National Geographic* May-June: 66-73.

Norman, J. 1988. *Chinese.* Cambridge, UK: Cambridge University Press.

People's Daily. 2009. Chinese characters, the complicated or the simple? *Xinhua News* [updated April 9, 2009]. Available at http://news.xinhuanet.com/focus/2009-04/09/content11154357.htm (last accessed Apr. 3, 2010).

Providing process of Hangeul, The. 2010. The National Academy of the Korean Language available at http://www.korean.go.kr/eng_hangeul/supply/001.html (last accessed Apr. 16, 2010).

Ricon, P. 2003. Earliest writing found in China. *BBC News* [updated April 17, 2003]. Available at http://news.bbc.co.uk/2/hi/science/nature/2956925.stm (last accessed Apr. 3, 2010).

Sima, Q. 1993. *Records of the grand historian: Qin Dynasty.* Translated by B. Watson. Hong Kong: The Research Centre for Translation, The Chinese University of Hong Kong, and Columbia University Press. Available at http://www.guoxue. com/shibu/24shi/shiji/sjml.htm (last accessed Apr. 3, 2010).

Wikipedia. *Debate on traditional and simplified Chinese characters.* Available at http://en.wikipedia.org/wiki/Debate_on_traditional_and_simplified_Chinese_characters#cite_note-Gunde.2C_Richard_2002-6 (last accessed Apr. 3, 2010).

Wu, J. and L. Guo. 2009. China to regulate use of simplified characters. *China View* [updated August 12, 2009]. Available at http://news. xinhuanet.com/english/2009-08/12/content_11871748.htm (last accessed Apr. 3, 2010).

Xianghong, N. 2009. Birthplace of Chinese characters. *China National Geographic* May-June: 53-65.

Xu, X (ed.) 1963. *An analysis and explanation of characters.* Beijing: Zhong Hua Book Company.

❧ 7 ❧

Straight Off the Deep End in Adventure Learning

*James Coben, Christopher Honeyman & Sharon Press**

Editors' Note: Numerous contributors to our 2009 book argued strongly for getting at least part of negotiation teaching out of the classroom and into real environments. So we tried it – in Istanbul, a famously negotiation-centric environment on many levels. In this introduction to a series of analyses of what happened and how adventure learning might be used in the future, the organizers take responsibility for a string of errors – each of which, it turned out, contributed usefully to everyone's education in the end.

"The policy of being too cautious is the greatest risk of all." (Jawaharlal Nehru)

Introduction

In this project's first book, *Rethinking Negotiation Teaching* (Honeyman, Coben, and De Palo 2009a) and companion publication in *Negotiation Journal* (Honeyman, Coben, and De Palo 2009b), more than a few contributors (see, e.g., Alexander and LeBaron 2009; LeBaron and Patera 2009; Nelken, McAdoo, and Manwaring 2009; Shmueli, Warfield, and Kaufman 2009) expressed frustration with the assumption that so practical a discipline as negotiation ever should

---

* **James Coben** is a professor of law and senior fellow in the Dispute Resolution Institute at Hamline University School of Law. His email address is jcoben@hamline.edu. **Christopher Honeyman** is managing partner of Convenor Conflict Management, a consulting firm based in Washington, D.C. and Madison, Wisconsin. He has directed a twenty-year series of major research-and-development projects in conflict management and is coeditor of The Negotiator's Fieldbook (ABA 2006). His email address is honeyman@convenor.com. **Sharon Press** is an associate professor of law and director of the Dispute Resolution Institute at Hamline University School of Law. Her email address is spress01@hamline.edu.

have been thought of as teachable almost entirely in a traditional classroom setting. We were struck by the vigor of these critiques and realized we were about to have an unusual opportunity for some experiments in a new direction. The venue of the second conference of our series – Istanbul – offered the tempting prospect of combining the strongly-desired cross-cultural elements, also argued for by many of our contributors, with some new procedural approaches to teaching.

In particular, we sought to address the post-Rome-conference critique that negotiation teachers: 1) over-rely on "canned" material of little relevance to students; and 2) share an unsubstantiated belief that role-plays are the best way to teach. Our solution was declared explicitly in the conference agenda:

> Provide a "learning lab" to explore an adventure learning thesis: "authenticity as priority." This suggests that all participants...experience directly some "real" negotiations as part of the meeting, and test existing perceptions against self-reflection on that experience (including not only "cognitive/rational" responses, but also emotional responses).[1]

Much of the planning for the Istanbul meeting involved our first, and as the reader will see in the chapters to follow, flawed attempts to make good on this challenge. If we were talented cartoonists we would insert a latter-day version of the famous *New Yorker* "Back to the Old Drawing-Board" cartoon here; but the reader will just have to imagine it.

Planning for the "Unplannable"

As soon as we realized the level of interest among our 2008-09 contributors in getting away from traditional teaching venues, an overwhelming image presented itself: the Grand Bazaar of Istanbul, one of the world's most storied environments for negotiation, going back half a millennium. It was irresistible.

It was also wrong. It was not until we arrived in Istanbul, and actually paced out the territory we expected our negotiating teams to cover, that we realized the Grand Bazaar was altogether too grand for our purposes, which involved getting teams of professional negotiation teachers to actually negotiate for something. The basic problem was that the 4,000 shops in the Grand Bazaar were heavily tilted toward the expensive, with numerous jewelry emporiums and a plethora of rug dealers. We could not reasonably expect our academic colleagues to invest hundreds or thousands of dollars in pursuit of our exercise.

Fortunately, an alternative became readily apparent. Down the hill from the Grand Bazaar is the Spice Market, which as its name implies, deals in more rapid trading of less costly goods. For our purposes, it was ideal. Or so we thought at the time. In retrospect, while there was ample learning to be had, the environment was still so special as to raise questions about replicability, under more normal circumstances and in more ordinary cities.

Still, as the following chapters will show, the environment served at least one purpose extraordinarily well – it inspired our colleagues to analyze, to invent, to create, and to write. Mostly, our colleagues begin by describing our Istanbul efforts in some detail, to set the context for each author's own take on the subject. So we will focus our discussion here differently, in order not to be repetitive. In particular, we will comment on our design decisions and the considerations which led to them, and discuss what we see as the particular results we encountered, warts and all. But our discussion of the activities themselves will be relatively brief, and we rely on the succeeding chapters to give the reader a sense of just how many ways the same activity could be experienced and interpreted.

The Gory Details

The two activities chosen, after much discussion, were a traditional negotiation in the marketplace (with a few twists) and a more "oblique" exercise intended to cause an internal negotiation within a team. (For a helpful conceptual framing of these assignments as "orienting" and "disorienting," see McAdoo, Manwaring, and Cheldelin, *Orientation and Disorientation*, in this section.) The activities were designed to devalue the cognitive, to encourage creativity, and to focus on emotion.

Negotiating the Spice Market (and Grand Bazaar): Adventure Learning/Praxis Activity I

Participants were given from 12 noon until 3:30 pm to complete the marketplace exercise. We provided mini-bus transportation to and from campus, which we thought of as merely a precaution against the threatened rain. But this turned out in retrospect to have "normative" consequences too – no one eligible for the free ride wanted to miss it, and everyone made it back on time. The next day, as we will see, was different.

The exercise followed a brief welcome/introductory plenary session and (assigned) break-out groups, on topics which were both follow-up sessions from the Rome conference and intended to set the tone for the activity which followed.[2] For the first exercise, participants were assigned to groups[3] and instructed to go to the Spice Market and/or the Grand Bazaar[4] and accomplish the following tasks as a group:

1) Negotiate a purchase of food (the group's contribution to what the entire conference will share during the adventure learning debrief upon return from the market);
2) Negotiate for whatever else anyone in the group wants to buy;
3) Observe negotiations (including, of course, those conducted by the group members); and
4) Interview seller(s) as to their concerns, experiences and strategies.

In creating the assignment, we sought to provide an opportunity for participants to experience "real" cross-cultural negotiations directly, with the outcomes having at least some consequence for the group (e.g., quality of the food at the next break) – in other words, an exercise of *authenticity* (see LeBaron and Patera 2009: 59). Of course, in retrospect, we can easily see the folly in labeling as "authentic" the wanderings of multiple small groups of five or six academics through a confined marketplace interviewing people and bargaining (sometimes inadvertently with the same seller)! But as detailed by Melissa Manwaring, Bobbi McAdoo, and Sandra Cheldelin (*Orientation/Disorientation*, in this section), there are many aspects of authenticity. At the very least, the assignment took us out of the conference facility and required participants to bargain "as themselves" as opposed to pretending to be a character in a role-play.

Negotiating Images of Istanbul: Adventure Learning/Praxis Activity II

The second exercise was designed to be more oblique (i.e., its relevance to negotiation theory and practice was intended to be less immediately evident to participants). We instructed teams (this time self-selected, but with the exhortation to "stay diverse") to go out and about in the city (where and how was left up to the group, but they were instructed to avoid the predictable and places where tourists usually go) and accomplish the following:
1) Agree on a photo taken by the group that the group believes best represents the crossroads of the sacred and the secular.
2) Agree on a photo taken by the group that the group believes represents the most dangerous thing you have seen during your walk about the city.
3) Agree on a photo taken by the group of the building that the group believes is most likely to be the "unmarked" CIA headquarters in Istanbul.
4) Agree on a self-portrait that best captures the essence of the group.
5) Add or change one thing about this assignment (before it is done) that would make this exercise a more effective learning experience for students of negotiation.

Our hope was that the "oblique" nature of the assignment (and its focus on creativity) would stimulate implicit learning, "knowledge gained without awareness" (Carey 2009).

The Unbearable Lightness of Being a Heavyweight Scholar

We found a good deal to celebrate in the experience as well as much that deserved self-criticism. The bazaar exercise might be hard to replicate in a more typical city, but it certainly has ignited plenty of thinking as to what might take its place (for helpful suggestions on implementation and variations, see Cohn and Ebner, *Bringing Nego- tiation Teaching to Life*, in this volume), and the discussions of culture that resulted have been richly satisfying to read. We think that as a single experiment, the exercise was well justified, even if one or an- other of the replacements becomes more appropriate for future ef- forts in the same direction.

Unlike the Negotiating the Spice Market exercise, which seemed generally well accepted (within the critiques which follow), the in- tra-team Negotiating Images of Istanbul exercise drew decidedly mixed results. If our bazaar exercise made us rethink our preconcep- tions the day before it was to run, our other exercise made us re- think our premises afterwards. In assigning people we think of as serious colleagues to perform a fun exercise, we made a bonehead error, in an area where any negotiator or negotiation teacher should know better: timing. We scheduled the exercise in the middle of the third day of a four-day meeting – in other words, after the group had already been together for a substantial time – and at a point in the day when they would have to come back and report on the same day. This resulted in a rueful lesson for us, as our wonderful col- leagues proceeded to do exactly what they felt like for as long as it turned out to take.

Not only did some of the teams almost blow off the exercise en- tirely, by deciding that they deserved a good lunch and taking the time for it out of the exercise time, but our goal of an intensive group debrief in cleverly-managed randomized regroups fell apart, as the working groups straggled back at whatever time each group in- dividually could bear to get itself back into a university building. Chaos reigned, at least for a while. Moreover, from our own observa- tion, many (though not all) of the photos taken were trite, the prod- uct of discussions that were often nowhere near the level of intensity and commitment we had hoped for.

CIA Secret Headquarters: Group One

CIA Secret Headquarters: Group Two

CIA Secret Headquarters: Group Three

CIA Secret Headquarters: Group Four

CIA Secret Headquarters: Group Five

Such problems, mostly self-imposed through our failure to anticipate just how many things could go wrong, are themselves valuable learning for the future. One adaptation that seems mandatory in future adventure learning design is to be prepared for a less controllable, less predictable experience than is normal in the classroom – and to prepare, in particular, to be ready to teach whatever aspects of negotiation are reinforced or unearthed by the particular students' idiosyncratic experiences with such an exercise. That, in and of itself, seems a development worth having for our next generation of negotiation teaching.

Learning by Doing It (Wrong)

The hard lessons learned from this first set of experiments included:

- The importance of "field testing" the assignment prior to its use, including an effort to replicate the actual expected conditions. By definition, adventure learning takes place outside of the classroom, and therefore is impacted by all kinds of elements outside the control of the instructor. Issues to be considered include: What happens if it rains? Is the activity planned during rush hour, when getting anywhere on time is impossible? Is the market even open on the day and time of the activity?

- The need to provide sufficient time for the activity. If the activity is to be completed over a traditional mealtime, build in extra time, because there will be some groups who will use the allotted time to eat at a sit-down restaurant, thereby losing valuable time for the work.

- The need to "position" the activity at a time that allows for the eventuality that participants will complete the assignment at different rates.

- The need not only to plan a significant debrief but to ensure that its timing will actually work for the group as a whole (for incisive critique on this issue, see Panga and Grecia-de Vera, *A Look at a 2.0 Negotiation Classroom*, in this volume).

- The need to recognize that adventure learning activities, because they are "authentic," may actually chill, rather than inspire some negotiation students (see Kamp, *A "Semi-Student" Perspecctive*, in this volume). As observed by Roy Lewicki during a debrief the evening after our first such exercise in Istanbul, you could "smell the fear" in the room as assignments were given out (and, keep in mind, the recipients were experienced negotiation scholars and practitioners, not typical students).

- The risk that adventure learning might chill, rather than inspire, pales compared to the unintentional harm caused by failing to consider accessibility issues in adventure learning. As outlined by David Larson (*Not Everyone Gets to Play*, in this section), risks of exclusion are not just physical, but also carry ethical and moral dimensions. Indeed, the ethics issues raised by adventure learning got relatively little attention in this first round of writing. Perhaps post-Beijing conference writers will have more to say on this point.

Conclusion

Our analysis right after the successes and failures of our Istanbul experiments suggested that it would be well worth trying at least the oblique/conceptual exercise again as soon as possible, in a version that would attempt to remedy the more obvious errors of our first try. Fortunately, wonderfully diverse opportunities soon emerged, starting within weeks.

In December 2009, Sharon Press and Christopher Honeyman (see *Second Dive Into Adventure Learning*, in this volume) ran a version of the orienting and disorienting activities with graduate students from twenty-one different nations, all attending a European Union-funded masters program in transnational trade law and finance at the University of Deusto in Bilbao, Spain. And, in spring semester 2010, as detailed by Manwaring, McAdoo, and Cheldelin (*Orientation and Disorientation*, in this volume), Sandra Cheldelin did the same with thirty students in her graduate-level, semester-long course on Reflective Practice, located in the greater Washington, D.C. area.

Suffice it to say, borrowing a phrase from William Faulkner, "[a]ll of us failed to match our dreams of perfection." But we hope you will agree that both chapters suggest extremely promising futures for adventure learning outside the negotiation classroom. Other writers in this section offer more incremental stages, including some strategies for achieving some of the same results within (or close to) the classroom.

Notes

[1] Our conference agenda declared a second objective as well – that participants "produce scholarship that challenges the field to think more about adventure learning opportunities (and how to implement them in typical instructional settings)." Given the eight chapters in this book on the subject, we deem it fair to claim "objective met."

[2] The sessions included: Finding Common Ground in the Soil of Culture, presented by Phyllis Bernard; Negotiation Philosophy in Chinese Characters, presented by Andrew Lee and Vivian Feng; Know Your Students: Variations on How to Begin Trainings, presented by Maude Pervere and Melissa Nelken; and Building an "Emotional Vocabulary," presented by Mario Patera.

[3] Groups were structured to create the most diversity possible. Characteristics considered included: gender, discipline, ethnicity, nationality, and immediate past influence (i.e., which session someone had attended in the morning.)

[4] Transportation to the Spice Market was provided via mini-bus, but once there participants could walk or take public transportation to the Grand Bazaar. In a test of the activity the day before, program organizers started in the Grand Bazaar and then walked to the Spice Market.

References

Alexander, N. and LeBaron, M. 2009. Death of the role-play. In *Rethinking negotiation teaching: Innovations for context and culture*, edited by C. Honeyman, J. Coben, and G. De Palo. St. Paul, MN: DRI Press.

Carey, B. 2009. How nonsense sharpens the intellect. *New York Times* (October 5), available at http://www.nytimes.com/2009/10/06/health/06mind. html (last accessed June 24, 2010).

Honeyman, C., J. Coben, and G. De Palo (eds.) 2009a. *Rethinking negotiation teaching: Innovations for context and culture*. St. Paul, MN: DRI Press.

Honeyman, C., J. Coben, and G. De Palo (guest eds). 2009b. Special section of eight articles: Second generation global negotiation education. *Negotiation Journal* 25(2): 141-266.

LeBaron, M. and M. Patera. 2009. Reflective practice in the new millennium. In *Rethinking negotiation teaching: Innovations for context and culture*, edited by C. Honeyman, J. Coben, and G. De Palo. St. Paul, MN: DRI Press.

Nelken, M., B. McAdoo, and M. Manwaring. 2009. Negotiating learning environments. In *Rethinking negotiation teaching: Innovations for context and culture*, edited by C. Honeyman, J. Coben, and G. De Palo. St. Paul, MN: DRI Press.

Shmueli, D., W. Warfield, and S. Kaufman. 2009. Enhancing community leadership negotiation skills to build civic capacity. *Negotiation Journal* 25(2): 249-266.

᪐ 8 ᪑

Orientation and Disorientation: Two Approaches to Designing "Authentic" Negotiation Learning Activities

*Melissa Manwaring, Bobbi McAdoo & Sandra Cheldelin**

Editors' Note: *The authors here build on their 2009 writings for this project, which were influential in setting an "adventure learning" agenda. In their new effort, they argue that adventure learning devolves into mere entertainment if it lacks authenticity, and they frame two contrasting approaches to achieving a sense of the real and the consequential.*

Introduction

A prevailing characteristic of Western negotiation education over the past several decades is the emphasis on experiential learning – that is, learning by doing – as a significant or even predominant complement to other approaches such as presentations, case analyses, or video demonstrations. While the role-play[1] is perhaps the most common experiential activity in negotiation courses, the Rethinking Negotiation Teaching initiative[2] explicitly questions a perceived over-reliance on role-plays, asking whether they fall short in giving students an authentic learning experience – that is, one that reflects the richness, complexity, and unpredictability of actual negotiations in which students engage outside of the classroom.

---

* **Melissa Manwaring** is a lecturer and director of learning assessment at the F.W. Olin Graduate School of Business at Babson College. Her email address is mmanwaring@babson.edu. **Bobbi McAdoo** is a professor of law and senior fellow at the Dispute Resolution Institute at Hamline University School of Law. Her email address is bmcadoo@hamline.edu. **Sandra Cheldelin** is the Vernon M. and Minnie I. Lynch professor of conflict resolution at the Institute for Conflict Analysis and Resolution at George Mason University. Her email address is scheldel@gmu.edu.

Authenticity is, of course, a complex concept. Should a negotiation learning activity – whether a role-play, game, or other exercise – be true-to-life or "authentic" in terms of the factual context? In terms of the roles students play or the behaviors they are expected to apply? In terms of the strategic, ethical, psychological, or other issues the activity elicits? What about authenticity in the way in which the negotiation is (or is not) labeled or framed? By their very nature, planned learning activities cannot be authentic in *every* way that a real-world negotiation is – and indeed, there are often powerful pedagogical reasons for certain elements of artificiality (Crampton and Manwaring 2008; Susskind and Corburn 1999). At the same time, it is worth examining whether some experiential activities might offer different forms of authenticity than role-plays do, and if so, whether they might be better-suited than role-plays for certain learning goals.

To support the emergence of thinking and scholarship about alternative pedagogies – particularly those that strive for authenticity – the organizers of the October 2009 Istanbul conference devoted significant time to experimentation with "adventure learning." Adventure learning activities (described in more detail below) typically comprise direct, active, authentic, engaging, and collaborative experiences that take place outside traditional classroom settings, involve some element of real or perceived risk, and involve the whole person (not just the cognitive). The conference participants (predominantly negotiation instructors) took part in two adventure learning activities with quite different design philosophies, referred to herein as "orientation" and "disorientation." In the orientation approach, participants are given direct, explicit instructions about what they should do and why. Just as "to orient" means "to cause to become familiar with or adjusted to a particular situation or circumstance" (Webster's 1999: 772), an orienting learning activity acquaints students with the nature and purposes of the activity. In the disorientation approach ("to disorient" meaning "to cause to lose one's sense of direction, position, or relationship with one's surroundings") (Webster's 1999: 328), students are *not* explicitly told the nature and purposes of the activity in advance. Instead, they may be given incomplete, oblique, or misleading instructions, or no instructions at all.

In this article, we summarize the constructivist and experiential underpinnings of the widespread role-play usage in Western negotiation education, along with more recent theories of the situated nature of learning that endorse authenticity and encourage authenticity-oriented educational approaches such as adventure learning.

We describe the implementation and results (including participant reflections) of the orienting and disorienting adventure learning activities with conference participants in Istanbul and with graduate students in a replication of these activities in Washington, D.C. We examine the more and less authentic aspects of the orientation and disorientation designs and discuss the benefits and limitations of each. We conclude that "authenticity" is multifaceted; that learning activities that explicitly orient the learner to their nature and purpose tend to be authentic in very different ways than more oblique activities designed to disorient the learner as to their purpose; and that negotiation instructors seeking to design or select "authentic" adventure learning activities should consider which specific types of authenticity best meet their learning goals.

In Search of Authenticity: Constructivism, Situated Learning, and Adventure Learning

As mentioned above, role-plays have been a mainstay of most Western academic and professional negotiation courses for decades (see, e.g., Buntz and Carper 1987; Spoormans, Cohen, and Moust 1991; Williams and Geis 1999; Lewicki 1999; Susskind and Corburn 1999; Fortgang 2000). This is not surprising: in addition to being fun, engaging, efficient, and easily replicable activities that tend to result in positive student evaluations (Wheeler 2006; Movius 2008; Alexander and LeBaron 2009; Patton 2009), the common pedagogical justifications for role-plays are rooted in some of the most prevalent themes of 20th-century education theory: namely, constructivism and experiential learning (Lewicki 1999; Susskind and Corburn 1999; Patton 2009).

Grounded in the work of Lev Vygotsky, Jean Piaget, and others, constructivist philosophy posits that learners actively create (and recreate) their own understandings through experiences rather than passively receiving understanding from a teacher (Fosnot 2005). Experiential learning – or learning by doing – is a natural application of constructivist philosophy, and heavy use of role-plays would seem to be a natural application of these principles to a negotiation curriculum.

More recently, however, negotiation educators have begun to criticize a perceived over-reliance on role-plays and other classroom simulations as a teaching tool (*e.g.,* Alexander and LeBaron 2009; Kovach 2009). A key criticism is that role-plays – while useful for certain pedagogical purposes – are nevertheless too artificial to maximize student learning and skill building.[3] While traditional role-plays need not be discarded entirely, the argument goes, they at least should be supplemented with more authentic learning activities situated in a more realistic negotiation context (Volkema 2007; Weiss 2008; Alexander and LeBaron 2009; LeBaron and Patera 2009).

Implicitly or explicitly, many concerns about over-reliance on role-plays resonate with two themes prevalent in contemporary experiential learning theory: the situated/contextual nature of learning and the corresponding value of authenticity in learning activities (*e.g.*, Vygotsky 1978; Brown, Collins, and Duguid 1989; Lave and Wenger 1991; Wilson 1993; Young 1993; Doolittle 1997; Petraglia 1998; Reeves, Herrington, and Oliver 2002; Driscoll 2004). According to situated learning theorists, learning is not only constructed through experience; it is inextricably related to the context of that experience (Brown, Collins, and Duguid 1989). "Context," like authenticity, is incredibly complex, and can include such factors as the physical, emotional, social, and cultural context (Doolittle 1997). From this perspective, "authentic activities" – or learning activities that re-create as closely as possible the context (key dynamics, challenges, emotions, etc.) of real-world activities – are critical to making learning relevant and transferable (Crampton and Manwaring 2008). Effective education will "provide complex learning environments that incorporate authentic activity" (Driscoll 2004).

In some disciplines, situated learning through authentic activities has long been a pedagogical staple. Classic examples include the residency for medical students, student teaching placements for education students, and flight simulators (followed by actual flights) for aviation students. In others – notably the legal field – alternative pedagogical models such as case discussions have historically dominated, and educators have only recently begun to incorporate more authentic learning experiences that reflect more accurately what professionals actually do in practice. In 1992, for instance, the MacCrate Report by the American Bar Association critiqued law schools for doing too little to teach the skills and values that actual lawyers need (American Bar Association 1992). More recently, legal educators have been challenged anew by the Carnegie report to synthesize the theory, practice, and professionalism aspects of legal education better so that students are ready to practice law when they graduate (Sullivan et al. 2007). While law school negotiation courses traditionally have been more experiential and skills-oriented than most other law school courses (and perhaps more than other courses in the other disciplines in which negotiation is taught, such as management, international relations, or planning), it is nevertheless worth considering whether negotiation educators can do still more to prepare students to negotiate effectively outside the classroom by providing them with highly authentic learning experiences.

So what exactly are authentic learning experiences? Synthesizing the work of numerous researchers and theorists, Thomas Reeves, Jan Herrington, and Ron Oliver enumerated the following characteristics of "authentic activities" in an academic environment:

1) Authentic activities have real-world relevance...match[ing] as nearly as possible the real-world tasks of professionals in practice rather than decontextualised or classroom-based tasks.

2) Authentic activities are ill-defined, requiring students to define the tasks and sub-tasks needed to complete the activity....[They] are open to multiple interpretations rather than easily solved by the application of existing algorithms....

3) Authentic activities comprise complex tasks to be investigated by students over a sustained period of time....They require significant investment of time and intellectual resources.

4) Authentic activities provide the opportunity for students to examine the task from different perspectives, using a variety of resources....The use of a variety of resources rather than a limited number of preselected references requires students to detect relevant from irrelevant information.

5) Authentic activities provide the opportunity to collaborate. Collaboration is integral to the task, both within the course and the real world....

6) Authentic activities provide the opportunity to reflect...on their learning both individually and socially.

7) Authentic activities...encourage interdisciplinary perspectives and enable diverse roles and expertise rather than a single well-defined field or domain.

8) Authentic activities are seamlessly integrated with assessment...in a manner that reflects real world assessment, rather than separate artificial assessment removed from the nature of the task.

9) Authentic activities create polished products valuable in their own right rather than as preparation for something else.

10) Authentic activities allow...a range and diversity of outcomes open to multiple solutions of an original nature, rather than a single correct response obtained by the application of rules and procedures.

(Reeves, Herrington, and Oliver 2002: 563-565) (citations omitted).

While some highly complex "mega-simulations" may fit all of these criteria (see, e.g., Weiss 2008), many typical negotiation role-plays fall short in some ways or others. By their nature, for instance, few role-plays have "real-world relevance...rather than [comprising] decontextualised or classroom-based tasks." With their bounded sets of instructions, few are "ill-defined, requiring students to define the tasks and sub-tasks needed" or require "use of a variety of resources rather than a limited number of preselected references." Few "create polished products valuable in their own right rather than as preparation for something else."

Whether or not a learning experience meets the criteria for "authentic activities," however, misses the point. Activities with intentional elements of artificiality can provide powerful learning experiences (see Crampton and Manwaring 2008); and even activities that meet all the criteria for authenticity are irrelevant if they are incompatible with the teachers' and students' learning goals. Rather than asking "how authentic is this activity?," an instructor should ask "in what ways is this activity authentic – and does that matter with regard to our learning goals?" Two seemingly "authentic" learning activities can nevertheless differ substantially in the *ways* in which they are authentic – and thus in the specific learning goals they are likely to support. As Karen Barton, Patricia McKellar, and Paul Maharg observe:

> One theme running through the many contemporary versions of experiential learning is that of "authenticity" – the correspondence, in some way or other, of learning to the world of practice that exists outside of teaching institutions. The concept is an important one, for it lies at the heart of the attempts by educators since Dewey to address the relationship between learning and life. In dealing with it, we must acknowledge that there are many factors that affect authenticity of task such as context, learner motivation, task, feedback, social interaction, and social presence... (Barton, McKellar, and Maharg 2007: 145).

Turning to the negotiation education context, there are many forms of possible "authenticity" in learning activities: the physical environment; the interpersonal communication and relationships; the resources involved (e.g., "real money"); the emotions and motivations; the availability of external resources; the boundedness of the problem (or lack thereof); and so forth. Given practical and ethical constraints as well as the unique cultural dynamics of a formal academic environment, it is virtually impossible to replicate every single element of negotiation authenticity in such an environment. So, which elements of authenticity *can* be replicated in a negotiation learning exercise? And how? And what are the implications – pedagogical, practical, and ethical? We examine these questions in the context of a particular approach to authenticity in education.

Authentic activities can take many forms: clinical programs, residencies, internships, apprenticeships, moot court, and so forth. Many of these forms are far from new: for instance, lengthy periods of apprenticeship were required for entry into medieval craft guilds (see Larson, *Not Everyone Gets to Play*, in this volume). A more recent manifestation of the authentic learning approach is adventure education.

Adventure education (also referred to as adventure learning) involves "direct, active, and engaging learning experiences that involve the whole person and have real consequences," and that bring learners "out of their comfort zone...no matter where the location and how physically risky or active the mode of learning may be" (Prouty, Panicucci, and Collinson 2007: 4). The key characteristics are as follows:

- Adventure learning is *experiential*: participants do something that engages the "whole person" (Prouty, Panicucci, and Collinson) and goes beyond traditional cognitive academic activities such as analysis and discussion. The activity often involves some element of physicality that "raises levels of conscious alertness in the group and allows the subconscious, with its ways of knowing beyond the rational, to directly engage with deeper personal challenges" (Alexander and LeBaron 2009: 187). In the context of a negotiation course, for instance, an adventure learning activity would almost certainly involve students physically leaving the classroom and engaging in some type of negotiation (possibly among other activities such as navigating an unfamiliar city).
- Moreover, the adventure learning experiences must be *"authentic" and "real"* in some meaningful sense (Alexander and LeBaron 2009; Doering 2006) – though "authenticity" is highly complex, as discussed above.
- Adventure learning activities are often set "beyond traditional teaching spaces into environments where existing classroom power dynamics no longer apply" (Alexander and

LeBaron 2009) and "traditional hierarchical classroom roles are blurred" (Doering 2006). This need not involve trekking through the jungle or dogsledding across the tundra, but it does generally mean getting out of the usual educational space (e.g., the physical classroom or the online course discussion board), the situated learning dynamics of which can have their own gravitational pull.

- Adventure learning activities also generally involve some element of real or perceived risk (Alexander and LeBaron 2009: 187). In some learning contexts, this may be physical or emotional risk; it may also involve putting something of monetary or other value at stake (see Volkema 2007).

- Finally, adventure learning activities are typically collaborative endeavors: students are offered "opportunities to explore real-world issues through authentic learning experiences within collaborative learning environments" – including both face-to-face and online learning environments (Doering 2006).

Adventure Learning with Negotiation Instructors in Istanbul

In Istanbul, we engaged in two different types of adventure learning activities: negotiating in a bazaar and navigating the city to produce a series of photographs. For the bazaar negotiations, the organizers grouped the roughly sixty participants (primarily negotiation educators and practitioners from around the world) into groups of five or six, striving for diversity in terms of nationality, gender, age, and academic discipline. The groups were given several hours to travel from the conference site to the Grand Bazaar and/or the Spice Bazaar,[4] to negotiate a purchase of food to share with the rest of the conference participants, and if desired, to negotiate for anything else the group (or any individual in the group) might like to buy. For the photography activity, conducted on the following day, participants were invited to form their own groups and given several hours to travel to a neighborhood of Istanbul with which they were unfamiliar, with instructions to have lunch and produce a series of photographs. The photographs were to represent the group consensus on the best representation of the intersection of the sacred and the secular, the most dangerous thing the group saw, and the most likely location for Istanbul's Central Intelligence Agency headquarters, along with a group self-portrait. The groups were also told that they should make one change to their instructions (e.g., by eliminating, adding, or changing a theme). Each group's photographs would be shared with the other conference participants.

Both activities were authentic in some of the same ways: for example, everyone negotiated "as themselves" and not in an assigned role; the stakes (though small) were real, in that we were spending real money and/or ending up with real photos; and the setting was outside the classroom/conference room – what some might consider the "real world." Yet on closer inspection, the two activities were designed quite differently, and implicated different aspects of authenticity.

The bazaar negotiations, on the one hand, were clearly labeled as negotiations – in the conference agenda and in the oral instructions. We were told that we were going to conduct a real negotiation. Moreover, the very context (Istanbul bazaars) primed us to think about bargaining and negotiation. Many of us planned strategies or experiments on the way there – e.g., "I'm going to try especially hard to learn what I can [or apply what I've learned] about relationship-building" or "Let's set up an experiment to see whether different members of our group receive different first offers from the same vendor for the same piece." So, one could say that the participants were very much *oriented* toward the fact that this was a negotiation activity.

The photography assignment, on the other hand, was not framed explicitly as a negotiation exercise. In the facilitator's words, it was a more oblique activity than the bazaar negotiation. We were not told that the point was to go off and negotiate; we were told to go to an unfamiliar neighborhood of Istanbul and to come back with a set of photos that reflected specific themes. The context in which we did this (heading off to various non-touristy neighborhoods of Istanbul) was less likely to prime us to think about negotiations than a setting like the bazaar, in which negotiations are constant and expected. Thus, while the instructions for the bazaar negotiations explicitly oriented us to the negotiative nature of the exercise, the photography assignment was more of a dis-orienting activity. Given that the participants were mostly negotiation instructors, and that the context was a negotiation pedagogy conference, it is probably safe to say that most participants quickly intuited that there would be some negotiation embedded within the activity. Nevertheless, it is also safe to say that there was less explicit framing/priming toward the negotiative nature of the photography activity, compared with the bazaar activity, and that the stated purpose and context of the photography activity was less likely to prime negotiation schemas.[5] Immediately upon return from both the bazaar negotiation and the photography activity, the Istanbul conference participants debriefed their experiences in facilitated small groups.

Interestingly, some of us commented during the second debriefing session that the negotiations that emerged from both assignments were authentic, but in quite different ways – even though the bazaar negotiations seemed at first glance to be the more authentic negotiation activity. Though we were not directly primed to think about and plan for negotiations in the photography activity, negotiations naturally emerged over all sorts of issues, such as where to go and how to get there; what the best photography subjects would be; where and how long to stop; how quickly to continue moving; and when and where to stop for lunch. While none of these were particularly weighty issues, they emerged based on authentic individual interests, preferences, and motivations, and not based on externally-imposed motivations. Moreover, there was an authenticity to the way in which our photography negotiations emerged – naturally and organically, without explicit labeling or priming – which is how most day-to-day negotiations emerge.

At the same time, the seemingly ultra-authentic bazaar negotiations had at least two elements of artificiality. First, the primary motivation/interest (i.e., to negotiate a purchase of food) was externally imposed; and second, we were very explicitly primed to view this as a negotiation activity (which is probably atypical of most negotiations). These contrasts should not be overstated – for instance, the motivation to take certain types of photos was also externally imposed; and the bazaar negotiations did leave room for the emergence of intrinsic preferences/interests around what to buy – but the pedagogical distinction is important. One activity was directly and explicitly framed as a negotiation, with high contextual priming; the other was much less directly framed as a negotiation, with lower contextual priming.

Curious about whether others believed that the differently-designed adventure learning activities had led to qualitatively different experiences and learning outcomes, we invited all conference participants to post summaries of their adventure learning experiences and debriefing sessions to the conference website after the conference. After eight of approximately sixty participants responded, we followed up with a six-question online survey,[6] and communicated directly with many colleagues to try to boost the number of responses and increase the richness of our data about their adventure learning experiences. Eighteen participants responded to the online survey (some of whom had also contributed summaries of their experiences). Based on our own experiences and multiple informal conversations with colleagues, we believe that the responses capture a reasonably accurate impression of participant experiences in Istanbul.

Learning From the "Orienting" Activity: Negotiating in Istanbul's Famed Bazaars

A consistent theme in participant reflections on the bazaar negotiations was excitement about the opportunity to apply academic theory to a "real" negotiation. Many consciously experimented with or watched for particular dynamics, such as rituals for breaking the ice; trust-building moves; the effect of first offers and ultimatums; the role of gender, age, and other observable traits in first offers; and techniques for creating value. When asked what they learned from a participant/student perspective (as opposed to an educator perspective), the participants cited a range of observations, including the pervasiveness of negotiation in everyday life, relevance of communication facility or barriers (especially given the range of primary languages among the conference participants and their negotiating counterparts), the concrete effects of relationships (both within negotiating groups and with counterparts in the bazaar), environmental influences (such as whether business at the vendor's stall was slow or busy), the role of informal and nonverbal communication, and the confirmation and/or disconfirmation of culturally-based assumptions.

From an educator's perspective, most conference participants were positive about the idea of incorporating adventure learning into a negotiation course. When asked what they saw as the primary pedagogical purposes of an orienting activity such as the bazaar negotiation, most cited the unique opportunity to introduce negotiation concepts in an authentic manner. More specifically, they commented on the opportunity to connect theory and practice by giving students the opportunity to plan, conduct, and debrief a "real" negotiation, to expose them to authentic dynamics stemming from gender, culture, and language issues, to experience authentic psychological aspects of negotiation such as feelings, worries, empathy, body language; and to increase students' awareness of their own role in a negotiation.

For those who were not as certain that the bazaar negotiation worked, the questions raised generally centered on the lack of clear learning objectives, making it impossible to assess whether they had been achieved. Moreover, several reports mentioned that the debriefing activity was not sufficient for nuanced reflection on the overall learning of the activity. A few raised the question of whether there is evidence that this potentially time-consuming approach is more effective than a good in-class simulation.

Learning From the "Dis-orienting" Activity: Navigating and Photographing Istanbul's Neighborhoods

Several reports suggested that the negotiations that naturally emerged during the "oblique" or "dis-orienting" negotiation assignment (i.e., the assignment to go to an unfamiliar neighborhood of Istanbul and take a series of thematic photographs) were highly authentic in their own ways, with reference made to the give-and-take in group negotiations about where to go and the factors relevant to how individuals influenced their groups' choices (such as who happened to have a map or a car; who had a strong preference about where to go; cultural norms; etc.). When asked what they learned from this activity from a participant (not an instructor) perspective, the participants cited insights different from those that followed the bazaar negotiations, such as that meaning-making systems are personal, that images can say more than words and evoke strong emotional reactions, that cultural differences can affect perspectives on both images and words (e.g., what does "dangerous" mean?), and that risk-taking and creativity are natural elements of negotiation.

When asked about the primary pedagogical purpose for assigning an oblique, dis-orienting activity such as the photography assignment in a negotiation course, the Istanbul conference participants focused less on the explicit connections of theory with practice (as they had with the bazaar negotiations) and more on the relevance of group dynamics and how the diversity of a group will require participants to explore different ways of thinking. The purposes they cited included: understanding different perspectives, especially given that the same assignment yielded very different results in terms of the photographs; highlighting the importance of framing, partisan perceptions and the "language" of symbols; challenging student curiosity and awareness; presenting students with an activity where they are not explicitly focused on the types of interactions that will be used for purposeful reflection; teaching intra-group negotiation; and highlighting the human factors in negotiation.

Adventure Learning with Graduate Students in Washington, D.C.

While we valued the reactions from Istanbul conference participants to the two adventure learning activities, we also recognized that conducting these activities with educators at a negotiation pedagogy conference might produce somewhat different results than conducting them with students in a negotiation course. We hypothesized that the negotiation educators at the conference – being familiar with negotiation theory and hyper-conscious of negotiation dynamics in action – would be more likely than most to plan for, experiment with, and purposively attempt to influence overtly labeled negotiations. We also assumed that the educators would be more likely than most to anticipate, notice, and participate intentionally in the negotiations that emerged organically from the more oblique photography activity – thus not being truly "dis-oriented" regarding the activity's purposes, particularly in the context of this conference.

A few months after the Istanbul conference, therefore, Cheldelin ran versions of the orienting and disorienting activities with her graduate-level, semester-long course on *Reflective Practice*, located in the greater Washington, D.C. area. The course comprised thirty students in a graduate program on conflict analysis and resolution, most of whom had not yet had any formal training in negotiation theory or practice.

The first of several "practices" in Cheldelin's course was a three-week module on negotiation, during which students were asked to form self-selected groups of three or four and, on their own time: 1) conduct a negotiation; and 2) produce a photograph that reflected the intersection of the secular and the sacred. Each student submitted a brief reflection paper on their experiences, and the students debriefed both within their adventure learning groups and as a whole class: our analyses of their experiences draws from each of these sources. Like the Istanbul activities, the Washington, D.C. activities were conducted outside the classroom in small groups, involved "real" negotiations and stakes, and included one activity that explicitly oriented students to the negotiation elements, as well as a more oblique activity intended to disorient students regarding the negotiation elements. There were a few structural differences between the two sets of activities: the D.C. graduate students conducted both exercises in the same groups and on the same day while the Istanbul conference participants did so in different groups on different days; and the graduate students focused on a single theme for their photography exercise while the conference participants sought photographs depicting multiple themes. In most significant respects, however, the pairs of activities in D.C. and Istanbul were similar, except for the critical fact that the Istanbul participants were familiar with negotiation theory and highly attuned to negotiation dynamics (particularly in the context of a negotiation pedagogy conference), whereas the D.C. participants – sophisticated as they may have been in other areas – were generally unfamiliar with negotiation theory and presumably substantially less attuned to negotiation dynamics.

Learning From the "Orienting" Activity: Negotiating In and Around Washington, D.C.

In response to the general instruction to "go out and negotiate something," Cheldelin's graduate students conducted a range of real-world negotiations. These included bargaining over the purchase of scarves and other clothing articles at local markets, bargaining over used book prices, securing the lowest-priced hotel package for a weekend in New York, replacing a lost cell phone, and procuring an alcoholic beverage without providing proper identification. The students' reflection papers demonstrated that they understood there were many negotiations taking place – not just the intended negotiation over a purchase or service, but also the intra-group negotiations over how much money was going to be spent, who would spend it, what they wanted to buy, and where they would go. As one student noted, "The planning phase was initially a negotiation between the group members to determine what we were going to purchase and where we were going to purchase the item."

Several additional themes emerged from the reflection papers, demonstrating the broad learning potential of the direct, orienting activity. For instance, some students identified cultural constraints on negotiation – sometimes associated with their own anxieties about negotiations that involved money – as reflected in two remarks:

- I was nominated to negotiate on behalf of the group as I had previous experience in such matters back home in Ghana. I was a bit surprised though when both Mary and Michelle informed me they were pretty bad negotiators when it came to making purchases but I guess in a country where most of the prices of items are fixed there will not be much opportunity for anyone to haggle on the price for goods and services.
- I have been responsible for negotiating tremendous contracts in the oil industry, but have never actually negotiated the price for something to purchase for myself. We do not have the bargaining culture in my family.

Several others identified gendered issues in negotiations and wanted to explore them, especially the extent to which gender matters when paired with other strategies such as building rapport:

- We wondered why it was so easy for the woman in our group to get a 20 percent discount, while the man struggled for a number of minutes. We postulated that this could be a consequence of sex/gender, culture and strategy. Perhaps the foreign woman merchant responded better to a foreign woman buyer who spoke to her in a friendly manner.
- I think that because I [being a male] was personable with the old man, that I had been to his village...we were able to create a positive relationship.
- Even under these rigid circumstances where price could not be easily negotiated, it did appear that certain gender issues – feminine characteristics such as warmth, and a non-threatening manner – can also be used to soften the setting of negotiation.

In addition to highlighting cultural and gender influences on negotiation, the orienting exercise deepened the class discussion about key negotiation dynamics and processes. Sample themes in their reflections included:

- Agency: As a third party, depending on the nature of the object and the stakes, I would do my best. But if I had to negotiate for myself, especially for some goods or services, I would certainly need someone to do it on my behalf. I guess this is all due to the way I have been brought up, and due to other factors. [This launched a full-class discussion of various factors involved in conducting a successful negotiation.]
- Ethics: At the conclusion her positive attitude towards the situation made me feel horrible about even having the audacity to ask her to risk her livelihood for one beer beverage. [This launched a class discussion about ethics and negotiation. Throughout the course "the beer incident" became a metaphor for ethical issues.]
- Interests and relationships: All she really wanted was for us to go away so she could take care of other customers. It was an interesting negotiation piece, and the biggest thing I learned from it is there is no real way to cover all the variables, no way to always know what the positions and interests are, unless you have a deeper connection with the person you are negotiating with, deeper than ours with the stall lady anyway. [This became part of the full discussion of prioritizing variables.]

Like conference participants in Istanbul, overwhelmingly these students enjoyed the exercise (even though some were anxious about having to negotiate):

- I felt we had a very positive experience and good value for the money; ...I was also happy that the girls had purchased something from Ecuador since I knew the money would go back to this man's family back in his country; we all agreed that the experience was positive and that the negotiation was easy.
- I feel as though the negotiation was an overwhelming success for my group.
- I was not really interested in getting an extremely good deal, as much as I was in completing the assignment and moving on with my life!
- I must say that I was euphoric that we had accomplished our group goal – and had a good time doing it.
- In retrospect, I am reminded how my own fear of incompetence sometimes gets in the way of trying new things that may actually be successful. I also sometimes assume the worst outcomes will happen when there is no real indication that is the case....I am anxious to hear how it went for the other groups.

One student, in particular, was able to articulate her concerns about the assignment and use them to consider her own areas for growth and development. She was part of a group that went to the Eastern Market in Washington, D.C. to negotiate for outerwear for children from an Ecuadorian vendor:

I had been dreading the prospect of having to conduct a purchase negotiation ever since we were given the assignment. I didn't want to have to go through that kind of situation. I've negotiated prices before but only when I've had to (e.g., living in post-Soviet Russia) or really wanted something....In retrospect, there are all sorts of things I could reflect on: how helpful it was that my comrades spoke Spanish and that one of them had been to the country; how well the three of us got along and worked together; how nice it was to discover that market there. However, I keep coming back to the thought that it feels to me that I came unprepared by not having enough money. I wonder if subconsciously I did that on purpose. Almost like I thought it would mean I wouldn't have to do the dreaded negotiation. While I could ruminate uselessly over that shameful thought, perhaps it is more useful to wonder how other parties sabotage negotiations – purposefully or subconsciously – so that they damage or delay the process....But I keep coming back to me...what does this all mean for me for future negotiations? What if it's not just during market negotiations that I freeze up? And I also keep thinking to myself that I wish I'd held eye contact a little longer when saying goodbye. I've thought about that several times since the transaction.

This student shared her concerns with the class and it resulted in a lengthy and thoughtful discussion about emotions, preparation, language, culture and sabotage. Though these were her personal reflections, other students were able to relate to the conversation and offer their experiences or perspectives on the issues.

Learning From the "Disorienting" Activity: Photographing the Secular and the Sacred Around Washington, D.C.

In addition to conducting a negotiation, the Washington, D.C. graduate students were instructed to work with the same group members to produce a photograph representing the intersection of the sacred and the secular.[7] This "disorienting" activity was intended to elicit intra-group negotiations, though the activity was not framed as a negotiation and students were not explicitly primed to notice the negotiations that arose.

In their reflection papers – the subject of which was supposed to be the entire group outing, including the explicit negotiation and the photography activity – only two of the thirty students addressed the photography activity. Most of the students may have been sufficiently "disoriented" as to the purpose of the activity – even though it occurred during a three-week unit titled "Negotiation" – as to not recognize the negotiations either as they occurred or during their individual reflections.[8] The two students who did address the emergent negotiations in the photography activity demonstrated awareness of their own thinking about negotiation, as well as of the negotiations themselves:

> Our first class activity, forming groups to find a photo that represents the intersection between the sacred and the secular and to negotiate a purchase, *led me to realize that negotiations – big and small – are a part of our everyday interactions.* Forming the groups themselves was really the first negotiation. This was followed by negotiating a mutually convenient time to meet and then negotiating with my boyfriend to reschedule the shopping and cleaning we had planned to do on the night that worked best for my group to get together.

When my group met, negotiations continued *[emphasis added]*.

We actually negotiated about a number of things on Saturday – what time and where we would meet – what item we would negotiate a price for – where we would eat lunch – what our image of the intersection of sacred and secular would be – how we would get to Arlington Cemetery – *and the dual concern model came to mind each time we agreed [emphasis added]*.

After submitting their reflection papers, the students sent their photographs to the teaching assistants who in turn enlarged them to poster-size and displayed them around the classroom. The photographs reflected varied and interesting images, with the U.S. Capitol building representing a recurring secular symbol (compared with the mosque as a dominant sacred symbol in the Istanbul photographs). For nearly two hours student groups presented their images to the other groups and discussed the processes by which they had selected, created, and interpreted the images. Cheldelin observed that most of this discussion focused on the intra-group negotiations, demonstrating awareness *at this point* of the negotiations that had occurred during the activity – even though there was little evidence that students had recognized the negotiations as they were happening, or even as they wrote their individual reflections. The discussion included observations on the benefits of brainstorming and collaboration, and on the processes by which they resolved disagreements over which image would best represent the assigned theme.

In general, both the reflection papers and the class discussion indicated that students found the exercises useful. They were able to recognize explicit negotiations as they occurred and more organic, emergent negotiations in retrospect (if not in real time), as well as demonstrating an understanding of the negotiation concepts and dynamics in play.

Implications for Negotiation Instructors

Based on our own experiences, the participant summaries, and the participant survey responses from the adventure learning activities at the Istanbul conference, and based on student reflection papers and class discussion from the parallel activities in the Washington, D.C.-area graduate course, we have developed the following tentative conclusions about what two different approaches to adventure learning can offer negotiation students or scholars of different levels of sophistication.

Learning Opportunities From "Orienting" Activities

Direct adventure learning negotiation activities that explicitly orient participants to the negotiative nature of the exercise (such as the bazaar negotiations in Istanbul or the more open-ended "go negotiate something" activity in Washington, D.C.) can offer:

- Multiple forms of authenticity, particularly environmental/contextual authenticity, authenticity of interpersonal dynamics such as gender and cultural issues, authenticity in the counterpart's motivations and behavior, and in some cases, emotional and psychological authenticity (such as the potential anxiety or exhilaration of conducting a real negotiation). For participants relatively new to the study of negotiation, and particularly if the activity is conducted early in the course, this might serve to highlight the complexities of negotiation, to reinforce the relevance and utility of negotiation theory, and/or to provide a shared experience – a shared reference point – with which to connect concepts and issues that arise later in the course. For more sophisticated participants – or if the activity is conducted late in the course, perhaps as a capstone – the activity could provide an authentic context in which to notice or test theories and/or to apply particular skills – which leads directly to the second learning opportunity:

- An opportunity for participants to be highly intentional about how they approach the negotiation aspects of the activity, because they are oriented to its nature and purposes. For instance, they could (at the direction of the instructor or of their own accord) watch for particular dynamics such as anchoring or relationship-building moves, consciously attempt to apply particular skills or techniques, or even conduct mini-experiments.[9] Less advanced students might simply try to observe certain dynamics or their own behaviors and reactions; more advanced students might be more purposeful about participating in the negotiation, as mentioned above.

- An opportunity for students to collaborate in a meaningful way and build relationships, particularly at the beginning of a course. Participants in both the Istanbul and the Washington, D.C. activities commented on the intra-group bonding effect the activities created.

Comments from Istanbul participants reinforced the notion that an orienting adventure learning activity can offer different opportunities early in a course (or with less advanced students) than later in a course (or with more advanced students). Several observed that the intra-group relationship-building effect would probably be more useful and relevant early in a course or workshop rather than at the end. Others noted that, with the rich array of negotiation concepts that might arise from such an activity, it might be most appropriate as a capstone experience, because students will have more ability to articulate their experiences in negotiation terms at the end of a course than at the beginning.

Learning Opportunities From "Disorienting" Activities

On the other hand, the more oblique, indirect activities that intentionally disorient students as to the negotiative elements – or that at least leave those elements implicit – seem to offer somewhat different forms of authenticity, such as authenticity regarding the unpredictable and organic way in which negotiations often arise – *without* framing or labeling or opportunity for preparation, as well as authenticity in the interests motivating those negotiations and in the emotions and psychological reactions that accompany them.

Because the negotiations that arise in a disorienting activity are less expected than those in an orienting activity, the disorienting activity provides a context in which to assess participants' attunement to negotiation opportunities. Early in a course – particularly with introductory students such as those in the Washington, D.C. course – the disorienting activity can also offer a baseline for student self-assessment: How do they really behave when a negotiation (or negotiation opportunity) arises naturally, without the neat frame of role-play instructions? Do they notice the opportunity? Do they recognize it as a (potential) negotiation? Do they consciously employ analytical, relational, cognitive, or other negotiation skills? With more advanced participants such as those at the Istanbul conference (or later in a course), a disorienting activity can provide a vehicle for assessing the extent to which participants have developed their ability to notice, recognize and exploit negotiation opportunities – in other words, their ability to apply in authentic practice what they have already learned in theory, and perhaps in the more framed and primed context of role-plays.

The following charts summarize some benefits and drawbacks of the orienting and disorienting adventure learning approaches, and compare them to more traditional classroom experiential activities:

Orienting Activities	In-classroom setting	Out-of-classroom / adventure learning setting
Definition	Learning activities in which the nature and/or purposes are explicit; students understand what they should try to do and why	
Examples	-Role simulation with explicit instructions to apply particular concepts/skills (e.g., presentation/readings on value creation techniques followed by a role play in which students are instructed to attempt to create value). -"Deliberate practice" drills in which students practice particular micro-skills, receive feedback, and refine their attempts.	Adventure learning activity in which students are instructed to conduct a "real" negotiation with someone outside of the course (e.g., to purchase something at a market, to negotiate the interest rate on a credit card, etc.)
Benefits	Opportunity for conscious application and practice of theory/advice. Classroom exercises can be tailored to highlight particular issues or dynamics. Use of the same exercise for all students facilitates instructor and group understanding of the context as well as cross-student comparisons. Compatible with "deliberate practice" approach to behavioral skill-building.	Opportunity for conscious practice and application of theory / advice. Certain aspects of the activity (e.g., non-student negotiation counterparts, "real" stakes, possible great discretion in how to prepare for and conduct the activity, inherent unpredictability and complexity) may more closely replicate "real" negotiations. Can serve as icebreaker / relationship-building exercise.
Limitations	Can raise concerns about applicability in the "real world." Opportunities for preparation and practice may be limited by the nature of the exercise (e.g., students may not have the option to conduct additional research or preparation beyond the bounds of the instructions).	Can pose logistical and ethical challenges. Variations in context and experiences can make cross-student comparisons difficult.

Figure 1 – Orienting Activities

		In-classroom setting	Out-of-classroom / adventure learning setting
Disorienting activities	**Definition**	Learning activities with at least some oblique or hidden purposes; students are not explicitly told (or are only partially told, or are misled about) what they should try to do and why	
	Examples	-"Unfreezing" exercises (e.g., Argyris & Schön's X-Y Exercise) -Iterated Prisoner's Dilemma exercises (e.g., Oil Pricing or Populator) in which the stated goal of the exercise (e.g., to maximize profits) may mask additional purposes (e.g., to highlight interrelationships among behavior, trust, and reputation) -Role simulations with hidden/non-obvious "twists" (e.g., simulations in which both parties have a strong incentive to negotiate but which are structured such that no deal is possible that is better than both parties' BATNAs)	Adventure learning activity in which the stated goal of the exercise may mask additional purposes (e.g., students may be told that the goal is to explore an unfamiliar neighborhood in small groups and return with a series of themed photos, while the unspoken purpose is to reflect on the negotiations that arise organically within the groups)
	Benefits	Can generate powerful "a-ha" moments. Can predictably (from the instructor's standpoint) highlight particular dynamics and insights. Can help assess negotiation "executive function": i.e., capacity to recognize negotiation opportunities and apply negotiation skills without explicit direction.	Can offer authenticity in motivation, emotions, interests, and "organic emergence" of negotiation opportunities. Can help assess negotiation "executive function": i.e., capacity to recognize negotiation opportunities and apply negotiation skills without explicit direction. Can serve as icebreaker / relationship-building exercise.
	Limitations	Can generate resentment; repeated use can raise students' suspicions and incent them to "game" simulations by looking for "the catch." May be more appropriate for current skill assessment and making a memorable point than for practice / development.	May be difficult to justify or explain exercise; may be difficult to motivate students. May be more appropriate for current skill assessment than for practice / development.

Figure 2 – Disorienting Activities

Challenges to Incorporating Adventure Learning Into Negotiation Teaching

In addition to the benefits and opportunities described above, there are, of course, challenges to the use of adventure learning in negotiation teaching. While most of the Istanbul conference participants were positive about their experiences and about the potential to use adventure learning for negotiation teaching, a small number of participants questioned whether the activity accomplished any more than building group rapport and camaraderie. They noted that it may not have been worth the time commitment required for its execution, and it was generally conceded that this activity might be impossible in a short (one- or two-day) training format, given the requisite time commitment.

In response to survey questions about how likely they were to use adventure learning and about challenges they foresaw in doing so, the Istanbul conference participants identified a number of considerations, including:

- The potential difficulty of making the adventure learning activity relevant to teaching and learning objectives, and determining the right time in the course (sequencing) for an adventure learning activity to be meaningful. We attempt to address these concerns above, identifying specific learning opportunities for both orienting and disorienting activities either at the beginning or at the end of a course.

- The complex and uncontrollable nature of a "field" experience, in which the dynamics are far less predictable than those in a role-play. This characteristic of authenticity means that the instructor should have a clear plan for debriefing the exercise – whether that plan involves focusing on particular concepts and dynamics such as the influence of culture, or whether it involves working with whatever questions, observations, and reflections the students bring from the experience. Without some sort of reflective debriefing activity – whether a discussion, reflection paper, group presentation, or other follow up – the learning activity runs the risk of being reduced to a fun field trip.

- The need for a suitable environment (e.g., an alternative to Istanbul's Grand Bazaar, for those based further afield) or context in which to conduct the activity – particularly a direct negotiation activity. Cheldelin's experiment in the Washington, D.C. area indicates that students need not have access to a traditional bazaar in order to engage in real-world negotiations: they demonstrated substantial creativity in finding negotiation opportunities, ranging from an attempt

(by a student old enough to legally drink alcohol) to purchase beer at a campus bar without the requisite photo identification, to attempts at bargaining over the prices of
various goods and services (clothing items, hotel reservations), to an attempt to negotiate a free or discounted replacement for a lost cell phone.

- Other opportunities might include inviting students to negotiate for a reduction in their credit card interest rates[10] or to
create the most value possible from one dollar.[11] A disorienting adventure learning activity poses a slightly different
problem: it is not particularly difficult to find an environment in which students might take photographs, for instance, but it might be a challenge to frame the activity so
that students are sufficiently disoriented regarding the negotiation aspects while still being adequately motivated. One
educator at the Istanbul conference suggested having groups
of students take photographs of the "best" and "worst" negotiators they saw – which permits not only reflection based
on the explicit activity of representing negotiators in images
(e.g., the relevance of identifying characteristics such as
race, age, gender, and attractiveness; attention to context,
such as negotiating bail versus resolving a marital dispute;
and/or noting stereotyping or in-group preference tendencies) – but also reflection based on the more oblique activity:
the inevitable, organic, intra-group negotiations over whom
to photograph, and how and why.[12] Another educator suggested looking to locally significant places or events for ideas
on how to frame a disorienting activity. She noted that her
law school building was about to be demolished to make
room for a new building, and that she planned to ask student teams to take photos of their favorite locales in the old
building – not revealing until later that a secondary (or even
primary) purpose of the activity was to elicit intra-group negotiations and to assess students' real-time attunement to
these negotiations.[13]

- Ensuring that adventure learning is (and is perceived to be)
a legitimate graduate level activity, including careful consideration of how to grade it, how to make it a significant challenge, and how to frame the assignment so the activity is
taken seriously by students and faculty peers. As many of
the Istanbul participants commented, it is particularly important for the instructor to be clear (at least to himself or
herself) about the goals and objectives for adventure learning activities, to provide for some form of reflection or de-

briefing, and to have a plan (perhaps even a rubric) for the way in which student work will be analyzed and/or assessed. With clear goals for the activity and reflection – even if these are not disclosed to the students until later – the instructor can facilitate student meaning-making from the experience. Disorienting activities in particular may risk appearing frivolous to others – at least at the outset – but grounding them in clear learning goals and assessment criteria can help ensure their relevance as well as their perceived legitimacy.

Conclusion

We believe, based on our own experiences as adventure learning participants and on the debriefing sessions and written data from the Istanbul and Washington, D.C. experiments, that adventure activities can offer powerful learning opportunities for negotiation students. Accordingly, they are well worth considering as a supplement to (not necessarily a replacement for) more traditional teaching tools such as role-plays and case analyses. Not all adventure learning activities are created equal, however, and negotiation instructors interested in using them should bear in mind the following:

- First, designing an "authentic" negotiation learning activity is not as simple as it may sound. There are many forms of authenticity – including environmental, behavioral, psychological, motivational, and developmental – and it would behoove instructors to consider which elements of authenticity would best serve the learning needs and goals for the particular group of participants.

- Second, a negotiation instructor may wish to consider the pros and cons of a more direct, explicit, "orienting" adventure learning activity (like the bazaar negotiations) versus a more indirect, oblique, "disorienting" learning activity (like the photography assignment). Why might an instructor choose one over the other? What are the implications of each, from a curriculum design perspective? In general, more direct, orienting activities seem to be more useful for prescriptive purposes (such as conscious attention to particular dynamics or deliberate application of certain skills), while more indirect, disorienting activities seem better-suited to descriptive purposes (such as assessing students' ability to notice and/or act on organically emergent negotiations and negotiation opportunities).

- Third, an instructor should consider the best point or points in a course to incorporate adventure learning. Applied earlier in a course, adventure learning can provide a baseline for assessing students' current capacities, ground the course content and provide a reference point to which students can connect concepts and theories learned later in the course, motivate students to learn more and improve their skills, and create a cohesive, relationship-building experience that can influence the class dynamic for the remainder of the course. Applied later in the course (perhaps as a capstone experience), it can offer opportunities to connect theory and practice, to assess students' abilities to transfer their learning from the classroom to the outside world, and to enrich students' understanding of various concepts and theories and the complexities of how they arise in authentic practice.

- Finally, regardless of how, when, or with whom an instructor uses adventure learning, he or she should have a clear set of learning goals in mind (whether or not these are made explicit to the students), along with a plan for debriefing or reflecting on the exercise. This helps ensure that the activity is a basis for learning, in addition to being a fun and perhaps relationship-building experience.

In sum, adventure education can offer different forms of authenticity depending on whether students are explicitly oriented to the activity's nature and purposes or whether they are intentionally disoriented through more oblique instructions. Negotiation educators can maximize the learning opportunities from these "authentic experiences" by tailoring their design and timing to fit the participants and their learning goals. No travel to Istanbul – "that fabled bridge between east and west" (Gloom 2005) – is required for orientation and disorientation, or for the adventure.

Notes

[1] By "role-play" we refer to an exercise in which two or more students are given instructions to assume certain facts, goals, and other information regarding a particular "role" – such as that of a buyer or seller – and are asked to negotiate with each other based on those instructions. While some role-plays are designed to be highly dynamic and complex – in some cases, directly connected with real-world events – most are relatively static in that students are bound by the instructions they are given, and somewhat predictable in that they are designed to elicit particular dynamics (though human factors ensure that they are never completely predictable) (see Weiss 2008). The term "role-plays" in this article refers to the latter form. For examples on negotiation-oriented role-play, see the Program on Negotiation Clearinghouse, http://www.pon.org/catalog/index.php (last visited May 14, 2010); and the Dispute Resolution Research Center,

http://www.kellogg.northwestern.edu/drrc/teaching/index.htm (last visited May 10, 2010).

[2] A multi-year effort to critique contemporary negotiation pedagogy and create new training designs, spearheaded by Hamline University School of Law in cooperation with the JAMS Foundation (www.jamsadr.com/jams-foundation), JAMS International ADR Center (Italy) (www.jamsadrcenter.com), and *Negotiation Journal*. This project – which pays particular attention to cultural considerations in the content and design of negotiation education – centers around a series of workshops for negotiation educators and practitioners in Rome, Istanbul, and Beijing; the October 2009 conference at Bilgi University in Istanbul was the second of the three. See http://law.hamline.edu/dispute_resolution/second_generation_negotiation.html.

[3] Other concerns about role-play use stem from lack of empirical evidence regarding the transfer of in-class learning to authentic out-of-class negotiations (see Movius 2008) and culturally-situated assumptions about learning styles and preferences (see LeBaron and Patera 2009).

[4] See generally, Istanbul Government (English) website http://english.istanbul.gov.tr/ (last visited May 14, 2010). Both the Spice Bazaar (sometimes called the Egyptian Spice Bazaar or Mısır Çarşısı) and the Grand Bazaar (also known as the Covered Bazaar or Kapalıçarsı) are located in the historic center of Istanbul, on the European side of the Bosphorus, and are famed both for the variety of merchandise on offer and for the constant, overt bargaining processes (many items are not labeled with prices, particularly in the Grand Bazaar). The Spice Bazaar dates to the seventeenth century; the Grand Bazaar dates to the fifteenth century and is one of the oldest and largest continuously operating covered markets in the world. See http://english.istanbul.gov.tr.

[5] Other researchers have demonstrated the significance of framing to the way in which participants are likely to interpret, approach, and experience the exercise: for instance, the framing of an iterated Prisoner's Dilemma game as "The Community Game" or "the Wall Street Game" was far more predictive of students' approach to the game than their perceived collaborative or competitive tendencies (see Ross and Ward 1996). Here, too, the framing was different: the trip to the bazaar was framed as a negotiation, while the photography activity was framed as a photography activity.

[6] The six questions were: 1) Please answer the following as though you were a negotiation student who had just participated in the Day One adventure learning activity from Istanbul ("Negotiating the Grand Bazaar"), and were reflecting on the experience for your professor: What were two or three things you learned or had reinforced from your "Negotiating the Grand Bazaar" experience? 2) Please answer the following as though you were a negotiation student who had just participated in the Day Two adventure learning activity from Istanbul ("Negotiating Images of Istanbul" – the photography activity), and were reflecting on the experience for your professor: What were two or three things you learned or had reinforced from your "Negotiating Images of Istanbul" (photography activity) experience? 3) Now put your negotiation teacher hat on. What would be your primary pedagogical purpose(s) in assigning an activity comparable to the Day One adventure learning activity ("Negotiating the Grand Bazaar")? 4) Please

keep your negotiation teacher hat on. What would be your primary peda-gogical purpose(s) in assigning an activity comparable to the Day Two ad-venture learning activity ("Negotiating Images of Istanbul" – i.e., the photography activity)? 5) How likely are you to use adventure learning in your negotiation teaching, and why/why not? 6) Please speculate as to what you think the biggest challenge would be for you to use adventure learning effectively in teaching negotiation.

[7] This replicates one piece of the "dis-orienting" activity in Istanbul, which involved self-selecting groups, navigating to an unfamiliar neighborhood, taking a series of five to six themed photographs (one of which was to rep-resent the intersection of the sacred and the secular; others involved themes such as a group self-portrait, the most dangerous thing the group saw, and the place most likely to be the Central Intelligence Agency headquarters in Istanbul); and changing at least one of the rules.

[8] It is also possible that some students misunderstood the assignment, as-suming that the reflection paper was the work product for the explicit nego-tiation activity and that the photograph itself was the work product for the more oblique photography activity. As these were not the instructions, however, it seems unlikely that twenty-eight out of thirty students had the same misunderstanding. More likely, at least some of them simply did not notice the intra-group negotiations over the photographs or did not con-sider them negotiations worth analyzing – though it became clear in the full-class debriefing sessions that multiple intra-group negotiations did oc-cur.

[9] As an example, one group in Istanbul experimented with a variation on Ian Ayres' well-known study (Ayres 1991) on car dealerships in Chicago, where white male experimenters received the best (lowest) offers and black female experimenters received the worst (highest) offers. Members of the group – which was quite diverse in terms of age, gender, ethnicity, and na-tional origin – separately approached the same Grand Bazaar stall to inquire about the price for the same carved wooden box, to find out whether they would receive different opening offers (see Schneider 2009). The group members' familiarity with the Ayres research and curiosity about its cross-cultural implications undoubtedly contributed to this approach to the activ-ity.

[10] We thank Professor Clark Freshman of Hastings School of Law for this example, which he uses with his own negotiation students.

[11] For instance, a student might negotiate with a local restaurant for a $20 gift certificate, in exchange for the dollar and a promise to distribute the restaurant's takeout menus to the entire class (an idea inspired by a similar feat by Professor Robert Bordone of Harvard Law School, whom we grate-fully acknowledge).

[12] Thanks again to Professor Clark Freshman of Hastings School of Law.

[13] We thank Professor Andrea Schneider of Marquette University Law School for this example.

References

Alexander, N. and M. LeBaron. 2009. Death of the role-play. In *Rethinking negotiation teaching: Innovations for context and culture*, edited by C. Honeyman, J. Coben, and G. DePalo. St. Paul, MN: DRI Press.

American Bar Association, Section of Legal Education and Admissions to the Bar. July 1992. *Report of the Task Force on Law Schools and the Profession: Narrowing the Gap. Available at http://www.abanet.org/legaled/publications/onlinepubs/maccrate.html (a.k.a. the MacCrate Report)* (last accessed May, 14, 2010).

Argyris, C. 1982. Reasoning, learning, and action: Individual and organizational. San Francisco: Jossey-Bass.

Ayres, I. 1991. Fair driving: Gender and race discrimination in retail car negotiations. *Harvard Law Review* 104: 817-872.

Barab, S. A., K. D. Squire, and W. Dueber. 2000. A co-evolutionary model for supporting the emergence of authenticity. *Educational Technology Research and Development* 48: 37-62.

Barton, K., P. McKellar, and P. Maharg. 2007-2008. Authentic fictions: Simulation, professionalism and legal learning. *Clinical Law Review* 14(1): 143-93.

Brown, J. S. and P. Duguid. 2000. *The social life of information.* Boston, MA: Harvard Business School Press.

Brown, J. S., A. Collins, and P. Duguid. 1989. Situated cognition and the culture of learning. *Educational Researcher* 18(1): 32-41.

Buntz, C. G. and D. L. Carper. 1987. A conflict management curriculum in business and public administration. *Negotiation Journal* 3(2): 191-204.

Crampton, A. and M. Manwaring. 2008. Reality and artifice in teaching negotiation: The variable benefits of "keeping it real" in simulations. *Teaching Negotiation* 2(1) (copies accessible at http://tinyurl.com/ye4ywzx) (last accessed May 14, 2010).

Dewey, J. 1938/1997. *Experience and education.* New York, NY: Touchstone.

Doering, A. 2006. Adventure learning: Transformative hybrid online education. *Distance Education* 27(2): 197-215.

Doering, A. Adventure learning: Situating learning in an authentic context. *Innovate* 3(6). Available at http://www.innovateonline.info/index.php?view=article and id =342 (last accessed May 14, 2010).

Doolittle, P. E. 1997. Vygotsky's zone of proximal development as a theoretical foundation for cooperative learning. *Journal on Excellence in College Teaching* 8(1): 83-103.

Driscoll, M. P. 2004. *Psychology of learning for instruction*, 3rd edn. Needham Heights, MA: Allyn and Bacon.

Ebner, N. and Y. Efron. 2005. Using tomorrow's headlines for today's training: Creating pseudoreality in conflict resolution simulation games. *Negotiation Journal* 21(3): 377-394.

Fortgang, R. 2000. Taking stock: An analysis of negotiation pedagogy across four professional fields. *Negotiation Journal* 16(4): 325-338.

Fosnot, C. T. (ed). 2005. *Constructivism: Theory, perspectives, and practice.* 2nd edn. New York: Teachers College Press.

Friedman, V. J. and R. Lipshitz. 1992. Teaching people to shift cognitive gears: Overcoming resistance on the road to Model II. *Journal of Applied Behavioral Science* 28(1): 188-136.

"Gloom with a view," review of *Istanbul,* by Orhan Pamuk. *Economist* (April 19, 2005) 375:71.

Herrington, A. and J. Herringtong. 2005. *Authentic learning environments in higher education.* Hershey, PA: Information Science Publishing.

Houde, J. 2007. Analogically situated experiences: Creating insights through novel contexts. *Academy of Management Learning and Education* 6: 321-331.

Kenworthy, A. L. 2010. Service-learning and negotiation: An educational "win-win." *Journal of Management Education* 34(1): 62-87.

Koo, G. 2007. *New skills, new learning: Legal education and the promise of technology.* Berkman Center for Internet and Society Research Publication Series, No. 2007-4. Available at http://cyber.law.harvard.edu/publications/2007/New_Skills_New_Learning (last accessed May 14, 2010).

Kovach, K. 2009. Culture, cognition, and learning preferences, In *Rethinking negotiation teaching: Innovations for context and culture,* edited by C. Honeyman, J. Coben, and G. DePalo. St. Paul, MN: DRI Press.

Lave, J. and E. Wenger. 1991. *Situated learning: legitimate peripheral participation.* Cambridge, UK: Cambridge University Press.

LeBaron, M. and M. Patera. 1999. Reflective practice in the new millennium. In *Rethinking negotiation teaching: Innovations for context and culture,* edited by C. Honeyman, J. Coben, and G. DePalo. St. Paul, MN: DRI Press.

Lempereur, A. P. 2004. Innovation in teaching negotiation: Toward a relevant use of multimedia tools. *International Negotiation* 9(1): 141-160.

Lewicki, R. J. 1999. Teaching negotiation and dispute resolution in colleges of business: The state of the practice and challenges for the future. In *Teaching negotiation: Ideas and innovations,* edited by M. Wheeler. Cambridge, MA: PON Books. Originally published in 1999 in *Negotiation eclectics: Essays in memory of Jeffrey Z. Rubin,* edited by D. Kolb. Cambridge, MA: PON Books.

McAdoo, B. and M. Manwaring. 2009. Teaching for implementation: Designing negotiation curricula to maximize long-term learning. *Negotiation Journal* 25(2): 195-215.

Movius, H. 2008. The effectiveness of negotiation training. *Negotiation Journal* 24(4): 509-531.

National Research Council. 1999. *How people learn: Brain, mind, experience, and school,* edited by J. Bransford, A. Brown, and R. Cocking. Washington, DC: National Academy Press.

Patton, B. 2009. The deceptive simplicity of teaching negotiation: Reflections on thirty years of the negotiation workshop. *Negotiation Journal* 25(4): 481-498.

Peterson. R. A. 2005. In search of authenticity. *Journal of Management Studies* 42(5): 1083-1098.

Petraglia, J. 1998. *Reality by design: The rhetoric and technology of authenticity in education*. Mahwah, NJ: Lawrence Ehrlbaum Associates Inc.

Prouty, D., J. Panicucci, and R. Collinson. 2007. *Adventure education: Theory and applications*. Champaign, IL: Human Kinetics.

Reeves, T. C., J. Herrington, and R. Oliver. 2002. Authentic activities and online learning. In *Quality Conversations: Proceedings of the 25th HERDSA [Higher Education Research and Development Society of Australasia] Annual Conference, Perth, Western Australia, 7-10 July 2002*: 562-567.

Ross, L., and A. Ward. 1996. Naïve realism: Implications for social conflict and misunderstanding. In *Values and knowledge*, edited by T. Brown, E. Reed, and E. Turiel. Hillsdale, NJ: Lawrence Erlbaum Associates.

Schneider, A. 2009. Does the Ayres study work in Istanbul? *ADR Prof Blog*. Available at http://www.indisputably.org/?p=622 (last accessed May 14, 2010).

Spoormans, H., J. Cohen, and J. Moust. 1981. The course on negotiation at the faculty of law, University of Limburg, Maastricht, The Netherlands. *Negotiation Journal* 7(3): 331-337.

Sullivan, W., A. Colby, J. Wegner, L. Bond, and L. Shulman. 2007. Educating lawyers: Preparation for the profession of law (a.k.a. the "Carnegie Report"). San Francisco: Jossey-Bass.

Susskind, L. E. and J. Corburn. 1999. Using simulations to teach negotiation: Pedagogical theory and practice. In *Teaching negotiation: Ideas and innovations*, edited by M. Wheeler. Cambridge, MA: PON Books.

Taylor, D. 1994. Inauthentic authenticity or authentic inauthenticity? *TESL-EJ* 1(2): A-1.

Volkema, R. J. 2007. Negotiating for money: Adding a dose of reality to classroom negotiations. *Negotiation Journal* 23(4): 473-485.

Vygotsky, L. S. 1978. *Mind in society: The development of higher mental processes*. Cambridge, MA: Harvard University Press.

Webster's II New College Dictionary. 1999. Boston, MA: Houghton Mifflin Company.

Weiss, S. E. 2008. Mega-simulations in negotiation teaching: Extraordinary investments with extraordinary benefits. *Negotiation Journal* 24(3): 325-353.

Wenger, E. 1998. *Communities of practice: Learning, meaning and identity*. Cambridge, UK: Cambridge University Press.

Wheeler, M. 2006. Is teaching negotiation too easy, too hard, or both? *Negotiation Journal* 22(2): 187-197.

Whetten, D. A. 2007. Principles of effective course design: What I wish I had known about learner-centered teaching 30 years ago. *Journal of Management Education* 31: 339-357.

Williams, G. R. and J. M. Geis. 1999. Negotiation skills training in the law school curriculum. In *Negotiation eclectics: Essays in memory of Jeffrey Z. Rubin*, edited by D. Kolb. Cambridge, MA: PON Books.

Wilson, A. L. 1993. The promise of situated cognition. *New Directions for Adult and Continuing Education* 57: 71-79.

Young, M. F. 1993. Instructional design for situated learning. *Educational Technology Research and Development* 41(1): 43-58.

⋙ 9 ⋘

Bringing Negotiation Teaching to Life: From the Classroom to the Campus to the Community

*Lynn P. Cohn & Noam Ebner**

Editors' Note: Taking your students to the Grand Bazaar of Istanbul, Cohn and Ebner point out, is educational all right, but it is expensive. So they turn their attention to what might be done with adventure learning in the immediate environment of a university. A whole menu of options, it turns out, is readily available.

Introduction

Negotiation, by its very nature, is a practical endeavor. It is a real-world phenomenon, encountered and practiced numerous times in the course of a single day.[1] Reflecting this, negotiation pedagogy always maintains a bridge connecting what is being taught in the classroom with the world students encounter outside of it. Depending on teaching goals, this bridge might be considered a major element of the curriculum (such as in an executive training course) or a less significant one (such as in a course focusing primarily on negotiation theory); but it is always there.

Various teaching methods are used to relate negotiation theories and concepts to real-life situations, such as case studies, eliciting of stories from students' own experiences, analysis of current events or of scenes from television series or popular movies, and other techniques. However, no single method enjoys the same widespread use as that of the simulated negotiation referred to as a "role-play."[2] [2a]

* **Lynn P. Cohn** is the director of the Program on Negotiations and Mediation and a clinical associate professor of law at the Northwestern University School of Law in Chicago, Illinois. Her email address is l-cohn@law.northwestern.edu. **Noam Ebner** is an assistant professor at the Werner Institute at Creighton University's School of Law, where he chairs the online masters program in Negotiation and Dispute Resolution. His email address is noamebner@creighton.edu.

In addition to their value for mediating between theory and reality, role-plays are valued by negotiation teachers for a variety of reasons, including their contribution to concept learning and to student interest and motivation.

However important these goals of role-play might be, the common wisdom that role-play is the *best* method to satisfy these aims has been critiqued from different perspectives in recent years (see Ebner and Kovach, *Simulation 2.0*, in this volume). These include challenges from inside the world of negotiation pedagogy, such as Nadja Alexander and Michelle LeBaron's (2009) critique. They noted (among other issues) the cultural challenges and implications of assuming another's identity; student resistance to role-play for a number of reasons; the difficulty of disassociating one's self from the experience; and the challenge of transferring the experience to real life (Alexander and LeBaron 2009). Additional challenges emerge from the wider literature on use of simulation as an educational tool in the social sciences, where extensive research shows that while role-play certainly delivers the goods in terms of student motivation, the actual *content learning* benefits teachers tend to associate with simulation do not play out in reality (Druckman and Ebner 2008; also see Druckman and Ebner, *Enhancing Concept Learning*, in this volume); students' understanding of concepts they learn through simulation is no better than, for example, the understanding they gain from a classroom lecture.

While it is unlikely – and inadvisable – that role-play would be completely banished from the negotiation teaching agenda as a result of the critique mentioned above (this point is elaborated on by Ebner and Kovach, *Simulation 2.0*, in this volume), the challenge of moving forward and exploring new ways to augment and support the gains of simulation with other types of learning is intriguing. Alexander and LeBaron suggested that teachers begin using a wider array of experiential learning methods, particularly the use of "adventure learning" modules. Adventure learning in the context of negotiation teaching can be defined as participation in a real negotiation experience rather than a simulated role play, coupled with the opportunity to reflect and debrief the experience following the negotiation.

We agree that the resources currently dedicated to simulation should be shared between a wider range of methods. In this chapter, models of learning that allow participants to have *authentic* experiences in real life contexts are suggested. Particularly, we will focus on the use of adventure learning for bridging theory to practice and preparing students for competence in their future interactions.

Adventure learning in negotiation might take on many forms; it could be a direct negotiation assignment, such as the "Go out to the Bazaar and negotiate for something" instructions given to the participants in the Istanbul Rethinking Negotiation Teaching conference in October 2009. Alternatively, it might be assigning students to a task that obliquely engages them in implementing and reflecting on concepts related to negotiation, such as team building, collaboration, emotions and trust. Common examples of such indirect activities might be a ropes course or a survival mission.

In this chapter, we will explore incorporating adventure learning into a course offered in any higher educational setting including a business school, law school, undergraduate or graduate program.[3] The goal is to create a menu of adventures that complement and reinforce the learning in such classes. The following categories of learning modules range from adding some adventure to classroom experiences to ranging outside of the classroom setting to the campus or surrounding community:

1) A classroom experience with real implications for the student;
2) A role play set in a real-world setting, in which students engage with professional negotiation opposites;
3) An assignment in which students negotiate for themselves;
4) An assignment that involves the student applying a key concept from the course out-of-class;
5) An opportunity to observe or participate in real-life negotiations of others; or
6) An out-of-class experience not involving negotiating directly but which allows the student to transfer learning from the adventure to their understanding of negotiations.

In crafting activities involving adventure learning, we suggest looking at venues and resources close at hand. While taking your students to Istanbul's Grand Bazaar might be a wonderful idea, few institutions have the resources to permit such a trip; moreover, for adventure learning to be practical and motivating, the focus should be on participating in the exercise rather than on costly travel to a distant location. And, as it turns out, the average university campus and surrounding community offer multiple venues and opportunities for adventure learning. Providing students with close-at-hand training grounds, by means of changing the way they approach familiar surroundings and interactions, is likely to heighten motivation, in addition to reducing the investment of time and effort necessary to participate in the activity.

Creating Real Implications for Classroom Experiences

When involved in a traditional role play simulation, students take on the interests, character and judgment of a fictitious persona. Students report that the separation of themselves from the person they portray at times allows them to avoid responsibility for the judgment calls which they make on this other's behalf: "While I would never have done that, my role allowed or even encouraged that choice." Being in character may also give students the sense that extreme bargaining choices and ethical calls do not have significant consequences since the negotiation "was not real." The fact that role plays typically involve outcomes with pretend benefits and losses furthers this disconnect. Some teachers use a range of methods to incorporate a dose of real-world stick-and-carrot in simulations.[4]

Below, we take this further, suggesting that teachers overcome this disassociation from the negotiation experience by augmenting their curriculum with small, but real, negotiation experiences that have real implications for the students and in which they must act on their own behalf, right there in the classroom.[5] If course participants actually experience the consequences of their decisions, they may engage more authentically in both the negotiation and the learning that flows from the exercise.

Negotiating for Food/Drink

Every teacher knows the value of providing food and drink to the class. Students are notorious for always being hungry, thirsty and broke. Allowing the students to negotiate over food and drink choices to be enjoyed during the class provides an immediate sense of what good negotiation skills can accomplish (Press and Honeyman, *Second Dive into Adventure Learning*, in this volume).

In the *Trading Up* negotiation created by Jay Folberg, participants value what different food items in the drink, candy, fruit and pizza categories are worth to them based on their own preferences. Items from these categories are then randomly distributed to the students and they are then allowed to engage in several rounds of negotiation with an increasing number of counterparts each round. Following the final round, each student can see how they were able to increase the value of their items through the process of negotiation.

Negotiating a Team Contract

Negotiation courses often involve team exercises or projects. For example, in the Negotiation Workshop at Northwestern University School of Law, participants work in teams of six throughout the semester to explore a key negotiation concept which must be tested outside of class, written up and presented to the class. Invariably team members complain that others did not carry their weight in terms of ideas, work and time invested in the assignment.

Leigh Thompson, an expert on effective teams, has created a team contract which can be used by students to commit to expectations about team members' behavior and consequences for breach of the contract (Thompson 2007). Underlying this contract is the notion that as students themselves design and impose the consequences, the repercussions of failing to live up to the agreement might be more effective than externally decided penalties. Examples of consequences students agree on include grade penalties or the obligation to feed the group.

Negotiating for Your Grade

Some teachers try to bring home the insights of the negotiation course in a very direct way: by having students negotiate for their grades. One teacher shared that for the students' final project in his negotiation course, he has students negotiate with each other, in groups of three to five, over the number of points they will each receive for the final project itself. As the final project is worth about thirty percent of the final course grade, students' negotiation skills can significantly impact their overall course grade. To drive home the point that sometimes in the real world, to counter-phrase an old adage, "it's not how you play the game, it's whether you win or lose," students are not graded on the negotiation skill they display – but they are awarded the amount of points agreed on, directly reaping their negotiation outcome.

A different take on this type of activity was reported by Roger Volkema. Rather than have students negotiate with each other, he had them negotiate with him, their teacher, for their grades (Volkema 1991).[6]

In order to be true learning opportunities, we suggest that these experiences must be accompanied by a debrief process reflecting on what transpired and what might be learned from that. If not, this is simply a real-life negotiation.

Role Playing with an External Opposite

Participants in a negotiation course get to know each other very well throughout the class. They become comfortable with each others' negotiating styles. Sending students to participate in an exercise with a counterpart who is not a classmate can add an element of surprise and the unknown to the negotiation experience.

While there are ways to do this that are simply enhancing the role-play (such as having students negotiate with students from another class, or another university; see Ebner and Kovach, *Simulation 2.0,* in this volume), other approaches might upgrade this into a more effective learning exercise with higher degrees of realism and motivation. For example, law students can be assigned to negotiate the role-play with a real lawyer from the surrounding community.[7] While the scenario is still technically a role play, the fact that the students will go to a law firm, government office or other professional setting to meet with a stranger with more exposure to the real world gives the experience an importance and authenticity which is different from in-class exercises. Multiple real-world motivations are triggered: facing the challenge, succeeding at a challenging task and achieving or maintaining "face" vis-à-vis the professional, the teacher or the rest of the class.

This type of exercise can be an effective last class experience for students for a number of reasons. First, students, perhaps mistakenly, often believe that professionals who have graduated and been in the workforce will be effective negotiators regardless of their training or approach. Thus, facing them as counterparts is a great challenge and confidence builder. For some, seeing good negotiators in action creates a desire to continue to develop their negotiation skills as a professional. Other students come to the realization that as a result of their skills coupled with their understanding of negotiation theory, they are far ahead of those with work experience who negotiate without this understanding or training.

Using Students' Real-Life Negotiations
Negotiation teachers routinely remind students that negotiations are constantly occurring in their lives. Some teachers encourage students to bring their real life negotiations to class in order to create or drive home this relevance. This might be done by inviting students to present stories that will be used as learning opportunities for the class. Another, more structured approach might be to start each class with a student report on a real negotiation in order to reinforce how the learning can be practically applied. By having students prepare for and analyze these actual negotiations just as they do the simulations, the opportunity is more likely to ensure that the students will be able to apply the principles learned in the classroom beyond the context of the simulation in which the principles were first learned. The following is just a partial list of the types of real life negotiations that many students face:

1) Negotiating with a landlord or Housing Office
2) Negotiating with a roommate over coexisting
3) Negotiating with students on a class project

4) Negotiating with the school administration regarding a policy or decision
5) Negotiating with a student group regarding a policy or decision
6) Negotiating with the Financial Aid Office
7) Negotiating with a future employer
8) Negotiating with a business for a donation, discount or benefit

Alternatively, some teachers use these real life experiences as a basis for a written assignment, in which students analyze their own negotiation using the principles learned in class.

While these are worthy exercises in their own right, they are not in our opinion "adventure learning" unless a stronger tie-in is created between the real-life negotiation and the classroom discussion. One way to do this is to follow a student's story presentation and class discussion with the class offering specific recommendations. The storyteller might choose to adopt a certain course of action based on these recommendations, and volunteer to tell the class, in the next lesson, how this played out in reality. The second session will include a discussion of the effect the chosen actions had on the negotiation dynamics. We would recommend that teachers using such a method add on a very clear caveat, warning students not to conduct experiments on issues that are of significant importance to them.

Designing a Real Negotiation Experience to Challenge a Student

The typical negotiation course sets out clear learning objectives for the class. Once these goals are identified, a syllabus is created to achieve these learning targets. Requiring that students go out into the world to practice and apply the key learning concepts will provide an enjoyable, practical and most likely memorable experience, a true "adventure."

However, motivation is only one of the pedagogical reasons justifying this type of adventure learning. Here are some other considerations that in our experience tip the scales in favor of incorporating at least some adventure learning activities into a negotiation course:

- The progression formed, presenting students with incrementally challenging situations – learning skills in class, practicing them in theory (on paper or in class discussion), trying them out on each other in simulations and, finally, taking the opportunity to practice these skills in the real world.

- The saving of in-class time by assigning out-of-class activities. This type of exercise is easy to set up and conduct between lessons without sacrificing class time.
- The degree of empowerment students often undergo by seeing the concepts play out in real life. In our experience, even if a student's real-world attempt turned out to be unsuccessful, their newfound ability to explain *why* they were not successful in the interaction has positive effect.
- The opportunity for group-building (a powerful side-effect of real-world experiences on classmates). Students often self-organize into pairs or small groups to gain support and motivation for engaging in these activities. Teachers can encourage or require this.

In this section we will suggest three ways of structuring this type of activity:

1) An activity in which students experience a particular course concept or a specific element of negotiation;
2) An activity in which students practice a particular negotiation skill; and
3) An activity in which students engage in a full-blown real-life negotiation process for the purpose of learning from the adventure.

1) Experiencing and exploring individual course concepts

This type of assignment requires that students engage in an interaction in which they will experience and manage a key lesson from the curriculum. For example, if the desired teaching goal is to teach students that money is not the only, or even the main, interest in all negotiations, have them go out for lunch in teams without any money. To amplify the challenge, students could be instructed that they may not disclose that they are doing this for a class. If the desired teaching goal is to have them explore the value of understanding the other's point of view before being understood, ask them to identify a problem or decision that they are facing with someone in their lives. They should plan to schedule a session with this person during which they may not speak about their own perspective, but rather listen to where the other is coming from and reflect back on their understanding. In the class debrief, the instructor could explore how the students' understanding of the situation changed and whether new approaches for dealing with the situation emerged. Just as important, students could identify their own feelings during the listening session as well as any challenges. [8]

2) Practicing specific skills

Teachers can identify very specific micro-skills or micro-dynamics for students to practice in the real world. For example, if you want to have students practice assertive behavior – including its potential positive and negative effects – have students go to a restaurant and return something they ordered to the kitchen, or make a phone complaint to a service provider.[9] Roger Volkema (2007) described an activity in which he gave students a package of sponges he bought – and instructed them to attempt to return them, without a receipt, to a retail store – without knowing where the sponges had been bought. Students went to a store of their choosing, which in all likelihood was *not* where the sponges had been purchased, and attempted to return the sponges.[10]

Alternatively, it might be something you can send students out to do, on campus, in a thirty to forty-five minute timeframe in the middle of class. For example, if you want to have them practice asking for concessions, assign them to ask someone standing at a photocopying machine if they can cut ahead of them for just a few pages. If you want them to practice information gathering, assign them all to engage a stranger in conversation and learn three things about the other.

Another advantage of incorporating the real-world practice of individual skills in our classes is that this type of assignment can be tailored to suit the needs of individual students. Ideally, students in negotiation courses are encouraged to reflect on their individual strengths and challenges throughout the course. Some of these attributes are evident from their pre-class lives and some emerge as they learn to apply the negotiation theory presented in the class. Along these lines, in the spirit of full adventure learning, negotiation teachers and students could partner to create individualized challenges to address the participant's learning needs.

There are a number of approaches to designing individualized challenges. The instructor could meet with each student in order to explore specific needs and options. Alternatively, the students could partner with each other and as an assignment, identify each other's needs, create the challenge, and provide a written analysis of how it worked.

To illustrate the concept of individualized challenges, let us meet Christine, an undergraduate student enrolled in a twelve-week negotiation workshop. Christine is proficient at creating rapport, exchanging information and breaking impasse once negotiations are underway. She reports that she is uncomfortable negotiating with counterparts who raise their voices, interrupt her or put her on the spot with questions or tough bargaining. In the challenge creation phase, exploring her history with these behaviors and their impact on her negotiation choices would be helpful. Identifying alternative strategies and coping techniques is key. At this point, Christine identifies people in her life who display the behaviors that stress her. Her challenge is to approach one of them with a request and implement an alternative approach when faced with the other's challenging behavior. The experience can then be debriefed in an individual session with her teacher or assignment partner and perhaps the whole class.

Students are always asking for more feedback on their individual skills and judgments in their negotiations. The concept of personalized challenges meets this request head on. Students examine themselves as people and negotiators and work to reach a new level of effectiveness.

Christine's example calls attention to another element always present, to one degree or another, in adventure learning – risk. Interacting with a real counterpart raises the stakes considerably. The outcome of the interaction has implications well beyond the classroom and into the future, for better or worse (see also Honeyman and Coben, *Half-Way to a Second Generation*, in this volume).

3) Negotiating for the adventure: whole-process activities

A structured way to have students bring negotiations they conduct in the real world into the learning process would be in the form of an ongoing assignment. Ask students to commit, a few lessons into the class, to holding a particular negotiation, which they will engage in as a class requirement. They will have to submit a brief write-up of the context/situation for approval ahead of time (this will enable the teacher to evaluate that it is an interaction of suitable scope and meaning for the purposes of the assignment on the one hand, and to conduct a risk assessment on the other). The chosen negotiation might be one of the student-typical interactions noted in the previous section, or any other: at work, at home, with a mobile phone provider or credit card company, etc. You might ask them to announce their intentions in class (although, depending on the nature of the proposals, you might exempt some of them for personal reasons, or just skip this step altogether).

Depending on how much time you consider suitable to devote to this adventure exercise, or have available for this purpose, you might then assign students to conduct a breakdown of strategy analysis and negotiation elements as preparation, either in a one-page paper, in a small group discussion or in a five to ten minute presentation to the whole class. Students can be given a time frame in which to conduct these negotiations, ranging from "by the next lesson" to "over the course of the next three weeks" or so. Finally, students will have to conduct a post-negotiation analysis, in the form of a paper or a class presentation. This structure might be expanded or reduced, based on the number of students in class, time available, etc.

This teacher-initiated adventure-negotiation might turn out to be much more valuable than a semi-structured, ad-hoc "case-study" of a story a student decided to raise in class, or a "choose a negotiation you've experienced and write about it" assignment – due to the degree of mindfulness and deliberation involved in the planning, consulting, implementation and debrief.

An Opportunity to Observe or Participate in the Negotiations of Others

Once students are grounded in negotiation theory, the opportunity to understand its application is invaluable. One method used in many educational contexts, but less so in the negotiation context, is giving students the opportunity to learn from watching and participating in the negotiations of professionals. For example, doctors, therapists and teachers must complete internships or student teaching which provides them with real life experience and the support of an expert in the field.

This observation need not take place over a long period of time; watching even one negotiation could be meaningful. Students could be given the opportunity to observe a settlement conference or mediation in order to examine the application of negotiation skills in the dispute context. On the deal side, witnessing a real estate agent work through the sale of a house from start to finish would bring many necessary skills to light, as would sitting behind the one-way glass in a police interrogation room or a used-car dealership.

A truly novel learning prospect would involve connecting students to groups or individuals in need of negotiation expertise who cannot afford to obtain such assistance in the marketplace. On the dispute side, this could be accomplished in a mediation advocacy clinic like that at Hamline University School of Law, where law students provide free representation to alleged victims of employment discrimination in cases where the Equal Employment Opportunity Commission has offered early intervention mediation. To obtain experience negotiating transactions, students could partner with small business clinics like that at Northwestern University School of Law, or local centers that provide professional advice.

Facilitating Negotiation Insights From "Non-Negotiation" Activities

The study of how people negotiate has crossed into many disciplines including psychology, neurology, physiology and biology. Clearly, there are many experiences which may not directly involve negotiating which can offer insight into negotiation.

Professor Leonard Riskin has challenged participants in his classes and workshops to become mindful of their feelings and thoughts (Riskin 2009). He gives each class participant a raisin and invites them to experience the raisin on various levels for a period of time. This awareness of the raisin's texture, feel, taste and appearance makes the experience of eating the raisin surprisingly rich. This experience opens the group up to a discussion regarding how individuals experience the practice of negotiation, mediation or conflict resolution in terms of self-awareness. Professor Riskin encourages the class to use mindfulness in their negotiation and mediation practices.

Similarly, those who are able to incorporate meditation and breathing techniques into their negotiation practice may have an advantage in terms of patience, endurance and dealing with emotions. Yet, these practices are far from ubiquitous in the average negotiation course. Or, perhaps, we are just looking at the wrong side of the world.

Several articles have done comparative analysis of how negotiation relates to other creative disciplines. For example, our esteemed colleague Judge Jack Cooley examined what jazz music (Cooley 2007) and magic (Cooley 1997) could teach about best practices in negotiation and mediation. Ranse Howell, a negotiation specialist based in London who also happens to be a professional ballroom dancer, has explored the connection between learning how to dance and learning how to negotiate (see Howell and Cohn, *Two to Tango*, in this volume).

Students are likely to come forward with similarly creative suggestions, once this idea has been broached with them. While you might not be qualified or inclined to expound on any of these, you might consider having students conduct their own adventure learning experience regarding them. For example, if a class discussion identifies three to four different fields/disciplines/activities which students connect metaphorically or practically to negotiation, you can them ask them to divide into groups according to these activities. Students will choose to participate in the group whose topic interests them the most. The group will plan an activity involving that other field and participate in it. For example, if students raise martial arts as a related field, they could go to an aikido lesson. Finally, each group would then hold a discussion drawing parallels between the activity and negotiation concepts.

Conclusion

Surely this article only scratches the surface of the possible adventure learning opportunities that negotiation teachers can include in their courses. Adventure learning also requires that we be adventure *teachers*, with a willingness to let go of a rigid script and to go with the flow of authentic experiences and validation of feelings inherent in this model. As we open up to the concept of adventure, the journey will take us away from controlled content, out of the classroom and into disciplines where negotiation courses have dared go not.

Notes

[1] That is not to say that the field of negotiation lacks a theoretical body of knowledge. Rather, we argue that negotiation theory, which has provided us with numerous perspectives on how to capture this type of human interaction in frameworks and models, is, for the main part, grounded in observations of practice, and ultimately aimed towards improving practice.

[2] Interestingly, this prevalence of role-play holds true even in courses purporting to be purely theoretical, and not focused on skill-building – in such courses, educators use role-play to advance conceptual understanding by immersing students in a real-life, albeit simulated, experience in which these concepts play out. In courses focused on skill-building, it seems almost redundant to comment on the degree to which simulations fill this theory-to-practice role.

[2a] In this chapter, we use the terms "simulation" and "role-play" as generic references to experiential-learning-oriented activities, commonly labeled "simulations," "games," "simulation-games" and "role-play." While the literature on simulation and gaming differentiates between various terms (see Crookall, Oxford, and Saunders 1987), the literature on negotiation, for the most part, does not. Our usage of the terms is not intended to influence the debate on the way these activities are conducted or the delineation between them.

[3] We are focusing on this setting due to the wide degree of latitude and teacher discretion it provides, and – as we shall stress – the ready-made training-ground provided by the university campus. In the non-academic setting, such as the executive training workshop, more thought and experimentation needs to be done regarding the method's suitability and possibilities for its implementation; we hope to address that in a successor edition to this book. Open questions include what potential adventure learning modules might look like in such a time-condensed training setting, whether including such modules will affect the popularity or marketability

of such trainings, and how facilitators can be sure that key concepts are covered.
[4] One easily incorporated approach to creating small consequences for negotiation choices involves upgrading simulations into something with real consequences by means of rewarding students who performed well in their simulations with in-class perks (such as scheduling priority or the opportunity to dictate the snack for the following session). One instructor allows students to pick from a gift bag which typically contains a mix of gag gifts and books or calculators that might be useful in future negotiations. This system creates an enjoyable and positive association with negotiation choices and injects a reflection of real-world motivation into the simulation environment. Another teacher offers $10 to each of the two best-performing individual students in a simulation. As the simulation regards distribution of money, this reward is an even closer reflection of the simulated negotiation outcome. Negotiation choices also result in negative consequences and the possibility of penalties associated with those choices could also be employed. Possible penalties include requiring a student to collect or distribute material, bring a snack, or report on an outside reading. We are not aware of any faculty using such a direct penalty approach. However, Volkema (2007) describes a series of activities running through his course in which students do pay a symbolic price for poor outcomes. And, as we shall discuss, some teachers create systems in which students lose out as a result of poor negotiation – not as a penalty, but simply as they did not achieve their goal. Of course, the instructor must determine what behaviors or outcomes warrant the perk or penalty. A student who uncovers her counterpart's interests through good questions and active listening would be a candidate for a perk while a student who makes unwarranted concessions might warrant a penalty. Yet there are often many potential "right" or "wrong" choices in a given negotiation, depending on the context created by the parties. One option is to allow the class to vote on who they learned the most from each week, whether from a good or poor judgment call. Another is to focus on negotiation outcome. Still a third is to have each simulation observed by a scorer, who would be instructed to award points for certain moves and tactics. For other ways of adding real-life motivation into a simulated exercise (for example, through the simple method of grading students on their performance and outcomes and including this as part of their overall course grade), see Coben, Honeyman, and Press, *Straight Off the Deep End*, in this volume.
[5] While not "true" adventure learning as per the definition above, this is somewhere in between adventure learning and role-play. The real-life ramifications of the role-play are intended to mobilize reactions and thinking patterns that would characterize real-life interactions – even if these are only implemented on a reflection of a real-life interaction.
[6] In this article, Volkema discusses many issues that came up in his experiments with negotiating for grades: the power differential between teacher and students, the need to be very clear on the negotiated agreements, issues

of fairness, the tendency of students to delay having the negotiation and more (Volkema 1991). In addition, he discusses other issues such as the ethical ramifications of involving unwitting third parties in adventure learning (e.g., a landlord with whom a student is assigned to negotiate, without a real intent to rent) that are relevant both to his chapter and to others in this book.

[7] Of course, this exercise involves the teacher securing the assistance of quite a few external participants. This assignment would certainly be an easier proposition in small classes as opposed to larger ones. Teachers might send a call out to alumni practicing locally, or assign a teaching assistant the task of tracking down and securing assistance. The number of lawyers needed might be cut in half if the teacher asks them if they would agree to conduct a role-play twice. Another possibility is designing a role-play in which the story-line incorporates a party with two participants (e.g., husband and wife, two business partners, etc.) negotiating with a second party flying solo (the lawyer); designing a three-party negotiation simulation, in which students play two roles and the lawyer a third, is yet another option. Another approach is to have the students do the legwork – assigning them to find a local lawyer or businessperson to negotiate with. In our experience, this usually works quite well; the teacher's administrative role is reduced to approving the opposites, once students bring in their agreement, and sending out role information. Sometimes, the teacher will need to use her own network to land opposites for a few students who were unable to secure one for themselves. But the approach to "opposites" could itself be structured as a gradable exercise.

[8] Of course, this exercise could be – and in most courses, is – done with classmates; however, experiencing the benefits and challenges of active listening in a conflict that is impacting the student's life will surely be more meaningful and a next step towards capacity to implement this tool naturally in unplanned interactions.

[9] Doubtless, some of the suggestions we made here have ethical dimensions. We are detailing specific activities just for examples of what could be done, without taking a stance on what *should* be done. For an overview of ethics challenges, hopefully many of which will be systematically addressed in book three of this multi-year project, see Honeyman and Coben, *Half-Way to a Second Generation*, in this volume.

[10] "Students achieved a range of outcomes, including some who obtained a refund higher than what Volkema had originally paid!" (Volkema 2007: 479).

References

Alexander, N. and M. LeBaron. 2009. Death of the role-play. In *Rethinking negotiation teaching: Innovations for context and culture*, edited by C. Honeyman, J. Coben, and G. De Palo. St Paul, MN: DRI Press.

Cooley, J. 1997. Mediation magic: Its use and abuse. *Loyola University Chicago Law Journal* 29: 1-75.

Cooley, J. 2007. Mediation, improvisation, and all that jazz. *Journal of Dispute Resolution* 2007: 305-385.

Crookall, D., R. Oxford and D. Saunders. 1987. Towards a reconceptualization of simulation: From representation to reality. *Simulation/Games for Learning* 17(4): 147-170.

Druckman, D. and N. Ebner. 2008. Onstage, or behind the scenes? Relative learning benefits of simulation role-play and design. *Simulation & Gaming* 39(4): 465-497.

Folberg, J., D. Golann, L. Koppenberg, and T. Stipanowich. 2005. *Resolving disputes: Theory, practice, and law*. New York: Aspen Publishers.

Riskin, L. 2009. Awareness and ethics in dispute resolution and law: Why mindfulness tends to foster ethical behavior. *Texas Law Review* 50: 493-503.

Thompson, L. 2007. *Making the team: A guide for managers*, 3rd edn. Upper Saddle River, NJ: Prentice Hall.

Volkema, R.J. 1991. Negotiating for grades: Theory into reality in the classroom. *Journal of Management Education* 15(1): 46-57.

Volkema, R. 2007. Negotiating for money: Adding a dose of reality to classroom negotiations. *Negotiation Journal* 23(4): 473-485.

❧ 10 ❧

A Look at a Negotiation 2.0 Classroom: Using Adventure Learning Modules to Supplement Negotiation Simulations

Salvador S. Panga, Jr. and Gwen B. Grecia-de Vera [*]

Editors' Note: *Panga and Grecia-de Vera analyze initial experiences with adventure learning from a Philippine perspective. They conclude that in a number of ways, the experimental exercises showed serious flaws – and yet demonstrated the potential of adventure learning to provide authenticity, risk, challenge, and context.*

> "All...by nature desire to know. An indication of this is the delight we take in our senses; for even apart from their usefulness they are beloved for themselves....With a view to action, experience seems in no respect inferior to art, and men of experience succeed even better than those who have theory without experience." (Aristotle)

Introduction

One highlight of the Rethinking Negotiation Teaching conference in Istanbul was the introduction of adventure learning activities, which we took as forming part of "Negotiation 2.0 Apps" – pedagogical applications that may be used whether in relation to Negotiation 1.0 or 2.0 theory and practice. The conference organizers explained that these activities were designed in response to the conference outcome in Rome[1] the previous year. While conference participants appeared

---

[*] **Salvador S. Panga, Jr.** is secretary general of the Philippine Dispute Resolution Center, Inc. His email address is sspanga@phpeplaw.com. **Gwen B. Grecia-de Vera** is director of the Institute of International Legal Studies and an assistant professor at the University of the Philippines College of Law. Her email address is ggdevera@up.edu.ph.

to have enjoyed the trip to the Spice Market and being accompanied to various places of interest in Istanbul, some have expressed a variety of concerns about employing adventure learning in negotiation training. (See the other chapters in this volume.)

In our contribution to this volume, we explore what adventure learning is, how it can contribute to both the teaching and learning experience in the context of the negotiation classroom and executive training session, and what lessons in the four stages of the adventure learning cycle can be used to enhance other experience-based tools that are already in use for negotiation teaching and training. We will begin by sharing what brought us to Istanbul, including why we are particularly interested in exploring adventure learning and what we understand adventure learning to be, and discuss its early applications. With these as backdrop, we share what our adventure learning experience in Istanbul was like and, taking these experiences, discuss what we perceive as its limitations. We will conclude with our perspective on bringing adventure learning to the negotiation classroom or executive training course, with a brief account of how it might be received in the Philippine setting, and on what particular elements can be appreciated and taken to contribute to what is already taking place in negotiation training.

Our Journey to Istanbul: Exploring Philippine Themes in Negotiation

We joined the Istanbul conference with several specific goals. The Institute[2] for which we are working had earlier made a decision, consistent with our law school's vision of engaging in research and capacity building relevant for its stakeholders, to seek linkages with other academic institutions with a view to mutual learning, exchange of information and possible collaborative opportunities. Among those areas we wanted to explore was how recent developments in ADR theory and practice could be applied to our local concerns, whether in the areas of public policy dispute resolution, environmental management, economic development and policy formulation, or in the conduct of private transactions.

On a lesser scale, but no less important, we also wanted to see to what extent these new perspectives could inform our own understanding of the field, both in the way we perceived it and in the way we conveyed our appreciation of it to others. In particular, we hoped that the initiatives to review Western and interest-based negotiation theory and subsequently develop a second generation curriculum might present a unique opportunity for us to impart a Philippine, and perhaps Asian, perspective, provide a venue for pilot-testing any modules, courses or programs that may be developed, and participate in any post-program evaluation. With these goals in mind, we approached the organizers to allow us to participate and we were gratified by their quick and positive response.

We came upon quite interesting results as we began our preliminary work in preparation for our participation in the Istanbul conference. With a little over three months between receiving project approval[3] and the October conference in Istanbul, we moved quickly, without forsaking deliberation, to organize a set of activities that would allow us to examine local and primarily academic literature on negotiation theory and practice, and survey the availability of negotiation content in various Filipino academic institutions (specifically in law and business). In September 2009, we called a consultative meeting involving participants from government, private sector and academe to see whether there are perspectives to negotiation different from the philosophy, viewpoints and approaches of the Western, interest-based model; approaches and processes that participants have found particularly helpful in their respective fields; and whether there are principles and processes participants would like to include in designing a Filipino negotiation curriculum or training program. We were fortunate that our invitation to the consultative meeting was warmly welcomed; participants from different sectors, including private companies and law firms, affirmed the importance of thinking and talking about negotiation, whether as a mode of alternative dispute resolution or a transactional tool.

Most participants acknowledged having been involved in one form of negotiation or another, whether at home with their family, in the workplace with a co-worker or superior, in school or in the law firm. Significant thinking on negotiation that came out of the consultative meeting (which we hope to discuss extensively in a post on our blog at http://iilsclaw.blogspot.com or in a separate publication) helped us understand the perception and uses of negotiation and negotiation training in our local context.

Dean Antonio G. M. La Vina, lead negotiator on the United Nations Collaborative Programme on Reducing Emissions from Deforestation and Forest Degradation in Developing Countries (REDD) at Copenhagen, after reflecting on his extensive experience negotiating public issues (from environmental concerns to peace process), led the conversation on what happens when consensus fails and differences prove irreconcilable. He shared his perspective on the imperative of reaching an agreement on process in negotiations involving public issues, which can be, as he calls them, "perpetual negotiations" (considering how negotiations of international agreements have lengthened).

Professor Evelyn (Leo) Battad, Director of the University of the Philippines College of Law, proposed a rights-based approach in negotiation (as opposed to interest-based) when developmental issues are involved. She added that this may also be the approach that applies in a collectivist culture such as the Philippines (it is interesting to note, however, that some participants disputed the claim that the Philippines is a collectivist culture). They were joined by experienced negotiators in stressing the importance of turning to disciplines in psychology, technology and leadership in developing "Negotiation 2.0" thinking and teaching methodology.

Despite the presence of experienced negotiators among the participants and the recognition of the centrality of negotiation to many undertakings in the public sector, we were surprised to find that our survey disclosed only two full texts on negotiation, with only one discussing Filipino values applied in the context of negotiation and that, of the major law and business schools in the National Capital Region, only three offered negotiation courses.[4] Representatives from two public agencies confirmed having received training in the interest-based approach.[5] One participant, a member of a local law firm, affirmed the importance of lawyers having negotiation skills, but gamely shared that, after reading all the chapters of *Rethinking Negotiation Teaching*, he was overwhelmed by the discussion of a second generation negotiation or "Negotiation 2.0," while he remained unsure of what the current theories and practices are.

This led our project team to identify the following as areas requiring the Institute's intervention: 1) development of a negotiation curriculum for the law school classroom; 2) design of training module/s for government trade negotiators; conduct of seminars and workshops to aid our government negotiators in learning (and teaching) how to articulate the national interest and design consultative methods to ensure that stakeholders are engaged; and 3) a study of how indigenous methods of negotiation and dispute resolution may be adopted to form part of the current thinking on negotiation theory and practice.

Professor Nieves Confesor[6] of the Asian Institute of Management described our endeavor in the field of negotiation as contributing to the creation of a community of practice. We are hopeful that our efforts will indeed be fruitful and meaningful. Our interest in learning about "Negotiation 2.0" and adventure learning as an output of the new thinking in negotiation is inspired by our desire to understand the development of negotiation theory and practice in the global setting to the extent that it can inform and improve negotiation teaching, training and learning in the Philippine context. While at the Istanbul conference, we were keen on not only making a contribution to what might become "Negotiation 2.0," but also in observing what tools we can integrate in the negotiation classroom we will be developing for our law school, and possibly for other institutions. We are interested in learning about adventure learning, having experienced it ourselves in Istanbul, and what it brings to negotiation teaching and training and if we might make use of it in the Philippine negotiation training classroom.

Understanding Adventure Learning and its Applications

Unlike other forms of experiential learning modes, adventure-based learning is a type of educational or therapeutic program in which activities or pursuits that are physically and/or psychologically demanding are used within a framework of safety and skills development to promote interpersonal and intrapersonal growth (Luckner 1994: 57, citing Bagby and Chavarria 1980). Adventure learning draws on the work of many education scholars, including David Kolb who, in 1984, suggested a circular model of learning involving four stages that flow from each other. These four stages involve: 1) concrete experience; 2) reflection on the experience on a personal basis; 3) abstract conceptualization (whether through the derivation of general rules describing the experience or the application of known theories to it); and 4) active experimentation, or the construction of ways of modifying the next occurrence of the experience, which then leads to the next concrete experience and so forth (Kolb 1984: 68-69). Kolb defined experiential learning as "the process whereby knowledge is created by the transformation of experience [and] results from the combination of grasping and transforming experience" (Kolb 1984: 41).

Drawing on Kolb's work, Aaron Doering sought to merge the concept of "experience-based learning" with "inquiry-based learning" (or learning derived from the student's pursuit of answers to their own questions rather than memorizing facts) and called it "adventure learning" (Doering, citing Bransford, Brown and Cocking 2002; National Research Council 1999). Doering used adventure learning in the context of online experience. A team of educators and explorers conducted various adventure learning activities, such as a 3,000-mile dogsled trip in 2004 from Yellowknife, Northwest Territories, Canada, to the north end of Baffin Island, stopping at seven Inuit communities along the way, while primary and high school students worldwide interacted online directly with the participants, several subject matter experts, the native community members and their own instructors.[7]

The emphasis on authenticity, participation, collaboration, dialogue and openness to inquiry explains adventure learning's attraction as a negotiation training tool for scholars of the Rethinking Negotiation Teaching project, one stated objective of which is to "critique contemporary negotiation pedagogy and create new training designs." Indeed, the project's main purpose is to compel us to revisit our understanding of the concepts, ideology and approaches underlying negotiation theory; evaluate the extent to which they are, or remain to be, applicable and relevant across cultures, nationalities and contexts; and explore new ways by which these can be improved in the twenty-first century.

Much of the scholarship that came out of the first conference in Rome produced a thoughtful and incisive analysis of current negotiation philosophy. Summarizing the incredibly rich and insightful scholarship that came out of Rome, the following core themes stand out:

1) The first-generation negotiation model envisions the negotiation process as linear, methodical and sequential, one that involves moving the negotiation along a rational and strategic process (Fox 2009: 22).

2) First-generation negotiation philosophy is characterized by the following key principles, namely:
    a) Explicit communication and direct confrontation;
    b) individualist perspectives on agency and autonomy;
    c) competitive assumptions that people will act to maximize individual gains and can be assisted to extend this behavior to maximizing joint gains if their interests are not compromised;
    d) action-orientation at the expense of focus on being or inaction;
    e) analytic problem-solving;
    f) sequential orientation to time;
    g) universalist ideas about the international applicability of interest-based negotiation; and
    h) emphasis on agreement as central measure of success (LeBaron and Patera 2009: 48).

3) The linear and sequential first-generation model does not accurately capture the real nature of negotiation, which "is a dynamic and emergent process where every communication move potentially changes everything that follows" (Fox 2009: 22). Consequently, the "modularization of negotiation training" (defined as a "desire to encapsulate its precepts and processes into sequential flows of ideas and trainable modules") (LeBaron and Patera 2009: 49), a concept that

naturally follows a linear view of the negotiation process, would not work well in a system that conceives of negotiation as a complex/nonlinear process.

Central to all these themes is the idea that emotion, nuance, context and culture are as essential to negotiation (and as critical to its outcome), as logic, reason, interest identification and value-maximization.

Apart from critiquing the philosophical and ideological underpinnings of contemporary negotiation theory, several Rome conference scholars have also sought to address the perceived inadequacies in the delivery and teaching of negotiation content, and suggested alternative approaches to negotiation training. Notably, Nadja Alexander and Michelle LeBaron identified the limitations of role simulations, in which students are asked to assume certain identities, and to learn negotiation concepts, strategies and techniques while in these roles. Apart from the fact that assuming identities other than one's own may be perceived in some communities and in certain contexts as disrespectful or nonsensical (Cohn et al. 2009: 333), they point out that role playing "takes people 'out of their skins' into a synthetic situation that may have little relevance to their lives, and limited transferability to actual negotiations" (Alexander and LeBaron 2009: 183). They argue that continuous self-evaluation and reflection, the internalization of new approaches and the ongoing implementation of new strategies, are key to effective learning. These, in turn would be enhanced not by asking students to assume identities that they may only have had a few minutes to familiarize themselves with, but rather to undergo real, authentic experiences involving risk, challenge and genuine emotions in situations that may have real meaning to them, thus ensuring that the experience and lessons learned will be retained (Alexander and LeBaron 2009: 183-184).

As an alternative, or at least as a supplement, to the inherent artifice of role plays, they propose using the adventure learning model as a means to boost the negotiation experience, introduce authenticity and genuine emotion to the exercise and encourage reflection and self-awareness. In their words,

> [a]dventure learning activities take participants beyond traditional teaching spaces into environments where existing power dynamics no longer apply...in their new environment, a range of skill sets are in demand and participants must negotiate their place in the new world order" (Alexander and LeBaron 2009: 188).

Taking Part in Adventure Learning

Taking off from Alexander and LeBaron's criticism of the inherent artifice of role plays, the Istanbul conference organizers designed two negotiation exercises as a learning laboratory to explore adventure learning possibilities. The central theme for these two exercises was "authenticity as priority." Both required the participants to leave the classroom and engage in real-life negotiations with their colleagues based on certain tasks assigned.

In the first exercise, the conference participants were placed in groups, pre-selected to maximize diversity in nationality, gender, age and race, and given the following instructions: go to the Spice Market as a group, and together decide what food to buy, then negotiate a purchase, and bring it back to the university to share with the rest of the conference participants during debriefing. Groups were also asked to be mindful of and observe any perceived rituals and contexts that underlay the bargaining. The organizers suggested that groups may engage the sellers in conversation regarding their concerns, experiences and strategies, to test whether the sellers' responses would differ if they were told that the group was interested in making a purchase or informed that there was no intention to conclude any transaction.

It seemed to us that conference participants welcomed the exercise and were delighted at the prospect of exploring a place characterized in the travel guidebooks as a "must see." The Spice Market proved to be an appropriate setting for the first adventure-based learning activity. Located next to the Yeni Mosque, right at the southern end of the Galata Bridge on the Golden Horn in the Eminonu District, and accessible by taxi from the conference cite (Bilgi University), its vast number of goods – from spices, dried fruits, nuts, seeds, to the colorful and fragrant Turkish delights, as well as its diversity of merchants, ensured almost immediately that the experience would be rich and memorable.

In the second exercise, the conference participants were again asked to form groups, this time self-selected. Each group was then tasked to choose any neighborhood in the city with which its Turkish member was not intimately familiar. The groups were then given the following instructions:
1) Agree on something that represents the crossroads of the sacred and secular, and take a photo of it.
2) Agree on and photograph something that the group believes represents the most dangerous thing seen during the walk around the city.

3) Agree on and photograph something that the group believes is the most likely to be the "unmarked" Central Intelligence Agency (CIA) headquarters in that part of Istanbul.
4) Agree on a self-portrait that best captures the sense of the group.
5) Add or change one thing about the assignment that would make it a more effective learning experience for negotiation students.

Both exercises appear to have been designed to explore the negotiation process on several levels. In the first exercise, the groups needed to engage in a multi-issue conversation to consider, among others, the following: 1) what to buy; 2) how to make the selection (i.e., should we agree on the item first, and then check out the stores to see who offers the best product at the most reasonable price, or should we explore the bazaar first, see what's being offered, and *then* decide what to buy?); 3) deciding on a reservation value; 4) agreeing on a negotiation strategy or several strategies; 5) identifying one or more negotiators for the group; and 6) deciding which seller or store to buy from. Moreover, they needed to agree on the *process* for reaching agreement, by deciding on a facilitator and agreeing on a procedure to resolve any disagreement or debate arising from the consideration of any of the foregoing.

It was only after resolving these issues that the group could move on to the next set of negotiations to pursue their principal goal of securing a food purchase. In this negotiation, another multiple set of issues was involved. Participants had to consider whether in the context of Turkish bazaar negotiation dynamics, 1) bargaining was an accepted or even expected part of the sale; 2) there were certain types of goods whose prices were considered fixed and non-negotiable (e.g., bar-coded items); 3) it was expected to engage the seller in a conversation before making a purchase; 4) it was considered good form to haggle with a merchant, then defer closing the sale in order to see whether another merchant is able to offer a better price for the same item; or 5) how many offers and counter-offers would be considered permissible before a final offer would be accepted.

The participants also had to contend with commercial practices different from what they were used to. Instead of the expected negotiation dance from merchants of offers and counter-offers, many of the sellers seemed willing, even eager, to engage the buyers in a conversation, and appeared genuinely curious to find out where the buyers came from. On one hand, participants felt uneasy and a bit wary of the glib and charming sellers who seemed able to assess the participants' aptitude and endurance for bargaining based on their respective nationalities. One merchant explained that Americans were by far the easiest to sell to, as they seemed embarrassed to bargain, and would at most engage in only one round of offer and counter-offer. The Canadians were next, as they would only bargain for three rounds at most, while Russians were at the far end of the scale, since they preferred to chat for several hours before even making an offer. On the other hand, the impression that the majority of the merchants were nice, and were willing to engage customers in a lengthy conversation created a moral dilemma for many participants, as they felt they had an obligation to purchase something from the merchants' shop (even if they had not wanted to do so originally), to compensate him for his time.

The second exercise was also intended to be a lesson in communication and group dynamics, where the participants were supposed to engage in a process of reaching common agreement or consensus on the foregoing tasks. However, unlike the first exercise, the tasks that the participants were asked to agree on appeared to be pointless and disjointed, and did not seem to trigger any particularly intense emotion or debate that would have converted the assignment into a meaningful exercise. As this exercise was being debriefed, the general sense from the participants was that since very few identified with the questions posed, and since the objectives of the exercise were neither clearly delineated nor readily ascertainable, no one felt particularly invested in them to have a strong opinion or position either way. The result was that, for many groups, the participants simply took advantage of the down time to enjoy a casual chat, a nice lunch and generally have a good time with the group. Although the instructions were complied with, there was no active discussion or engagement by the participants, and choices were agreed upon simply by acclamation without close scrutiny or examination.

While the designated tasks were potentially emotionally charged and controversial, this promise did not translate well on the ground. Several reasons predominated: either the themes did not resonate with the participants; or there were no challenges to overcome or penalties sustained by ill-considered or erroneous negotiation decisions; or the learning objectives were not readily ascertainable; or for some, the exercise did not work simply because, despite the intermittent rain, it was a beautiful day in Ortakuy and it seemed wrong to waste it on what appeared to be a meaningless exercise. While the last reason may seem frivolous or superficial at first blush, it underscores the need to design adventure learning exercises that challenge the participants emotionally and intellectually.

In the Spice Market exercise, the participants were parting with their own money, and they needed to make certain that what they bought was worth it, that they did not feel shortchanged or cheated, and that they, along with the rest of the conference participants, would eventually enjoy the food purchased. Moreover, since in the debriefing they would be expected to recount their adventure learning experience, it was also psychologically important for the participants to have a meaningful negotiation so that they would not feel compelled to relate that they were pushovers. Challenge of the same degree, however, was not attached to the second exercise. There was nothing to win or lose, whether materially, psychologically or emotionally, so there was no pressing need for the group members to engage either in competitive or collaborative behavior to achieve an objective. This made it so much easier for the participants to simply go out and have fun. Some of the conclusions we have are consistent with the findings of Melissa Manwaring, Bobbi McAdoo, and Sandra Cheldelin, who provide a detailed critique of the Istanbul conference adventure learning activities, as well as a subsequent replication of those activities with graduate students in Washington, D.C. (Manwaring, McAdoo, and Cheldelin, *Orientation and Disorientation*, in this volume). They identify authentic and artificial elements and describe the first adventure learning as "direct, explicit, "orienting," as against "indirect, oblique, disorienting." They offer negotiation instructors guidance on designing adventure learning activities, taking into consideration these characteristics.

Our Evolving Thinking on Adventure Learning
From what we experienced and observed in Istanbul, the adventure learning model appears to offer significant opportunities for robust student/trainee participation, collaboration and engagement. The activities in which we participated demonstrated and confirmed the potential of adventure-based learning to provide authenticity, risk, challenge and context identified by the Rome conference scholars as necessary in making training relevant and promoting transferability to actual negotiations.

How did we feel about adventure learning? Is it indeed a negotiation 2.0 app and a tool that we would consider integrating into a law school course on negotiation? Did we find a new lamp for our old one during our stay in Istanbul? In answering these questions, we first take the day one training session offered by Kenneth Fox and Manon Schonewille as a typical executive negotiation course (attempting some new content and methods as well as showcasing best practices of "Negotiation 1.0"), and then the ideas from the

Rome conference to assess how adventure-based learning exercises may contribute to the delivery of the negotiation training content.

Experience-based learning has been part of the negotiation training toolkit for some time, whether in the form of simulation and role-plays or games. Means have been explored on how to enhance these activities. Writing nearly fifteen years ago, John Barkai shared how he ran a combination of simulation and observation learning by video demonstration, using the story of the orange which he called the Ugli Orange Negotiation (Barkai 1996). Though simple, he was able to use the simulation to introduce two major negotiation and ADR themes,[8] and explore the importance of communication, by the use of creative debriefing activities (Barkai 1996). Similar strategies were employed by Fox and Schonewille throughout the sample training course, which covered negotiation concepts and skills training, including discussion of basic negotiation concepts (Shell's bargaining style, unassisted negotiation, best alternative to a negotiated agreement (BATNA), worst alternative to a negotiated agreement (WATNA)) and employed various activities, such as group dynamics, fish bowl, games and even negotiating lunch. It is difficult for us to see how these activities, also experience-based, cannot have continued relevance in the training classroom of the future. Indeed, Alexander and LeBaron explained "[e]ven if role-plays are kept in the standard toolkit of trainers, varying experiential vehicles to address different elements of a negotiation would facilitate learning by those with diverse learning styles and ways of paying attention" (Alexander and LeBaron 2009: 185, citing Sogunro 2004).

We agree with the observation made by some Rome conference scholars that "[n]egotiation training is ready to graduate to its second generation [and that] this advancement requires retention of past best practices but also moving forward with new approaches to influence the future of negotiation [skills] training" (Cohn et al. 2009: 330). Discussions in the Istanbul Conference, as well as those in the Rome Conference, indicate an ever-growing list of areas that ought to be covered – negotiation across cultures, the role of psychoanalysis and social psychology, negotiation training for leadership, and understanding the role of emotions. It does not seem adequate then to approach adventure learning as part of the 2.0 environment without considering in which areas of negotiation training it can have the most efficient impact.

According to John Dewey, "all genuine education comes about through experience (but)...not all experiences are genuinely or equally educative" (Dewey 1939: 25). It is not enough to design a few hours of adventure, challenge and risk for a measure of authenticity to be achieved or to attain the transformation of the experience that makes for the creation of knowledge and acquisition or enhancement of skill. The preparation that is poured into developing a negotiation course involving various models that primarily include or make use of adventure-based learning does not culminate in having covered safety parameters and logistical concerns. Adventure-based learning activities can deliver powerful structured experiences. But as John Luckner and Reldan Nadler point out, "to merely provide an experience, albeit a powerful one, and to expect the student to return home and to sort it out for himself is to invite failure" (Luckner and Nadler 1991).

We need only reflect on the second exercise during the Istanbul conference to validate this point. Groups were asked to agree on a photograph that best represents the sacred and the secular. This is a loaded question, particularly since each group had members from different countries and cultures. But without a clear sense of the learning objective, whether from the trainer or participant end, the possibilities presented by the exercise were not exploited and participants were left to reflect on their own. Remember that the emphasis of some of the Rome scholarship is on the delivery of authenticity. But this is not authenticity for authenticity's sake. Adventure-based learning and its potential for providing authenticity is looked upon as a negotiation 2.0 app because of what can be accomplished in completing its four stages – the creation of knowledge and skill through the construction and transformation of experience, consistent with the conception of negotiation as a dynamic process where "every communication move potentially changes everything that follows" (Fox 2009: 22).

It is worthwhile to revisit here the four stages, widely accepted as noted above, for experience-based learning: the delivery of a concrete experience, an opportunity for personal reflection, abstract conceptualization and active experimentation, and construction of ways of modifying the next occurrence of experience. While each stage is essential, it is suggested that planning and processing are key elements. The importance of adequate planning cannot be overstated when it comes to integrating adventure learning in negotiation training. When we speak of planning, we refer to a wide range of concerns, stretching from determining and setting out clear learning objectives and perhaps learning outcomes, to training the program designer and the trainers, moderators and facilitators involved. While trainers or leaders in adventure-based learning experiences are generally and primarily tasked to oversee safety, provide skills instruction and facilitate interaction and engagement, they are also often charged with preparing the training design, program and specific modules. In the same way that a variety of interventions are available to the outdoor adventure learning activity (for team-building and similar applications), there is a range of ideas to help the trainer design a program and prepare one for a negotiation setting. We emphasize importance not only of trainer preparation (see Ebner and Efron, *Get Ripped and Cut Before Training*, in this volume), but thorough planning, even to the extent of briefing participants before they get to the training seminar or classroom. Planning must also consider framing for transfer (of knowledge and skills), an essential component of experience-based learning.

Certainly insights about transfer gleaned from the training literature are also relevant to adult educators who work in a wide range of contexts. As Rosemary Caffarella points out, "training is an element of the [planning] process that is receiving increased attention as both participants and sponsors of education and training programs demand more concrete and useful results" (Caffarella 2002: 205). Unfortunately, the adult education literature also suggests that few education and training programs actually account for transfer in either the planning or implementation phase of programming. Too often the application of what is learned in education programs has been left to chance (Caffarella 2002: 209).

This aspect of planning is particularly important because, as Luckner and Nadler (1991: 19) stress, adventure-based learning activities lend themselves to creation of a condition of disequilibrium that is critical to the notion of transfer (real life skills transfers) and "durable cognitive and affective shifts." Planned chance events are catalysts in this regard.[9] Sufficient thought and effort invested in the planning of an adventure-based learning activity, of whatever dimension or duration, will consider questions of inclusiveness, the physical ability of participants to take part in the activity, any additional financial cost which may hinder either actual participation or impact the process of negotiation, or necessity of employing a certain gender, age or race mix. It is helpful to recall here that for the first adventure learning activity in Istanbul, participants were asked to break into pre-selected groups for both the activity itself and the following debrief. (We queried the organizers as to the intention behind the grouping and whether, in their view, the goal, whether learning objective or otherwise, was achieved. They responded "We deliberately structured debriefings so that the debriefing group would have perspectives from multiple adventure learning teams, reasoning that the groups themselves would individually debrief during transit. The structure for debriefing the second exercise collapsed, however, when the groups returned at such diverse times.")

(For more, see Honeyman and Coben, *Half-Way to a Second Generation*, in this volume.)

The pretense in role-plays allows dissociation, and in certain instances, invites the participant to review his action and reaction with a degree of detachment. The detachment provides an objective space for the participant to consider how he might improve upon his performance, particularly if he is considering an application of learning in a real negotiation. But if adventure-based learning activity gets us so close to what is real, will we have the detachment to assess objectively how our knowledge can be broadened, our skills enhanced, or our performance corrected? This concern and our examination of adventure-based learning as a teaching or training tool also led us to materials emphasizing the importance of processing.

During the Istanbul roll-out of adventure learning, the activities were each designed to conclude with a period of debriefing. It is interesting to compare the debriefing sessions which were conducted right after the completion of each exercise. For the Spice Market activity, conference participants were assigned to debriefing groups whose composition was intentionally different from that with which they explored the Spice Market. Each debriefing group had a facilitator who managed discussions and the exchange of stories. The debriefing for the second adventure learning activity was done with all conference participants together. Photographs taken were flashed on the screen, and a representative from each group explained how the decision to present the particular photograph was reached. In the particular sessions in which we participated, we found the discussion interesting, but not directed. One participant with an interesting story to tell can easily "capture" the debriefing. While this may provide the entertainment adequate for trainees to fill in their "happy sheets," it misses the opportunity for transference. These observations lead us to suggest not only specific preparation for the trainer or the acquisition of certain set of skills and traits for a trainer involved in debriefing, but also designing debriefing with specific goals. What Alexander and LeBaron argue for in approaching role-plays, we believe is also true for adventure learning – "debrief specifically and completely;" "resist the tendency to relegate debriefing to an afterthought or a rushed invitation for general comments." The primary reason for processing is that adventure-based learning experiences are rich in symbol, metaphors, feelings, mixed with typical behavior patterns. Participants involved in adventure-based activity are engulfed and at times overwhelmed with new stimuli. "Processing teases out the richness of the experience so it stands out and apart, like the important lines of a page underlined with a yellow highlighter" (Luckner and Nadler 1991: 3). Processing is a developmental endeavor of discovering patterns and unique outcomes of the participants. It is a liberating and generating process that helps construct a new reality or make up new meanings from their experiences.

For the Istanbul conference activities, we feel that participants could have benefited from further meaningful, specific and constructive feedback, but wonder how this can be made possible when monitoring of the activity was not pursued, and participants and their respective groups engaged in the activity without a facilitator, instructor or coach accompanying them. We also note literature on adventure-based learning activity emphasizing the need for "follow-up" – to check on the participants and the application of knowledge beyond the training program.

Here we turn to the "gold standard" for training evaluation developed by Donald Kirkpatrick in 1959. The Kirkpatrick assessment measures trainee reaction to the (negotiation) program, accomplishment of learning goals, application of improved negotiation skills, and improved outcomes in negotiations (Kirkpatrick: 1994). In the Kirkpatrick model, we note that one form of measurement is using evaluation forms to determine trainee reaction to the negotiation program. As explained by Lynn Cohn and her colleagues, "typically, feedback from trainees is obtained solely from evaluation forms that participants fill out after each session. These sheets are often referred to as 'happy sheets' due to the tendency for trainees to express positive feelings about the training, particularly if they have been entertained" (Cohn et al. 2009: 336). We agree with Cohn and her colleagues that "[t]hese evaluations are clearly important but do not capture both qualitative and quantitative analysis" (Cohn et al. 2009: 336).[10] Where negotiation training incorporates adventure-based learning activity, Kirkpatrick's model ought to be revisited, and proper processing included, not only as part of the four-part cycle embedded in adventure-based learning activity, but as a measurement tool, if not at Level 1, perhaps throughout the four levels.

Bringing Adventure Learning within Philippine Themes in Negotiation

Our discussion of adventure learning would not be complete without bringing it closer to our local concerns and taking it within our context and culture. For this purpose, we recently organized a small group meeting involving three negotiation teachers, one from a business school and two from different law schools. In our conversations with them we encountered the same questions which Alexander and LeBaron posed:

[h]ow do trainers legitimize the use of non-mainstream learning experiences, especially in "serious" disciplines such as business and law? How do we avoid making fools of ourselves? And what about the students? Are we not placing them in an extremely vulnerable situation? What if they just aren't artistic or adventurous? Even worse, what if we aren't? (Alexander and LeBaron 2009).

Apart from these questions, our local context provides a unique challenge to negotiation thinking and the design of training programs or classrooms, particularly for our Institute, since we have been tasked to develop training modules specifically for the law school classroom (and possibly clinical legal program) and for government agencies dealing with sensitive and at times controversial public issues. Current literature, particularly from the West, acknowledges that negotiation training has become widespread – whether in its two-day executive form or in various disciplines (particularly law and business):

The ability to negotiate effectively is now recognized as a core skill for professionals, union/management teams, government officials and community leaders. During the past several decades, negotiation training programs have flourished. These trainings are popular in part due to the universal relevance of the skills taught. Furthermore, negotiation trainings can be extremely entertaining and interactive while providing learning opportunities. Typical negotiation programs are one to two days in length, cover the essential theory of negotiation, and provide opportunities for trainees to participate in negotiation simulations (Cohn et al. 2009: 329-330).

Negotiation training is not as widespread in the Philippines, however, and the added challenge for us is the state of negotiation training in the Philippines – not widely available, possibly costly, and not consistently delivered. (See Grecia-de Vera, *Can We Engineer Comprehensiveness?*, in this volume.) Some of the methods employed in negotiation training that have already been found tiresome, or oblique, may not be viewed in the same way when used in the Philippine context. Nor does it appear that any one method has gained consistent usage, with the effort to simultaneously ensure that materials put to actual use are suited for cultural and social aspects that are uniquely Filipino. While one trainer sources her materials from Harvard's Program on Negotiation, another tries to develop her own case studies, drawing from Philippine sources; while some public issues are negotiated using indigenous methods,[11] some public sector negotiators are learning to grapple with national and sectoral interests from foreign experts. The rather basic research we have conducted thus far discloses that we have yet to derive the shape of what the negotiation classroom or training session is for the Filipino and, perhaps, the Filipino overseas. But it seems we have not even fully explored the current tools that were extensively reviewed in the Rome conference, and we have yet to apply the same critical review of interest-based approaches in the Philippines.

With Sikolohiyang Pilipino[12] and related social psychology theory informing interpersonal, and even organizational, relationships in the Philippines, the application of adventure learning, indeed all experience-based learning activities, must be viewed in the context of and with sensitivity towards culture. True, role-plays, for example, have been shown to be disrespectful and nonsensical in some cultures, but an ill-designed adventure-based learning activity can also implicate problems of culture. Let us take that Spice Market exercise. Whether participants correctly received it as primarily involving bargaining and haggling, such a perception can deter participants from participating. In certain cultures, bargaining and haggling are not permitted, or are viewed with some disdain; yet in others, individuals would simply feel uncomfortable engaging them even in the context of the marketplace.

One of the Filipino negotiation teachers to whom we presented ideas from the Istanbul conference shared her personal view of negotiation as self-reflection, and working with that framework in mind, remarked that in the Philippine context it is not the bargaining setting or reality in the classroom that will work to surface her concept of negotiation, but rather activities given to self-reflection. Another joined the conversation to say that an activity similar to the Spice Market adventure will not necessarily present a degree of risk or challenge that will complete the cognitive shift, since Filipinos are culturally accustomed to settings involving bargaining and haggling.

Conclusion

We count ourselves fortunate to have been part of the Istanbul conference and to have seen firsthand adventure learning models in the context of negotiation training. We see that negotiation scholars will be examining this new application with great interest. But from what we experienced, we are quite confident that, if not adventure learning activity as a whole, certain elements can be taken to enhance the classroom for negotiation, by also reviewing first generation tools and incorporating second generation elements including, for example, the important lessons on planning and processing. Our experience in the Istanbul conference and the collaborative efforts that were established as a result, as well as our encounter with adventure learning, are now part of our thinking as we continue to explore indigenous modes of dispute resolution and forms of negotiation practices that can inform or otherwise be integrated in mainstream negotiation training and the application of adventure learning in three settings: our law school classroom, in locally delivered executive negotiation courses involving private transactional concerns and disputes, and in the development of theory, practices and tools specifically for the public sector, for high impact issues of national and public importance.

Notes

[1] The Rethinking Negotiation Teaching project, a four-year project to develop "second generation" global negotiation education, was launched in 2008 in Rome, Italy. During the four-day Rome conference, the first two days were used to showcase the best of a traditional twelve-hour executive negotiation course, which then served as a learning laboratory for participating scholars to review towards the creation of "second generation" negotiation training designs. See Honeyman, Coben, and De Palo (2009).
[2] Institute of International Legal Studies, part of the University of the Philippines Law Center.
[3] To prepare and make meaningful our participation in the Istanbul conference, a project proposal involving a consultative conference, research particularly in the area of indigenous modes of negotiation and dispute resolution, and preparation of negotiation course curriculum for the law school and a three- to five-day training course for government trade negotiators, had to submitted and approved.
[4] These are the Asian Institute of Management, the Ateneo de Manila University School of Law, and the University of the Philippines College of Law. We are currently validating the information we earlier received based on our survey.
[5] A set of government negotiators in the area of international environmental law received training on mutual gains approach from Professor Lawrence Susskind of the Massachusetts Institute of Technology in the late 1990s.
[6] Prof. Nieves Confesor is a core faculty member of the Center for Development Management, Asian Institute of Management. Her areas of teaching and research include strategic negotiation and conflict management, public policy, and leadership and management of change. In 2005, she was appointed member, and later Chairperson, of the Philippine Government Panel in negotiations with the Communist Party of the Philippines-National Democratic Front-National People's Army. She served as Secretary of the Department of Labor during the administration of the late President Cora-

zon C. Aquino (http://www.aim.edu.ph/faculty2.aspx?id=60&cat=fulltime) (last visited May 14, 2010).

[7] Some of the project activities included an "education day," where team members worked together to create multimedia-enhanced reports (including trail updates, photographs, audio and video clips and interactive movies) for posting to the website, weekly chat sessions, where the online students communicated directly with the expedition members or with subject matter experts; and regular student interactions through collaboration zones available through the web site. School instructors were also provided a pedagogical framework (consisting of a curriculum and activity guide containing instructional materials, discussion questions and learning activities for different modules) pertaining to different activity levels appropriate for varying grade levels).

[8] The two major negotiation and ADR themes John Barkai referred to in his article "Teaching Negotiation and ADR: The Savvy Samurai Meets the Devil" are the themes of underlying interests and communication.

[9] Planned chance events refer to indirect experiences that the student has not actually self-selected, yet which occur because they have agreed to participate on the course (Luckner and Nadler 1991).

[10] We would have happily filled out a happy sheet following the first day of the conference.

[11] Among the Kalinga, negotiators are called *mansasakusa*. During the consultative conference on negotiation practices held by the UPLC-IILS (see footnote 3), Basilio Wandag at the legal affairs office of the National Commission on Indigenous Peoples shared that a *mansasakusa* assumes the role only upon being accepted by the community and after undergoing certain rites and rituals.

[12] Sikolohiyang Pilipino is anchored on Filipino thought and experience as understood from a Filipino perspective. The most important aspect of this definition is the Filipino orientation. "Filipino behavior has been analyzed and interpreted in the light of Western theories. Since these theories are inevitably culture-bound, the picture of the Pilipino has been inaccurate...." The lesson from psychology may be true for negotiation. "Reservations regarding the appropriateness and applicability of Western models in the Third World setting have been expressed by a growing number social scientists. The Philippines experience has proven that approaching psychology using these models cannot encompass the subtleties of Asian cultures" (Pe-Pua and Protacio-Marcelino 2000).

References

Alexander, N. and M. LeBaron. 2009. Death of the role-play. In *Rethinking negotiation teaching: Innovations for context and culture*, edited by C. Honeyman, J. Coben, and G. De Palo. St. Paul, MN: DRI Press.

Andres, T. 1998. *Negotiating by Filipino values*. Manila: Divine Word Publications.

Bagby, S. and L. S. Chavarria 1980. *Important issues in outdoor education: ERIC/CRESS mini reviews*. Las Cruces, NM: ERIC Clearinghouse on Rural Education and Small Schools.

Barkai, J. 1996. Teaching negotiation and ADR: The savvy samurai meets the devil. *Nebraska Law Review* 75: 704-749.

Bransford, J., A. L. Brown, and R. R. Cocking (eds). 2002. *How people learn: Brain, mind, experience, and school.* Washington, DC: National Academy Press.

Caffarella, R. S. 2002. *Planning programs for adult learners: A practical guide for educators, trainers and staff developers,* 2nd edn. San Francisco: Jossey-Bass.

Cohn L., R. Howell, K. Kovach, A. Lee, and H. de Backer. 2009. We came, we trained, but did it matter? In *Rethinking negotiation teaching: Innovations for context and culture,* edited by C. Honeyman, J. Coben, and G. De Palo. St. Paul, MN: DRI Press.

Cooney, L. and L. Epstein. 2001. Classroom associates: Creating skills incubation process for tomorrow's lawyers. *Capital University Law Review* 29: 361-381.

Dewey, J. 1938. 1938. *Experience and education.* New York: Macmillan.

Doering, A. 2007. Adventure learning: Situating learning in an authentic context. *Innovate* 3(6), available online at www.innovateonline.info.pdf/vol3_issue6/Adventure (last accessed June 18, 2010).

Fox, K. 2009. Negotiation as post-modern process. In *Rethinking negotiation teaching: Innovations for context and culture,* edited by C. Honeyman, J. Coben, and G. De Palo. St. Paul, MN: DRI Press.

Gastardo-Conaco, C. 2007. Filipino social psychology. In *General psychology for filipino college students,* edited by L. A. Teh and M. E. J. Macapgal. Quezon City, Philippines: Ateneo de Manila University Press.

Higgs, J. (ed). 1988. *Experience-based learning.* Sydney: Australian Consortium on Experiential Education.

Honeyman, C., J. Coben, and G. De Palo (eds). 2009. *Rethinking negotiation teaching: Innovations for context and culture.* St. Paul, MN: DRI Press.

Jacobs, B. 2008. Teaching and learning negotiation in a simulated environment. *Widener Law Journal* 18: 91-112.

Kirkpatrick, D. L. 1994. *Evaluating training programs: The four levels.* San Francisco: Berrett-Koehler.

Kolb, D. 1984. *Experiential learning: Experience as the source of learning and development.* Englewood Cliffs, NJ: Prentice Hall.

Lao, F. and P. Lao. [need year]. *Profitable negotiating techniques: Strategies for getting what you want while helping others get what they want.* Pasig City, Philippines: Anvil Publishing, Inc.

LeBaron, M. and M. Patera. 2009. Reflective practice in the new millennium. In *Rethinking negotiation teaching: Innovations for context and culture,* edited by C. Honeyman, J. Coben, and G. De Palo. St. Paul, MN: DRI Press.

Luckner, J. 1994. Effective skills instruction in outdoor adventure education, *Journal of Physical Education, Recreation and Dance* 65(1): 57-61.

Luckner, J. and R. Nadler. 1991. *Processing the adventure experience: Theory and practice.* Dubuque, IA: Kendall/Hunt Publishing.

Luckner, J. and R. Nadler. 1997. *Processing experience: Strategies to enhance and generalize learning*. Dubuque, IA: Kendall/Hunt Publishing.

Menkel-Meadow, C. 1984. Toward another view of legal negotiation: The structure of problem solving. *UCLA Law Review* 31: 754-842.

Merriam, S. and B. Leahy. 2005. Learning transfer: A review of the research in adult education and training. *PAACE Journal of Lifelong Learning* 14: 1-24.

Nelken, M. 1996. Negotiation and psychoanalysis: If I'd wanted to learn about feelings, I wouldn't have gone to law school. *Journal of Legal Education* 46: 420-429.

Nelken, M., B. McAdoo, and M. Manwaring. 2009. Negotiating learning environments. In *Rethinking negotiation teaching: Innovations for context and culture*, edited by C. Honeyman, J. Coben, and G. De Palo. St. Paul, MN: DRI Press.

Nelken, M. 2005. The myth of the gladiator and law students' negotiation styles. *Cardozo Journal of Conflict Resolution* 7: 1-25.

Pe-Pua, R. and E. Protacio-Marcelino. 2000. Sikolohiyang Pilipino (Filipino psychology): A legacy of Virgilio Enriquez. *Asian Journal of Social Psychology* 3(1): 49-71.

⚛ 11 ⚛

Is What's Good for the Gander Good for the Goose? A "Semi-Student" Perspective

*Adam Kamp**

Editors' Note: "Smell the fear?" Kamp forces us to consider how the shock-and-awe of adventure learning might shut down, rather than inspire, negotiation students. He offers practical tips, from his own unique "semi-student" perspective, to help ensure that activities beyond the classroom actually meet the prime objective: making students active participants in their own educational experience.

A View from the Fringe

It is a truism in adult education that ideal teachers are students as well, who in the course of educating are themselves educated by the various experiences their students bring to the table. This is doubly the case when the teachers themselves are asked to join in adventure learning, where the true education comes afterward in reflecting on our own experiences and those of others. The newness of the experience provides an education for anyone willing to learn.

But let us not get carried away. Consider: I have been immersed in negotiation theory and its pedagogy for the last three years. I can recite chapter and verse from articles we hope are at the cutting edge of the profession. And yet, not only have I never taught a class on the subject, but not once in between my first exposure to *Getting To Yes* (Fisher, Ury, and Patton 1991) and the second Rethinking Negotiation Teaching conference in Istanbul had I even once engaged in any significant formal economic bargaining that the paying public is seeking to master by taking a negotiation class. Maybe all people are students (or should be), but some people are more students than others.

---

* **Adam Kamp** is a Bakken fellow and law student at Hamline University School of Law. His email address is ajkamper@gmail.com.

Still, my situation of having one foot in each world provides us with an opportunity. As a novice in real-world situations, my impressions of the adventure learning sessions in Istanbul should be relevant to planning negotiation classes for students, particularly those who are in an academic program taking a class as preparation for a career, rather than in executive seminars for those who are already using formal bargaining in their daily lives. Only a year passed between my taking a semester-long negotiation class and going to Istanbul; many of my attitudes towards our adventure learning were not those of an educator trying something new, but rather those of a student facing one in a series of assignments.

Nonetheless, I come from the camp of the educator as well: though I am currently a law student, my previous life experiences include a host of graduate work, academic study, and teaching at the college level. So I understand the necessities involved in trying to help students explore and learn in the classroom. I believe that my in-between status – not quite one or the other – provides a useful lens for teachers evaluating the effectiveness of the adventure learning exercises we undertook in Istanbul. Though informed by some knowledge of the theories involved and pedagogical experience, I still see the world from the perspective of a student.

Smell the Fear:
Dodging Negotiation in a Turkish Bazaar

It was reassuring to see that, upon learning we would be going to the Istanbul Spice Market in teams and negotiating with its denizens for snack food, many of the teachers in our group had just as much fear and trembling as I.[1] We were tasked in groups of eight, which proved a cumbersome way to work through not only the crowds at the bazaar, but the distractions of rose-scented Turkish Delight, silver jewelry, densely-woven rugs, and above all else ostentatious heaps of ground spices: sharp cumin, rich cinnamon, saffron in bright red and gold. Perhaps a veteran of the bazaar would have remained unseduced; our group splintered. We did retain one veteran, who had lived in Turkey for a number of years and was less overwhelmed by the setting. Nevertheless, the interest in actually doing our assignment with the verve and energy it needed started to wane, as we spent more time exploring and window-shopping.

At one point, I tried to personally negotiate for a few vanilla beans in what could be best described as a parody of principled or even rational negotiation; unnerved by the presumably vast experience of the merchants, I picked a reservation point quite at random, offered a somewhat lower price, and was offered in return a price much higher. When the seller seemed uninterested in coming down further (pointing out that I was seemingly refusing to negotiate even another Turkish lira, about sixty cents), I panicked, refused to think about whether I actually wanted the beans at that price, and walked out in a hurry. So much for negotiation theory. Eventually, in an effort to fulfill our obligations quickly, we found a set of treats that our informal guide insisted were excellent, offered a slight reduction in price as a nominal negotiation, and continued on our tourist ways.

What did our group learn about the practice of negotiation and culture? Not so very much, other than confronting our own recalcitrance towards negotiation in that setting. What we did discover is that the value of an external exercise, even more so than in the formal atmosphere of the classroom, is entirely dependent on the kinds of people who take part in it. Especially when students are forced to confront the unfamiliar, it becomes clear that adventure learning works best for *adventurers*. What is a fascinating opportunity for some kinds of people could be nearly excruciating for others.[2] This will not come as a surprise to experienced teachers, since the idea that students have vastly different learning styles and therefore need a variety of stimuli in order to thrive has been fully accepted for decades (Joyce 1987). Nevertheless, an exercise that might work wonderfully for a cross-section of negotiation educators could fail to reach many students in a formal program, all with different motivations for taking part in the class.[3] With such a diverse group, there is a variety of factors that will need to be resolved in redesigning the bazaar exercise for use in the semester-class context.

Extroversion vs. Introversion

According to one study, forty-eight percent of students in law school negotiation classes are introverted, as measured by the Myers-Briggs Type Indicator (Peters 1993: 19). Determining how best to deal with introverts in a structured format such as the classroom setting is not an insuperable obstacle; for example, the reflection paper instead of, or in addition to, an in-class debrief is an excellent device to help these students, who might not be comfortable developing their ideas in a group setting, reap the most from their negotiation experiences. However, the essence of the bazaar exercise is exploration by way of social interaction – highly appealing to the extroverted, but problematic for people who do not draw their energy from such interaction.[4] One task for the exercise designer, therefore, is including people who find this kind of learning uncomfortable. (For more on inclusion issues, see Larson, *Not Everyone Gets to Play*, in this volume.)

Conflict Management Styles

The Dual Concerns model suggests that there are five different kinds of general preferences for managing conflict, plotted by measuring one's concerns for one's own outcomes against concerns for one's counterpart (Pruitt and Kim 2004).[5] Though rarely does one use the same kind of strategy for every conflict one enters, some people may generally be avoidant of conflict; yielding; competitive; problem-solving; or compromising. Of course, each type will have a different reaction to being forced to negotiate, in real life, for an assignment, and that diversity provides an excellent opportunity to understand our own learning styles.

Yet, just like the extroversion/introversion divide, this difference can complicate getting wholesale participation in the project. Many students in a negotiation class will find the act of negotiation itself appealing: these are the types of people who are likely to have very engaged methods of dealing with conflict, such as problem-solving or competitive bargaining. But, especially in the semester-long law school format, students will be taking a negotiation class for many reasons: to fill a course requirement for some sort of practical experiment, as part of a broader dispute resolution program where the overall focus is on managing conflict instead of seeking it out, or even for self-protection when they are forced to negotiate. These people may well be generally accommodating or avoidant, and may not want to actively seek negotiation. (Such a perspective would explain the dynamic of my own splintered group, where there was no appetite to actually negotiate; we may have been in the minority among educators, but quite possibly less so in a law school classroom.[6]) A persistent question will be to ask to what extent reluctant students should be *required* to be active negotiators.

Experience/Inexperience

This is not to discount the nervousness of the educators who also went into the bazaar, but for people who may have never conducted an economic negotiation of any significant scale (a distinct possibility in college-age Americans, where negotiation for most items is not part of the culture), to be pitted against sellers who haggle on a daily basis would be quite a sharp introduction to the field. (For reports on such exercises, see Press and Honeyman, *A Second Dive into Adventure Learning* and Manwaring, McAdoo, and Cheldelin, *Orientation and Disorientation*, in this volume.)

Even though in this case the stakes were extremely low from a financial standpoint (unless, I suppose, the negotiation went dreadfully wrong), the emotional stakes involved are sufficiently high to frighten the novice. Some people, again, are excited by this kind of adventure, but some have no appetite for it whatsoever. There may be cultural dynamics at play too: people from different cultures may have different attitudes towards negotiation that they bring to the table, and the design of a "go-and-negotiate" exercise should be designed to maximize that diversity of personal experience.

Indeed, part of what made the negotiations at the Spice Market such a terrifying experience was the cultural shock. We were already well outside our comfort zones, taking on the mores of a new world, trying to bring our own theories and preconceptions of negotiation into a place that we suspected would have very different rules. Could that same sense of culture shock be brought to a similar adventure in one's home country? That might depend on the extent to which negotiation is common in one's own culture: in a society where bargaining is ever-present there will be little difficulty finding an adventure to equal the Spice Market; in a place like the United States almost any kind of economic bargaining could be unusual. Part of the design of a U.S.-based adventure learning assignment could be whether to allow parties to choose negotiation in contexts with which they are familiar, or to require an unusual and unsettling context, whether in a different subculture (such as an ethnic street market) or by bringing negotiation into an arena where it is not usually encountered.

Personal Investment

In addition, though this was not a dynamic at our conference, the position of a student with respect to such an "assignment" is very different from that of a teacher. When we were in Istanbul, we engaged in the adventure learning as an exploration of a teaching tool and of our own nature as negotiators; in other words, we were co-participants. In a student's position, the very same project becomes an assignment – something required by an authority figure. In the words of Mark Twain, "Work consists of whatever a body is obliged to do. Play consists of whatever a body is not obliged to do." A student in the situation of being required and expected to negotiate may be less willing to do so than someone who is a full partner in the adventure. Obviously, this is a problem in or out of the classroom, and it is quite possible that the difference between the normal school environment and real-world negotiation can provide that investment, replacing a mediocre interest in the subject matter with an interest in newness. It was that newness which induced me to try negotiating for vanilla beans that I did not even particularly need; how many chances does one have to buy something in the Spice Market of Istanbul? Though for me the adventure enabled me to get over my reticence (to a degree), to another student it might provide motivation that counteracts disinterest in the subject matter itself.

Full Involvement in Adventure Learning

For all these reasons, in many cases the use of bazaar-style adventure learning will have to overcome some significant avoidant behavior. A group of eight traditional law students will not react in the same way as a group of eight teachers – some, even many, may need more prodding out of their comfort zone. It is not difficult to imagine a situation where, with such large groups, there is one bold person who eventually does the negotiation while seven people stand around, slightly abashed, but deeply unwilling to take part: some trusting others to do the assignment adequately (especially in a market or bazaar where a host of distractions await); others who took a negotiation class so they could defend themselves in the horrible circumstance that they should be forced to protect their interests, but absolutely not interested in going out in seeking that conflict; and still others who would make fine negotiators, but are too shy, introverted, or unassertive for cultural reasons to want to take that step. Either way, the formal negotiation is being done by just a few, while the observers are many.

To borrow a metaphor from the technology sector: is this behavior a bug, or a feature? One approach to designing these adventure learning exercises would be to accept the different roles as a function of different learning styles. After all, if introverts are likelier to learn less from social interaction and more from internal review afterwards, then let them take part in the intra-group negotiations regarding how best to fulfill the assignment, observe the negotiations carefully, write reflection papers, and stay essentially within the role they prefer. This way, they will not be forced to take an approach that is unfamiliar to them, and they will get more out of the exercise. People who are uninvested for other reasons may be drawn in by allowing them more input into the design of the exercise (Nelken 2009; Nelken, McAdoo, and Manwaring 2009; Druckman and Ebner, *Enhancing Concept Learning*, in this volume). Either there could be a classroom discussion on the sorts of materials that are to be negotiated for and what the negotiation's goals are going to be, or the options could be more free-form: if the admonition is merely that the parties should choose something interesting to negotiate, but nothing more specific, that in itself may be sufficient to induce buy-in and personal investment on the part of students who otherwise might not be willing to engage.

But is enabling people to *not negotiate* a good idea for a negotiation class? One of the underlying tropes of the modern negotiation classroom is that conflict, and negotiation about that conflict, happens all the time. That understanding is reflected in the interest in discussing the intra-group negotiations in the adventure learning exercises: these are the sort of non-economic discussions of interests and perceptions that are a part of everyday life in many of our relationships. Understanding such negotiations is valuable. But adventure learning – in this case, integrating real-life negotiation into the classroom – is a unique opportunity to bring true, formalized economic negotiation into the curriculum. Unless a course is comprised largely of such elements, opportunities to hone one's skill in actual bargaining situations will be limited. In such a case, it seems like a disservice to design the assignment in such a way that there are fewer primary negotiators and more observers. Many of the students will have taken the class precisely so they could succeed in formal bargaining situations: as educators, we should give the students what they are asking for.

Moreover, in many of the cases it is precisely those students who are less likely to take the role of primary negotiator in a larger group who most need to practice their skills in such a setting. Socially reticent, conflict-avoidant, or yielding-style students may have been less likely to find themselves in this formal setting, because it is less appealing to them. Students just out of college may not have had the opportunity to take part in significant economic negotiations, and may be unwilling to take that risk now for the first time. Kevin Avruch (2009: 164) suggests that teaching, as compared to training, should have the effect of unsettling the assumptions of the learners and forcing them to confront new ideas and ways of behaving. An assignment where the parties are allowed to stay in their comfortable roles, instead of practicing the skills that the class is supposed to teach, may be less helpful to new negotiators. Of course, this is an admonition from personal experience: those of us who for various reasons are less likely to seek out experiences that test us should, at least once, be forced to do so.

A Sample Lesson Plan

The following adventure learning exercise is designed to work relatively late in the semester, after the parties have been introduced to the basic theories and understandings of negotiation and have perhaps participated in a simulation or two, to familiarize themselves with the basic structure of such interaction. It would function best over two or three weeks, to allow the students to choose a negotiation, act on it, and debrief/reflect on it.

- Students would be divided into pairs. If at all possible, it would be helpful to have the members of each dyad be different in personality or negotiating style, though that might be difficult to accomplish. Using pairs would require both parties to be equal partners: since there is only one negotiator and one observer at any time, there is no opportunity to avoid any of the responsibilities.

- Outside of class, the two people should determine two situations that they each will negotiate. There is an array of restrictions that the teacher could use to make this more pertinent to their lives. If there is a possibility of classic, market-style negotiation in the area, then the professor could simply require that all the parties do at least one if not both of their negotiations in that setting. In Istanbul, of course, the plan was to negotiate snack foods: if time and setting allowed, that could be used here as well, or other items could be used.[7] Another restriction the teacher could use, in order to make the negotiation take on more meaning to the students, would be to require it to be in an unusual area, something outside of the students' comfort zone. If they are accustomed to bargaining in a market, perhaps they would have to bargain in a department store instead. That newness would force people who might otherwise try to avoid new situations to confront those fears and test their own skills.
- Of course, while one student negotiates, the other will observe – since there will be two negotiations, for the second the roles will switch.
- Within a week or two, there could be an in-class debriefing, followed by a reflection paper, making sure that students who learn best by either method would get the most out of the post-experience breakdown.

The primary advantage to this lesson plan, of course, is that it expects everyone to be an active participant: rather than relying on the real-world nature of the adventure learning itself to induce investment, it is set up so that people who might otherwise not want to stretch their boundaries are forced to. Students are allowed to come up with their own preferred negotiation (within certain limits), further enhancing their own buy-in to the process – and there is no reason that the class as a whole could not run an in-class contest for best negotiation. And if possible, it expects exactly the sorts of economic negotiation that students, especially younger students in the United States, might not have had the opportunity to undertake in the past, and gives them the chance to practice precisely the skills which many have taken the class in order to master.

Conclusion

As a student, by the end of my own negotiation class, the entire matter began to take on a surreal abstraction. Simulations can only teach so much: while they may serve a purpose, they fail to capture the richness of real-world negotiation. Adventure learning, as the other articles in this section of the book demonstrate, hopes to transcend that by making the stakes and the class work real and pertinent to the students' lives. I believe that for a semester-long class, these exercises may be the best way to make the nature of negotiation real. But because of the independent nature of such learning, adventure assignments, for any number of reasons, risk allowing students to avoid taking active roles in the work – not because they are bad students, but because to be an active negotiator would be difficult and unsettling in those circumstances. In order to avoid that danger, adventure learning using formalized negotiation as a foundation should follow a few simple rules. Such an exercise should:

- Try to maximize student input into the design of the adventure.
- Use small groups – dyads or triads – in order to ensure that everyone is forced to take an active role.
- Actively seek to put students into negotiating roles with which they are uncomfortable; the newness of the experience may force learners to test their beliefs instead of merely confirming them.

Settings like the Spice Market provide a crucible in which many of our beliefs about negotiation and about ourselves as negotiators may dissolve and lose their structure, challenging us to find formulations that can resist the heat and pressure. While we cannot expect every classroom to have such a place available to them, the suggestions above may help to provide a workable equivalent.

Notes

[1] Roy Lewicki, at the debrief of our exercise, described the atmosphere with the pungent comment in the section header.

[2] See, e.g., Larson, *Not Everyone Gets to Play*, in this volume. Though he describes the more extreme concern of Asperger's Syndrome and other disabilities, even "unusually high reticence" or what might be called the lack of an adventuresome spirit, in an environment where one is not absolutely required to take affirmative action, can completely shut down one's role in the exercise.

[3] This is not to suggest that negotiation educators are not at least somewhat diverse in their personalities and interests, merely that they are somewhat less so than the population of students as a whole. The population of people who go in for teaching negotiation is far from random.

[4] This is simplified somewhat. Arguably, many people may still be excited by a negotiating adventure even if they do not draw energy from social in-

teraction, and even extroverts may be shy in unusual social situations. But, insofar as introversion and social reticence are at least somewhat related, we can use the former as a stand-in for the latter.

[5] For a more in-depth exploration of the Dual Concerns model and how it is used in negotiation pedagogy, see Ebner and Kamp, *Relationship 2.0*, in this volume.

[6] Consider, for example, the student of Sandra Cheldelin's who did not bring enough money, in the hope of avoiding the negotiation at hand (Manwaring, McAdoo, and Cheldelin, *Orientation and Disorientation*, in this volume). The intra-group negotiations in that exercise provide one of the ways, of course, that the students who might want to avoid the primary bargaining around which the assignment is centered nonetheless can gain from the exercise.

[7] If the market did not serve food, one could think of other games – e.g., parties could go in with no more than a small amount of cash and try to come out with the object that by class vote was deemed the most valuable (to which any leftover cash would be added). If a grade bonus were given to the winners, then the stakes of the negotiation would be higher for the parties as well.

References

Avruch, K. 2009. What is training all about? *Negotiation Journal* 25(2): 161-169.

Fisher, R., W. Ury, and B. Patton. 1991. *Getting to yes: Negotiating agreement without giving in*, 2nd edn. New York: Penguin.

Joyce, B. 1987. Educational perspectives, then and now. *Theory into Practice* 26: 416-428.

Nelken, M. L. 2009. Negotiating classroom process: Lessons from adult learning. *Negotiation Journal* 25(2): 181-194.

Nelken, M. L., B. McAdoo, and M. Manwaring. 2009. Negotiating learning environments. In *Rethinking negotiation teaching: Innovations for context and culture*, edited by C. Honeyman, J. Coben, and G. De Palo. St. Paul, MN: DRI Press.

Peters, D. 1993. Forever Jung: Psychological type theory, the Myers-Briggs Type Indicator, and learning negotiation. *Drake Law Review* 42: 1-121.

Pruitt, R. and S. Kim. 2004. *Social conflict: Escalation, stalemate, and settlement*, 3rd edn. New York: McGraw-Hill.

❧ 12 ❧

Adventure Learning: Not Everyone Gets to Play

David Allen Larson*

Editors' Note: Larson analyzes the initial experiments with adventure learning in Istanbul, a setting replete with long staircases, narrow winding alleys, and user-hostile transportation (at least to Westerners with mobility problems.) He concludes that the post-modern agenda of excitement and authenticity in learning carries a serious risk of running smack into the post-modern agenda of openness to all, characterized by the Americans with Disabilities Act. The risks are not just physical; some of the "disabilities" students may encounter have an ethical or moral dimension. Larson offers a number of cautions for future applications.

Introduction

Educators, or at least the educators with whom I am familiar, try very hard to be inclusive. But try as we might, sometimes we adopt learning strategies and approaches that turn out to have the opposite effect. We understand that when students are excluded, the entire educational enterprise suffers. The Second Generation Negotiation program in Istanbul, Turkey was remarkably interesting and productive on many levels. But it reminds us that unless we are careful, the programs we develop may exclude participants because of disability, ethical issues, cultural differences, spirituality, and religion.

---

* **David Larson** is a professor of law and senior fellow in the Dispute Resolution Institute at Hamline University School of Law. His primary email address is dlarson@hamline.edu. Professor Larson reviewed and revised the proposed Regulations and Interpretive Guidance for the Americans with Disabilities Act when he was the "Professor in Residence" in the Office of General Counsel, Equal Employment Opportunity Commission headquarters (1990 – 1991).

Adventure learning, which was a central theme for the program in Istanbul, encourages students to physically leave the classroom in order to experience how theoretical models and principles apply in the "real" world. Adventure learning admittedly has substantial value. But the initial rush of enthusiasm witnessed during the Second Generation Negotiation project in Istanbul must be tempered. When participants are directed to venture out of the classroom in order to perform certain tasks, persons with disabilities, persons with certain values or beliefs, and persons from different cultures may find it impossible to complete those assignments.

Pedagogical approaches entirely unrelated to adventure learning also may be problematic. It is not surprising that educational programs typically are delivered using methods familiar to the instructors. Effective as these approaches may be when teaching in one's own country, these methods may be quite nation-centric. Information and ideas may not be communicated effectively when the methods of delivery, and the language used, are not as familiar to the participants as they are to the instructors. If instructors do not become familiar with their students' values, traditional approaches to problem-solving, cultural practices and, in some instances, religion, then instructors not only may fail to communicate effectively with program participants, they also may risk discouraging and even alienating participants.

Problems with Adventure Learning

When a student, without warning or notice, suddenly is confronted with the fact that an essential part of the learning experience will be experiential, and consequently impossible for him or her to complete, then all participants are harmed. The student certainly will be disappointed, if not angered, and the purpose of the learning exercise will not be accomplished. The student will be isolated by the abrupt and complete separation from the group. The characteristic that makes this student different from the rest of the group will be highlighted in a dramatic fashion. Unique insights attributable specifically to the experiential nature of the exercise will be unavailable to the student. Although the rest of the students who can participate in the adventure learning exercise likely will report their experiences to the entire group once that group is reassembled, the fact that the excluded student only can *hear* about an adventure learning experience emphasizes the fact that the excluded individual(s) did not *share* this learning opportunity.

The harm is not restricted to the excluded individual(s), however. To the degree that we believe that diversity has inherent value and that different perspectives are important, an adventure learning exercise can exclude someone as effectively and completely as a bold lettered "No '__s' Allowed" sign (feel free to fill in the blank). Unique perspectives that may be valuable for the entire group will be lost.

Furthermore, adventure learning exercises often lead to more intense and multidimensional experiences than one can have in the classroom. Shared experiences of this nature help create connections, and perhaps even friendships, among those who participate. Individuals who are excluded, however, not only miss the experience itself, they miss the opportunity to build connections with their fellow participants. Particularly when it comes to programs that last only a few days, this loss can be impossible to overcome and the excluded individuals may be relegated to the periphery of the group.

Potential Legal Liability

And one should not underestimate the fact that an adventure learning program may result in legal liability. Although one easily could write an article dedicated exclusively to the fact that adventure learning can result in unlawful disability discrimination prohibited by statutes such as the Americans with Disabilities Act,[1] this article will not focus primarily on legal and statutory analysis. This article instead will identify potentially problematic situations and suggest how those situations can be avoided. Nonetheless, program planners and educators should be aware that relevant statutes require virtually all public venues and classrooms selected to host programs be accessible for individuals with disabilities.[2]

In the United States, for example, programs utilizing venues identified in Title III of the Americans with Disabilities Act may have to ensure accessibility regardless of whether the program planners own the property or simply have made arrangements to use the property temporarily.[3] Physical barriers may have to be removed, for instance, if that is "readily achievable."[4] And if ADR education is being offered to children in the United States through the school system, then an entirely new set of accessibility requirements may apply.[5] Although countries may have widely divergent requirements regarding disability discrimination,[6] or may have no formal requirements at all,[7] educators and program planners must make themselves aware of the relevant legal environment.

Benefits of Adventure Learning

But if adventure learning is so problematic, why should we even consider using this approach? We all are familiar with scenarios where students sit passively at their desks while the speaker at the front of the classroom drones on. Perhaps you, and undoubtedly I, have been that dreaded "droner." And we have watched our students try to pretend how carefully described characters would react in a precisely scripted simulation when, in fact, they have little or nothing in common with those imaginary characters and they never have experienced the hypothetical circumstances themselves.

Adventure learning, in contrast, offers an opportunity to apply theories and principles essentially on a first-hand basis. Students do not have to assume contrived personalities or imagine how they would behave if confronted with a set of wholly unfamiliar circumstances. When students are asked to put theory into practice in a real-life situation, this approach can create a level of excitement sorely lacking in the lecture and simulation scenarios described above. The lessons that students learn will be retained because it is likely that the entire experience will be remembered, often quite vividly and specifically.

Students may be asked to go to a retail establishment and negotiate the price of a particular item, for example. They will act only as themselves while interacting with an actual merchant.[8] Students can be given the very real goal of completing the transaction, or they may be asked to try to establish the beginning of a long term relationship. The possible scenarios are almost limitless.

Students today are bombarded with relentless multimedia stimuli and, out of necessity, they are learning to manage, and ultimately embrace, those stimuli (Larson 2006).[9] Much of the information being communicated in today's world is presented in a multimedia format and students may now expect, and even demand, that formal educational material be presented in a similarly stimulating manner. As educators we are coming to accept the fact that time-honored and traditional methods of teaching, such as lecturing and simulations, may not resonate with a technology-weaned generation. Accordingly, one cannot be dismissive of an approach such as adventure learning that offers the opportunity for students to be fully engaged intellectually, emotionally, and physically.

But we have to be careful. It was rather surprising to see the degree of excitement generated by the idea of adventure learning at the Istanbul Second Generation Negotiation Conference. The atmosphere, frankly, had a "kid in the candy store" quality to it, including the same sense of naiveté. It almost appeared as though adventure learning had not been reviewed thoroughly or critically but that, instead, it was being heralded as a remarkable, new, exciting discovery.

Historical Context

The fact is, however, that experiential learning in higher education has a long history. This author had the good fortune to spend a semester participating in the Comparative European Studies program offered by Antioch College,[10] an institution that has been a pioneer in experiential education.[11] The College describes itself as follows:

> Antioch College has been a pioneering and values-driven secular institution since it was founded in 1852. ...In the 20th century, Antioch College redefined liberal arts education by initiating an entrepreneurial and experiential curriculum through the development of its hallmark cooperative work program. Many of the now-common elements of today's liberal arts education – self-designed majors, study abroad, interdisciplinary study, and portfolio evaluation – had an early start at Antioch College.[12]

Experiential learning and what is best termed as its subset, adventure learning, is not a new approach, and substantial literature is available from subject areas distinct from ADR (Manwaring, McAdoo, and Cheldelin, *Orientation and Disorientation*, in this volume).[13] It may be helpful to put adventure learning into a historical context.

Legal education in the nineteenth century, for example, was conducted primarily through experiential learning methods, specifically apprenticeship (Moliterno 1996: 78). Although students likely read various legal treatises, students principally were educated by observing a practitioner as he consulted with clients and appeared in court, or provided basic legal services such as the drafting of wills, pleadings, and real estate documents (Moliterno 1996: 71).

In the early twentieth century, a revolution in legal education took place, spearheaded by Christopher Columbus Langdell of Harvard University, in which classroom-based appellate case reading replaced the apprenticeship as the dominant means of legal instruction (Moliterno 1996: 82-83). Although appellate case reading is not intuitively classified as experiential learning, Langdell's revolution was part of a broader transformation at Harvard designed to lessen the role of reading and lectures in professional education and expand experiential learning opportunities (Moliterno 1996: 84).

In medical education, this transformation took the form of laboratories, field experiences, and the establishment of teaching hospitals (Moliterno 1996: 84). In the area of legal education, however, both Langdell and Harvard University President Charles W. Eliot concluded that the law library was to the budding lawyer what the teaching hospital was to the emerging physician (Moliterno 1996: 85-86).

Eliot actually may have preferred to create a teaching institution for legal education comparable to a teaching hospital, but he determined that it was not possible. Legal education's experiential education history consisted of individually arranged apprenticeships. In contrast, medical education's experiential education history was institutionally based and offered a more standardized experience from which reform could proceed (Moliterno 1996: 87). Additionally, medicine's clear relationship with "hard science" distinguished the profession from, and elevated it above, more common "trades." Law had no similar relationship. It consequently was left with the choice of being regarded as one of the less respectable social sciences or, instead, presenting itself as its own science (Moliterno 1996: 87-88). The result was that the varied experiential learning methods characteristic of the apprentice system were replaced by a form of legal instruction that focused exclusively on the "experience" of appellate case reading for the purpose of extracting legal doctrine, understanding legal theory, and developing the skills of legal analysis (Moliterno 1996: 83).

Today, the experiential component of law school often is limited to summer employment opportunities, externships, and moot court or law review participation. Law schools frequently run legal clinics that serve actual clients, however, and these clinics can provide extraordinarily rewarding experiences. But clinic enrollment typically is severely restricted and many students never have a clinical experience.

Experiential learning is based on the idea articulated by Carl Rogers that "the only learning that really sticks is that which is self discovered" (Moliterno 1996: 80). Experiential education achieves the goal of self-learning through a process, outlined by John Dewey among others, in which the teacher explains the theory behind an activity to a student and then provides the student with an opportunity to experience that activity (Moliterno 1996: 81). The student evaluates his or her experience and its relationship to the relevant theory, and then forms a new or modified theory consistent with the knowledge gained through participation in the activity (Moliterno 1996: 81). The student subsequently tests his or her new theory through additional experiences and the theory evolves accordingly (Moliterno 1996: 81). The unique value of experiential education is its ability to provide the student with an internal locus of evaluation (Moliterno 1996: 81). This model for iterative learning through experience enables the student to self-learn in a manner that is transferable to diverse activities and theoretical frameworks (Moliterno 1996: 81).

Despite the many positive aspects of experiential learning, however, it has drawbacks even beyond those already discussed. The fact that an adventure learning program may exclude persons with physical disabilities seems quite obvious. Persons with mental impairments also quite obviously may be affected adversely. Additionally, persons with particular personality traits who do not have impairment, but who feel significant discomfort in certain social situations, also may find themselves unable or unwilling to complete a particular adventure learning assignment.

A Critical Look at the Istanbul Program

During the two-day Istanbul Second Generation Global Negotiation Program, for example, attendees were asked to participate in two adventure learning exercises. The first half day exercise required participants to walk around the Spice Market and the Grand Bazaar and negotiate with vendors. Participants were encouraged to experiment with different negotiation techniques, to interact with multiple vendors, and to compare and contrast those experiences. Attendees were assigned to small groups and transported to the markets to complete this exercise.

The exercise required the participants to spend a substantial amount of time on their feet and to walk over ancient, and therefore not surprisingly, rough and uneven surfaces. Because of the physical demands, at least two of the attendees were unable to participate in this exercise.

For the half day adventure learning exercise planned for the second day, attendees again were assigned to small groups. The groups were asked to travel around Istanbul and take photographs that captured visual images in response to specific questions proposed by the conference planners. Again, one of the two individuals who were not able to participate in the first adventure learning exercise also was unable to participate in this exercise because of the physical demands. Neither of these individuals was aware prior to the conference that he or she would be required to engage in these physical activities in order to participate fully.

Physical disabilities are not the only reason why participants may be excluded. Asperger's syndrome, for example, is a developmental disorder that affects one's ability to socialize and communicate effectively with others.[14] Individuals with Asperger's syndrome may be employed, highly functioning and truly exceptional when it comes to solving complex tasks, but they also may exhibit social awkwardness and an all-consuming interest in specific topics.[15] And they, like many other employees and students, may be interested in participating in a program described rather simply as a dispute resolution training program.

It is not difficult to imagine how an individual who is uncomfortable in social settings may find an assignment difficult or even impossible when he or she is dispatched to negotiate with strangers in an unfamiliar location. This may be the outcome regardless of whether his or her unusually high reticence rises to the level of what some would call "an impairment."

As someone who has been a full time faculty member at four different universities across the country and who has taught thirteen different courses ranging from Torts to Employment Discrimination Law to Municipal Corporations, this author honestly can say that most ADR instructors with whom he is familiar are unusually sensitive and responsive to inclusion concerns. The fact that adventure learning exercises may exclude certain individuals almost assuredly is a result of the fact that certain characteristics such as disability are not always immediately apparent. And as a society, at least in the United States, we still are not automatically conditioned to be alert for, and to accommodate, certain characteristics such as disability.

Including persons with disabilities never has been the highest priority. One only need recall that race, color, religion, sex and national origin discrimination was prohibited in the United States as a result of national legislation over forty-six years ago.[16] Similarly, age discrimination was outlawed in the United States only two years later.[17] Disability discrimination, in contrast, did not receive comparable protective federal legislation until twenty-six years after passage of the Civil Rights Act of 1964.[18]

While upon reflection it becomes obvious that persons with disabilities may be excluded from adventure learning, persons with characteristics that have nothing to with disability also may be excluded. For example, an unexpected opportunity presented to participants before the Istanbul Second Generation Negotiation program officially began involved a program known as the Interfaith Dialogue.

Program participants were invited by gracious local Turkish hosts to travel to the hosts' office or workplace to see how and where each person worked. Once we arrived at the different destinations, we had an opportunity to sit down and describe our jobs and learn about our hosts' vocations. We then were able to explain how spirituality enters into our work lives and to listen as our hosts explained the role spirituality plays in their lives.

If you are a spiritual person, then this was a remarkable opportunity. But if you do not believe in a higher being or an afterlife, but you nonetheless were very interested in Turkish working life, then you may have been frustrated as the conversation turned to topics in which you have little interest, and for which you may have little patience.

Now admittedly, the individuals who attended the Istanbul Second Generation Global Negotiation Program have an orientation that would make it very unlikely that they would be offended by a conversation of this nature. But as noted earlier, this author believes (and genuinely appreciates) that dispute resolution educators are an unusually empathetic and tolerant group. It is difficult to believe, however, that we all have not witnessed situations or circumstances where the introduction of religion or spirituality into a discussion had a negative impact on that conversation.

An adventure learning exercise that directs students to explore how real-life merchants' or professionals' spirituality manifests itself in their vocational life may be alienating for individuals who reject the idea of a higher authority or a god. An individual with minimal dispute resolution experience who thought that he or she was signing up for a class or a short program simply to learn a little bit about, and only about, negotiation may be (at the least) surprised when the focus turns to spirituality. Accordingly, if an instructor plans to explore the role and influence of spirituality and religion in negotiation then, similar to the suggestions with regard to physical activities and planned social interactions, it would be helpful to inform prospective attendees in advance that this topic will be explored.

A student also may feel his or her personal ethics are being challenged or compromised by an adventure learning assignment. For instance, a student asked to negotiate a purchase for purposes of an educational experience may be quite uncomfortable imposing on a merchant for whom the negotiation is anything but an academic exercise. For the merchant, time is money and his or her financial livelihood depends upon whether or not actual sales are completed. Students may be very uncomfortable negotiating with a merchant knowing that they have no intention to actually purchase an item. Or if students are instructed to complete the sale and purchase the item, then they may be unhappy that they are being asked to spend their typically limited resources on such a frivolous purchase.

What Can We Do?

There certainly is no need to abandon adventure learning. But at a minimum, program planning should be transparent. Because surprises tend to grab peoples' attention and because most people appear to enjoy surprises, program planners may be tempted to withhold certain information. The planners may hope that program attendees, who may be losing interest as the day wears on, will be energized by a new, unanticipated learning opportunity – particularly one that engages them physically as well as intellectually.

But information can be communicated that need not spoil the surprise. It may be enough simply to advise potential participants that the planned activities will involve an extended period of standing or walking. If this fact will be troublesome or challenging for some individuals, then the planners should request that they be contacted in order to explore possible accommodations. If an accommodation simply is not possible (in the United States accommodations must be made only when reasonable and when they will not create an undue burden),[19] then at least the potential participant will not be surprised, after the program already has begun, with the fact that he or she cannot participate in core activities. Furthermore, reasonable accommodations often are less expensive and more achievable than one might think, and sometimes all it takes is awareness and planning.[20]

When it comes to issues of spirituality and ethics, it also may be advisable to provide information regarding planned activities. When potential participants are alerted in advance about adventure learning exercises that may involve religious or spiritual issues, they can make the individual determination as to whether they want to participate before the program has begun. This can and should occur before individuals suddenly are forced to decide whether they will participate without any time for reflection. The Istanbul Second Generation program, it must be noted, did provide significant notice and information to participants about this dialogue opportunity well in advance.

Conclusion

Without a doubt, few teaching opportunities are as exciting as the chance to teach negotiation to a global audience. Not only will the instructors be challenged in their preparation and planning in ways they never may have been challenged before, they also will be able to learn seemingly limitless information about culture, values, and dispute resolution practices. Although we tend to be sensitive about the existence of cultural differences, we may not invest sufficient energy to appreciate the details and extent of those differences. Once we begin, we often learn that the challenge is much more than we anticipated.

As we search for new teaching models appropriate for a diverse global audience, we need to be attentive to the myriad ways in which individuals can be excluded. Some of the characteristics that can lead to exclusion are fairly obvious, but others are not immediately apparent. If we are going to adopt multidimensional learning approaches like adventure learning that engage students intellectually, physically, ethically, and perhaps even spiritually, then we have to be responsive to the danger that students may be excluded and unable to participate because of characteristics relating to any one of those dimensions.

Notes

[1] 42 U.S.C. § 12101 et. seq. (2009). The Americans with Disabilities Act ("ADA") was passed by the United States Congress in 1990 to remedy the effects of systemic and individual discrimination against Americans living with a variety of physical and mental impairments. Id. The most recent amendments to the ADA became effective on January 1, 2009, and broadened the statutory scope of protection for these individuals. Id.

[2] 42 U.S.C. § 12181-12189 (2009). Title III of the ADA, entitled "Public Accommodations and Services Operated by Private Entities," establishes the minimum standards of accessibility that private entities must provide when they are engaged in a wide array of commercial activities considered to be "public accommodations." Id. Under Title III,

> The following private entities are considered public accommodations...if the operations of such entities affect commerce: (A) an inn, hotel, motel, or other place of lodging...(B) a restaurant, bar, or other establishment serving food or drink; (C) a motion picture house, theater, concert hall, stadium, or other place of exhibition entertainment; (D) an auditorium, convention center, lecture hall, or other place of public gathering; (E) a bakery, grocery store...shopping center, or other sales or rental establishment; (F)...[the] office of an accountant or lawyer, pharmacy, insurance office, professional office of a health care provider, hospital, or other service establishment; (G) a terminal, depot, or other station used for specified public transportation; (H) a museum, library, gallery, or other place of public display or collection; (I) a park, zoo, amusement park, or other place of recreation; (J) a nursery, elementary, secondary, undergraduate, or postgraduate private school, or other place of education; (K) a day care center, senior citizen center, homeless shelter, food bank, adoption agency, or other social service center establishment; and (L) a gymnasium, health spa, bowling alley, golf course, or other place of exercise or recreation.
> 42 U.S.C. § 12181 (2009).

[3] See generally 42 U.S.C. § 12181-12189 (2009). See also 28 C.F.R. § 36.201-36.203; 36.304 (2009). The United States Department of Justice ("DOJ") is responsible for enforcing Title III of the ADA. Id. The DOJ regulations governing Title III enforcement stipulate that both landlords and tenants bear the responsibilities of ensuring accessibility:

> Both the landlord who owns the building that houses a place of public accommodation and the tenant who owns or operates the place of public accommodation are public accommodations subject to the requirements of this part. As between the parties, allocation of responsibility for complying with the obligations of the part may be determined by lease or other contract 28 C.F.R. 36.201 (2009).

Furthermore, these parties are responsible for providing accessibility and services in as seamless a manner as possible to facilitate ease of use: "A public accommodation shall afford goods, services, facilities, privileges, advantages, and accommodations to an individual with a disability in the most integrated setting appropriate to the needs of the individual." 28 C.F.R. 36.203 (2009).

[4] 28 C.F.R. § 36.304 (2009). In fact, the DOJ regulations essentially make mandatory the removal of such barriers, defining "readily available [as] easily accomplishable and able to be carried out without much difficulty or expense." Id. Section 36.304, the regulation governing the removal of barriers, provides a non-exhaustive list of examples to illustrate the ways in which barriers should be removed and, furthermore, provides guidance on the order of priority for removal. Id. Compliance with Section 36.304 requires, among other things,

> (1) Installing ramps; (2) making curb cuts in sidewalks and entrances; (3) repositioning shelves; (4) rearranging tables, chairs, vending machines, display racks, and other furniture; (5) repositioning telephones; (6) adding raised markings on elevator control buttons; (7) installing flashing alarm lights; (8) widening doors; (9) installing offset hinges to widen doorways; (10) eliminating a turnstile or providing an alternative accessible path; (11) installing accessible door hardware; (12) installing grab bars in toilet stalls; (13) rearranging toilet partitions to increase maneuvering space; (14) insulating lavatory pipes under sinks to prevent burns; (15) installing a raised toilet seat; (16) installing a full-length bathroom mirror; (17) repositioning the paper towel dispenser in a bathroom; (18) creating designated accessible parking spaces; (19) installing an accessible paper cup dispenser at an existing inaccessible water fountain; (20) removing high pile, low density carpeting; or (21) installing vehicle hand controls. Id.

The order of priority focuses first on external accommodations (designating parking spaces, building ramps, etc.), second on internal accommodations, (lowering display racks, rearranging tables, etc.), third on restroom facility accommodations (widening stalls, installing grab bars, etc.), and fourth on "any other measures necessary to provide access to the goods, services, facilities, privileges, advantages, or accommodations of a place of public accommodation." Id.

[5] The rights of students with disabilities are governed by the Individuals with Disabilities Education Act ("IDEA"). 20 U.S.C. § 1400 et seq. (2009).

The United States Congress pursued legislation to protect the rights of disabled students after determining that: "Improving educational results for children with disabilities is an essential element of our national policy of ensuring equality of opportunity, full participation, independent living, and economic self-sufficiency for individuals with disabilities." 20 U.S.C. § 1400(c)(1) (2009). To this end, Congress originally passed IDEA with the intent to:

> [E]nsure that all children with disabilities have available to them a free appropriate public education that emphasizes special education and related services designed to meet their unique needs and prepare them for further education, employment, and independent living...ensure that the rights of children with disabilities and parents of such disabilities are protected; and...assess, and ensure the effectiveness of, efforts to educate children with disabilities 20 U.S.C. § 1400(d) (2009).

[6] In Australia, for example, the country's Disability Discrimination Act ("DDA") not only protects *individuals* with disabilities from discrimination, but also protects *associates* of individuals with disabilities from discrimination (Australian Human Rights Commission). The DDA is relatively broad in scope, including in its definition of disability the use of corrective lenses, stuttering, and even allergic reactions to cigarette smoke. Id. In contrast, Germany amended its constitution in 1994 to include a prohibition against disability discrimination, but has yet to codify this mandate into a single, comprehensive legislative scheme (see e.g., Degener 2006, explaining that, "The concept of disability varies according to German criminal, civil, education, and social law... Even within one legal subject area, such as social law, there is no universal definition of disability covering all social welfare and social security laws"). In the context of employment, for example, German law protects only those individuals classified as "severely disabled ... persons whose degree of disability is at least 50%...." Id. Within social law, on the other hand, disability protection extends to individuals "if their physical functions, mental capacities, or psychological health are highly likely to deviate for more than six months from the condition which is typical for the respective age and whose participation in the life of society is therefore restricted." Id.

[7] Bolivia, for example, has enacted a series of laws that explicitly include individuals living with disabilities as citizens entitled to rights such as "employment, health care, rehabilitation, vocational training, and access to public spaces" (Center for International Rehabilitation 2004). Yet these laws neither prohibit discrimination nor ensure the enforcement of these rights. Id. In fact, the government itself discriminates against certain people with disabilities: "The [Bolivian] Civil Code declares that 'deaf-mute and mute persons are incapable of making a will.' They are likewise deemed 'incapable' of serving as a witness, as are people who are deaf." Id. Notably, however, certain provisions of the country's criminal law impose harsher sentences for crimes against disabled persons: "Individuals who commit a crime against a person with disabilities [such as] rape, etc., may be sen-

tenced...to a longer [imprisonment] period due to the aggravating circumstances." Id.

[8] Even in simulation debriefing, students approach the experience as "not in the real world."

[9] See also Ojeda-Zapata (2010) (reporting that an increasing number of schools across the United States are incorporating mobile technology devices, such as the iPod Touch, into their curricula).

[10] After more than a century and a half, however, the Board of Trustees for Antioch University decided to close Antioch College in July, 2008 (Antioch to Close Main College 2007). See also Goldfarb 2007 (describing an alumnus' perspective on the demise of the college).

[11] In light of the closing of Antioch College, one might question whether the verb should be present or past tense; "has been" or "had been." But loyal and determined alumni formed the Antioch College Continuation Corporation, are planning to reopen Antioch College in 2011, and consider the closing to be an opportunity to reorganize and regroup, see generally http://antiochcollege.org/ (last accessed June 7, 2010).

[12] See generally http://antiochcollege.org/about/mission_and_history.html (last accessed June 7, 2010).

[13] One always should keep in mind, of course, that dispute and conflict resolution cannot be taught without exploring human behavior. Theoretical studies alone will not be sufficient.

[14] See MAYO CLINIC, ASPERGER'S SYNDROME DEFINITION, available at http://www.mayoclinic.com/health/aspergers-syndrome/DS00551 (last accessed June 7, 2010). Asperger's syndrome characteristics include "engaging in one-sided, long-winded conversations; displaying unusual non-verbal communication, such as lack of eye contact, few facial expressions, or awkward body postures; showing an intense obsession with one or two subjects, such as baseball statistics, train schedules or snakes; and having a hard time reading other people or understanding humor" (Voigt 2009). Asperger's syndrome typically is grouped with other conditions that are called autistic spectrum disorders or pervasive developmental disorders and generally is considered to be at the milder end of this spectrum (Voigt 2009).

[15] Id.

[16] 42 U.S.C. 2000e et seq. (2009). Since its original adoption in 1964, the Civil Rights Act has been amended several times, with its most comprehensive amendments in 1991. Id.

[17] 29 U.S.C. § 623 et seq. (2009). The Age Discrimination in Employment Act (ADEA) protects people 40 years of age and older from employment discrimination based on age. 29 U.S.C. § 623 (2009). The ADEA states that it is illegal for an employer:

> (1) [T]o fail or refuse to hire or to discharge any individual or otherwise discriminate against any individual with respect to his compensation, terms, conditions, or privileges of employment, because of such individual's age; (2) to limit or segregate or classify his employees in any way which would deprive or tend to deprive any individual of employment opportunities or otherwise adversely affect

his status as an employee, because of such individual's age; or (3) to reduce the wage rate of any employee in order to comply with this chapter. Id.

[18] 42 U.S.C. § 12101 et. seq. (2009). As mentioned above, the ADA was passed in 1990 and was a remedial measure to address Congress' finding that:

> [H]istorically, society has tended to isolate and segregate individuals with disabilities, and, despite some improvements, such forms of discrimination against individuals with disabilities continue to be a serious and pervasive social problem; [and further] unlike individuals who have experienced discrimination on the basis of race, color, sex, national origin, religion, or age, individuals who have experienced discrimination on the basis of disability often had no legal recourse to redress such discrimination 42 U.S.C. § 12101 (2009).

[19] 42 U.S.C. § 12182 (2009). Under the ADA, it is unlawful discrimination if an entity fails:

> [T]o take such steps as may be necessary to ensure that no individual with a disability is excluded, denied services, segregated, or otherwise treated differently than other individuals because of the absence of auxiliary aids and services, unless the entity can demonstrate that taking such steps would fundamentally alter the nature of the good, service, facility, privilege, advantage, or accommodation being offered *or would result in an undue burden* ... Id (emphasis added).

[20] See supra note 4 (discussing the types of accommodations required by the ADA). In the employment context, for example, one study found that "most accommodations sampled required little or no cost – more than 75% required no cost; somewhat less than one quarter cost less than $1,000; and less than 2% cost more than $1,000. The average direct cost for accommodations was less than $30" (Blanck 1999: 280).

References

Age Discrimination in Employment Act 29 U.S.C. § 623 et seq. (2009).

Americans with Disabilities Act 42 U.S.C. § 12101 et seq. (2009).

Australian Human Rights Commission, *Frequently asked questions: Who is protected by the DDA?* Available at http://www.hreoc.gov.au/ (last accessed June 7, 2010).

Blanck, P. D. 1999. Empirical study of disability, employment policy, and the ADA. *Mental & Physical Disability Law Reporter* 23: 275-280.

Center for International Rehabilitation, *International disability rights monitor country report – Bolivia* 2004. Available at http://www.ideanet.org/ content.cfm?id=5254 (last accessed June 7, 2010).

Degener, T. 2006. The definition of disability in German and foreign discrimination law. *Disability Studies Quarterly* 26(2). Available at http://www.dsq-sds.org/issue/view/33 (last accessed June 7, 2010).

Goldfarb, M. 2007. Where the arts were too liberal. *The New York Times* June 17, 2007. Available at http://www.nytimes.com/2007/06/17/opinion/17goldfarb.html (last accessed June 7, 2010).

Gunsalus, C. K. and J. Steven Beckett 2008. Playing doctor, playing lawyer: Interdisciplinary simulations. *Clinical Law Review* 14: 439-463.

Individuals with Disabilities in Education Act 20 U.S.C. § 1400 et seq. (2009).

Jaschik, J. 2007. Antioch to Close Main College. *Inside Higher Ed.* Available at http://www.insidehighered.com/news/2007/06/13/antioch (last accessed June 7, 2010).

Larson, D. A. 2006. Technology mediated dispute resolution (TMDR): A new paradigm for ADR. *Ohio State Journal on Dispute Resolution* 21: 629-686.

Moliterno, J. E. 1996. W. M. Keck Foundation Forum on the Teaching of legal ethics: Legal education, experiential education, and professional responsibility. *William and Mary Law Review* 38: 71-123.

Ojeda-Zapata, J. 2010. iPods and educational applications have Minnesota students giddy about learning. *Pioneer Press.* Jan. 11, 2010. Available at http://www.twincities.com/education/ci_14045406 9 (last accessed June 7, 2010).

Voigt, R., M.D. 2009. Mayo Clinic medical edge: Asperger's likely has a genetic link. Available at http://www.northjersey.com/news/health/68827487.html (last accessed June 7, 2010).

ം 13 ൠ

A Second Dive into Adventure Learning

Sharon Press & Christopher Honeyman *

Editors' Note: Back into the potentially treacherous waters of adventure learning just weeks after Istanbul, Press and Honeyman provide a detailed account of a "next try" that was explicitly built to respond to the first critiques of the Istanbul exercise. It shows how rapidly the initial problems with adventure learning are being addressed – even while some new ones are being revealed.

"The definition of success is: lack of failure."
(Robert Louden[1])

Introduction

The preceding chapters in this section amply demonstrate both how much our first tryout with adventure learning inspired others to think and write about the topic, and how much rueful head-shaking it inspired – among ourselves, as well. Fortunately, a second chance to get it right came within weeks. As we will discuss here, adventure learning is not out of the woods just yet, but it is improving.

Our second opportunity to try out adventure learning presented itself when several of the organizers of the Istanbul conference were invited to teach an ADR module at the University of Deusto in Bil-

---

* **Sharon Press** is an associate professor of law and director of the Dispute Resolution Institute at Hamline University School of Law. Her email address is spress01@hamline.edu. **Christopher Honeyman** is managing partner of Convenor Conflict Management, a consulting firm based in Washington, D.C. and Madison, Wisconsin. He has directed a twenty-year series of major research-and-development projects in conflict management and is coeditor of *The Negotiator's Fieldbook* (ABA 2006). His email address is honeyman@convenor.com.

bao, Spain, as part of the European Master in Transnational Trade Law and Finance (EMTTLF), an EU-supported Erasmus Mundus program.[2] The EMTTLF is described as

> [a] flexible, semester-based, international, multi-site program that offers
> - A formative, problem-oriented, multidisciplinary itinerary with the most advanced competencies of technical and procedural analysis and judicial and economic rationality,
> - An innovative itinerary in transnational trade law, which aims to develop high level professional competencies and analytical skills, offering a professional and a research track.[3]

The program is open to graduate students of all nationalities. Candidates for admission must have completed at least a "first cycle" degree in a discipline related to law or business administration, as well as recognized qualifications in the languages of the universities where they will study.[4] In 2009 the nearly thirty EMTTLF students included at least one student each from Albania, Algeria, Brazil, Chile, China, Costa Rica, Dominican Republic, Ecuador, El Salvador, Iran, Iraq, Mexico, Moldova, Russia, Rwanda, Spain, Taiwan, Thailand, Ukraine, Venezuela, and Yemen. This extraordinary diversity was balanced by a rather high degree of consistency in two other respects: these highly selected students (more than 500 had applied) were not only very bright, but were more adapted to working outside their own cultures than most students are.

The program is structured such that the students spend their first semester (September to February) studying Private International European Union Law at the University of Deusto in Bilbao, Spain.[5] Among the courses completed during this semester is the module entitled Arbitration and Alternative Methods of Solving Conflicts in the European Union. This nearly one-month-long module has traditionally included sections on negotiation, mediation and arbitration – and relatively less of the latter than the title might imply – and has been taught during the month of December, after the students have studied together for several months and just prior to the winter break when many students return home for the holidays.

This year, the faculty[6] for the module agreed that the first week would be focused on traditional negotiation theory and exercises, and the second week would be devoted to mediation theory and practice. The third week would include international arbitration and the conclusion of the mediation section, along with some additional bits and pieces on negotiation including "heuristics and biases" and an online negotiation exercise. The final two days of the program would be devoted to the "new negotiation material" – specifically, an adventure learning activity.

The Adventure Learning Assignment

Since this chapter is the only one in this book which will describe the Deusto adventure learning experiment, we will include more nuts-and-bolts detail here than in the related chapter that begins this section, discussing Istanbul. The instructors decided that the more oblique exercise would be adapted, incorporating the lessons learned from Istanbul. The class was divided into five groups.[7] The groups were instructed to take the following photographs:

1) Agree on and photograph whatever you find that the group believes best represents the *crossroads of the sacred and the secular*.
2) Agree on and photograph the *most dangerous thing* you see.
3) Agree on and photograph the door or any other entryway that the group agrees is most likely to be the "unmarked" *CIA headquarters* in Bilbao.
4) Arrange a self-portrait that best captures *how your group is different* from other student groups.
5) Agree on and photograph one thing that *should not be where it is*.

In addition, each group was to bring back one snack for the class for the end-of-class celebration, which was to be "different from what all other groups bring" – *without* discussing it with any other group. (The learning objective for this portion of the assignment was to highlight how decisions must often be made in the face of imperfect information and based on speculation as to what others will do.)

The groups were given the following additional instructions:

- Designate a reporter for the group (the reporter was not permitted to participate in the decision-making, so that s/he could objectively observe the dynamics of the group and report back fully on the negotiations).
- Determine a process for how decisions will be made (multi-party negotiation, mediation or arbitration).[8]
- Determine where you will go as a group to complete the project.
- Make one *addition or change* to this assignment (before you do it) to create a more effective learning experience.

Unlike in Istanbul, this exercise was used as part of an academic program, and was therefore graded. As an experiment to follow up on a strongly argued point in our 2009 book, i.e., that students would learn more if given more control in negotiation courses (Nelken, McAdoo, and Manwaring 2009), the students were informed that those in each assignment group would be graded as a group *by the rest of the class* based on the quality of the decisions made by the group (best choice of photo subjects, best snack, most creativity, etc.) and also on how consistent the group was in its use of the group's own chosen decision-making process. The professors reserved the right to modify the grades up or down if appropriate (discussed in more detail below).

The activity took place on Monday, December 21, which happened to be the date of the famous Santo Tomas Festival in Bilbao. On this day, hundreds of stalls are set up along the river as a traditional country market festival. This annual event dates back to the nineteenth century, when the villagers would come to town to pay the landlords their rent, and took the opportunity to sell their home-produced goods. The festival is marked by strolling musicians playing traditional instruments, large crowds, and lots of drinking. Students were encouraged to consider the Festival as an option for their picture taking excursion.

Over the weekend, the hard-working students had taken their exam for negotiation, mediation and arbitration, and had also participated in an online negotiation exercise. Class began on Monday at 10:00 a.m. with an hour spent debriefing the online negotiation which the students had completed over the weekend. The following thirty minutes were spent explaining the adventure learning activity, assigning the class into groups, and having the groups meet to decide on a reporter, on the dispute resolution process they would use, on what change they would make to the exercise, and on where and when they would go to complete the task. Instructions were provided in writing to all of the students and were also reviewed orally along with a PowerPoint slide. Prior to their leaving the room, each group had to inform the instructors of the change they were making to the exercise, what process they would use to make decisions, and the reporter's name.

Every group opted to use multi-party negotiation. One group further specified that if they were unable to reach agreement through multi-party negotiation, they would use arbitration, and designated one of the members to serve as the sole arbitrator. This same group decided that they would videotape their negotiation (and possible arbitration), in order to observe the techniques used and to be able to "identify the important negotiation issues." Two of the groups requested permission to have the reporter participate in the decision-making as the change to the exercise. (The instructors did not allow this change, in order to ensure that someone was paying attention to the interactions and would be in a position to report on them thoughtfully during the debrief.)

In other respects, each group approached the task differently. One group, for example, went to a café to develop a plan on how to approach the assignment – specifically, whether the group should split up and each take photos, which would then be shared online and culminate in an online negotiation as to which photo to select, or should the group stay together, take several photos for each required item, and then choose which one to use for the assignment.

Another group stayed in the classroom long after the other groups were gone, in an attempt to reach consensus on what to take pictures of before beginning the adventure. Other groups went right to the Santo Tomas festival and worked from there. The resulting negotiated images included these examples:

Crossroads of the sacred and the secular: exterior of Parroquia de los Santos Juanes Church, where a street artist has set up for business.

The most dangerous thing seen by one group: reporter from one of the groups, considering ending the exercise early.

The "unmarked" CIA headquarters in Bilbao.

Self-portrait of one group – represented entirely by *items* the rest of the class associated with each of them.

One thing that should not be where it is: a student trying to improve on the first shot, and about to be reduced to two dimensions himself.

The class reconvened at 10:00 a.m. the next morning for the last class of the module (also the last class of the semester).[9] One student from each group in turn sat with one of the instructors and downloaded and renamed all of the pictures, so that two sets of photographs were created: 1) a collection of all five photos (one from each group) for each of the *requirements* and 2) a set of all five photos from each of the *groups*. This was so the class could review each group's photo set while the reporter described the group's negotiation and rationale for the photos chosen, but could also review the pictures for each topic together, to compare for creativity, etc.

During this organizational time, the other instructor had the students answer a series of questions about the last portion of the ADR module generally and the adventure learning exercise in particular. Students were asked to respond to the following questions:

1) Was the adventure learning activity a useful exercise for class? Consider the time it took to participate in this activity and what might have been covered if you remained in the classroom instead.
2) Did you learn anything new in the adventure learning activity? If so, what?
3) Where any ADR concepts reinforced in the adventure learning activity? If so, which ones?
4) Were there aspects of the adventure learning activity that did not work? If so, what were they?
5) If you were teaching negotiation, would you incorporate an adventure learning activity?
6) If yes, would you change this exercise? If so, how?

Once all of the pictures had been downloaded and organized, the reporter from each group presented the group's work and discussed how decisions were made. The rest of the class was encouraged to ask questions of the group under discussion, in order to determine what grade to assign to the group. Much of the debrief time was devoted to looking at the pictures and to comments about whether the responses met a sufficient level of creativity. (Some, but not all, of the students were bracingly critical of the less distinguished efforts.) After each group had presented its results, each student assigned a grade to each group of which s/he was not a part, on a scale of 1 - 10. Students were permitted to talk with their classmates while deliberating on the grades to assign, but each student gave an independent grade to each group.

The grades assigned by the students were as follows:

- Group 1: average grade of 7.52 with a low of 4 and a high of 10.
- Group 2: average grade 8.15 with a low of 6 and a high of 10.
- Group 3: average grade 8.18 with a low of 6 and a high of 10.
- Group 4: average grade 7.8 with a low of 6 and a high of 10.
- Group 5: average grade 8.78 with a low of 7 and a high of 10.

While some students gave tens across the board, most students differentiated between groups. The instructors reflected on the work of the group and their own perceptions, which were broadly consistent with the students' results, and saw no reason to alter the student-granted grades. These grades were factored in with the grades given for the other portions of the ADR module. It should be noted that the structure of the course meant that these last two days did not account for a high percentage of the overall grade, lessening the risks involved in this experiment.

What Worked and What Did Not
The aspects of this adventure learning activity that worked well for this iteration were:

Clarity of Assignment
The combination of providing written explanations along with oral description of the exercise seemed to be effective. The students, in general, understood what they were required to do and were able to complete the tasks.[10] It is clear that for such an exercise to be effective, instructors must do sufficient pre-planning (e.g., field-testing the assignment, determining who has the ability to take pictures which could be downloaded, assigning groups, producing written instructions, etc.).

Group Formation
The size and composition of the groups were appropriate and effective for the exercise. The class of 27 was divided into five multinational groups (each group had at least five participants and two groups had six participants). The number of groups created a sufficient number of pictures and presentations to be able to form a comparison on approaches. The number of participants within each group and the make-up of the groups provided enough different ideas so that students had to use negotiation principles.[11]

Design of the Exercise
For the most part, we think the design of the exercise was effective. It provided an opportunity to use theory that had been taught in the prior weeks, in a "real" situation.[12] From Istanbul, we had learned that the activity should be planned in such a way that students have sufficient time to complete the exercise *and* have the flexibility to spend different amounts of time doing so. Unlike how the exercise was structured when completed in Istanbul, the students in Bilbao were given the assignment at the end of the structured class period for that day. They were instructed to report back to class with the assignment complete the next morning. When and how they completed the assignment was up to the groups to decide (negotiate). The benefit of structuring it in this manner was that when class started the next morning, all groups were present at the same time, and with completed assignments.[13]

Negotiation Theory Reinforced

Students identified the following concepts as either newly recognized or reinforced as a result of the adventure learning activity:

- "I learned to work around the edges when consensus is required..."
- "I learned that it may be possible to have other people [at] the table or in the room of negotiation. For that, I don't have to be scared by any extra eye on the table or in the room which may cause me to negotiate the way I would not have done if they were not there."[14]
- "...it is very difficult to find a compromise when we deal...not only with logic but with creativeness."
- "I learned how to manage the issue when it came to be a multi-party negotiation [and] ADR concepts could be applied to any...procedure depending on [the] level of disagreement..."
- "We all have different ideas and concepts of what we think should be done. At first you try to convince or persuade the others [then] at a certain point you have to decide if you want to give up, for the sake of the group."
- "I could experience a real process of negotiation, whereby I was responsible myself for deciding on the techniques to use, approach of negotiation and conflict handling myself.... I reinforced the integrative approach, brainstorming and also to handle the tension between empathy and assertiveness."
- "... different perspectives when seeing the same thing."
- "...every phenomenon has a lot of points of view"
- "I learned how...concepts in ADR can be applicable outdoors, like negotiating common decisions, for example where to make a stop and have a coffee or a snack."
- "...it is an interesting 'field experience' to implement what you have learned in the 'real world.'"
- "...outside the room you have to deal with external factors that make the activity more challenging."
- "I confirmed that deciding in a group is a hard task and that every opinion counts and must be respected and tried to be understood."
- "I understood how it is very difficult to make [a] final decision for people who have different choices, different backgrounds but finally it [becomes] very easy when you agree on one important and common interest."
- "The concepts of interests were reinforced as well as the integrative approach."

- "The multi-party negotiation was seen one more time from a different perspective and in a different environment where we had pressure to decide on where to go because we were in the middle of a lot of people."
- "We understood that we came from different cultures but we have similar perspectives of the world."

There were also aspects of this adventure learning activity that (in our opinion and/or the students') did not work well, but could probably be improved in another "run." These include the following:

Timing of the Exercise

The adventure learning exercise took place at the conclusion of the three and a half week ADR module, which was itself the last module the students completed before winter break. The students had been together in classes and socially (some even lived together as roommates) for several months. Several students commented that while they enjoyed the activity and got something out of it, it would have worked better earlier in the term, before they all knew each other so well[15] and before they had already learned the concepts of negotiation and had so many opportunities to practice them within the classroom.[16] There was a split among the students as to whether being so close to the Christmas holidays was a positive[17] or a negative.[18]

There was another consideration, however; the instructors from the *prior* year were supportive of the alternative exercise, partly because, they reported, it was very difficult to hold the students' attention during the final days of the semester when teaching such an intensive course in a traditional manner. The final relevant aspect of timing was the day chosen for this exercise, the Basque festival of Santo Tomas. While the lively crowds made it more entertaining for the students, some remarked that the crowds also made it more difficult to accomplish the tasks.[19]

Insufficient Conflict in the Exercise

The most critical response from a student was that

> [t]he whole exercise didn't work because it's a banality that is detached from real-life scenarios and from theory explained in class. There [were] no real negotiations going on; students just agree[d] immediately.

While others were not as critical (and/or had a different experience), suggestions for improving the exercise included requiring more negotiations with strangers, locals or people on the street;[20] having each person in the group take their own pictures, then conduct a negotiation and arbitration to decide which one would represent the group; having the instructors assign the decision-making process so that the class would have to apply every method of ADR learned in class; "[putting] someone in the group to contradict the choices to improve the discussion;" making the exercise more competitive; and giving the individuals in the group contradictory personal interests. Interestingly, one student indicated she would "definitely incorporate an adventure learning activity in class," but suggested it should be "something related to a real negotiation out of class using real objects."

The implication appears to be that for many of the students, this exercise design still did not elicit a "real" negotiation. When asked to assess the usefulness of the adventure activity considering the time it took as compared to having additional classroom time, one student noted that he liked the activity but "it would be better to have more time for activities and…more feedback for the activities."

Importance of an Effective Debrief

Several students noted the importance of the debrief.[21] Unfortunately for purposes of analysis, the students completed their course evaluations before the debrief session,[22] so the comments cannot be directly correlated with the effectiveness of the debrief. From the instructors' perspective, we do not think that the debrief was as effective as it could be or should be. Given the short amount of time and the focus on grading the groups based on creativity, much of the presentation by the reporters and the questions by the class focused on *what* was selected as opposed to *how* it was selected. We would change this for a future run.

Clarity of Goals

The learning objectives for the exercise were deliberately not made explicit prior to the activity. The intent was to assess the effectiveness of the exercise and what the students learned without giving them a preconceived notion of what we wanted them to learn. The students were only told that this activity was being done as part of a larger effort on rethinking how negotiation is taught. As a result, some students reported being unclear as to what the purpose of the activity was.[23] In addition to standard negotiation theory, students reported learning about new places in Bilbao and more about the Basque Country, learning more about classmates, improving their ability to find "unusual" stuff, and learning collaboration and team-building.

Additional Considerations

When using an exercise for a grade, some kind of contingency plan must be created for the probability that one or more students will miss the exercise through no real fault of their own, or will be physically unable to complete it (see Larson, *Not Everyone Gets to Play*, in this volume.) In Bilbao, we had one student who missed the entire exercise and a second student who was able to participate with her group in the adventure learning, but was not at class the next day for the presentations and debrief.

We decided that this situation offered its own experimental opportunity. Both students were asked to do the following:

1) The student would submit a short paper (2 – 4 pages long), describing a real-world negotiation which she had as a result of leaving campus. In the paper, she would analyze how the teachings of the course applied or did not apply to that negotiation. The time invested should be comparable to what other students invested in the final exercise, i.e., several hours.

2) The student would then meet with an instructor[24] in order to demonstrate to the faculty member that she had learned as much by being away as she would have by participating in the adventure learning exercise. (For a detailed discussion of such exercises, see Cohn and Ebner, *Bringing Negotiation Teaching to Life*, in this volume.)

The first student chose a negotiation she had with her landlord, about her need to leave the apartment she was renting prior to the date specified in her lease. She described her negotiation in detail, including how the landlord was initially set in his position and unwilling to change, and how after she pointed out the disadvantages for both of them if they were unable to reach an agreement, he changed his position. In the end, they negotiated a new contract which called for the student to pay half a month's rent if the landlord was unable to find another tenant (with the student's assistance). Her paper demonstrated a clear understanding of negotiation principles and their application to a real problem.

Specifically, the student outlined her approach as follows:
Firstly, [the student] identified the problem. Secondly, she focused on the interests of the parties, [the student's] interest was to not pay one additional month rent, [the] landlord's interest was to have a tenant in order to not lose one month's rent. Once identified…[the student] tried to focus on generating possible solutions suitable to both parties. After generating the solution, she evaluated the alternatives according to the parties' interests and needs.

The student also discussed the importance of clarity in the opening and the special effort she made since she did not speak Spanish very well and the landlord only spoke Spanish, tying it to the lessons on negotiating in a multi-cultural environment. Finally, she described how she considered where to hold the negotiation, and opted for it to be in her apartment over tea and homemade apple pie(!) in order to "demonstrate to the landlord that she was keeping the house in very good condition."

The second student described a negotiation with her roommate, with whom she was having difficulties about the upkeep and use of their apartment. Her paper contained a lot of negotiation vocabulary. She described the benefits of "interest based bargaining" and a "collaborative manner" and that her counterpart was engaging in "positional bargaining," and "a competitive negotiation and adversarial negotiation and resource claiming negotiation." However, she did not seem to really understand how to integrate the principles into practice. She described trying to explain to him that "both of [them] should try our BATNA" but "his way of negotiating was bringing [them] unfortunately close to [their] WATNA," indicating a lack of real understanding of these concepts. She also simplistically described the negotiation as follows:

> Knowing and being aware of all these consequences and based on my integrative mindset position I went on putting in practice the four primary integrative elements and I tried to separate him by his problem by listening carefully to him and trying to understand his point of view. I focused on his interest and his needs by asking what [did] he really need. I gave him several options that could function for both of us by trying to be inventive inspired from our common problems and I insisted that we both should focus on the objective criteria for each of us so we both could achieve the goal of this common agreement that would satisfy both of us.

This negotiation, however, ended by the student moving out and sharing a more expensive flat with a close friend.

To us, the comparison of the two papers (and their appropriately different grades, not to mention the substantive results of the respective negotiations) suggests that such an assignment is a tenable alternative to adventure learning. Although the papers were approximately the same length, the students' respective understanding of negotiation principles and how they operationalized them were easy to differentiate.

Conclusion: Next Steps in Adventure Learning

Our personal assessment is that adventure learning is a valuable addition to negotiation teaching, well worth the inevitable struggle to make it reliable. Based on the lessons learned in Istanbul and Bilbao, for the next try or tries (and knowing we are still in the early stages of what are likely to be many iterations) we would restructure such an activity as follows:

Timing

Run the activity early in the course, rather than late during the time the students/participants are together. Assign the activity to take place outside of the regular instruction time, such that students complete the assignment prior to the start of the next scheduled gathering time.

Group Formation

Groups should have between four and six members and should be assigned by the instructor, to ensure a cross between manageable size and diversity of as many different kinds (e.g., gender, ethnicity, field of specialization) as possible.

Content

Include both a "concrete" negotiation (with strangers) and an "oblique" negotiation (by which we mean, one that requires reaching a conceptual agreement among a group). Specifically, students should be required to negotiate with someone who is not part of the group, and also to participate in decision-making *as* a group.

- Given the importance of tapping into creativity, retain the picture taking element (or an equivalent gambit that requires a conceptual negotiation but not expenditure of significant funds – which students tend to *consider* scarce, even when they dress better than the professors). But rather than have the group negotiate on which pictures to take (and/or which pictures to use to represent their assignment group), it may be more effective to require each group to take a set of multiple pictures that respond to each prompt, and then conduct a more intentional negotiation between the group as to which picture to use. As an alternative to requiring each group to have a reporter who does not participate in the decision making, the groups could be required to record the negotiation. (Whether this works in practice or creates too many technical foul-ups can only be tested empirically. On another level, such recording might work better if combined with student-to-student grading, as logically *other students* then listen to the tapes, freeing the instructor from what could be daunting extra hours of labor.)

- To increase the stakes even more for the students, grades could be assigned based on two aspects: 1) the highest possible grade for (the relevant percentage of) the course would go to the group which, as a group, had the "best" pictures[25] and 2) within the group, based on whose pictures were selected to represent the group. For example, the student with the greatest number of pictures selected would get the highest grade, the student with the next highest number of pictures selected would get the next highest grade, and so on. This combination of grading (we think, without having tried it yet) could create an incentive for the group as a whole to choose the best pictures to represent the group – while each individual would also have a stake in having his/her personal picture(s) chosen. Depending on the grading value chosen, this could help resolve an identified problem with our early efforts by adding more tension to the intra-group negotiation, which, as our students (and fellow teachers) commented, often went too easily in these first experiments.

Structure the Debrief

In order to get the greatest benefit from the exercise, the goals should be clearly articulated to the participants in advance, and participants should be prompted to identify where theory and practice intersected. In addition to a structured debrief in class, participants could be assigned a reflection paper, to be handed in at the start of the debrief class period. This would enable a more authentic assessment of what each participant learned from the exercise. The debrief should include a report from each group, which would include specific examples of observed negotiation theory-in-practice from both aspects of the assignment (the negotiation with someone outside the group, and the intra-group negotiation to choose the pictures).

We have no doubt that such modifications will not represent a "six-sigma" nearing of perfection, or anything close. After all, we are still in the initial phase of what will probably be many years of development of adventure learning in our field. Even after that, adventure learning will involve a level of risk of the segment failing its intended purpose that is inherently greater than the more predictable, controllable classroom. In preparing students for the unpredictable, hard-to-control world of real negotiations, though, we believe this game is more than worth the candle: it is essential.

Notes

[1] Robert Louden served as the first-ever commanding officer of the renowned Hostage Negotiation Team of the New York Police Department. The following excerpt (Cambria et al. 2002: 338) says it all:

> Bob Louden....was negotiating a rather difficult, very long and ongoing hostage situation. The chief of detectives said, "Hey Louden, seems like you aren't having any success here." Bob said, "I think we are." The chief says "What's your definition of success then?" Bob says "Lack of failure." That's it in a nutshell. As long as you haven't failed, the implication is that you are succeeding.

[2] The EU's Erasmus Mundus program offers financial support for institutions and scholarships for individuals to participate in European joint Masters and Doctorate programs (see http://eacea.ec.europa.eu/erasmus_mundus/index_en.php).

[3] European Master in Transnational Trade Law and Finance; program brochure available at http://www.transnational.deusto.es/emttl/index.html (last accessed May 27, 2010).

[4] According to the Program Brochure, "[s]election criteria include motivation, academic qualifications, language skills, research experience, and professional experience."

[5] The second semester of the program is in International Sources for Transnational Trade Law and is completed at Tilburg University. Students have the option of studying European Business Law (Strasbourg University), Law and Finance (Institute for Law and Finance), or Industrial and Intellectual Property (Strasbourg University) during their third semester. The fourth semester of the program is either a research project or an internship.

[6] The team, though all-American, had significant experience with Deusto. All three U.S. institutions, represented mostly by the same individuals, have been collaborating with Deusto for more than seven years, beginning with a multi-year, joint U.S./EU project which was one of the precursors to the Rethinking Negotiation Teaching project. These years of coordination among the team made the rotation of six instructors less confusing to the students than it might first appear. Ken Fox, Associate Professor, Hamline University taught the first week in negotiation. Joseph Stulberg, John W. Bicker Professor of Law, The Ohio State University, Michael E. Moritz College of Law; Lela Love, Professor and Director, Kukin Program for Conflict Resolution, Benjamin N. Cardozo School of Law, Yeshiva University; and Sharon Press, Associate Professor of Law, Hamline University, taught the mediation portion. Ellen Deason, Professor of Law, The Ohio State University, Michael E. Moritz College of Law taught the arbitration portion of the course. And Christopher Honeyman and Sharon Press taught the final segment.

[7] The prior week, the instructor had identified which students had access to a camera or cell phone to take digital pictures which would be downloaded. In assigning the groups, the instructors ensured that each group had at least one person who had that capability.

[8] If the groups selected mediation or arbitration, they also had to agree on who would serve as the "neutral."

[9] By the last class (three days before Christmas), two students had already departed and the others were making plans to depart soon after class. Although one of the students had participated in the activity and only missed the debrief, both students completed a make-up exercise, which will be described below.

[10] One student did report that the instructions were not clear, but added that this was possibly due to insufficient English proficiency. With a class of students from more than twenty cultures, however, we might have anticipated that some might have such difficulty, and taken extra steps to make sure no one was left in doubt.

[11] "Our group was composed of people from four continents: Africa, Asia, America, and Europe and it was very possible to not agree on something..."

[12] "The Adventure activity was a useful exercise because it is [a] practical part of what we learnt in class in this past three weeks." "[W]e had the opportunity to work on our own and practice the concepts that we have learned during this module."

[13] It should be noted that five students suggested in their evaluations that having still more time would have improved the exercise. One thought the team needed more time "so that students would be able to use different ADR methods and then to debrief them in their report." Another suggested that the exercise would be improved if the exercise developed over a couple of days, which would "increase the challenge and to actually create opportunities for conflict resolution." The other three students did not provide a context for their statements. It is a little puzzling as to how they thought that the exercise could be designed to provide more time in the particular setting, given that the students had approximately 22 hours from when the assignment was given to when it was due. If they felt there was insufficient time, that appears to have been a decision made by the group of how much time to spend on the activity, and therefore was more appropriately a topic to discuss in the debrief, i.e., how the decision was made about how much time to spend on the activity. (See Druckman 2006 for an example of a longer exercise, but in a very different setting.)

[14] Student added that the learning came from sometimes having to take "funny" positions for photos in public "where everyone was looking...surprised."

[15] Student reactions included: "These two days of classes would have been better to take place [at] the beginning of the course as a natural introduction of students to the negotiation teaching field." "... this exercise would serve its purpose better if organized before the negotiation training in class." Another student reported in response to the question, "did you learn anything new...?" "It was really funny, but it was like a friends' meeting." Two students suggested it would have been more effective in the middle of the course (not the end). Another student suggested running an adventure learning activity at the beginning of the course "when nobody has devel-

oped a friendship or relationship" and then again at the end to "compare results."

[16] "Although I believe it was a learning exercise, its effect on us was not as significant as we were already trained very well in negotiating skills and many aspects of ADR in [the] classroom...Moreover, we already worked in groups and practiced a broad range of negotiation skills and behaviors in class..." "We actually did not have any problem getting into agreements with the multi-party negotiation system, it just came very natural for all of us." "... if I had worked with [other] people the experience could be different. We know each other and we knew which are the required skills to negotiate."

[17] "It was effective in the sense that everyone was looking forward to the holidays. Frankly speaking, when you have students with lower motivation about learning, it was considered effective that this adventure made everyone go out, do things, and negotiate." Another student reported, "[it] could be a very good idea to be relaxing after the long time working intensely."

[18] "The last two days of class were effective but I think we would have enjoyed [them] more if they were [at] a different time of the year, because placing them right before Christmas/holidays were very hard to concentrate..." "There was not [much] discussion. Everybody was tired and wanted to agree as soon as possible with the pictures in order to finish the work." The timing, just before Christmas, was not good because "people were nervous about packing and couldn't concentrate sometimes during the activity."

[19] One student identified the challenge of all of the activity in the city as useful to learning about dealing "with people in the street" and "external factors" that may make a negotiation more challenging. He noted that "sometimes you have to negotiate with people in the street to ask for help."

[20] See Cohn and Ebner, *Bringing Negotiation Teaching to Life*, in this volume, for some ideas in this vein.

[21] One student wisely noted, "to determine [the] usefulness and applicability [of the exercise], it is important to rely on the class discussion which we have not had yet." In response to the question, "would you incorporate an adventure learning activity" if you were teaching negotiation?, one student remarked "yes, only if the development of the course would allow a thorough analysis of the experience." Another student noted that if the time had been spent in class, "we would be able to analyze and debrief our negotiation or arbitration."

[22] This was done for efficiency reasons, so that students had a task to complete while the reporters were downloading their pictures and the instructor was preparing them for the presentation. In retrospect, it was a bad idea, because we lost valuable feedback on the exercise as a whole, which should have included the debrief.

[23] One student noted "...if the purpose of the activity was 1) time management, 2) organizing a negotiation without assistance of teachers and specific information (as we had in the role plays) and 3) while performing the

activity, be ourselves (and not simulating or representing other parties), I think the adventure learning fulfilled its goals and I would not change it."
[24] See Nelken, McAdoo, and Manwaring (2009) for the pedagogical basis for this gambit. In this circumstance, the assignment was designed so that the student would meet face-to-face (or via telephone if the student had already left Bilbao) with one of the permanent professors at Deusto who were ultimately responsible for the program once the U.S.-based instructors for the class were no longer in Europe. This of course demanded an extra effort from Professor Luis Gordillo, the faculty member who volunteered, to whom we are grateful.
[25] For this double-tiered grading approach to work, each student would produce a set of pictures, from which the group would select a final set to represent the group. Sufficient clarity would have to be provided as to how "best" would be defined. Possible options include most creative, most responsive, etc.

References

Cambria, J., R. J. DeFilippo, R. J. Louden and H. McGowan. 2002. Negotiation under extreme pressure: The "mouth marines" and the hostage takers. *Negotiation Journal* 18(4): 331-343.

Druckman, D. 2006. Uses of a marathon exercise. In *The negotiator's fieldbook: The desk reference for the experienced negotiator*, edited by A. K. Schneider and C. Honeyman. Washington, DC: American Bar Association.

Nelken, M., B. McAdoo, and M. Manwaring. 2009. Negotiating learning environments. In *Rethinking negotiation teaching: Innovations for context and culture*, edited by C. Honeyman, J. Coben, and G. De Palo. St. Paul, MN: DRI Press.

❧ 14 ☙

Get Ripped and Cut Before Training: Adventure Preparation for the Negotiation Trainer

*Yael Efron & Noam Ebner**

Editors' Note: In this entertaining closing piece to the Beyond the Classroom section, Efron and Ebner argue that adventure learning cannot work unless the instructor is "up" for it. Using a metaphor from the world of professional bodybuilding to provide a useful acronym ("RIPPED & CUT"), they prescribe nine practical pre-training exercises to inspire negotiation teachers to be at their best.

Introduction

As described elsewhere in this book, the 2009 Istanbul Conference highlighted different uses of adventure learning for expanding the students' learning area beyond the classroom. Participants experimented with direct exercises, such as negotiating in a bazaar. In addition, they participated in indirect exercises, such as being given a team assignment, unrelated to negotiation, to complete around the city, in order to later examine intra-team negotiation processes. In this manner, the conference challenged participants to reach beyond the constraints set or implied by the classroom setting.

As we participated in the exercises, and on our own journeys to the conference and back home, it struck us that the type of real-life exercises that are the basis of adventure learning may serve yet another purpose. While the value of different types of experiential learning has been explored (both in *Rethinking Negotiation Teaching*

* **Yael Efron** is assistant to the Dean of the Safed College School of Law. Her email address is yaele.law@gmail.com. **Noam Ebner** is an assistant professor at the Werner Institute at Creighton University's School of Law, where he chairs the online masters program in Negotiation and Dispute Resolution. His email address is noamebner@creighton.edu.

(Honeyman, Coben, and De Palo 2009), the product of the 2008 Rome Conference, and other chapters in this book) in the context of enhancing *student learning*, we suggest that it may have implications for a relatively untouched corner of the negotiation training workshop: *trainer preparation*.

As evidenced elsewhere in this book, an important element of the new approach to negotiation workshops and training developing in Negotiation 2.0 involves taking a step away from some of our more constraining practices, in terms of both workshop content and style. These constraints would include, for example, use of off-the-shelf generic material, or applying a trainer's individual style across an undifferentiated range of training situations (see Lewicki and Schneider, *Instructors Heed the Who*, in this volume). It would seem that there is a clear shift towards preferring a student-focused approach in both design and implementation: tailoring workshop content to students' particular needs and context, and running the training sessions using pedagogical methods that appeal and speak to the students we are working with. Instead of hearing calls to focus on "what do we want to teach them, and how do we do that best," we are hearing a call to focus on "what do they want to know, and how do they want to learn it?"

While these two questions might be partially answered by preparation (such as conducting preliminary talks with the client organization, sending preliminary questionnaires out to students, etc.), the most important elements of the answers might only be available, ultimately, in the classroom itself. In order to receive this information, though, a trainer must be prepared to elicit it, and be open to receiving it. How can we attain this degree of openness and curiosity? We suggest that a pre-training exercise, aimed at buffing up the trainer's level of curiosity, openness to new information and adaptability might be a good way for trainers to spend their time on the way to the training room.

The road from the trainer's home to the training venue presents many opportunities for this type of "tuning-up" exercise. The list presented below was originally formulated in the context of the airport setting in which this chapter was originally mapped out and planned, but each individual exercise can be adapted for implementing while driving alone or with others, while riding a bus, or over the course of a five-minute walk from a hotel to the training site.

This new model of preparation requires a bit of a change in habits for some trainers. No longer is the long and winding road leading to the training room "down time," in which you may, at best, be able to clear a few emails out of your inbox. This road is, in fact, your inner prep and setup time. The moment you start your journey, you are engaged in the game.

Of course, many trainers do in fact use this time to prepare by going over their prepared notes for the training. We are certainly not suggesting you forego reviewing your notes! However – if you *only* go over your notes, you will probably walk in to the room and conduct the training you prepared. We are suggesting that you go over your notes at home, but spend the journey priming yourself to engage with your students.

A metaphor providing a useful acronym for this exercise comes from the world of professional bodybuilding. Before competitions, bodybuilders attempt to reach a peak of being "ripped" and "cut" to have maximum impact on audiences and judges. While sometimes used interchangeably, "cut" involves achieving a balance between being lean and bulging: stripping the body of excess body fat while retaining maximum muscularity. "Ripped," on the other hand, is a condition connoting extremely low body fat with superior muscle separation and vascularity. It focuses on discrete definition of each and every visible element of the physique.

Playing with this metaphor, we are looking for preparation that combines the power of the content we are about to deliver, with an enhanced degree of clarity and an increased ability to notice and appreciate distinctions. Side benefits may include our own enhanced motivation, and, of course, a story or two to tell in the classroom in the venerated "an interesting thing happened to me on the way to the classroom this morning..." tradition.

RIPPED & CUT

How do we get RIPPED & CUT? By performing some (or all!) of the following exercises incorporated in this acronym as we make our way to the training venue. Depending on your level of motivation and energy, this can be done in two forms:

- Passive: noticing when these interactions occur to you, or to others in front of you, and conducting a conscious self-debrief; or
- Active: setting yourself missions, targeting people for interactions, purposefully engaging with them and conducting self debrief.

1) *Relationship*

Engage with another in a way that enhances your relationship. This may be a minor interaction, or a more substantial piece of relationship building. Examples:

- Choosing a stranger on the street or riding the bus with you, and seeking to engage them in a conversation.
- Deciding that you will somehow make the person selling you a cup of coffee smile at some point during your interaction.
- Attempting to make a bystander respond to you by sharing a thought or an observation with them (weather and traffic comments are suitable for this purpose in some cultures, sports in others, etc.).

The mental channel we hope to clear through this exercise is the relational channel, the part of our brain that appreciates the complexities of interpersonal interactions, particularly those in which there is a confusing mix of assumptions, perceptions and interdependence – a mix that well characterizes negotiation training.

2) Information

Gain a piece of information from someone else. At a basic level, this may involve asking a person filling a mundane role a contextually suitable question (such as enquiring at the information desk "Excuse me, where is gate 216?"). A more advanced exercise would be targeting a stranger and giving yourself a mission ("My goal in engaging with that person is to make her share something about her family").

This exercise seeks to prime us for engaging in an elicitive, learning mode as opposed to a top-down, imparting mode.

3) Problem Solving

Identify someone having trouble or needing assistance. Ask the person if you can help them, and choose between assisting passively (doing what the other tells you to do) or assisting proactively (making suggestions, doing things unilaterally). Alternatively, you might self-debrief a situation in which you tried to solve a problem of your own, asking yourself what approach you took and what stages did your process go through.

This exercise will prepare us to notice problems as they arise, including clashes between students and between their goals and ours, and prime us for engaging with them through different approaches.

4) Pretend to Be Someone Else

In the training room, you will be stepping into a role and on to a stage. You will be focusing on the needs of the role, not the needs of the actor. Prepare doing this consciously and practice interacting with others consciously "through" the role. Here are some things you can do:

- Speak to people while faking an accent.
- Ask for something you don't need.
- Lie about something.

5) *Entertain*

Like it or not, the reality of negotiation training is that part of what we do is entertain our audience. However, not everybody is looking to be entertained, and not everything we consider entertaining (and therefore, do by rote after our first few dozen trainings) will resonate with any given audience. Entertainment, as a source of motivation and engagement for students, is something worth doing right. This includes consciously considering how someone else may (or may not) consider you to be entertaining. This priming will serve us well in the classroom. Exercises you might consider:

- Make someone smile.
- Tell a stranger a joke.
- Play with a kid on the street or with a baby on the bus.

6) *Describe*

Watch an interaction between two people: ask yourself "How would I tell that story to my students?" This primes you for story-telling mode. Next, ask yourself "How would I like to *hear* that story?" – to transition into a story-hearing mode. Finally, you might ask "How do I think my students would like that story told?" Many of the themes in Negotiation 2.0, as presented in this book as well as the previous volume, require that teachers travel a linguistic and mental journey from focus on self to connecting to others via their preferences and needs. Storytelling is a powerful tool for making this journey explicit.

7) *Curiosity*

Adopting a curious stance towards your students – as opposed to assuming curiosity directed at you from their side – seems to be a central theme emerging in Negotiation 2.0, mirroring the notion of adopting a curious stance towards a negotiation counterpart (for more on this notion, see Guthrie 2009). Given the internal pressures involved in initiating the first steps of a training (and the early morning hour at which this may occur), it may be difficult to achieve this "curiosity frame." We suggest you give this ability a warm-up on your way to the training room. Here are some exercises you might enjoy:

- Choose a stranger on the street. Be curious about them: Ask yourself a question about them, make up a story about them, or guess what they might be doing.
- Zoom in on a phenomenon on the street: traffic suddenly halting, people moving quickly in the same direction, etc. Ask yourself about this phenomenon ("why is everybody running?") and give several answers.

"Applied curiosity" might incorporate the "information" and "relationship" exercises discussed above. After noticing the phenomenon, ask a stranger to explain it to you. Perhaps, invoking the "Take" exercise (see below), ask for their advice, or even help, in dealing with it.

8) *U*

Take care of you. Our most important training prop is ourselves. Checking the hardware – the room, the seating arrangements, the computer and audiovisual equipment – is something we do proactively, as is checking the software (such as presentations, movie clips, etc.). Internalizing this, trainers need to give their own physical and emotional energy status a quick going over. If either of these is weak, recharge! Eat, drink, do something calming, smile, meditate – whatever the source of the energy leak is, find a way to plug it and stock up on what is missing. Training while off-balance, you might naturally gravitate towards your "certainty zone" – your prepared training plan and notes. Student input might be internally perceived as an attempt to push you further off balance, and perhaps result in pushback and defensiveness rather than listening, considering and adapting.

9) *Take Something From Someone*

As trainers, we have many goals in conducting training. We might want to affect people's perceptions, achieve change, impart knowledge, enjoy a spotlight, have fun, earn a living – or any number of other goals. Likewise, trainees participate in negotiation training for a variety of reasons. However, it is safe to assume that students (in the executive training programs this book is centering on) will usually share one primary purpose: to gain. Participants are *probably* there at least in part because they want to learn skills that will help them gain resources. By practicing *taking* before walking into class, we are putting ourselves in our students' shoes, and opening up a channel to connect with their goals and motivations.

We are not, of course, prescribing theft. However, engaging with another for the explicit purpose of gaining something for ourselves is a valuable exercise. Here are some possibilities:

- Ask a stranger for a cigarette.
- Ask a sales clerk for a discount.
- Ask someone at the bus stop, or at the copying machine, if you can go before them.

Whether or not the interaction results in your actually obtaining that advantage or resource is of secondary concern; the core activity which will keep you congruent with participants' state of mind is the *attempt* to gain.

Get RIPPED and CUT, and your engagement with students is bound to include a new level of give-and-take, of mutual learning and of decentralized process- and content- related decision-making.

References

Guthrie, C. 2009. I'm curious: Can we teach curiosity? In *Rethinking negotiation teaching: Innovations for context and culture*, edited by C. Honeyman, J. Coben, and G. De Palo. St. Paul, MN: DRI Press.

Honeyman, C., J. Coben, and G. De Palo (eds). 2009. *Rethinking Negotiation teaching: Innovations for context and culture*. St. Paul, MN: DRI Press.

ca 15 ba

Simulation 2.0: The Resurrection

*Noam Ebner & Kimberlee K. Kovach** *

Editors' Note: *Ebner and Kovach consider the critique of role-plays previously offered in this series (see particularly, Alexander and Le-Baron 2009) – and reject it. They argue that what is needed is not to move away from simulations, but to use the critique to devise more efficient, more convincing, more authentic, and more sensitive simulations. They outline a series of tactics within this strategy.*

"The reports of my death are greatly exaggerated."
(Mark Twain)

The Widespread Use of Role-Play in Negotiation 1.0

If there is any one teaching method that seems to be universally accepted in the trainer's manual for Negotiation 1.0, it would be the use of simulation-games and role-plays.[1] Noam Ebner and Yael Efron summed up the ubiquity of the use of simulation-games in negotiation training as well as in other related contexts:

> It seems almost unnecessary to note the degree to which conflict resolution trainers rely upon the use of simulation games as a training tool. The literature singles out simulation games as a particularly effective method of education in negotiation (Meerts 1991; Winham 1991), mediation (Moore

* **Noam Ebner** is an assistant professor at the Werner Institute at Creighton University's School of Law, where he chairs the online masters program in Negotiation and Dispute Resolution. His email address is noamebner@creighton.edu. **Kimberlee K. Kovach** is the director of the Frank Evans Center for Dispute Resolution and a distinguished lecturer in dispute resolution at South Texas College of Law. Her email address is k2kovach@yahoo.com.

2003) and peacebuilding (Truger 2001). This, combined with legislation making simulation games a mandatory element of professional training in several countries,[2] merely reinforces what conflict resolution trainers have known all along: practice makes perfect. Successes, as well as failures, occurring in a controlled, debriefed environment enable the most efficient learning process (Ebner and Efron 2005: 378).

In a recent piece, published in *Rethinking Negotiation Teaching*, Nadja Alexander and Michelle LeBaron put this more succinctly, suggesting that "[u]sing role-plays in negotiation training has become as common as Santa at Christmas...or drinking beer at Oktoberfest... or expecting snow in a Canadian winter" (Alexander and LeBaron 2009: 180).

Why does role-play enjoy the popularity it does? In order to understand this more completely, we must step back and take note of the fact that conflict resolution educators are not the only ones who have had a long term relationship with role-play, and hold it in the same high regard.

Role-play – It's Not Just Us!

Role-plays and simulation are considered important educational tools in a variety of educational fields, such as the natural sciences, management studies and the social sciences, and we would do well to learn from the experience and best practices associated with design and implementation of these activities in other fields.[3]

One source of positive attitude towards role-play is adult learning theory. While much study and research throughout the years has been focused on pedagogy, it has been only in the last few decades that a similar interest in andragogy or adult learning theory arose. For example, Malcolm Knowles in 1973 was one of the first educators to explore the differences in the ways that adults learn (see Knowles 2005). Since that time, others have taken the core concepts of adult learning to serve as a basis for designing and constructing classes and teaching methodologies in professional education, including business and law schools as well as in social work and nursing.

Exploring andragogy in the context of legal education, for example, Frank Bloch noted that clinical legal education, (the representation of actual clients by students under supervision) had its foundation in adult learning (Bloch 1982). Much of the use of experiential education, which often includes simulations along with actual practice, is derivative of innovation in adult learning principles. When one applies elements of adult learning, particularly those of self-directed learning and the need for immediate application of learning, it is easy to see why experiential education-based simulations have become integral in teaching negotiation courses. For the most part, these courses have been taught primarily in graduate and professional schools as well as executive courses – aiming, therefore, at an adult audience.

Additional reasons exist for why role-play, as an instructional method, enjoys the popularity it does. Cathy Stein Greenblat, a leading writer on the subject of simulations and games, attempted to capture and categorize the many claims made about this type of instructional method by its proponents and enthusiasts (Greenblat 1981b). She found that the inventory of claims could be broken down into six categories. Simulations and games are claimed to:

1) Enhance motivation and heighten interest (in the activity itself, the topic being learned, the course being taken and in learning in general).

2) Promote cognitive learning (of factual information, procedural sequences, general principles, real-life structures, best practices, etc.), decision-making skills and systematic analysis.

3) Make changes in the character of future course work (more meaningful participation, more sophisticated and relevant inquiry and greater participation).

4) Trigger affective learning towards the subject matter (changed perspectives and orientations, increased empathy with others).

5) Enhance affective elements of learning (increased self-awareness and self-confidence).

6) Promote changes in classroom structure and relations (better student-teacher relations, greater freedom to express and explore ideas, higher degree of student autonomy, greater degree of student peer acceptance, etc.) (Greenblat 1981b: 141-143).[4]

With such potential promise being articulated for simulations and games in the formative years of negotiation pedagogy, perhaps it should come as no surprise that negotiation education embraced these methods from the beginning. But does role-play deliver on these claims?

Critique of Teaching with Role-Play

Alexander and LeBaron suggested that while subjecting negotiation pedagogy to general review, it might be time to cut down on the role that role-play plays. Suggesting that perhaps the time has come for "The Death of the Role-play" (although they were quick to revive it themselves in the same article), some of their critique of the use of role-play centered on the following points:

1) Students push back against being set up to behave in certain ways.
2) In some cultural settings, taking on others' identities may be disrespectful, or nonsensical.
3) Role-play invites participants to rely on stereotypes in playing unfamiliar identities.
4) The degree of transferability of skills from role-play to actual negotiations is questionable.
5) Over- or under-identification by one participant with the role they were assigned to play can undermine the effectiveness of the activity for an entire group.

Alexander and LeBaron are not the first to question the use of role-play, although the focus of their critique (particularly the cultural focus) certainly brings up original questions which tie into wider concerns about negotiation pedagogy discussed in this book and the previous volume in the series.

Previous challenges to the use of simulation-games and role-play tended to focus on various elements of efficacy, suggesting that role-playing did not live up to the reputation built for it by educators employing it. Greenblat (1981b) commented that most of the support for the assertions made regarding the value of role-play tended to be anecdotal rather than theory-based or scientifically grounded. Indeed, some of these assertions have never been properly researched – and some of those assertions that have been examined have been found to be overreaching, if not actually mistaken.

In a recent meta-review, Daniel Druckman and Noam Ebner (2008) examined a wide body of research encompassing dozens of studies to measure the efficacy of educational simulation-games in the social sciences, conducted since simulation-games began enjoying popularity in the 1960s. While there is some variation in the data and in the testing methods, there is little variation in the results. The large majority of these studies indicated that there were no *learning* benefits associated with learning through means of participation in simulation-games, beyond those associated with other teaching methods. Students did not show enhanced understanding, a better grasp of concepts or any other measurable learning indicator, as compared to the teaching methods that simulations were being compared to.[5]

On the other hand, this same body of research supports the notion that simulation enjoys advantages over other methods in two areas: learning through simulation, students tend to retain the material better over time, and in addition their interest, motivation and engagement are enhanced. According to Druckman and Ebner, "a pattern can be discerned across many types of studies: Most social-science simulations do not improve student learning; however, they are useful tools for retaining the material and stimulating interest."[6] (Druckman and Ebner 2008: 467).

To be sure, these findings fly in the face of anecdotal reports extolling the learning benefits of simulation, as well as in the face of many teachers' intuition (ourselves included) regarding this method's value. Many teachers might consider this intuition one reason to delay the burial of the role-play. Another reason might be that we would do well to remember that even if role-play does not live up to the reputation built up for it, it has *not* been shown to be an *ineffective* method. The findings above simply change the equation: instead of one catch-all method that provides maximum learning and maximum motivation at the cost of a given amount of time and resources, we need to reconsider a variety of teaching methods capable of achieving these goals, and use them in a thoughtful manner meant to achieve maximum return in any individual setting.

It may be that students benefit greatly from a varied teaching approach. Rather than teach directly to a particular learning style, which has been urged in many instances, controversial new research claims that students may not derive greater benefit from matching learning approach or style (Glenn 2009). Rather, learning is enhanced more by the use of diversity in approach, or in other words, by progressing through the learning cycle (Kolb 1984).

Alexander and LeBaron likewise called for diversifying the teacher's toolbox by adding in multiple types of experiential learning. Some of those, such as adventure learning, are examined at length in this book (see, e.g., Manwaring, McAdoo, and Cheldelin, *Orientation and Disorientation*; Coben, Honeyman, and Press, *Straight Off the Deep End*; Ebner and Cohn, *Bringing Negotiation Teaching to Life*). We would add a caveat: *Any* experiential method employed to fill the gap left in the instructional toolbox due to the critique on role-play *needs to be subjected to the same examination that cleared this space*. In other words, it needs to be examined for cultural and contextual suitability on a course-by-course or training-by-training basis, and also tested for its efficacy regarding content learning, student motivation and material retention. The variety of methods used for testing the efficacy of role-play might give some idea on how to conduct such studies.[7] For one such experimental examination of an alternative method, see Druckman and Ebner, *Enhancing Concept Learning*, in this volume).

Rebirthing the Role-Play

With some of the pressure taken off the role-play by other methods, we can now take the opportunity to revisit the role-play and aid in its resurrection by making suggestions to improve educational gains through improving their design and usage. Coupling the vast amount of experience Negotiation 1.0 education has with using role-play with the critique described above, what can we recommend for using role-play in Negotiation 2.0?

Based on the critique presented above, and on other identifiable trends in the transition from Negotiation 1.0 to 2.0, we would suggest some overarching considerations for using role-play, broken down into four parts:

1) Preliminary considerations: Should role-play be used at all?
2) Simulation choice/design: What needs to be carefully considered in the design process?
3) Playing it out: Conducting role-plays.
4) Making sense of it all: How should feedback, assessment and debrief be tailored to maximize the benefits of role-play use in learning?

This will be followed by a list of suggestions for new modes/types/models of teaching with role-play that emanate from these general considerations.

1) The Negotiation 2.0 Simulation: Preliminary Considerations

The critique presented above dictates that we can no longer automatically assume that role-play is a "good," "tried-and-tested" or even "safe" teaching method for every situation. Careful consideration should be given to the question of whether use of role-play is suitable, given the culture and context of the educational setting and the participants.

Teachers, reconsidering the efficacy of role-play as a teaching tool, need to reconsider the amount of time dedicated to it, the topics they teach with it and its congruence with other teaching methods, including other experiential methods.

Specifically, some insights from the discussion of efficacy might be:

a) Role-play does not teach actual content or concepts better than other methods such as a classroom lecture. On the other hand, a role-play intended to elicit a number of negotiation elements might be much less costly in terms of time than a class lecture and discussion regarding each point. Teachers need to reconsider their division and allocation of time, and the specific teaching goals.

b) Role-play's biggest advantage as a teaching tool is in the area of student interest and motivation. Role-plays might best be interspersed throughout a course rather than concentrated in blocs (as some courses currently schedule them), and scheduled for times/topics prone to attention- and motivation- deficiency, such as after lunch.

c) Role-play is associated with heightened material retention. While, of course, "everything is important" and must be retained, role-play can be used to target those concepts teachers consider most important. Additionally, role-play might be used to highlight material which students will need to rely on later on in the course. For example, if an adventure learning activity is scheduled at the end of the course, in which students will need to rely on their positional bargaining skills, and positional bargaining is discussed at about the midpoint of the course, teachers might do well to include a positional bargaining role-play as part of the lesson plan, in order to enhance retention of the material.

d) The role-play can also be used to "pull together" both distinct and related concepts – which may have been dealt with in lecture or discussion individually – into a more cohesive idea or model. This "pulling together" might have special importance in those not-uncommon situations in which training is conducted by teams of two or more individuals, or in which students need to learn to implement material from more than one course or workshop. We suggest that role-play might assist in overcoming learners' tendencies towards compartmentalization and segregation.

e) Role-plays also provide a superior method for engagement in self-reflection, and can even be more effective in that regard if recorded for later playback and review.

2) The Negotiation 2.0 Simulation: Design Considerations

In their paper discussing the desired degree of proximity between simulation and reality in role-play design, Ebner and Efron (2005) suggested that:

> ...the design process of educational simulation games for conflict resolution *training* purposes has largely been neglected, and it seems that no theoretical models or paradigms have been developed for designing what is, in practice, the field's leading training tool. Successful models would be those designed to incorporate the knowledge gained in simulation game study into the unique dynamics and frameworks familiar in negotiation...simulation games. We propose that developing such models through increased

writing, analysis, discussion, and refinement would enable taking conflict resolution training – and with it, practitioners' abilities and skills – to the next level (Ebner and Efron 2005: 379).

Taking this challenge to heart, it would seem that the themes running through Negotiation 2.0 now present us with – if not a unique design process – a new set of parameters or guidelines which should be taken into account while designing simulation-games:

a) Take students' cultural background, learning habits and preferences into account.
This might include conducting more active research regarding the student population than we traditionally do. This also places on the negotiation educator an onus of constant creativity, adapting and tailoring, who may have fallen into the habit of using the same simulation materials over and over, across wide spectrums of context and culture.

b) Consider engaging students in the design process.
Having students design simulations is an activity of great educational value affecting concept understanding and integration, material retention and student motivation (see Druckman and Ebner, *Enhancing Concept Learning*, in this volume). Taking this one step further, incorporating students into the design process of simulations that will actually be role-played in class – such as by having two groups of students design role-plays centered on several specific negotiation concepts, and having each perform the role-play written by the other group – might increase gains in all of those categories; however, this suggestion has yet to be substantiated by experimentation. Even if one does not go through the design-swap-play process described above (it is certainly a time-costly exercise!), engaging students in the design process by asking the group, or individual students, their opinions about what topics, negotiation concepts and role-play communication medium would appeal to them might be of great value. This suggestion is an operationalization of the approach set forward by Melissa Nelken, Bobbi McAdoo, and Melissa Manwaring (2009), advocating engaging students in the process of designing their negotiation course, partially or in its entirety. Such an exercise is also quite consistent with the adult education component of self-directed learning.

c) Take into account other experiential methods used in the course.

The role-plays should be designed to integrate with, and comple-ment, those other methods. If some form of adventure learning is to be used, a simulation reflecting either the concepts underlying that experience (e.g., positional bargaining skills), or the setting of that environment (e.g., a marketplace setting) might serve both to teach the immediate topic and to prepare students to make the most out of their upcoming experience. Other experiential methods such as providing peer feedback and even teaching a component of material can also be easily adapted and integrated in simulation activity.

d) Take into account the question of proximity to reality.

This issue encompasses several aspects, which have been given at-tention in recent years (see Crampton and Manwaring 2008). In-creased attention to cultural and contextual suitability makes tailoring existing simulations, or creating unique simulations, for a particular audience more likely. Tailor-made simulations are likely to be set in particular contexts, and reflect particular realities, making attention to the desired balance between reality and play more acute. Trainer-designers need to be aware of the ramifications of us-ing scenarios with close proximity to real life.

Noam Ebner and Yael Efron (2005) noted that the closer a sce-nario comes to reflecting participants' own experiences, the current events of the day or the context in which the training is being con-ducted, the more likely it is to trigger participant motivation and engagement, mediated by identification with the situation and with individual roles. However, this does not mean that the closer to real-life a scenario is, the better the learning returns. On the contrary, Ebner and Efron note that negative effects – over- or under-identification with role, disruptive group dynamics and suspicion regarding the teacher's motives – might prove to be disruptive. Ac-cordingly, they recommended that in cases calling for role-play sce-narios closely related to real-life, teachers utilize not reality, but "pseudo-reality." Using this method, scenario designers might bor-row storylines, settings, or supporting material (such as newspaper articles, maps, etc.) from real-world events, or from participants' immediate context; however, they should do so only to the degree that this serves to support learning by enhancing identification and interest. When real-world facts, events or details might undermine these, or cause students to lose focus from the concepts and content the role-play is meant to teach, designers should replace them, ig-nore them or actively write them out of the story, forming an alter-nate reality or "pseudo-reality" (Ebner and Efron 2005).[8]

Another way of adding a dose of reality into role-play is by breaking the glass wall between the participant and the role they are playing, by making negotiation outcomes achieved in the role-play have real-world effect. Howard Raiffa conducted much of his early research by having students role-play with each other, with each student's outcomes scored, totaled, and calculated in a manner that accounted for one-third of the student's final course grade (Raiffa 1982). Roger Volkema (2007) describes a similar experiment with ascribing monetary value to role-play results; students paid a $20 "player's fee" at the beginning of the course, and their outcomes in a series of role-play activities affected whether they were allowed to keep the money or whether it remained "in the kitty."[9]

In another take on incorporating students' negotiation skills into their grade, law professor Charles Craver discusses utilizing a method of class ranking. For example, in a negotiation between lawyers representing a plaintiff and a defendant, the greater the amount received by plaintiff's counsel, the higher the ranking; conversely, of course, defense counsel rankings are the inverse. This class ranking is then used as a substantial criterion of the final grade (Craver 2000).[10]

Another type of activity involves students negotiating directly for their grades. Rick Voyles, a teacher of negotiation at Sullivan University and at the Keller Graduate School of Management, related to us how for the students' final project in his negotiation course, he has students negotiate with each other, in groups of three to five, over the number of points they will each receive for the final project itself. As the final project carries considerable weight (about thirty percent of the grade, similar to the points dedicated to the role-play outcomes in Raiffa's courses), students' negotiation skills can help them improve their final course grade, in a very real way. Students are not graded on the skill they display – they are awarded the amount of points agreed on. A different take on this type of activity was reported by Volkema, who assigned students the activity of negotiating with him, their teacher, for their grades (Volkema 1991).

In our opinion, students negotiating for grades (assuming that the teacher is serious about this being part of the grading system) is in no way role-play. It might be adventure learning (we prefer to leave that to other writers in this book, who will no doubt attempt to define adventure learning and map out what types of activities fall under this category). It might simply be "negotiation."

e) Create engaging and relevant role-play materials.
Despite the incredible advances made in word-processing, image manipulation, desktop publishing and Web 2.0 technology, we think

it is a safe guess that most role-plays utilized by negotiation teachers are still contained in the familiar medium of a sheet of paper handed out to Party A, and another sheet of paper handed out to Party B.

We suggest that teachers would do well to consider a general upgrading of participants' interface with the role-play. Instead of a sheet of paper, role information and background can be presented in many different ways. In an international negotiation role-play, a student might be presented with a complete case file including text documents (e.g., a briefing prepared by the State Department for the negotiator, a treaty relevant to the negotiation), maps (which might be real maps, or real maps with alterations such as a fictitious cease-fire line), or newspaper clippings (which can be realistically generated online).[11] In a negotiation between two parties already engaged in litigation, participants can be handed a "real" case file containing all of the pleadings filed on both sides, together with any confidential documents each party may have. They would then be instructed to learn the case and prepare their approach based on the file along with any independent research they wish to conduct. A dispute between two singers over the rights to a song currently topping the charts could be introduced by a news report about the dispute (which can also be easily generated online), and reproductions of email exchanges between each participant and the singer retaining them, so that they know what they have "done" before initiating the negotiation itself. More enterprising teachers might also include a link to the song's lyrics, or to an actual song.

Of course, material design needs to be congruent with the general objectives of the role-play. Artifacts that contribute to the role-play's proximity to reality, that create role identification, that trigger motivation and interest, are all of value (keeping in mind the caveats presented above regarding the potential negative effects of reality and identification). On the other hand, not all that glitters is gold. If role-play-supporting material necessitates that students spend extensive time just to access it, or if it is dependent on technological equipment or know-how, it might be counterproductive. Similarly, over-producing material might cause students to focus on the wrong thing; if the bells-and-whistles take center stage during their preparation, they might not focus on the information they need to know, the analytical process they need to conduct, and the tactical preparation they need to do before engaging in the role-play.[12]

f) Design simulations suitable for the communication medium the negotiation is conducted through.

In a previous piece, we have suggested that the content of negotiation courses needs to change to reflect the fact that a great deal of our negotiation processes are not conducted "at the table" in any physical sense, and courses must incorporate units or content regarding negotiation conducted at-a-distance (Ebner et al. 2009). Such a shift will likely include having students conduct role-plays through online communication channels (for more on the why and how of incorporating such simulations, see Matz and Ebner, *Using Role-Play in Online Negotiation Teaching*, in this volume). For reasons pertaining to realism and student motivation we would suggest using scenarios which incorporate distance between the parties, or some other reason for e-communication, as part of the storyline. Role-playing a negotiation between two neighbors regarding the exact placement of their joint property line by email would seem arbitrary and out-of-place, and might cause some dissonance between participants and the simulation environment. On the other hand, a storyline regarding a dispute between a buyer and a seller on an online auction platform, or a negotiation between the buyer and seller of a web domain name, might be a good mesh of storyline and medium (for examples of such simulations, see Manwaring 2005 and Ebner 2009).

g) Consider student-oriented media.

Continuing the previous point, do not limit yourself to the communication media you are used to communicating through. If your students discuss interactions they have through a medium which you are not fully familiar with (e.g., Facebook, Myspace, or Twitter), view that as an opportunity for engaging them in the design process – both course-design, and simulation-design. If your students are constantly instant messaging, consider asking students to design a simulation contextually suited for being conducted through this medium. If they are the type who are constantly checking in to Facebook or other social networking venues (in the world of wireless internet, there is a good chance you will see this going on in class, tipping you off to this valuable opportunity for engagement and practice), see if there is any topic or issue they might consider suitable for negotiating through this medium, and let them run with the design process. If your students bring their experiences in Second Life as examples of recent negotiation interactions they have had, consider creating a negotiation between avatars in that venue. If they seem comfortable "tweeting" their status in the middle of class, engage them in a discussion of whether there are any issues which they find themselves negotiating in up to 140 characters at a time – and lead them through a simulation design and conduct process.

h) Design some of the simulations to mirror real life experience of the trainers or their colleagues.
After the simulation, a discussion of the actual outcome can serve as the basis for a discussion of how certain factors – often thought to be insignificant – can influence and change an outcome. This again provides students with a bridge connecting the simulation with the real world.

i) Integrate the assessment or evaluative component of the course within the design.
Give thought, at the design stage, to ways of stressing the particular elements you will be focusing on in debrief. In particular, when using videorecording, invite student input for the recording and playback portions. When students are not only informed of the methods through which review will occur, but are also given a part in selecting certain skills to isolate or focus on in the recording, they may prepare more extensively and perhaps in a more focused manner, enhancing their ensuing learning.

3) Playing It Out: Conducting the Negotiation 2.0 Simulation
In addition to new issues to consider regarding method choice and simulation design, the critique of role-play, the experience gained with this method over the past few decades and the new issues in negotiation teaching raised in Negotiation 2.0 lead us to suggest that the actual conduct of the role-play needs to be reconsidered. Awareness as to context, culture, medium, learning style and teaching goals all necessitate careful attention to simulation initiation and conduct, going far beyond the familiar format of "I'm going to break you down into pairs, and give you each role information." Here is an initial list of issues and suggestions emanating from our previous discussion:

a) Utilize modes of simulation that cut down on use of class time.
Some of the critique of role-play centered on the time taken from other means of learning. The calls for widening the spectrum of experiential activities are likely to place still heavier demands on already-overtaxed class time. This dictates that we need to look for ways to save actual class time in any way possible, without eliminating necessary exercises. Some initial recommendations for consideration are:

- Give students role-material for preparation ahead of time, instead of on-the-spot in class. In addition to saving time, this might alleviate some of the pressure associated with students feeling put on the spot. By asking students to not only read and prepare their role but to rewrite it or personalize it in some way, problems related to under-identification might be pre-empted (Ebner and Efron 2005).

- Assign students to conduct a negotiation out of class, such as over lunch or in the evenings. This method certainly presents challenges related to evaluation and debriefing, and teachers might consider different methods for overcoming these, such as innovative self-reflection or group reflection practices, or use of video (see below).

- Assign students to conduct a negotiation out of class, on their own time, through email. This allows students more flexible scheduling. Additional benefits are the practice of negotiation through the online media and the facilitation of evaluation and feedback through use of the recorded text transcript.

- Consider following up on an out-of-class simulation with an in-class debrief, to achieve specific teaching goals as well as to stress the joint-but-separate experience of the negotiation groups, transforming them back into one large learning-group after their individual, external, exercise.

b) Use communication media that reflect the multiple channels through which negotiation takes place in today's technologically-mediated world.

While many negotiations do take place in the face-to-face mode, this is quickly changing. We have already recommended incorporating email negotiation into negotiation courses (Ebner et al. 2009). Taking this one step further, teachers might attempt to replicate the reality of modern interactions in which a negotiation process might be conducted using multiple methods for message interchange. For example, preliminary information may be exchanged through email or fax, while opening discussions take place in person. Subsequent offers and responses may also take place through email or other means such as a phone conversation, texting or instant messaging. Providing methods for students to experience this variety within a single case or simulation provides the means to increase the realism of the simulation, in addition to practicing negotiation through a variety of media (for more on conducting role-plays at-a-distance, see Matz and Ebner, *Using Role-Play in Online Negotiation Teaching*, in this volume).

c) Anticipate and recognize reasons for student distress or under-participation.

This potential downside to simulation use should be addressed early. Often, students in executive courses are unable or unwilling to detach from their work, and find themselves returning a call to a client or engaging in an actual negotiation for the purchase of real estate even as they are supposed to engage in a simulated negotiation. This distraction is one of the reasons for under-participation and lack of preparation. By directly addressing the situation at the simulation's initiation, this might be avoided or the effects diminished. Another by-product might possibly result: this addressing of potential distractions is an opportunity for instructors to learn more about the participants, perhaps leading to the creation of more realistic and meaningful role-plays, or to variations created on the spot.

d) Provide more direction in role-plays.

One concern raised about using role-plays was that the participants over-acted, or, conversely, did not seem to be engaged in the simulations in a way that was particularly helpful to learning. Simulations are either not played out or over-exaggerated (Alexander and LeBaron 2009). Providing more detailed instructions, and addressing issues of identification, role-acting and the relationship to the participant's real life persona will lower anxiety rates and result in more authenticity and realism. This will be beneficial in a number of ways, both for simulation conduct as well as for skills and knowledge transferability to real-life situations.

In some instances specific instructions for a role-play might include certain reactions and/or emotions, which are helpful in demonstrating and isolating particular points or situations – for example, the cognitive barrier of optimistic overconfidence. In many other instances, however, simulations can be much more realistic if the participants are instructed to "be themselves" and act and react as if the situation described actually happened to them. Not only does a more realistic situation result, but the participants are then in a better position to provide more accurate (at least from their standpoint) feedback to others.

e) Devote more time to preparation.

Devoting more time to the preparation segments of the simulation may be one way that not only produces more realistic role-plays, but also provides learning about a stage of negotiation that is often overlooked in reality, as it is under-taught in trainings: preparation for negotiation. Often, students are provided the simulation information immediately preceding the role-play. This leads to rushed preparation, in which students attempt to quickly learn enough to play, as opposed to carefully consider and internalize their role, strategize, and plan specific tactical moves. When possible, role information should be provided well in advance. Teachers can hand out preparation sheets to be filled out, either aimed at teaching students a particular model of preparation or at focusing them on particular elements which are the actual learning goals of the exercise. Providing role information in advance also makes it possible to provide much more information, such as an entire case file, as mentioned earlier. As a result, the participants would have more time to review and become familiar with the material, as well as designing the approaches they plan to take. Simulations can be designed to allow students to take advantage of this preparatory stage for *in-role* preliminary activities, such as reaching out to potential allies (in a multiparty simulation), obtaining additional information through independent research, etc.

f) Don't limit yourself to the class participant list.

There are many ways in which you can arrange to have your students negotiate with people who are not their current classmates. One option may be to engage local professionals, for example from business and law, and pair your students with them to simulate a negotiation drawn from their area of actual practice. This might include sending students to these professionals' office or place of business, adding a shot of reality to the exercise (see Cohn and Ebner, *Bringing Negotiation Teaching to Life*, in this volume). In frameworks in which the instructor has recurring courses, she might call on alumni of previous courses to engage in simulations with current students. Other ways to provide students with unfamiliar opposites might be to hire professional actors, engage your university's drama department, match up two negotiation classes of your own, or invite last year's students in for a simulation. This lack of familiarity with the other will serve to increase the degree of realism in the role-play, contributing to transferability of lessons learned. In addition, this method can be used in order to generate potential for cross-cultural issues to manifest, providing unique learning opportunities. An interesting and motivating way to do this is to form a partnership with another negotiation teacher, perhaps from another country, and have your students conduct a simulation with each other at a distance.

g) Integrate assessment, to some degree.

While we address assessment in detail in the following, separate section, methods of integrating evaluative means should also affect simulation conduct considerations. Yet most of us think of the terms evaluation and assessment in terms of a final or course ending activity (see, for example, Cohn et al. 2009) Recently educators across disciplines have been placing additional focus on formative assessment, that is, the use of assessment tools *during* the learning process (Sullivan et al. 2007).

Most of the discussion on assessment we provide below centers on video use as an assessment or evaluation tool, whether done by the instructor, peers or self-evaluation. How might this same method enable formative assessment? A simple and often used example through which simulations are used in formative assessment is with feedback provided during, or immediately after, the roleplay. To increase and incorporate video self-review can increase the effectiveness of formative assessments. One way would be to record part of the role-play, stop the recording, review it, either alone or with another, whether it be peer or instructor, and then use what has been learned to improve performance and increase understanding in continuing the simulation or in a subsequent one. Thus, the simulation can be recorded at several intervals during the course.

This opportunity to revise a simulation mid-course provides a uniquely rich learning opportunity for students by broadening the use of formative assessment means and increasing the effectiveness of experiential education. Simulations may also be designed with an eye toward conducting them with the use of recording, with a variety of specific goals in mind. Often absent in the design of simulations is specificity of the particular points which are to be highlighted. For example, if the instructor intends to demonstrate the cognitive barrier of optimistic overconfidence and perhaps the related concept of partisan perceptions, the simulation can be written with language and instructions to highlight these barriers. When such focus is made during the simulation, participants are able to actually see and note the changes in what they are doing. As we have noted, priming students in advance can improve formative assessment. If time allows, this design can provide additional avenures for learning. In the context of optimistic overconfidence, rather than having just one opportunity to test methods to overcome this barrier, with video, playback, and the ability to "take two," students can have more than one learning experience.

This is obviously more time-consuming in the course as a whole, as well as time-intensive for instructor. We never said it would be easy. After all, as we are learning, Negotiation 2.0 is all about deliberately making hard choices.

4) Making Sense of Things: Debriefing and Assessing the Negotiation 2.0 simulation

A crucial issue in improving learning and retention gains from use of simulation is providing the best feedback, assessment and evaluation possible. In trying to capture the general state-of-the-art regarding key features of a basic feedback session on a negotiation simulation, we would say the following:

- It is usually the trainer, coach or facilitator who observes the simulation and then provides – or guides – the feedback.
- This feedback is generally provided in a public forum – that is, in front of the class or at a minimum the other role-players.
- Feedback is most often given at the conclusion of the simulation (although some trainers choose to conduct simulations in a "stop-comment-start" mode).
- Encouraging and providing opportunities for self-reflection during feedback is a critical component.

We suggest teachers consider all of these elements, as they have potential for great effect on the teacher-student relationship, the depth of feedback and opportunity for change during the role-plays, among other issues.

Undoubtedly, room for improvement exists with regard to evaluation, and we need to search for ways to best utilize this element of simulation for insight capturing and for highlighting transferability between simulation and real-life. In this regard, we suggest three distinct uses of video which can improve the assessment methodology. The reason we are stressing video in this chapter is that this is one area in which a huge jump has been made over the past few years, which has barely at all been reflected in the classroom. Ten years ago, videotaping a simulation required a special room, special equipment and a technician. Today, most cell phones can record decent-quality video-clips (albeit limited in length), many students possess digital cameras which they can bring to class, and good quality webcams built into laptops might also be used to record simulations. Many students will be skilled at downloading the movie from the camera, editing it in various ways and perhaps uploading it to the Internet where it can be accessed by all students in the class. With this advance in technology and economy, let us examine the benefits of using video recording for feedback and assessment.

Reviewing video recording of a simulation provides the student-participant a very accurate (and nearly indisputable) picture of exactly what they did. This allows the trainer/critiquer to point out the various aspects of performance that were conducted well, as well as to raise questions regarding needed or helpful changes to improve effectiveness in negotiation. For some time now, the use of recording for evaluation purposes has been explored and advocated, particularly where such courses are graded, as in university settings (Kovach 1996). As mentioned earlier, simulations can also be recorded in segments, allowing students to make changes during the simulation. Recordings can also be structured to allow students to engage in self-reflection and assessment, a vital component of professional development (Schön 1987).

Recording of the simulation allows the students to see for themselves how they conducted the negotiation. Rather than receive comments from external sources (even the coach, with copious notes, may not remember or see/observe everything), the recording provides an accurate picture for review. In addition, it also provides a mechanism to *continue* to review – perhaps after waiting some time to allow an increased comfort level. This is not to say that telling an individual how they conducted themselves is not beneficial; however, it is only beneficial if they are open to it. Some students, particularly when coming off of the emotional and identity rollercoaster that a simulation sometimes is, may feel defensive and not be willing to accept the feedback, perceived as criticism. However, an accurate observation of themselves by themselves can often break through the resistance (Rosenberg and Petersen 2008).

Another benefit of recording is that it allows others, at a later time, to provide feedback. Receiving multiple assessments can be helpful – as well as allowing students to understand some of the variation in negotiation approaches, which easily illustrates the absence of a complete right or wrong way to approach the process. One concern about evaluation of skill performance is that it is inherently subjective in nature. As often the review is done by only one individual, even where a specific rubric is used, the assessment necessarily includes that individual's personal preferences. Multiple assessments or evaluations provide greater breadth of feedback.

With the use of actual recordings, students are able to see for themselves just how they conducted the negotiations, on a move-by-move level. They are able, for instance, to determine if planned strategies and tactics were implemented effectively. Perhaps even more important, they are able to view their reactive moves, those parts of the process which cannot often be planned for (unless the negotiators work with each other on a continual basis).

Through watching themselves on video, participants are able to *relive* the moments, producing a better ability to understand and remember just what was going on, cognitively, when particular moves were made. This contributes to greater accuracy in self-reflection and analysis. An important element of professional education is the ability to accurately engage in self-reflection (Schön 1983). To accurately self-assess is a necessary component of a learning process; yet, sometimes offering those opportunities can be difficult (Schön 1987). Often, part of self-reflection is developing an understanding of how and why action is taken. Without the aid of a recording, we sometimes remain stumped: we are asked why we did something and try to remember, but have difficulty doing so. With the use of a recording, however, watching the action can stimulate memory. Moreover, in some self-reflection without the aid of a recording, students are either too critical (when suffering from low self-confidence), or conversely (when suffering from an excess of the same), do not appreciate the need for improvement. In this context, the value of a recorded simulation provides not only an opportunity to view oneself, but also to allow a more accurate and hence effective picture to view.

This self-reflection does not need to be immediate, and it does not need to be teacher-driven. The video can be commented on by the participants themselves, in small-group work or in individual assignments; immediately following the simulation, or over the days following class. Software allowing the inclusion of text sidebars, or voice-overs with commentary, can enable students to comment on specific moments and moves, provide a play-by-play or reflect on emotional undercurrents of the negotiation dynamics, and allow for several viewpoints regarding the same moment or interaction examined (for an example of teaching with such software, see Williams, Farmer, and Manwaring 2008. For other suggestions on using video for giving feedback to students, see Matz and Ebner, *Using Role-Play in Online Negotiation Teaching*, in this volume.)

Conclusion

Returning from the grave has never failed to enhance reputation, and simulations are no exception to this. The critique posed to simulation, rather than bury it, will serve to improve it – if its lessons are taken to heart.

Notes

The authors wish to thank Rick Voyles, of Conflict Resolution Academy, LLC, for his enthusiasm and ideas.

[1] In this chapter, we use the terms "simulation" and "role-play" as generic references to experiential-learning-oriented activities commonly labeled "simulations," "games," "simulation-games" and "role-play." We use the term "role-players" to denote participants in a simulation activity who play out roles based on information and instructions they are given, such as in

the experimental condition described below. These decisions are not intended to influence the debate on the way these activities are conducted or the delineation between them. For an in-depth discussion of this issue, see Greenblat (1981a) and Crookall et al. (1987).

[2] This is exemplified by mediator certification rules in, for example, the state of New York (New York State's Office of Court Administration 2003: 12) and in Israel (Israel Court Administration 1999: 12). *(footnote in the original)*.

[3] A good starting point for exploring the uses of simulation and gaming across various educational fields is provided by David Crookall's guide to the literature (Crookall 1995: 167-9)

[4] Alexander and LeBaron suggested several other reasons which may explain why role-playing resonates with negotiation trainers: They are animating, they are popular with students and they can be used multiple times with little or no revision.

[5] This varied from study to study. While usually compared to conventional, frontal-lecture-type classroom study, simulation was also measured against the case-study method and others.

[6] For discussion of one method that was found to give better returns than role-play not only in concept learning but in motivation as well, see Druckman and Ebner, *Enhancing Concept Learning*, in this volume.

[7] For a listing of some of these studies, and some critique of their design, see Druckman 1995 and Druckman and Ebner 2008.

[8] For an example of a simulation designed utilizing the pseudo-reality method, see *"Converging! September 2007 in Israel/Palestine"* (Ebner and Efron 2007).

[9] Of course, one would do well to remember that at a certain point along the proximity-to-reality spectrum, an activity ceases to be role-play, and becomes something else. One of Volkema's activities was to have students attempt to return a package of sponges without a receipt to a retail store – without knowing where the sponges had been bought. Students went to a store of their choosing, which in all likelihood was not where the sponges had been purchased, and attempted to return the sponges. While they received a monetary reward or penalty vis-à-vis their "player's fee," this activity – requiring students to go out into the real world and engage with it – is much closer to adventure learning than role-playing. Yet, as students negotiate every day, (although many do not realize or acknowledge it) spending more time and focus on the real negotiations they are involved in can not only connect the class work to reality, but also provide additional foundation for the design of additional simulations. Students could also inform instructors of a negotiation they will be engaging in, such as a lease agreement, and the instructor could create an *ad hoc* simulation as a "dress rehearsal."

[10] Craver does, however, provide students an option of a pass/fail grade. An interesting note is that more and more students are opting for the pass/fail grade option. See also Craver (1999).

[11] For examples of such material, see Ebner and Efron, *supra*. note 8.

[12] This is particularly important in the context of the "executive course" which by design is short, and where balancing time constraints is always a challenge. One option is that the preparatory element of the simulation

would take place in the evenings of the course. Clearly, a new balance needs to be struck.

References

Alexander, N. and M. LeBaron. 2009. Death of the role-play. In *Rethinking negotiation teaching: Innovations for context and culture*, edited by C. Honeyman, J. Coben, and G. De Palo. St. Paul, MN: DRI Press.

Bloch, F. S. 1982. The andragogical basis of clinical legal education. *Vanderbilt LawReview* 35: 321-353.

Crampton, A. and M. Manwaring. 2008. Reality and artifice in teaching negotiation: The variable benefits of "keeping it real" in simulations. *Negotiation Pedagogy at the Program on Negotiation E-Newsletter* 2(1). Available at http://archive.constantcontact.com/fs079/1101638633053/archive/1102208945307.html#LETTER.BLOCK6. (last accessed on Apr. 13, 2010).

Craver, C. B. 1999. Gender, risk taking and negotiation preference. *Michigan Journal of Gender and Law* 5: 299-352.

Craver, C. B. 2000. The impact of student GPAS and a pass/fail option on clinical negotiation course performance. *Ohio State Journal on Dispute Resolution* 15: 373-389.

Crookall, D. 1995. A guide to the literature on simulation/gaming. In *Simulation and gaming across cultures: ISAGA at a watershed*, edited by D. Crookall and K. Arai. Thousand Oaks, CA: Sage.

Crookall, D., R. Oxford, and D. Saunders. 1987. Towards a reconceptualization of simulation: From representation to reality. *Simulation/Games for Learning* 17(4): 147-170.

Druckman, D. and N. Ebner. 2008. Onstage, or behind the scenes? Relative learning benefits of simulation role-play and design. *Simulation & Gaming* 39(4): 465-497.

Ebner, N. 2009. Email negotiation simulation: Live8. In *Negotiation: Readings, exercises and cases*, edited by R. Lewicki, D. Saunders, J. W. Minton and B. Barry, 6th edn. Burr Ridge, IL: McGraw-Hill/Irwin.

Ebner, N. and Y. Efron. 2005. Using tomorrow's headlines for today's training: Creating pseudo-reality in conflict resolution simulation-games. *Negotiation Journal* 21(3): 377-394.

Ebner, N. and Y. Efron. 2007. Converging! September 2007 in Israel/Palestine. *E-PARC's Top 5 Teaching Simulations of 2007*, Program on the Analysis and Resolution of Conflicts, The Maxwell School of Government, Syracuse University. Available at http://www.maxwell.syr.edu/parc/eparc/simulations/converging.asp (last accessed Apr. 14, 2010).

Ebner, N., A. Bhappu, J. G. Brown, K. K. Kovach and A. K. Schneider. 2009. You've got agreement: Negoti@ing via email. In *Rethinking negotiation teaching: Innovations for context and culture*, edited by C. Honeyman, J. Coben, and G. De Palo. St. Paul, MN: DRI Press.

Glenn, D. 2009. Matching teaching style to learning style may not help students. *Chronicle of Higher Education*. Available at http://chronicle.com/article/ Matching-Teaching-Style-to/49497/ (last accessed Apr. 14, 2010).

Greenblat, C. S. 1981a. Gaming simulations for teaching and training: An overview. In *Principles and practices of gaming-simulation*, edited by C.S. Greenblat and R. D. Duke. Beverly Hills: Sage.

Greenblat, C. S. 1981b. Teaching with simulation games: A review of claims and evidence. In *Principles and practices of gaming-simulation*, edited by C. S. Greenblat and R. D. Duke. Beverly Hills: Sage.

Israel Court Administration, Advisory Committee on Court Mediation. 1999. Report (2). Jerusalem, Israel.

Knowles, M. S., E. F. Holton, and R. A. Swanson. 2005. *The adult learner*, 5th edn. Amsterdam: Elsevier.

Kovach, K. K. 1996. Virtual reality testing: The use of video for evaluation in legal education. *Journal of Legal Education* 46(2): 233– 251.

Kolb, D. A. 1984. *Experiential learning: Experience as the source of learning and development*. Englewood Cliffs, NJ: Prentice-Hall.

Manwaring, M. 2005. *Lattitude.com*. Available at http://www.pon.org/catalog/product_info.php?products_id=374 (last accessed Apr. 14, 2010). Cambridge, MA: Program on Negotiation Clearinghouse.

Nelken, M., B. McAdoo, and M. Manwaring. 2008. Negotiating learning environments. In *Rethinking negotiation teaching: Innovations for context and culture*, edited by C. Honeyman, J. Coben, and G. De Palo. St. Paul, MN: DRI Press.

New York State Office of Court Administration. 2003. Standards and Requirements for Mediators and Mediator-Trainers, Training Curriculum Guidelines for Initial Mediation Training.

Raiffa, H. 1982. *The art and science of negotiation*. Cambridge, MA: Harvard University Press.

Rosenberg, L. B. and G. J. Petersen. 2008. Time-lapse video as a self-reflection tool for collaborative learning projects. *Journal of Research of Educational Leaders* 4(2): 4-16.

Schön, D. A. 1983. *The reflective practitioner: How professionals think in action*. London: Temple Smith.

Schön, D. A. 1987. *Educating the reflective practitioner: Toward a new design for Teaching and Learning in the Professions*. San Francisco: Jossey Bass.

Sullivan, W. M., A. Colby, J. W. Wegner, J. Welch, L. Bond, and L. Shulman. 2007. *Educating lawyers: Preparation for the practice of law*. San Francisco: Jossey Bass.

Volkema, R. J. 1991. Negotiating for grades: Theory into reality in the classroom. *Journal of Management Education* 15(1): 46-57.

Volkema, R. J. 2007. Negotiating for money: Adding a dose of reality to classroom negotiations. *Negotiation Journal* 23(4): 473-485.

Williams, G. R., L. C. Farmer, and M. Manwaring. 2008. New technology meets an old teaching challenge: Using digital video recordings, annotation software, and deliberate practice techniques to improve student negotiation skills. *Negotiation Journal* 24(1): 71-87.

⊂ℜ 16 ℘

Enhancing Concept Learning:
The Simulation Design Experience

Daniel Druckman & Noam Ebner[*]

Editors' Note: Druckman and Ebner carefully review a large number of studies which conclude that simulations (in all fields, not just negotiation) typically fail to live up to their promise. One quirk of the studies, however, drew their particular interest and inspired their own research: it seemed that students who designed simulations learned more than those who participated in them. Druckman and Ebner use this clue to develop a different kind of negotiation simulation – one in which the student plays the role of a teacher, and designs an exercise.

Introduction

Role-plays and simulations[1] have long been considered a central element in negotiation pedagogy, as well as that of the wider field of conflict resolution (Ebner and Efron 2005, Druckman and Ebner 2008, Alexander and LeBaron 2009). Perhaps one reason for this is the fact that the early roots of negotiation education developed during a period, beginning in the 1960s, in which experiential learning began to gain momentum and acceptance, particularly in the social sciences. Indeed, some of the earliest examples of widely used simulations in the social sciences included either negotiation or specific related elements such as cooperation vs. competition, interdependence and communication.[2]

[*]**Daniel Druckman** is a professor of public and international affairs at George Mason University and distinguished scholar at the University of Southern Queensland's Public Memory Research Centre in Australia. His email address is dandruckman@yahoo.com. **Noam Ebner** is an assistant professor at the Werner Institute at Creighton University's School of Law, where he chairs the online masters program in Negotiation and Dispute Resolution. His email address is noamebner@creighton.edu.

As simulations are intended primarily to enhance learning benefits for the role-players participating in them, a top-down approach was adopted regarding their design; teachers or simulation-experts designed simulations for student-participants. By providing realistic, but controlled, environments in which students are guided by implicit rules, as well as explicit constraints, teachers provide students new venues to accomplish learning objectives by applying a body of theoretical knowledge in practice.

Precise design of these venues is paramount, in order to ensure that students are exposed to designed stimuli that encourage them to acquire the key concepts of the subject area being taught or the specific technical skills for which they are being trained. The effort to conceptualize what needs to be considered while designing educational simulations is evident in several early treatments of the design process by Richard Duke (1974, chapter 5), Cathy Stein Greenblat and Duke (1975, part II), Michael Inbar and Clarice Stoll (1972, chapter 17), Henry Ellington and colleagues (1984), and Ken Jones (1985). These authors provide systematic step-by-step guidelines for conceptualizing, constructing (scenario development), and implementing simulations. For the most part, the focus is on the educator-designer who, familiar with learning goals and participant proficiency, creates a training world for his or her students. However, as important as the issue of the perfect design process is, a more fundamental question demanded (and continues to demand) center stage in the literature on simulation games: is learning with simulations and games really effective?

Simulations as Teaching Tools: Do They Deliver the "Goods?"

In the fields of negotiation and conflict resolution, the question of the efficacy of simulation-games seems almost moot; ask any negotiation educator whether use of simulation as a training tool is beneficial, and odds are they will tell you it is. This is obvious from any review one could make of course syllabi and training plans. However, while little has been done to measure the effectiveness of simulations for learning in this field, there is a large body of research focusing on this in the literature of the fields of education and the social sciences, and a large number of evaluation studies have provided information about the learning and motivational outcomes of simulation participation. In a recent review conducted on the research regarding simulation evaluation, we discussed the overall themes presented by these studies (Druckman and Ebner 2008).

In brief, the findings we presented showed that an overwhelming majority of studies conducted since the mid-1960s indicate that simulations do *not* live up to the notions held in their regard by the many educators who use them (for more on these notions, see Kovach and Ebner, *Simulation 2.0*, in this volume). Students learning through simulation showed no better outcomes than students learning through other methods regarding the degree of learning or thinking critically about the material. Simulations *did*, however, enjoy an advantage in two important areas: some studies suggested that students learning through simulations retained the material longer than students learning through other methods. Additionally, simulations repeatedly scored higher on student motivation. "Motivation" has been approached in different ways, in separate studies; this term seems to be wide enough to capture elements such as student interest, commitment, positive attitude towards the material, and desire or willingness to engage in a similar activity again (see Cherryholmes 1966; Pierfy 1977; Bredemeier and Greenblat 1981; Randel et al. 1992; Ellington, Addinall, and Percival 1998; Druckman and Ebner 2008).

Facing the challenge of improving students' learning through simulation, teachers would do well to improve the effectiveness of their employment of this method. A variety of suggestions have been made for improving the contribution of simulations to learning: what must we do to make the exercises work? Examples are clarifying learning objectives (Bredemeier and Greenblat 1981), providing more conceptual background on the subject prior to the simulation activity (Druckman and Robinson 1998), creating time for reflection on the events and getting feedback (McLaughlin and Kirkpatrick 2005), and providing participants with conceptual maps and graphics that reflect the game's purpose (Duke 1974). Other suggestions regarding use of simulations have been made through the evolving perspective provided by Negotiation 2.0 in this book (Kovach and Ebner, *Simulation 2.0*, in this volume), as well as in the previous volume (Alexander and LeBaron 2009).

Improving the way we structure and use simulation is, however, only a partial response to the research described above. It challenges teachers to revisit their intuitive notions regarding simulation. Given the body of research showing that most social-science simulations do not improve student learning – but are, on the other hand, useful tools for retaining the material and stimulating interest, it would seem clear that the use of simulation needs to be targeted more carefully than it currently is, and that other modes of learning be considered. While suggestions have been made for incorporating a wider spectrum of experiential methods, relieving simulation of its center-stage role (Alexander and LeBaron 2009), we want to focus on something a bit closer to home. Long-time enthusiasts and designers of simulations ourselves, we will move on to suggest another mode of learning that does not take us too far away from the previous discussion: employing student *design* of simulations as a learning tool.

Benefits of Design

It would seem as if the learning benefits of design were by no means ignored by veteran simulation designers; however, few took the step of actually implementing this well-known secret in a classroom setting and most settled for mentioning it as a reflection or an anecdote regarding their own learning process. In the literature, some designers comment directly on why these activities are likely to enhance an understanding of the concepts being simulated. Others make the learning advantages apparent in their descriptions of the design process.

The theme of simulation design as a learning device is highlighted in these treatments. Daniel Druckman (1971) provides examples of how designers learn to conceptualize system processes. Cleo Cherryholmes, after conducting what may have been the first comprehensive study showing relatively few benefits to simulation participation over other forms of learning, suggested that students be given "the task of designing a simulation before playing it, either re-designing an existing game or constructing a simple game of their own" (1966:7). In discussing students' experiences in playing Simulated Society (SIMSOC), William Gamson remarked that: "Playing a game may be a more active experience than listening to a lecture, but developing a game is more active still" (1972: 67). He went on to decry game playing as an experience that (for most students) contributes little to analyzing the events in a detached manner. In contrast, design contributes to analysis by identifying critical elements with clarity, encouraging a search for concreteness, synthesizing the elements (roles, goals, resources, and rules), and leading to new analytical questions (Greenblat 1975), as well as having designers take all these into account while considering relational and identity-based issues (Ebner and Efron 2005). Attention to the design process remains popular as evidenced by the game-building exercise featured at the 2007 International Simulation and Gaming Association (ISAGA) conference at Nijmegen in the Netherlands and in several sessions of the 2009 ISAGA conference in Singapore. It is also evident in the recent book by Chris Bateman and Richard Boon (2006).

If simulation design is such an effective learning tool, why do we not often encounter it in the classroom? We would suggest two reasons. First, the top-down approach mentioned above is evident in the simulation literature, which assumes a teacher/designer-planned and -driven activity. Second, the comments extolling design are mainly opinionating and anecdotal. The efficacy of design as a teaching tool was not considered, measured, or reported. All of the evaluation data, such as those studies commented on above, explored the effectiveness of *participation* in simulations; none of them measured the learning effectiveness of *designing* them.

Elsewhere in this book, it is suggested that modest learning returns in simulation-based classrooms are one of the reasons for diminishing its role in negotiation education and developing a new range of experiential methods to serve as learning vehicles. If so, then it stands to reason that each of these new methods be subjected to the same type of systematic evaluation that has been done routinely with simulation techniques. If not, we are replacing a tried-and-tested method with known benefits and recognized downsides with what might turn out to be, at best, a set of well-intentioned but unevaluated ideas (Ebner and Kovach, *Simulation 2.0*, in this volume).

Taking this line of thinking seriously, we decided to experiment with the method of role-play design, testing its value as a teaching tool. We decided that design would be compared to the most widely researched teaching method in the field – learning through participation in simulation games as role-players. A literature review showed that despite the comments mentioned above, simulation-design as a teaching tool was not discussed much, and certainly little examination of its efficacy was conducted in the realm of negotiation pedagogy. Generally speaking, only a few attempts have been made to compare approaches for learning negotiation skills. Druckman and Victor Robinson (1998) assessed the learning that occurs in each of three roles: analyst, strategist, and designer. The authors did not compare designers with role-players. The more recent study by Raphaël Mathevet and colleagues (2007) assessed learning processes during the negotiating phases of a complex environmental simulation. They did not, however, compare learning in different simulated environments. Other studies have used simulations as platforms for evaluating a variety of less-active learning approaches to negotiation (e.g., Spector 1995; Nadler, Thompson, and Boven 2003). They did not examine the active learning features of simulating, or raise the notion of design as a learning activity.

In order to compare the benefits of the two methods, we set up the following experiment. Students heard a similar lecture regarding three negotiation concepts: alternatives, time pressure and power. They were then randomized into two groups. One was charged with designing a simulation that incorporated these three concepts into the storyline and instructions. The second group was then assigned to role-play these simulations.[3] At the end of each group's activity – design/role-play – they were asked to fill out a questionnaire regarding learning and motivation. A third group served as a control: they heard the lecture and, without partaking in any further activity, filled out the questionnaire. In addition, students in all groups were asked to fill out the same questionnaire one week later, during the next meeting of their class. The experiments were replicated with multiple groups, in Australia and Israel. For a full description of the experimental design and a discussion of the considerations behind it, see Druckman and Ebner (2008).[4]

The experiment resulted in four major findings regarding learning and motivational impacts of simulation role-players and scenario designers:[5]

1) The process involved in designing scenarios enhances short-term concept learning more than playing roles in those scenarios; role-playing did not improve perceived learning over the control group.

2) The relation among the various concepts learned is understood better by designers than by role-players or controls. Further, role-players did not understand the conceptual relationships better than the controls who only listened to the lecture.

3) Designers retain their understanding of the concepts better than role-players.

4) Designers demonstrate *higher* degrees of motivation than role-players.

To summarize, working "behind the scenes," designers learn more about negotiation concepts than their "onstage" role-play counterparts, and enjoy the play more. These results were obtained both in Australia and Israel.[6]

These results challenge a long-held belief by negotiation teachers and trainers about the advantages of role-playing. The role-players in this study indicated less understanding of the concepts in both short and retention assessments and were less creative in their brief essays about relations among the concepts – but showed equivalent understanding in their essays on each of the separate concepts. They also showed less motivation in both short-term and retention assessments. Perhaps the motivation finding is most surprising. Designers were highly motivated by the task, more so than role-players. As we have already commented, enhanced motivation is the one consistent advantage simulation enjoys over other teaching methods; that designing trumps role-play participation on its home turf is very telling, in our opinion, regarding the pedagogical value of incorporating designing activities in negotiation courses.

The spread of results from this experiment provides empirical support for the intuitive observations made by the professional designers cited above. However, there is no clear, accepted, cause accounting for the advantage of design over role-play. Three possible mechanisms have been suggested. One is encouraging active involvement with the material. This is referred to also as concreteness (e.g., Greenblat 1975; Crookall 1995). Another is synthesis or seeing connections between ideas and processes (e.g., Druckman 1971; Duke 1974), including an appreciation for the long-term consequences of how the designed system is likely to evolve (Toth 1995). A third refers to generating analytical questions. All of these elements contribute to linking abstract thinking with concrete implementation in the form of a simulation. All are likely to result from a design experience to a higher degree than they are likely to manifest during a role-play. They may differ, however, on their relative contribution to learning (synthesis), retention (question generation), and motivation (concreteness). Other explanations may exist, or are waiting to be suggested.

Among the four findings, and of the explanations for design advantages discussed above, we were struck in particular by the finding that designers displayed a better grasp of the relation between concepts than role-players. Synthesis is particularly important in studying the field of negotiation. One well-accepted approach is that the negotiation process is not sequential but is rather a tension between various elements formed by the way these influence each other over time (see Ebner and Kamp, *Relationship 2.0*, in this volume). The interaction and relation between the various elements are what make each process unique, and pose the negotiator with his or her greatest opportunities for gain and perhaps jeopardy for loss.

To demonstrate the importance of understanding relations among concepts, let us consider a negotiation between management and union representatives during a strike. Positions taken by the parties at the bargaining table are influenced by an interplay among the following factors: state of the economy, current administration policy on unemployment, the wage-price spiral, community standard of living, going rates at other companies, company budget and costs for alternative agreements, union funds/strike costs, and the history of the strike including factors that generated the grievances. Defining these factors in a simulation scenario is one design challenge. Conceptualizing relationships among them is another. For example, going rates at other companies in the industry depend on the state of the economy as well as company profits and the community's standard of living. The going rates are also alternatives for employees who must balance opportunities against the costs of striking and time pressure. The challenge of creating a scenario that ties these concepts together enables the designer to appreciate complexity, which includes also changing relationships among them through time.

Concept synthesis is a negotiation teaching goal, which designing seems to achieve at a unique level. Why does design enhance synthesis? David Crookall illuminates the key features of design: "(a) Design is concrete – you can touch the results; (b) it is creative – you develop an object, and (c) it is involving – you develop understanding in a passionate and intimate way" (1995: 161). These features are further developed in Duke's (1974) earlier chapter on the simulation design process. Taking the process through a sequence of stages, Duke provides clues to learning. Most important to the synthesis issue, perhaps, is the first stage, referred to as "generating the conceptual map." Questions asked include: What is to be conveyed (themes, issues, problems) by the simulation? How is the message to be transmitted to the role-players? These questions are answered by expressing the conceptual map with text and graphics, gauging the correspondence between the map and reality, ascertaining an appropriate level of abstraction, and implementing the map through simulation construction. This process encourages designers, first, to view the system from above and, second, to work out the details (including role definitions and assignments) for play – thereby capturing Crookall's features of creativity, involvement, and concreteness at a whole-system level, as the designer carries around a mental web of all the elements and concepts involved – and the connectedness and tensions between them.

Greenblat specifically recognized synthesis as a reward of designing: "... a gaming-simulation may be a more productive way of conceptualizing elements and relationships, whether one's purpose is teaching or refinement of theory" (1975: 93). This point is reinforced by the authors in Part II ("Elements of Design and Construction") of her 1975 book edited with Duke. In Greenblat's more recent book on game design, she claimed that design "primarily (satisfies) the need for systemic understanding – seeing the connections among roles, goals, resources, constraints, and contingencies." She adds: "Thus you may design your gaming simulation to instruct others, but you learn a great deal yourself!" (1998: 34).

Experiments on Conceptual Relationships

Based on this literature and on our findings, it is clear that simulation design promotes synthesis. It seemed to us that if we could crack the code of what it is, precisely, about design that enhances synthesis, we would be able to improve design exercises and instructions to students. Our aim was to take advantage of the synthesis-related benefits that this method has to offer.

The first step was to discover whether synthesis is affected by explicit priming, which was not done in the earlier experiments. The questions asked are: Does highlighting the designer activity of thinking about relationships among the concepts increase the amount of synthesis achieved in the exercise? Is there room for improvement beyond that achieved in the earlier experiments? These questions are one-sided: they suggest either improvement or no difference due to priming. A two-sided question could also be asked: Does priming actually decrease the amount of synthesis achieved? Conceivably, priming could backfire by focusing designers' attention on a particular activity rather than on a whole-picture view of negotiation. These alternative hypotheses were investigated, namely, that priming either improves or hinders synthetic thinking.

But other factors may be at play in the design process. One of these factors is the type of scenario that is designed. We observed that some designer teams created scenarios based on their own negotiating experiences while others created situations that were less experiential or more generic. This distinction is similar to that made between situated and non-situated learning. By situated we refer to the use of personal experience as a referent for scenario design. Non-situated means relying on knowledge about negotiation not rooted in personal experience. The former has been shown to enhance concrete (situation-specific) learning and is promoted in the context of on-the-job training programs. The latter is regarded as being beneficial for concept learning and is promoted in the context of academic education. (See Klatsky and Reader 1994, for a review of the debate and issues.) Implications for design are suggested by the difference between situated or non-situated scenarios and concept learning. That difference takes the form of a hypothesis: concept learning is enhanced by the process of designing non-situated scenarios. This hypothesis was evaluated by the experiment to be described next.

Both priming and "situatedness" were included in the experiment. A 2 x 2 design consisted of the four combinations of these variables: instructions with and without priming were crossed with situated vs. non-situated instructions. The priming condition asked designers to "consider the relationships between the three elements (alternatives, time pressure, and power)." The situated designers were asked to "choose a negotiation situation in which you were personally involved." These instructions were reinforced orally by the instructor. No other changes were made from the original design condition. The results, obtained from responses to the appended questionnaire, can be summarized.

Only a few statistically significant effects occurred for either of the two variables. Even the directional effects favored neither the primed or situated conditions: eight questions showed more learning for the primed condition, nine favored the non-primed condition; similarly, eight questions favored the situated condition while nine favored the non-situated condition. However, the differences that did occur were on the open-ended questions concerned with meaning and application of the concepts: five of the eight questions that favored priming were open ended; four of the eight that favored learning effects for "situatedness" were open ended. This is interesting because of the general lack of effects on these questions in the original experiment that compared designers with role players.

The overall lack of differences suggests the possibility of ceiling effects for the original designer condition. There may be limited room for further improvement on learning. However, they may also have been due to: 1) a weak manipulation of the variables; 2) a lack of theoretical justification for the variables; 3) implementation problems; or 4) unmotivated subjects (as suggested by answers to the questions on effort and satisfaction). These concerns led us to design and implement another experiment with the Israeli student population.

This experiment primarily addressed the issue of a weak manipulation for the priming variable. The key addition was the following instruction for the priming condition:

> Consider how you might craft your scenario such that these relationships could emerge and influence the way the simulation develops during role play. Please make this a priority in your design. A good simulation, for the purposes of this simulation-writing exercise, will be one which helps role players to understand the interplay among the three ideas. Their actions should be affected by this interplay.

In contrast, designers in the non-primed condition were told to "incorporate each of the three concepts into the simulation." These instructions were reinforced orally by the lecturer. Both conditions were run with the generic, non-situated instructions for the type of scenario being constructed. The results differed considerably from those obtained in the previous priming experiment.

Seventeen of the nineteen immediate forced choice and open-ended assessments favored the priming condition; identical means were obtained for two of the open-ended questions. Nine of the nineteen differences were statistically significant, with effect sizes ranging from .32 to .55.[7] The priming condition means were also considerably higher (more self-reported learning) than those obtained for priming in the previous experiment. Further, for most questions asked in both the immediate and retention assessments, the mean obtained from the original (non-primed, non-situated) designer condition fell between those for the primed and non-primed conditions of this experiment. Thus, indeed, there was room for improvement; the original designer results did not hit a ceiling.

Eighteen of the nineteen one-week retention questions favored the priming condition. Thirteen of the nineteen differences were statistically significant, with effect sizes ranging from .39 to .71. Thus, the retention results were somewhat stronger than the immediate assessments, including those obtained for the open-ended questions about the meaning of alternatives and time pressure as well as how to deal with alternatives in a negotiation.

Another evaluation of condition effects was in terms of an index of percent increase in learning. The index consisted of a ratio of the average across the learning questions divided by the length of the scale, which was six steps for all the questions. The priming condition ratio for immediate learning was .83. The non-priming condition ratio was .65, a difference of .18.[8] The original designer condition ratio (from the Druckman and Ebner 2008 experiment) fell between at .75. The priming condition ratio for retention learning was also .83 while the ratio for non-primed designers was .67, a difference of .16. Again, the original designers fell between with a ratio of .75.

Together, the findings obtained from these analyses suggest that a strong priming manipulation works. It produces a similar across-the-board sweep of findings as were obtained in the Druckman and Ebner (2008) comparison of designers with role players and controls. However, the strong designer priming exaggerates the differences further. Encouraging designers to focus attention on relationships among the concepts improves learning.

A question of interest is the extent to which explicitly priming conceptual relationships improves designer learning. Two assessments bear directly on this question. One is the question, asked also in the earlier experiments, about "the extent to which the exercise helps you to understand the relationships between the three concepts." Clear results were obtained with primed designers "out-learning" non-primed and original designers. Another question, added for the priming experiment, asked about "the extent to which you feel that placing special emphasis on relationships between the concepts contribute to learning about them." This question was also asked on a six-step scale with six indicating maximum relational learning. Significant differences between the conditions occurred for both the immediate (Mean [primed] = 5.5; Mean [non-primed] = 4.4) and retention (Mean [primed] = 5; Mean [non-primed] = 4) assessments. Primed designers were aware of the connection between conceptual relationships and learning. The priming strengthened these perceived connections.

Our results reinforce the observations made by simulation theorists: synthesis is part of the design process. But, our findings go a step further. They suggest that the hypothesized learning benefits are increased when designers are told to prioritize this particular feature of scenario design. The practical implication of this finding is clear, namely, prime the relational feature in design assignments. The theoretical implications are more complex. Several questions are raised for further research:

1) Are the learning differences obtained in these experiments limited to concept learning? Would learning effects for role players be stronger on tactics than on concepts?

2) To what extent do the priming findings reflect expectations for learning (referred to also as demand characteristics) rather than actual learning?

3) Do the effects obtained with negotiation concepts also occur in other substantive domains?

4) Do role players learn more when they implement professional designs? Do they learn more when they play different roles and versions of the same scenario?

These are questions to be addressed in a next generation of experiments. Before concluding the chapter, we turn to a discussion of implications of the findings for teaching.

Applications

The findings reviewed in this chapter suggest that design activities enhance concept learning in general and relational learning in particular. This conclusion has implications for teaching applications. In this section we discuss four ways in which designer exercises can be implemented in the classroom. Each has been used by us and by colleagues familiar with the research findings. The teaching methods can be arranged in terms of increasing complexity or levels of analysis as follows:

- Teaching individual negotiation concepts
- Teaching sets of concepts
- Comparing different models
- Integrating the material from an entire course

Each approach is summarized briefly followed by suggestions for conducting the exercises.

Teaching Individual Negotiation Concepts

Using design to teach one element at a time can be done in a relatively short period of time. After explaining the negotiation concept, students are instructed to write a brief story about a negotiator who is considering that element. It is advisable to keep other creativity-requirements to a minimum at this stage, until they understand the basic structure of design; they can be told to write a story about a particular context or situation instead of making up situations on their own. For example, regarding the concept of alternatives, students can be asked to write a brief story about a person who is negotiating for a used car, in which the element of best alternative to a negotiated agreement (BATNA) comes into play. A few students should read their stories to the class, so as to make sure that the concept of BATNA is embedded in them (and, perhaps, to make a couple of design-focused comments along the way). They may also write the opposite role – in this case, a used car salesperson with a van on their lot – incorporating the concept of BATNA on this side as well.

A good form of design-related feedback for teaching single element designs is to ask students to alter existing scenarios. For example, after teaching the concept of alternatives, students are asked to retrieve their copy of a simulation conducted the previous week. Then, add two sentences, referring to alternatives, that would have changed the negotiation dynamics significantly.

The party-by-party design exercise can be completed in half an hour, whereas the scenario-alteration exercises can be completed in less than ten minutes. This is a good investment of time, particularly if more extensive design is planned as an activity later in the course.

Teaching Sets of Concepts

We have shown that simulation design is a powerful method for learning about relationships between concepts, particularly when students are primed to take these relationships into account. In our experiments, students were encouraged to incorporate three concepts in their scenarios – alternatives, time pressure, and power. However, any set of concepts may be used: for example, culture, emotions, and integrative agreements; a variety of concepts can be drawn from the research as summarized by Druckman and Robinson's (1998) sixteen thematic narratives.

The instructions that were used for the experiment can be adapted for use in conjunction with any designer exercise. Few changes would be needed for any set of negotiation concepts. The key instruction is to

consider how you might craft your scenario such
that relationships between the concepts could
emerge and influence the way that the simulation
develops during a role play. This is a priority in your
design. A good simulation, for the purpose of this
exercise, will be one that helps role players understand the interplay among the three ideas. Their actions should be influenced by this interplay.

Instructors would be available to field questions from designers
about relational challenges that arise during the writing period.

Comparing Alternative Theories

The simulation design method can be applied on a larger scale. For
example, it can be used to allow students to develop a full "elements" model of negotiation. Such an exercise is preceded by considerable learning of the model, and usually involves students
developing more extensive role information. Students prepare a full
scale simulation keeping all of the model's elements in mind, and
giving thought to how they can be incorporated into the simulation.

Another large-scale application of this method would involve using simulation-design as a vehicle for comparison *between* theoretical
models. Students might be assigned to choose two models from a
menu of theories studied during a course, and tasked with designing
a simulation in which elements related to them are embedded such
that they are likely to be called into play in the negotiation situation.
After a break, the designers then attempt to incorporate the other
theory in their scenario. The class debrief focuses on comparing the
strengths and weaknesses of the two models in relation to the case.
An example is to contrast positional bargaining with interest-based
bargaining (Fisher, Ury, and Patton 1981). Another example is the
difference between alternative game-theoretic models referred to as
transaction costs and discounting (Cramton 1991). These models
posit different choices leading to equilibrium solutions to the bargaining problem. Other contrasting negotiation approaches, drawn
from class readings and discussion, could be highlighted in the exercise as well.[9]

Integrating the Material of an Entire Course

Another way of using simulation design for learning, which benefits
greatly from the power of design to clarify relationships between
discrete elements, is assigning simulation design as a course's final
project. At this point, students are at the peak of their negotiation
knowledge and are also experienced with negotiation simulations –

how they are constructed and how they play out. If small design exercises have been assigned along the way, students have this to build on as well. We have found that students approach this assignment enthusiastically and creatively, as evidenced by the quantity of material produced, the creative production of support material, the intricacy of the story lines, and by their direct feedback.

Designers are asked to develop a complex simulation that incorporates ideas learned in class. Sample instructions include the following: "…build a scenario comprised of familiar elements…be sure to include stages of conflict escalation or of relationship change, leaving room for further development by the role players…the basic elements of negotiation learned in class should surface in the scenario." Further, "such processes as coalition forming, intra-team dissension, trading on multiple issues (logrolling), and communication barriers should emerge…these processes were demonstrated in the class video and discussed by the authors of your assigned readings."

Choices to be Made
The following choices often confront designers of simulations in any of the four approaches discussed above. Guidance is provided by our answers.

Should Designers Work by Themselves or in Pairs?
We have conducted these exercises both ways, and have observed that task motivation and creativity (but not concept learning) are enhanced when designers work in pairs. However, team-work adds a dimension of coordination which increases the time needed to complete the exercise. Of course both formats can be tried and, perhaps, leaving the decision up to the students is reasonable.

Should the Exercise be Conducted in Class, or Outside of Class-hours?
The smaller-scoped versions, as we have mentioned, are quite suitable for in-class work. The experimental task discussed above was completed in an hour, not including time for a de-briefing. One does, however, need to keep in mind that writing is a creative task, which needs a suitable amount of time and a certain frame of mind. As a result, the wider the scope of the assignment, the more it will be suitable to let students design simulations on their own time, perhaps as a take-home assignment. We have used this assignment in a distance-learning course, where students complete work at their own pace. We have also conducted online exercises, in asynchronous formats, that allow students to complete their work over several

days. These longer assignments are suitable as well for longer course-end projects.

What Should Designers Write About?

One question that often arises is whether students should base their scenarios on situations they have experienced or invent fictional scenarios based primarily on their knowledge of negotiation. As we noted earlier, our research thus far has not shown differences in learning outcomes between the two types of scenarios. As a result it would probably be best to tell students to choose whichever they prefer and hope that this freedom will have a positive effect on motivation.

What Types of Groups Should Conduct These Exercises?

It is important to stress that, in our experience, not all students enjoy the design exercise. Some felt that they were being pressured to produce original material in a short period of time. It will be helpful to explore a variety of procedures for conducting design writing, including allotting more time and perhaps other types of support. More compelling, perhaps, is that the exercise may be problematic in some cultures or contexts. Like any classroom innovation, the receptiveness of students or trainees is important to take into account. More generally, teacher mindfulness and specific preparation for each group are advised.

Conclusion

The learning advantages shown for designers suggest that class role plays should be supplemented with design exercises. Several of us have been doing this for a long time and have developed alternative approaches for implementing the exercise, as discussed in the previous section. We now have empirical evidence to support this pedagogical decision. Further, we have discovered that relational thinking may be the key: stronger effects for the design experience occurred when conceptual relationships were primed and this occurred on both the forced-choice and open-ended questions. It occurred also for both situated and generic scenarios. Yet, the weaker effects obtained on many of the open-ended application questions serve to reduce our enthusiasm to an extent. The difference between perceived and demonstrated learning remains an issue for further research. (For more on this issue, see Druckman and Ebner 2008.) So too does the need for comparisons with other teaching techniques and among a variety of student and professional populations. But, research also needs to address the implication drawn from our findings – that role plays are less useful than previously thought.

Although it may be that role-playing is not the preferred approach for enhancing concept learning, it is likely to contribute in important ways to negotiation practice. Role-playing may well be the method of choice for gaining experience and feedback from employing a variety of tactics. It may also contribute to the design experience by providing designers with insights into the way a simulation is structured and managed. (See also Winham 2002, for other practical advantages of role-plays.) These contributions bolster the case for complementary – and sequential – uses of role-play and design. For example, simulation design may enhance the understanding of such concepts as alternatives while role-playing in simulations may be a better method for learning when and how a negotiator might disclose his or her alternatives to a negotiating opponent.

Notes

[1] In this paper, we use the term "simulation" as a generic reference to experiential-learning activities commonly labeled "simulations," "games," "simulation-games," and "role-play." We use the term "role-players" to denote participants in a simulation activity who play out roles based on information and instructions they are given, such as in the experimental condition described in this chapter. These decisions are not intended to influence the debate on the way these activities are conducted or the delineation between them. For a detailed discussion of this issue, see Crookall, Oxford, and Saunders (1987).

[2] This interplay of elements, familiar to any negotiation trainee, is the hallmark of Inbar and Stoll's (1972) guide to simulation design, one of the first texts on this subject. Using a conflict simulation as their example, these authors provide a step-by-step guide to designing a simulation. They emphasize goal setting, structuring of constraints, and allocating resources. Each is an essential feature of negotiation. By goals, they refer to structuring the game outcomes to allow for one or many winners. Four constraints include legitimacy, interdependence or common fate, patterns of communication, and coalition formation. By allocating resources, they refer to designing an exchange process for transferring resources.

[3] A question can be raised about whether amateur designs provide a quality learning experience for role-players. It may well be that simulations designed by professionals would provide a better learning experience. However, it is also the case that the designers were also amateurs whose learning experience would have been enhanced by prior design opportunities. Symmetrical experience provide an apples-to-apples experimental comparison. It would have been more problematic to match amateur designers with role-players who implement professional designs or to compare experienced designers with amateur role-players. Further research is needed to evaluate relative learning benefits from amateur vs. professional designs.

[4] The questionnaire addressed learning in two aspects: Perceived learning (or, how students evaluate their understanding of a concept) and demonstrated learning (students' explanation of a concept being assessed by an expert reader). In our 2008 article we discuss the reasoning behind adopting this dual form of measurement and also discuss some interesting discrepancies between the two sets of data. Motivation was only measured by subjective means, but we probed this issue from various directions (e.g., satisfaction with outcome, desire to engage in such a task again, etc.).

[5] These findings are reported here in brief. For a more precise discussion about the statistical significance of each finding, see the original article.

[6] The focus of these experiments is on indicators of learning/motivational benefits derived from the activities of design and role-play. We do not assess competence in scenario writing or in role-playing. Further, participants are told that "we will not use your scenarios (or role-plays) to evaluate your negotiating or literary skills."

[7] The effect size (ES) expresses the amount of variation accounted for in the dependent variable (learning) by the independent variable (priming vs. non-priming). In these analyses, the ES is a conversion of a t test significance level to a correlation coefficient (see Wolf, 1986 for the conversion formulae).

[8] A ratio of .83 means that priming-condition designers reported achieving more than four-fifths of the distance on the six point scale (where six is maximum learning), with an average mean of 5. A difference of .18 between the condition ratios indicates that primed designers reported 18% more learning than non-primed designers (a mean of 3.9 on the six-step scale).

[9] Thanks go to Atalia Mosek of Tel Hai College, Israel, who developed this application of teaching by simulation-design after hearing about our experimental work. For detailed instructions used with each of the approaches discussed in this section, contact the authors at dandruckman@yahoo.com or noamebner@creighton.edu.

References

Alexander, N. and M. LeBaron. 2009. Death of the role-play. In *Rethinking negotiation teaching: Innovations for context and culture*, edited by C. Honeyman, J. Coben, and G. De Palo. St. Paul, MN: DRI Press.

Bateman, C. and R. Boon. 2006. *21st Century Game Design*. Hingham, MA: Charles River Media.

Bredemeier, M. E. and C. S. Greenblatt. 1981. The educational effectiveness of simulation games: A synthesis of findings. *Simulation & Games* 12(3): 307-332.

Cherryholmes, C. 1966. Some current research on effectiveness of educational simulations: Implications for alternative strategies. *American Behavioral Scientist* 10(2): 4-7.

Cramton, P. C. 1991. Dynamic bargaining with transaction costs. *Management Science* 37(10): 1221-1233.

Crookall, D. 1995. A guide to the literature on simulation/gaming. In *Simulation and gaming across disciplines and cultures*, edited by D. Crookall and K. Arai. Thousand Oaks, CA: Sage.

Crookall, D., R. Oxford, and D. Saunders. 1987. Towards a reconceptualization of simulation: From representation to reality. *Simulations/Games for Learning* 17(4): 147-170.

Druckman, D. 1971. Understanding the operation of complex social systems: Some uses of simulation design. *Simulation & Games* 2: 173-195.

Druckman, D. and N. Ebner. 2008. Onstage, or behind the scenes? Relative learning benefits of simulation role-play and design. *Simulation & Gaming* 39(4): 465-497.

Druckman, D. and V. Robinson. 1998. From research to application: Utilizing research findings in training programs. *International Negotiation* 3(1): 7-38.

Duke, R. D. 1974. *Gaming: The future's language*. New York: Halsted Press.

Ebner, N. and Y. Efron. 2005. Using tomorrow's headlines for today's training: Creating pseudo-reality in conflict resolution simulation-games. *Negotiation Journal* 21(3): 377-394.

Ellington, H., E. Addinall, and F. Percival. 1984. *Case studies in game design*. London: Nichols Publishing Company.

Fisher, R., W. Ury, and B. Patton. 1991. *Getting to yes*, 2nd edn. New York: Penguin Books.

Gamson, W. A. 1971. SIMSOC: Establishing social order in a simulated society. *Simulation & Gaming* 2(3): 287-308.

Greenblat, C. S. 1975. Gaming-simulation and social science: Rewards to the designer. In *Gaming-simulation: Rationale, design, and applications*, edited by C. S. Greenblat and R. D. Duke. New York: Halsted Press.

Greenblat, C. S. 1998. *Designing games and simulations: An illustrated handbook*. Newbury Park, CA: Sage.

Greenblat, C. S. and R. D. Duke. 1975. *Gaming-simulation: Rationale, design, and applications*. New York: Halsted Press.

Inbar, M. and C. S. Stoll. 1972. Designing a simulation. In *Simulation and gaming in social science*, edited by M. Inbar and C. S. Stoll. New York: The Free Press.

Jones, K. 1985. *Designing your own simulation*. London: Routledge.

Klatsky, R. and L. Reader. 1994. Transfer: Training for performance. In *Learning, remembering, believing: Enhancing human performance*, edited by D. Druckman and R. A. Bjork. Washington, DC: National Academy Press.

McLaughlin, R. G. and D. Kirkpatrick. 2005. Online text-based role-play simulation: The challenges ahead. *SIMTECT Papers 2005*. Available at http://www.siaa.asn.au/library_simtect_2005.html (last accessed May 17, 2010).

Mathevet, R., C. Le Page, M. Etienne, G. Lefebvre, B. Poulin, G. Gigot, S. Proreol, and A. Mauchamp. 2007. BUTOSTAR: A role-playing game for collective awareness of wise reedbed use. *Simulation & Gaming* 38: 233-262.

Nadler, J., L. Thompson, and L. V. Boven. 2003. Learning negotiation skills: Four models of knowledge creation and transfer. *Management Science* 49: 529-540.

Pierfy, D. A. 1977. Comparative simulation game research, stumbling blocks, and steppingstones. *Simulation & Games* 8: 255-268.

Randel, J. M., B. A. Morris, C. D. Wetzel, and B. V. Whitehall. 1992. The effectiveness of games for educational purposes: A review of recent research. *Simulation & Gaming* 23: 261-276.

Spector, B. I. 1995. Creativity heuristics for impasse resolution: Reframing intractable negotiations. *The Annals of the American Academy of Political and Social Science* 542(1): 81-99.

Toth, F. L. 1995. Simulation/gaming for long-term policy problems. In *Simulation and gaming across disciplines and cultures*, edited by D. Crookall and K. Arai. Thousand Oaks, CA: Sage.

Winham, G. R. 2002. Simulation for teaching and analysis. In *International negotiation: Analysis, approaches, and issues*, edited by V. Kremenyuk, 2nd edn. San Francisco: Jossey Bass.

Wolf, F. M. 1986. *Meta-analysis: Quantitative methods for research synthesis*. Beverly Hills: Sage.

Appendix

Learning About Your Experience

We are interested to learn about your experience. Please provide feedback by answering the following questions. Note that some ask you to provide an "X" on a scale, while others ask you to provide more detailed information. Thank you very much for your participation.

Regarding the Concept of "Alternatives":

1. How much did the exercise contribute to your understanding of this concept? (Check one box)
   - ☐ Very much
   - ☐ Pretty much
   - ☐ Somewhat
   - ☐ A little
   - ☐ Not much
   - ☐ Not at all

2. To what extent did the exercise provide added value to your understanding of the concept presented in the lecture? (Check one box)
   - ☐ Added considerably
   - ☐ Added pretty much
   - ☐ Added somewhat

☐   Added only a little
☐   Did not add much
☐   Did not add anything at all

3. What is meant by "alternatives"

_____
_____
_____

4. How would you use or deal with this concept in the course of a negotiation?

_____
_____
_____

Regarding the Concept of "Time Pressure":

5. How much did the exercise contribute to your understanding of this concept? (Check one box)
☐   Very much
☐   Pretty much
☐   Somewhat
☐   A little
☐   Not much
☐   Not at all

6. To what extent did the exercise provide added value to your understanding of the concept presented in the lecture? (Check one box)
☐   Added considerably
☐   Added pretty much
☐   Added somewhat
☐   Added only a little
☐   Did not add much
☐   Did not add anything at all

7. What is meant by "time pressure"?

_____
_____
_____

8. How would you use or deal with this concept in the course of a negotiation?

_____
_____
_____

Regarding the Concept of "Negotiating Power":

9. How much did the exercise contribute to your understanding of this concept? (Check one box)
☐   Very much
☐   Pretty much

☐   Somewhat
☐   A little
☐   Not much
☐   Not at all

10. To what extent did the exercise provide added value to your understanding of the concept presented in the lecture? (Check one box)
☐   Added considerably
☐   Added pretty much
☐   Added somewhat
☐   Added only a little
☐   Did not add much
☐   Did not add anything at all

11. What is meant by "negotiating power"?

_____

_____

_____

12. How would you use or deal with this concept in the course of a negotiation?

_____

_____

_____

13. To what extent did the exercise help you to understand the relationships between the three concepts? (Check one box)
☐   Very helpful
☐   Pretty helpful
☐   Somewhat helpful
☐   A little helpful
☐   Did not help much
☐   Did not help at all

14. How do you think these concepts are related in negotiation?

_____

_____

_____

General Observations
15. More generally, we would like to know how much you enjoyed the exercise: (Check one box)
☐   Very much
☐   Pretty much
☐   Somewhat
☐   A little
☐   Not much
☐   Not at all

16. How much effort did you put into the tasks? (Check one box)
- ☐ A lot
- ☐ Pretty much
- ☐ Somewhat
- ☐ A little
- ☐ Hardly any

17. Would you do it again? (Check one box)
- ☐ Yes
- ☐ No
- ☐ Maybe

18. How satisfied were you with the results? (Check one box)
- ☐ Very much
- ☐ Pretty much
- ☐ Somewhat

19. What did you enjoy most about the exercise?

_____
_____
_____

20. What did you enjoy least?

_____
_____
_____

21. Do you think that you would have learned more, less, or the same by performing the other role (either scenario writer or role-player)? (Check one box)
- ☐ Would have learned more
- ☐ About the same
- ☐ Would have learned less

Thanks again for your time!

ଔ 17 ଼

Using Role-Play in Online Negotiation Teaching

David Matz & Noam Ebner*

Editors' Note: Matz and Ebner consider the impending collision be-tween teachers' strong desire to use role-play and other simulation ex-ercises, and the rise of online teaching, in which the students may never see each other. Can the advantages of simulation teaching and the advantages of online teaching be brought together to improve both?

Introduction

If there is a trend in higher education in which all arrows point in the same direction, it is the growth of online education. While dis-tance learning has been available, in various forms, for the past 200 years (see Holmberg 2005), the accessibility provided by the Internet has created a boom over the past decade.[1]

This trend has not skipped over the fields which most commonly serve as homes for negotiation courses: management and dis-pute/conflict resolution programs. Business degrees are among the most commonly offered online degrees, and conflict resolution pro-grams are also increasingly going online, in their entirety or through offering individual courses.

Negotiation courses' third natural home, law schools, have so far largely resisted the surge towards online education, primarily due to objections raised by the American Bar Association and other bar as-sociations around the world. But this is changing. With the advent of accredited online law schools in the United States and Australia, and with shifting global trends both in education and in the way

* **David Matz** is a professor in the Graduate Programs in Dispute Resolution at the University of Massachusetts/Boston in Boston, Massachusetts and principal at The Mediation Group in Brookline, Massachusetts. His email address is davidematz@gmail.com. **Noam Ebner** is an assistant professor at the Werner Institute at Creighton University's School of Law, where he chairs the online masters program in Negotiation and Dispute Resolution. His email address is noamebner@creighton.edu.

people view technology, law schools are beginning to offer courses online.

In short, if you are a negotiation teacher and you are not yet teaching online, chances are that you will be. This will be a matter of choice for some, of circumstance for others, and perhaps of downright coercion for a few – but, in any event, it is coming.

For most negotiation teachers, role-play[2] is a crucial tool. Whether this is due to teachers' association of learning benefits with this method (Ebner and Kovach, *Simulation 2.0*, in this volume), to their appreciation for the motivational benefits associated with it (Druckman and Ebner, *Enhancing Concept Learning*, in this volume), or simply to the fact that this is the way teachers have been doing it for so long, simulations enjoy a reserved table in the restaurant of negotiation course design.

Role-Play – Online? Really?

The centrality of role-play in negotiation pedagogy presents significant challenges when viewed through the perspective of online teaching. Here is a loose framing of some of these challenges:

- Transferability: Can negotiating in an online venue prepare students to negotiate at the (real) table? No matter which medium (text, audio, video) is chosen for conducting simulations at-a-distance, aren't the negotiation dynamics inevitably distorted by the medium through which they are conducted (Ebner et al. 2009)?

- Limited skills-building: What is the value of a teaching process in which key elements of human interaction, such as personal presence, tone and contextual cues, are diminished if not eliminated? How can we teach students to communicate if many elements of communication are eliminated?

- Administration: In the face-to-face classroom, there is nothing simpler than saying "Everybody – grab an Other" and handing each party a sheet of paper. How does one set up simulations at-a-distance, without a great deal of technical know-how and a prohibitive investment of time?

- Control: Engaging participants in role-play and maintaining the simulation "bubble" around the exercise is difficult enough in the classroom. How can teachers ensure that students participate in the role-play, take it seriously and dedicate the necessary amount of time and effort to it, when they and the negotiating students are all at a distance from each other?

- Observation and debrief: Teachers accustomed to running the "role-play relay" between several simulating groups, observing the negotiation dynamics and elements playing out in each one, and connecting classroom points to very specific occurrences in the simulations might wonder how, in the online environment, can they observe students' experiences in a way that will allow them to add value by providing guidance, insight and assessment?

These are the primary questions we have heard in thinking about teaching role-plays online. And we would add two more:

- Advantages: Is online teaching of role-plays in some ways *better* than teaching them live?
- Compensation: If some things are lost in online role-play teaching, are there ways to compensate for these losses?

To answer these questions, we did three things. First, we reviewed the literature focused on online teaching in general, and on online teaching of analogous skills (e.g., interviewing.) Second, we interviewed thirteen teachers teaching negotiation online – asking them what they do with regards to role-play, how well it works, and what they would like to do. We rounded this out by holding discussions with several students who have taken part in role-plays in the course of studying negotiation online. Finally, we consulted our own imaginations as teachers, teachers with some experience in the online teaching world. This chapter is a report of our findings.[3]

Teachers Talk

Many of the insights gained from our interviews with teachers will be incorporated later on. However, at this stage, two important findings regarding teachers should be made:

1) Several teachers (around one-fifth of those we spoke to) reported that they did not use simulations when teaching negotiation at a distance – although they would (and do) employ it while teaching similar courses face-to-face. Teachers stressed different reasons for avoiding role-play, reasons mentioned in the questions listed above, with the difficulty of following the role-play and giving feedback topping the list.

2) Teachers employ different media for conducting role-plays, as will be discussed below. However, we found that besides the question of "which medium should we use?" teachers had different approaches to the question of "does it *matter* what media we use?" Some teachers chose (or developed) a specific media platform in order to utilize its characteristics for pedagogical goals. For example, some teachers require students to negotiate by email (in order to keep a clear record of the conversation for debrief purposes); others prefer to use discussion forums, so as to enable viewing by a larger group and to allow multiple modes of student input. However, other teachers are indifferent to the communication

method employed, so long as the simulation is completed. From their point of view, choice of method is up to students, and is a matter of convenience and familiarity; students can speak over the phone, communicate by email, or meet in person to negotiate over a cup of coffee if they are fortunate enough to share a locale.

The first finding – that some teachers shy away from using role-plays in courses taught at-a-distance – reinforced our motivation to write this piece. We hope that by providing some answers to the "how" questions, negotiation teachers will be able to choose to incorporate role-plays without concern about distance, or the online environment, hampering use of this method. Moreover, we will go beyond that to suggest some teaching benefits *unique* to online role-play, which might encourage teachers to dedicate time to online role-play – even in blended (online and face-to-face) and face-to-face classes.

The second finding, regarding the range of different media teachers employ, led us to structure this piece according to different types of media. The three primary technology categories that teachers are currently using for conducting role-play are text, audio and video. We have organized the report so that a teacher can review each technology and decide if there is something in it that he/she would like to try. For each technology, we have tried to address each phase of role-play teaching:

- organizing the role-play (distributing the parts, pairing the teams, etc);
- conducting the negotiation;
- evaluation by students of their work;
- evaluation by faculty of student work;
- teaching a class about the role-play;
- evaluating the role-play as a learning experience.

And finally, going beyond the three technology categories, we took a stab at predicting where imagination and technology might be going in teaching role-plays online in the future.

Text-Based Teaching

Many of the teachers we interviewed relied either solely or largely on text when they taught role-plays online. By text they meant email (inside their course management system or through students' own email), threaded forum posting, instant-messaging, or documents posted online. While some teachers reported using a synchronous method such as a dedicated chat room, most teachers tended to employ asynchronous communication, through email or a dedicated discussion forum thread.

Setting Up

Setting up text-based role-plays is easily done, more easily than neophytes tend to expect. Much as in face-to-face settings, some teachers prefer to decide the pairing up by themselves, and others leave it for students to decide. Students receive their role-play instructions, either via email or via some function of the course management system. Either way allows for giving all students designated as Party A quick access to that party's role information. Teachers might set up a dedicated forum or email list, allowing students playing the same role to discuss issues with each other at the preparation stage (McKersie and Fonstad 1997).

Conducting the Role-Play

The most common criticisms raised regarding the asynchronous, text-based role-play approach are that the players have no experience observing body language, have only a diluted sense of the personality of the Other, and thus only a dim sense of relationship; in short, they miss large parts not only of what is most beneficial, even central, to face-to-face negotiation, but of what is beneficial in live role-plays.

Two students added another dimension. They said that when the course was a hybrid (incorporating both online and face-to-face elements), they found text-based role-plays to be troubling. As they knew the Other from classroom interaction, they found themselves imagining what that person would be thinking and they missed his/her personality. But when the course was solely online, they found that text-based role-play gave them the comfortable opportunity to imagine a full personality for the Other.

Some students have observed that text-based role-playing is not only less intense than live role-playing, but that they tend to multitask (checking their Facebook accounts while waiting for the Other to respond), causing them to give less thought to the next move. Others have commented conversely, saying that participating in the role-play according to their own schedule allows them to clear time to concentrate. We would observe that the potential for distraction is more likely in synchronous text-based negotiation if scheduling has not taken account of students' home schedules (though this is difficult to do with students in different time zones), and particularly if the teacher is not "present" in some way, observing the simulation's development.

The challenges to relationship posed by the text medium offer teachers two distinct paths; one is to focus on them as content-matter in their own right, opening room for discussion of best practices in real-life e-negotiation situations, and for discussion of the role of relationships in face-to-face negotiating. Some teachers, for example, direct students to focus the first part of the negotiation on getting acquainted online. They suggest that students introduce themselves, in role, and try and get to know the other through questions. These tactics, or variations on them, might also be useful in real-life online negotiations. Another approach is to try to mitigate these challenges in order to allow students to practice traditional negotiation skills without the online medium getting in the way.[4] Adopting this approach, teachers might have students introduce themselves (for real, out-of-role), and perhaps exchange pictures of themselves, before initiating the actual role-play; this has the effect of eliminating perceived distance, and of humanizing students playing opposite each other. A couple of teachers noted that they sometimes simply instruct students to ignore the online medium, and picture the role-play as taking place across a table (although they are aware of the difficulties this suggestion poses).[5]

Some argue that there are additional advantages of text role-playing over face-to-face. The latter, in this view, puts *too much* emphasis on the interplay of personalities, diminishing the ability of students to focus on strategy and the use of concepts in action. Some students feel intimidated by (or overly engaged by) the presence of the Other, and thus feel less able to think "on their feet." Using only text, student learning is enhanced by the asynchronicity, leaving them time to assess the negotiating situation and to formulate a next move.

Some teachers are concerned that live cross-cultural role-play (negotiating with someone who really is from another culture) runs the risk of over-emphasizing cultural stereotyping. In this view, students using such stereotypes can find it more difficult to envision and use the flexibility that we know exists within them. The use of text can mask those characteristics of the Other that might give rise to such stereotyping, and thus enable the student to focus only on the negotiating behavior itself, not on his/her own cultural expectations. (Students have asserted the same masking effect even when negotiating within one culture, reducing dynamics such as bias and intimidation.) Taking this a step further, some students find that by mid-way in a term they know many of their classmates so well that negotiating in new roles is increasingly, and perhaps distortingly, influenced by what they already know about the Other (see Coben, Honeyman, and Press, *Straight Off the Deep End*, in this volume); a text-based role-play can be arranged so that students negotiate anonymously. (For more on the effects of computer-mediated communication in cross-cultural negotiation, see Kersten, Koszegi, and Vetschera 2003.)

A modest further advantage of online role-play teaching is that the professor can modify the instructions during the role-play by sending all students – or all students playing one side – a notice (e.g., one side's best alternative to a negotiated agreement (BATNA) just declined in value).

Finally, text role-play, as we have mentioned, allows students to practice text-based negotiation, an interaction that is becoming ubiquitous in the real world but is still not given enough attention in negotiation courses. For example, students need to practice the art of asynchronous communication, and be familiar with media effects associated with the scarcity of contextual clues, such as the absence of tone of voice, body language, etc. (Ebner et al. 2009).

Observing Role-Play

The value of teaching role-play via text is pronounced for the process of observing the role-play as it unfolds, and providing input. During the role-play the teacher can tune in to one or both sides; can comment as the role-play evolves, to both sides or one; and other students also can observe the negotiation as it proceeds, and they too can comment. This affords an online approximation of a live fishbowl, with the advantage that the comment can be made public to the whole group or just "whispered" to one negotiator. This online fishbowl, when conducted asynchronously, enjoys additional benefits: students – participants and observers – can carry on conversations on the sidelines, and can relate what is going on in the role-play to reading material (Douglas and Johnson 2008; Douglas and Johnson 2009).

But clearly the most dramatic advantage of teaching role-playing via text is the automatic creation of a full transcript. As this can be reviewed by a participant, by other students, and by the faculty, it enhances precision in reflection. Its presence eliminates the problem of faulty memory inherent in reviewing live role-plays.[6] The transcript introduces the need for a fundamentally new skill for teachers: learning, and teaching students, how to learn from a transcript. This will begin with helping students recognize in print the negotiating ideas taught in class, or via the reading, prior to the role-play. It will also need to focus on their absence. It will provide the opportunity to focus on interactivity: how did each student respond to the move of the other. One professor asks students to identify in the transcript emotionally significant moments that made a difference in how things proceeded. Another gives a list of terms, asking students to identify sentences or message interchanges exemplifying these terms. The transcript will enable a teacher to call attention to patterns of behavior over time, by either the student or the Other. It also will provide fine grist for a final paper. Transcript analysis is, however, very time-consuming for the student and the teacher, so scheduling needs to be done with care.

Debriefing of a text role-play can be done in many ways, including:

- A threaded discussion, where all students discuss their own experience with it, or all discuss one example selected by the teacher. The focus for this can be one transcript. It might also be a PowerPoint created by a student acting as observer and note taker in a text-based role-play.
- A written assignment in which students comment on their own negotiation transcripts, or those of others, relating interactions to specific negotiation concepts.
- A forum/paper in which students compare two negotiation processes.
- A discussion forum in which the teacher opens thematic discussion threads, each focusing on a different negotiation concept.
- A review by a (rather ambitious) teacher of all text negotiations looking for patterns and characteristic problems or surprises.

Role-Play Online: Audio

Most online courses incorporate some means for real-time audio conversation. This might be part of the course management system, or rely on external software. It might enable a teacher or student to speak to the whole class, the teacher to speak to individual students, individual students to talk to each other, and students to speak in a group. Each of these communication channels is useful for teaching role-play.

Some course management systems incorporate an integral audio or Voice over Internet Protocol (VoIP) – technologies for delivery of voice communication over the Internet. Familiar examples of freely accessible VoIP applicaticions include Skype and Google Talk. However, as most course management platforms are still text-oriented, many institutions offer teachers use of other software such as webconferencing platforms (e.g, WebEx, WIMBA, Elluminate). Of course, to use audio communication, one is not limited to software platforms provided by the university, or, indeed, to software platforms at all. One can use telephone, VoIP, or other commercial communication systems like ooVoo. Each has advantages: telephone is ubiquitous; Skype is free; ooVoo allows three or more parties to communicate simultaneously.

As discussed below, audio is not usually used as a stand-alone medium for role-play. The teachers we interviewed who use online audio, always combine it with various text elements.

Setting Up

At the organizing and set-up phase of a role-play, the audio feature adds little. Distributing role-play instructions, setting up teams, handing out roles, and answering questions can all be done just as well or better with text.

Conducting the Role-Play

However, conducting the role-play itself is a different matter; here the audio medium enjoys several important advantages.

Audio communication is almost always synchronous. It privileges those students who are most comfortable in oral interchange, though without each seeing the other there is still some protection for the shy or the anxious. Of course, there are media effects to be anticipated, such as increased contentiousness in contrast to face-to-face interactions (Drolet and Morris 2000), and reduced trust, (Raiffa 1982) perhaps producing a higher rate of impasse outcomes. However, when compared to text interactions, audio enjoys two major advantages. First, it includes voice tone, inflections, and the "music" of voice in general, all of which are the source of many of our conversational inferences, often made without the listener being aware of it (Tannen 1986). In addition, the synchronous conversation, combined with the audio message exchange contributes to a stronger sense of the social presence of the Other. As a result, these media effects will distort less than those encountered in text-based communication, leading to the conclusion that adding audio to the conduct of the role-play goes a long way toward re-introducing the feel of a face-to-face role-play.

An online technique teachers might consider employing would be to combine audio communication with use of a whiteboard (an online shared screen, often found in video- and data-conferencing software, which allows all viewers to view (and in some cases post and even mark up in real time) files such as documents and presentations). It is our experience that when data is presented visually and audibly, the impact is greater than when presented only audibly. Thus if students are taught to use whiteboard to record the pattern of offers and concessions, or to keep a list of the topics being negotiated, the negotiation will be different. The range of these differences is far from clear, but, for example, when engaging in Prisoner's Dilemma–type simulations, such as PEPULATOR, OIL PRICING, or PASTA WARS students are clearly more competitive when they see the comparative score unfolding on a blackboard than when that visual aid is not used. Similarly, the visual components would allow one-text editing, detail clarification (e.g., including pictures, maps and charts) and increased social presence of the negotiators. One teacher who uses webconferencing for conducting an audio-oriented *facilitation* role-play told us that his students *always* used some of the additional features of the platform – whiteboard, document uploading, etc. – to add a visual component. In a facilitation, of course, "making things visible" comes as naturally as breathing. Negotiation teachers who have used this report lower rates of student initiated usage. An additional issue to consider in this regard is students' familiarity with the tools at hand. The teacher told us that the degree to which students utilized these visual elements differed, based on their familiarity with the tools – including the degree to which they had read the tutorials provided and conducted trial runs. This would seem to support the suggestion that negotiation teachers should not only point out the visual potentialities of the platform (and perhaps explicitly recommending or assigning their use), but also help those students get accustomed to using them through written or videorecorded tutorials and perhaps a facilitated practice session.

As with any synchronous technique, if the course is fully online there is the likelihood that students will be in different time zones, and if the differences are extreme, scheduling audio conversations can be a hurdle.

Debriefing

The debriefing of traditional face-to-face role-playing ordinarily ignores certain dimensions related to communication, such as: voice, tone, pace and vocabulary. This is because much of our interpretation of such matters is unconscious and because we have no record, other than memory, to refer to. Online audio (so long as it is more advanced than telephone communication) will often have a recording device built in. Thus the students can review their own performance, the teacher can review the record, and the teacher can use all or part of the record in a subsequent class.

Students might be asked to keep a log (including time-stamps) of turning points, emotional outbreaks or any other elements teachers choose to focus on. There is, of course, a history of teachers having students tape-recording their face-to-face negotiations for review; we can now do this in role-play at a distance.

Whatever the method of recording used, teacher review of such records is a very time consuming process, and we are unaware of any readily available software designed to assist in identifying cognitive moves or tonal styles. Creating such software would be a great step forward in helping role-play reviewers focus on previously unattended communication.

A teacher can, however, take one or a few such audio records and play them at the next synchronous class (on- or off-line), stopping and starting, in a kind of post-hoc fishbowl process. In addition, teachers can post recordings of several negotiations online following the simulation, asking students to choose one simulation in which they did not take part, and provide insight and feedback.

And, finally, the ambitious teacher can review all the recordings to see if there are patterns in the ways students are learning the material or participating in the role-play. This can be valuable as part of a class in that course, and as grounding for teaching the class (and using that role-play) in the future.

Role-Play Online: Video

Video has made its way into face-to-face classrooms in many ways over the past few years. Many teachers show students professionally prepared videos of negotiations, and others have their students videorecord their own role-plays. There is, in addition, very good – if not very easy to use – software that helps the students and teachers assess the videos the students record. However, of the teachers we spoke to, we found no teacher using real-time, interactive video for role-plays on line. Or, to be more exact – while some teachers allow their students to interact through video, and still others wish they had the technical ability to incorporate this method, none of the online teachers assign students to role-play specifically through use of video-conferencing. Four reasons seem to stand out as driving this slow transition to video:

1) Some teachers do not feel themselves technologically competent to figure out how to conduct role-plays through this medium, let alone set them up and administer them.

2) Some teachers worry that some students will not be technologically adept, causing them to gain less from the simulation as well as placing a burden on the Other and on their teacher.

3) Some teachers are very concerned about the lack of direct teacher observation of the interactions in real-time, and feel as if the use of video-conferencing does not allow them the opportunity to provide helpful feedback and input.

4) Some teachers commented that the freeware videoconferencing platforms available on the market today are not high-quality, and are not reliable. Conversations get cut off; video comes out unclear or out of synch with audio.

Interestingly, this last concern did not seem to be of primary concern for most teachers regarding video. We will relate to it first, however, as we feel it might now be a secondary concern that will raise its head once some of the other concerns are dispelled.

There is some truth to the quality and reliability concerns; despite everything futurists and dot-coms have been promising for years, the "video phone," even in its computer version, is far from ubiquitous. This directly affects the average student's skill and familiarity with the available platforms. True, this might be solved by having universities provide students with access to video-conferencing services using high-end technology, providing good quality and reliability; however, this is still too expensive for most universities.

Moreover, the high-end technology on the market is aimed primarily for conference-room-to-conference-room communication, and does not provide a complete answer for the needs of online education, requiring that students be able to operate from home. Even if universities would purchase comprehensive video-conferencing platforms to be used by students at home, the quality and reliability is then lowered by low-quality end-user hardware (webcams, computer systems) and software (operating systems, webcam and audio drivers, etc.) and by end-users' bandwidth limitations.

As new uses for videoconferencing take root at the personal and small business level (examples related to our field that come to mind are teletherapy, online mediation and telecoaching), the demand for inexpensive, reliable video technology using personal computers should, as with other communications technologies, improve quality, bring down cost and drive solutions to work around bandwidth limitations. When will this happen? Probably soon is a safe, if amorphous, bet.

As we have said, when reliable video is available, some of the concerns regarding online role-play will disappear. Let us discuss some of the top-level concerns raised earlier, and then move on to make suggestions for incorporating the use of video in role-plays.

Teachers' Familiarity and Competence with the Medium

This is, of course, an important concern. It involves both capability (to deal with the medium, conduct the simulation through it, explain it to students, and field any questions they may have) and also, perhaps, identity and image (teaching in an unfamiliar environment is a risky step where the student may be more adept than the teacher.) The good news is, using simple videoconferencing programs (such as Skype or ooVoo) is simpler than many people imagine. Teachers can practice with a friend, or even on their own. One need not be an expert: competence with the basics is good enough. Additionally, there is a decent chance that in any university there is someone in the IT support department who can tutor faculty.

Students' Familiarity and Competence with the Medium

Most online programs are currently text-based; even those that incorporate video are primarily concerned with teacher-student video (pre-recorded or live video-lectures). As a result, even for many students in online programs, video is the "final frontier" of communication. In our experience and that of the one teacher we spoke to who did incorporate videoconferencing in his course, it would seem that providing students with guidance and training is vital. It is unwise to toss students into the water by telling them "download this program, and interact through it." Student participation is directly related to student preparation for interacting through the medium: provide students with an introduction to the software, a link to its help and frequently asked questions (FAQs) pages; if possible, prepare a tutorial, using a text document, a presentation with screen shots, or a video-recorded tutorial including screen captures. Perhaps one can have someone from the university's instructional design or information technology support departments construct and/or conduct the training.

One concern related to students' skill is the concern that their lack of familiarity with the medium stems from their lack of proper equipment for video-conferencing. Assigning a video-conference role-play might stress economic differences in class or put an unnecessary financial burden on students. This concern is certainly worth considering on a case-to-case basis, particularly when deliberating whether to assign an online role-play to students in a face-to-face class. If students are already studying in an online program, chances are that this concern is minimal.

Lack of Real-Time Feedback
We heard from several teachers that lack of real-time feedback is the primary reason they avoid using video for role-play. On this issue, we would make two comments.

First, the issue of real-time intervention and feedback is an issue of pedagogy and teaching style; many teachers prefer not to intervene even when they are physically able to, and there are many ways of debriefing an exercise that do not include an immediate gathering of the group for discussion. Teachers might use this opportunity of exploring role-play in a new environment to experiment with methods of giving input which they have not previously tried. Teachers who usually observe every phase of a role-play and lead the debrief might experiment with methods for student self-debrief, or peer-debrief. Teachers used to giving immediate feedback might experiment with delayed feedback, given after viewing a recording of the role-play or part of it.

Second, familiarity with video-conferencing software might allow the teacher to choose the platform that is most suited to his or her intervention/debriefing style, as well as to use it in the most beneficial way possible. For example, some platforms allow for three-way video calls, allowing the teacher to be present in real time. In order to reduce the teacher's presence, and its artificial effect on the negotiation, the teacher might let students know that s/he is there, but not turn on a webcam.

Some videoconferencing platforms allow for videorecording and archiving of the entire interaction, forming a video transcript of the negotiation to be debriefed in the ways we have suggested above in the discussion of text-based teaching.

Setting Up

As we have discussed above regarding audio role-plays, video role-plays are best set up through other methods, primarily text. The text material can include a link leading students into the video meeting-room, or a link to the site where the software platform can be downloaded and installed. Instructions and tutorials can also be sent as attachments.

Conducting the Role-Play

Conducting the role-play is of course the phase in which the use of video is most significant. Commercial teleconferencing has reached a level that ordinarily reduces or even eliminates awareness of the intervening technology. But not all the problems are solved. The presence of the camera will influence all but the most self-assured students, though many relax after a while. This sensitivity is enhanced with the awareness that a recording of the interchange may be used by the faculty member later. It will constitute a breakthrough of some significance when the two parties to a negotiation have lunch "together" via video. If the technology is truly flexible (like Skype) then both sides can schedule more than one session as easily as scheduling multiple session phone calls. (Though, again, time zone differences may intrude.)

Debriefing

Video can also be used as a tool for debrief, with students asked to watch others' negotiations, to compare specific moments or dynamics, etc., as described above regarding use of various types of transcripts. Teachers able to master basic video-editing tools can splice together important moments to show in class, or create a single video clip incorporating scenes from several negotiations (particularly enterprising teachers can incorporate "We Can Work it Out" as background music).

The Future

Though considerable research about the process of negotiation has filled journals and books over the last twenty years, the basic con-tent of negotiation teaching has stayed stable. It may be, however, that this is about to change. One major influence will be the set of conferences of which this publication is a part (see Honeyman and Coben, *Half-Way to a Second Generation*, in this volume). Another may be the impact of online teaching on the process of teaching itself.

Though we have tried to be clear in this chapter about the challenges inherent in online role-play teaching, we have also tried to be clear that for some purposes online is already also better than face-to-face. Now, we would like to describe some learning advantages of teaching role-plays online: coming soon to a computer near you.

The Record

Although audio and video equipment have long given students a chance to hear/see how they "really" perform, and to get around all the issues of working from memory, they have been awkward to use for focused teaching on skills. Online technology may develop to solve this problem.

An online role-play done via audio or video can be recorded by just pressing the buttons on the computer. The quality and reliability of the video is still variable, but there is little doubt that this technology will improve dramatically in the next five years. A role-play done via text, of course, automatically creates a transcript of both sides' participation, which can be archived, edited or exported, depending which text platform was employed.

There is, however, the question of how to use these records, whether video, audio or text. The old-fashioned way still has value: student (with his/her Other, with other students, with the teacher, with someone unfamiliar with the role-play, etc.) reviews the record and seeks out important insights. Those insights can come from the observer's own sense of what is important in the record, from the teacher's agenda of negotiation concepts (e.g., what reframing occurred and how effective was it?), or from a more generic set of foci (e.g., were there turning points? were there messages sent but not received?). These insights can then be shared with the class via the whiteboard or conversion to a PowerPoint slide.

Some computer technology has already been developed in order to help with this task. Video annotation software such as MediaNotes[7] allows the teacher to specify things to look for, and then allows the student to find those significant moments in the video and to enter comments in the margin (see Williams, Farmer, and Manwaring 2008). The student can send his/her notes to the teacher; the teacher can enter comments on the student's comments and send them back, etc. Indeed this approach allows teacher-student dialog about both the student's quality of analysis and the student's quality of negotiating performance. Though its payoffs are significant, MediaNotes can still be cumbersome to use.

As technology makes it easier to access moments and patterns in the records of the role-plays, questions will arise: What do we want students to focus on? What do we want to highlight? We do have a vocabulary for such effort (e.g., reframing, options) but these tend to focus on specific moments. There is of course great value in such focus, and the field of microteaching has been developed to exploit that. But this approach does not capture that part of the reality of negotiating that involves patterns of behavior, a gestalt, an attitude. How can the record be exploited to explore the creation, destruction, or repair of trust? To consider relationship building in general? If a core idea in our canon has to do with the interaction of collaboration and distribution, how can we use the record of a role-play to capture that interaction and how it is managed over time? Put another way, a strategy aimed at collaboration will at any given moment have to take into account the past and the future in deciding on the present: can a record be used to help students see how their behavior reflected, well or poorly, this continuum?

In the future, as software develops for measuring variables in human interactions, it might be possible to assess some of these notions. A "trust barometer" might serve to assess parties' comfort with taking risks on each other's reciprocal actions; a relationship thermometer might be able to score a party's attitude towards another and a "cooperation gauge" might measure collaboration. These tools might develop out of existing codings and instruments used in content analysis. In audio records, they may benefit from developments in assessing the psychological state of a speaker based on voice analysis. In video records, software for body language analysis might add yet another layer of meaning.[8] A technological generation down the line, integration software might be able to compare these three archives of meaning, decoding interactions at a very sophisticated level.

Asynchronicity

Students studying negotiation together at a distance are, in many cases, separated not only by distance but also by time. Many learning activities are structured so that students can access and engage in them at their own convenience – unencumbered by the need to be accessible and dedicated to the course at a specific time or place. This characteristic of asynchronicity is where much of the appeal, and promise, of distance education lies. But it certainly poses challenges to teachers used to classroom teaching. In traditional negotiation courses, perhaps the most "synchronous" activity, the one which is nearly impossible to "make up" by any alternative method is participating in role-plays (indeed, this serves as the justification for many negotiation teachers' strict class-attendance policies). Does this imply that in teaching at a distance, teachers need to find a method to replicate this synchronicity when conducting role-plays? Or – might there be value in asynchronicity?

In teaching at a distance, teachers can choose between various media, offering different degrees of synchronicity. A streaming video web-cast of two students simulating a negotiation, which the entire class must watch in real-time, might be the most synchronous method, whereas students engaging in a simulation through email exchange is a decidedly asynchronous method.

Classroom teachers of negotiation are familiar with the advantages of synchronous role-play. This tries to simulate the interpersonal interaction of a live negotiation: the multiple cues and clues;

the subtleties of personality; the impact of personality on process and relationship. Perhaps most important, it simulates the task of being able to respond immediately to the last thing the opponent said or did. It thus emphasizes quickness and spontaneity, and it gives a student a feel for his/her own personality when challenged by such immediacy. This immediacy is useful in that it gives a student an insight into him/herself and it gives practice in learning to be responsive quickly.

These elements of spontaneity and quickness are neutralized when the simulation is performed asynchronously. However, teachers might find new potential gains enabled by asynchronous role-play that have remained largely untapped in the traditional classroom role-play. Asynchronicity, inherent in many forms of communication through text (including email, forum posting, document exchange, etc.), gives the respondent an opportunity to think before responding. It separates the stare of the other from the time to consider the right response. And in doing so it can give a student the opportunity to reflect on what has been taught in class, absorbed from the readings (or perhaps do or re-do the readings), and to decide among various alternative moves. Indeed a teacher may exploit this interval between a student receiving an email and sending a response by requiring a journal submission describing the choices the student sees as available and the decision process he/she uses to select among them. The teacher may even respond to the student's journal, all before the student actually does respond to the other. Other students can also make suggestions on tactics, provide additional reading material, or just give moral support. This approach will privilege the cognitive process within the role-playing process. (For suggestions on using these methods and others in online fishbowl simulations, see Douglas and Johnson 2008; Douglas and Johnson 2009.)

A variation on this approach, already used by one of us (Ebner, with Bernie Mayer and Eileen Barker), is a form of microteaching (or of teaching micro-skills) in which the teacher provides the negotiating problem (in this case, reframing) in online text, and asks each student to reframe it. The student then provides a reframe to the teacher, who responds either with critique or rejoinder that provokes yet further reframing. This process can continue for several rounds. Supporting this teaching is a worksheet provided for the student with a checklist of desirable characteristics for a reframe. Similar processes can be conducted for the reflecting component of active listening, or for teaching the use of "I-messages."

The point of this section has been that teaching by asynchronicity has some advantages over teaching role-play live, and that this approach can help a student when he/she later has to negotiate face-to-face. An added benefit of incorporating asynchronicity in teaching is that it is highly transferrable to real-life situations in which negotiations are conducted asynchronously (e.g., email). Teaching asynchronously can thus simulate "real" negotiating by focusing on issues of pacing, messages inferred from pacing, messages one wants to send via pacing, etc.

Of course, one can incorporate asynchronous methods in face-to-face teaching – the method is not absolutely dependent on the online medium. However, asynchronous methods are usually not incorporated into negotiation courses, as they do not mesh naturally with the classroom flow; online teaching presents us with a natural environment in which to conduct such exercises.

Automated Negotiation Opposite

Another approach (which is not, strictly speaking, restricted to online teaching but which is especially suited to it) is the use of automated negotiation Others. By this we mean any application which simulates a human decision-maker, against which a student can negotiate (analogous to playing chess against a computer). The most impressive of these are done with Flash animation: each student is presented with a basic storyline (e.g., buying an antique clock), after which he/she sees an animation in which the other party speaks, presenting the student with an offer, asking a question, etc. The animation then cuts off, and the student is presented with several choices for his/her next move. After clicking one of these, the animation resumes, with the virtual Other responding to the student's move. The animation continues until another decision point, at which it cuts off again to give the student a chance to choose his/her next move. The negotiation progresses in that fashion. At different points in the animation, or at the end of the negotiation, the animation can advise the student on the wisdom of each move. The teaching core of this approach lies in the choices provided for the student, the subtlety of the differences among them, and the plausibility of the consequences following from each choice.[9] These animations might be based on general, everyday scenarios for teaching broad concepts, or serve as an easily-accessible interface with more complex concepts (such as those described by Jones 2009).

Of course, this approach can be used in a live classroom, with teachers asking students to respond to vignettes, and continuing to the next connected vignette based on a pre-constructed model.[10] However, whether done through text or through Flash animation, this exercise is particularly suited to the online environment, in which the student interacts with an artifact and not with live counterparts. Like a role-play, this exercise gives a student the chance to practice both negotiation analysis and decision making without the need to cope with the personality/relationship of the other.

Immersive Media

In addition to text, audio and video individually, the online venue offers technology that uses two or all three of these, and allows parties to feel as if they are actually in some "new" place together with their Other. Parties can be immersed in the sensation of being in a meeting with the Other, so much so that they forget they are at a distance at all.

Some corporate boardrooms provide for webconferencing that reaches this level of immersion. Some communication companies promote the use of holograms as a means of projecting not only audio and video, but also some form of physical presence, immersing parties in the sense of being in the same room with each other.

Though it will take a while before home webconferencing equipment reaches this level, an immersive negotiation experience can now be attained by interaction in virtual worlds, such as Second Life. Such "worlds" are really software platforms in which users – represented by on-screen bodies called "avatars" – interact with each other in a 3D environment. Participants can interact, explore, manipulate objects, buy and sell virtual or real-world goods and services and much more. When interacting with others, one can see their avatar's movements, hand motions and gestures, in addition to speaking with them vocally, and add text as well. This all gives a very powerful sense of being "in" the environment – the multiple-sensory illusion fools the brain into perceiving reality. Even the distractions the environment provides add to this sense – while speaking, one can look around, and see other interactions going on, observe people meeting and talking, or just look at the view. [11]

Negotiating in this environment, one gets a strong feeling of the social presence of the Other, making this experience, in many ways, a good replica of a face-to-face interaction. However, the opportunities provided by the platform go beyond this. Traditional classroom simulations rely on participants pretending that they are characters in a given scenario – even though everything else about the environment screams otherwise. In the end, it is always students, dressed as students, with equipment that students have, in a classroom of some sort, with a piece of paper in their hand, sitting down and talking. If those students are role-playing a car accident conflict scenario, where is the sound of the crash, the smoking vehicles, the flashing lights, the approaching sirens? In a negotiation between two executives on merging their companies, where is the corporate boardroom, the mahogany table or the pricey suits? In most role-play material, these environmental elements are left out; students are not even asked to imagine them. While we will leave the issue of "how real is too real" for other pieces (see Ebner and Efron 2005; Ebner and Kovach, *Simulation 2.0*, in this volume), clearly, creating a realistic environment will engage students' minds in the situation to a higher degree, leading to more natural responses and therefore, arguably, to higher levels of transferability. In the virtual world, one can have the students not only role-play a scenario; the scenario can be created around the students. With a click of the teacher's mouse, students role-playing executives can be clothed in fine apparel and have their hair cut to conform to the corporate style of the day. They will then enter an impressive boardroom, and sit on impressive leather seats around a heavy round table. If the teacher has a teaching assistant handy, he or she could enter (in avatar-form) and serve virtual coffee. With this level of immersion, interactions we are used to seeing in the classroom change noticeably. And, perhaps, topics now taught poorly in face-to-face role-plays, like trust and relationships, can take on levels of reality approaching those of real negotiations. (For more on the issue of authenticity in negotiation learning experiences, see Manwaring, McAdoo, and Cheldelin, *Orientation and Disorientation*, in this volume.)

Of course, there is a learning curve and a technology curve involved in getting students accustomed to interacting in a virtual world – and in getting the teacher accustomed to administering these interactions. However, as we found out, it is easier than one may think – and well worth the effort. (For one discussion of using a virtual world platform for negotiation simulations, see Miglino, Di Ferdinando, Rega, and Benincasa 2007; for another description of training in virtual worlds, see Hax 2009.)

Negotiation Support Systems

As the field of Online Dispute Resolution (ODR) expands, many interesting software applications are being developed to assist disputing parties. ODR service providers utilize a wide array of technological platforms, based on communication media ranging from simple, forum-type posting boards to real-time broadband video-conferencing. One way of categorizing these platforms (known as Negotiation Support Systems) is to break them down according to their primary function: some platforms are passive conveyers of information or messages; others are a more active participants in the process. This is a question of system choice and design. The first type includes platforms providing communication means ranging from simple message-exchange forms that provide fields for entering information, complaints and offers which will be conveyed to the other side, to dedicated forums or chat rooms in which parties can meet and exchange information and offers. The latter type are platforms designed to support not only communication but decision-making as well; such software aids parties in comparing offers, analyzing their preferences and making suggestions for optimal solutions (Rule 2002; Ponte and Cavenagh 2005; Koeszegi, Srnka, and Pesendorfer 2006; Ebner 2008).

In essence, these platforms are ready-made training-grounds for negotiation teachers wanting students to conduct role-pays online. As noted, they span the technologies we have surveyed in this chapter. Using them would certainly add a jolt of motivation into the course. Additionally, teachers would not have to invest much time in set up, as the platforms are designed specifically for this type of use. Finally, conducting simulations on such platforms allows students to learn negotiation as well as to expand their familiarity and experience with technological tools which may become regular features of the negotiation field in the future.

Teachers can make contact with service providers, asking for co-operation in running a series of simulations with their students in return for good publicity and perhaps feedback on users' experience with the platform. If not, perhaps a low-cost arrangement could be found. (For a description of how both types of platforms described above can be integrated into a course, see Koszegi and Kersten 2003).

Conclusion

Teaching negotiating role-plays online has obvious disadvantages and some surprising advantages. And predicting how technology will evolve is obviously not a secure pastime. But one bet is a good one: online teaching now, and in the foreseeable future, generally requires teachers to become more precise and more reflective about what they want to teach and what they want students to learn. That, we believe, is undeniably a good thing, and may well be the biggest impact of teaching role-plays, and anything else, online.

Notes

The authors wish to thank the negotiation teachers we interviewed, who shared not only their time and ideas but also their enthusiasm and support as this chapter developed. In addition, our thanks to Melissa Manwaring, whose comments on a draft of the chapter were – as always – extremely valuable and much appreciated.

[1] In a 2006 study of enrollment at universities in the United States conducted by the U.S. Dept. of Education, the university with the largest number of enrolled students was an online university (the University of Phoenix). At 150,000 students, this number was over triple the number of students enrolled at the university in second place on this list (U.S. Dept. of Education 2006). Only three years later, this figure has itself tripled, and the same university is closing in on half a million students at the time of writing (Stern 2009). In addition, ninety-six percent of the largest academic institutions in the United States offer, at least, individual online courses (Sloan 2006). Though it is not easy to be precise, the annual rate of growth

in this area is about twenty to thirty percent. With online education con-tinuing to expand despite the financial crash of 2008, and with the Obama administration considering dedicating hundreds of millions of dollars to fund online course creation at the college level, there is no reason to expect this explosive growth trend to end anytime soon (Sloan 2006; Stearn 2009).

[2] In this chapter, we use the terms "simulation" and "role-play" as generic references to experiential-learning-type activities commonly labeled "simu-lations," "games," "simulation-games," and "role-play." We use the term "role-players" or "participants" to denote participants in an activity who operate in simulated environments based on information and instructions they are given. In the literature on simulation-gaming, there is much dis-cussion of the delineation between different types of activities (such as "role-play," "simulations," and "games"), the way they are conducted and the pedagogical implications of each one. Our somewhat irreverent inter-changing of the terms is not intended to influence the debate on the way these activities are viewed or conducted, or to detract from the importance of refining understanding regarding each individual type. For in-depth dis-cussions of this issue, see Greenblat (1981), Crookall, Oxford, and Saunders (1987) and Ellington, Fowlie, and Gordon (1998).

[3] Some faculty teach role-play fully online; some teach part of it online and part of it live. We have organized this chapter so a teacher can identify tools to be used in any combination he/she wishes.

[4] For more on the value of relationship building in the specific context of text-based negotiation, see Ebner et al. 2009. For more on the relational elements of teaching negotiation online, see Bhappu et al. 2009.

[5] In negotiation, when we discuss relationship we often mean trust. And when we say trust we mean one or more of three things. We mean: 1) that the opposite will tell us the truth; 2) that if we share information, strategi-cally or unintentionally, the opposite will not use that sharing to damage or exploit us; or 3) that if we make a deal, the opposite will comply with it.

At first glance face-to-face negotiating would provide the advantage that one can watch the opposite and draw inferences from body language, tone of voice, etc., but this is questionable: students as role-players are not very good actors when it comes to conveying emotions and personality, so the cues we pick up from them may well be misleading. Moreover, as one goal of role-playing for students is to try new approaches to negotiating, the opposite may well be testing out his/her capacity to lie or puff. The other bases from which we create our willingness to trust (reputation, incre-mental concessions) are not necessarily different in a face-to-face setting than they are in a text setting. Thus a student may draw a more reliable judgment about trust from text-based negotiating because he/she is less likely to be misled by false clues. Overall, however, though building or act-ing on trust (in one or more of its forms) can be absolutely essential to ef-fective negotiating, it is probably the most difficult aspect to teach. By, in effect, removing trust from focus in a role-play we are presenting an artifi-cial picture of negotiating, one manufactured for teaching purposes.

[6] For a good discussion of the value of accurate role-play data, see Peppet 2002.

[7] For more on this software, see http://w.cali.org/medianotes/features (last accessed May 18, 2010).

[8] For one example of the inroads being made in this area, see this report on work done by researchers at the Department of Artificial Intelligence of the Universidad Politécnica de Madrid's School of Computing and Madrid's Universidad Rey Juan Carlos, who have developed an algorithm that is capable of processing video and recognize – and categorize – their facial expressions in real time. http://www.sciencedaily.com/releases/2008/02/080223125318.htm (last accessed May 18, 2010).

[9] See http://www.sfhgroup.com/ca/training/online-training/online-negotiation-course.php for a description and sample of how this works as produced by the Stitt Feld Handy Group of Toronto.

[10] This might also be done in book form, styled similarly to the Choose Your Own Adventure™ series, and assigned to students for out-of-class work. Another mode of low-tech engagement with a scenario can be found on the BeyondIntractability.org website at http://www.beyondintractability.org/action/essays.jsp?nid=5124 (last accessed May 19, 2010).

[11] We are referring to virtual worlds in which people participate, via their on-screen avatars, in interactions including, *inter alia,* casual conversation, commerce and education. Other virtual worlds have central themes such as worlds that are in essence a platform for a MMPORG (a Massively-Multiplayer Online Roleplaying Game) and are less suitable for online teaching; however, there is a lot to be learned in them. Many of the most popular of these, such as World of Warcraft, though focused on raiding and competition with anonymous strangers around the world, also require an emphasis on team building and maintenance. One program (Heavy Rain), brand new at the time of this writing, though not focused on negotiation at all, suggests how – with enough money – one could make a very powerful interactive negotiation simulation. See http://www.heavyrainps3.com/#/en_US/home for their website demonstration. The authors of this note were unable to test this program themselves as all their younger relatives are of the Wii persuasion and Heavy Rain communes at the altar of PlayStation 3.

References

Bender, T. 2005. Role-playing in online education: A teaching tool to enhance student engagement and sustained learning. *Innovate* 1(4). Available at http://innovateonline.info/pdf/vol1_issue4/Role_Playing_in_Online_Education:A_Teaching_Tool_to_Enhance_Student_Engagement_and_Sustained_Learning.pdf (last accessed May 19, 2010).

Bhappu, A., N. Ebner, S. Kaufman, and N. Welsh. 2009. The strategic use of online communication technology to facilitate relational development in executive training courses on negotiation. In *Rethinking negotiation teaching: Innovations for context and culture*, edited by C. Honeyman, J. Coben, and G. De Palo. St. Paul, MN: DRI Press.

Crookall, D., R. Oxford, and D. Saunders. 1987. Towards a reconceptualization of simulation: From representation to reality. *Simulation/Games for Learning* 17(4): 147-170.

Douglas, K and B. Johnson. 2008. The online mediation fishbowl: Learning about gender and power in mediation. *Journal of the Australasian Law Teachers Association* 1: 95-109.

Douglas, K. and B. Johnson. 2009. On-line role plays as authentic assessment: Five models to teach professional interventions. *Proceedings of the ATN assessment conference*, edited by J. Milton, C. Hall, J. Lang, G. Allan and M. Nomikoudis. Melbourne, Australia: RMIT University Learning and Teaching Unit.

Drolet, A. and M. W. Morris. 2000. Rapport in conflict resolution: Accounting for how nonverbal exchange fosters communication on mutually beneficial settlements to mixed motive conflicts. *Journal of Experimental Social Psychology* 36(1): 26-50.

Ebner, N. 2008. Online dispute resolution: Applications for e-HRM. In *Encyclopedia of Human Resources Information Systems: Challenges in e-HRM*, edited by T. Torres-Coronas and M. Arias-Oliva. Hershey, PA: Idea Group Reference Publishing.

Ebner, N., A. Bhappu, J. G. Brown, K. K. Kovach, and A. K. Schneider. 2009. You've got agreement: Negoti@ing via email. In *Rethinking negotiation teaching: Innovations for context and culture*, edited by C. Honeyman, J. Coben, and G. De Palo. St. Paul, MN: DRI Press.

Ellington, H., J. Fowlie, and M. Gordon. 1998. *Using games and simulations in the classroom*. London: Routledge.

Greenblat, C. S. 1981. Gaming simulations for teaching and training: An overview. In *Principles and practices of gaming-simulation*, edited by C. S. Greenblat and R. D. Duke. Beverly Hills: Sage.

Hax, M. 2009. Negotiation training in Second Life. *CNN iReport* [updated November 12, 2009]. Available at http://www.ireport.com/docs/DOC-356373 (last accessed May 19, 2010).

Holmberg, B. 2005. The evolution, principles and practices of distance education. In *Studies and reports from the Center for Distance Learning Research at the Carl von Ossietzky University of Oldenburg*, edited by U. Bernath, F. W. Busch, D. Garz, A. Hanft, T. Hülsmann, B. Moschner, W. D. Scholz, and O. Zawaki-Richter. Oldenburg, Germany: BIS-Verlag, Carl von Ossietzky University of Oldenburg. Available at: http://www.mde.uni-oldenburg.de/download/asfvolume11eBook.pdf (last accessed May 19, 2010).

Jones, G. T. 2009. Designing heuristics: Hybrid computational models for teaching the negotiation of complex contracts. In *Rethinking negotiation teaching: Innovations for context and culture*, edited by C. Honeyman, J. Coben, and G. De Palo. St. Paul, MN: DRI Press.

Kersten, G. E., S. T. Koszegi, and R. Vetschera. 2002. The effects of culture in computer-mediated negotiations. *Working Paper*: School of Business, Economics, and Computer Science, University of Vienna. Available at http://zsu-schmelz.univie.ac.at/fileadmin/user_upload/orga/working_papers/ OP2002-08.pdf (last accessed May 19, 2010).

Koeszegi, S. T. and G. E. Kersten. 2003. On-line/off-line: Joint negotiation teaching in Montreal and Vienna. *Group Decision and Negotiation* 12(4): 337-345.

Koeszegi, S. T., K. J. Srnka, and E. M. Pesendorfer. 2006. Electronic negotiations: A comparison of different support systems. *The Business* 66(4): 441-463.

McKersie, R. B. and N. O. Fonstad. 1997. Teaching negotiation theory and skills over the internet. *Negotiation Journal* 13(4): 363-368.

Miglino, O., A. Di Ferdinando, A. Rega, and B. Benincasa. 2007. SISINE: Teaching negotiation through a multiplayer online role playing game. In *Proceedings of the 6th European Conference on e-Learning*. Reading, UK: Academic Conferences Limited.

Peppet, S. 2002. Teaching negotiation using web-based streaming video. *Negotiation Journal* 18(3): 271-283.

Ponte, L. and T. Cavenagh. 2005. *Cyberjustice: Online dispute resolution (ODR) for e-commerce*. New Jersey: Prentice Hall.

Raiffa, H. 1982. *The art and science of negotiation*. Cambridge, MA: Harvard University Press.

Rule. C. 2002. *Online dispute resolution for business: B2B, e-commerce, consumer, employment, insurance, and other commercial conflicts*. San Francisco: Jossey-Bass.

Tannen, D. 1986. *That's not what I meant: How conversational style makes or breaks relationships*. New York: Random House.

Williams, G. R., L. C. Farmer, and M. Manwaring. 2008. New technology meets an old teaching challenge: Using digital video recordings, annotation software, and deliberate practice techniques to improve student negotiation skills. *Negotiation Journal* 24(1): 71-87.

‹∞ 18 ∞›

What Travels: Teaching Gender in Cross-Cultural Negotiation Classrooms

Andrea Kupfer Schneider, Sandra Cheldelin & Deborah Kolb [*]

Editors' Note: *Our cross-disciplinary team tackles the inconsistencies of gender teaching as seen from the perspective of law, business, and peace studies negotiation courses. In the process, they reconsider gender in the context of culture, demanding a forthright and coherent approach to topics now too often cut up into little boxes of "content."*

"I am not hindered by my gender; I use it to my advantage – being cute, young and naïve – to get better deals for my clients." (Israeli lawyer)

"The likeability-competence stereotype doesn't fit the Turkish experience – the choice of competence is not one women can even consider – all leadership positions are held by men." (Turkish psychologist)

"How do we help our students? In one class of all women, the professor failed half the class." (Turkish academic)

[*] **Andrea Kupfer Schneider** is a professor of law at Marquette University Law School in Milwaukee, Wisconsin. Her email address is andrea.schneider @marquette.edu. **Sandra I. Cheldelin** is the Vernon M. and Minnie I. Lynch professor at the Institute for Conflict Analysis and Resolution at George Mason University in Arlington, Virginia. Her email address is scheldel@gmu.edu. **Deborah Kolb** is the Deloitte Ellen Gabriel professor for women and leadership at the Simmons College School of Management in Boston, Massachusetts. Her email address is kolb@simmons.edu.

Introduction

The comments above were typical of the responses we received following our presentation on gender made at the Rethinking Negotiation Teaching conference held October 2009 in Istanbul, Turkey. Reflecting some of the current work on gender and negotiation, our presentation focused on the most recent findings on the stereotype content model, and the relationship between this model and gender issues in negotiation (Cuddy et al. 2009; Bowles, Babcock, and Lai 2007). Using examples from the 2008 U.S. presidential elections and research on law students, we focused on the "likeability" vs. "competence" dichotomy that women have faced in negotiations, particularly those concerning compensation (Bowles, Babcock, and Lai 2007; Wade 2001; Stuhlmacher and Waters 1999). We illustrated how the dichotomy is operative for women in certain situations (the U.S. presidential elections and the portrayal of Hillary Clinton and Sarah Palin) and not in others (particularly in certain professions, e.g., lawyers, and under certain conditions) (Tinsley et al. 2009; Schneider et al. 2010).

We were simultaneously intrigued and surprised at some of the responses from colleagues, especially of other cultures, to our presentation on gendered perceptions of likeability and competence in negotiations. We surmise that we must include factors that we had not previously considered, such as religion, family, power, voice and position; even when working within the likeability v. competence dichotomy, how these factors and culture affect behavior is an increasingly evident question. In retrospect, we are not shocked at the responses because our previous international experiences have repeatedly demonstrated that trainings applicable to an audience in the United States are often not fully appropriate in other countries (Honeyman and Cheldelin 2002). Still, for some attendees, the dichotomy resonated. There were similar examples of this dichotomy evident within their own cultures (Israeli presidential elections) and similar professional contexts (lawyers in Spain). Others, however, argue that the dichotomy cannot be found at all – that it already assumes a certain gendered order in which women could be seen as professionally competent and in which working women have certain legal rights, backed by societal acceptance. Moreover, in many countries, the concept of a woman's "Best Alternative to a Negotiated Agreement" (BATNA) is irrelevant when the conditions under which women find themselves are not at all negotiable. In Ethiopia, a group of women reported they had already attained the best scientific jobs available to them (and that they considered themselves lucky in that accomplishment) so there was nothing left to negotiate. In the post-conflict environments of Bosnia and Liberia, women consider themselves extraordinarily fortunate if they are able to obtain employment at all. To these women, talking about negotiating salary or benefits seems irrelevant.

As we reflect on this feedback and consider the most current research on gender, especially negotiated order, a number of questions arise. Women are subject to more negotiations than men in the United States (Kolb and McGinn 2009), and this fact is also true in other societies. In the United States, our tendencies are to look at gender *differences* – even stereotypes – in negotiation, but what contributions or dimensions can other societies offer to our analysis of gender and negotiations? As an example, we know *identity* matters and is salient to negotiation. In the United States, we have a relatively narrow view of gender (does being female result in different treatment?) and yet there are multiple dimensions of *identity*, including family, religion, and class, which are rarely considered in the United States. Our colleagues from other cultures spoke of the important differences regarding their roles within their families, their religion, and their culture – these are all present within the negotiation context. What are the cues of salient identity aspects or shifts that can help us understand their impact during negotiations?

In reconsidering how we teach and talk about gender, we draw on different theoretical and empirical perspectives that, generally, have not been a part of the discourse on gender and negotiation as it has taken place in the Western academy. We focus on three approaches – the organizational, cultural, and individual – to frame how gender can impact negotiations (Risman 2004; Deaux and Major 1990; Kolb 2009):

1) Organizational or institutionalized expectations and assumptions create the negotiated order within which negotiation occurs. These expectations and assumptions reflect power differentials and position negotiators differently (Kolb and McGinn 2009).

2) Social and cultural expectations activate status-based stereotypes based on different dimensions of identity. These expectations affect the range of individual actions in the context of negotiated interactions (Ridgeway and Correll 2004).

3) Individuals have choices in the roles they take up in a negotiation and these roles are quite fluid and variable, reflecting the *intersectionality* of gender with other dimensions of identity (McCall 2005).

Based on these frameworks, we suggest how these three approaches might be incorporated into a pedagogy that can travel outside of the United States.

Second Generation Gender Issues, Social Roles, and the Negotiated Order

One perspective, when considering how gender (in all its complexity) plays out in negotiations, includes consideration of the institutional factors, or negotiated orders, which shape negotiated interactions. From this perspective, institutions and organizations are not locations where gender differences occur, but rather the sites where gendering occurs. Two theoretical perspectives are relevant to understanding the role negotiated orders play in setting the context for negotiation. The first perspective is a role theory that focuses on gendered role expectations based on the distribution of men and women into different social roles both in society generally, and in organizations and professions (Eagly 1987). The second perspective is based on a consideration of *second generation gender issues* – a particularly relevant consideration as we move the pedagogy of teaching gender and negotiation forward. Second generation gender issues appear neutral and natural on their face, but they result in different experiences for, and treatment of, women and men (Tinsley et al. 2009; Sturm 2001; Acker 1990). As distinct from first generation discrimination involving intentional acts of bias, second generation gender practices appear unbiased in isolation, but they reflect masculine values and the life situations of men who have dominated the public domain of work (Flax 1990; Fletcher 1999). As a result, the negotiated order of most organizations privileges masculine and discounts feminine practices and assumptions.

Social roles can position men and women differently in the home, in the workplace, and often in the community – an implication for how they fare in negotiations. Disproportionately, women in most cultures have larger responsibilities in the family than their partners, and in some cultures, that responsibility has been labeled the *second shift* (Hochschild and Machung 1997). A recent group of studies has considered these social roles – in particular, how pregnancy, birth, maternity leave, and work schedules position a mother differentially than those women who are not mothers (Dau-Schmidt et al. 2009; Correll, Benard, and Paik 2007; Roth 2006). In Western cultures, mothers are routinely offered less desirable assignments and lower compensation than women without children (Stanford 2009). For example, in the 2004 U.S. Federal Circuit Court case *Lust v. Sealy*,[1] the plaintiff, a woman, was not considered for a promotion solely because the promotion entailed moving her family, which included her two small children, from Madison, Wisconsin to Chicago, Illinois. Mothering roles in other societies may be even more prominent, making it a challenge to negotiate at work and in the community (Al-Dabbagh 2008).

Social roles are translated into a sex-based division of labor, prominent in most industrial societies. Labor market structure often pushes men and women into different industries and occupations – with different pay structures. Within organizations, sex segregation can position women in staff roles and men in supervisory positions; different groups may find themselves at the bottom of the organization structure with little opportunity for advancement (Reskin and Roos 1987). These patterns apply to leadership roles as well, where there is an incongruity between gender role behaviors and the definition of leadership (Eagly and Johannesen-Schmidt 2001). Consequently, opportunities for leadership are less likely to be offered to women and, when offered and accepted, women may be less likely to achieve success in those leadership roles. These effects are even more pronounced for African American women whose legitimacy is more likely to be challenged (Bell and Nkomo 2001).

The study of second generation gender issues unearths challenges to gender in workplace practices. Building from social roles, Joan Acker (1992) suggests that there are four processes that render organizations gendered, positioning men and women differently when they negotiate. They are: 1) structural gender divisions that subordinate women; as well as 2) organizational symbols that justify these divisions; 3) interactions that often reproduce them; and 4) the organizational members' "mental work" that constructs and maintains an appropriate, gendered organizational persona. Together, these processes serve to render organizations "masculine," consequently disadvantaging those persons who do not fit the ideal of masculinity – women, and certain groups of men.

This gendering of organizations position negotiators differently. Jobs and opportunities are gendered in the sense that certain people are seen to "fit" a job and others are not. These issues of "fit" are often complicated by race, class, and ethnicity. Issues of "fit" apply to workers in a wide variety of professions – from shop floor supervisors to prison guards to Wall Street bankers to lawyers (Pierce 1995; Wilkins and Galuti 1999; Britton 2000; Roth 2006; Skuratowicz and Hunter 2007). Negotiated orders define what constitutes work and how it gets valued. Joyce Fletcher (1999) described the unrecognized work of women engineers who try to anticipate problems before they happen, seek to integrate the work of others, and try to build a team (see Mumby and Putnam 1992). These examples, found within contexts in which masculine approaches to work tend to be highly valued and feminine approaches to work underrated (Valian 1998), suggest that claiming the value of one's work so that it is recognized and rewarded is part of the gendering of negotiation because it occurs in a variety of workplaces (Martin 1994; Ashcraft 1999). But recognizing this unseen, unvalued work can shift the traditional notions of how jobs and roles are defined (Fletcher 1999). Furthermore, when women seek to succeed by adhering to the masculine ideal, they will suffer backlash because of their refusal to adhere to the feminine stereotype. In the U.S. Supreme Court case *Price Waterhouse v. Hopkins*, Deborah Hopkins was denied partnership and told that she needed to wear more makeup and attend "charm school."[2] In the pending U.S. Federal District Court case *Kirleis v. Dickie, McCamey & Chilcote,*[3] law firm partner Alyson Kirleis was told that she worked too hard and should be home more with her two children (Schneider et al. 2010).

Status, Hierarchy, Power and Privilege

A second perspective by which to examine gender is to attach gender to status and hierarchy. Negotiations occur in institutional contexts that position negotiators differentially. Cecilia Ridgeway's work on status construction theory (e.g., Ridgeway and Erikson 2000) provides evidence of how widely held beliefs about the assumed rightful status of members of any identity group spread through interaction. Existing structural conditions within organizations and society reflect a status ordering that places some groups higher than others. This creates a self-reinforcing system that attaches status and provides advantage to individuals because of their group identity. This also explains the backlash when women attempt to move into new professions – e.g., witness women in the U.S. presidential campaign.

When gender status beliefs are operative in interactions, they manifest men's status value as superior and more competent than women. According to Ridgeway (2001), gender status beliefs have three implications for inequality, particularly in employment. First, they create expectations that men will be more competent than women. These expectations can become self-fulfilling prophecies that affect assertiveness and confidence in negotiation, both of which are necessary for effectiveness (Schneider 2002). Second, gender status beliefs can position men over equivalent women, as more deserving of benefits and rewards. Finally, those who are advantaged by gender status beliefs are less likely to attend to information that might challenge that belief. These status beliefs can be quite difficult to dislodge, often requiring multiple rounds of disconfirming evidence. This clearly has implications for how negotiators are positioned to negotiate.

Gender, Identity, and Intersectionality

In the popular view, gender is an individual characteristic. Gender is reflected in who people are, how they behave, and how they see themselves (Wharton 2005). This perspective is embodied in sex difference research, where the issue of differences between all men and all women overwhelms the study of intra-group differences. Embedded in this field of work is the notion that one's gender is an essential and stable attribute of the individual and that the "master" category of gender represents the experience of most men and women (Shields 2008).

Feminists have argued that rather than being an essential property of the self, the degree to which a negotiator takes up a gendered role and how that role is expressed is likely to be fluid and fragmented and differentially assumed (Deaux and Major 1990; Ely and Padavic 2007). Individuals have multiple, intersecting, identity memberships that can lead to qualitatively different meanings and experiences that enable (and constrain) their actions within a negotiation. Typically, these dimensions include physical markers such as sex, race, age, and ethnicity, and personal identity markers such as social class, religion, sexual orientation, and social roles in the family, community, and at work.

The intersectionality of gender builds on both gendered order and positioning theory. From our perspective, gender status beliefs need to be elaborated beyond just men and women to consider what happens at the intersection of gender with other aspects of identity. Robin Ely and Irene Padavic (2007) suggest that working class masculinity (brawn) is contrasted to upper class masculinity (brains) and with femininity. Raewyn Connell (2002) describes "subordinated masculinity" as one too closely identified with femininity. Similarly, Ely and Padavic (2007) suggest that stereotypes about women of Asian descent as extremely feminine, for example, place them far from masculine images of success– which center on assertiveness and self-confidence – and therefore disadvantages their career prospects. The process differs for women of color, particularly African American women. When they act competently, assertively, and with self-confidence, they often are perceived as controlling, manipulative, and aggressive (Bell and Nkomo 2001; Collins 2004). These stereotypes can limit their success. Indeed, research suggests that different stereotypes are evoked when gender and race are considered together than when they are considered separately; when we invoke the stereotype of woman, it is white women who are likely to be overrepresented (Warner 2008).

A major challenge for the feminist perspective expressed above is that although intersectionality conceptually makes sense, it is complex both to study, and to implement in practice (Warner 2008; McCall 2005). The reason for this complexity is that one can find herself making a long list of categories – e.g., she is a white, married, middle class, Christian woman – and then whom do we compare her to – e.g., a white, married, middle class Christian man, or an African American, married, middle class Christian woman, or do we start to change categories of class, sexual orientation, religion, and so on? Because men and women vary on so many dimensions – race, social class, religious beliefs, age, abilities, cultural background – it is important to be clear about which categories of identity are of interest. Some identities matter most of the time while others become more crucial in particular historical moments or contexts (Warner 2008). The former have been called "master" categories, while others might be more emergent (McCall 2005).

More recently, Joan Acker (1992) has expanded her view of gendered organizations to explicitly include intersectionality. She makes this expansion by focusing on what she calls "inequality regimes" (Acker 1992: 565-569). These are defined as the interlocked practices and processes that result in continuing inequalities along the lines of class, race, gender, sexuality, religion, and physical disability, among others, as they play out in work organizations. Case-based examples demonstrate the ways these inequality regimes work in practice and the possibilities for changing them. Telling new stories and making alternative narratives visible can be an intervention for changing dominant organizational discourses (Kolb et al. 2002; Ely and Meyerson 2000).

Teaching Gender in a Cross-Cultural Negotiation Classroom

Since organizations more and more reflect a global community with multi-cultural constraints, we need to prepare ourselves and our students better to be culturally sensitive to gender-based issues in negotiations. We offer a few suggestions framed within various contexts considering how gendered issues play out in negotiations: social roles, negotiated order, status, hierarchy, power and privilege, identity and their intersectionality.

We know that second generation gender issues may, on the surface, appear gender neutral, yet there are distinctly different experiences for women and men; although intentional bias is not so much the focus (as in first generation issues), masculine values dominate the public domain of work. When gender status beliefs are operative, they reflect men's status as superior and more competent than women. The implications for inequality are critical – men are perceived as more competent and more deserving of rewards (and therefore less likely to relinquish this status). Creating case-based examples to demonstrate the "inequality regimes" in work practices will highlight the students' understanding of the implications of these regimes when trying to negotiate change.

We suggest two cases. The first, *Marisol's Mandate,* was developed by Fleur Weigert (2000) under Deborah Kolb's supervision. Marisol is a director of programs for an agricultural research and development organization and is responsible for managing several of the agency's international portfolios. She is dealing with a struggling seed dissemination initiative in Peru, working in collaboration with a local partner and her organization's regionally-based representative, both of whom are men. In the process of working on the problems she is surprised to find herself sidelined and bypassed. The dynamics reflect gender, power and conflict avoidance issues. The *Marisol* case can lead to an interesting class discussion and might conclude by having students consider alternative strategies to the gender-status dilemma. In addition, ask students to consider the same case but have Marisol as a man (and therefore, too, working with all men). In what ways would the issues be different? Or, what if Marisol's local partner was a woman? Would that difference likely change the dynamics and if so, in what ways and why?

The second case, *Allison's Arrangement,* was developed by Deborah Kolb (2001). Allison is a senior research scientist working at an international center with its home base in Europe. Her husband works in North Africa and she is now pregnant. She wants to arrange a long-distance telecommuting schedule (from North Africa), but finds the workplace has no work and family policy, and that her boss is reluctant to agree to her proposal. Allison's case has leading questions for students, and forces them to consider what one does to prepare for negotiating under these conditions – how to get her boss to take her seriously – and to develop proposals that would meet the parties' needs. The case could be modified to focus on gender and culture by placing Allison in different places around the world – in Africa or South America or Asia, etc. – and see how students would view the case. Like the modification of the *Marisol* case, what if Allison was a male Ali – how would the students respond differently? Would Ali face even more backlash for following his spouse?

Teaching Gender Status, Hierarchy, Power and Privilege

Most faculty teaching negotiation are familiar with power-based simulations such as *StarPower*[4] (Shirts 1969) that offer students ways to progress through various levels of society by acquiring wealth. Ultimately, those with the most resources are able to make the rules for the entire group; usually, those with fewer resources experience resentment and frustration. Most of the power-based simulations work; gender can be superimposed on the same games where women have limited abilities/access to wealth.

To begin a discussion on gendered issues related to status, hierarchy, power and privilege, ask students to consider the possibility that they will awaken tomorrow as a person of the opposite sex. What would be different in their daily lives, and why? After they articulate these likely differences, focus the discussion on issues of power and privilege.

Though more complicated, we encourage replicating or creating variations on the experiments by Catherine Tinsley and her colleagues (2009) that demonstrated ways women and men are treated differently based on the likeability vs. competence dimension. Tinsley put together a series of videos manipulating the behavior of a director (alternatively male and female) to two situations: a work-related technology crash and a family-related sick child problem. The director either stayed at work to deal with the information technology crisis or went home to care for the child. The students then rated the director on questions related to likeability and competence. Female directors were rated more competent if they stayed at work, but less likeable, and were rated less competent if they chose to go home, but more likeable. The ratings for the male directors were consistent: they were always judged competent and likeable regardless of staying at work or going home.

Similarly, a teacher could divide the class into four groups, have them read a similar scenario and instruct the class to rate the director on likeability v. competence. These types of simulations and experiments, where students see ways their own ratings are influenced by gender, enrich the discussion that should follow. Guide student reflection by asking them such pertinent questions as: how did it feel to be able to make the rules for the entire group? What were the reactions of the others? What would you do to negotiate on behalf of those persons who are less powerful?

Teaching the Intersectionality of Gender With Other Aspects of Identity

There are a number of ways educators and scholars can teach how gender intersects with identity. Scholars have captured the complexity of intersectionality by focusing on individual narratives and stories. As Aida Hurtado has suggested, when different groups of women, in her case, Latina, tell their stories, they can shift from one group's perception of social reality to another, and at times, are able simultaneously to perceive multiple social realities without losing their sense of self-coherence (Hurtado 1989). These stories can bring to light alternative accounts and perspectives that might not otherwise be obvious. Individual stories shift experiences from that of a "generalized other" to a "concrete other," enabling people to connect in ways more abstract accounts do not (Benhabib 1992; Cobb 2000). If a class is sufficiently diverse, ask students in small groups to tell their stories about experiences that reflect this intersectionality of gender and identity. If the class is not diverse, case studies can capture intersectionality, particularly if they reveal different perspectives on the same phenomenon. In this way, comparisons among groups can be made.

Another approach is to use cultural scripts around certain social phenomena of interest (Holvino 2009). For example, one can consider a factor like "being emotional" and consider its meanings for different groups – white women (upset), black men (hostile), Asian women (reserved) (Warner 2008). These approaches, in capturing the simultaneity of different identities, help us appreciate their dynamic character. Identities are not static; instead, they are repeatedly negotiated as people take action. Each of these ways of approaching intersectionality has implications for teaching about the "who" in negotiation.

At the Istanbul conference, we engaged in several experiential activities. Divided into small teams with diverse membership – by gender, nationality, religion – we were given assignments to conduct a negotiation in the spice market, to purchase something for the group's afternoon snack, to capture an image on camera that reflected something dangerous, and to capture an image that reflected the intersection of the sacred and the secular. These activities – called *Adventure Learning* – worked because the subsequent debriefing provoked a number of responses that ultimately led to writing about various topics pertinent to second generation teaching. With greater intentionality regarding the conference assignment, these activities can become gender-based learning. For example, in what ways does the spice market, though public, reflect the underlying task of women purchasing food for the family (private domain)? Are women just as capable or successful in their negotiations as men at the market? Do cross-cultural partnerships (Turkish and American women) make a difference, and in what ways? Do men and women translate "danger" in different ways? What about differences in the meaning of sacred and secular? Add dimensions of religion, ethnicity and race with gender. What happens? Though spice markets are not so available in most of our cities, there are farmers' markets, flea markets, hotel chains, restaurants, etc., where students could experiment with these complexities as they conduct negotiations in the field. (For a "post-Istanbul" experiment, see Manwaring,

McAdoo, and Cheldelin, *Orientation and Disorientation*, in this volume.)

Cases and experiments allow students to speculate on ways negotiations can address these gendered complexities, domestically and cross-culturally. Telling the stories and articulating the narratives of actors across different axes of power and identity practices is an important intervention for changing dominant organizational discourses. The process of story-telling brings to light alternative narratives that seldom find their way into mainstream accounts and organizational mythologies (Calás and Smircich 1999; Ely and Meyerson 2000).

Faculty should encourage students to think broadly about ways negotiation is changing (second generation). For example, returning to the situation in Turkey where a male faculty member failed half of his all-women class, what could the female students have done? If half of an all-male class had failed, what would the male students have done? Are the same options available to women? (Schneider 1994) Why or why not? Perhaps the students should enlist allies, seek assistance from a third party, or advocacy group – for example, by enlisting the parents of the female students. This kind of discussion can also lead to considering ways to avoid backlash (advocating on behalf of a group rather than individual cases, or seeking assistance from a third party or advocacy group) and being more effective in that particular gendered order (Tinsley et al. 2009).

Conclusion

Our intention with this article is to articulate ways to move away from the dominant approach of teaching gender (first generation) – often viewed as "fixing women" or dealing with stereotypes – to providing a smorgasbord of approaches that faculty can use to raise gender issues as they travel around the world (second generation). We have presented three different models – gendered orders, power and hierarchy, and intersectionality – with the hope that faculty will be able to raise with their students a variety of issues around gender that both women and men must address within different cultures, and to provide a richer context for gender (along with culture, religion, ethnicity, and education) as it plays out in negotiations.

Notes

[1] *Lust v. Sealy*, 383 F.3d 580, 583 (7th Cir. 2004).
[2] *Price Waterhouse v. Hopkins*, 490 U.S. 228 (1989).
[3] *Kirleis v. Dickie, McCamey & Chilcote*, 560 F.3d 156 (2009).
[4] Available for purchase through Simulation Training Systems, http://www.stsintl.com/ (last accessed June 20, 2010).

References

Acker, J. 1990. Hierarchies, jobs, bodies: A theory of gendered organizations. *Gender and Society* 4(2): 139-158.

Acker, J. 1992. From sex roles to gendered institutions. *Contemporary Sociology* 23(5): 565-569.

Al-Dabbagh, M. 2008. The context for intergroup leadership among women's groups in Saudi Arabia. *Working Paper Series*. Dubai, UAE: Dubai School of Government.

Ashcraft, K. L. 1999. Managing maternity leave: A qualitative analysis of temporary executive succession. *Administrative Science Quarterly* 44 (2): 240-280.

Bell, E. L. J. and S. M. Nkomo. 2001. *Our separate ways: Black and white women and the struggle for professional identity*. Boston, MA: Harvard Business School Press.

Benhabib, S. 1992. *Situating the self: Gender, community and postmodernism in contemporary ethics*. New York: Routledge.

Borzak, L. (ed.) 1971. *Field study: A source book for experiential learning*. Beverly Hills: Sage.

Bowles, H. R., L. C. Babcock, and L. Lai. 2007. Social incentives for gender differences in the propensity to initiate negotiations: Sometimes it does hurt to ask. *Organizational Behavior and Human Decision Processes* 103(1): 84-103.

Britton, D. M. 2000. The epistemology of the gendered organization. *Gender and Society* 14(3): 418-434.

Calás, M. B. and L. Smircich. 2009. Feminist perspectives on gender in organizational research: What is and is yet to be. In *Handbook of Organizational Research Methods*, edited by D. Buchanan and A. Bryman. London: Sage.

Cobb, S. 2000. Imagine co-existence: Narratives from fieldwork in Rwanda. *CGO Learning Seminar*. Boston: Center for Gender in Organizations, Simmons School of Management.

Collins, P.H. 2004. *Black sexual politics: African Americans, gender, and the new racism*. New York: Routledge.

Connell, R. W. 2002. *Gender*. Malden, MA: Blackwell Publishers.

Correll, S. J., S. Benard, and I. Paik. 2007. Getting a job: Is there a motherhood penalty? *American Journal of Sociology* 112(5): 1297-1338.

Cuddy, A. J. C., S. T. Fiske, V. S. Y. Kwan, P. Glick, S. Demoulin, J. Ph. Leyens, and M. H. Bond. 2009. Stereotype content model across cultures: Universal similarities and some differences. *British Journal of Social Psychology* 48(1): 1-33. Available at http://www.people.hbs.edu/acuddy/2009,%20cuddy%20et%20al.,%20BJSP.pdf (last accessed May 18, 2010).

Dau-Schmidt, K. G., M. S. Galanter, K. Mukhopadhaya, and K. E. Hull. 2009. Men and women of the bar: The impact of gender on legal careers. *Michigan Journal of Gender & Law* 16(1): 49-145.

Deaux, K., and B. Major. 1990. A social-psychological model of gender. In *Theoretical perspectives on sexual difference*, edited by D. L Rhode. New Haven, CT: Yale University Press.

Eagly, A. H. 1987. *Sex difference and social behavior: A social role interpretation.* Hillsdale, NJ: Lawrence Erlbaum Associates.

Eagly, A. H., and M. C. Johannesen-Schmidt. 2001. The leadership styles of women and men. *Journal of Social Issues* 57(4): 781-797.

Eagly, A. H. and L. C. Carli. 2007. *Through the labyrinth: The truth about how women become leaders.* Cambridge, MA: Harvard Business School Press.

Ely, R. J. and D. Meyerson. 2000. Theories of gender in organizations: a new approach to organizational analysis and change. *Research in Organizational Behavior* 22: 103-151.

Ely, R. and I. Padavic. 2007. A feminist analysis of organizational research on sex differences. *Academy of Management Review* 32(4): 1121-1143.

Flax, J. 1990. Postmodernism and gender relations in feminist theory. In *Feminism/postmodernism: Thinking gender*, edited by L. J. Nicholson. New York: Routledge.

Fletcher, J. K. 1999. *Disappearing acts.* Cambridge, MA: MIT Press.

Hochschild, A. R. and A. Machung. 1997. *The second shift: working parents and the revolution at home, 2nd edn.* New York: Viking Penguin.

Holvino, E. (forthcoming). Intersections: The simultaneity of race, gender and class in organization studies. *Gender, Work and Organization (special issue on gender and ethnicity).*

Honeyman, C. and S. Cheldelin. 2002. Have gavel, will travel: Dispute resolution's innocents abroad. *Conflict Resolution Quarterly* 19(3): 363-372.

Hurtado, A. 1989. Relating to privilege: Seduction and rejection in the subordination of white women and women of color. *Signs* 14(3): 833-855.

Kolb, D. A., and R. Fry. 1975. Toward an applied theory of experiential learning. In *Theories of group process*, edited by C. Cooper. London: John Wiley.

Kolb, D. M., J. K. Fletcher, D. Meyerson, D. Merrill-Sands, and R. J. Ely. 2002. Making change: A framework for promoting gender equity. In *Reader in gender, work, and organization*, edited by R. J. Ely, E. G. Foldy, and M. A. Scully. Victoria, Australia: Blackwell Publishing.

Kolb, D. M. and K. L. McGinn. 2009. Beyond gender and negotiation to gendered negotiations. *Negotiation and Conflict Management Research* 2(1): 1-16.

Kolb, D. M. 2001. *Allison's Arrangement.* Unpublished case, available from author at the Center for Gender in Organizations, Simmons Graduate School of Management.

Kolb, D. M. 2009. Too bad for women or does it have to be? Gender and negotiation research over the past 25 years. *Negotiation Journal* 25(4): 515-531.

Koller, V., S. Harvey, and M. Magnotta. *Technologically based learning strategies.* Oakland, CA: Social Policy Research Associates. Available at http://www.business-access.com/about/techbasedlearningstrategies.pdf (last accessed Apr. 2, 2010).

Martin, J. 1994. The organization of exclusion: Institutionalization of sex inequality, gendered faculty jobs and gendered knowledge in organizational theory and research. *Organization* 1(2): 401-431.

McCall, L. 2005. The complexity of intersectionality. *Signs* 30(3): 1771-1800.

Miller, J. B. 1976. *Toward a new psychology of women.* Boston: Beacon Press.

Mumby, D. K. and L. L. Putnam. 1992. The politics of emotion: A feminist reading of bounded rationality. *Academy of Management Review* 17 (3): 465-485.

Pierce, J. 1995. *Gender trials: Emotional lives in contemporary law firms.* Berkeley, CA: University of California Press.

Reskin, B. F. and P. A. Roos. 1987. Status hierarchies and sex segregation. In *Ingredients for women's employment policy*, edited by C. Bose and G. Spitze. Albany, NY: State University of New York Press.

Ridgeway, C. 2001. Gender, status, and leadership. *Journal of Social Issues* 57(4): 637-655.

Ridgeway, C. and S. Correll. 2004. Unpacking the gender system: A theoretical perspective on gender beliefs and social relations. *Gender and Society* 18(4): 510-531.

Ridgeway, C.L. and K. G. Erickson. 2000. Creating and spreading status beliefs. *American Journal of Sociology* 106(3): 579-615.

Risman, B. J. 2004. Gender as a social structure: Theory wrestling with activisim. *Gender and Society* 18(4): 429-450.

Roth, L. M. 2006. *Selling women short: Gender and money on Wall Street.* Princeton, NJ: Princeton University Press.

Schneider, A. K. 1994. Effective responses to offensive comments. *Negotiation Journal* 10(2): 107-115.

Schneider, A. K. 2002. Shattering negotiation myths: Empirical evidence on the effectiveness of negotiation styles, *Harvard Negotiation Law Review* 7: 143-233.

Schneider, A. K., C. H. Tinsley, S. I. Cheldelin, and E. T. Amanatullah. 2010. Likeability v. competence: Why political candidates face it but lawyers do not. *Duke Journal of Gender Law and Policy* (forthcoming).

Shields, S. A. 2008. Gender: An intersectionality perspective. *Sex Roles* 59(5-6): 301-311.

Shirts, R. G. 1969. *StarPower: A simulation for understanding power and empowerment.* Del Mar, CA: Simulation Training Systems. Available at http://www.stsintl.com/ (last accessed June 20, 2010).

Skuratowicz, E. and L. W. Hunter. 2004. Where do women's jobs come from? *Work and Occupations.* 31(1): 73-110.

Stanford, H. B. 2009. Do you want to be an attorney or a mother? Arguing for a feminist solution to the problem of double binds in employment and family responsibilities discrimination. *Journal of Gender, Social Policy & The Law* 17(3): 627-657.

Stuhlmacher, A. F., and A. E. Walters. 1999. Gender differences in negotiation outcome: A meta-analysis. *Personnel Psychology* 52(3): 653-677.

Sturm, S. 2001. Second generation employment discrimination: A structural approach. *Columbia Law Review* 101(3): 458-568.

Tinsley, C. H., S. I. Cheldelin, A. K. Schneider, and E. T. Amanatullah. 2009. Women at the bargaining table: Pitfalls and prospects. *Negotiation Journal* 25(2): 233-248.

Valian, V. 1998. *Why so slow?* Cambridge, MA: MIT Press.

Wade, M. E. 2001. Women and salary negotiation: The costs of self-advocacy. *Psychology of Women Quarterly* 25(1): 65-76.

Warner, L. R. 2008. A best practices guide to intersectional approaches in psychological research. *Sex Roles* 59: 454-463

Weigert, F. 2000. *Marisol's Mandate.* Unpublished case available from Deborah Kolb, Simmons Graduate School of Management.

Wharton, A. S. 2005. *The sociology of gender: An introduction to theory and research.* Malden, MA: Blackwell.

Wilkins, D. and G. Mitu Gulati. 1996. Why are there so few black lawyers in corporate law firms: An institutional analysis. *California Law Review* 84: 493-625.

०ॐ 19 ॐ०

Emotions – A Blind Spot in Negotiation Training?

*Mario Patera & Ulrike Gamm**

Editors' Note: "We must teach about emotions," say Patera and Gamm. We see in emotions, we think in emotions, we remember in emotions. There's no way around it, and our field is increasingly irresponsible in trying to maintain the pretense that things are otherwise. Patera and Gamm offer criteria for really grappling with a topic that makes many teachers, let alone students, uncomfortable (see, e.g., the next chapter).

Introduction: From Blind Spots to New Perspectives

We see primarily what we believe in. Every act of perception produces its own specific blind spots. These are usually not accessible to the person doing the seeing. Conscientious motorists, alert to the dangers of blind spots and dead angles, ensure a smooth and safe ride by using rear-view and side mirrors almost automatically. But where are the specific blind spots in today's negotiation trainings? What has received little or no attention in approaches to date, both methodically and content-wise? Which rear-view and side mirrors will be needed in the next generation of negotiation trainings?

Based on general observation of the field and particular observation of the Rethinking Negotiation Teaching project's two "benchmarking" conferences in Rome and Istanbul, one aspect seems

---

* **Mario Patera** is a tenured social scientist at the Faculty of Interdisciplinary Studies and Continuing Education at the University of Klagenfurt's Vienna, Austria center. He introduced the topic of "Mediation" to five Austrian universities and works as a certified psychotherapist, coach and mediator. His email address is mario.patera@univie.ac.at. **Ulrike Gamm** is working as an organizational consultant and mediator in Austria. She is the co-founder of Konfliktkultur. Her email address is: ulrike.gamm@konfliktkultur.com.

particularly clear: a failure to address emotions both in the course of negotiations and in negotiation trainings can be regarded as a possible blind spot. Shutting out emotions does not, however, refer to a lack of competence on behalf of the individual. Rather, this behavioral pattern can be attributed to the specific context of negotiation training and its inborn logic. Accordingly, any credible "Rethinking" of negotiation training, should, in our opinion, challenge common patterns of perception. What do different persons in negotiation training actually focus on? To what aspects is there depth of focus? In relation to emotions, what aspects are but superficially taken into account, or not perceived at all? What extension of perception is required, and which assumptions and approaches can be linked? For us, these issues are not just aspects of individual reflection. Doubting one's own ability to perceive and assess when talking about emotions needs to be institutionalized as part of negotiation training, both with regard to trainers and trainees. In this respect it may be helpful to summarize (see below) some recent findings from the field of neurobiology which redefine the correlation between rationality and emotionality.

Numerous other questions arise as a result of our failure to deal openly with emotions. What additional topics – and more important, what other stances and approaches – does negotiation training need in order to integrate emotions as a central governing authority? Which emotions of the parties involved (whether openly expressed or just guiding in the background) would such a change process in the Rethinking Negotiation Teaching project need to grapple with? To what extent have the previous two conferences and the discussions and reflections within the conferences contributed to questioning our assumptions concerning emotions? Below, we will attempt to address some of these in at least preliminary fashion.

The organizational theorist Karl Weick called for professionals to "Drop your tools" in order to see without prejudice the special qualities and skills of social systems for self-organization (Weick 1996). In terms of negotiation trainings, this plea does not seem to have been heard very often. What should new negotiation trainings look like, without a standard formula?

In order to change ourselves, we as trainers need to have the opportunity to observe our own perception instead of obtaining more and more training tools. Many colleagues in Rome and Istanbul experienced themselves as actively creative in dealing with emotions, even if external observers had different perceptions and reached different assessments. But it is not enough to have outsiders, consultants or researchers perceiving certain dynamics or patterns. For further development and changes in dealing with emotions in negotiation trainings, the persons involved have to develop new forms of self-observation. "If we cannot perceive, then we cannot recognize the future. We therefore do not know what now needs to be done" (Foerster 1993).

Perhaps more fundamentally, we should ask ourselves the question: why do we need all this effort of explicitly integrating emotional intelligence into negotiation training? From the multitude of possible and meaningful answers, we would like to highlight a few:

- The most important reason arises from the neurobiological realization that there is no separation of emotions from rationality or objectivity in our thinking. Our brains store all of our experiences in pictures; it is an illusion to have a thought without emotions. From a neurobiological perspective, to deny or suppress feelings, to attempt to focus on substantive issues, to try to separate thoughts and feelings and to attempt the removal of the body from the mind simply makes no sense. Gerald Hüther (2008: 31) has illustrated that our feelings are messages to ourselves which are indispensable for orientation in our everyday lives. They provide us with information about whether what we are experiencing makes sense in the context of what we have experienced up till now.

- The second argument draws on the professional self-conception of negotiators. Each negotiator is ultimately his/her own instrument. Hence to be knowledgeable about one's own instrument seems to be essential; how else would something such as "authenticity" be possible as a source of power and self-direction in negotiations? To be able to direct negotiations self-confidently, knowledge of one's own emotional state is necessary. If we try to ignore, suppress or repress emotions, then an external control takes over. Emotions are subconsciously controlling the room as long as they are not perceived and addressed.

We will proceed next to some significant elements of emotion.

Emotions: Some Basics

In our everyday professional and private lives, emotions – despite the large number of hollow claims to the contrary – are still generally seen as interfering factors. In the 400 years since the birth of Réne Descartes ("Cogito ergo sum"; "I think, therefore I am") and his (later) fateful separation of body and mind, little has changed in this regard. Emotions continue to be a taboo in many Western professional contexts.

In contrast to ideas, strategies or actions, which can be discussed in public, emotions are generally classified as private matters, part of our intimate sphere. We can speak more or less openly about unsuccessful projects, inefficient meetings, unsatisfactory negotiation results, etc., but not about the emotions of disappointment or aggravation that arise from those occurrences. When emotions do emerge in day-to-day business, or when they are even addressed directly in conversation, then there is a tendency to push those perceptions (and conversations about them) into the background by means of rationalization, explanation or other actions.

Much of what we know about emotions in the Western world has arisen from research on people with mental illnesses. Accordingly, many of the proposed means of dealing with emotions are rooted in this context – which is hardly an incentive to engage with the issue in an everyday situation. Such interventions are usually spot-focused (What is the quickest way for me to pull myself out of this depression?), and do not change the general mind-set in approaching and dealing with one's individual emotions. Until the beginning of this century, there were no comprehensive concepts at all for working with and on emotions (Lammers 2007: 10). In the last two decades, the understanding of emotions as well as their origins and functions has changed drastically, especially due to the impact of neurobiology. A glance at conflict management literature on the subject (see, e.g., Deutsch and Coleman 2000; Schwarz 2001; Cloke 2008; Tries and Reinhardt 2008), however, shows that unfortunately, little attention has so far been paid to these new insights. This material states that – just as in a negotiation context – emotions should be controlled or managed (Maiese 2005). The main focus is on "strong emotions" that usually have negative connotations, and are often automatically associated with aggravation, anger, rage, etc., although the term itself primarily points to the intensity of an emotion or its expression.

The numerous individual disciplines in research on emotions have various ways of differentiating between affect, emotions and feelings, as well as the relationships between emotion, cognition and motivation. As a general orientation, therefore, we would like to formulate seven theses that, in our experience, are useful in dealing with one's own emotions, and on that basis dealing with emotions in interaction, especially in negotiations.

Thesis 1: Emotions are a Combination of Body and Mind
Emotions are often described as the antithesis to rationality, reason, etc. But this appreciation can no longer be sustained, as emotions

are in fact much more a combination of, or even a bridge between body and mind.

Emotions consist of several components (Lammers 2007), each of which holds a different significance for work in this area:

- A somatic response (quickened pulse, muscle tension, etc.); that is, emotions can be perceived physically and are experienced in the body differently by each individual (somatic markers);
- Behavior (or behavioral changes), for example in one's facial expression, voice, gestures or behavioral responses such as fleeing, yelling, etc.;
- Cognitive processes (assumptions about oneself and one's environment, interpretations, appraisals);
- Motivational components, which refer to the orientation toward individual needs;
- A subjective component, i.e., the individual perception of an emotion (= feelings) (Damasio 2002).

It is the last component of emotions listed above – subjective perception (= feelings) – which draws the individual's attention to the overall dimensions of his/her own emotions. This perception, this attentiveness is the prerequisite for the conscious shaping of potential changes (and thus also the prerequisite for, and the most difficult part of, "emotional intelligence," (Goleman 1996) a buzzword used frequently in recent years), which will in turn have effects on emotional experience. Therefore, "having an emotion" is not the same as "recognizing a feeling." However, this recognition is required in order to assume individual control and individual responsibility for feelings as well as the corresponding cognitions and actions. Without this perception, recognition and attentiveness, navigation is impossible.

Thesis 2: Differentiate Between Emotions and Expression of Emotions

The expression of emotions is a social construct that takes different forms in various cultures. A smile can be an expression of contentment in one culture, or an expression of grief in another. This gives rise to a sense of insecurity: What is the appropriate way to express emotions here, in this context, in this culture? Which emotions can we actually show? The differing intensities with which emotions are expressed and realized reveal nothing about how intensively emotions are experienced by the individual in question.

In many professional and organizational cultures (examples include professions such as law or medicine, or organizational cultures such as universities), expressing emotions is generally regarded as a sign of weakness and is frowned upon by society, or even considered taboo by professional standards. But what fear, what worry lies behind the desire (which is shared by many managers, negotiators and trainers) to be able to block out or control emotions? What we are addressing here is a central area of tension in which many myths can still be found: the conflict between certainty and uncertainty.

What does this mean? Emotions are unpredictable in terms of when they arise as well as their intensity, their form of expression and the effects they may trigger. Emotions disrupt and interfere with our (implicit) assumptions about controlling processes. In many expert professions, certainty is defined as the ability to predict, to foresee the next step. However, it is time to depart from this myth of linear control once and for all. As negotiators and trainers, we are not the ones who control what happens next or what effects our interventions (questions, looping, etc.) will achieve. This is an easy statement to make, but when things become difficult, when we are under pressure, we fall back on these linear models time and again. But if the assumption of predictability cannot create certainty, what then can help in this storm of emotions?

As an alternative safeguard in dealing with uncertainty, people attempt to rely on models, techniques or checklists. Clear instructions and process steps are meant to create (would-be) certainty, to provide orientation in dealing with the unpredictable. These are again usually based on linear logic, and increase the pressure on parties involved in emotionally-charged situations that often cannot be directly acted upon. This attempt to recall techniques and guidelines, and focus on structures, results in a loss of authenticity. Authenticity and congruency in contact with others and the use of one's own emotional resources become considerably more difficult, if not entirely impossible. However, the fear of losing control hinders people from making authentic contact and allowing emotions – in conflicting parties as well as ourselves.

In what other way should we work with emotions, if we wish to regard them not as a barrier between ourselves and the conflicting parties, but as a valuable resource for cooperation? As always, the work necessary for this purpose begins with ourselves, with a new inner attitude, with our ability to allow, withstand and even shape emotions. Awareness of our own emotions is a prerequisite for perceiving emotions in others and shaping emotions in interaction. For this purpose, the pages that follow provide a number of suggestions from practice.

Thesis 3: There are No Positive or Negative Feelings
At this juncture, we would like to point out a key difference in our understanding: research and literature frequently postulate a di-

chotomy between negative (e.g., anger, fear, disgust, disdain, grief) and positive emotions (e.g., happiness). Despite its widespread popularity, for example in the much-discussed work *Beyond Reason* by Roger Fisher and Daniel Shapiro (2007), this dichotomy is problematic in multiple respects. First, it conceals the differences between the emotions within both of the sub-groups. Second – and this is where we see the far more serious disadvantage – so-called negative emotions are subject to a social taboo due to moral judgments, a fact which makes it far more difficult to express, perceive and come to terms with these emotions. Finally, what are often referred to as "unpleasant emotions" are not perceived as unpleasant in all cultures. In Chinese medicine, for example, anger is regarded as an essential energy, as a drive for self-realization and growth, as a healthy desire to expand and to rise up against a restrictive environment (Hammer 2000). Indeed, as Jean-Paul Sartre once wrote: "Every single emotion changes the world" (Sartre 1939).

Emotions steer our attention and behavior in certain directions: unpleasant emotions warn us of potential dangers to our own well-being and prompt us to avoid them. Emotions that are perceived as pleasant provide a signal that something conducive to our own well-being is occurring, thus stimulating us to continue toward the goals currently pursued (increased motivation). Thus, a great part of our behavior is motivated by our pursuit or avoidance of specific emotions. In this way, emotions trigger important adaptive responses on the physiological, cognitive and behavioral levels at every moment of awareness.

Thesis 4: Differentiate Between Basic and Reflexive Emotions

According to Paul Ekman (2007), basic emotions refer to those emotions which have been selected in the course of evolution due to their benefits in ensuring human survival, and which are found in every human. These emotions are shown in the same facial expressions across all cultures and can therefore be interpreted universally all over the world. Basic emotions are categorized as follows:

- Grief
- Anger
- Surprise
- Fear
- Disgust
- Disdain
- Happiness

Basic emotions are innate, so they do not require learning processes and can be activated without complicated cognitive processes.

In contrast, reflexive emotions such as envy, hope, insecurity, shame, guilt, pride, loneliness, and jealousy result from learning processes. First, they are a judgment of oneself as a person: how do I experience myself with regard to my surroundings? Second, they regulate human interaction and help to maintain community. They control how we co-exist with others by stimulating us to make contact, by triggering guilt and shame when social rules are violated, and by releasing (aggravation) and regulating (uncertainty) energies in disputes.

The individual shaping of reflexive emotions is linked to attachment experiences in one's own socialization process. One substantial difference lies in the fact that unpleasant reflexive emotions such as guilt and shame are more easily triggered than pleasant reflexive emotions (Leary and Tambor 1995). For negotiators, it is important to be familiar with both basic and reflexive forms of emotions, so that they can be dealt with appropriately in a negotiation process.

Thesis 5: Emotions Perform Important Functions
In summary, four central functions of emotions can be identified:

Ensuring survival
Emotions have emerged in the course of evolution in order to allow us to respond more quickly to decisive, vitally important events. External stimuli, for example, pass through the emotional regions of the brain even before they are perceived consciously and processed cognitively. In the case of very intense and basic emotions, automatic responses triggered by subcortical areas of the brain may arise. Intense fear, for example, can prompt people to run away immediately, and then consider other possible responses only once they have distanced themselves from the stimulus which triggered the fear.

Decision-making
The emotional processing of sensory perceptions is faster than cognitive processing, and therefore has a paramount impact on cognitive processes and decisions. This is even the case when the preceding emotion was subjectively imperceptible (as a feeling), possibly due to its low intensity and short duration. This lack of perception contributes to one of the most persistent misconceptions: the myth of purely rational decisions. Appeals such as "Please try to remain rational," "Let's stick to the facts," etc. are, in our opinion, nothing more than an illusion arising from an insufficient knowledge of neurophysiology. Therefore, it is high time we abandoned the assumption that decisions can be made on the basis of rational analyses alone. Even emotions which are merely anticipated have an impact

on decision-making (i.e., we think what we feel, and we feel what we think).

Fostering learning and development

The memory stores key events in life as emotions, and it influences our assessment of new situations by means of emotional schemata (i.e., intuitive decisions based on emotional memory). Indeed, we do not remember past events in a purely cognitive manner, but always in an emotional manner as well. Learning processes such as those that take place in negotiations and negotiation trainings are therefore anchored in the cognitive as well as the emotional level.

Reinforcement of community

In addition to the unifying and regulating social functions outlined above, expressing emotions in a community informs others about one's own state as well as potential dangers from the environment, thus affecting the behavior of others in the community. Moreover, emotions are perceived as belonging directly to the person expressing them. Thus they convey an impression of authenticity and identity, which is a crucial element of credibility.

Thesis 6: Emotions Also Have Costs

However, emotions cannot always be regarded as an appropriate guide for decision making. The complexity of everyday life also requires us to supplement and regulate emotional processes with cognitive processes. In many cases, emotional reactions would otherwise prevent us from making certain decisions that are associated with unpleasant emotions in the short term but are highly beneficial to us in the long term.

Thus, there are emotions that are rooted in experiences from the past, which are stored in our emotional memory (LeDoux 2001) and which are reactivated in current situations. Due to changing conditions as well as our own development, however, these emotions may no longer enable appropriate assessments or actions.

In addition to the danger of insufficient orientation through automated assessment mechanisms and (on that basis) avoidance strategies, strong emotions in particular are detrimental to perception, interpretation and assessment. Emotions change our view of the world and our interpretation of others' behavior. With the onset of a strong emotion, there is a refractory period in which our memory filters our existing knowledge and experience in such a way that only that information is available which serves to nourish the emotion we are experiencing. In this state, we assess all information from our external and internal environment in such a way that it can be brought into line with our perceived feeling. The stronger the feeling is, the more effective this mechanism becomes. This is the case with pleasant emotions (e.g., idealization, by blocking out certain parts of a person when we are in love), as well as unpleasant emotions, for example in escalated situations of conflict in which aggravation, disappointment and fear prevail.

This means that the same mechanism that provides us with orientation in our environment also prevents us from taking in new information which we cannot reconcile with our inner experience, and from accessing contradictory knowledge gained and stored in the past.

However, this means that in escalated situations of conflict, for example, neither recourse to previously concluded agreements (e.g., regarding procedure; stored knowledge) nor content-based arguments (new information) are helpful in shaping the process, as this information cannot be perceived and integrated. In our view, it also means that the suggestion put forth by Fisher and Shapiro (2007: 203) that one should "address the concern, not the emotion,"[1] in escalated conflicts with strong emotions, will probably not be very useful, as the cognitive requirements can neither be met nor even comprehended by the clients.

Gaining a critical distance to one's own emotional experience is a long and difficult process. It is easier to act or think differently than to feel differently. Thoughts which carry a strong emotional charge can only with great difficulty be changed by "objective" counterarguments. As a result, we sometimes feel the desire simply to eliminate the triggers for certain emotions; in a sense, we wish to have a "Delete" button for our own emotional schemata.

Nevertheless, emotions do not lead to compulsive behavior or automatism in everyday life; rather, they control a behavioral disposition, an inclination to behave in accordance with emotions. As soon as we are aware that a feeling has taken control of us, we can distance ourselves, dissociate, re-assess the situation and develop new options.

Thesis 7: Emotions Have Their Own Logic and Their Own Grammar

The nature of rationality is that one must always have or find a reason for something. The Grammar of Emotions (Baer and Frick-Baer 2008) chooses not to follow this type of logic; it has its own logic and totally different "grammar." Here are some examples of this grammar:

Emotions are beyond all measure

The extent or measure of emotions is radically subjective, the experience of emotions is not comparable; emotions are therefore measure-less. When expressing emotions there are cultural regulations of measure. This sometimes leads to a contradiction between our inner experience ("I am fuming with rage") and social, cultural norms (to show no emotions).

Emotions do not need a reason, at most an occasion

According to rational logic, everything has a cause; without cause it is cause-less and therefore meaningless, irrational. There are often no causes assigned to emotions, but there are occasions, signals that (e.g.) give rise to associations with situations in the past. Some events can be identified, whereas others remain hidden. Sometimes a scent, a certain posture is enough.

Emotions disappear from our perception – yet still remain

Emotions that are not (allowed to be) lived disappear from our perception, yet remain in our subconscious and keep resurfacing in different forms. Unexpected mood swings, or fascination for people who let out the emotions that we do not live ourselves, are just two examples of this.

Emotions are interchangeable

Helplessness is experienced in the form of anger; grief manifests itself as annoyance. When emotions are unable to find resonance, emotions disappear into thin air. Repeated experience of this lack of resonance then becomes a heavy burden. This means that the original emotion gets hurdled and instead gets "bypassed" with another feeling that is easier to express (e.g., anger instead of disappointment).

"And" in the world of emotions

Emotions connect opposites. This could mean, for example, that in a premature termination of a project, feelings of both sadness and relief about its end can be felt, along with frustration and hope for a new beginning. Instead of "either–or," the rule in the logic of emotions is: "as well as."

Emotions form chains and landscapes

Emotions are not separated from one another, but rather are interweaved together in various ways. In emotional chains different feelings are lined up one after the other in a process of experience: I am shocked by a comment of my negotiating partner, am then annoyed, then react very angrily, am then ashamed of my reaction, withdraw, and am sad about the loss of contact. In emotional landscapes the number of emotions are not perceived as occurring one after the other, but they stand side by side, with or without a connection to each other.

Ideas for Integrating Emotions in Negotiation Training

The previous section should have clarified what could potentially be highlighted in an emotionally conscious negotiation training session. The following PAAT model, which we use as the backbone for our training to sharpen people's awareness of emotions, has four steps:

- P = Perception of emotions
- A = Acceptance of emotions
- A = Addressing of emotions
- T = Transformation of emotions

This model requires participants in the training process to deal with their own emotions as an important prerequisite for designing ways of dealing with emotions in difficult negotiation situations. These four steps also provide instructions of how emotions are outlined in professional roles, such as in negotiation or mediation. By listing various exercises we would like to illustrate the implementation of these educational steps.

1) Perceiving Our Emotions

In order to perceive the emotions of others, I should be able to perceive my own emotions. This attentiveness is a prerequisite for a fair treatment of our own emotions.

> Exercise: Take time for a moment of contemplation twice a day. Find out which emotions you are able to perceive. Are there any others going on that you are not immediately aware of? (More than one emotion is usually present.)

In our training, participants actively deal with somatic markers, i.e., those parts of the body where we perceive different emotions (our own, but also those of other people) particularly strongly. These somatic markers are important "feelers" or sensors for the perception of emotions, and it is possible to practice working with them.

> Exercise: Draw the outline of a human body on a piece of paper. Which emotions do you feel where? On which parts of your body, and according to what changes in your body do you feel your emotions?

Since we rely primarily on experiential learning in our training approach, the evaluation of exercises or role plays usually begins by paying particular attention to one's own emotions (in different roles, in different phases of exercises). A better perception of our own emotions helps us to improve our understanding of our own behavior modes, such as strategies in role plays, as well as in real life negotiation situations (see above: function of emotions in decision-making processes). If I have better awareness of my own emotions, then I have a greater chance of self-control. This is also true for the role of the trainer in negotiation trainings. If I devote attention to my own insecurities and fears, then I have a better understanding about which of my interests needs special attention.

Perception of other people's emotions, in our opinion, requires using all of our senses. In addition to observing changes in skin color, facial expressions and posture, it also has to do with finding resonance with the emotions of your negotiating partner. This act of finding resonance is very often seen as dangerous. Negotiators are often afraid of being drawn into emotionality, letting themselves become influenced, losing control of themselves and then no longer being in control of the process. Or as a negotiator, there is the concern that by resonating, one may become biased. However, resonance and empathy are important resources for dealing with our emotions, and should be used consciously in our work. What assumptions do we make and what must be taken into account in this context?

Our everyday lives are full of spontaneous resonance phenomena: a yawn is just as contagious as a charming smile. Wherever people come together, moods are transferred with great regularity. But how do empathy and resonance work? In recent years, neurobiology has revealed fascinating new insights in this area (Bauer 2006; Hüther 2006; Iacoboni 2009). The system of mirror cells represents the neurobiological basis for mutual emotional understanding. When we observe the emotions of another person, the networks of neurons in our own brains resonate, reflecting the emotions of the other in our own experience. The ability to feel empathy is based on the fact that these mirror cells spontaneously reconstruct those emotions which we perceive in another person (Bauer 2006: 51). However, this capacity for resonance is not confined just to emotions, it also includes our intuitive understanding of actions. Even if we only perceive partial sequences of an action, this perception sets our mirror neurons in motion, which then spontaneously construct the overall process. For this purpose, they use the learning experiences the individual has undergone with typical situation sequences. Even imagining a possible action activates our mirror cells in the same way as if we were carrying out that action ourselves, thus also activating the attendant emotions.

Through emotional contagion between people who come into contact with one another, there is a creation of continuous, synchronous attentiveness (→ joint attention, Bauer 2006). This means that resonance causes the attention of the parties involved to be drawn in the same direction, thus giving rise to intense contact. Resonance and empathy therefore promote a deeper understanding of the other side, and in our opinion are extremely conducive to controlling the process. In addition, they also act as facilitators because they support enhanced understanding on the clients' part.

Therefore, our mirror neurons allow us to understand things intuitively, as we can perceive the emotions of the other side in our own bodies. We can then offer this emotional resonance to our clients in the form of a question. In this process, it is important not to interpret, but simply to offer them our perceptions. If the client does not take us up on this offer, we can leave it at that for the time being.

Fear, tension and stress drastically reduce the signal rate of our mirror neurons and thus weaken our ability to empathize, to understand others and to perceive them along with their differences. In situations of conflict, therefore, the parties' ability to empathize is drastically reduced.

Consciously creating resonance is a process of opening and closing oneself. Creating resonance does not mean losing oneself completely in empathy or losing one's distance. It is important to treat perceived feelings in such a way that we do not identify with them. Therefore, we have to develop our own dissociation strategies. This can be a conscious physical change (standing up, walking over to the flip-chart, shifting one's chair), a conscious transition to the cognitive level in the process (e.g., by summarizing what we have heard so far), or the formation of an internal hypothesis (What does this feeling of X reveal to me about the interactions between the conflicting parties, or between the conflicting parties and me?).

2) Accepting Emotions

The second step of accepting emotions as a resource in negotiations sounds easy, but takes on the rejection of feelings, which has been going on for centuries (see "Emotion: Some Basics" above). But how can I accept the emotions of others in negotiating situations when I cannot accept, or only partially accept, my own emotions? Take a moment to check which of your own emotions you accept and which ones you reject. How do you feel, for example, when you are ashamed? What would you try to do in order to achieve a higher level of acceptance?

A first step could be to welcome every emotion – so take a deep breath and let them come. I see my emotions as an important source of information that can inform me about the state of my well-being at any time. "Emotions follow a natural rhythm, they come and go, swell and fade, if we allow them to come and don't try to block them out or avoid them" (Greenberg 2006: 121).

Exercise: Dealing with our own emotions is a learned behavioral pattern, so in our training sessions we invite participants to grapple with their own patterns. In an individual exercise (following a relaxation exercise), participants take time to remember important people from childhood. Which emotions can be seen in these persons? How did they deal with these emotions? Which emotions were expressed and how? How did they speak about feelings? Who expressed emotions particularly intensely, which reactions could be observed as a result? What does this mean for you when dealing with your own emotions? The impressions of this individual exercise are then reflected upon further in order to detect one's own pattern.

---

3) Addressing Emotions

Emotions become more intense and are expressed more strongly if they go unnoticed over a longer period of interaction, or if the need underlying these emotions is not addressed. To address these emotions we recommend taking four aspects into consideration:

a) Many negotiators shy away from addressing emotions because they are afraid of bringing out the full intensity of the emotions and losing control of the process.

However, our experience has shown that such "excluded elements" always find a way of making themselves visible again. The harder we try to eliminate emotions, the larger the "stage" becomes on which this excluded element will reappear, hoping to be perceived. Addressing emotions involves showing our counterparts that we perceive their emotions and notice changes in their emotional state. This feedback from perceptions is a fundamental part of satisfying the individual need for "being taken notice of," which itself has a substantial impact on a person's self-esteem – a concept that Virginia Satir drew our attention to decades ago (Satir and Banmen 2000: 42). However, addressing emotions does not mean diagnosing their triggers, causes, etc. This would require a special role or a specific task (such as a psychotherapy session). Working with emotions specifically in negotiations calls for addressing emotions only in a differentiated manner.

b) It is rare for people to describe their feelings directly; instead they express them indirectly through voice, facial expressions and gestures.

This means that this indirect expression has to be articulated in words, to make sure that we have perceived it correctly. Here careful wording is essential, like in the form of a question ("For me that felt as if you were very hurt, is that your experience too?"). Then we can find our interpretation corrected ("It is not frustration, but I feel completely drained and exhausted"). This is not a criticism of our suggested hypothesis, but is rather a sign that our counterpart, the client, has at this moment assumed responsibility for the precise designation of his/her feelings.

c) In his film "Scenes from a Marriage," the famous Swedish filmmaker Ingmar Bergman included a highly memorable statement: "We are emotional illiterates" (Bergman 1974).

Unfortunately there is virtually no training seminar where we can learn to express our own emotions and those of others appropriately. It is important to distinguish between sentences that express feelings and those that only describe what we think about ourselves or others (e.g., "I feel incapable...") or how others behave toward us (e.g., "I feel misunderstood" or "I feel ignored").

Sentences that begin with "I feel..." frequently do not harbor emotions, but interpretations, assessments or statements about the motives of the other side:

- The statement "I feel that this idea is useless" is not a feeling, but an assessment of an idea.
- The statement "I feel that you are not qualified for this job" is also not a feeling, but an assessment of another person.
- The statement "I do not feel appreciated by my co-workers" is likewise not a feeling, but a statement indicating my assessment of the relationship between myself and others (Rosenberg 2005).

This commingling and non-precise use of language is problematic because of the masking effect it has of suppressing emotions. We give the illusion of having spoken about feelings and are not aware of our own masking effect.

d) The articulation of emotions is differentiated.

From hypnotherapy and NLP we know that the body reacts very sensitively to different terms and experiences them as being appropriate or incongruous (semantic reaction, Korzybski 1958). This is especially the case when addressing emotions, but also when addressing interests and needs. One explanation for an emotion (e.g., fear) can be experienced much too strongly by a dialog partner, while a weaker choice of wording (e.g., worry, uncertainty) is acceptable. These gradual differences in language are based on the individually perceived intensity of feelings as well as on different cultural contexts (contextualization of language). In many professional and organizational cultures the dose of emotions that is acceptable in public is very small, even if the inner experience is very strong. An insult may not be acceptable, but a disappointment is. Unfortunately, we still only have a very limited vocabulary to be able to express emotions in their differentiated nuances.

Exercise: The dictionary of emotions. In our training, we expand our vocabulary in the form of a group exercise. Working in small groups, the participants put together a mind map and assign one emotion (basic emotion or reflexive emotion) to each main branch respectively. They then add different nuances of these emotions to the sub-branches. In the following pooling of ideas of the visualized results ("gallery"), a "dictionary of emotions" becomes visible which is more or less extensive. When evaluating the exercise we first focus on the emotions perceived personally during the exercise (key questions: How did I personally feel during this exercise? What could I observe and perceive about myself?), and the participants can use their expanded vocabulary here. During the content analysis part, there is often a display of regret regarding loss of differential expression.

In our professional roles we try to communicate in a recognizable manner: this is a place where emotions are important, where emotions are perceived and appreciated. Yet this perception of emotions (and interests) does not usually take place in conflicts between the parties, as there is a concern that perception and understanding from the other party could immediately be interpreted as acceptance/consent or weakness. Therefore it is particularly important that an external third party is the person doing the perceiving and addressing as a substitute for the parties doing this themselves, allowing the conflicting parties themselves to let these levels flow back into their communication and interaction.

4) Transformation of Emotions
The transformation of emotions goes in two different directions: one is the direction of understanding the actions controlling needs and

interests, the other is the direction of greater acceptance of the responsibility for one's own thoughts and actions. Albert Einstein once wrote: "Everything that has been written or imagined by persons, serves the satisfaction of perceived needs" (Vaas 2008: 92). For Marshall Rosenberg (2005), emotions are the bridges to needs and interests. In short, emotions provide an indication of whether perceived stimuli contribute to the satisfaction or frustration of needs. Accordingly, this results in experiencing either pleasant or unpleasant emotions. So when perceiving emotions in a negotiation situation, it means that the communication either takes place in the direction of meeting these needs, or moves away from them. Perceiving and addressing emotions is therefore an essential pillar for interaction in interest-based negotiation. The above-mentioned somatic reactions (changes in breathing pattern, changes in skin color, etc.) let us know immediately if a need, or interest, has been addressed. In our experience, in difficult communication situations it is not possible to address "core concerns" (Fisher and Shapiro 2007:15) straightaway, since these cannot be heard, because of the emotional burdens of the negotiating partner (from a neurobiological perspective). Cognitive understanding is only possible when understanding has been established on an emotional level.

The second aspect of the transformation makes a learning process possible for the negotiation partners by allowing them to have a better understanding of their own stake in the emergence of their emotions. As illustrated previously, emotions always have a cognitive element, both in the emergence of emotions (interpretation and evaluation of a situation), as well as in choosing appropriate coping strategies (we think how we feel and we feel how we think!). All of these crucial assumptions about ourselves and our surroundings make up the part of emotional processes which we have access to.

For this purpose we use reflexive questions that contribute to a better understanding of our own perceptions, expectations, worlds of explanation and a subsequent redesign of our own mental model. Reflexive questions bring partners into contact with their own way of thought.

Reflexive questions offer two major benefits in working with emotions: first, they provide clients with an opportunity to depart from their emotions for a certain period of time, thus providing them with relief by allowing them to distance themselves. Second, the clients take on a meta-position and receive support in the process of understanding their own thinking and assumptions. These assumptions support the subjective assessment of whether a piece of information, a decision or a certain type of behavior contributes to satisfying one's own needs and interests, which means that the clients recognize their own internal emotional triggers.

In many difficult situations, where unpleasant feelings exist, people attempt to hold another person (or that person's behavior) responsible for their own feelings. ("I am very disappointed because you didn't answer.") In our view, others can only be the trigger for our emotions, not the cause. Especially in the case of unpleasant reflexive emotions (i.e., emotions where we place ourselves in relation to our environment (e.g., envy, inferiority, jealousy), responsibility is often shifted to the environment: "Your constant reproaches caused me to lose my composure." Therefore, self-deprecation through shame (deprecation of a behavior type in a situation) or guilt (deprecation of oneself in a situation) frequently leads to externalization, that is, shifting the blame to others. In contrast, our own part in originating the emotion (known as internalization) remains unseen.

Both transformation steps are aimed at enabling the negotiating partners to interact more self-confidently with themselves and their surroundings in negotiation situations by involving their emotions.

Conclusion

In our opinion, the next generation of negotiation training requires a fundamental change in stance, which should start at an individual level but also requires the context of negotiation training to address four key points:

1) There is No Sustainable Learning Without Emotions

Emotions are always a part of the interactions between participants and trainers. How then can we succeed in integrating experiential learning into training, where the here and now of the participants can be picked up on? How can existing learning concepts that include learning improvement via external feedback be enriched through perceiving and understanding one's own emotions? How can participants and trainers be made to experience how their own emotions direct their concrete actions in negotiations? Which new stances need to be developed on the side of the trainer? How can this change in learning be supported in a professional context (law, economy, university), where emotions are still very often regarded as irrational?

2) Competencies Can Only be Developed through Experience-Based Learning

Competencies that are necessary for negotiation can only be developed in concrete action, which therefore requires experience-based learning. Video-based learning does not compensate for personal experience. It is also not enough to receive feedback on role plays from experienced negotiators. Many roads lead to Rome, according to the European proverb; it is important that the trainees understand which assumptions and emotions have led them individually to certain actions in role plays. This understanding enables change. Experiential learning, however, also contains risks, e.g., the dangers of coming into contact with unpleasant experiences. How can we encourage participants in training to experience delight in failure? What other stances do trainers need to adopt, in order to enable participants to get in contact with their inner resources and internal barriers in dealing with emotions?

3) Experiential Learning Needs a Different Time Frame

Creating experiences and reflecting upon these experiences, as well as grappling with one's own emotions and assumptions, is not something that can be accelerated. As the European saying goes: "Olives won't grow any quicker if you pick them." We are sometimes astonished to read which goals and what content should be addressed and attained in just a two-day basic negotiation training session. Even if the session is offered by highly renowned and qualified trainers, whose personal competence is without question, the possibility of accelerating experiential processes is very limited. If experience-based learning is to succeed, then the following applies: less is usually more.

4) At What Point Does the Tail Begin to Wag Its Dog?

What are the implications if a description of a negotiation training programm offers less content and promises more modest objectives than the competition? What institutional reactions are then to be expected? And how do those responsible for the training deal with their own fears?

We are wondering who should adopt responsibility in the future for the development and implementation of quality standards in training. Or formulated in a more pointed manner: should the tail wag the dog or does the dog empower itself to wag its own tail? In the course of many conversations with those responsible for training programs, it was repeatedly emphasized that top managers could not be expected to spend more than two days in training, and that everything had to be packed into this time period. The market would not permit a different approach.

At this point we would like to remind all those responsible for training of the law of the 18th century French economist Jean Baptiste Say, a law founded on the notion that the supply of goods and services creates its own demand. Therefore, we would like to encourage all those interested in a new level of quality in negotiation training to have the confidence to create new market niches.

Notes

Authors' Note: This chapter was inspired by experiences Mario Patera gained in conferences in Rome, 2008 and Istanbul, 2009 as part of the Rethinking Negotiation Teaching Project, where he had the opportunity to observe top-flight teachers of negotiation during their training, talk with them about their assumptions, and work with them in a workshop he led entitled "Building an Emotion Vocabulary." His initial impressions of this exciting work were published in "Reflective Practice in the New Millennium" (Le-Baron and Patera 2009), after an intensive process of co-creation with Michelle LeBaron. This current chapter continues the exploration of the commonalities and differences between the practices of many negotiation trainers and the approaches we have developed in our training approaches in Austria. This article may well serve as a kind of "eye test," which helps us to see what may potentially be of interest on the subject of emotion and negotiation training, or rather should be focused on, in the opinion of the authors. Our approach is based on our experiences in German-speaking countries, and is therefore to be understood as the work of non-lawyers, non-Americans, and not primarily in support of scientists/trainers in the field of negotiation.

[1] This suggestion was made by Fisher and Shapiro, as they believed that conscious interaction with emotions is difficult – an assumption that comes pretty close to a self-fulfilling prophecy. We believe that their alternative approach is at a disadvantage because out of the five suggested core concerns, only three have the character of needs. Based on our understanding, status and role merely represent strategies for the satisfaction of underlying needs.

References

Baer, U. and G. Frick-Baer. 2008. *Das ABC der Gefühle*. Weinheim: Beltz Verlag.

Bauer, J. 2006. *Warum ich fühle, was du fühlst: Intuitive Kommunikation und das geheimnis der Spiegelneuronen*. München: Heyne Verlag.

Bergman, I. (dir). 1974. *Scenes from a marriage*, DVD. Criterion Collection (2004).

Ciarrochi, J. and J. D. Mayer. 2007. *Applying emotional intelligence: A practitioner's guide*. New York: Psychology Press.

Cloke, K. 2008. *Conflict resolution: Mediating evil, war, injustice and terrorism*. Calgary, AB: Janis Publications.

Damasio, A. 2002. *Ich fühle, also bin ich: Die Entschlüsselung des Bewusstseins*. Stuttgart: List Verlag.

Deutsch, M. and P. T. Coleman. 2000. *The handbook of conflict resolution: Theory and practice*. San Francisco: Jossey-Bass.

Ekman, P. 2007. *Gefühle lesen: Wie sie Emotionen erkennen und richtig interpretieren*. München: Spektrum Akademischer Verlag.

Fisher, R. and D. Shapiro. 2007. *Beyond reason: Using emotions as you negotiate*. London: Penguin.

Foerster, H. V. 1993. *KybernEthik*. Berlin: Merve Verlag.

Goleman, D. 1996. *Emotionale Intelligenz*. München: Hanser-Verlag.

Greenberg, L. 2006. *Emotionsfokussierte Therapie: Lernen mit den eigenen Gefühlen umzugehen*. Tübingen: dgvt-Verlag.

Hammer, L. 2000. *Psychologie und Chinesische Medizin*. Sulzberg: Joy Verlag.

Hüther, G. 2005. *Biologie der Angst: Wie aus Stress Gefühle werden*, 7th edn. Göttingen: Vandenhoeck & Ruprecht.

Hüther, G. 2006. *The compassionate brain: How empathy creates intelligence*. Boston: Trumpeter.

Hüther, G. 2006. *Die Macht der inneren Bilder: Wie Visionen das Gehirn, den Menschen und die Welt verändern*. Göttingen: Vandenhoeck & Ruprecht.

Hüther, G. 2008. Die biologischen Grundlagen der Spiritualität. In *Damit das Denken Sinn bekommt: Spiritualität, Vernunft und Selbsterkenntnis*, edited by G. Hüther and W. Roth. Freiburg: Herder Verlag.

Iacoboni, M. 2009. *Woher wir wissen, was andere denken und fühlen: Die neue Wissenschaft der Spiegelneuronen*. München: DVA.

Korzybski, A. 1958. *Science and sanity: An introduction to non-Aristotelian systems and general semantics*, 4th edn. Lakeville, CT: International Non-Aristotelian Library Publishing Co.

Lammers, C. H. 2007. *Emotionsbezogene Psychotherapie: Grundlagen, Strategien und Techniken*. Stuttgart: Schattauer.

Leary, M. and E. S. Tambor. 1995. Self-Esteem as an interpersonal monitor: The sociometer hypothesis. *Journal of Personality and Social Psychology* 3: 518-530.

LeBaron, M. and M. Patera. 2009. Reflective practice in the new millennium. In *Rethinking negotiation teaching: Innovations for context and culture*, edited by C. Honeyman, J. Coben and G. De Palo. St. Paul, MN: DRI Press.

LeDoux, J. 2001. *Das Netz der Gefühle*. München: dtv-Verlag.

Maiese, M. 2005. Emotions: Beyond intractability. Available at www.beyondintractability.org/essay/emotion (last accessed June. 22, 2010).

Patera, M. 2001. Reflexionskompetenz – Qualitätskriterium für (künftige) MediatorInnen. *Zeitschrift für Konfliktmanagement* 5: 226-229.

Rosenberg, M. 2005. *Nonviolent communication: A language of life*. Encinitas, CA: PuddleDancer Press.

Sartre, J. P. 1939. *Skizze einer Theorie der Gefühle in: Die Transzendenz des Ego*. Reinbeck: Hamburg Rowohlt Verlag.

Satir, V. and J. Banmen. 2000. Das Satir-Modell. Familientherapie und ihre Erweiterung, 2nd edn. Paderborn: Junfermann Verlag.

Schwarz, G. 2001. *Konfliktmanagement: Konflikte erkennen, analysieren, lösen*, 5th edn. Wiesbaden: Gabler.

Tries, J. and R. Reinhardt. 2008. *Konflikt und Verhandlungsmanagement: Konflikte konstruktiv nutzen*. Berlin/Heidelberg: Springer.

Vaas, R. 2008. *Schöne neue Neuro-welt: Die Zukunft des Gehirns*. Stuttgart: Hirzel.

Weick, K. 1996. Drop your tools: An allegory for organizational studies. *Administrative Science Quarterly* June: 301-313.

❧ 20 ❧

If I'd Wanted to Teach About Feelings, I Wouldn't Have Become a Law Professor

Melissa Nelken, Andrea Kupfer Schneider & Jamil Mahuad[*]

Editors' Note: "Oh no, do we have to?" is these authors' mock-horrified initial reaction to the previous chapter. Their second response, however, is "Well, if we have to, we'd better get good at it." They go on to analyze how a series of exercises already widely used for other purposes could be adapted to perform double duty, to make students really think about their emotions.

Introduction

Fifteen years ago, Melissa wrote an article entitled "Negotiation and Psychoanalysis: If I'd Wanted to Learn about Feelings, I Wouldn't Have Gone to Law School" (Nelken 1996). The article discussed how the typical law student reacts when faced with a discussion of emotions and feelings in a negotiation class. Since that article, negotiation courses have dramatically increased their coverage of related areas – communication and listening, cognitive psychology, behavioral economics, etc. Yet despite the burgeoning interest in the "softer" aspects of negotiation skills, many law teachers remain

[*] **Melissa Nelken** is a professor of law at the University of California, Hastings College of Law in San Francisco, California, faculty chair of the Hastings Center for Negotiation and Dispute Resolution, and a practicing psychoanalyst. Her email address is nelkenm@uchastings.edu. **Andrea Kupfer Schneider** is a professor of law at Marquette University Law School in Milwaukee, Wisconsin. Her email address is andrea.schneider@marquette.edu. **Jamil Mahuad** is a co-founder and senior advisor to the Harvard International Negotiation Program at the Program on Negotiation, Harvard Law School. He teaches executive education programs on the use of emotions in negotiations based on his experiences as Mayor of Quito (1992-1998), President of Ecuador (1998-2000) and Nobel Peace Prize nominee (1999). His email address is jmahuad@law.harvard.edu.

hesitant at the prospect of bringing feelings into the room when teaching negotiation. At the recent Istanbul conference on "next generation" negotiation teaching, there was general agreement that emotions/psychology/feelings were important topics to address in a negotiation class – and yet there has been considerable reticence in the legal academy about writing on any of these topics (despite notable recent contributions by Leonard Riskin, Peter Reilly and Daniel Shapiro (Riskin 2010; Reilly 2005; Shapiro 2004).

This reluctance may stem from various sources. Perhaps we worry that negotiation classes are already so different from typical doctrinal courses that talking about emotions (rather than preparation, best alternative to a negotiated agreement (BATNA), or other "hard" numeric issues) will lead to more perceptions of "touchy-feely" teaching; perhaps we take "separate the people from the problem" to mean that with an understanding of interests and good listening skills we can avoid most emotions; perhaps we worry that our own lack of comfort or knowledge about psychology and emotions will undermine our authority in the classroom. However we rationalize it, it also reflects our own discomfort as professors and human beings in dealing openly with our emotions in a public setting.

In a sense, this reluctance is not surprising; those of us currently teaching negotiation were almost all trained at a time when most law schools did not offer negotiation classes, and many did not have clinics or skills classes other than trial and appellate advocacy. Without models based on our own experience, we have to make a conscious effort – and invest in considerable intellectual retooling – to move from acknowledging the theoretical importance of non-rational, unconscious factors in negotiation to exploring them in real time in the classroom. Our goal in this article is to provide law professors, and others, with concrete tools for teaching (and feeling better about teaching) the importance of emotions in understanding negotiation.[1]

Feelings, Psychoanalysis, and Where We Are Now

Melissa's earlier article addressed the lack of preparation in law school for dealing with actual flesh and blood clients and for dealing with the strong emotions that legal disputes evoke in people. The article noted that students are often drawn to the legal profession thinking that it will provide a set of clear rules and principles to guide them and that logic and analytic reasoning will suffice to produce optimal solutions for legal problems. Legal education, outside of clinics and skills classes, operates largely in an abstract universe, removed from the actual people whose disputes engender the appellate opinions that are the core of learning in law school. And since appellate courts address only legal questions, these opinions are peculiarly distant from the messy factual situations that give rise to legal disputes in the first place. In short, learning "to think like a lawyer" has traditionally favored cognition and ignored the powerful role of emotions in all human undertakings.[2]

Given the focus on the cognitive in legal education, it is no easy matter to switch gears and to introduce feelings into the picture. Some students will bristle at the thought that their prized rationality will be undermined by attention to feelings, and some (like the student whose comment became the title for Melissa's earlier article) will resist the notion that feelings have any place in a lawyer's education. Indeed, students have been taught that in order to think like lawyers – to be sufficiently detached to function productively on behalf of clients – they have to be emotionally disconnected from them and their concerns. An entire first-year curriculum built around briefing the appellate opinion versus the actual problem, understanding the holding versus understanding the client, and focusing on the court's decision versus the client's decisions leaves no room for feelings – and many teachers reinforce this with class discussion that prizes detachment and discourages emotions of any kind. (Imagine a discussion, instead, focusing on how Mr. Marbury felt about his last minute executive appointment (in Marbury v. Madison[3]) or how Mrs. Palsgraf (of Palsgraf v. Long Island Rail Road[4]) must have reacted to an exploding package – and how these feelings must have played a role in motivating their lawsuits.) A mistaken detachment from feelings can result in a sterile, distanced form of representation that is not satisfying for either lawyer or client. By running away from the dangers of personal over-involvement in a case, lawyers can easily end up in the equally treacherous territory of disconnection.

One of the goals of focusing on feelings in a negotiation class is to help students learn that they can be emotionally engaged with clients and, therefore, with their own work as lawyers without becoming identified with them. Lawyers who understand clients at an emotional level are better able to represent the client's needs. And a lawyer who is sensitive to the emotional cues of his counterparts in a negotiation is better able to navigate the tricky waters of dispute resolution in a way that satisfies his client's needs without riding roughshod over the other parties involved.

Much of what needs to be taught about the centrality of feelings in negotiation is no more foreign to students (or their teachers) when they begin a negotiation class, than negotiation itself is foreign to them. As social animals, humans are hard-wired to pick up subtle emotional cues from others in order to maintain the social fabric. What is novel in the approach we are encouraging is the explicit focus on these cues in order to develop the capacity to pay conscious attention to them. When we train ourselves to notice when we or others feel afraid, excited, or humiliated, for example, we can use that information to be more effective in negotiation.

As discussed below, there is an extensive literature on the psychology of negotiation. As negotiation scholarship has become more interdisciplinary, scholars have familiarized themselves with, for example, the broad social psychology literature on negotiation, decision making, emotional intelligence and the role of positive emotions. They have introduced many concepts from that literature into the legal/business literature on negotiation, and law and business schools now have social psychologists on their faculties who focus in these areas.

Familiarity with the psychology literature is crucial to an informed understanding of how emotions and irrational mental processes affect negotiating and negotiation outcomes. But reading about feelings can take a negotiator only so far. At some point, students have to confront their own conflicting feelings and learn how to deal with them without either imploding or exploding at the negotiation table. Without a first-hand, real-time struggle with their own strong emotions, students, and professors, are inclined to keep what they read at an abstract and distant level that is hard to draw on when the going gets rough.

Recent Literature on Emotions

When Melissa published her article, psychology had already entered negotiation pedagogy. The importance of learning about listening, cognitive biases, and partisan perceptions had been well-documented and integrated into many textbooks. More often today law students can understand (and law professors can teach from their own experience) the importance of seeing the client's perspective or learning how to listen better in order to get more information from clients. This mild acceptance of some aspects of psychology, however, does not readily extend to really dealing with the feelings that negotiators bring to the table. But in the fifteen years since Melissa's article appeared, the "feelings" part of the scholarship has greatly expanded.

The development of literature on emotions has occurred in three primary streams. First, as psychologists continued to run experiments on mood, law professors picked up this approach to emotions and integrated it into emerging negotiation pedagogy. Positive moods (induced by cartoons or chocolate, for example) have been shown to lead to more creative and more integrative outcomes.

Negative or angry negotiators are less likely to reach an agreement at all, and if they do, they reach less integrative outcomes (see, e.g., Freshman, Hayes, and Feldman 2002). The importance of tone and mood in email negotiations, in particular, has also been much addressed (Ebner et al. 2009; Morris et al. 2002).

Second, in a response to the often misinterpreted *Getting to Yes* (Fisher, Ury, and Patton 1991) phrase, "separate the people from the problem," Roger Fisher and Daniel Shapiro (2005) outlined in their book, *Beyond Reason*, a new approach for dealing with emotions in negotiation. As Fisher and Shapiro assert, negotiators need to recognize that human beings are in a state of perpetual emotion – and trying to ignore these emotions or eliminate them from negotiation is impossible. It is understandable that negotiators try to control emotions – after all, runaway negative emotions can divert your attention from substantive concerns, open you up to manipulation, lead to substituting feelings for material gains, and take charge of the negotiation. Rather than suppressing these emotions, negotiators need to find ways of effectively communicating about their emotional state. Fisher and Shapiro focus on five core sensitive concerns – appreciation, affiliation, autonomy, status and role – that give rise to emotions in negotiation. For example, when one party threatens the autonomy of another party to the negotiation through a take it or leave it offer, negative emotions are likely to arise. The reverse is also true – bolstering autonomy leads to positive feelings. In his chapter contribution to *Beyond Reason*, Jamil illustrated how intuitively paying attention to the emotional needs of the multiple parties involved in a high level international negotiation was crucial to avoiding a war between Peru and Ecuador and signing a definitive peace treaty.

Third, Leonard Riskin has, almost single-handedly, brought the meditation concept of mindfulness into lawyer training (see, e.g., Riskin 2002; Riskin 2004; Riskin 2010). He argues that less conscious self-awareness can lead to less effective negotiation behavior. If a negotiator can be more mindful in a negotiation, the negotiator will be better able to focus attention on a given subject, to deal with stress, to develop an understanding of himself and of others, and to feel compassion and empathy. Mindfulness also helps implement an understanding of mood and of the gamut of emotions that a negotiator might feel in the course of a negotiation – and Riskin notes that mindfulness will help a negotiator deal with these emotions (Riskin 2010).

Exercises on Emotions

In this section we outline a series of exercises that can bring out feelings and help foster classroom discussion about how best to deal with emotions in negotiation. We start with some more traditional ideas that many will have seen before – journals and active listening exercises – and then explore some exercises based on the new literature on emotions described in the previous section.

Journaling – Practicing What You Preach

Melissa's earlier article proposed that one way to counter law school's emphasis on rationality is to encourage students to become more self-observant in the context of developing negotiation skills – to become more aware of the multiplicity of feelings and motivations that affect their approach to different sorts of negotiations with different people. Increased self-awareness helps a beginning negotiator learn what works well for her and when she is likely to get in trouble in a negotiation. Self-reflection through weekly journal writing develops an appreciation for the myriad feelings that get stirred up in negotiations – excitement, fear, anxiety, aggression, pleasure, etc. – and journals continue to be a valuable way for negotiators to get to know themselves in the process of negotiating.

By keeping a written journal – similar to the ones that students keep to reflect on their negotiations – about her observations in the classroom, a teacher can also increase her capacity to pick up on subtle emotional cues in the room and refine her approach to teaching, just as her students refine their negotiation skills through self-observation. Student participation in simulated negotiations and group discussion are central to the way most of us teach negotiation. Without the structured format of a lecture or a Socratic dialogue, the teacher is herself involved in a negotiation with her students in every class session. She has to respond to the ebb and flow of student attention and motivation in a way that keeps the possibility of a satisfactory resolution – the sense of having taught/learned something of value – alive for all parties.

Teaching in this way requires willingness to relinquish certain aspects of control in favor of a more flexible and fluid approach that responds to the dynamics of the particular group in the room (see generally Nelken 2009). By attending to these dynamics – noting in her journal how the "weather" in the room and her own personal weather affect how well or poorly the lessons of the day are given and received; when discussion is generative and when it is merely gap-filling; when a topic catches fire and when it falls flat – a teacher can develop an appreciation for the myriad emotional contingencies that impact all negotiation outcomes. These real-time observations contribute to a deeper and more immediate understanding of the role that feelings play in any negotiation, and they help the teacher learn how to address them fruitfully with a particular group of students. Most centrally for the topic of this article, a teacher's written self-reflection can build conviction about the importance of grasping the psychological dynamics of negotiation as a means of achieving the negotiator's goals.

Thinking about teaching as a negotiation also creates an opportunity for one's teaching to reinforce the material being taught:

> The more the *way* in which one teaches models *what* one teaches, the more deeply the lessons will be learned. Students will learn what it means to listen closely, to take the other parties' interests into account, to care about their perspectives on the situation, to seek joint gain, and to adapt strategy flexibly if this is what the teacher models in the classroom in the way he structures discussion and attends to students' comments and questions (Nelken 2009: 190-191).

Listening Exercises

For many people, conversation is like a ping-pong game, with each player more focused on returning the ball than on hearing the other party out. But if bargaining for information is an important aspect of negotiation, then learning to tune in to the information being communicated by one's counterpart is essential. Part of developing skill as a negotiator and as a representative of clients in negotiation involves honing the skill of listening well. A negotiation pedagogy that values the content of what others have to say has to start by helping students learn to listen well rather than simply to prepare their next conversational volley. There is a difference between hearing and listening. According to the dictionary, to hear is "to perceive with the ear the sound made..." To listen is "to give one's attention to a sound...," "make an effort to hear something;" "take notice of and act on what someone says..." We hear the rain but do not generally listen to it. We need to train our students to understand the difference.

Active listening involves attending to what the other person has to say, then demonstrating your understanding by paraphrasing it in your own words, reflecting back both the content expressed and the feelings behind it. Sometimes those feelings are explicit; other times they are picked up by the listener from tone of voice, gestures, or other nonverbal signals. It is common wisdom to say that we communicate with words. That is why we pay a lot of attention to wording the right messages. However, we communicate more and in a more powerful way through our body language and our facial expressions. People do this all the time, but we do not always consciously register the subtle messages that are being communicated. Developing more awareness of the many layers and shades of meaning and feeling in seemingly simple communications is a valuable practice that can make the difference between a "tone deaf" negotiator who runs into a stone wall and a sensitive one who finds her way around obstacles to resolution.

As an exercise, active listening can be practiced in less than ten minutes' time, by pairing students and having them take turns being speaker and listener, talking, for no more than a minute each, about any topic about which they have strong feelings. After the listener reflects back what he or she has heard, the speaker confirms the listener's understanding or clarifies points or feelings that were misunderstood. This simple exercise alerts students to:

1) How hard it is to listen closely, even for a minute, without speaking;
2) How interference or "noise" in the listener's head ("Will I remember everything?" "When will it be my turn?" "Why does she think that?") makes listening, even for a minute, difficult; and
3) How impoverished our vocabularies of feelings often are ("you are upset/frustrated/sad/glad") unless we focus on them ("is she furious/livid/angry/annoyed/bothered?")

Another exercise is exactly the opposite: instruct students to listen poorly to their counterparts – to interrupt, to give advice without being asked, to blatantly daydream, etc. – by giving them private instructions in advance. In debrief, students who were the "talkers" will note how frustrated or hurt or annoyed they were. And, for the "listeners," they may discuss how hard the bad behavior was to enact or may, in fact, be surprised at how easy it was and/or be surprised at the reactions of the talkers.

Once students have been introduced to the basics of active listening, they can try a more extended exercise in which each member of a pair talks about an actual problem – personal or school/work-related – that she is currently dealing with. The exercise proceeds like the first one, except that the conversation goes on for five minutes or so. The listener gives intermittent feedback about what she has understood about the speaker's problem, and the speaker confirms or clarifies the listener's understanding after receiving feedback. In addition to giving students further practice in active listening, this exercise demonstrates how active listening often deepens a conversation, leading from more superficial issues to more nuanced ones as the listener repeatedly reflects back both the content and the feelings expressed by the speaker. When the speaker feels understood by the listener, she is often able to see the problem in a new light and to feel less conflicted about how to deal with it.[5] For law students, who often believe that a lawyer's job is to "solve" clients' problems, it is valuable to discover how much help they can provide simply by listening well and demonstrating their understanding of what the speaker says. For many of them, it is a revelation and a relief to learn that having all the answers is not a necessary requirement of the job; and that realization in itself reduces anxiety and enables them to listen better and understand more.

Fostering Constructive Dialogue

Once students grasp the basics of active listening, they can begin to put it to productive use. In addition to listening well, negotiators need to express themselves in ways that further dialogue between the parties, rather than create barriers to understanding. Both brief and extended exercises can help students learn how to frame and reframe messages to increase the likelihood of their being understood and accepted instead of mistaken and rejected. A number of popular books, including *Getting Past No* (Ury 1993), *Difficult Conversations* (Stone, Patton, and Heen 1999), and *Tongue Fu!* (Horn 1996), provide examples of how to choose words that open up discussion rather than shutting it down. For law students trained in one-sided argumentation aimed at persuading a third party rather than their counterparts, these texts offer a particularly useful perspective on how to foster agreement and understanding without resort to language of rights and power.

Learning to phrase things in ways that other people can hear and take in is an invaluable skill for a negotiator, yet many law students resist the idea that how they say something can actually change its perceived meaning. They are surprised at how habitual some negative expressions are in their everyday speech and at the difference in tone that can result from changing a few words in a sentence. *Tongue Fu!* author Sam Horn's "words to use and words to lose," scattered throughout her book, are a good basis for a class exercise that illustrates these points. Working in groups of three or four, students rewrite sentences, for example, to acknowledge others' concerns with "and" rather than negating them with "but" ("I'd like to help you, but I'm busy right now" becomes "I'd like to help you, and I will as soon as I finish this task") (Horn 1996: 71-76) or to focus on desirable future change rather than past error ("You shouldn't have revealed how desperate you were to buy the widget" can become "Next time, try to get a sense of how eager the owner is to sell her widget before revealing your need for it") (Horn 1996: 71-76). Criticism that is backward-looking induces shame and a sense of defeat; forward-looking comments assume both the ability and a desire to improve. They are thus less harmful to people's self-esteem and less likely to make them shut down.[6]

Difficult Conversations Exercises

A different exercise based on reading *Difficult Conversations* (Stone, Patton, and Heen 1999) can bring home to students in a personal way how powerful its method can be in increasing understanding in conflict situations. Students are instructed to think of a real person with whom they are involved in a conflict and come to class prepared to attempt a conversation with that person, played by one of their classmates (the "partner"). The class is divided into groups of four or five, each with a coach, so that everyone gets a chance to be speaker, partner and observer. When the exercise begins, the first speaker describes the characteristics of the other person to his partner, who is instructed to respond in role as the conversation proceeds. The speaker starts from the "third story," describing the conflict as objectively as possible, and then proceeds to explain his story to his partner. After a few minutes, when the conversation ends, the speaker, the partner, and the observers each give feedback about their observations: what fueled or reduced the conflict, when and how emotions shifted during the conversation, etc.[7]

Despite the "as if" nature of these conversations (in the absence of the actual other party to the conflict), the exercise often gives students increased understanding of the conflict itself and of their own contribution to it, as well as increased understanding of the other party's point of view. Because the subject matter is real to the participants, they also gain a conviction about the value of undertaking such difficult conversations that no amount of reading or exhortation could instill.

Andrea uses the preparation sheet from *Difficult Conversations* with the Casino exercise[8] in order to demonstrate how "regular" preparation differs from one that focuses on identity and feelings. The Casino exercise is a workplace conversation between a supervisor and worker with undertones of sexism and poor supervision and in which both parties have the potential for strong feelings. (Of course, professors could run this preparation with different exercises.) For Andrea's class, students can prepare using a classic Seven Elements preparation sheet or can prepare using the *Difficult Conversations* sheet (in which the identity and feelings conversations are each identified). At the debrief of the exercise, students then discuss how they chose to prepare, why, and how that affected the negotiation. Different ways of thinking about the negotiation – the standard lawyer approach versus one that includes more explicit preparation on the emotions – are easily compared and brought to light. This type of preparation about the identity and feelings conversations can also be used in real-life scenarios as outlined above.

Mood Exercises

There are several different ways that professors can bring the points about mood into the class. First, students could journal how they felt going into the negotiation, what the rest of their day had been like, what mood they were in when the negotiation started and ended. Second, professors could also run exercises in class where some groups of students are given chocolate (perhaps the class is separated into two rooms for ostensible space reasons but then only one section is given chocolate.) Andrea also had one student discuss the impact of meal time in a negotiation – one could suggest that students try, in the course of a semester, doing a negotiation when really hungry, to see how that affects the outcome. Most importantly, the key for students is to learn that mood does matter and that they need to be aware of this in order to manage their surroundings, the timing of the negotiation, etc.

Beyond Reason Exercises

Jamil has been teaching (and co-teaching with Daniel Shapiro) executive programs for people from various backgrounds focused on "Nemotiating: Using Emotions in Negotiations." Students start off by using a 5 x 5 matrix. This matrix takes the five elements of negotiation focused on the content or substance of the negotiation from *Getting to Yes* (Fisher, Ury, and Patton 1991) and then, on the other axis, uses the five sensitive concerns from *Beyond Reason* (Fisher and Shapiro 2005). Every student writes an actual emotional situation that requires a negotiated agreement to move forward and is stuck at some emotional level. In the course of the workshop, Jamil invites the student to re-visit and re-interpret that particular personal case with the new tools he is learning. Throughout, students are given moments of silence for personal self-assessment and insights. Students also view film clips to see each individual concern in action and foster in-class discussion about the concept and practice of that concern and the subsequent emotional unfolding/escalation. (By unfolding, Jamil means discovering tensions, how the problem is composed, and how it comes to the surface. He compares this process to a Hitchcock movie in which the audience is allowed to see what is about to happen before the character can.) Discussions in private journals, small groups and plenary session promote awareness about the relevance of the theory to understanding interactions in the group and the process the group is actually ("here and now") going through. Finally, to prove the method's worth and applicability to any difficult situation, Jamil uses the Peru-Ecuador negotiation process in 1998. After a short presentation of the facts, he invites the students to play the role of advisers and make suggestions about how to handle the emotionally charged first encounter between President Fujimori and him. Then he describes what actually happened, and the students can judge the relevance of their suggestions.

Mindfulness Exercises

Some teachers start every class by ringing a bell and asking students to focus for a minute on their breath as a way of calming the mind in preparation for the day's class. Although many of us would be uncomfortable teaching students meditation practices unless we had been trained in doing so, it can be a useful exercise to try something unfamiliar and talk with students, not as an expert but as one of the beginners. It would be especially helpful if everyone had read one of the articles on mindfulness in negotiation beforehand. In addition, one can encourage students to try out workshops offered by others (sometimes even through the law school) and to report back to the group.[9] Short of training in mindfulness, the concept of building awareness, finding quiet time before negotiations, and centering oneself before starting a conversation are all fruitful activities in which the students could engage.

Conclusion

Our goal in this article is to equip negotiation professors better with the ability (and desire) to address feelings more fully as an important topic in negotiation. The literature in emotions and psychology continues to expand, with more and more empirical evidence to support what we already know is true – those who are able to manage their own emotions, understand their client's motivations, and work with the emotions of their counterpart will be more effective negotiators. The second part of this article outlined a variety of exercises that are designed to support each of the streams of literature. While we do not expect that each professor will use all of the exercises, we hope that the array demonstrates how easy it can be to introduce a discussion and to add this to our repertoire.

Notes

[1] A similar shift has occurred in economics scholarship, where the field of behavioral economics has rejected the "rational actor" of classical theory and sought instead to take account of the often irrational ways that people actually make economic decisions.

[2] Of course, many talented lawyers learn about emotions intuitively through years of practice and become quite good, for example, at reading their clients' emotions in order to better counsel them or playing on the emotions of the jury in order to better persuade them. Our point is that – in law school – the importance of feelings is often downplayed, if taught at all.

[3] 5 U.S. 137 (1803).

[4] 162 N.E. 99 (N.Y. 1928).

[5] Additional listening exercises and an active listening worksheet are available by emailing Andrea at andrea.schneider@marquette.edu.

[6] There is an obvious lesson here for negotiation teachers as well, since providing feedback to novice negotiators also calls for tact in phrasing comments constructively.

[7] Teachers interested in trying this exercise can obtain an instruction sheet (including an advance written preparation exercise for speakers) by emailing Melissa at nelkenm@uchastings.edu.

[8] Case is available for purchase from Program on Negotiation at Harvard Law School, http://www.pon.harvard.edu/.

[9] One of Melissa's recent students also studies the martial art of Aikido, and he did a fascinating final project presentation on how the central principles of that discipline can be applied to negotiation.

References

Ebner, N., A. Bhappu, J. G. Brown, K. K. Kovach, and A. K. Schneider. 2009. You've got agreement: Negoti@ting via email. In *Rethinking negotiation teaching: Innovations for context and culture*, edited by C. Honeyman, J. Coben, and G. De Palo. St. Paul, MN: DRI Press.

Fisher, R., W. Ury, and B. Patton. 1991. *Getting to yes: Negotiating agreement without giving in,* 2nd edn. New York: Penguin.

Fisher, R. and D. Shapiro. 2005. *Beyond reason: Using emotions as you negotiate.* New York: Penguin Group.

Freshman, C., A. Hayes, and G. Feldman. 2002. The lawyer-negotiator as mood scientist: What we know and don't know about how mood relates to successful negotiations. *Journal of Dispute Resolution* 2002(1): 1-79.

Horn, S. 1996. *Tongue fu!: Deflect, disarm, & diffuse any verbal conflict.* New York: St. Martin's Griffin.

Morris, M., J. Nadler, T. R. Kurtzberg, and L. Thompson. 2002. Schmooze or lose: Social friction and lubrication in e-mail negotiations. *Group Dynamics* 6(1): 89-100.

Nelken, M. 1996. Negotiation and Psychoanalysis: If I'd wanted to learn about feelings, I wouldn't have gone to law school. *Journal of Legal Education* 46(3): 420-429.

Nelken, M. 2009. Negotiating classroom process: Lessons from adult learning. *Negotiation Journal* 25(2): 181-194.

Reilly, P. 2005. Teaching law students how to feel: Using negotiations training to increase *emotional* intelligence. *Negotiation Journal* 21(2): 301-314.

Riskin, L. 2002. The contemplative lawyer: On the potential contributions of mindfulness meditation to law students, lawyers, and their clients. *Harvard Negotiation Law Review* 7: 1-66.

Riskin, L. 2004. Mindfulness: Foundational training for dispute resolution. *Journal of Legal Education* 54: 79-90.

Riskin, L. 2010. Further beyond reason: Emotions, the core concerns, and mindfulness in negotiation. *Nevada Law Review* 10 (forthcoming). Available at SSRN: http://ssrn.com/abstract= 1568644 (last accessed June 15, 2010).

Shapiro, D. 2004. Untapped power: Emotions in negotiation. In *The negotiator's fieldbook: The desk reference for the experienced negotiator*, edited by A. K. Schneider and C. Honeyman. Washington, DC: American Bar Association.

Stone, D., B. Patton, and S. Heen. 1999. *Difficult conversations: How to discuss what matters most*. New York: Viking Penguin.

Ury, W. 1993. *Getting past no: Negotiating your way from confrontation to cooperation*, rev. ed. New York: Bantam Books.

❦ 21 ❧

Relationship 2.0

*Noam Ebner & Adam Kamp**

Editors' Note: Ebner and Kamp examine the treatment of relationships in typical negotiation teaching, and conclude that critics of our field and its doctrines have a point: in several ways, our doctrines set students up for failure when dealing with "hard" bargainers, because of a tension that is not only unresolved but unadmitted. The authors argue that the first thing needed is for teachers to be transparent about "relationship doctrine" – because actually doing something different is going to be a daunting task. They go on to explain why.

Introduction

The way the concept of relationship is taught in contemporary negotiation education leaves students with an unclear, and often conflicted, picture of its nature and role. We believe that negotiation teachers prime students to consider a positive relationship between negotiators as a value in itself, for reasons that might be based either on our grasp of ethics and fairness, or on the relational framework we would prefer to see transactions and interactions based on.

We suggest that the place of this advocacy in negotiation education should be closely examined. We do so here by critically looking at three primary pedagogical "tools:" 1) *Getting to Yes*, which serves as a textbook or as a set of precepts underlying much of negotiation education; 2) the Dual Concerns or Bargaining Styles graph; and 3) the Prisoner's Dilemma game. All three tools – or the way they are used in the classroom – advocate for a *particular* mode of relationship

* **Noam Ebner** is an assistant professor at the Werner Institute at Creighton University's School of Law, where he chairs the online masters program on Negotiation and Dispute Resolution. His email address is noamebner@creighton.edu. **Adam Kamp** is a Bakken fellow and law student at Hamline University School of Law. His email address is ajkamper@gmail.com.

and interaction, without teaching students how to differentiate between situations and apply approaches aimed at getting them the best deal possible for themselves in each situation. Negotiation teachers who use these tools without acknowledging their limitations are unintentionally setting up students to lose by paying a substantive price in return for maintaining a "positive" relationship.

The Negotiation 1.0 Relationship

In attempting to capture the essence of the concept of relationship in Negotiation 1.0, one would do well to start off with Roger Fisher, William Ury, and Bruce Patton's (1991) *Getting to Yes*.[1]

Getting to Yes purports to address a core problem: negotiators often find themselves cornered into a trade-off. Making concessions in the deal itself in return for the other maintaining a positive relationship is a constant possibility. By exerting pressure on two fronts at once, demanding a better deal while threatening to withhold or damage a good relationship, negotiators try to maneuver their opposites into a concession on the former in return for an easing of the pressure in the latter. However, making these concessions or being "nice," as the authors state correctly, is no answer. On the contrary – it may make a negotiator vulnerable, perceived as weak, and open to manipulation (Fisher, Ury, and Patton 1991: 8-9).

In essence, this is a relationship problem, and in that perspective one might say *Getting to Yes* is a relationship-oriented book. In order to avoid the relationship/substance trade-off, the *Getting to Yes* model suggests that negotiators *separate the people from the problem*. By dealing with their opposite in a respectful and open manner, while not going any easier on the substance of the deal, negotiators can avoid paying a price for relationship.

Separating the people from the problem is, in essence, the core framing of relationship in negotiation in the *Getting to Yes* model. Relationship exists *alongside* the substance of the negotiation. It should be a *working* relationship, one whose costs might be measured in terms of time, patience and communication, but not in concessions on the substance of the deal. Taken in context of the complete model the book presents, the essence of a "good" negotiation relationship would then be one that supports open communication, sharing of interests, exploration of options, and presentation of and comparison of standards.

Whether educators expressly teach the *Getting to Yes* model or simply borrow some of the relational elements, it would be a fair guess to say that two core notions – maintaining a good working relationship and separation between relationship and substance – are commonly encountered principles in Negotiation 1.0 education.

The Problem

We suggest that in attempting to create a clear scheme for students to follow ("Form a good working relationship with the other without paying a price for it") we are actually sweeping a very challenging tension under the carpet. This separation between relationship and substance is a very tricky precept to master, practically speaking. As the *Getting to Yes* authors themselves state, negotiators are humans, and human nature and the dynamics of negotiation challenge our ability to separate relationship and substance. Manipulative negotiators you face – be it your boss or your three year old daughter – will *always* attempt to tie the two elements of relationship and substance together. More challenging, manipulative negotiators will often be supported in their behavior by internal and external forces affecting you. By assuming that the tension is always easily overcome by one approach, regardless of context, regardless of culture, regardless of personality, we are not preparing students to analyze, recognize, contextualize, and choose how to manage this tension situationally.

Furthermore, we suggest that there is more being said about relationship, through other elements of a negotiation course or an executive training, that affects the way a student grasps this tension and the ways to resolve it. As we will detail below, the sum total of input we present our students with regarding the concept of relationship in negotiation presents them with a confusing, unbalanced – perhaps even lopsided – grasp of the concept and its operationalization.

What are we teaching students about relationship in negotiation? We will try to uncover this by examining three commonly employed teaching tools which deal with relationship either directly or obliquely. Negotiation teaching has always relied upon mixing multiple methods for enhancement of learning; a danger, rarely explored, is that our covert or unintended messages are reinforced by this multiplicity of methods. To show how the messages regarding relationships permeate negotiation pedagogy, we will focus on three different types of teaching tools – a book, a model, and an interactive exercise:

1) *Getting to Yes* (the book itself, and/or training materials structured around it)
2) The Dual Concerns / Bargaining Style model
3) The Prisoner's Dilemma game

Getting to Yes

In this chapter, we will consider the book as a teaching tool, due both to its prevalence as required reading in negotiation courses, and to its influence as the basis for training structure and material.[2]

As discussed above, *Getting to Yes* attempts to lay out a clear picture of the negotiation relationship, as a vehicle for carrying the negotiation along productively without interfering with the substance of the deal.

However, it would seem that no sooner have we been offered a way out by striving towards a separation between people and problem, than we are once again sucked back into people-issues. Instead of leaving this notion of separation as a stand-alone, overarching precept, the authors attempt to simplify things by becoming prescriptive, breaking down just how this separation might be accomplished. We suggest that in this breakdown of do's and don'ts, the authors lead negotiators along a relationship-tightrope walk, along which human nature beckons them to fall into relationship-traps (or to use Fisher, Ury, and Patton's own terminology, situations in which negotiators will be tempted to pay a substantive price for maintaining the relationship) at every turn.

The *Getting to Yes* authors recommend four things regarding relationship:

1) You need to listen well, allowing the other to express themselves as best as they can (Fisher, Ury, and Patton 1991: 34);

2) You need to give the other space and allow them to vent, without reacting to emotional outbursts (Fisher, Ury, and Patton 1991: 31-32);

3) You need to step into the other's shoes, enabling yourself to see things from their perspective, and then reconsider your position (Fisher, Ury, and Patton 1991: 23-24); and

4) You need to view the other as a partner, not a competitor or enemy (Fisher, Ury, and Pattton 1991: 37).

Each of these recommendations (intended to be "universally applicable") is hazardous to some extent in itself; in the aggregate, they are almost certain to cause the negotiator to fall into the very relationship traps he or she is attempting to avoid. We will briefly discuss some of the reasons we consider each of these recommendations to be hazardous, and then focus on the list as a whole.

Listen

Can it really be that the prescription to listen is *always* suitable, context notwithstanding? For example, this approach assumes an honest, straightforward speaker, and one who lacks the self-awareness to doctor one's statements for the benefit of one's counterpart. This is hardly the case. Such uncritical listening to a manipulative negotiator frames the entire discussion in a context that may have little bearing to the counterpart's actual reality, and can build sympathy for a situation that is in fact mostly or entirely illusionary. While it may of course be possible to counter this, later on, through reframing, it is setting the negotiator up for the challenge of applying that complex skill successfully. In any event, few teachers of negotiation discuss any potential value in *not* listening to the other party, or consider other models of discussion.

Allow venting, avoid reacting

Not only is the expectation that we try to forego emotionality in the face of a heated outburst a sheer impossibility, but here in particular the suggestion that negotiators should allow the other party emotions they deny themselves has the result of valuing the other's feelings over their own. If venting serves a purpose in negotiation, then it might be something we should consider allowing ourselves to do as well – passing the onus to be accepting, understanding, forgiving (and perhaps even conceding) over to the other party. While there may be an advantage to recognizing a counterpart's emotions and stake in the game, this should not come at the cost of one's own emotional interests – yet that might be just the result of such a one-sided process-concession.

Recognize partisan perceptions

In a sense, this is a third variant of the same theme: where in the first suggestion the negotiator may adopt the other's factual scenario, and in the second the other's emotional state, here the unwitting negotiator is asked to inhabit the other's perceptions. This is by no means an uncommon message; any negotiation class spends a great deal of time teaching students to recognize that our perceptions are flawed, from counting the number of times a letter appears in a simple sentence and reaching different conclusions each time,[3] to counting basketball passes in a video – completely overlooking something normally thought of as much more arresting (a gorilla passing by).[4] Multiple generations of women are drawn, from a single image, and mobilized to demonstrate the notion that people can view the same issue differently in the physical world, much more so in the world of ideas and opinions.[5] But – despite the *Getting to Yes* authors' protestations that one can understand another's perception without adopting it – is that necessarily true? Remember, we are being advised to understand the other's perception in a reality in which the other might not be concerned about understanding our own. This creates an imbalance: two parties understand Party A's perceptions, but only one party understands Party B's perceptions. Might this not have the effect of shifting the balance towards Party A's perceptions – which both parties can appreciate? For example, consider that better outcomes are generally a product of setting high values for oneself (see Schneider 2006; Freshman and Guthrie 2009). When the *Getting to Yes* authors suggest that understanding another's perceptions may cause one to re-evaluate the merits of one's own claim, doing so is counter to keeping one's own goals high, and may result in unnecessarily lowering one's expectations.

Of course, whether one has a competitive or a cooperative bargaining style, one might still find it useful to understand the other's perceptions in order to better cast one's own response in terms one's counterpart may understand (Brown 2009). But without clarifying the dangers of understanding those partisan perceptions so profoundly that they become the dominant frame of the conflict, this advice might lead the unwary reader awry.

Partner-ize the other

This is potentially the most dangerous trap, because it assumes mutuality of purpose. If the other side is treating you as a partner, then in most cases the most productive solution is going to be to treat the other as a partner as well. The book treats the creation of trust necessary to create such a partnership as simple, taken in stride. However, especially when considering an experienced and manipulative negotiator, those same overtures can be used to create a false sense of partnership; the trappings of trust-building, such as gifts or friendly statements, can lead us to make concessions based on preserving the relationship that we have assumed to exist.

Aggregate hazards

Taken all together, these recommendations lead students down an even more hazardous path regarding relationship, owing to the potential implication of one party adopting this general mode of behavior regardless of their opposite's actions. If these recommendations (and others offered in chapter two of *Getting to Yes*) were made by a mediator speaking to both parties at once, or if one could promise that all negotiators would read *Getting to Yes* and adopt it to the same degree, these would be wonderful recommendations. As the authors say in their introduction to the method:

> Dealing with a substantive problem and maintaining a good working relationship need not be conflicting goals if the parties are committed and psychologically prepared to treat each separately on its own legitimate merits (Fisher, Ury, and Patton 1991: 21).

However, these recommendations are made to *individual negotiators*, who (in the rest of the chapter following the above quote) are charged with taking responsibility to conduct an effective negotiation for *both* parties, to ensure effective and productive communication between *both* parties, and for understanding the other party and where they are coming from. As a cluster of recommendations, this package seems highly likely to send the average negotiator (and, in particular, the average negotiation trainee or student – our target audience as negotiation educators) right back down the path of being *more concerned about the relationship than the other* – and falling into the same old trap of paying a price for it.

The risk associated with these recommendations might well be worthwhile if following them could be guaranteed to deliver the desired combination of a working relationship with no associated substantive costs, and the best deal possible for the individual negotiator following them. Obviously, that cannot be guaranteed in any individual case. Moreover, even the suggestion that these recommendations are *applicable* in all cases (and beneficial in most) seems to be predicated on certain relational assumptions, which might be called into question:

Assumption #1: relationship always matters. "Any method of negotiation may be fairly judged by 3 criteria: It should produce a wise agreement, if agreement is possible. It should be efficient. And it should improve or at least not damage the relationship between the parties" (Fisher, Ury, and Patton 1991: 4). This top-level depiction of the desired correlation between a negotiation method and the concept of relationship is well laid out – but where does it come from? It seems to be an outcome of the authors' more general assumption about relationship *always* being an interest of individual negotiators:

> Every negotiator wants to reach an agreement that satisfies his substantive interests. That is why one negotiates. Beyond that, a negotiator also has an interest in his relationship with the other side. An antiques dealer wants both to make a profit on the sale, and to turn the customer into a regular one. At a minimum, a negotiator wants to maintain a working relationship good enough to produce an acceptable agreement if one is possible given each side's interests. Most negotiations take place in the context of an ongoing relationship where it is important to carry on each negotiation in a way that will help, rather than hinder future relations and future negotiations ..." (Fisher, Ury, and Patton 1991: 19-20).

This is certainly often true. However – it is often *not* true. Sometimes the relationship does *not* matter. And sometimes, relationship matters in quite the opposite way of what the authors intended (i.e., "maintaining a good relationship matters"). Sometimes, the only relationship I may want with someone is to squeeze all I can out of them. Perhaps I, as an individual negotiator, want a relationship dynamic that will produce an acceptable agreement *without* taking the other's interests into account. Perhaps (in the context of an ongoing relationship) I want to set up an uneven dynamic in this negotiation, so that we will continue to play it out, reflexively, in future negotiations.

Teaching students that the future always matters and that relationships always matter is purposely telling them only half the story; more important, we need to teach students how to assess the value of a relationship or gauge the shadow the future should cast.

The premise that relationship always matters leads to the second assumption, also evidenced in the excerpt quoted above:

Assumption #2: a positive relationship is always a good thing. This is also only a partial portrayal of reality, which might be misleading to students. Sometimes a vague relationship, unsettling to the other party, might play out in our favor. Sometimes maintaining a highly-visible bad relationship with another will pay off for us by serving as a warning to external partners of the cost of not giving in to us.

In addition, and perhaps most importantly in the context of this chapter, this assumption undercuts the basic principle of "separate the people from the problem" even as it aims to support it. It is hard to imagine how with this precept in mind, we will be able to avoid falling into relationship traps in order to maintain something that is "always positive."

Assumption #3: a shield, not a sword. Relationship being used manipulatively is something you need to be on guard against, and defend yourself from. It is *not* something you should use yourself, to gain advantage from another.

Fisher, Ury, and Patton themselves state that, "If your response to sustained, hard bargaining is soft positional bargaining, you will probably lose your shirt" (Fisher, Ury, and Patton 1991: 8-9). Taking this prescriptively, it would seem as if someone with a knack for hard bargaining would do well to consider employing this very approach, when he or she finds themselves (lacking a shirt and) dealing with a negotiation opposite adopting a soft approach. However, no such recommendation ("If you are skilled at hard bargaining – and we will be learning how to bargain well – use it to take the other's shirt") is made, or is likely to be made by those teaching Negotiation 1.0 (see Ebner and Efron 2009).

Assumption #4: adopting this approach to relationship cannot hurt you. Striving for a working relationship, based on separating the people from the problem, will not have a negative effect. If you etch "separate the people from the problem" on the inside of your skull, you can engage in unavoidably relational activities without risking falling back into relationship traps.

In this context, we might share a war-story: Bargaining in Istanbul's Grand Bazaar during the 2009 Istanbul Conference, one of our colleagues inquired as to the price of a small carpet. The merchant replied that it costs $100, but that for her he would make it $80. She told the merchant she might return, and left. Over lunch, she related that she really wanted the carpet, but that the price was prohibitive. She did not want to spend more than $30-35 on a carpet. When advised to return to the stall and offer the merchant $20 for the carpet, she turned a horrified face and said "I couldn't do that! It would be so insulting!" Her colleagues asked her three questions:

1) How do you know that would be insulting? (You are in a foreign culture, assuming relational norms about a person you have known for ten minutes.)

2) Why do you care if it is insulting? (Assuming that if the price range remains anchored to the merchant's opener, you are not going to buy the carpet anyway – and will never see this merchant again – so why does the relationship matter to you?)

3) Do you think the carpet merchant was afraid of insulting *you* by highballing you with the initial $100 price and with the transparent manipulation of giving you a "discount?" (What is the cost of only one party caring about the relationship?)

Had our colleague really been able to separate the people from the problem, offering $20 would not have posed a problem at all. However, her overarching desire to avoid forming a negative relationship with the merchant by insulting him negated her ability to separate the people from the problem. This occurred despite the fact that this was a textbook one-shot interaction, with astronomical odds against the two of them ever meeting up again interdependently. This elementary people-trap was overwhelming, despite the fact that having taught negotiation for thirty years, she had probably said the sentence "separate the people from the problem" a thousand times. Falling into a simple people-trap, she found herself deliberating between two disadvantageous options: avoidance – not returning to the stall and losing out on a beautiful carpet for her home – or making an offer that she felt would not insult the merchant – $40 (which was, itself, beyond the reservation point she had set for spending in the bazaar, and which certainly would have been countered by the merchant with a higher figure of his own, such as $65). If a deal had been reached in this fashion, it would probably have been for about $50-55 – leading our colleague to pay much more than her carpet budget for the dubious "value" of a maintained good relationship with the merchant.[6]

Having understood these dynamics, and being of adventurous spirit, she agreed to return to the stall and offer $20 for the carpet. As expected, rather than declaring a blood feud between them as a result of a horrible insult, the merchant countered with a concession of his own; the deal was sealed for $35.

The final two assumptions, while not directly focused on relationship, have to do with two issues which are, as we shall see, tightly interwoven with this issue in the framework laid out by *Getting to Yes*: interest-based bargaining and cooperation.

Assumption #5: it is always possible to avoid the trade-off. A fundamental premise underlying the approach laid out in *Getting to Yes* is that negotiators can, and should *always*, engage in interest-based bargaining in order to avoid paying for relationship with concessions: "If you do not like the choice between hard and soft positional bargaining, you can change the game" (Fisher, Ury, and Patton 1991: 9).

This is not always possible, or practical, for a number of reasons.

- *The stakes are too low.* In a situation with limited time and limited value, the time spent exploring interests is in itself a concession, and the item bargained for is simply not worthwhile. In a later work, one of the authors admits this might be the case (Fisher 1984).

- *Interests are directly oppositional.* In the Turkish bazaar, what other interests were directly implied by the negotiation? The merchant would certainly prefer to be treated with respect and fairness, but when it came to the price of the rug, those interests were clearly secondary to getting the highest possible price for the rug. This is especially true in the case of a tourist; the expected return in making a concession on price in order to aim for the slim chance of accumulating repeat business is meager. In such a case, the interests available to the negotiator are mostly those that can be reached via positional bargaining.[7]

- *The other party flatly refuses.* Fisher, Ury, and Patton are alert to this possibility, and suggest a number of ways that positional bargaining can be deflected. But in the case of negotiators who determine that they are more likely to get a better outcome via positional than interest-based negotiation (possibly due to one of the above factors), then if one values the object of the negotiation sufficiently (or has too low a best alternative to negotiated agreement (BATNA), one will have to accept (and excel at) positional bargaining in order to meet one's personal objectives.

Assumption #6: competition is bad. A general reading of *Getting to Yes* leaves one with the sense that applying power – the underlying dynamic of most competitive moves – is somewhat dirty; it is the type of thing the positional bargainers do and which the interest-focused negotiators must sidestep and reframe. The only "acceptable" purpose of applying power is not to get a better outcome for oneself, but to enable a fair outcome for both parties; therefore, hard bargaining is only acceptable to the point that it enables a resolution on the "merits."

Put simply, a competitive approach to negotiation endangers relationships; this statement is left as an obvious evil that needs no further justification (Fisher, Ury, and Patton 1991: 6).[8] In fact, many situations might make taking a competitive approach a reasonable action, either trading the damage to the relationship for other gains or not actually causing harm to a relationship at all:[9]

- *When the stakes are too high.* It is sadly not too difficult to imagine situations where one's interests in the outcome are so high that the relationship is only valuable insofar as it gets you the best result for this negotiation alone: a hostage situation with a kidnapper operating alone, for example. A lesser example might be an item that is rare or unique and deeply valuable for objective or personal reasons.

- *When there is no relationship to speak of.* The tourist negotiator might be an example of a one-shot deal in which allowing a false sense of relationship to affect our actions might be self-defeating.[10] We might also note cases of "negative relationship" – in which one's negotiation opposite, by either poor reputation or actual broken promises, has elicited one's distrust. [11]

- *When the other party is not highly motivated.* If our counterpart has low motivation regarding the value we are trying to obtain or extract from them, early competitive action might cause them to withdraw from the playing field and abandon the prize to us.

- *When relationships in one's counterpart's culture are not harmed by competitive bargaining.* The critique of *Getting to Yes'* universal application in light of recognition of the different negotiating values of different cultures is an ongoing discussion (see

Bernard 2009, LeBaron and Patera 2009; Bernard, *Re-Orienting the Trainer to Navigate*, in this volume), and not the primary intent of this article. Still, we must note that one of the primary drawbacks ascribed to competitive negotiation in the book's framework is that it is harmful to relationships. At the very least this assumption must be interrogated with respect to culture: most likely, it simply does not apply in many parts of the globe, and trying to use a paradigm of integrative negotiation may even smack of cultural imperialism. One may still apply some of the lessons of principled negotiation as a matter of self-protection, but to add an additional concern of respecting the relationship itself may be costly and unnecessary.

For all these reasons, then, the foundational text for many negotiation classes is very much incomplete in the picture it paints of relationship. It admonishes readers not to pay a price for a good relationship – yet, at the same time, it extols the value of a good relationship to such an extent that it seems it is worth paying almost *any* price in order to obtain one! In a real-life situation, this might easily translate into even the most wary "separate the people from the problem" novice making seemingly small concessions in the deal in order to obtain a good relationship. This is not an insuperable obstacle; any number of teaching tools are capable of dealing with this weakness. Too often, though, those tools are used, not to soften this overemphasis on relationship, but to reinforce it.

Dual Concerns Model/Bargaining Styles Model
While negotiation teaching has offered several frameworks for conceptualizing the negotiation process, no particular model describing and analyzing the entire process seems to have been generally accepted by the field.[12] As a result, in seeking out a model to explore for overt and implied messages regarding relationship, we decided to discuss a model that seeks not to describe negotiation in its entirety, but rather one important aspect of the process: strategies that negotiators adopt to guide them through their interactions with the other.

The model we will discuss enjoys different names and different purposes, but in one form or another it shows up in every negotiation course the authors are familiar with.[13]

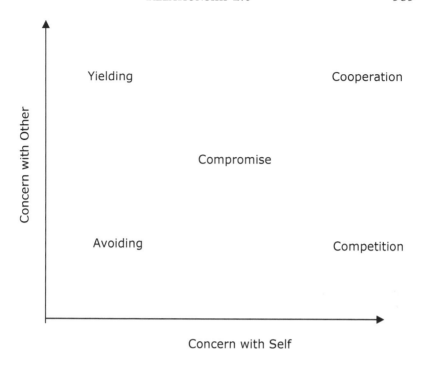

Figure 1 - The Dual Concerns Model

The Dual Concerns Model was originally developed as a conflict style or conflict orientation framework, presenting a theory of individual predilection for action in conflict situations. The notion that people have a tendency to act in similar patterns when encountering conflict, context notwithstanding, is an eye-opener for many, in that it contradicts our strongly held beliefs regarding rational decision making on a case-specific basis. This theory has been supported by several studies, and as a result has become the basis for instruments (such as the popular instrument developed by Kilmann and Thomas (1977) aimed at gauging an individual's style (Pruitt and Kim 2004).

Another form this model takes is that of a framework for choice of conflict management approach, whether by a dyad (e.g., two opposing parties deciding to attempt cooperation) or by an individual (e.g., someone engaged in conflict deciding to yield).

Finally, this model is often used to capture the range of *strategies* a negotiator might adopt in a given situation. In other words, in any particular situation, with a specific opposite, within a given context, an individual negotiator must design an overall gameplan, to be implemented through specific moves in the negotiation process. In this process of conscious strategic choice, the dual concern model presents five possible approaches from which to *choose* (Pruitt and Kim 2004).[14]

This multiple usage of the Dual Concerns Model does little to contribute clarity to negotiation teaching, particularly in that it often blurs the distinction between orientation and strategy, or between instinct and choice. Having said that, it is perhaps the most commonly encountered framework in negotiation teaching and – so long as the teacher is very explicit regarding just what it is being used to describe – a very useful tool.

Assuming that this framework is being taught to help students understand and improve their decision-making process with regard to negotiation, what are the implied messages of this model with regard to the role of relationship?

First of all, the model can be – and sometimes is – taught without any reference being made to relationship. The focus, then, is on "concern with my gains" vs. "concern with other's gains." While this might seem to simplify things by taking this model out of the realm of relationship-related material students are exposed to, the opposite might be true. What are the implications of a student expressing zero concerns with another's outcome, and giving *no* thought to the relationship? This might be a very dangerous proposition. As a result, discussion of relationship usually finds its way into study of the model, particularly as the cooperation-zone of the graph is discussed. In some teaching and training material, the chart itself includes "concern for the relationship" as part of the graph – treated either as synonymous with, or instead of, "concern for other's gains" (see, e.g., Filley 1975).

While it is hard to pin down specific messages always discussed regarding relationship, the following are some themes that we are certain most teachers will recognize from this point in a negotiation course:

- There is a correlation between a good relationship and cooperation.
- Cooperation is facilitated by a positive relationship (resulting in the trust, and risk-taking, that cooperation often requires).
- A good relationship is, in itself, a trigger for cooperative behavior (as parties prefer working together to rocking the boat).

These themes are all valid – but they are only a partial depiction of the picture. The questions they raise would require a more complex discussion of cooperation and relationship than most classrooms currently provide. This is compounded by teachers' gravitation towards certain areas on the chart. In a typical classroom, no more than a few sentences will be said regarding accommodating, or avoidance – as if these are things come naturally to us and have negative connotations; so why learn about them? Actually, of course, many situations merit choosing those strategies, but we do not engage in analytical or prescriptive discussion about them. Of course, a discussion about when to choose a yielding or accommodating strategy would be a wonderful opportunity to contrast concession-making due to high concerns for the other's goals, with "separate the people from the problem." And yet, this opportunity is usually lightly passed over, or perhaps avoided.

Perhaps even more troubling is the somewhat intuitive placement of "compromise" in the center of the chart. From this placement, students are led to believe that all parties to a compromise feel something along the lines of "If we were able to come to a compromise and not go all-out against each other, we must have some ability to work together; we're not viewing each other negatively, and we can go home and live our lives without harboring ill-wishes to one another." In short, we compromise because we place at least some value on the relationship itself.

This is wrong even on a strictly goals-focused level: in the real world, we usually do not compromise because we are concerned with the other's goals, but because we are concerned about the other's power and the damage they might do to our outcome. In reality, many people choose (or are dragged kicking and screaming into) compromise even though they feel that the other is taking advantage of them, or even stealing what is rightfully theirs, and wish that the other would get hit by a bus upon leaving the conference room.

Placing "compromise" in the middle is not a depiction of concerns but of outcomes. On the level of outcome analysis, similarly, many people leave a compromise feeling not that they gained half of what they expected, and that they have a halfway good relationship with the other – but rather, that they lost half of what was theirs and that the other is to blame.

If we were to tell the outcome-oriented narrative of compromise instead of the simplistic centering on the Dual Concerns chart, a very different story of relationships would emerge, in which finding common ground is as much a function of power as of personal connection, and where an agreement that fits both parties' economic needs (and may even be maximally Pareto-efficient!) might not be accompanied by a positive relationship at all when each party thinks the other is being unfair or unjust.[15] At the very least, it would ensure that the connection of "good relationships equals good outcomes" is not so clearly drawn.

Teachers tend to gravitate towards the "cooperation" area of the chart. Usually, they do so through comparison of this strategy with a competitive strategy. For reasons we will discuss later on, cooperation is usually given the spotlight, and the advantages of cooperation are usually driven home at this point with a simulation (such as *Ugli Orange*[16]), or with a story (such as about two industrious sisters with strong ties to a particularly challenging piece of citrus fruit[17]), or a game such as the arm-wrestling game described below. Different ways of cooperating are discussed, and integrative, pie-expanding thinking is stressed.

This typical discussion lacks two components. First, the discussion fails to examine the different factors to be considered when choosing between strategies. What contextual and situational elements need to be taken into account in order to make the best strategic choice possible – yielding or competing, compromising, accommodating or cooperating? Second, the discussion omits the role of relationship as one of those factors. To what extent should we allow a past or desired relationship to affect our choice of strategy? How can we factor this in with other elements, which might be leading us in different directions? How do we avoid paying a price for relationships?[18] While negotiation theory provides us with a substantial body of knowledge for discussing and analyzing these issues, negotiation teaching tends to gravitate towards a "do whatever you can to achieve cooperation, whenever you can" – leaving students at a loss regarding elements to consider, contextual deliberations, and benefits of other strategies.

Relationship should never be detached from strategy, and strategy needs to remain an approach to achieving self-interest premised on choice. If we teach anything that breaks this chain, we are not teaching what we say we are teaching. At the heart of the discussion of strategic choice in negotiation, where we should be teaching students the negotiation version of Kenny Rogers' famous gambling advice ("You've got to know when to hold 'em, know when to fold 'em; know when to walk away and know when to run"), we teach them, instead, to play the same hand, again and again. This theme is so pervasive that, even when another ubiquitous teaching tool, the Prisoner's Dilemma game, would seem to dictate the necessity of changing one's strategy as needed, the tool is used to teach just the opposite.

Prisoner's Dilemma

Elsewhere, we have commented on the position simulation-games enjoy as the field's favorite teaching-tool (Druckman and Ebner, 2008; Druckman and Ebner, *Enhancing Concept Learning*, in this volume; Ebner and Kovach, *Simulation 2.0: The Resurrection*, in this volume). One of the most (if not *the* most) commonly encountered type of simulation-game is that in which students participate in a game rigidly structured around a Prisoner's Dilemma (for more on the Prisoner's Dilemma, see Axelrod 1984; Schelling 1960).

To describe this type of activity in brief, students find themselves in a situation in which they have the ability to cooperate or to act non-cooperatively (this latter behavior is referred to as "defecting") towards one another. The game structure presents participants with predetermined payoffs, dependent on the aggregate of all the players' choices regarding cooperation/defection. The interaction is iterated, and communication between participants is limited and controlled by the teacher.

The precise way in which these simulation-games are conducted varies, according to the game used and the teachers' preferences. Two differentiating factors include game size and the use of storyline. Some games, such as Roger Fisher's *Oil Pricing,*[19] are structured around multiple games going on in the classroom at the same time. Others, such as Ebner and Winkler's (2009) *Pasta Wars*, provide for a shared experience in which an entire class, broken down into four teams, participates in one large game (for a more complex, four-player Prisoner's Dilemma), gaining the effect of one shared experience for debrief. Another differentiating feature between different games is the question of whether the game is embedded in a storyline, or whether it is laid out as a simple set of rules to follow. In simulation-gaming parlance, some examples of these activities are simulation-games, others are just games. *Pasta Wars* (Ebner and Winkler 2009) is a simulation-game; the oft-encountered *Win As Much As You Can* (WAMAYC), which provides no background story, is a game.[20]

When Prisoner's Dilemma games are used in class, whatever the specific game is, the post-game structure is usually the same. The class gathers again and debriefs. Scores are compared, and while there might be some instances of successful cooperation that have led participants to score many points together, other participants have forged the sort of resentment that lasts entire careers, either due to a mutually competitive approach or due to one party's unreciprocated cooperation. There will invariably be at least one case of deception or dishonesty, and at least one individual pointed out by several others as being the root of all evil (often premised not even by specific knowledge of disruption but merely by the presumption thereof).

The mix of primary lessons taught with the Prisoner's Dilemma game may depend on the teacher's goals or on the way the game played out. One primary lesson might be that of communication;

parties who are able to discuss their plans (and thereby avoid the lack of information on which the classic Dilemma is premised) can avoid negative outcomes. In games allowing for more inter-party communication, the issue might be trust, and how it relates to the concept of relationship; how can one develop the relationship necessary to ensure that the other parties will cooperate with you? When you breach trust, what happens to your outcomes? How do relationships, either pre-existing or as part of the exercise, affect this trust relationship?

What does not vary is the underlying message of the game, which is always voiced (and sometimes oft-repeated), by students or teachers: all players' outcomes will be better if they can find a way to cooperate.

No matter how often this message is repeated, far too little is said *about* it. True – in the context of the game, this is mathematically correct. However, in a discussion aimed at affecting the way students view interdependent interactions and the way they might act in them (and the Prisoner's Dilemma game, as used by negotiation teachers, undoubtedly has this underlying goal and/or effect) – this is simplistic. Shouldn't we be questioning this message, casting doubt upon this assumption?

It is a truism that the applicability of game theory to real-life negotiations is limited; when turning contextualized negotiations into arithmetical problems, much of the complexity of human interaction is lost in transition. Nevertheless, the very choice to teach with Dilemma exercises legitimizes them in the eyes of students, and a half-hearted apology for the necessary oversimplification in the game does nothing to defuse the implicit preference for cooperation. As an ideology, this is certainly appealing; as an accurate assessment of reality, it is lacking.

For a specific pedagogical example, consider the well-known game *Win As Much As You Can* (WAMAYC). This game might the simplest Prisoner's Dilemma game of them all, in that it does not involve a simulation, a storyline or background scenario; participants are asked to choose between "cooperate or defect" (which might be reflected by "green and red," "rabbit and snake," "X and Y," or any number of variations trainers have come up with) and score points based on the aggregate of their decisions (for a further explanation of WAMAYC, see Gold 2009). In a typical debrief of the game, cooperation is privileged over competition: groups that manage to cooperate will get better outcomes than those who do not; rarely will someone who competes score as well as members of a group who cooperate well. The focus is on the negative effects of competition; students arguing that they did well for themselves by competition might find themselves the target of persuasion by their teacher to accept that they might have done better, had they cooperated. The negative effects are framed as losses, joint (or aggregate) losses are spotlighted (without deep justification for this) and the beneficiary of those losses (if one exists in the game) is pointed out as a manifestation of the evils of competition ("We fought, so *he* was able to take *our* money"). If the game is not analyzed any more deeply, it remains a demonstration of the value of cooperation. The layers of complexity inherent in the game are ignored or paid lip service.

Here is an example of that complexity: In the last round (if a "last round" is identifiable within the game), the interaction transforms from an iterated to a one-shot Prisoner's Dilemma. Since within the context of the exercise there will be no future punishment for defecting, the risks of doing so are significantly less; in fact, your outcome will always be better if you defect than if you cooperate. A professor might overlook this aspect, or might mention it in passing. But a teacher might just as easily ask, "Okay, so you could have done better if you had defected here; in what circumstances in real life might that also be the case?" The WAMAYC game provides an opportunity to teach the viability of deliberate competitive action as another tool in the negotiator's skill set. Yet few negotiation teachers use the game for this purpose, because it seems so at odds with the fundamental cornerstones of the field – cooperation and its close companion, relationship-building. Once again, we ask: By avoiding the opportunity to teach contextual considerations of strategy and relationship, are we not shortchanging students?

In some courses, the teacher takes the concept of the Prisoner's Dilemma beyond the game, and teaches a bit about it, including some supplemental material and/or discussion on the topic. Unfortunately, in these as well, the supplement often focuses on a particular theme, and discusses it in such a way that the preference for cooperation is further reinforced. For example, a textbook might start with a brief explanation of how the Dilemma works, and then relate a story also popularly described by teachers: Axelrod's work with the iterated Prisoner's Dilemma tournaments, where different strategies are pitted against one another. The strategy that works best in Axelrod's simulations is *Tit For Tat*, a very simple strategy: On the first turn of the game, it cooperates; thereafter, it does what the other strategy did on the last turn. When pitted against one another, both these programs cooperate, and succeed very well. Against a defector, it defects in turn and minimizes losses. By cooperating with cooperators and losing little with defectors, the program does exceedingly well in the long run.

In our experience, this is about as "in-depth" as discussions of Prisoner's Dilemma exercises get. What messages are implied in this discussion? The first is that cooperative behavior can arise from self-interest, which is entirely reasonable. Frequently, students have the perception that self-interested behavior and cooperation are at odds; the story of the Prisoner's Dilemma and *Tit For Tat* should dismantle that perception. Moreover, it subtly augments the message of *Getting to Yes*: one can achieve better outcomes by cooperation, and the likelihood of better outcomes improves as more people choose cooperation over competition. But, by leaving this story without significant context, it also underscores the privileged status attributed to cooperation – and, by extension, to relational concern. The *Tit For Tat* strategy relies on the principle of reciprocity: one must be able both to meet cooperation with cooperation, and also to defect when the other party has done similarly. However, such reciprocal defection (taking the form of competitive actions, when translated into negotiation situations) is devalued by the tone and subtext accompanying the classroom presentation of the dilemma. Put more simply: by not teaching our students how to *Tit* effectively (and to feel legitimate in doing so), we are setting them up to be steamrolled by the other's *Tat*!

We have demonstrated the way in which the Prisoner's Dilemma game supports and reinforces the underlying messages discussed above, regarding *Getting to Yes*. In order to complete the triangle between the three teaching tools we have spotlighted in this chapter, let us take a look at the connection between the Prisoner's Dilemma game and the Dual Concerns model. Of course, some connections are obvious: in the Prisoner's Dilemma game, participants choose between the strategies the model describes, and the language used to debrief the game, contrasting "competition" with "cooperation" as well as "win/win" with "win/lose," is the language the model is often presented in. Sometimes, the connection between the game and the model is not only done explicitly such as through content and language, but is intimated through pedagogy and course flow. In some training courses, due to lack of time, the Prisoner's Dilemma game is condensed to a quick-setup win/win game such as the well known arm-wrestling exercise. Students, in dyads, face each other, take hold of each other's hands, and are charged to score as many points for themselves as they can; points are scored when the back of their opposite's hand touches the table. Often, this exercise is used in *addition* to the Prisoner's Dilemma game, in order to stress the same points for emphasis (e.g., at the beginning of the next lesson).

In some of the trainings we have observed (and conducted), this same exercise has then been debriefed for a totally different purpose: teaching the Dual Concerns model. Asking students how they acted in the game, teachers elicit the five negotiation strategies that form the content of the Dual Concerns model, and insert them in their place on the chart. Whereas students who remained red-faced and deadlocked are shown to be epitomizing the strategy of competition (and exemplifying its downside – the 0/0 clash of the titans, or the "winner's" relatively low score), students who *let* their opposite bang their hands down repeatedly are demonstrating a yielding or accommodating approach. Participants who decided not to play, or left the room, or talked about something else, are choosing avoidance. The spotlight then captures those students who found ways to exchange points and scored relatively high (such as by rapidly banging down one participant's hand and then swinging over to the other side, to score one point for each); this is shown to be a ("successful") example of a cooperation strategy, and the students gain status as being those who "succeeded" in implementing "win/win." We mention this as a further example of how these three teaching tools interact and sometimes merge with one another. Students learn about strategies they can purportedly choose between, even while they are being taught, at the same time and with the same tools, to value relationship and to beware of competition.

In effect, using the Prisoner's Dilemma game, the Dual Concerns model and *Getting to Yes* in the classroom, we fall into similar patterns. All of these teaching tools are premised on enlightened self-interest; the appeal of cooperation is to get better outcomes for ourselves. However, when we actually teach the material, we start to erase the self-interest aspect from the equation. Teachers become so focused on the relationship with the counterpart that, on occasions where true self-interest should be placed above the needs of the other, we have not properly trained our students to take this action. Saying "consider using *Tit For Tat*," like teaching "separate the people from the problem" and like recommending "choose between these five strategic approaches" is how we, as teachers, give our students a challenging task – which we then proceed to make nearly impossible.

Worldview, Advocacy, and Negotiation Teaching

It would seem that the typical alumni of Negotiation 1.0 may have a vague, confused or conflicted view of what relationship means in the context of negotiation, and of how to operationalize the concept. Relationships are viewed as a tool used by manipulative negotiators in order to trip us up in a particular deal. At the same time, they are viewed as the foundation upon which this particular deal and future deals are dependent. The dangers of relationship notwithstanding, students are not advised against relationship – on the contrary, they are taught to take responsibility for building, maintaining and preserving the relationship. Rarely, if ever, are students taught to contextualize relationship, to avoid (in practice) the costs of relationship, to capitalize on a relationship in a one-sided manner or to avoid relationship. Why then do we sustain this unbalanced, confusing portrayal of relationship?

First, there is an overarching problem with terminology. In the literature as well as in the classroom, the terms regarding relationship and strategy are used interchangeably, and are broken down into two broad categories: competitive, distributive, and positional on the one side; contrasted with cooperative, integrative, and interest-based on the other.

This dichotomy has served the negotiation field well, insofar as it depicts individual moments, turning points, decisions or actions within the negotiation process (see, for example, Lax and Sebenius 1986). However, when it is called upon in order to describe processes and approaches in the widest possible view, this division seems to be serving a different purpose altogether. Particularly so, when *positive value* is ascribed to one side of the dichotomy, and *negative value* to the other.

It has been suggested, both briefly in the previous volume of this series (Ebner and Efron 2009) and at length elsewhere in the wider literature on dispute resolution (epitomized by Condlin 2008) that as a field, we are engaging in advocacy, and in doing so, paying a price in limiting the knowledge and skills imparted. This advocacy certainly extends to the concept of relationship as well as to other issues raised in this critique (such as the embracing of interest-based negotiation over positional bargaining). In fact, seeing this worldview as an underpinning of Negotiation 1.0 goes a long way towards explaining some of the conceptual difficulties we have described in this piece.

We would suggest that this worldview is aimed at broad social change, through advocating cooperation. How might this change come to fruition, given the solidly competitive nature of the very arenas targeted for change – such as business, divorce, or international relations? Once again, we turn to game theory (keeping in mind our own caveat about real-world applicability).

In Robert Axelrod's (1984) discussion of how cooperation gains a foothold and takes root in a non-cooperative environment, he describes how this will only happen if the cooperative players do better, in the aggregate of all their interactions, than the non-cooperative players. Once the cooperative strategy is recognized as more beneficial, non-cooperative players will need to consider adopting this strategy. But, given that [Axelrod says] in individual interactions between cooperative and non-cooperative players the non-cooperative will usually score better, how can this situation ever occur? The answer lies, Axelrod explains, in having cooperative players "invade" a non-cooperative environment as a *group*. Now, each player has interactions with both non-cooperative and cooperative players. If the payoff for mutual cooperation is sufficiently high, it will only take a relatively small amount of interactions between cooperative players to compensate for their detrimental interactions with non-cooperative players. If a few other cooperative players join in the "game," cooperative players are now scoring so high from their mutual interactions that they are starting to gain more in the aggregate than the non-cooperative players – even though these last score higher than them when the two types interact in individual encounters. At this stage, non-cooperative players must begin to reconsider their chosen strategy and perhaps give cooperation a try.

In these terms, it would seem as if Negotiation 1.0 incorporated an effort – perhaps mainly unorchestrated – to achieve that critical mass of cooperative players needed to change the game played in key arenas and in human interactions in general.

What is the role played by relationship in this worldview? In an approach promoting cooperation over competition, and interests over positions, relationship is a central support; if not a keystone, then at least a load-bearing wall. Relationship affects the ebb and flow of interparty trust. This in turn directly affects interparty communication, impacting the information flow so crucial for interest-based negotiation. One's approach to relationship dictates whether one focuses on a particular interaction, or zooms out to take the future into account. Relationship is the lubricant allowing cooperation when positions and needs seem to be opposed.

As a result of all this, relationship is an element that needs to be portrayed so that it supports the cooperative worldview being advocated. However, doing so is not easy, as we remain aware of the perils of a non-contextual approach to relationship. Instead, as we have seen, little more than lip service is paid to that danger, and Negotiation 1.0 continues to promote such a non-contextual approach due to the effect this has on the way students accept and begin to practice a new, cooperatively-oriented, mode/method of negotiation.

Indeed, Negotiation 1.0 took a chapter out of Axelrod's book – a chapter he titles "How to promote cooperation" and opens with the words "This chapter takes the perspective of a reformer" (Axelrod 1984: 124). Axelrod suggests taking five strategic steps:

1) enlarge the shadow of the future;
2) change the payoff structure;
3) teach people to care about each other;
4) teach reciprocity; and
5) improve recognition abilities (so that players recognize other players and connect them with their acts in the past).

Obviously, issues of relationship permeate all of these steps, and they have all found their place within the teachings of Negotiation 1.0, with one exception: Negotiation 1.0 utterly fails to teach reciprocity for both cooperative *and* competitive behavior. And reciprocity – as Axelrod stresses – is *vital* for keeping cooperation running.

The result? Our field is casting our students into the world of negotiation relationship, having taken away (by omission) two key skills: contextualizing and reciprocity. Here, we have used the terms "confused," "vague" and "conflicted" to try and capture the effect this has on students. However, going back to Negotiation 1.0's roots, perhaps it can best be portrayed by quoting the opening sentences of *Getting Together*, another sequel to *Getting to Yes*:

> *What we want and what we need in a relationship are unclear*
> Our assumptions about relationships are often inconsistent with the kind of relationship we need to get what we want. These inconsistencies lead to confusion about our objective (Fisher & Brown 1988: 3).

A generation later, we would suggest, this description is apt. And we are part of the problem, not part of the solution.

We suggest that by not questioning – and perhaps by creating – this state of inconsistency and confusion, we have ignored the "do no harm" rule. What harm might be inherent in advocacy for a cooperative, integrative, positive-relationship oriented approach? We suggest there are two types of potential harm we need to be aware of: harm to individual practitioners, and harm to the fields of negotiation and dispute resolution.

Focusing on individual practitioners, the question of whether we are helping them to achieve the goals they set for themselves when they undertook to be our students would seem to be a fair – and even important – question for us to ask ourselves as teachers. Are we engaging in advocacy? And if so, will the system we are advocating pay off for students at least as well as any other system that we are aware of? Encouraging our students to focus on relationship and cooperation might indeed be a worthy attempt at enabling individuals and groups to evolve beyond the Tragedy of the Commons (Hardin 1968) that characterizes so many human interactions at the micro and macro levels. Still, Axelrod's model promises low returns and poor results for the first small groups of cooperative players invading competitive environments. Is this what we are setting our students up for? It certainly is not what we are promising them!

In certain situations, these gaps between what students expect, what they are taught, and their real-world interactions are extreme and troubling (Ebner and Efron 2009). More generally, to believe that we can actually denude most negotiations of their distributive aspects, as the Negotiation 1.0 paradigm might have us do, ignores the range of situations where an adversarial attitude may be unavoidable, culturally normal or even simply desirable: for example, where there is a justified sense of victimhood or a true conflict over scarce resources (Mayer 2004). Borrowing from the parlance of our field – sometimes *both* scientists want only the juice of the *Ugli Orange*.

We certainly do not mean to imply that we should be treating competition as more valuable, or even as valuable, as cooperation. We are not suggesting substituting the present dominant worldview with any other. We are reminding all of us to focus on our students. Many, perhaps most, students take classes on negotiation in order to determine how best to get positive outcomes for themselves. The same can be said for business people engaging in corporate training. Is it the instructor's job to teach the method that he or she finds more socially, culturally, ideologically or personally appealing, or to teach all methods known for their ability to help one achieve positive outcomes for oneself, and to let the individual student determine the moral weight of cooperation versus competition?

Concededly, it may be impossible for the instructor to occupy an ideology-free space or to try to teach a subject without bias and preference. But in that instance, out of respect for the expectations of the students if for no other reason, that ideology needs to be made explicit. If a teacher finds it difficult to discuss the value of competition in certain circumstances, this issue needs at least to be named and described, and the educator's stake in rejecting it should be made transparent.

Looking at the potential harmful effects on the fields of negotiation and dispute resolution in a more general sense, we might say that the revolution advocated for by Negotiation 1.0 has worked too well – in the sense that it has permeated our own field overwhelmingly, to the point that it is holding us back. This would seem to be happening on two levels: first, we are only engaging in conflict in certain ways, and through certain lenses. Like Paul Simon's one-trick pony, we have based our entire practice, including our revenue, on the limited set of moves that derive from our narrowed approach. Second, we are often viewed and described by outsiders through a lens which is not that far removed from our worldview – as well intentioned do-gooders.

This situation is probably connected to the fact that many teachers of Negotiation 1.0 have roots and connections in the wider fields of conflict resolution and ADR – fields that are struggling with these same issues of identity, ideology and worldview. These issues are at the core of the crisis these fields have been going through over the course of the past decade. In his book *Beyond Neutrality*, Bernard Mayer (2004) discusses the reasons that the field of conflict resolution has not yet lived up to the potential that so many people saw in it. It has not achieved wide recognition or a strong consumer base except in limited geographic or subject matter areas, has not greatly affected public policy or substantially altered society – despite having the potential to do all of those. Mayer lists "Ten beliefs that get in our way."[21] Among those, he lists the following beliefs, so common to those working, writing and studying in our field:

> *Belief #2: Competition is bad, cooperation is good*
> *Belief #3: Our goal is a Win-Win situation*
> *Belief #4: Interests are in, positions are out*

These beliefs did not arrive out of the blue – they are an outcome of the way Negotiation 1.0 advocacy affected the development of the dispute resolution field in its developmental stages. And they are supported by another, important, widespread belief:

> *Belief #8: Good relationships are our goal, adversaries our problem*

Summarizing the challenges we have raised in this section, we found we could not put it better than Mayer's own summary:

> All of the beliefs...have merit, and the approaches they imply have their place. Many of the beliefs are simple representations of values that are worthwhile holding onto and tactics that are often worthwhile employing. But we have built a great deal of our practice and our field around the notion that these values or beliefs represent reality and that these tactics are the cornerstone of our profession. In doing so, we have often limited the potential role we can play with people in conflict, and we have also raised suspicions about how realistic we are about the real nature of conflict or the actual way people experience conflict....

If these concepts have been comforting and helpful on one level, they have been restrictive and misleading on another. To move our field forward, we have to give up or at least significantly modify some of the ways we have understood our work and approached conflict..." (Mayer 2004: 147).

Return to Relationship: Implications for Teaching

Teacher Self-Awareness

The questions raised above are not just posed as a critique of Negotiation 1.0; they are an acknowledgement of how negotiation educators' worldviews affect their teaching and their teaching goals. We are spotlighting this not to constrain pedagogical freedom of negotiation teachers, but rather to hold up a mirror in which teachers should examine their pedagogy and course content in light of their worldviews. Should worldview and ideology inform negotiation pedagogy? We would suggest that they should not, but will not delve deeper into this in order to not trigger the debate regarding whether this is at all possible. That debate might detract from the *main* discussion that needs to take place, after a generation and more of Negotiation 1.0: identifying worldviews, discussing them, developing them, and investigating their place in the classroom. Viewing negotiation teaching and training as an arena for social change through shifting beliefs was a largely *unspoken* element permeating the Negotiation 1.0 worldview. One of the first things that needs to be done in Negotiation 2.0 is to expose these underlying beliefs to our own scrutiny, and to that of others. This does not mean that the worldview will evaporate, or lose its legitimacy; indeed, the view that shifting beliefs is a training goal has been expressed in Negotiation 2.0 as well (see Alexander and LeBaron 2009). However, it means that worldviews will now become part of the debate – and benefit, evolve and grow as a result.

We expect that as worldviews and teaching approaches become clarified, it will become easier to share coherent views regarding relationship in negotiation with students. The current complexity of the topic is in no small way a result of our effort to present conflicting elements as a congruent picture. Any clarity added to our top-level thinking will pay off in clear messages to our students in the classroom.

New Conversations About Relationships

In order to share those messages, new conversations regarding negotiation relationships need to take place in our classrooms. In these conversations, contextualizing should be encouraged, and world-view-related approaches (both teachers and students) should be – if not checked at the door – clearly labeled.

How might these new conversations get started? Inviting complexity into the classroom is never a simple thing to do. In addition, raising complexity is sometimes time-consuming, and we are painfully familiar with the all-too-limiting time constraints of negotiation courses and workshops. We will make a few suggestions here, and hope that in the future we or others take on the challenge of designing new lesson plans or teaching materials for this topic.

Assign Relationship-Related Reading Material

In order to counterbalance the covert messages much of the Negotiation 1.0 material conveys about relationship, teachers can assign the class an article/book chapter that takes a different perspective.[22] This does not necessarily have to be a piece directly on negotiation; depending on the context of the course/workshop, it might be a piece dealing with marketing, customer relations, or online dating – so long as it raises perspectives that can be contrasted in class with other material students have read.

Address Relationship Head On

As we have seen, relationship is often taught as an important theme under wider topics: as a part of conflict, a part of strategy, etc. Teachers might consider ways in which this concept can be addressed head on – naming it as a primary concept that affects conflict, strategy, communication, etc. – in effect, reversing the way it is taught. In this way, teachers might feel very comfortable with presenting its complexity and the way it affects negotiation dynamics in seemingly incongruent ways. This discussion might be reinforced by an experiential exercise such as a role-play or adventure learning activity targeting relationship as the primary learning objective.

Ask New Questions

Once the necessity of portraying relationship as a complex issue is grasped, raising new questions in the class – and thereby opening the door for students to ask new questions – should be fairly intuitive. Ask students if they ever use relationship in order to get what they need – and how that use works for them. Ask students who have participated in a Prisoner's Dilemma game if they regret not having defected more often. After observing a simulation in which one of the parties got the better of the deal, at the expense of the other, explore in the class what relationship-oriented elements assisted them in achieving this – and discuss whether this might be a good idea to try in the real world. These are just a few of the paths we usually do not take in class, worried about where they might lead us – but they are well worth walking down.

Conclusion

We have been presenting students with a confusing picture of the notion of relationship in negotiation. At the source of this tendency is the fact that relationship is needed as a supporting column, reinforcing some of the unspoken ideological underpinnings of Negotiation 1.0. We hope that the insights of a generation will allow for new classroom conversations regarding this elusive concept, one that presents it in a more complex light and one that might turn out to be more beneficial to students.

Notes

[1] The cited book's effect on the field of negotiation needs no introduction from us. We chose it as representative of Negotiation 1.0 because its effect on negotiation teaching is at least as great as its effect on the practice of negotiation. Nowhere was this more obvious than at the "Best of Negotiation 1.0" baseline negotiation training showcased at the 2008 Rome Conference, in which the book's influence was tangible – including regarding the topic of relationship.

[2] In terms of multiple methodologies, parts of the *Getting to Yes* method are often taught through more than one technique. Students might be assigned the book to read, and in addition hear a lecture, view a presentation, have the points exemplified through a video clip, apply them in a simulation and have them re-stressed in debrief.

[3] In this exercise, students are asked to count the number of times a letter appears in a sentence – and for various perception-related reasons, come up with quite varied answers, despite their all viewing the same sentence. See an example at http://www.bouldertherapist.com/html/humor/WordPlays/f's.html (last accessed May 18, 2010).

[4] In this exercise, a teacher's instruction to focus on the task of counting repetitions of an occurrence causes students to have "tunnel vision," completely tuning out other things happening on-screen. See examples of this at http://viscog.beckman.illinois.edu/flashmovie/15.php and http://www.break.com/index/awareness-test.html (last accessed May 18, 2010).

[5] In this exercise, students are presented with a drawing in which they perceive a young woman. Often, their brain "flickers" to allow them to see another figure drawn in the same picture, from a different angle: this one an old woman. See examples at http://mathworld.wolfram.com/YoungGirl-OldWomanIllusion.html (last accessed May 18, 2010).

[6] For different approaches to the element of relationship in the context of the Turkish bazaar, see Bernard, *Reorienting the Trainer to Navigate – Not Nego-*

tiate – Islamic Cultural Values, in this volume and Docherty, *Worldviews and Negotiation Generation 1.5 and 2.0,* in this volume.
[7] See above, note 3.
[8] In Ury's follow-up *Getting Past No,* this lesson is repeated, but again with an incomplete exploration of the issues, placing the means on the same footing as the ends and implying a universality to this argument when there are many situations in which a victory in a power struggle might be more effective than using power merely to even the scales in order to attain a collaborative agreement (*see,* Ury 1991, chapter five).
[9] For an example of a detailed discussion regarding choice between strategic approaches to negotiation, see chapter two of Pruitt and Kim's (2004) Social Conflict: Escalation, Stalemate and Settlement. Such a contextual and analytical discussion of choosing between cooperation and competition is noticeably lacking in *Getting to Yes.*
[10] In one sense, the tourist negotiator is not just a one-shot deal: the effect that the tourist's behavior might have on the perception of one's entire nation (by the merchant, by groups of merchants, etc.) is potetially relevant. Arguably, *Getting to Yes* relies on this extension of relationship: if we model interest-based negotiation, then the behavior may spread and negotiation will become easier as a result. Whether one chooses not to compete (and possibly accept a worse outcome) based on this belief may depend on whether one finds this scenario likely.
[11] Of course, distrust in no way means that a relationship is always negative or unimportant; distrust can be contextual and exist simultaneously with a great deal of trust. Take for example a car sales representative whom one might trust completely in a social context but not at all when buying a vehicle. Roy Lewicki (2006) provides a summary of how trust and distrust can exist side-by-side in an existing relationship. Nevertheless, some relationships (based on few interactions or reputation alone) may be actively negative, a dynamic that may well be in play in the bazaar where fear of the other culture could play a role in how a tourist approaches the negotiation.
[12] One divide that seems to stand out is whether a model of negotiation should be chronological or sequential ("We start with this, and then we do that") in its depiction, or whether it should be atemporal, focusing instead on elements always present and at play within a negotiation process. These models tend to vary in their precise content based on teachers' and authors' preferences, worldviews and experience. For example, a sequential model might include six stages beginning with preparation and ending with agreement, or it might divide up the process into ten stages beginning with the awareness of a need and ending with implementation of the agreement. An atemporal approach might focus on four principles (as in the original *Getting to Yes* model), seven elements (as in the popular Harvard Negotiation Workshop model), three crucial variables (as Herb Cohen (1980) highlights), ten elements (as one of the authors prefers to use) or any other way of dissecting the forces at play in the process. While some approaches are more popular than others, it would seem that there is no one negotiation framework that has been largely canonized. Although, if one would combine the book sales of *Getting to Yes* with the ubiquitous training programs modeled on the Harvard training program, one might guess that the atem-

poral model introduced in the former and expanded (from four elements to seven) in the latter is probably the model most commonly encountered.

[13] Perhaps we should comment that even in courses where the graphic depiction itself is not used, the approaches it contains are laid out as a spectrum of possibilities to choose from, further widening the ubiquity of the model. We have certainly seen this approach in many training settings and university courses. However, as it is challenging to "cite" a course (as the reader cannot check this out for themselves), we might mention that we encounter the five behaviors/strategies/styles without their breakdown into the dual concerns scheme in the negotiation literature as well. See, for example, the discussion about "bargaining styles" opening Richard Shell's *Bargaining for Advantage: Negotiation Strategies for Reasonable People* (2006).

[14] Pruitt and Kim (2004) limit this to four possible choices. In their opinion, compromise is not a distinct solution but rather "a kind of 'lazy' problem solving, involving a half-hearted attempt to find a solution serving both parties' interests" (Pruitt and Kim 2004: 41). We included compromise here, viewing it, as many others do, as a distinct strategy in its own right; however, we dispute that its proper place on the graph is in the center, equidistant from the other strategies, as we will discuss.

[15] For information on how two parties may differ on whether a given value is fair, see Welsh 2006. As for the idea that in some situations a midpoint in both parties' zone of agreement may make the most economic sense (explaining the concept of Pareto efficiency therein), see Korobkin 2000.

[16] In this popular simulation, two parties have seemingly incompatible interests: they both need a supply of a rare fruit in order to develop a cure for an impending disaster. However, careful reading of the instructions, and cooperative process-behavior (including sharing interests, divulging information, etc.) might lead them to a cooperative solution, as they each really need different parts of the fruit to achieve their goals; one party needs the peel, and the other the juice.

[17] This oft-told tale, attributed to Mary Parker Follett, incorporates a theme similar to that discussed above. Two sisters fight over an orange, not realizing they need different parts to achieve their separate goals: one needs the fruit to squeeze into juice, while the other needs the peel to make jam.

[18] A third component, noticeably lacking, is a discussion of how to compete effectively, if that strategy is chosen. The reasons for this are detailed in the discussion section below.

[19] Available at http://www.pon.org/catalog/index.php?manufacturers_id= 14&osCsid =3e6a69b3b364dff9579f06d1dbc61241 (last accessed May 18, 2010).

[20] There are many other variations of the game, which are teaching variations as opposed to structural variations. For example, some teachers conduct a single exercise between four students, in a fishbowl observed by all students. Some teachers tweak the amount of communication students are allowed to have, or throw in relational data relevant to the storyline, to affect the interactions. Different versions of this game, with teaching manuals, can be found at: http://media.wiley.com/assets/manual/sample_download.pdf; http://www.ag.ohio-state.edu/~bdg/pdf_docs/h/TB9A.pdf; and

http://nationalqualitycenter.org/files/17179/08%20Win%20as%20 Much %20as%20You%20Can%20Game.pdf (last accessed May 18, 2010).
[21] Mayer's use of the word "our" invokes the wider field of conflict resolution (including negotiation), and this critique is only partially relevant to negotiation itself, the focus of this book. Still, the development of alternative dispute resolution and that of the approach to negotiation encapsulated in Negotiation 1.0 are undeniably intertwined, and we feel that drawing on Mayer's insights is certainly appropriate here.
[22] A good example of a different presentation of relationship that is more complex yet still packaged neatly into a model of its own would be Roberge and Lewicki, *Should We Trust*, in this volume.

References

Alexander, N. and M. LeBaron. Death of the role-play. In *Rethinking negotiation teaching: Innovations for context and culture*, edited by C. Honeyman, J. Coben, and G. DePalo. St. Paul, MN: DRI Press.

Axelrod, R. 1984. *The evolution of cooperation*. New York: Basic Books.

Bernard, P. 2009. Finding common ground in the soil of culture. In *Rethinking negotiation teaching: Innovations for context and culture*, edited by C. Honeyman, J. Coben, and G. DePalo. St. Paul, MN: DRI Press.

Brown, J. 2009. Addressing partisan perceptions. In *Rethinking negotiation teaching: Innovations for context and culture*, edited by C. Honeyman, J. Coben, and G. De Palo. St. Paul, MN: DRI Press.

Cohen, H. 1980. *You can negotiate anything*. New York: Bantam.

Condlin, R. J. 2008. Every day and in every way, we are becoming *meta* and *meta*, or how communitarian bargaining theory conquered the world (of bargaining theory). *Ohio State Journal on Dispute Resolution* 23: 231-299.

Druckman, D. and N. Ebner. 2008. Onstage, or behind the scenes? Relative learning benefits of simulation role-play and design. *Simulation & Gaming* 39(4): 465-497.

Ebner, N. and Y. Efron. 2009. Moving up: Positional bargaining revisited. In *Rethinking negotiation teaching: Innovations for context and culture*, edited by C. Honeyman, J. Coben, and G. De Palo. St. Paul, MN: DRI Press.

Ebner, N. and Y. Winkler. 2009. Pasta Wars. *Simulation & Gaming* 40(1): 134-146.

Filley, A. C. 1975. *Interpersonal conflict resolution*. Glenview, IL: Scott, Foresman & Co.

Fisher, R. 1984 Comment to "The pros and cons of *Getting to yes*." *Journal of Legal Education* 34: 120.

Fisher, R. and S. Brown. 1989. *Getting together: Building relationships as we negotiate*. New York: Penguin Group.

Fisher, R., W. Ury, and B. Patton. 1991. *Getting to yes: Negotiating agreement without giving in*, 2nd edn. New York: Penguin.

Freshman, C. and C. Guthrie. 2009. Managing the goal-setting paradox: How to get better results from high goals and be happy. *Negotiation Journal* 25(2): 217-232.

Gold, J. 2009. Cultural baggage when you "win as much as you can." In *Rethinking negotiation teaching: Innovations for context and culture,* edited by C. Honeyman, J. Coben, and G. De Palo. St. Paul, MN: DRI Press.

Hardin, G. 1968. The tragedy of the commons. *Science* 162(3859): 1243-1248.

Kilmann, R. H. and K. W. Thomas. 1977. Developing a forced-choice measure of conflict-handling behavior: The "mode" instrument. *Educational and Psychological Measurement* 37: 309-325.

Korobkin, R. 2000. A positive theory of legal negotiation. *Georgetown Law Journal* 88: 1789-1831.

Lax, D. A. and J. K. Sebenius. 1986. *The manager as negotiator.* New York: Free Press.

LeBaron, M. and M. Patera. 2009. Reflective practice in the new millennium. In *Rethinking negotiation teaching: Innovations for context and culture,* edited by C. Honeyman, J. Coben, and G. De Palo. St. Paul, MN: DRI Press.

Lewicki, R. 2006. Trust and distrust. In *The negotiator's fieldbook: The desk reference for the experienced negotiator,* edited by A. K. Schneider and C. Honeyman. Washington, DC: American Bar Association.

Mayer, B. 2004. *Beyond neutrality: Confronting the crisis in conflict resolution.* San Francisco: Jossey-Bass.

Pruitt, D. and S. Kim. 2004. *Social conflict: Escalation, stalemate, and settlement,* 3rd edn. New York: McGraw Hill.

Schelling, T. C. 1960. *The strategy of conflict.* Cambridge, MA: Harvard University Press.

Schneider, A. K. 2006. Aspirations. In *The negotiator's fieldbook: The desk reference for the experienced negotiator,* edited by A. K. Schneider and C. Honeyman. Washington, DC: American Bar Association.

Shell, R. 2006. *Bargaining for advantage: Negotiation strategies for reasonable people.* New York: Penguin Group.

Ury, W. 1991. *Getting past no: Negotiating your way from confrontation to cooperation.* New York: Bantam Books.

Welsh, N. 2006. Perceptions of fairness. In *The negotiator's fieldbook: The desk reference for the experienced negotiator,* edited by A. K. Schneider and C. Honeyman. Washington, DC: American Bar Association.

03 22 80

Bazaar Dynamics: Teaching Integrative Negotiation Within a Distributive Environment

*Habib Chamoun-Nicolas, Jay Folberg & Randy Hazlett**

Editors' Note: These authors take a very different perspective from the previous chapter. Comparing Istanbul's Grand Bazaar to a pawnshop in East St. Louis and a wedding dress shop in Mexico, they find a great deal less that is "distributive" than is typically thought of each environment, and a great deal more of relationship-building. They outline a series of recommended steps that the supposed "one-shot" customer might adopt, or be taught to adopt in a negotiation course, which would work better for the customer than typical behavior does.

Introduction

Relationship building and establishing reputation are common to successful negotiators, irrespective of culture. Even in a distributive negotiation environment where repeat business is not necessarily expected, such as a bazaar catering to tourists, a pawnshop, or a wedding dress store, there are opportunities to generate positive relationships and value to the clients. Our experience and observations suggest that negotiation in such settings involves more than simply the exchange of money for goods. The seller may deliver a quality buying experience, even in a one-off deal, and benefit through indirect reciprocity and reputation building. Furthermore, bargaining in

---

* **Habib Chamoun** is an honorary professor at Catholic University of Santiago Guayaquil-Ecuador and an adjunct professor and member of the executive board at the Cameron School of Business at University of St. Thomas in Houston. His email address is hchamoun@keynegotiations.com. **Jay Folberg** is a professor emeritus and former dean of the University of San Francisco School of Law and now a mediator with JAMS. His email address is jfolberg@jamsadr.com. **Randy Hazlett** is president of Potential Research Solutions and Christian Artist's Workshop in Dallas, Texas. His email address is rdhazlett@sbcglobal.net.

bazaars or markets can be a rich, viable external classroom experience in teaching negotiation, provided students are trained on what to look for and how value is created. We suggest an outside-of-the-classroom adventure learning exercise to a local farmers' market where students can observe bazaar dynamics and put theory into practice.

Relationship Examples

What do the Grand Bazaar in Istanbul, a pawnshop in East St. Louis, and a wedding dress store in Nueva Rosita, Mexico have in common? Perhaps more than one would think, given the variety in products, geographic separation, and cultural imprint. We examine these three mercantile examples for commonality.

Istanbul's Grand Bazaar

If one visits the Grand Bazaar in Istanbul, one finds well-trained sellers and negotiators in every corner. Not only do they know how to handle objections, but they have a time-tested system of external attractors, including barkers, sidewalk displays, and outside taste tests, as a strategy to get potential customers inside the store. Once inside, the store owner defers immediate business with hospitality, e.g., a nice cup of tea. Eventually, the customer can browse the merchandise, often of high quality and price, such as carpet and fine scarves, in a relaxed manner. Even if no goods are sold, store owners do not get mad, for they accomplished one of their goals – generating a great shopping experience. There is a culture of customer service, even though the client may never come back. Shop owners rely on the one human invention that elevates us above the rest of creation – gossip (Siegfried 2006: 87), the willful distribution of second-hand, unconfirmed information, experiences and impressions. Hospitable behavior builds a good business reputation that, together with trust, is critical to effective negotiations within a relationship (Lewicki, Saunders, and Barry 2006).

In the bazaar, there is also a sense of the business as an extension of the family. Even small bazaar owners have business cards, and surprisingly, some have professional degrees. Many businesses have been passed down from parent to offspring over multiple generations. Sons and daughters go off to college and come back to take care of the family business. This generates credibility, according to Henry Mills (2000) and Robert Cialdini (1993).

Is there opportunity for integrative solutions in such an environment? Identifying potential value creation is part of the negotiation process. When several of the Grand Bazaar owners were questioned on how they feel about haggling, their responses were similar.

If a foreigner haggles, they enter the game. The merchants, however, never lose sight that they have a fixed minimum price point. If the buyer feels good bargaining, the merchants participate, because they want the buyer to leave with the item feeling good about the price and the experience. Still, they prefer to give customers value rather than focus only on price. Prices are generally not posted, because pricing is not fixed. The shop owner makes an effort to build a relationship with the customer, since as Roy Lewicki et al. (2006) point out, relationship issues can dramatically change the approach to negotiation and tactics. Once an item interests a customer, they can discuss terms of sale as friends. Thus, sellers in Istanbul's Grand Bazaar engage in a relationship even with a short term sale client, implying that the parties expect a future relationship or at least want to be civil in the present relationship. The merchant may also seek some "intangible" value of a pleasant interaction in addition to a decent price. These are not exactly the same. We can argue that what is going on here is a mixture of both the "good feeling" (i.e., not beating the other up, not making the other angry, and acting in a way in which one can judge oneself as fair, honorable, etc.), which Lewicki describes as "short term relationship mode" (STRM), and also long term relationship building. Even in many short term transactions, both buyer and seller seek to assure STRM satisfaction; the interesting question is how much of the need to assure a positive STRM is actually traded off against incremental price improvement.

An East St. Louis Pawn Shop

In a second example, we examine the inner workings of a pawnshop in East St. Louis, owned and operated by the father of one of the authors. Jay Folberg recalls his father as a good "schmoozer" who listened more than he talked. This is a cornerstone in interpersonal relations, and it helped him establish a personal connection with customers. Jay's father would suggest that customers visit the jewelry store down the street and then do the BABULEW – which stood for "Best Alternative to Buying Used from Lew." The pawn broker sometimes made "exploding offers" by introducing deadlines into a negotiation as a way to create a perception of a vanishing opportunity.

In a pawnshop, repeat business is a possibility, but cannot be counted on. Clientele may, as in a bazaar, be transient. However, customers usually thought they did well, were treated with respect, and had some fun bargaining with the pawnbroker. Even if they did not come back again, they spread a good word about the pawnshop.

A Wedding Dress Store in Nueva Rosita, Mexico

Another author recalls standard practice in his mother's wedding dress store in Nueva Rosita, Mexico. Mrs. Chamoun had invested resources in a quality inventory, but she always listened carefully to the bride's family and especially to the bride's demands, knowing that tailoring to needs and expectations was always a possibility. She would entertain the customer with a beverage and light snacks and not rush to sell. After showing her wares, she stressed that this was one of the most important occasions for a bride and recommended that the client visit the seller's competitors to make sure the bride was getting the right dress at the right price. Most brides returned to make the purchase. She could do this because she believed in her product and knew her competition. What she was selling, however, was not just a nice wedding dress for that special occasion. In what is surely a stressful planning period, the client could trust the details of customization and alteration to be done according to specifications in a timely and professional manner. Furthermore, when the bride was ready to pay, Mrs. Chamoun would give them a wedding ornament as a token of appreciation for the sale.

This bride would not be a return customer anytime soon, so why place so much emphasis on a customer relationship? Her strategy was building a reputation by giving things without expecting anything further from this client directly. However, a satisfied client has friends and family who will someday be in the market. Social networking (Durlauf and Young 2001) brings new clientele based upon independent experience. This is a form of indirect reciprocity (Nowak and Sigmund 2005).

Sending clients to competitors shows high confidence in her products and services and further builds credibility. Not only does the client have a positive experience to relate to her social network concerning Mrs. Chamoun's shop, she also has formulated lesser opinions regarding alternatives. From her small Mexican town, Mrs. Chamoun even exported dresses to very prestigious stores in the United States. Today, long after her death, people remember her as a great business woman with a caring heart, leaving a reputation that persists into the next generation. Reputation fuels business.

Reputation and Indirect Reciprocity

Direct reciprocity is repayment in kind for past behavior. Indirect reciprocity is the repaying of a debt owed by someone else. Robert Trivers (1971) calls this reciprocal altruism. According to Martin Nowak and Karl Sigmund (2005: 1291-1298):

Cooperation through indirect reciprocity, captured by the phrase "I help you, someone else helps me," requires the evolution of reputations and communication of those reputations among the larger group (as in the human instinct to gossip), cognitive abilities beyond being able to identify relatives (required for kin selection) or the individuals who have cooperated with you in the past (required for direct reciprocity).

A can do well to B and not get anything in return; however, the transaction may not remain private. C may choose to conduct business with A because of that information string, whether C has relationship ties with B or not. If A continues a pattern of behavior, A builds a history known to the whole community. A builds a reputation, though A does not control its use directly. A reputation can be either positive or negative. As seen in our examples, the only way to establish and maintain a reputation is to treat each customer as a carrier of information derived from the present shopping experience. Our information age has further empowered the consumer and heightened the role of reputation. The internet makes reputation as a "long term relationship mode" (LTRM) element far more valuable. Social networking sites and "rate this seller" features create strong, but indirect, reputational consequences.

Gerald Ferris and his colleagues (2003) have performed a systematic examination of reputation as it has been investigated in the accounting, sociology, economics, marketing, and organizational theory and strategy fields. The authors offer the following definition of personal reputation:

> Reputation is a perceptual identity reflective of the complex combination of salient personal characteristics and accomplishments, demonstrated behavior, and intended images presented over some period of time as observed directly and/or as reported from secondary sources (Ferris et al. 2003: 8).

We note the Arab proverb, "Do good things and throw them in the sea." This has four dimensions of meaning. First, the sea is so wide that no one will see you doing well unto them. Second, because of the extensiveness of the sea, you will not see them either. Third, the openness of the sea will make you always do well through the end of your life. Last, the sea is always dynamic in movement; without expectation, a wave of happiness and wellness will come back to you.

This business philosophy creates indirect reciprocity, and thus, is part of creating a reputation.

Reputation and Credibility

According to Harry Mills (2000), there are two things that build credibility: expertise and trust. The current work on trust suggests that there are three critical dimensions on which parties judge trustworthiness: the other party's ability (skills, knowledge, capability), benevolence (how nicely he/she treats me), and integrity (does he walk his talk, keep his word, etc.). All three work to strengthen credibility. Perhaps we all can name a relative whom we trust. However, we still may not endorse a hiring decision for this relative if his credentials and expertise do not match the job description. Likewise, a person with expertise whom you do not trust is unlikely to get a good recommendation. Credibility is produced by adding the parts. In the story of the wedding dress store, creating a trusting environment by sending customers to competitors would fail if they found better quality goods at reasonable prices elsewhere. That customers would return affirmed the shopkeeper's expertise. Similarly, we are reluctant to assume the risk of transacting business in an atmosphere of distrust, regardless of the perceived expertise. The combination builds credibility.

Offering product samples before buying likewise generates credibility. The hospitality fosters trust, while the customer is allowed to assess quality with his own personal taste. A token gift before the sale yields credibility, while a gift after the sale affirms it. Such gifting, however, must be of reasonable quality or meet a client need; otherwise, the gift loses its value and can even generate negative feelings (Chamoun and Hazlett 2009). Two of the authors, as students of history, are quick to point to the ancient Phoenicians as a model for repetitive sales based on a reputation of fair trades, quality products, and interest in long-term client needs (Chamoun and Hazlett 2007).

Teaching Negotiation and Bazaar Dynamics

According to Leandro Barretto (2009), *Ontological Coaching* is a very effective way of teaching, since the coach promotes the student's ability to discover on his own what he needs to learn in order to achieve a specific skill. Along these lines, classroom teaching can be enhanced by high-level, interactive, marketplace experiences with coaching. When we asked Istanbul Bazaar store owners how they learned to negotiate, the answer was overwhelmingly by watching and observing their parents and relatives from an early age. This is, likewise, true for the authors with pawn shop and wedding store experience. Despite cultural and geographic differences, the similarities in successful styles are remarkable. Sending students into the marketplace to observe, catalog, and practice behaviors from the buyers' perspective augments classroom teaching and promotes ownership of principles. A template to aid students in such an adventure learning experience at the marketplace is included in the appendix.

Bazaar Negotiation Process
Student observation and participation at a bazaar can demonstrate that long-term benefits can be created by attention to the following steps.

Prospecting
Consider a good value outcome for you and the other. For this, identify potential customers and culture, including being able to communicate in the customer's own language, if at all possible. The ability to select and identify prospects who are most likely to buy will give the shop owner leverage early in the negotiation. On the other hand, the buyer should not disclose his level of interest prematurely. The buyer should be empowered by the seller to bring something more than money to the table, such as the joy of negotiating and getting the deal. The store owner's initial objective is to get buyers into the store without being annoying. Buyers should realize that once inside, there will be a shift in strategy. With multiple prospects, owners will pay more attention to those perceived as buyers over browsers. Buyers can give cues or withhold them, depending upon their readiness to negotiate.

Creating and Claiming Value
Creating and claiming value are the challenges to the negotiator. At the Grand Bazaar, one store posted a sign outside the entrance indicating "FIXED PRICE" on a pile of displayed products. When asked, "How fixed was the fixed price?" the store clerk replied, "Very fixed." When asked if purchase of a substantial quantity would merit a better price, the answer was negative. The store owner was firm that quantity was not a viable negotiation tactic for this merchandise. However, if combined with a purchase inside the store, the price of displayed items was no longer immoveable. The outside products were hooks with little or no room to negotiate price. Once inside, the zone of possible agreements (ZOPA) for the items there was suddenly wider. By changing the environment, the prospective buyer can change the negotiation situation. Educated buyers must realize price ranges are already set by the owner and be prepared to

claim the value through negotiation. However, in cross-cultural exchanges within tourist markets, buyers are usually totally naïve as to price and cost, unless they have systematically shopped this particular item across several different merchants, which is generally rare. Buyers generally have little insight into how much price flexibility a seller has.

Store hooks can be seasonal or situational. Outside the Chamoun general merchandise store, toys and candies were placed outside for Christmas holidays to motivate parents to go inside, where many more products were available for their family. Similarly, the Folberg pawnshop used nylons and jeans, price-controlled items in short supply after World War II, as storefront hooks (Folberg 2008). Buyers should look for ways to widen the scope of negotiations, realizing there may be non-uniform margins across shop merchandise.

Relationship Building

Tasting products in the Grand Bazaar can induce feelings of obligation and a need to reciprocate with a purchase. If samples are offered freely, it can simply be a hook or a means to generate credibility. As cited, accepting samples fulfills an objective of the store owner. However, in the Grand Bazaar, if a sample is requested, rather than offered, and the customer moves on to sample similar wares of competitors, feelings of disloyalty are generated, and we have observed that the shop owner prefers not to sell to the returning customer. Their attempt to build a relationship with you was thwarted. Buyers must recognize relationship building overtures on behalf of sellers and respond in a culturally sensitive manner so as to maintain trust while establishing the value of a seller's goods. The seller is trying to establish credibility with expertise and trust. The interests of the buyer and seller extend beyond the immediate transaction. The seller's best deal will be through relationship, as it offers pricing to the customer that will support the shopkeeper's goal of reputation building, while the buyer, although looking for the best price, also has an interest in a quality experience.

Questioning

While the Socratic method of questioning is traditionally upheld as an effective method to learn about a counterpart and understand their needs, in Istanbul's Grand Bazaar, excessive questioning can generate hostility. Some cultures view questions as challenges, particularly to the credibility of the person being asked. In Turkey, buyers must be creative in getting information without aggressive questioning techniques commonplace in Western culture. As an example of when asking questions can be a deal breaker, one of the authors was trying to sell in the Grand Bazaar, rather than purchase. After trying unsuccessfully to place his trade books with multiple bookstores at the Grand Bazaar, one of our authors finally got a deal with one store owner to purchase five books. When the author returned with the inventory the next day at the mutually agreed upon time, the owner was absent. His brother-in-law indicated the shop owner would be back in an hour. With motive of being congenial while filling the wait time, the author engaged the brother-in law in conversation with ice-breaker questions concerning his home town, family size, and current business climate. Suddenly, the brother-in-law terminated the terms of the book exchange and escorted the author out of the store. The author consulted an eyewitness, the son of a neighboring shop owner, to gain insight into what transpired, who said the brother-in-law grew weary of too many questions. What can be a deal-maker in one culture could be a deal-breaker in another. We noticed at the Great Bazaar that asking questions when purchasing something is not considered as aggressive to the Turkish people as when you are selling to them.

Make Connections

People use gestures, questions, looks or touch to connect with others. According to John Gottman and Joan DeClaire (2001) there are five steps to strengthen your relationship with others:

1) Analyze the modes you use to connect and how you respond to attempts of others,

2) Discover how your brain's emotional command system affects your engagement process,

3) Examine how your emotional heritage impacts your ability to connect with others and your style of engagement,

4) Develop your emotional communication skills, and

5) Find shared meaning with others.

Each of the settings described included means to make a personal connection with clients, whether the customer bought or not. Relationship is first and foremost, even for a short term sale. In fact, the mindset of these negotiators was that each deal, even if a one-time transaction, has long term ramifications and potential ongoing value. Recalling Roy Lewicki's comments, there is intangible value to negotiators in believing you got a good deal (often not an objective determination), treating the other well, behaving fairly, etc. In fact, these dynamics may be greatly enhanced in "cross-cultural" negotiations, for many reasons. The buyer (let us presume, an American) is often outside of his own country, outside of his comfort zone with language and cultural familiarity, and, moreover, on the seller's turf.

The buyer is less comfortable with negotiation, because in *his* culture, merchants are not as aggressive at bringing buyers into their shop (the Grand Bazaar experience). The buyer is unable to objectively determine whether he is getting a good deal (who knows how much that box of chocolates should really sell for?), facing someone who negotiates for a living, and does not want to be seen (in his own eyes or that of his spouse or friends) as the cultural stereotype of an "Ugly American." Given this psychological mindset, you can imagine how vulnerable a culturally different negotiator really is in these transactions. Not all of this matters to every buyer, but enough does that it introduces significant psychological discounting into the process.

We recommend following the five steps described by Gottman and DeClaire (2001) to make sure we connect. Sellers may make quick gestures to initiate trust, but these overtures can be fragile. Buyers should be aware that the objective was to make the customer happy regardless of whether a purchase results.

Showing Respect

Owners may politely walk you to the door of the store regardless of sales. There is an overall air of loyalty to customers, including courtesy, smiling, sincerity, and enjoying the process. Buyers should reciprocate in a similar manner, although non-native buyers often see this as more aggressive compared to their own culture, in which merchants may only approach buyers once they are in the shop. How does a naïve buyer distinguish this from "aggressive hustling" (leading to defensive protectiveness on the part of the buyer)? These are the types of questions we should be raising to students in preparation to negotiate with other cultures.

Leveraging Expertise

Often, end-users are not equipped with either the time or information necessary to properly evaluate opportunities. While trust could be generated with any number of shop owners, the expertise element to establishing credibility may be lacking for both buyer and seller for specialty items. For example, one of our colleagues wanted to fix or replace a broken watch at the Grand Bazaar. Rather than deal directly with individual shop owners and be subject to decisions regarding shop expertise and reliability, the buyer decided to hire an expert from the Bazaar to find the best solution. At the end of the day, the expert concluded a replacement option was best and brought several watches to the hotel for the buyer's final choice. Buyers must discern when and when not to enter a negotiation directly. Sometimes the best choice is to delegate to another knowledgeable individual, though this creates agency problems well known in the literature (Docherty and Campbell 2006a; Nolan-Haley 2006).

Elevating the Relationship

The relationship does not always end at the point of sale. After a purchase, you may be invited for a cup of tea, or owners will give you an extra gift. This is what Chamoun and Hazlett (2007) call Tradeables, not to be confused with pre-sale nibble tactics. This can elevate the relationship above the present deal.

Suggested Outside-the-Classroom Adventure Learning Exercise

While cultural immersion is a key element in the Istanbul Grand Bazaar experience, a microcosm of bazaar dynamics amenable to student learning can be found in many local farmers' markets where multiple vendors sell fresh produce in a designated area. In some places, these may be alternatively called people's markets. In a farmers' market, shoppers will typically find a mix of posted-cost and unlabeled items. There may be freely offered samples of many items. Shoppers may also find a blend of hired workers, family members, produce growers, and middlemen who buy from others to resell. Frequently, shoppers may find an increase in cultural diversity among sellers at such markets, lending an additional dimension to the negotiating exercise.

At a farmers' market, students can practice how to look for and generate value in negotiations with a relatively modest investment. We suggest that students be allocated a fixed sum, perhaps $10, and given a predetermined shopping window, say one to two hours, depending on market size. Students should be sent in pairs or triads with common purchasing criteria. For example, students could be instructed to purchase at least one red, green, and yellow item. Their purchases could be expected to include at least one fruit and one vegetable. Only one item can be negotiated directly, focusing on price. Others must generate and create value aside from price. One student negotiates purchases, while the others observe. At appointed time intervals, they switch roles. Returning to class, students will compare results and bring their lessons learned from these experiences. In the debriefing session, students will collectively determine who made the best deal.

Students should be encouraged to develop criteria for vendor selection, to establish a relationship, to sample the products they purchase, and to find creative solutions to sweeten the deal. Students must look not only for the best deal, but also recognize who has the authority to negotiate better terms. Students may create value other than their monetary buying power to leverage a win-win scenario, such as making referrals.

While we encourage those teaching negotiation to develop an in-depth checklist to guide students through their farmers' market negotiation experience, the beginning pieces of one are offered in the attached Appendix. This checklist should include how to create and seek value generation, what to look for in a negotiation, and how to approach the counterpart, among other things. The farmers' market can provide a low budget opportunity rich in bazaar dynamics to put classroom teaching into hands-on practice.

Conclusion

Integrative, long-term negotiation strategies can be created in a distributive environment, such as a bazaar, a pawnshop, or a wedding dresses store. As Antoine de Saint-Exupéry (1943) in his famous book *Le Petit Prince* mentioned, "the essential is invisible to the eyes." In a distributive negotiation, we do not see the essentials, because we focus on the trade. We can find the essentials of the integrative negotiation by empathizing, understanding our bids and others, entering and respecting relationship-building overtures, and looking for ways to increase the scope and vision of negotiation to a bigger dimension – a long term one. Buyers and sellers should contemplate every transaction as though it has longer term consequences and use an integrative mindset, even if no future direct interaction is envisioned.

Classroom teaching of more effective integrative negotiations can potentially be bolstered by giving students more real experiences. Students should be coached on expectations, strategies, and behaviors, with particular attention to cultural context, in order to maximize lessons learned from negotiation exercises outside the classroom. Outlined bazaar dynamics apply across many cultures and geographic locations, suggesting that augmenting student curricula with marketplace experiences is a globally attractive addition to teaching negotiation for a working knowledge of integrative and distributive negotiation theories. The authors suggest an outside-of-the-classroom adventure exercise to include in the negotiation curricula to engage students into active learning by doing.

Notes

The authors gratefully thank the editors. Special thanks to Gerald Ferris, who amply supplied his work on reputation. We appreciate the mentoring role provided by Roy Lewicki in the preparation and editing of the manuscript.

References

Barretto, L. 2009. The role of ontological coaching on assuring quality: An approach for the professional competencies of the employees. Masters thesis, Universidad Autónoma de Tamaulipas.

Blickle, G., P. B. Schneider, Y. Liu, and G. R. Ferris. A predictive investigation of reputation as mediator of the political skill - career success relationships. *Journal of Applied Social Psychology* (in press).

Campbell, M. C. and J. C. Docherty. 2006. What's in a frame? In *The negotiator's fieldbook: The desk reference for the experienced negotiator*, edited by A. K. Schneider and C. Honeyman. Washington, DC: American Bar Association.

Chamoun, H. and R. Hazlett. 2007. *Negotiate like a Phoenician*. Houston, TX: KeyNegotiations.

Chamoun, H. and R. Hazlett. 2009. The psychology of giving and its effect on negotiation. In *Rethinking negotiation teaching: Innovations for context and culture*, edited by C. Honeyman, J. Coben, and G. DePalo. St. Paul, MN: DRI Press.

Cialdini, R. B. 1993. *Influence: The psychology of persuasion*. New York: William Morrow.

De Saint-Exupéry, A. 1943. *Le petit prince*. San Diego, CA: Harcourt.

Docherty, J. S. and M. C. Campbell. 2006a. Consequences of principal and agent. In *The negotiator's fieldbook: The desk reference for the experienced negotiator*, edited by A. K. Schneider and C. Honeyman. Washington, DC: American Bar Association.

Docherty, J. S. and M. C. Campbell. 2006b. Negotiation, one tool among many. In *The negotiator's fieldbook: The desk reference for the experienced negotiator*, edited by A. K. Schneider and C. Honeyman. Washington, DC: American Bar Association.

Durlauf, S. N. and H. P. Young. 2001. *Social dynamics*. Washington, DC: Brookings Institution Press.

Ferris, G. R., R. Blass, C. Douglas, R. W. Kolodinsky, and D. C. Treadway. 2003. Personal reputation in organizations. In *Organizational behavior: The state of the science*, edited by J. Greenberg, 2nd edn. Mahwah, NJ: Lawrence Erlbaum.

Folberg, J. 2008. Negotiation lessons from the pawnshop. *Dispute Resolution Alert* 8(2): 1-7.

Gottman, J. M. and J. DeClaire, J. 2001. *The relationship cure*. New York: Three Rivers Press.

Hochwarter, W.A., G. R. Ferris, R. Zinko, B. Arnell, and M. James. 2007. Reputation as a moderator of political behavior – work outcomes relationships: A two-study investigation with convergent results. *Journal of Applied Psychology* 92(2): 567-576.

Lewicki, R. J, D. M. Saunders, and B. Barry. 2006. *Negotiation: Readings, exercises, and cases*, 5th edn. New York: McGraw Hill/Irwin.

Mayer, B. 2006. Allies in Negotiation. In *The negotiator's fieldbook: The desk reference for the experienced negotiator,* edited by A. K. Schneider and C. Honeyman. Washington, DC: American Bar Association.

Mills, H. 2000. *Artful persuasion: How to command attention, change minds, and influence people.* New York: AMACOM.

Nolan-Haley, J. 2006. Agents and informed consent. In *The negotiator's fieldbook: The desk reference for the experienced negotiator,* edited by A. K. Schneider and C. Honeyman. Washington, DC: American Bar Association.

Nowak, M. A. and K. Sigmund. 2005. Evolution of indirect reciprocity. *Nature* 437: 1291-1298.

Siegfried, T. 2006. *A beautiful math: John Nash, game theory, and the quest for a code of nature.* Cambridge, MA: Belknap Press.

Trivers, R. L. 1971. The evolution of reciprocal altruism. *Quarterly Review of Biology* 46: 35-57.

Zinko, R., G. R. Ferris, F. R. Blass, and M. D. Laird. 2007. Toward a theory of reputation in organizations. In *Research in personnel and human resources management, Vol. 26,* edited by J. J. Martocchio. Oxford, UK: JAI Press/Elsevier Science Ltd.

Appendix

Template/Checklist for Marketplace Adventure Learning Experience
Advanced Preparation and Market Observations

Y N

☐ ☐   Was there a purchasing objective (i.e., to get at least two different type of fruits for less than x dollars)?
If so, what?

_____

☐ ☐   Did the buyer set a target price, wish price and a walk away price?
☐ ☐   Did the buyer set a BATNA and WATNA?
☐ ☐   Did the buyer consider the other's BATNA and WATNA?
☐ ☐   Did the buyer make the first offer?
☐ ☐   At any point, did an anchor (nonnegotiable terms) form?
☐ ☐   Did the buyer identify and deal directly with the decision maker(s) with power to negotiate?
☐ ☐   Did the buyer identify cultural differences/sensitivities?
☐ ☐   Did the buyer develop empathy?
☐ ☐   Did the buyer sample products?
☐ ☐   Was there a seller's entrance strategy (to get potential buyers in the store)?
If so, identify tactics used:

_____

☐ ☐   Were there tactics to close the sale?
If so, identify tactics used:

_____

☐ ☐   Did the seller ask questions to obtain the buyer's needs?

☐ ☐ Did the seller attract the buyer's attention?
If so, identify tactics used:

☐ ☐ Did the seller demonstrate credibility?
☐ ☐ Did the seller successfully handle buyer objections?
☐ ☐ Were there concessions made? If so, were they:
    ☐   Made by the seller (vs. buyer)?
    ☐   Made quickly (vs. slowly)?
    ☐   Large (vs. small)?
☐ ☐ Was there a sense of value added?
☐ ☐ Was there a sense of relationship established beyond the immediate deal?
☐ ☐ Was there an attempt to widen the scope of the deal?
☐ ☐ Was there an attempt to increase the negotiation pie towards a win-win scenario?
☐ ☐ Was the buyer happy with the purchase?
☐ ☐ Would the buyer return to this place of business?
If no, why not?

⚝ 23 ⚝

Should We Trust Grand Bazaar Carpet Sellers (and vice versa)?

Jean-François Roberge & Roy J. Lewicki *

Editors' Note: *Roberge and Lewicki use Lewicki's previously published model of trust and distrust to analyze transactions in the Grand Bazaar of Istanbul, and conclude that the merchants are often acting quite differently, and with different motivations, than Western customers assume. They use this insight to develop the "TRUst-rElationship" (TRUE) model, a more convenient way of defining four different kinds of relationships, each of which is based on each party's prediction of the trustworthiness of the other.*

Introduction

Istanbul's Grand Bazaar is a mythic place for negotiation. Starting as a "caravan sérail" in 1453 under the reign of Mehmet II, it now hosts more than 2000 boutiques selling various textiles, handbags, carpets, jewelry, lamps, Turkish delight (a Turkish candy), etc. As we discovered it, the Grand Bazaar is a perfect place for negotiation adventure learning exercises, highlighting the role of trust and relationship building in negotiation. As many customers did for hundreds of years before us, we asked ourselves this crucial question during negotiations: should we trust Grand Bazaar carpet sellers? And they were probably asking themselves the same question about us. Should Grand Bazaar carpet sellers trust us as customers?

With this chapter, we hope to provide some answers to this ancient question. In the first part, we will share a real-life-inspired

* **Jean-François Roberge** is a professor of law and director of Graduate Dispute Prevention and Resolution Program at the University of Sherbrooke, Faculty of Law (Québec, Canada). His email address is: jean-francois.roberge@ usherbrooke.ca. **Roy J. Lewicki** is the Irving Abramowitz memorial professor in the Max M. Fisher College of Business at The Ohio State University. His email address is lewicki_1@fisher.osu.edu.

Grand Bazaar negotiation scenario, highlighting trust building and relationship building between customers and merchants. In the second part, we will propose a theoretical model, "TRUst-rElationship" (TRUE), to understand how trust and relationship interacts in this negotiation dynamic. According to the TRUE model, as relationships develop between negotiating parties, trust levels change, and as trust levels change, relationships further develop. We believe this relationship-trust dynamic has a significant impact on negotiation processes and outcomes. Inspired by the "Aladdin and the New Lamp" décor of the Grand Bazaar, we hope the TRUE model can be seen as a "New Lamp" shining light on and helping us to answer an ancient question.

Part One: The Grand Bazaar Carpet Sale Scenario

This carpet sale negotiation is based on a true story lived during an adventure learning experience in Istanbul's Grand Bazaar. First we will detail an "insider-customer" view of the negotiation factual context as we experienced it. Second, we will take an outsider observer's (negotiation professor's) perspective, and highlight the trust and relationship dilemmas faced by the customer and the merchant during negotiations. In this paper's first part, we hope to highlight bazaar dynamics to "stage" the TRUE model perspective on trust and relationship.

The Negotiation Context

The meeting step

James, a negotiation professor, is interested in buying a Turkish carpet at Istanbul's Grand Bazaar. He enters *Mamid's Treasury*, a small carpet store located in one central alley of the Bazaar. Azra, the smiling seller, welcomes the professor and invites him to sit down comfortably. Azra calls his assistant Birman, who appears from the back room. Azra asks James what he is interested in. James answers that he is interested in buying a carpet. Azra asks James if he already has a Turkish carpet. James answers no and says he would like to be well counseled before buying. Smiling, Azra tells the professor he is in the right place.

The selling demonstration step

Azra starts the selling demonstration. He asks his assistant Birman to unroll first one carpet, then a second and a third, all different in colors and details. He asks James which one he prefers. The professor points at one in particular. In a firm and determined way, Azra asks his assistant to unroll three other selected carpets among the few hundred in the store. Then Azra gives explanations about the carpets, starting with the one on top, and enters in a conversation with James.

Azra:	*This silk carpet was made 150 years ago. It is hand made and comes from the Antalaya region. Pure silk (with an enthusiastic tone of voice and a straight look at James).*
James:	*How can I be sure it is 150 years old? (with a dubious tone).*
Azra:	*Because I know (with a reassuring smile).*
James:	*How can I be sure you know? (re-emphasizing his dubious tone).*
Azra:	*Because we are in the business for four generations.*
James:	*How much is it?*
Azra:	*$6000 U.S. (with a firm convinced attitude).*
James:	*It is very expensive! (surprised).*
Azra:	*It is top quality fabric. Pure silk. Handmade. 150 years old. Real Turkish carpet can last forever! (with conviction).*
James:	*I like the shiny red one below the two others.*
Azra:	*This red one is ten years old. Handmade. From Ankara region. It is shinier than the oldest one because it is newer.*
James:	*How much is this one?*
Azra:	*$800. Very good quality.*
James:	*Well, I like this one. Give me your best price. You are the first shop I visit today. I do not want to shop around all day so I need your best price now.*
Azra:	*This is a good price and you are my first customer today. You bring me good luck.*

While James is talking to Azra, Birman the assistant at the back of the store subtly calls someone on his cell phone. Two minutes later, Omar, a tall man in his early forties wearing a nice jacket, enters the small store and introduces himself to James in perfect English. Azra immediately steps aside and leaves Omar full discretion to pursue the discussion with James.

The persuasion step

Omar:	*James, so you like this one?*
James:	*Yes, that is my favorite so far. What is your best price? You are the first store I visit today and I will only visit*

	one more store after yours. I want to compare prices and I will buy a carpet where I get the best deal.
Omar:	*It may be tough to compare. Let me propose you something else. I offer you to come to our bigger shop, two minutes from here. We have a lot more carpets there and we will make you the best deal we can. Come with me.*
James:	*Your time is precious. My time is precious. So give me your best price on this one and I will compare.*
Omar:	*James, where are you from?*
James:	*From the states.*
Omar:	*New York, California?*
James:	*California. San Francisco.*
Omar:	*I like California. I have friends there. San Francisco is a wonderful city. James, I see you have potential. I trust you. Here is my proposition. Bring the carpet you like to your home in San Francisco. You pay nothing now. Ask an expert in San Francisco to evaluate the price of the carpet and you will pay me what the expert estimates it is worth. What do you think about this proposition? Is it fair?*
James:	*Well, it seems fair. That is an interesting proposition. Let me think about it. (James then takes written notes of the proposition.)*
Omar:	*You seem very analytical. What do you do for a living?*
James:	*I am a professor.*
Omar:	*It shows, you are serious and intelligent. Come with me at our biggest store, we will offer you tea, lokums (a candy more commonly also known as Turkish Delight), and you will be comfortable to choose the right carpet for you.*
James:	*I do not want to waste your time and my time, and besides I need to ask my wife before I purchase such a pricey carpet. That is why I ask you for your best price.*
Omar:	*You can take the carpet with you to your hotel and if your wife does not like it, no problem, bring it back to the store and we will find the right one.*
James:	*I really need your best price on this carpet.*

The Negotiation Dilemma

Omar:	*I made a step forward with my offer. Now you need to make your step as well.*
James:	*Why not give me your best price?*

After a moment of silence, Omar looks James in the eye and asks him: "Do you have trust issues?" From that moment on, Omar makes the discussion a matter of trust and relationship. Omar changes the rhetoric from a substantive conversation about the rug and its price to the relationship itself. James is surprised and says nothing.

Omar: *I made a step forward. You did not. You have trust*
          issues, James. You should change....You would have
          a happier life...(with a judgmental tone and attitude).

From then on, the "newly built relationship" between Omar and James was at stake. Trust became a central issue of the negotiation. Clearly, relationship and trust between customer and seller are part of the negotiations and have an impact on process and outcome.

How any negotiator responds honestly to the question "Do you have trust issues?" is an important issue that has not really been addressed in negotiation writings. In this context, an honest and courageous James should say: "Yes I do, I do not trust you." In fact, James seems to have very reasonable trust problems. He is not an expert in rugs and does not know how to fairly assess the quality of the carpet and the fairness of the price. Cultural differences also seem to create misunderstandings that inhibit trust development. In James's commercial culture, sellers do not swap salespersons in mid-sale, serve tea, take you to another store, let you go home with goods without paying, etc. James may have stereotypes about merchants in other cultures and the way they sell rugs. In addition, James may experience negative emotions, like fear of being "taken" and looking foolish, generating defensiveness. Is the seller in cahoots with someone else? What and who will he find in that other store? Will James be able to walk away if he does not like the deal, or will the seller push the sale and try to trap him into making an agreement?

In order to reach an agreement, James should ask Omar to help him overcome the distrust, and vice versa. Otherwise, the seller's presumed friendliness gestures, performed to create positive feelings and identification with the buyer, will be perceived as inauthentic and as a strategic move to push for the sale at a price which is perceived to be overrated. Similarly, the buyer's repeated questions about the rug's quality and price can be perceived by the seller as excessive distrust, which will prevent the creation of a trustworthy relationship between them. The buyer asks for reliability in a "cost-benefit" assessment, as the seller expects reliability by knowing the buyer better and assesses his "reciprocal similarity" or reciprocity.

Buyer and seller would each like to trust the other, but each has a different set of trust problems that they cannot directly assess or discuss.

There are many things going on in this conversation. Not only is there a trust problem, but the parties switch "languages" or "frames" in the middle of the conversation. In negotiation, parties talk at least three "languages." One is the language of information, where each exchanges information about the substantive issues. A second is the language of persuasion and negotiation, attempting to use strategy and tactics to gain a competitive advantage. And the third is the language of relationship in which parties openly discuss how their process is affecting their ability to communicate with the other, trust the other, make progress toward an agreement, and affect the negotiation in the future.

The relationship conversation is often the most critical, but also the most difficult to have. Moreover, when one party changes the "language" of the conversation abruptly to this level, it can be very disarming – as our buyer discovers when Omar begins to talk about the "trust problem." Can parties actively take charge of a negotiation by mastering the interchange among these different conversations? This needs more reflection. In this paper, we will focus on these trust and relationship interactions.

Finally, analyzing this Grand Bazaar scenario raises many questions. Should the negotiation professor buy, or "bring home" the carpet? Should he trust the carpet seller (and vice versa)? Should the negotiation professor learn to be more comfortable with the seller (and should the carpet seller learn to be more responsive to the buyer – and what would it take for the parties to get to either state)? How did trust and their relationship interact and evolve over time? Why is trust and the parties' relationship so relevant in negotiation – even in a single transaction like a rug purchase? What was the impact of trust and relationship building on the negotiation process and outcome here?

The TRUE model we propose provides a framework to understand the evolution and interaction of trust and relationship during a negotiation. In the second part of this paper, we will now look at how the TRUE model, as a "new lamp," could help us better understand Grand Bazaar negotiation dynamics.

Part Two: A Trust-Relationship (TRUE) Model to Understand the Grand Bazaar Dynamics

Should we trust Grand Bazaar carpet sellers (and should they trust us)? Why? How? Our objective in this second part is to provide some answers. Negotiating in the Grand Bazaar generated a reflection on trust and relationship building in negotiations. Lessons learned led us to create the "TRUst-rElationship" (TRUE) theoretical model (see Figure One). This model's main origins can be found in the work of Roy J. Lewicki (2000, 2006) on trust in relationships, and William A. Donohue (2001) on the topic of communication and relationship. The TRUE model is strongly inspired from their work, and can be seen as a unique adaptation relevant to understanding the Grand Bazaar's dynamics.[1]

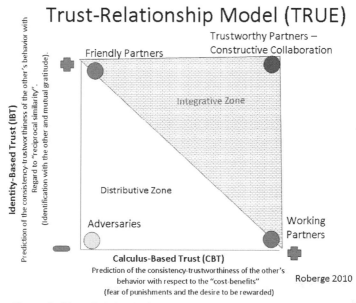

Figure 1. "Trust-Relationship" model (TRUE) with its four relationship types, based on their combined degrees of calculus-based trust (CBT)/identity-based trust (IBT) and their connection to the integrative/distributive negotiation zones.

In a nutshell, the "TRUst-rElationship" (TRUE) model helps to identify how one party perceives his relationship with the other party, based on that party's prediction of the trustworthiness of the other's behavior. The TRUE model addresses four types of relationships, developing during the course of a negotiation between two parties: adversaries, friendly partners, working partners and trustworthy partners. Each type of relationship is a relational state determined by the degree of "calculus-based trust" (CBT) and "identity-based trust" (IBT) each party predicts from the other party's behavior. These two types of trust are described extensively in Lewicki (2000, 2006) (see also Figure 1). Adversaries and trustworthy partners' relationship types (the lower left and upper right corners) are non-paradoxical relational states because parties have corresponding low CBT and IBT or high CBT and IBT states together. Friendly partners and working partners are paradoxical relational states because either type of trust (e.g., CBT) is high while the other type of trust is low (e.g., IBT), creating ambiguous communication between parties and making it difficult for one party to predict the other's behavior. This perception or prediction of the other's behavior can change over time according to interactions during the negotiation. Accordingly, relationship types are dynamic, and can move from one to another in paradoxical or non-paradoxical relational states.

The TRUE model we propose has multiple uses. First, we believe it can help us understand bargaining dynamics in the bazaar, and is transferable to other negotiation contexts. Second, the TRUE model can be used as a feedback tool for exercises that replicate the dynamics of the bazaar (i.e., yard sales or used car negotiations), or other similar negotiation contexts involving significant trust and relationship interactions. The Grand Bazaar factual scenario detailed in part one of this paper could even be formatted as such an exercise. Finally, the model can also be a theoretical framework for exploratory empirical research.

The TRUE model's fundamental principles will be explained in the form of answers to four questions:

1) What is our definition of trust and relationship?
2) How do trust and relationship interact?
3) What is the impact of trust and relationship in negotiation?
4) How do we build trust in negotiation?

What is Our Definition of Trust and Relationship?

One commonly accepted definition in the research literature on trust is that "trust is a psychological state comprising the intention to accept vulnerability based upon positive expectations of the intentions or behavior of another" (Lewicki 2006, quoting Rousseau et al. 1998: 335). Confident positive expectations have been defined as virtuous intentions attributed to another party on the basis of "an individual's belief in, and willingness to act on the basis of, the words, actions, and decisions of another" (Lewicki 2006: 440, citing McAllister 1995; Lewicki, McAllister, and Bies 1998). Lewicki emphasizes that "[t]he need for trust arises from our interdependence with others" and notes that "[a]s our interests with others are intertwined, we also must recognize that there is an element of *risk* involved insofar as we often encounter situations in which we cannot compel the cooperation we seek" (Lewicki 2006: 192).

Because of that risk, inherent as a consequence of our interdependence with others, we believe one party will trust another party based on the prediction party one makes of the consistency and trustworthiness of the other's behavior. Predictions can be made on the basis of two kinds of criteria. First are "cost-benefit" criteria (fear of punishment and the desire to be rewarded) leading to CBT. As noted by Lewicki and Wiethoff (2000),

> [t]his kind of trust is an ongoing, market-oriented, economic calculation whose value is determined by the outcomes resulting from creating and sustaining the relationship relative to the costs of maintaining or severing it....It is grounded in impersonal transactions, and the overall anticipated benefits to be derived from the relationship are assumed to outweigh any anticipated costs" (88; 92).

Second, predictions can also be made in regard to criteria of perceived similarity and commonality (identification with the other's desires, values and definition of self) leading to IBT. According to Lewicki and Wiethoff (2000: 93),

> [t]his type of trust exists because the parties can effectively understand and appreciate one another's wants. This mutual understanding is developed to the point that each person can effectively act for the other....It is grounded in perceived compatibility of values, common goals, and positive emotional attachment to the other.

Indeed, "[a]s the parties get to know each other and identification develops, the parties come to understand what they must do to sustain the other's trust" (Lewicki 2006: 194).

The second conceptual grounding for this model can be found in the work of Donohue (2001). Donohue states that "autonomy and affiliation are the two fundamental dimensions underlying interpersonal relationships" (2001: 28). Relationships are defined as the simultaneous combination of autonomy and affiliation between parties. Autonomy is defined as the desire to maintain social autonomy when people interact with others while affiliation is defined as the desire to be accepted and connected to others (Brown and Levinson 1978; Donohue 2001).

As Donohue (2001: 28-29) suggests, we think autonomy and affiliation function simultaneously in interpersonal communication and they can come into conflict with each other. This conflict gives a paradoxical nature to relationships as parties negotiate their interdependence (being tied to the other), dealing simultaneously with their desire to be unimpeded by others and yet be affiliated with others. The paradox has been studied by many communication researchers (Bateson et al. 1956; Watzlawick, Beavin, and Jackson 1967; Bavelas et al. 1990; Donohue 2001). Rawlins (1989, 1992) and Leslie A. Baxter (1990) explored the concept of paradox in understanding interpersonal relationships (Donohue 2001: 29). They conceive of relationships as dynamic, temporary resolutions of the competing tensions between simultaneous autonomy and affiliation as parties negotiate their interdependence (Donohue 2001: 29-30). The TRUE model conceptualizes the paradoxical nature of relationships into four relationship types.

How Do Trust and Relationship Interact?

Trust has been described as the "glue" that holds relationships together and enables individuals to perform more efficiently and effectively (Lewicki 2006: 191). We assume trust between parties has an impact on their relationship, and vice versa (Lewicki and Wiethoff 2000). As relationship develops, trust changes, and as trust changes, relationship develops. We believe people tend to approach others with some initial positive level of trust (McKnight, Cummings, and Chervaney 1998). "Many people approach a new relationship with an unknown other party with remarkably high levels of trust" (Lewicki 2006: 197). But relationships are also developmental, as parties share experiences, and multifaceted, as parties interact in different contexts (Lewicki and Wiethoff 2000).

As proposed in Figure 1, relationships between parties can be categorized according to the degree of CBT and IBT. This categorization addresses the paradoxical nature of relationships we discussed earlier where autonomy and affiliation interact simultaneously. Thus, friendly partners live in a competitive paradox. While they feel understood by the other party, they do not believe the benefits of working together will outweigh the costs. But working partners live in a cooperative paradox. While the parties believe that it is worth working together, they do not feel understood by the other party. Paradoxical relationship types involve equivocal ambiguous communication between parties and reinforce the difficulty of predictions.

A relationship type is a relational state (Donohue 2001). Each party lives in a certain mental state; sometimes parties will "live" in the same state and other times they will live in different states. Relational states evolve over time and can change according to the interaction between parties. We conceive friendly partners and working partners as paradoxical states in the sense that one party trusts the other party in a specific way, but at the same time does not trust him in another way. We see adversaries and trustworthy partners as nonparadoxical states in the sense that one party either does not trust the other at all, or fully trusts the other. There are, of course, also degrees in between each pair of states. In brief, we assume trust between parties determines the relational state they are in as categorized here, some of which are paradoxical and others non-paradoxical (see Figure 2). These paradoxes have an impact on negotiation dynamics, as discussed in the next section.

	Low Calculus-based trust Negative cost-benefit predictions	High Calculus-based trust Positive cost-benefit predictions
High Identity-based trust Positive reciprocal similitude predictions	Friendly partners Paradoxical relational state	Trustworthy partners Non-paradoxical relational state
Low Identity-based trust Negative reciprocal similitude predictions	Adversaries Non-paradoxical relational state	Working partners Paradoxical relational state

Figure 2. The four relationship types, as paradoxical or non-paradoxical relational state, based on their degree of combined calculus-based trust and identity-based trust.

What is the Impact of Trust and Relationship in Negotiation?

The TRUE model assumes that relationship types influence the negotiation approaches parties are more likely to adopt (see Figure 1). Literature on negotiation generally classifies negotiation processes as two different types: distributive (competitive) vs. integrative (collaborative) (Walton and McKersie 1965; Lewicki, Barry, and Saunders 2010). Relationships developed by parties can significantly affect their negotiation process (Greenhalgh 1987; Donohue 2001). The negotiator's dilemma is the tension between competing and collaborating desires experienced by every negotiator (Lax and Sebenius 1986). Collaborating is risky if one party cannot predict the other's behavior, as the game theory field has illustrated (Axelrod 1984). Yet it should not be surprising that paradoxical relationship types exist when parties struggle with desires to compete and collaborate at the same time.

Non-paradoxical relationship types (adversaries, trustworthy partners) can lead parties toward unambiguous distributive or integrative negotiation processes. The party that shares an adversary relational state with another is more likely to negotiate in a distributive way because CBT and IBT trust are both low. Parties will see each other as "adversaries," leading to competitive bargaining and focusing on the maximization of individual gains at the expense of the other. As noted by Donohue (2001: 33), "communication in this relational condition includes factual information sharing, attempts at bolstering one's own position and credibility, and messages about termination and withdrawal."

Conversely, if parties share the "trustworthy partners" relationship type, their CBT and IBT are high and they should be more willing to negotiate in an integrative way. Quality information sharing, potentially leading to generating creative solutions, is likely to happen when parties have greater expectations of trust (Lewicki 2006). Moreover,

> [g]reater information sharing tends to enhance effectiveness in achieving a good negotiation outcome (and less information sharing tends to diminish effectiveness in achieving a good outcome), although this effectiveness may not necessarily be the result of greater trust (Lewicki 2006: 198).

Trustworthy partners feel confident in their prediction of the other's behavior, based on their relationship cost-benefit ratio and in regard to their reciprocal similitude. They believe it worth risking the collaboration. Thus, according to Donohue (2001: 32), "when parties retain this relational condition for some time, they are expected to focus on exchanging information, proposals, and concessions while also avoiding the use of threats and other types of attacks." And, notes Lewicki (2006: 198), "[t]rust increases the likelihood that negotiation will proceed on a favorable course over the life of a negotiation."

Paradoxical relationship types (friendly partners and working partners) can lead either to distributive negotiation or integrative negotiation processes, depending on the context. "This paradoxical state can either hinder or improve the parties' ability to negotiate, depending on how they choose to resolve the relational paradox" (Donohue 2001: 34). Equivocal or confused communication may result from paradoxical relationship types, and it becomes difficult for a party to predict the other's behaviors. In these situations, one party's prediction of the other's consistent behaviors may not be clear or accurate enough to risk collaboration. Because CBT or IBT is low, they may distrust the other and act in a distributive way.

For example, members of the same working team may believe each one is able and willing to perform the task properly, leading to integrative negotiation when ordering or building goods or services. High CBT exists among these workers because each one trusts the other's abilities and capacities, and the overall anticipated benefits to be derived from the relationship are assumed to outweigh possible anticipated costs. At the same time, these workers may negotiate in a distributive way when decisions have to be made on how to share the profits, because they do not share the same sense of fairness or honesty; e.g., one believes in equality for everyone and the other believes in proportionally sharing based on who dedicated the most time to the construction of the goods. A low IBT exists among the workers. Their relationship type could then be defined as "working partners" (high CBT and low IBT). They live in a cooperative paradox, because they feel it worth sustaining the relationship relative to the costs of severing it, while they do not perceive or share compatibility in values, goals, or positive emotional attachment to the other. Equivocal communication may be used, meaning "I do not think you and I have a lot in common, but I am willing to work with you." At the same time, the nature of the negotiation tasks (distributive vs. integrative) can have an impact on how parties shape trust (Lewicki 2006). "In a more distributive context, trustors tend to focus on the risks they face, while those in a position to receive and then reciprocate the others' trust focus on the benefits that the trustors have provided them" (Lewicki 2006: 198).

How Do We Build Trust in Negotiation?[2]
While some authors may challenge this assumption, "bazaar" negotiations are generally considered distributive by nature. However, even in distributive negotiations, trust-building techniques can be used to improve both CBT and IBT levels and influence relationship development. We will explain how this can happen.

As Lewicki (2006) succinctly summarized,

> [t]rust building is a bilateral process that requires *mutual* commitment and effort, especially when attempting to deescalate conflict. While one party can initiate actions that may move the trust-development process forward, the strongest trust must be mutually developed and at a pace acceptable to both parties" (199).

Given the distributive, market orientation of bazaar negotiations, we can generally expect parties to primarily focus on CBT for trust building (Lewicki 2006). Let us not forget that IBT could also play an important role in sustaining a long-term relationship and to overcome the inevitable conflict that will occur over time. "Strong [CBT] is critical to any stable relationship, but IBT (based on perceived common goals and purposes, common values, and common identity) is likely to strengthen the overall trust between the parties and enhance the ability of the relationship to withstand conflict that may be relationship fracturing" (Lewicki and Wiethoff 2000: 102).

Lewicki (2006: 199-200) suggests actions to increase CBT and IBT. Here we provide a summary as a framework reference and invite you to read the original for details. To increase CBT, Lewicki proposes the following actions:

1) perform competently your duties and obligations;
2) create and meet the other party's expectations in a consistent and predictable way;
3) point out and reaffirm the benefits of creating mutual trust;
4) establish credibility with honesty and accurate, open and transparent communication;
5) show concern, respect and sensitivity for others;
6) share and delegate power and control over the process; and
7) develop a good reputation in creating the belief that you are trusting and act trustworthily.

To increase IBT, Lewicki (2006: 199-200) suggests that we work to:

1) develop similar interests;
2) identify similar goals and objectives;
3) act and respond similarly to the other in the same situation;
4) identify true common principles and values without compromising; and
5) "actively discuss your commonalities, and develop plans to enhance and strengthen them."

In addition, we find it relevant to highlight some similarities between ancient Phoenician merchants (2300 B.C. – 65 B.C.), known to be skillful negotiators, and contemporary bazaar shop owners. As Habib Chamoun-Nicolas and Randy Doyle Hazlett (2008) highlighted, Phoenicians used "tradeables" to develop trustworthy relationships in the particular context of market oriented negotiations. By tradeables, they mean either: 1) a set of ideas or actions that help leverage a deal without being part of the deal, or 2) "products and services that satisfy customer needs outside our own product line that are not in competition with our offerings" (Chamoun and Hazlett 2008: 1; see also Chamoun, Folberg, and Hazlett, *Bazaar Dynamics*, in this volume).

By using "tradeables," Phoenicians were able to create long-term relationships with their clients (Chamoun and Hazlett 2007). Phoenicians developed tradeables by following some or all of the following nine steps:

1) understand before being understood;
2) know the other party's rituals;

3) prepare before responding (e.g., visit the store prior to serious shopping);
4) take time to plan your strategy;
5) propose solutions;
6) make an accord;
7) verify the agreement;
8) execute the agreement;
9) confirm the agreement is complete and look for future discussions (Chamoun and Hazlett 2008: 115-163).

In analyzing Bazaar shop owners' negotiations with customers, we come to the conclusion that the trust building techniques they recommend appear to be very similar to the Phoenicians' "nine step culture of trade." Bazaar merchants, as the Phoenicians long before them, develop relationships with customers using a mix of CBT and IBT techniques, as we will illustrate using the nine step process:

Step 1: A Bazaar owner will first listen to the customer to find out their needs and interests.

Step 2: He or she carefully analyzes the customer to understand where they are coming from ("know the rituals"), carefully trying to listen to nonverbal as well as verbal cues. (These first two steps seem to correspond to Lewicki's proposed IBT actions 1, 2 and 3, where parties look for common ground and synchronicity.)

Step 3: He or she will get the customer inside the store, by all persuasive means, and particularly by showing expertise and product knowledge, thus building credibility.

Step 4: While this is going on, the Bazaar shop owner is preparing a strategy, smiling, offering tea or other beverages, and other sampling of products.

Step 5: Only then, after the customer is thoroughly comfortable, is a customized proposal developed.

Steps 6 and 7: An agreement is reached, but the merchant tries to verify what is included and if the customer needs anything else, potentially increasing the size of the negotiating pie. (CBT building actions 1 to 5, as mentioned earlier, seem to fit steps 3 to 7, where parties establish credibility, consistency, and predictability, and address expectations.)

Steps 8 and 9. Then the "Fait Accompli" is established and the merchant confirms that you have what you need and makes sure you are happy with the sale. The two last steps seem to be a mix of IBT action 5 and CBT actions 6 and 7, oriented to additional and/or future negotiations. Since the Phoenicians and maybe before, this seems to be a very old way of developing trust.

In summary, bazaar owners' trust-building techniques seem to focus on the development of IBT to create a "bond of partners" at the beginning of the negotiation. Then CBT actions are used to create a "mutually agreeable deal" between trustworthy, credible partners. After the deal, a "bond of trustworthy satisfied partners" is created, leading to a good mutual reputation for future rounds of negotiation later on.

Conclusion

Should we trust Grand Bazaar carpet sellers, or not? Should they trust us? The answer is complex. To answer that question, the TRUE model suggests identifying the relationship types that parties are experiencing. Predictions of the other's behavioral consistency, based on "cost-benefit" and "reciprocal similarity" criteria and corresponding levels of combined CBT and IBT, will determine the relationship type experienced. Paradoxical relationship types, namely friendly partners and working partners, will lead us to "cautious trust." Negotiations with Grand Bazaar carpet sellers in an integrative way will be limited, since collaborating moves, such as open information sharing, will appear to be risky. Non-paradoxical relationship types will lead us either to genuinely trust the other as trustworthy partners, or not at all, as adversaries. Again, negotiations with Grand Bazaar carpet sellers will be influenced by the relationship types experienced, leading to potentially integrative negotiation or purely distributive negotiation. Relationship types change over time as actions are taken to improve CBT and IBT. In proposing the TRUE model, we hope to create a "new lamp," lighting the crucial role of trust and relationship in negotiations practiced since "mille et une nuits" (A Thousand And One Nights).

Notes

[1] The actual paper adopts sometimes different premises than previous Lewicki and Donohue works. One difference from Lewicki's conception of trust is that here we split up the two dimensions of trust, "identity-based" and "calculus-based" trust, as co-existing and simultaneous instead of sequential, as this fits with the real-life negotiation experience between our Turkish sellers and American buyer. The co-existence of these two forms of trust may be more consistent with the co-existence of "calculative" and "relational" forms of trust as described by Rousseau et al. (1998).
[2] We are grateful to Habib Chamoun-Nicolas and Randy Hazlett for their contribution to this section.

References

Axelrod, R. 1984. *The evolution of cooperation*. New York: Basic Books.

Bateson, G., D. D. Jackson, J. Haley, and J. Weakland. 1956. Toward a theory of schizophrenia. *Behavioral Science* 1: 251-264.

Bavelas, J. B., A. Black, N. Chovil, and J. Mullett. 1990. *Equivocal communication*. Newbury Park: Sage.

Baxter, L.A. 1990. Dialectal contradictions in relationship development. *Journal of Social and Personal Relationships* 7: 69-88.

Brown, P. and S. Levinson. 1978. Universals in Language usage: Politeness phenomena. In *Questions and politeness: Strategies in social interaction*, edited by E. Goody. Cambridge: Cambridge University Press.

Chamoun H. N. and R. Hazlett. 2008. *Negotiate like a Phoenician: Discover Tradeables*. Houston: Keynegotiations.

Donohue, W. A. 2001. Resolving relational paradox. The language of conflict in relationships. In *The language of conflict and resolution*, edited by W. F. Eadie and P. E. Nelson. Thousands Oaks, CA: Sage.

Greenhalgh, L. 1987. Relationships in negotiations. *Negotiation Journal* 3: 235-243.

Lewicki, R. J. 2006. Trust and distrust. In *The negotiator's fieldbook: The desk reference for the experienced negotiator*, edited by A. K. Schneider and C. Honeyman. Washington, DC: American Bar Association.

Lewicki, R. J., D. J. McAllister, and R. J. Bies. 1998. Trust and distrust: New relationships and realities. *Academy of Management Review* 23(3): 438-458.

Lewicki, R. J. and C. Wiethoff. 2000. Trust, trust development, and trust repair. In *The handbook of conflict resolution*, edited by M. Deutsch and P. T. Coleman. San Francisco: Jossey Bass.

Lewicki, R. J., B. Barry, and D. Saunders. 2010. *Negotiation*, 6th edn. Burr Ridge, IL: McGraw Hill Higher Education.

Lax, D. and J. K. Sebenius. 1986. *The manager as negotiator*. New York: Free Press.

McAllister, D. J. 1995. Affect and cognition-based trust as foundations for interpersonal cooperation in organizations. *Academy of Management Journal* 38(1): 24-59.

McKnight D. H., L. L. Cummings, and N. L. Chervaney. 1998. Initial trust formation in new organizational relationships. *Academy of Management Review* 23(3): 473-490.

Rawlins, W. K. 1989. A dialectical analysis of the tensions, functions, and strategic challenges of communication in young adult friendships. In *Communication yearbook*, edited by J. Anderson. Newbury Park: Sage.

Rawlins, W. K. 1992. *Friendship matters*. New York: Aldine de Gruyter.

Rousseau, D., S. Sitkin, R. Burt, and C. Camerer. 1998. Not so different after all: A cross-discipline view of trust. *The Academy of Management Review* 23(3): 393-404.

Walton, R. E. and R. B. McKersie. 1965. *A behavioral theory of labor negotiations: An analysis of a social interaction system*. New York: McGrawHill.

Watzlawick, P., J. H. Beavin, and D. D. Jackson. 1967. *Pragmatics of human communication*. New York: Norton.

෬ 24 ෨

Navigating Wickedness: A New Frontier in Teaching Negotiation

Christopher Honeyman & James Coben*

Editors' Note: This short essay sets the context for the following three chapters, and introduces a remarkable group of contributors, surely one of the most extraordinary and diverse working teams we have yet seen in our field. In the chapters which follow, their collective experiences and stories are woven together for the first time. The result makes the case for enlarging our canon to include a sophisticated consideration of "wicked problems."

The final three chapters in this book epitomize its title: we are now "Beyond the Classroom" indeed. Here, practitioner-scholars with experience negotiating conflicts in some of the world's most troubled places join with others, whose less violent experience-settings are remarkable for other reasons, to analyze what might be done to teach people to negotiate "wicked problems."

Wicked problems, first described by public planners Horst Rittell and Melvin Webber (1973), exist in a messy space where technical planning processes and political decision-making intersect. For the purposes of this introduction (and the chapters to follow), we use the term "wicked" to describe problems that exhibit some combination of the following features:

* **Christopher Honeyman** is managing partner of Convenor Conflict Management, a consulting firm based in Washington, D.C. and Madison, Wisconsin. He has directed a twenty-year series of major research-and-development projects in conflict management and is coeditor of *The Negotiator's Fieldbook* (ABA 2006). His email address is honeyman@convenor.com. **James Coben** is a professor of law and senior fellow in the Dispute Resolution Institute at Hamline University School of Law. His email address is jcoben@hamline.edu.

- The problem is ill-defined and resists clear definition as a technical issue, because wicked problems are also social, political, and moral in nature. Each proposed definition of the problem implies a particular kind of solution which is loaded with contested values. Consequently, merely defining the problem can incite passionate conflict.
- Solutions to a wicked problem cannot be labeled good or bad; they can only be considered better or worse, good enough or not good enough. Whether a solution is good enough depends on the values and judgment of each of the parties, who will inevitably assess the problem and its potential solutions from their respective positions within the social context of the problem.
- Every wicked problem is unique and novel, because even if the technical elements appear similar from one situation to another, the social, political, and moral features are context-specific.
- A wicked problem contains an interconnected web of subproblems; every proposed solution to part or the whole of the wicked problem will affect other problems in the web.
- The only way to address a wicked problem is to try solutions; every solution we try is expensive and has lasting unintended consequences. So, although we have only one shot to solve *this* wicked problem, we will have plenty of opportunities to develop our skills as we deal with the wicked problems that we create with our attempted solutions.[1]

When dealing with wicked problems, we need to focus our energy on identifying and framing the negotiable problem, while also paying attention to the connection between efforts to solve the problem and the political and social context. To resolve wicked problems we must be creative; we need to adopt a stance of openness that facilitates continued learning and revision of our understanding of the problem and possible solutions.[2] We also need to monitor the ways our own actions reshape the problem and the context.

This stands in sharp contrast to the nature of problems that the planning profession has labeled "tame." As summarized by Ritchey (2005-2008: 1), a tame problem:

- Has a relatively well-defined and stable problem statement.
- Has a definite stopping point, i.e., we know when a solution is reached.
- Has a solution which can be objectively evaluated as being right or wrong.

- Belongs to a class of similar problems which can be solved in a similar manner.
- Has solutions that can be tried and abandoned.

"Negotiation 1.0," the contributors to this section assert, provides a valuable and useful set of theories and tools to understand and address so-called "tame" problems. In their experience, however, the same "conventional" negotiation theory and tools are not well-matched for problems with "wicked" characteristics. However, it is useful to recognize that even within a "wicked" problem, there may be subsets of issues that are relatively "tame." Successfully negotiating these subsets of "tamer" issues may contribute to helping bring changes necessary to transform the problem as a whole.

Nevertheless, all the authors of these chapters posit that the main theories and tools developed so far to support "Negotiation 2.0" will be, in and of themselves, inadequate to address wicked problems. "Negotiation 2.0" methods will still be focused on negotiating particular problems – including the "relatively tame" subsets of issues within a wicked problem. Managing wicked problems, in Jayne's and Leonard's view in particular, requires a dual attention to negotiating particular problems and engaging in processes for maintaining, or resisting and reshaping, patterns of power, privilege and communication that shape our collective lives. The authors call the interactive processes that create and reshape the context social negotiation.

Consciously engaging in social negotiation even as we negotiate particular problems requires high levels of contextual awareness and self-awareness; a capacity for critical thinking, strategic planning and action; and a focus on ethical reasoning and judgment. Beyond this, Howard argues below that the need for "1.0 skills" is inescapable, even on the more "wicked" elements, because the wicked elements are compound products that inevitably include parts that require those skills. This point is under debate, at present: Jayne takes the view that some of the "1.0 skill set" must be *unlearned*, or at least set aside, to allow the necessary degree of flexibility and creativity. The difference may or may not be resolved in future thinking and writing of this team, or of our colleagues as more of them grasp this particular nettle; it is simply too soon to say whether Howard and Jayne have identified a troublesome conceptual stage or an enduring philosophical divide. For now, we believe both views are well articulated in the discussion which follows.

From their experiences, the authors in this section report that wicked problems occur in a wide variety of contexts:

- Sometimes, wicked problems arise in situations where the context surrounding the specific problem being negotiated is volatile and changing rapidly, perhaps as part of a violent conflict.
- Some wicked problems, on the other hand, occur in situations where the context is apparently stable, with participants sometimes "stuck" in stalemates of mutual dissatisfaction, disaffection, or dysfunctional responses to shared problems.
- Some wicked problems arise in contexts which have discrete elements of stability combined with elements of instability; both elements need to be addressed.

As a consequence, parties addressing wicked problems may at times work toward stability as a part of their overall solutions to the problem. At other times, particularly as articulated in Jayne's view in *"Adaptive" Negotiation* (Chapter 26), they actually may seek to destabilize existing socially negotiated systems of power and privilege[3] which have contributed to "blocking" the participants in a frozen situation. (Indeed, as discussed in Chapter 27 by Leonard, the new "Design" doctrine of the U.S. Army contemplates just such a destabilization of a traditional socially negotiated system. When employed at the discretion of the commander for use in complex and ill-structured settings, Design doctrine modifies the commander's traditional responsibility for setting parameters and labeling problems that the staff is charged to solve, instead requiring commanders to collaborate with the staff and share the role of frame setting and problem identification.)

Regardless of their context, the authors in this section agree that wicked problems require an orientation and a toolkit beyond those of "Negotiation 1.0." In other words, even as we are developing "Negotiation 2.0" and the teaching methodologies associated with it, the extraordinarily diverse individuals writing the chapters in this section of the book are thinking about an even more complex problem: what must we do to ensure that "Negotiation 2.0" is robust enough to deal with wicked problems?

The authors have chosen to divide that particular problem into two parts, suggested by these questions:

- How can we ensure that the problem-focused negotiation skills developed and taught in "Negotiation 2.0" are suitable for use in the global context of multiple cultures, and thereby useful for working with both tame and wicked problems?
- How can we ensure that the pedagogy which grows out of "Negotiation 2.0" will provide guidance for using problem-focused negotiation in tandem with other interventions to

address wicked problems, and avoid the disastrous or even fatal results that can arise from an unexamined use of "Negotiation 1.0" in such settings?

On the first of these questions, we should note, many other writers in this volume and its immediate predecessor, as well as in the *Negotiator's Fieldbook* (Schneider and Honeyman 2006) have much to say. The second question, however, is being addressed almost for the first time in the chapters in this section – with an honorable mention to three predecessor writings in the *Negotiator's Fieldbook*, those by Peter Coleman et al., Daniel Druckman, and John McDonald.

We recognize, for all of these reasons, that our attention to the role of negotiation in wicked problems – including its implications for teaching – represents a new frontier in our field, and an important one. It is not, however, without antecedents. Most conspicuously, there is a decades-long history of practice and scholarship in environmental and public policy disputes (see, e.g., Forester 1980; Bingham 1986; Carpenter and Kennedy 1991; Forester 1999; Susskind, McKearnan, and Thomas-Larmer 1999; and Carpenter and Kennedy 2001). This sophisticated body of writings lays out the basis for, and many of the techniques of, a practice where a "negotiation" may involve many parties, many issues, and many ancillary and even competing processes in addition to bilateral negotiation, all in an environment of unstable rules, laws, players and politics (see also Pruitt, Rubin, and Kim 2004).

Yet for many years, that work and that sophistication failed to "scale up." A second antecedent, a series of symposia in 2005-2006 organized in four cities by Christopher Honeyman, Peter Adler, Sanda Kaufman, and Andrea Schneider, started with this premise: that on the most important U.S. national issues of the day – Iraq, Afghanistan, Social Security, immigration, health care, and others – there was, at the time, no visible evidence that much, if any, of the conflict resolution field's vaunted sophistication was actually being employed. The rueful if tentative conclusions (Kaufman, Honeyman, and Schneider 2007) assigned much of the causality to our field's own habits, expectations – and prejudices.

In the next chapter (*Negotiating Wicked Problems*) the following authors share stories about their attempts to use "Negotiation 1.0" when addressing wicked problems:

- **Calvin Chrustie** is a Royal Canadian Mounted Police officer with experience in international peacekeeping operations and negotiating complex conflicts for the United Nations and other agencies, including hostage crises and international kidnaps, as well as aboriginal and other volatile intractable community disputes in Canada, the Middle East, the Balkans, and Africa. Calvin also has done guest lectures and teaching for military, police, and government agencies within Canada and abroad.

- **Jayne Seminare Docherty** is a professor at the Center for Justice and Peacebuilding at Eastern Mennonite University, where she teaches civilian peacebuilders who have been working in volatile and often violent situations. She has also spent most of the past two years teaching leaders of ethnic groups that have been involved in a protracted violent conflict about the possibilities of using negotiation as an alternative to continued fighting, and coaching them as they try to adapt negotiation strategies to fit their situation.

- **Leonard Lira** is a U.S. Army officer who, among other experiences, has served two tours in Iraq; he is now an assistant professor in the Army's Command and General Staff College at Fort Leavenworth, Kansas, where he is both teaching and developing teaching strategies for preparing mid-career officers for the emergent problems they will face in the field.

- **Jamil Mahuad** previously served as Mayor of Quito, as a member of the Ecuadorian National Congress and later as President of Ecuador. He is now co-director of the Project on the Prevention of Global Violence, part of the Harvard Institute on Global Health (HIGH), under the office of the President of Harvard University. He also is the co-founder and a senior adviser of the Harvard International Negotiation Program; a member of the global advisory board of Mediators Beyond Borders; and a board member of Masar Ibrahim El-Khalil (The Abraham Path), a project aimed at creating a historical/cultural walking path in the Middle East retracing the footsteps of the Prophet Abraham.

- **Howard Gadlin** is the ombudsman at the U.S. National Institutes of Health. A former professor of psychology, he has also been ombudsman for the University of California – Los Angeles (UCLA), the Los Angeles County Museum of Art, and the University of Massachusetts, Amherst. While at UCLA he was also co-director of the Center for the Study and Resolution of Interethnic/Interracial Conflict, and he has many years' experience working with conflicts related to race, ethnicity and gender. Currently he is developing new approaches to addressing conflicts among scientists, and he is often called in as a consultant/mediator in "intractable" disputes.

In the three chapters which follow, our colleagues tackle one of the hardest challenges in our field: how to think about, how to formulate, and how to teach negotiation under the worst of circumstances. The depth of the challenge and its complexity raise a conundrum for our authors, and our field. As part of our journey to a second, or for that matter, a third generation of effective negotiation teaching and practice, must we discard large parts of "Negotiation 1.0" altogether?

On the one hand, initial training is a way of introducing novices to the basics, so that they build up a degree of skill and confidence they can draw on almost without thinking when they are in a complex situation that calls for a complex response (see Gladwell 2008). As Howard has said, "I've played tennis for 50 years, but I still do drills, and I still take lessons (trainings) in the basics, because that is the only way I can incorporate what I learn into the deep repertoire of strategies with which I try to play the game."

On the other hand, simply making additions to the "Negotiation 1.0" toolbox may not take seriously enough the claim that its foundational assumptions limit its applicability and effectiveness. Jayne (in *"Adaptive" Negotiation*, Chapter 26) suggests that we need to re-center the social negotiation that gave rise to "Negotiation 1.0," by building an awareness of other forms of problem-focused negotiation that arose in other contexts into "Negotiation 2.0" practice and teaching. As noted above, this tension is visible in the writings which follow, and we believe it will be some time before it can be resolved.

A Section Summary

Chapter 25 (*Negotiating Wicked Problems*) lays the foundation for discussion of negotiations in several varied contexts distinguished by the presence of "wicked" characteristics, as the authors relate stories from their respective personal experience.

In Chapter 26 (*"Adaptive" Negotiation*), Jayne identifies features that must be incorporated into "Negotiation 2.0," if we are to use negotiation as part of our toolkit for addressing wicked problems. In addition, she addresses the challenge of teaching negotiators to pay attention to social ethics and the role of judgment in their work.

In Chapter 27 (*Design: The U.S. Army's Approach*), Leonard describes the way the Army is now using principles from planning and architectural design, among other external fields, to address the wicked problems encountered in situations such as Iraq and Afghanistan.

Undoubtedly, a stream of work for these and other thinkers and practitioners is just beginning: we are nowhere near finality. But this is more than a preliminary sketch, and the contributions to this section now set forth an analysis, an agenda, and a challenge to our field. To borrow a famous formula, we believe this is "the end of the beginning." There is reason to believe that these chapters can launch some of the most exciting and significant work that might be done in conflict management anywhere. In the meantime, the process of working out just what *is* our subject has itself posed something of a "wicked problem" for our authors. We salute the zeal, intellectual integrity, and grace with which they have begun to tackle it.

Notes

[1] This composite set of characteristics of wicked problems is derived from Rittell and Webber (1973), Ritchey (2005-2008) and Conklin (2005).
[2] "Social problems are never solved. At best they are only re-solved – over and over again" (Rittell and Webber 1973: 160).
[3] There is a distinguished literature on the moral value of destabilizing a system, ranging from the writings of Saul Alinsky to the writings of family therapists. Consequently, the concept of destabilization in our context does not have to be considered as new, but can refer back to these antecedents.

References

Bingham, G. 1986. *Resolving environmental disputes: A decade of experience.* Washington, DC: Conservation Foundation.

Carpenter, S. L. and W. J. D. Kennedy. 1991. *Managing public disputes: A practical guide to handling conflict and reaching agreement.* San Francisco: Jossey-Bass.

Carpenter, S. L. and W. J. D. Kennedy. 2001. *Managing public disputes: A practical guide for government, business and citizen's groups.* San Francisco: Jossey-Bass.

Coleman, P. T., L. Bui-Wrzosinska, R. R. Vallacher and A. Nowak. 2006. Protracted conflicts as dynamical systems. In *The negotiator's fieldbook: The desk reference for the experienced negotiator,* edited by A. K. Schneider and C. Honeyman. Washington, DC: American Bar Association.

Conklin, J. 2005. Wicked problems and social complexity. In *Dialogue mapping: Building shared understanding of wicked problems,* edited by J. Conklin. New York: Wiley.

Druckman, D. 2006. Uses of a marathon exercise. In *The negotiator's fieldbook: The desk reference for the experienced negotiator,* edited by A. K. Schneider and C. Honeyman. Washington, DC: American Bar Association.

Forester, J. 1980. Critical theory and planning practice. *Journal of the American Planning Association* 46: 275-86.

Forester, J. 1999. *The deliberative practitioner: Encouraging participatory planning processes.* Cambridge, MA: MIT Press.

Gladwell, M. 2008. *Outliers: The story of success.* New York: Little, Brown.

Honeyman, C., J. Coben, and G. De Palo (eds). 2009. *Rethinking negotiation teaching: Innovations for context and culture.* St. Paul, MN: DRI Press.

Kaufman, S., C. Honeyman and A. K. Schneider. 2007. Why don't they listen to us? The marginalization of negotiation wisdom. In *Négociation et transformations du monde*, edited by C. Dupont. Paris: Éditions Publibook.

McDonald, J. W. 2006. A new future for Kashmir? In *The negotiator's fieldbook: The desk reference for the experienced negotiator*, edited by A. K. Schneider and C. Honeyman. Washington, DC: American Bar Association.

Pruitt, R., J. Z. Rubin, and S. H. Kim. 2004. *Social conflict: Escalation, stalemate, and settlement*, 3rd edn. New York: McGraw-Hill.

Ritchey, T. 2005-2008. *Wicked problems: Structuring social messes with morphological analysis.* Swedish Morphological Society. Available at www.swedmorph.org (last accessed June 28, 2010).

Rittell, H. W. J., and M. M. Webber. 1973. Dilemmas in a general theory of planning. *Policy Sciences* 4: 155-169.

Schneider, A. and C. Honeyman (eds). 2006. *The negotiator's fieldbook: The desk reference for the experienced negotiator.* Washington, DC: American Bar Association.

Susskind, L., S. McKearnan, and J. Thomas-Larmer (eds). 1999. *The consensus building handbook.* Thousand Oaks, CA: Sage.

☯ 25 ☯

Negotiating Wicked Problems: Five Stories

Calvin Chrustie, Jayne Seminare Docherty, Leonard Lira,
*Jamil Mahuad, Howard Gadlin & Christopher Honeyman**

* **Calvin Chrustie** is an Inspector of Police and has served as the lead negotiator and negotiation strategist for the Royal Canadian Mounted Police Conflict Negotiation Team, Province of British Columbia. He has also been engaged in a multitude of conflict situations abroad with the United Nations and other agencies in the Middle East, the Balkans, and Africa. His email address is cal.chrustie@rcmp-grc.gc.ca or calchrustie@hotmail.com. **Jayne Seminare Docherty** is a professor at the Center for Justice and Peacebuilding at Eastern Mennonite University in Harrisonburg, Virginia. Her first book *Learning Lessons from Waco* was an analysis of the Federal Bureau of Investigation's attempt at hostage negotiation with the Branch Davidian sect, and her subsequent work has frequently involved the intersection and relationships between uniformed forces and civil society, ethnic minorities, and religious groups. Her email address is jayne.docherty@emu.edu. **Leonard Lira** is a Lieutenant Colonel in the U.S. Army and an assistant professor in the Department of Joint, Interagency and Multinational Operations of the Command and General Staff College at Fort Leavenworth, Kansas. His email address is leonard.lira@us.army.mil. **Jamil Mahuad** is a co-director of the Project on the Prevention of Global Violence, part of the Harvard Institute on Global Health (HIGH), under the office of the President of Harvard University; co-founder and senior advisor to the Harvard International Negotiation Program at the Program on Negotiation, Harvard Law School; and a member of the Global Advisory Council of Mediators Beyond Borders and board member of the Abraham Path Initiative. He teaches executive education programs on the use of emotions in negotiations based on his experiences as Mayor of Quito (1992-1998), President of Ecuador (1998-2000) and Nobel Peace Prize nominee (1999). His email address is jmahuad@law.harvard.edu. **Howard Gadlin** has been ombudsman, and director of the Center for Cooperative Resolution, at the National Institutes of Health since 1999. Previously he served as ombudsman for the University of California – Los Angeles (UCLA), the Los Angeles County Museum of Art, and the University of Massachusetts, Amherst. His email address is gadlinh@od.nih.gov. **Christopher Honeyman** is managing partner of Convenor Conflict Management, a consulting firm based in Washington, D.C. and Madison, Wisconsin. He has directed a twenty-year series of major research-and-development projects in conflict management and is coeditor of *The Negotiator's Fieldbook* (ABA 2006). His email address is honeyman@convenor.com. The authors thank Roger Foster for his extensive and careful help in the editing of this chapter.

Editors' Note: Sometimes the problem to be negotiated is itself both obscure and deeply unstable; everything you do to try to improve the situation turns out to create a new problem, and sometimes, a worse one. In these settings, the authors conclude, traditional negotiation training has often not been enough: we need something new. The contributors offer a series of personal and dramatic stories from very different settings, which together illustrate how a new set of concepts and approaches is developing. The rest of the chapters in this section set out to define what that might consist of, and how it just might – at a starting level, and with a great deal of needed development only barely under way – begin to work.

Introduction

The unusual team of authors for this paper came together in stages, starting in Rome at the 2008 initial conference of the Rethinking Negotiation Teaching project. There, the first three authors (Calvin, Jayne, and Leonard) started sharing stories about their efforts to use negotiation in situations of violence and instability. In Istanbul, Jamil and Howard joined the team with stories of negotiating difficult problems in more stable and less violent settings. The sixth author, Chris, makes no claim to have negotiated wicked problems, but has served as the team's internal facilitator.

As we proceeded from discussion to writing, we agreed that the project needed to focus not only on developing new ways of teaching "Negotiation 1.0," but also on shifting the theories that support negotiation and the tools used by negotiators. We also agreed that in our experience negotiation as a term may stand for a whole array of processes which, in other contexts, are often treated separately. To choose a relatively straightforward example, when the United States and China are referred to as being in the process of "negotiating" a new trade relationship, those directly concerned are likely to understand this as involving much more than two "negotiators" sitting down at a table in Beijing or Washington. In this example, it would not be unusual to find such a bilateral meeting taking place on one issue even while the same parties are holding mediated talks on another aspect, litigating two or three more issues before the World Trade Organization, and sending complementary or contradictory negotiating signals by unilaterally enacting new import regulations on something else. In the situations we are concerned with, it is often arid and unhelpful to try to separate "pure" negotiation from the other activities; what counts is the whole package.

Experience drives our conclusion: "Negotiation 1.0" practices were designed to work best when dealing with situations where the *problem* is clear (and agreed upon by the parties) but the *solutions* are not evident. We, on the other hand, have been working on cases where the problem is *not* clear. Furthermore, any attempt to define the problem incites passionate conflict, in part because each definition of the problem implies solutions that carry social, political and moral consequences that are valued differently by various parties. In other words, "Negotiation 1.0" practices were well suited to dealing with "tame" problems; we have found them inadequate, except as component parts of something more evolved, when dealing with "wicked" problems (Honeyman and Coben, *Navigating Wickedness*, Chapter 24). We argue in the succeeding chapters that our field needs to develop more robust and adaptive negotiation *practices*, as well as more flexible and creative methods for *teaching* negotiation, if we want to prepare our students to deal with the myriad number of problems in the world that are correctly classified as "wicked."

The concept of tame versus wicked problems is imported from public planning; we find the distinction also useful for thinking about why negotiation works well in some situations but not in others. However, the terms cause difficulty, because while "wicked" problems have a flavor all their own, the term "tame" seems insulting as well as inaccurate for problems that can include the negotiation of multi-million-dollar deals or the settlement of complex litigation. It is important to acknowledge that "tame" is not a synonym for easy, and "wicked" is not a synonym for complex.

A more useful way to think about negotiating tame versus negotiating wicked problems is to consider the types of changes negotiators need to make when dealing with a problem. Tame problems can be very complex, but they are still amenable to "technical" solutions. To the extent that "Negotiation 1.0" focuses on linear movement through identifiable steps and stages (which of course has never been *entirely* the case), it can be analyzed largely in terms of "technical" change – with the negotiator or intervener applying an external set of tools to solve a problem. Wicked problems, on the other hand, require "adaptive" responses that require negotiators or intervenors to modify their own views and behaviors, rather than merely applying tools to a problem outside themselves (Kegan and Lahey 2009). To the extent that "Negotiation 1.0" was originally "developed in large part by relatively affluent Western white males culturally situated in a free-enterprise context" (Greenhalgh and Lewicki 2003: 2) with a focus on managing transactions rather than managing ongoing relationships (Greenhalgh and Lewicki 2003: 31), it does not lend itself to dealing with problems that require the negotiators to change themselves and their relationships in order to address problems. It is also important to acknowledge that "tame" is not another word for "nonviolent" and "wicked" is not another word for "violent." Three of the authors (Calvin, Jayne, and Leonard) work in situations dominated by violence or the potential for violence. The other authors (Jamil, Howard, and Chris) do not deal regularly with violence. Yet we all deal with problems that appear to be wicked; each of the cases exhibits some combination of the following features (stated in the previous chapter but repeated here for convenience of the reader):

- The problem is ill-defined and resists clear definition as a technical issue, because wicked problems are also social, political, and moral in nature. Each proposed definition of the problem implies a particular kind of solution which is loaded with contested values. Consequently, merely defining the problem can incite passionate conflict.

- Solutions to a wicked problem cannot be labeled good or bad; they can only be considered better or worse, good enough or not good enough. Whether a solution is good enough depends on the values and judgment of each of the parties, who will inevitably assess the problem and its potential solutions from their respective positions within the social context of the problem.

- Every wicked problem is unique and novel, because even if the technical elements appear similar from one situation to another, the social, political, and moral features are context-specific.

- A wicked problem contains an interconnected web of sub-problems; every proposed solution to part or the whole of the wicked problem will affect other problems in the web.

- The only way to address a wicked problem is to try solutions; every solution we try is expensive and has lasting unintended consequences. So, although we have only one shot to solve *this* wicked problem, we will have plenty of opportunities to develop our skills as we deal with the wicked problems that we create with our attempted solutions.[1]

A tame problem, by contrast, can be – more or less – separated from the surrounding context and dealt with as a discrete issue. (Again, we must emphasize, this does *not* mean that "tame" should be confused with "easy"; problems meeting this definition can include the settlement of complex litigation or the negotiation of multi-million-dollar deals.) As summarized by Ritchey (2005-2008: 1), a tame problem:

- Has a relatively well-defined and stable problem statement.
- Has a definite stopping point, i.e., we know when a solution is reached.
- Has a solution which can be objectively evaluated as being right or wrong.
- Belongs to a class of similar problems which can be solved in a similar manner.
- Has solutions that can be tried and abandoned.

Wicked problems cannot be separated from the surrounding context; any engagement with a wicked problem has its own implications for the larger social, political, and cultural order. But contexts are not all alike. Some are more or less stable while others are highly unstable. Consequently, we see wicked problems at work in several differing contexts in our stories.

Some wicked problems arise in situations where the context surrounding the specific problem for which one might consider using negotiation is unstable and, in some cases, prone to violence. Other wicked problems arise in situations where the context is more stable – perhaps even too stable. In other cases (see Jayne's story below), the context is a complicated mix of unstable and overly stable (or "stuck") features. Contextually-driven factors that should be investigated when dealing with a wicked problem include:

- It is difficult for the parties to sustain a stable definition of the problem.
- It is also hard to demarcate the boundaries of the negotiable problem in ways that prevent other issues from encroaching on the negotiation process.
- The negotiating parties find it difficult to reach agreement about the relative goodness or badness of the proposed solutions.
- Individually, the participants have difficulty articulating their best and worst alternatives to a negotiated agreement because it is difficult to calculate risk and opportunity against an uncertain future. [2]
- Deep-seated problems exist, but they are not being addressed. [3]
- Individuals who "see" the problem are dismissed as doomsayers, comparable to the hysterical protagonist in the Chicken Little fable who keeps proclaiming "the sky is falling!"
- The system or parts of the system may have to be destabilized – by leaders, mass movements, violence, or catastrophic events – before the wicked problem will be adequately recognized.

- The beneficiaries of the unsustainable or violent systems resist change or threaten to resist change that alters their privileges.

Common to all wicked problems is the need for negotiators to proceed with careful attention to both the processes and the ethical implications of social negotiations which they choose to engage, as well as an appreciative mindfulness of those social negotiations which are already in play. The reasons why will become evident as we examine the stories which follow.

Wicked Problems: Five Stories from Different Worlds

The following stories illustrate our varied attempts to use negotiation in response to wicked problems. Each story is followed by a brief analysis of specific problems associated with using "Negotiation 1.0" in that particular context.

Wicked Problems in Unstable Contexts

Negotiating prisoner of war and body exchanges, and kidnapping cases (Calvin Chrustie)

In the early 1990s, Calvin Chrustie was deployed with the United Nations Protection Force (UNPROFOR), the peacekeeping force mandated by the United Nations (U.N.) on February 21, 1992 to ensure conditions for peace talks and security in three demilitarized "safe-haven" enclaves designated as United Nations Protected Areas (UNPAs) located in the Republic of Croatia, in Western Slavonia and Krajina. As the situation deteriorated, the UNPROFOR mandate was expanded to include:

- Controlling access to the UNPAs and control of the demilitarization of the Prevlaka peninsula near Dubrovnik;
- protecting the Sarajevo airport, protecting humanitarian aid in the whole of Bosnia and Herzegovina, and protecting civilian refugees;
- interdicting military aircraft in the Bosnia and Herzegovina airspace in coordination with NATO forces;
- monitoring the "security zones" of Bihać, Sarajevo, Goražde, Žepa, Srebrenica and Tuzla; and
- in 1994 and 1995, monitoring cease-fires.

On March 31, 1995 UNPROFOR was restructured into three coordinated peace operations and the forces of UNPROFOR were incorporated into the NATO-led Implementation Force (IFOR), whose task was to implement the Dayton Peace Accords. We include this brief history of UNPROFOR within the former-Yugoslavia to illustrate the fact that negotiators in volatile contexts are often working in situations where the overarching mandate of the organization they work for is subject to constant revision in response to issues and circumstances that are far removed from their control.

Calvin's story involves a little-known but common use of negotiation even in the context of an active war. As in other war settings, the warring parties in the former Yugoslavia – working with the International Committee of the Red Cross (ICRC) as facilitator – had created formal negotiating structures called Exchange Commissions, to manage negotiations about the return to their home communities, or exchange, of prisoners of war (POWs), detainees, hostages, and the bodies of deceased individuals. Legally, these situations fall under Chapter II of the Annex to the 1907 Hague Convention and its updated version known as the Fourth Geneva Convention of 1949, which covers the treatment of prisoners of war and detainees and clearly states that even where there is not a conflict of international character, the parties must at a minimum protect those persons described as noncombatants; members of armed forces who have laid down their arms; and combatants who are *hors de combat* (out of the fight) due to wounds, detention, or any other cause. These persons shall in all circumstances be treated humanely, with the following prohibitions (Fourth Geneva Convention of 1949, Article 3, Section 1):

1) Violence to life and person, in particular murder of all kinds, mutilation, cruel treatment and torture;
2) Taking of hostages;
3) Outrages upon personal dignity, in particular humiliating and degrading treatment.

The ICRC and the warring parties wanted UNPROFOR to participate in and support the Exchange Commissions, but the UNPROFOR response was indifferent at best. Many U.N. representatives either viewed the issues as "off mandate" or as so complex and politically risky that they had no desire to involve themselves in the work of the commissions. The political risks included being blamed by the parties for any failed negotiation, and being used as a scapegoat if the failed negotiations resulted in further escalation of tensions. At an organizational level, many key U.N. peacekeepers and negotiators were working under contract, and failure in exchange negotiations – particularly if such failures were seen as the cause of escalating violence – could result in nonrenewal of their contracts, or hinder personal advancement within the U.N. system. In other words, the negotiations involved high risks, including the potential loss of life, and the organizational and personal consequences for failure were so high that UNPROFOR personnel adopted a "risk averse" mindset that led them to avoid working with the Exchange

Commissions. This left the ICRC with the lead role in a "facilitated mediation process" for managing the exchange issues, but ICRC personnel quietly recognized their inability to advance the process towards resolution in many instances. Consequently, they solicited non-sanctioned support from individual negotiators assigned to UNPROFOR. These UNPROFOR personnel sometimes provided the pressure or expertise necessary to secure and implement agreements about exchanges. However, the ambiguity of the process often created situations where a public negotiation process acted as a screen, "covering" real negotiations in closed rooms or in the hallways outside of the negotiation rooms. Achieving success in the exchange negotiations was not easy.

The warring parties themselves were ambiguous in their commitment to resolving the exchange issues during the course of the conflict. Many warring military and paramilitary groups continued to capture, kidnap and withhold the casualities of war because the prisoners and even the deceased were seen as valuable commodities at the various negotiation tables within the larger context of the conflict. In some instances, the warring parties would collect human beings and even the remains of casualties in order to build their own power vis-à-vis other negotiations. They used the fate of the human beings (alive or dead) under their control to advance their interests in negotiations over freedom of movement, ceasefires, claims to territory and other issues.

Even though some leaders of the warring factions were clearly violating the Geneva Convention, others among the leaders exhibited independent thinking similar to that shown by UNPROFOR personnel who tried to assist with the exchange negotiations. These leaders were genuinely seeking the international community's support and assistance in the mediation and resolution of the exchange issues. But the net result of the pressures against negotiating issues of exchange was the creation of a fragile and tenuous negotiation process that was subject to numerous negative influences.

The issues were not easy to resolve or even to frame effectively for negotiation. For example, the parties, including individual negotiators directly involved in the process, were torn between their long-term and short-term interests. POWs and hostages, if released and turned over, were potential witnesses to war crimes and other human rights violations. Even the deceased could provide evidence of mass murders and genocide. And the allegations were likely to be leveled at some of the key military and civilian leaders, including some individuals associated with the exchange process. Achieving the release of one's own people was a political coup, but releasing the people held by one's own group had the potential to create other problems, including an escalation of tensions and further violence when the evidence carried by the released individuals (alive or dead) came to light. Whether the resolution of a POW, kidnap or body exchange was defined as the "end game" or as a "means to an end," serving other negotiation objectives was also fluid. Most often, it was difficult to ascertain what the interests of the parties really were, due to the complex web of influencing factors that were ever-changing and unpredictable.

Generally speaking, negotiators are taught that a certain level of transparency and information sharing is one key to the negotiation process. But the exchange negotiations were complicated by the high levels of risk associated with sharing information. It is difficult to negotiate effectively when, as happened to Calvin, even telling Side A whom he was meeting with on Side B resulted in Side A mounting a large special forces operation to capture friends and family of the negotiator for Side B. This was a dramatic situation, but overall it was not unusual to have a negotiation process lead to other kidnappings or loss of life, as each party tried to use coercion and threats to alter the decision-making of the other party.

The behaviors described above are difficult to comprehend if they are not set in the context of history. Many of the parties involved as either hostages or family to the hostages, and even many of the negotiators, were survivors or first generation children of individuals who had survived the concentration and POW camps of World War II, including the extermination camp of Jasenovac. And if they were not affected by historical traumas, many of the negotiators had witnessed recent violence and experienced deep personal loss, including the murder of relatives, as a consequence of the ongoing war. The relatively fresh memories of death camps, torture, and brutality and the immediate experience of violence gave rise to intense feelings of fear and hatred amongst the parties. For example, a senior Serb civilian was kidnapped in a small village near Rajic. The brother of the elderly Serbian male kidnapped, his only living relative, sought Calvin's assistance in securing his brother's release. Both the hostage and his brother were in their late sixties.

Months of negotiation ensued, during which the brother of the hostage shared with Calvin that both he and the hostage were orphans from a local WWII concentration camp. When the camp was liberated in 1945 by the Allies, a Yugoslavian couple adopted them, because the boys had lost their family in the concentration camp. Half a century later in 1993, one of them *again* found himself in a detention camp. The tools of active listening and expression of empathy seemed wholly inadequate for working with such traumatized individuals. And the task of negotiating a resolution or series of resolutions capable of bringing the POW and kidnap crisis to an end seemed well out of reach of individuals equipped only with the tool-kit of negotiation skills provided in typical "Negotiation 1.0" courses and trainings.

Furthermore, a victim image frequently invoked by language used in discussions of negotiation teaching (e.g., in the paragraph above, deep personal loss/trauma/fear) can be inadequate or mis-leading to describe some of the people one must negotiate with, who may be better described in terms of "players." For example, Calvin recalls attempting to secure the release of a certain high-ranking Croatian military officer who was kidnapped in 1992. A meeting was set up with a senior Serbian military intelligence officer to secure a response from the Bosnian Serbs as to their willingness to release the Croatian general, then being held in a detention center. The meeting was with one of the aides to the infamous top Bosnian Serb General Ratko Mladic – to this day, wanted for war crimes in the Hague, but uncaptured. The Serbian Colonel started by asking, "Who was the first victim in World War II?" Calvin responded, "I don't know." The Colonel looked across the table and asked "Who was the first victim in the Korean War?" Again, Calvin responded, "I don't know."

The Colonel continued on with several more wars over several more decades, with the same response. He then sat up, and with a serious and respectful tone, through the interpreter, stated, "The first victim in all these wars is the same, the *truth*." A thirty-minute discussion ensued, which Calvin quickly realized would be unpro-ductive. What emerged (i.e., the message that General Mladic, via his aide, effectively delivered that day) was characteristic of Calvin's experience not only in the former Yugoslavia but in other conflict zones, including Iraq, Israel and East Africa: there is often layer upon layer of lies and misinformation, to protect the truth for a mul-titude of strategic reasons. The implication for conflict practitioners is that in these conflict-ridden environments, the ability to analyze the issues, the interests, the positions and most important, the truth is often difficult, if not impossible.[4]

Analysis: Calvin's wicked problem was set in an ongoing violent conflict. But that conflict was only one of the contextual features that made Calvin's efforts to assist with body exchange negotiations difficult. Other types of contextual instability and uncertainty af-fected the negotiations from start to finish.

First, while Calvin tells his story in reference to international humanitarian law, a 1993 ICRC publication noted that "in situations of internal disturbances, the rules of the international humanitarian law can only be invoked by analogy."[5] There was no clearly and fully legitimized guidance about the applicability of humanitarian laws in general or the Geneva Convention specifically as they might apply in the situation of a disintegrating state. Consequently, individuals were often left to decide on their own whether these negotiations were "on or off mandate." Their decisions may not only have been influenced by the merits of the claim or the needs on the ground; they may also have been shaped by another, somewhat unpredictable set of realities – the U.N. system for hiring, firing, and evaluating peacekeeping personnel. Faced with this wicked problem, individuals and groups likely made different choices. Some chose to help the ICRC try to carry out their perceived mandate; others chose to ignore the problem.

It is worth noting that the ICRC was viewed at times as taking something of a technical approach to this problem, applying the procedures they had developed elsewhere to the current situation. They may or may not have adequately considered the local contextual features that would make their standard procedures less than helpful in relation to the overall war. In this situation, unlike others, the war was raging between neighbors, and the groups still harbored hopes of driving the enemy out of the community they had been sharing. The exchange negotiations became one venue in which to advance that overall strategic goal. This was likely one of many strategic goals that were being considered.

These elements reflect only the experience of the individuals who were trying to facilitate the negotiations. The actual parties were experiencing similar contextual turbulence. They were involved in other negotiations to settle the larger conflict – or they were at least invested in the outcome of those negotiations. Consequently, they had a difficult time sustaining a stable definition of their negotiable problem. Were they trying to solve this immediate exchange problem or were they trying to gain advantage in other negotiations for the purpose of winning a larger conflict?

Even if they were able to craft a potential agreement, the contextual turbulence made it difficult for the parties to assess its costs and benefits. The consequences of reaching agreement would depend in large measure on the resolution of the larger conflict and the ways that individuals and groups would be held accountable for their actions during the war. So their best and worst alternatives to a negotiated agreement (BATNAs and WATNAs respectively) fluctuated in response to decisions taken elsewhere and in response to the vagaries of an ongoing war and stop-and-start negotiations to end that war.

Negotiating in a counter-insurgency operation
(Leonard Lira)

Leonard Lira and others deployed in Iraq experienced similar complexities in local negotiations as part of their effort to end a violent insurgency and help local leaders develop governance systems capable of overcoming decades of inter-group hostility. The policy failures that created a situation in which U.S. Army personnel and civilians deployed to Iraq were left trying to manage complex, entrenched and rapidly shifting situations of violence have been well documented (see e.g., Ricks 2006). There is also a growing body of literature about efforts to "win the peace" in Iraq after the fall of Baghdad. The stories include studies of life in the Green Zone, where private contractors negotiated contracts to administer the post-war reconstruction projects for Iraq (Chandrasekaran 2007), as well as front-line accounts of civil affairs units trying to rebuild Iraq one community at a time (Schultheis 2005) and stories of civilian government administrators such as Rory Stewart, who was sent by the British Foreign Office to serve as the deputy governorate coordinator of Maysan, a province on the border with Iran that is occupied by the "Marsh Arabs" who were treated brutally by Saddam Hussein (Stewart 2006). At all of these levels of organization, negotiations were the pervasive means by which policies set in faraway places were executed. As Stewart argues (2006: xii), "it was not grand policy but rather the meetings between individual Iraqis and foreigners that ultimately determined the result of the occupation."

As it was in the former Yugoslavia in the 1990s, so it was in Iraq. The mandate, mission and goals of the occupying forces changed significantly over time. The goal of removing Saddam Hussein, establishing an Iraqi government and getting out quickly gave way to other realities, and everyone on the ground had to shift strategy and tactics to meet changing political goals. This was particularly difficult for the U.S. military, which was well equipped and staffed for war-fighting but poorly equipped and staffed for stabilization, reconstruction, and state-building activities. Nor was the shift from a combat to a reconstruction mission smooth and clear. The ever-morphing insurgencies and factional violence required a continued focus on security, and involved ongoing combat missions while the longer-term political goals of establishing a legitimate Iraqi government demanded a focus on development, infrastructure repair, and establishing effective governance mechanisms. The entire experience became a classic example of the initial failure to recognize a wicked problem, and only after failure on-the-ground, coming to see the problem in a new light. At the core of this recognition is attending to and learning from the unanticipated consequences of the initial intervention. Those consequences helped to reveal how the initial statement of the problem or task represented a misunderstanding of the nature of the problem.

The lack of clarity about how to execute a reconstruction effort as large as Iraq set off complex negotiations among political leaders and top military commanders (Ricks 2006; Cloud and Jaffe 2009), negotiations that have led to a reorganization of various branches of the U.S. military, the development of an updated military doctrine on counterinsurgency (U.S. Army Field Manual FM 3-24; Marine Corps Warfighting Publication No. 3-33.5), and parallel attempts to articulate guiding principles for civilian agencies and organizations operating in Iraq and similar situations (United States Institute of Peace and United States Army Peacekeeping and Stability Operations Institute 2009).

Leonard's personal stories about negotiations in Iraq (see Lira, *Design: The U.S. Army's Approach*, Chapter 27) parallel those of Stewart, who recounts a tale of multiple rounds of negotiations with different sheiks. The goal was to gain support for the newly elected council and bring a local militia group under control. Stewart and his colleagues shuttled among various sheiks gathering support for their plan, making promises and trades along the way. After nailing down the support of the last sheik necessary, they arrived at the final meeting, where they expected everyone to ratify the agreement to support the council and help bring the militia under control. They were greeted by thirty middle-aged Iraqis who had been invited to resolve the problem, only to have all thirty men present, including those with whom they had reached agreements to support the council and oppose the Sadrist leader, Ali Zeidi, declare the council unacceptable and form a new council supported by Ali Zeidi himself (Stewart 2006: 306-313).

It is not that the Iraqis did not know how to negotiate. Stewart (2006: 402) shares some success stories where Iraqi political leaders "proved their capacity to compromise, control their militias, and cut deals with their armed opponents." We may or may not agree with Stewart's argument that the problem was the identity of the coalition forces, not the inability of the Iraqis to govern their own communities. He says the coalition forces lacked any legitimacy to serve as negotiating partners in the overall process of rebuilding Iraq. If this is true, it is clearly a significant issue. Nevertheless, until the troops are withdrawn, they are going to need to continue to use negotiation to work with local communities. Leonard is now working to develop training programs that can help members of the military prepare to achieve more successes than failures in unstable situations such as Iraq.

Analysis: Leonard and Rory Stewart faced wicked problems which were also set in unstable conditions of violent conflict, albeit in later stages than Calvin's situation. In Leonard's and Stewart's cases, the effects of a wicked problem show up in several ways. The lack of clarity about the mission and the nature of the problem itself parallel the situation in Calvin's story. Also similar is the way in which a change mandated at the top level impacts the local negotiations, for good or for ill, by reshaping the parties' assessment of the value of negotiating and their cost-benefit analysis of any possible agreement.

In this situation there was an added problem created by "competing venues" for negotiating problems. As Stewart learned, you can negotiate well only to discover you were negotiating in the wrong venue; your carefully crafted agreement has been set aside in favor of an agreement reached elsewhere using different negotiating processes.[6] Not only was the venue for real negotiation invisible to Stewart; its rules, methods and assumptions were equally opaque.

Competing social norms about negotiating difficult conflicts also appear in Leonard's story (in *Design: The U.S. Army's Approach*, Chapter 27) about trying to facilitate the negotiations to form a local reconciliation committee in Iraq. There, the nationally mandated decision to form reconciliation committees in every community ran up against the socially negotiated norms for dealing with violence. The parties could not articulate the past harms as part of the reconciliation process because in their culture acknowledging those wrongs evoked a requirement for blood retribution.

The need for the U.S. military to *remake itself* in order to deal with the task of negotiating ground-level implementation of the rebuilding of a country is further evidence that they were dealing with a wicked problem.

Preparing to negotiate an end to a protracted
civil conflict (Jayne Docherty)

Jayne Docherty was asked to work with armed Burmese groups that have not signed cease-fire agreements in one of the longest-running civil conflicts in the world. They wanted to understand negotiation better as a possible strategy for achieving their goals. After two consultations, she agreed to spend twelve months (later extended to eighteen months) working with representatives from the armed groups. The primary goals were to increase their understanding of negotiation, improve their negotiation skills, and explore ways to use negotiation to advance their goal of creating a society and government that were not based on cultural assimilation by an ethnic majority population. Three weeks before her first consulting visit, the leader of the organization she was scheduled to meet with was assassinated, not by the regime in power, but by a rival splinter group from his own organization. Such infighting, it turns out, is not uncommon, even if assassinations are not the norm. This kind of internal conflict and inability to negotiate within each ethnic group and among the ethnic groups is common to all of the armed groups that continue to resist the government.

Jayne suggested, and the groups agreed, that the workshops, trainings and consultations would focus first on learning to negotiate within their ethnic groups and between different ethnic groups, and only secondarily on negotiating with the regime they oppose. They also agreed that part of the consultation would involve figuring out together how to use negotiation to actually change systems, rather than just resolve discrete problems, and that participants would be drawn from both senior political and military leaders and their own civil society organizations.

All of these approaches contravened the existing norms of the ethnic groups. The participants in the first workshop included top political and military leaders, representatives from the ethnic group civil society organizations, and young interns from a program that brings emergent leaders out of the country for training. The participants had never participated in a discussion of their future that included these hierarchically differentiated groups; few had been exposed to the differences in perspective between those living inside the country and those in the bordering countries. They quickly discovered that while they came from the same ethnic groups, they did not necessarily see the world the same way. They had serious internal divisions that needed to be addressed in order even to think about dealing with "the enemy." The divisions were inter-ethnic and intra-ethnic based on generational, philosophical, and geographic location differences.

A new constitution passed in a referendum (May 2008), which most observers agree was flawed and incomplete, called for elections in 2010 and provided a plan for a "disciplined transition" to democracy, including the reduction of military control of the government. The issue of how the groups should respond to the constitution and impending elections created a constant undercurrent of conflict in the workshops. Taking this as a teachable moment, Jayne invited the groups to practice using some of their negotiation skills around the problem of devising an effective response to the upcoming elections. The groups were stuck in polarized camps regarding how they *should* respond to the constitution and impending elections. One camp argued: "We must resist this illegitimate constitution and boycott the elections or we will lose everything." The other groups said: "The constitution is flawed and the elections will not be fully fair, but this is an opportunity to increase ethnic group participation in governing the country. We should participate and use the opportunities that will come from participation to promote greater change."

Factors that appeared to influence (but not rigidly predict) an individual's position on the elections included location and generation. Generally speaking, group members living "far inside" the country and under the rule of the regime were more prepared to adopt a pragmatic approach to the elections. Group members living in the internal border areas (which are contested and usually ruled only indirectly by the regime) and in bordering countries were deeply divided about the issues. And group members living in "far exile" in Europe, the United States, or elsewhere were the most likely to demand that their compatriots boycott the elections completely.

Generational differences were less clear, and they manifested differently in various ethnic groups. In some groups the leaders were willing to be more pragmatic and the young people were more militant; in other groups these positions were reversed. However, in all of the communities, generational differences were difficult to address because the groups are organized hierarchically. Small groups of senior leaders who do not operate transparently and do not typically elicit the opinions of "junior" leaders make policy; junior leaders exercise authority under the constant corrective scrutiny of their elders. Whatever view was held by the younger people, it was typically marginalized within the groups.

Efforts to reconcile the divisions within each ethnic group were exacerbated by the actions of others, most notably donors. For twenty years, most donors had assumed that citizens inside the country living under direct control of the regime were unable to assert any autonomy, so they supported the groups in bordering countries. But in May 2008, when Cyclone Nargis struck the country, civil society groups inside Burma/Myanmar took the lead in early relief and recovery activities, often in direct opposition to government directives. In response to this previously unrecognized capacity, donor organizations were starting to shift their efforts to supporting internal groups, promoting incremental political change, and increasing the capacity of citizens to make the most of the opportunities presented by the upcoming election.

As the workshop participants focused on negotiating among the ethnic groups and within their respective groups, they suggested that the tools from "Negotiation 1.0" were not well suited to their problem. After watching them struggle, Jayne agreed with them.

The problems they were facing were not just about conflicting interests. They were attempting to address deep identity conflicts, exacerbated by individual and group experiences of trauma that kept them frozen in an oppositional stance in relation to the regime and sometimes to one another. The instinct to focus her intervention on the internal conflicts of the ethnic groups was a good one, but "Negotiation 1.0" tools had little to offer for addressing those conflicts.

Jayne got direct feedback on "Negotiation 1.0" methods, because the workshop participants had also agreed to help her develop a set of culturally appropriate negotiation training materials. They pushed for two significant changes. First, they inserted a strong emphasis on developing self-awareness, self-management, and empathy in the negotiators. They call this S.A.M.E., and they argue that their own cultures do not lay these basic foundations for negotiation.[7] Secondly, based on a trial workshop, they have asked for help developing culturally appropriate interventions based on techniques used in narrative mediation (Winslade and Monk 2000; Winslade and Monk 2008). Some of them have recognized that creating a new future will depend, in part, on telling a new story about the past and the present.

Analysis: Jayne's story is actually an interesting combination of several "wicked" elements which combine to form an overall wicked problem. Violence between the regime and the ethnic groups, between ethnic groups and within ethnic groups continues. Neither the regime nor the ethnic groups can win militarily; they have reached a mutually hurting stalemate. (See Zartman 2006.) The inter- and intra-ethnic violence is widely recognized as playing into the hands of the regime. Yet many of the ethnic organizations are stuck in patterns of internal conflict. They have been fighting for so long that they have developed rigid patterns of thinking; they are also responsible for allocating access to resources within their groups, and some members are now benefiting from continued conflict. One element of the wicked problem is that these groups are stuck and unable to respond effectively to current challenges and opportunities.

Another subset of the larger wicked problem centers on the lack of stability in the context, which complicates their cost-benefit analysis when they think about how to respond to opportunities. The context has been destabilized by the regime's scheduling an election and donor organizations altering their funding patterns. The armed groups cannot participate in the elections, but others can. They need to decide whether to support or condemn their compatriots who choose to run for office. But it is not easy to assess the relative merits of these choices when outside parties pressure them to "stand firm" against the regime – and promise rewards for doing so – and some inside parties and the regime pressure them to be pragmatic about change – and point out that they will be left behind and marginalized if they block this opportunity for change. How do you assess your BATNA and WATNA when you have no idea what will happen and what kind of system will be in place to reward or punish your choices?

As the workshop participants who developed the S.A.M.E. framework have noted, these problems require a renegotiation of relationships, self-identities, patterns of communication and privilege, if the ethnic groups are going to develop a robust coalition capable of grasping new opportunities and facing emerging challenges. This is a problem of "social negotiation" (see Honeyman and Coben, *Navigating Wickedness*, Chapter 24) that might benefit from problem-focused negotiations *if* the parties can identify useful problems on which to focus. But "Negotiation 1.0" techniques will not be adequate for this situation without the kinds of changes we are advocating for "Negotiation 2.0" theory, practice, and pedagogy. (See, in particular, Docherty, *"Adaptive" Negotiation*, Chapter 26.)

Wicked Problems in More Stable Contexts: Getting Systems Unstuck

In contrast with the Myanmar/Burma, former-Yugoslavia and Iraq examples where physical violence has been used in war contexts, Jamil Mahuad and Howard Gadlin next examine whether the concepts expressed in this chapter could be applied to understand complex "domestic" disputes. They posit that even mundane matters can present wicked problems – at least to a degree, and in the sense of the initial obscurity of the problem and the requirement for adaptive thinking, if not the potential for violence or sudden change in the underlying conditions such as the legal system or who controls the government.

High drama in a high city (Jamil Mahuad)

In 1992, the more than one million inhabitants of Quito defined public transportation as the preeminent problem of the city. Constrained by a range of mountains on the west and a river cliff on the east, at 2800 meters (9200 feet) above sea level, Quito's long and narrow shape resembles a centipede crawling at the foot of the Pichincha volcano. At that altitude, with less ambient pressure than at sea level, gas or diesel combustion is incomplete, generating emissions that cause the unique old city walls and temples to deteriorate, not to mention people's lungs. In the middle of Quito, the city's Colonial Centre – a U.N. Educational, Scientific, and Cultural Organization (UNESCO) Heritage Site that harbors the Presidential and Municipal Palaces – is crossed by most of the public transportation lines, an immense, disorganized, privately owned fleet of very old, highly polluting buses.

Quiteños were tired of traffic and congestion. There was an increasing public health concern due to the unacceptable levels of lead found in blood tests. Bus passengers felt abused and disrespected for other reasons; they complained about lack of service to many barrios, and up to three hours of commuting to work.

Public transportation, however, was not actually regulated by the municipality. Instead, it was within the purview of the minister of the interior and the national police. In the midst of public allegations that some retired generals of the police had vested interests because they owned buses, there was no perceived moral authority to regulate and control the system. Historically, the *transportistas* had also been the most powerful union; their rather frequent strikes have overthrown some Ecuadorian governments. They used organization and strikes to obtain increments on the tariffs, which otherwise, even in moments of high inflation, were only authorized when there was current political viability. Tensions and open confrontations have characterized the relationship between bus drivers and *quiteños* for decades.

In that context, Jamil campaigned to become mayor of Quito, promising an integrated public transportation system, with new rules, new routes, a fleet of trolleybuses, and changes in the law to give the municipality the exclusive right to regulation and control. The drivers' union was openly against Jamil and favored his main opponent. "Your rival will win, because he has the support of the powerful drivers' union," Jamil was told in a radio program. "I'll win, because I have the support of the passengers," he replied. He was subsequently elected.

The "too good to be true" proposed solution. Jamil's promise represented Quito's most complex public construction project ever attempted. The solution needed to be modern, technically functional, non-polluting, and economically viable. A subway was out of the question for both technical and economic reasons. New buses would not answer the pollution concern, and would have a "more of the same" flavor. A gas/electric dual-power trolley bus, however, would satisfy all the concerns except the need for fast movement. Exclusive dedicated lanes in the narrow streets in the Centre would resolve that hurdle.

This type of system is known today as Bus Rapid Transit (BRT), and by now, more than 300 cities in the world are building versions of it. A subway is considered a financial capital intensive product, while a BRT is a political capital intensive one – as the then-pioneering implementation of such a project in Quito was about to demonstrate.

Quito's trolley bus project required the application of overlapping decision-making, communication, and leadership skills along with the negotiation skills described in this chapter, though the latter were not yet circulating in teaching, or indeed even as theory except in a few specialized fields. Like the China-U.S. trade negotiation discussed at the outset of this chapter, the actual "negotiation" here involved multiple ancillary (and even contradictory) processes. Furthermore, success depended on leaders who could identify and negotiate tame problems inside of the overall wicked problem, while also managing a larger cultural change process that resulted in revisions of the "socially negotiated" patterns of power, privilege and influence tied to the existing bus system (Docherty, *"Adaptive" Negotiation*, Chapter 26.)

Problems that were part of the interlocking web of sub-problems that made up the overall wicked problem included relatively tame problems, such as:

- Organizing many simultaneous national and international bidding processes, covering everything from construction work (which interrupted Quito's main street traffic for months) to buying the trolleys;
- creating and staffing an office in charge of writing the new rules, drawing the new routes, awarding the operational permits and managing the system; and
- creating a public enterprise from scratch to *operate* the fleet of trolleys.

Other parts of the web of interlocking problems required facing much more complicated and adaptive challenges. These included:

- Overcoming the lobbying and resistance of the Police, to persuade the Ecuadorian congress to pass legislation creating the *Distrito Metropolitano de Quito*, with exclusive regulatory powers and control over Quito's public transit and transportation;
- profusely disseminating factual information about the whole project, its feasibility and benefits, in the face of a disinformation campaign; and
- creating a new culture (socially constructed) to give *quiteños* (as distinct from the municipal offices) moral ownership of their trolleys.

Still other problems required both technical and adaptive tools, to:

- Design the most efficient and effective project (technical aspect) and to get from the national government – controlled by a different political party – its commitment to finance the project (adaptive aspect); and
- establish the tariffs for the new integrated system (technical aspect) and get the city council's approval, as well as the acceptance of the population (adaptive aspect).

The trolley project faced innumerable risks. It was crucial for the daily life of hundreds of thousands of people, who were unofficial supervisors of the daily advance of the public works. At the same time, Ecuador has a prolific history of aborted bidding processes; unfinished public projects were numerous even when easier and smaller, and the country had conspicuous and traumatic experiences with "white elephants." The trolley project also had intrinsic difficulties.

It was a counterintuitive solution: there was no cultural understanding of what an integrated transport system even meant, and no popular understanding of what a "trolley" is (there had been no trolleys in Ecuador since the early 1900s). It required a leap of faith based on trust in the new mayor. And originally, it was seen as the "mayor's pet project," without local ownership and clear champions.

It also did not serve established Ecuadorian commercial interests: they were in the business of selling bus units, and did not approve the decision to build a new system without them. To top these off, there was political calculation: people's fear of the unknown and of suffering yet another frustration were exploited by certain politicians.

The action plan is formulated. The plan demanded simultaneous political, economic, social, and international actions across very different fronts. It was considered crucial to build alliances with both a wide variety of actors and agents (NGOs, environmental groups, opinion leaders, professional associations, engineers). This required carefully identifying beneficiaries and patiently explaining the benefits to them, in one-on-one or town hall meetings. Through an education campaign, the team consistently disseminated information to the population; corrected the most frequent errors; and answered "FAQs" with patience. Consultants were hired to help with both the technical and adaptive work. Finally, in the days leading up to the inauguration of the service, the mayor's office launched an advertising campaign targeted to children and teenagers highlighting this efficient, green and clean alternative. The strategy spilled over to whole families, rooting the project deeply in the public imagination and developing a sense of ownership of the project in the population at large.

An unexpected adaptive challenge: Quito is hijacked. Using its recently acquired legal authority, the municipality produced a new route plan; refused to extend operating permits to bus units that did not pass the emissions test; and negotiated, with many drivers, new contracts as "feeders" of the trolley. But the opponents were not done. They had one last "tour de force" available, and used it. The narrow streets of the Centre in Quito only have two lanes. One was needed for the exclusive dedicated trolley lane; the other was to be open to all traffic *except* buses – because they would have blocked the traffic. The drivers had been resisting this decision for weeks, but the municipality had been able to enforce all the technical decisions. One day, however, around noon and executing a well coordinated plan without any forewarning, the buses stopped wherever they were at that moment; the drivers asked the passengers to step down to the street. They turned off the engines, locked the doors and left the scene. In a masterstroke, the city was suddenly paralyzed. All cars were trapped, because the buses chose intersections to block all over the city, and there was no way around them.

The bus drivers demanded that Jamil agree to keep the bus routes as they were and give the buses the right to use the second lane in the Centre's narrow streets, as a precondition to moving the units and reestablishing general traffic and bus service. Had Jamil accepted, the trolley would never have begun service, and the authority of the municipality would be severely eroded.

The people, in the hope of enjoying better transport service, initially supported Jamil's stand. But when the situation became prolonged, after a few days this support began to dwindle. Ministers could not get to the Presidential Palace. Schools were suspended. Hospitals had difficulties with ambulances and supplies; patients could not reach their health services. Gas and food scarcity became a factor because freight could not be delivered. The municipality, however, lacked the technical means to move the units by force (there were just two tow trucks in the city with enough power to move a bus, and they could not reach most of the buses anyway because of gridlock). The police did not want a confrontation, and avoided acting; the national government (which was not under the control of the mayor's political party) simply did not know what to do, and suggested a "negotiated solution" – meaning, in this instance, a backing down of the mayor. It was the moment of decision; the turning point in whether Quito would move forward as a city, or back.

In Jamil's analysis, the only solution was to pressure the drivers to come back, turn on the buses and go, accepting the municipality's decision. But the drivers had a very strong BATNA. The only potentially game-changing move was in the hands of the national government: an ultimatum, threatening to bring in the armed forces and open the streets by force if the drivers did not back down. The government was hesitant at best. With the tensions compounding, Jamil "went public" and invited the people to make their voices heard. Radio stations were overwhelmed by telephone calls, letters, and people coming in directly to participate in live programs. In the end, the government agreed to issue the ultimatum. Threatened with the real possibility of having their buses shoved roughly out of the way by tanks, the drivers moved their units. The trolley was saved, and the new system and its rules were implemented.

Analysis: Jamil's story demonstrates that dealing with wicked problems requires strong leaders who are able to marshal support for a complex process of managing multiple interconnected change initiatives simultaneously or in sequence. This is true for all contexts, but in less stable contexts (the stories told by Calvin, Leonard, Jayne, and Rory Stewart), the difficulty of identifying leaders who are considered legitimate across deeply divided sectors of society makes the other problems even more difficult to address. The people of Quito knew they had a problem, but they could not see a solution. They could have been stuck in grumbling mode for decades. Jamil marshaled the energy and passion of the *quiteños* and resources from inside and outside the city while simultaneously taking actions that controlled the resistance of special interest groups in order to "pick off" specific elements of the problem. These smaller problems were handled in ways that resulted in significant changes in systems, institutions, patterns of behavior, and political norms. It was the cumulative effect of smaller negotiations and other activities that addressed the wicked problem.

The relative stability enabled Jamil and others to demarcate problems and isolate them from external disruption. They were also able to sustain stable definitions of discrete problems. In addition, the parties were able to identify and act on their interests and assess their respective BATNAs and WATNAs against a clearly delineated set of alternatives – fix the transportation system and reap all of the benefits of doing that, or continue to live with a broken system and pay the price associated with inaction. When an entrenched interest group attempted to prevent resolution of the larger conflict, Jamil was able to mobilize another party (the people) around a *narrative expression* of a desirable future. Rational, calculated statements of interests do not mobilize the masses; stories and images can.

Down to earth: In the depths of a U.S. federal agency (Howard Gadlin)

Anyone who has worked in an organization has experienced or witnessed failed attempts at producing organizational change. The example that follows comes from an effort by the U.S. National Institutes of Health (NIH) to cure an epidemic of problems with employee evaluations by adopting a pass-fail system of evaluation.

As an ombudsman, Howard Gadlin has responsibility, in addition to addressing grievances, problems and conflicts, to identify systemic problems within the organization, bring them to the attention of the appropriate people in the organization, and make recommendations for ways in which these problems might be addressed.

After he had been at NIH for some years, Howard included the following passage in a report to the NIH community:

Another striking feature of the organizational culture at NIH is the dissatisfaction that both managers and employees feel with regard to a range of administrative personnel issues. Most significant of these is the adoption several years ago, partly as a response to a variety of problems, of a pass-fail system of employee evaluation. While a pass/fail system might reduce the number of rating related conflicts and grievances it is our impression that it creates problems in the long run. A probably unintended consequence of this system is that it has severely reduced the requirement for managers to provide serious meaningful, substantive feedback to employees about their performance and their conduct at work. Consequently, when a manager does raise issues regarding an employee, it is often experienced as a personal attack, even when delivered in a thoughtful and sensitive way, which, we might add, is not always the case. A pass-fail system, then, removes a formal occasion for the sort of critical exchange between manager and employee that is the responsibility of every good manager. Further, supervisors' effectiveness as managers has to be evaluated at least as seriously as the other aspects of their performance. Thus, to the extent that managers lose an opportunity to be evaluated in a meaningful way in their capacity as managers, an unfortunate ripple effect commences throughout the organization. The pass-fail system minimizes the kind of effective feedback that supervisors critically need to develop comfort and skill in their managerial roles.

In a related vein, it is a matter of some concern that supervisors are more often promoted into management responsibilities as a result of their skill in substantive and technical areas as opposed to careful consideration of their fitness to assume, or interest in handling, supervisory responsibilities. Moreover, they typically receive little or no training on how to manage effectively, and they are most extensively evaluated on their handling of issues and concerns within their area of substantive expertise as opposed to their performance of supervisory responsibilities, including providing employees useful feedback and effective mentoring.

The original problem with the evaluation system was linked to a more widespread problem of difficulty in addressing poor employee performance in federal agencies generally. Naïvely, Howard's office assumed that if the employee evaluation system could be improved, the difficulties in addressing underperforming employees could be reduced or eliminated. Such an assumption that there is a straightforward technical fix to what is in actuality a complex organizational issue is fairly common within organizations, especially when a particular practice or policy can be identified as the apparent culprit for what is generally a problem deeply embedded in an organization's culture and structure.

Among the recommendations of the ombudsman's office that year were a call for a serious evaluation of the pass-fail system and a call to establish a system in which managers provide more detailed feedback and evaluation than a mere pass or fail. Although these recommendations were not initially met with widespread agreement by upper management, over the next several years several other sources of organizational feedback converged with them. Along with related changes in managerial philosophy, this did lead to the further overhaul of the employee evaluation system. The new system included a four-point grading system (unsatisfactory, minimally satisfactory, fully satisfactory, and outstanding), and it linked year-end bonuses and awards to performance evaluation ratings. Under the new rules, the highest bonus awards were reserved for employees with "outstanding" ratings and considerably lower awards were available for some, but not all employees who received "fully satisfactory" ratings. The new system also required managers to provide meaningful mid-year evaluations and guidance to lower level managers as to how to give substantive feedback to employees.

However, it would be hard to find many people in the organization today who see the new evaluation system as a significant improvement. In addition, there have been many unanticipated consequences of changing the policy. Under the old pass-fail system, a "fail" rating was rare, and was often responded to with a grievance or an EEO complaint. Under the new system, there are still few "fail" ratings; but unexpectedly, there are many grievances from people who receive "fully satisfactory" ratings, but who believe they deserve an "outstanding." In some ways this new system has introduced a level of tension and antagonism between managers and their *best* employees, because the new system limits the number of "outstanding" ratings that can be distributed.

There are other unanticipated consequences of the change in evaluation practices. In some units, aware of the discrepancy in the size of bonus awards between those with "outstanding" and those with "fully satisfactory" ratings, decisions were made to rotate the distribution of "outstanding" and "fully satisfactory" awards from year to year, thereby ensuring that everyone who is performing at a satisfactory or higher level benefits relatively equally from the reward system. In still other units the professional staff has decided to accept "fully satisfactory" awards so that the "outstanding" awards can be reserved for the lower paid support staff. These reactions illustrate one of the key features of complex organizational problems: the components of the organization are semi-autonomous, and it is not possible to predict fully how any particular change in policy or practice will be interpreted or implemented within those semiautonomous units.[8]

Although some aspects of this change in policy did not have the desired effect, other features of the change did. For example, management realized from the beginning that managers would need support and training in order to fulfill their supervisory functions better. Consequently, some excellent support materials and training programs were developed and delivered, and there have been, among many of those in supervisory positions, noticeable improvements in the sorts of evaluative feedback they provide to employees.

The effects of these changes also ripple through the entire organization, as employees come to appreciate that someone is aware of what they are doing and how they are doing, and that it matters. This change also improves the ability of supervisors, at least those who have begun to provide substantive feedback, to address problems with underperforming employees, because they now have on record detailed accounts of problems and managerial efforts to address them.

The entire episode well illustrates that organizations are incredibly complex. It is very rare that one can address a problem without also taking into account the organizational context in which it occurs, and the interconnections among the various constituencies within the organization which will be affected by the new policies and procedures. Put simply, the problem is almost never as straightforward as it seems to be.

Analysis: Howard's story is an interesting example of what happens when the parties address a wicked problem as if it were a tame problem. Each time we try to define a wicked problem, we implicate the solution to that problem *and* we also mask parts of the problem. Every way of seeing is also a way of not seeing. The relative stability of systems and structures in some contexts of wicked problems lures protagonists into framing their issues in terms of tame and technical problems. But formulating the problem as technical means we do not see it as moral, political and ethical. So, when NIH decided to treat problems with employee evaluations by adopting a procedural change (a technical fix), they failed to recognize that correcting wicked problems requires self-change (adaptive solutions). Furthermore, wicked problems implicate moral and ethical dilemmas, not merely technical problems. The failure even to ask the participants about issues of fairness and justice when constructing the new employee evaluation procedures left individuals and groups to take these issues into their own hands by administering the procedures in unforeseen ways.

Conclusion: Wicked Problems are Not New

The trolley system in Quito, dramatic as the case is, does not stand alone as a wicked problem in "domestic" affairs generally or civic life in particular. Quite the contrary: many of the larger problems faced by political leaders at all levels and in many countries (certainly, in all democracies) are wicked problems that have something of the qualities of this story. Indeed, many local and regional conflicts do, too – and experience negotiating and mediating such environmental and public policy conflicts has been building up over decades (see, e.g., Forester 1980; Bingham 1986; Carpenter and Kennedy 1991; Forester 1999; Susskind, McKearnan, and Thomas-Larmer 1999; and Carpenter and Kennedy 2001).

Wicked problems arising in unstable (and sometimes violent) contexts have come to our attention in recent decades with the development of peacebuilding interventions designed to meet the problem of violent conflict as it emerged in the post-Cold War era. Most violent conflicts are now *intranational* (within a single country) conflicts that have tended to *internationalize* "to the degree that some conflictants, particularly opposition movements, inhabit neighboring countries; weapons and money for the conflict flow in from the surrounding region and from more distant locations; and displaced refugee populations cross immediate and distant borders" (Lederach 1997: 11). The problem of violent conflict was no longer seen as primarily an inter-state issue that could be addressed using diplomatic negotiation practices, and many different actors started to improvise responses to this pressing problem.[9] They have learned many lessons about using negotiation to increase stability and peace, and they are building a repository of knowledge and skill sets that can be incorporated into "Negotiation 2.0" practices.

The stories we have shared here, and others like them, formed the basis for our consideration of negotiating wicked problems and have helped us frame the following questions:

- What role can negotiation play when we are dealing with wicked problems, and how does it need to be coordinated with other activities?
- What does "Negotiation 2.0" practice need to include if we want to use negotiation to address wicked problems?
- How do we teach others about using negotiation to address wicked problems?

In the next chapter (*"Adaptive" Negotiation*), Jayne Docherty takes on the second question. She suggests that problem-focused negotiation must be understood as more than just a way to handle discrete problems. Every negotiation encounter is a location where the participants choose to reinforce, change, or ignore socially negotiated norms, values and mores. As such, every negotiation is a potential location for the adaptive changes required when dealing with wicked problems, but only if we understand the constitutive role of culture and meaning-making in negotiation. She also argues that negotiators need to be taught about social ethics and not just their own professional ethics. This is particularly important when facing wicked problems which combine technical problems with moral, social, and ethical dilemmas.

Leonard Lira (*Design: The U.S. Army's Approach*, Chapter 27) shares one organization's efforts to help leaders know when and where to use negotiation effectively, when the overall goal is managing wicked problems of the most challenging variety: bringing stability and security to situations that are unstable and violent. "Design" is only one way to handle this problem. We still have numerous questions about when, where, and how to use negotiation as a tool for dealing with wicked problems, and this chapter ends with some of those questions.

Our conclusions, as the reader will see, are far from fully formed. Indeed, we have begun, but not yet completed, at least two further writings, to match Leonard's military "Design" discussion with a peacebuilding/civil society equivalent, and to pull together some ideas for teaching these new approaches to negotiation. By way of explanation, we offer simply that our subject is itself emergent. We look forward to having more to say in the concluding book of the *Rethinking Negotiation Teaching* series.

Notes

[1] This composite set of characteristics of wicked problems is derived from Rittell and Webber (1973), Ritchey (2005-2008) and Conklin (2005).

[2] Michael Wheeler and Gillian Morris (2002) have garnered some useful ideas for making decisions in the face of uncertainty by studying the U.S. Marine Corps Warfighting Manual. Ideas worth following up on include: managing friction (indecision or time pressure for example); preparing a Plan B for every scenario in order to manage uncertainty; developing balance and agility to benefit from the fluidity of negotiation; and learning to improvise in the face of disorder (3-5).

[3] The complex reasons why wicked problems go unidentified and unaddressed include, but are not limited to: a) the costs of an unsustainable situation are being externalized to parties that lack voice and power; b) the costs are being delayed for future payment; and c) well-meaning individuals and groups keep applying "technical fixes" to parts of the problem, thereby keeping the situation from reaching a crisis that would spur awareness.

[4] This, of course, is not unique to conflict professionals: anyone trying to analyze major conflict has the same problem. (See Knightley 2004.)

[5] See http://www.icrc.org/Web/eng/siteeng0.nsf/html/57JMJ9 (last accessed July 30, 2010).

[6] It is not that such things do not happen in stable contexts; "forum shopping" is often a problem when dealing with complicated conflicts. However, the parties are usually aware of the various venues, and they understand the options that are open to themselves and the other parties. Parties may have venue preferences, but overall the venue options are all considered legitimate. In Iraq, the venues for negotiation were unclear to the coalition forces (and perhaps to some of the locals), and various venues had been "captured" by interest groups so that they lacked widespread legitimacy.

[7] Jayne had shared a story about her father's return from Vietnam and her own involvement in the anti-war movement. She talked about their arguments, but also about their continued love and respect for one another. A top military leader said privately, "The most important thing you have told us was the story about your father. Our culture does not allow us to disagree and maintain our relationships. If we don't figure out how to do that, I don't think we can resolve our conflicts."

[8] Chris offers a story he witnessed as a junior professional at the Detroit office of the U.S. National Labor Relations Board (NLRB) in the 1970s. At the time, General Motors (GM) was the world's largest industrial corporation, and it epitomized the concept of a hierarchical corporate structure – on the surface. Its employees were mostly organized by the United Auto Workers (UAW). One year during that period, however, a single employee (who was not even in the union, but in an ancillary function) nearly triggered a nationwide auto strike.

A specialized union, that year, had petitioned for an election to "carve out" the company's skilled-trades employees, during a legal "window" for such challenges. There were thousands of skilled trades workers, spread across many dozens of plants. The head office did not even know who they were – the lists were kept plant by plant. The law was such that if GM and the UAW continued to bargain while the challenge was open, the challenger arguably could charge both of them with violations of federal labor law. So bargaining ground to a halt – in the face of a strike deadline. If the challenger could not show that it had authorization cards from thirty percent of the employees affected, however, it had no right to an election. The NLRB demanded a list of all the employees arguably involved, broken down in various combinations to allow for different legal scenarios. GM, or at least its upper management, credibly stated that it was eager to comply. And then everything ground to a halt – for weeks, while the strike clock continued ticking.

The NLRB's daily calls received answers that seemed evasive. Eventually it came out that the plant-by-plant records were, on each site, under the control of the computer people – still, in that era, a priesthood of technicians. Some of them turned out to have other priorities than responding to the increasingly strident screams of rage emanating from head office in distant Detroit.

Of course, no one in their right mind would have deferred to any such individual the power to cause a nationwide strike. But delay is not explicit deferral, and one or two such individuals were all it took to make the dynamic of the legal process grind to a halt, while the dynamic of collective bargaining continued to press toward a crisis. By the time the last part of the list was supplied, even though the challenger was then quickly knocked out of the box by proving to have less than thirty percent support in any relevant combination of plants and skills, the remaining time for bargaining was very nearly not enough. Thus may one supposedly low-level technician, in practice, have almost enough inadvertent power to cause a shutdown of the world's largest industrial company.

[9] Many of the so-called "new" conflicts were not new at all, but had been repressed and distorted by the superpower rivalry of the Cold War. Once that pressure was removed, the conflicts became more violent and more prone to expansion.

References

Bingham, G. 1986. *Resolving environmental disputes: A decade of experience.* Washington, DC: Conservation Foundation.

Carpenter, S. L. and W. J. D. Kennedy. 1991. *Managing public disputes: A practical guide to handling conflict and reaching agreement.* San Francisco: Jossey-Bass.

Carpenter, S. L. and W. J. D. Kennedy. 2001. *Managing public disputes: A practical guide for government, business and citizen's groups.* San Francisco: Jossey-Bass.

Chandrasekaran, R. 2007. *Imperial life in the Emerald City: Inside Iraq's Green Zone.* New York: Alfred A. Knopf.

Cloud, D., and G. Jaffe. 2009. *The fourth star: Four generals and the epic struggle for the future of the United States Army.* New York: Crown Publishers.

Conklin, J. 2005. Wicked problems and social complexity. In *Dialogue mapping: Building shared understanding of wicked problems,* edited by J. Conklin. New York: Wiley.

Forester, J. 1980. Critical theory and planning practice. *Journal of the American Planning Association* 46: 275-86.

Forester, J. 1985. *Critical theory, public policy, and planning practice.* Cambridge, MA: MIT Press.

Forester, J. 1999. *The deliberative practitioner: Encouraging participatory planning processes.* Cambridge, MA: MIT Press.

Greenhalgh, L., and R. J. Lewicki. 2003. New directions in teaching negotiations: From Walton and McKersie to the new millennium. In *Negotiations and change: From the workplace to society,* edited by T. A. Kochan and D. B. Lipsky. Ithaca: ILR Press.

Heifetz, R. 1994 *Leadership without easy answers.* Cambridge, MA: Harvard University Press.

Kegan, R., and L. L. Lahey. 2009. *Immunity to change: How to overcome it and unlock potential in yourself and your organization.* Boston: Harvard Business School Press.

Knightley, P. 2004. *The first casualty: The war correspondent as hero and mythmaker from the Crimea to Iraq.* Baltimore: Johns Hopkins University Press.

Lederach, J. P. 1997. *Building peace: Sustainable reconciliation in divided societies.* Washington, DC: United States Institute of Peace.

Ricks, T. E. 2006. *Fiasco: The American military adventure in Iraq.* New York: The Penguin Press.

Ritchey, T. 2005-2008. *Wicked problems: Structuring social messes with morphological analysis.* Swedish Morphological Society. Available at www.swedmorph.org (last accessed June 28, 2010).

Rittell, H. W. J., and M. M. Webber. 1973. Dilemmas in a general theory of planning. *Policy Sciences* 4: 155-169.

Schultheis, R. 2005. *Waging peace: A special operations team's battle to rebuild Iraq.* New York: Gotham Books.

Stewart, R. 2006. *The prince of the marshes: And other occupational hazards of a year in Iraq.* New York Harcourt.

Susskind, L., S. McKearnan, and J. Thomas-Larmer (eds). 1999. *The consensus building handbook.* Thousand Oaks, CA: Sage.

United States Institute of Peace, and United States Army Peacekeeping and Stability Operations Institute. 2009. *Guiding principles for stabilization and reconstruction.* Washington, DC: United States Institute of Peace.

Wheeler, M. and G. Morris. 2002. A note on maneuvering in war and negotiation. *Harvard Business School Note* 9-902-157.

Winslade, J., and G. Monk. 2000. *Narrative mediation: A new approach in conflict resolution.* San Francisco: Jossey-Bass.

Winslade, J., and G. D. Monk. 2008. *Practicing narrative mediation: Loosening the grip of conflict.* San Francisco: Jossey-Bass.

Zartman, I. W. 2006. Timing and Ripeness. In *The negotiator's fieldbook: The desk reference for the experienced negotiator,* edited by A. K. Schneider and C. Honeyman. Washington, DC: American Bar Association.

❧ 26 ❧

"Adaptive" Negotiation: Practice and Teaching

Jayne Seminare Docherty*

Editors' Note: Docherty argues that in addition to improved sensitivity to culture, argued in many of the writings in this series, it is time to demand that would-be negotiators and those who attempt to teach them become more sensitive to situations where the culture and norms are themselves in flux. What is needed, she says, is to re-center much of our teaching on the development of creative and critical thinking, including a critical awareness of the context, the self, the other, and the definition of the problem to be negotiated or negotiable. Docherty uses an ostensibly simple story of a negotiation in an Istanbul market to illustrate how a focus on the parties' different ways of "worldviewing" changes perception as to what is really going on, and what is possible to negotiate.

Introduction

In the previous chapter (*Negotiating Wicked Problems*), my colleagues and I share five stories of using negotiation as part of a strategy for dealing with wicked problems. (A detailed description of wicked problems as compared with tame problems is included in Chapters 24 and 25. The definitions themselves are reproduced for the convenience of the reader here in endnote one.[1]) In summary, tame

* **Jayne Seminare Docherty** is a professor at the Center for Justice and Peacebuilding at Eastern Mennonite University in Harrisonburg, Virginia. Her first book *Learning Lessons from Waco* was an analysis of the Federal Bureau of Investigation's attempt at hostage negotiation with the Branch Davidian sect, and her subsequent work has frequently involved the intersection and relationships between uniformed forces and civil society, ethnic minorities, and religious groups. Her email address is jayne.docherty@emu.edu. The author wishes to thank Roger W. Foster, a graduate student at the Center for Justice and Peacebuilding at Eastern Mennonite University, from whose editing, organizing, and reframing this chapter has benefited greatly.

problems are amenable to solutions that are deemed "technical," against a backdrop of socially negotiated norms that are institution-alized into organizations and social structures. Wicked problems arise when technical problems meet conditions of political, social, and institutional uncertainty or when the established ways of doing business are incapable of addressing the presenting problem. In both cases, dealing with the particular problem requires that we also consider how that problem interacts with socially negotiated norms and the attendant structures, organizations or social institutions that have become problematic.

The contextual problems can arise for a variety of reasons. A society may be in a period of instability and chaos: e.g., Iraq and the former Yugoslavia (Leonard's story and Calvin's story in *Negotiating Wicked Problems*, Chapter 25); or it may be facing problems that cannot be addressed successfully without renegotiating cultural norms and institutions: e.g., dealing with global warming, health care reform in the United States, or on a smaller scale, fixing the public transportation system in Quito (Jamil's story in *Negotiating Wicked Problems*, Chapter 25). In some cases, resolving the problem may require that we deal with chaotic violence in one part of the context while also shaking up entrenched patterns of behavior that are preventing creative problem solving in other parts of the context (Jayne's story from Burma/Myanmar in *Negotiating Wicked Problems*, Chapter 25).

Addressing these types of problems requires a post-modernist theoretical foundation that incorporates two levels of analysis: "social constructionism, which posits that meaning is embedded in society through patterns of social interaction" (Fox 2009: 20) and "relational or dialogic theories, which focus on the ways we co-create meaning through our specific interpersonal and social interactions" (Fox 2009: 21). Meaning-making is the common variable in the macro- and micro-levels of a process by which groups create their shared social world. I call the combined macro- and micro-level processes "social negotiation," and I have argued that every issue-specific negotiation occurs inside a negotiated reality (Docherty 2001; see Figure One.) The influence goes in both directions between the micro-level and macro-level. Every negotiation encounter is a location for enacting macro-level meaning systems. Every negotiation is also an opportunity to reinforce, challenge, or transform institutionalized meaning systems at the personal level (by changing behavioral norms) and at the social level (by changing organizations and social structures).[2]

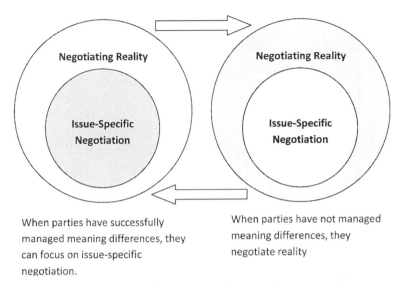

When parties have successfully managed meaning differences, they can focus on issue-specific negotiation.

When parties have not managed meaning differences, they negotiate reality

PARTIES MOVE BACK AND FORTH BETWEEN TWO TYPES OF NEGOTIATION

Figure 1: Two Interconnected Forms of Negotiation[3]

From this theoretical framework we can reconsider the nature of the negotiator. She is not just a value-maximizing, self-interested, rational actor engaging in solving a particular problem. She is also a relationally located meaning-maker capable of using her agency[4] to reinforce or challenge and renegotiate the social order, through the way she engages the process of negotiation and through the agreements she reaches with others. We can also reconsider the nature of negotiation itself. Negotiation is not just a tool for solving shared problems. Negotiation – whether focused on a tame problem or a wicked problem – is a social encounter rich with opportunities for remaking our social worlds.

These meaning-making aspects of negotiation, while present in all negotiations, are less obvious when we are dealing with tame problems. Tame problems are characterized by the fact that the parties tend to hold similar understandings of the problem, the frame for judging a good solution to the problem, and the "proper" way to negotiate. Or, put another way, tame problems are characterized by the fact that the parties have reached a level of "worldview détente" that enables them to agree on the nature of their problem, the process for negotiating a solution to their problem, and a sense of what constitutes a fair, just, acceptable, and/or appropriate solution to their problem. A problem is wicked, in part, because the parties do not define the problem in the same way *and* they reference incommensurate moral orders[5] for defining the "proper" way to negotiate and the "goodness" of possible solutions. In other words, negotiators dealing with wicked problems find themselves in significant world-viewing conflict[6] over the nature of their problem, the process for dealing with it, and the range of acceptable outcomes.

Consequently, parties dealing with wicked problems cannot choose to focus only on the presenting problem, or at least they cannot so choose without running the risk of doing great harm and making the problem even worse. They *must* negotiate problems related to the social order, which manifest in their conflict over defining the problem and in their conflict over judgment frames for assessing the legitimacy of their negotiation process, as well as the merits of proposed solutions. The negotiators must use a form of "double vision" in order to engage a process that is akin to a two-level game of chess; focusing on the immediate (problem-focused) negotiation, on the process of social (re)negotiation, and on the interplay between the two levels of negotiation.

Negotiating a specific problem is *one* venue in which the parties can engage in social (re) negotiation, but wicked problems cannot be resolved through negotiation alone. Even a series of such negotiations cannot address a wicked problem. As John Forester (2009) explains, public planning conflicts (which are often wicked problems) are addressed through a complex set of activities that includes but is not limited to negotiation. The goal is to promote "both inclusive representative participation *and* effective negotiations" (Forester 2009: 6), usually assisted by mediators. Furthermore, "skillful and wise practice involves a series of moves, phases, or even stages" rather than "just sitting down to make a deal" (Forester 2009: 4). The activities include: conflict assessment; convening the parties and their representatives; learning together about each other, the evolving context, and options for resolution; negotiation; and monitoring implementation of the agreement, followed by possible renegotiation (Forester 1985). These phases or stages are not neatly linear and they usually require the assistance of facilitative leaders and/or mediators. The ease with which parties can reach agreement about the process and viable outcomes correlates with whether the problem is tame or wicked.

To effect change at the level of social negotiation, this two-level problem requires a type of strategic planning to coordinate multiple interventions, which is not required for dealing with even the most complex tame problems. When our team of writers first started talking about "Negotiation 2.0," we were conflating the question of what needs to change in the way we negotiate specific problems and the process of thinking strategically about the overall intervention for dealing with a wicked problem. We have since concluded that it makes more sense to separate these problems, by asking:

- What needs to be changed in the way we think about and teach problem-focused negotiation, if we are going to prepare negotiators to recognize and deal adequately with wicked problems? We are now calling this "Negotiation 2.0."
- What needs to be *added* to problem-focused negotiation if we are going to use negotiation as one part of our strategy for dealing with wicked problems? We can think of this as a "guidance system" for using problem-focused negotiation ("Negotiation 2.0") when facing a wicked problem.[7]

Leonard Lira addresses issues of strategic planning for dealing with wicked problems in *Design: The U.S. Army's Approach* (Chapter 27). We know that there is much more to say on this question, and we have some partially written but not-yet-ready-for-publication chapters that we look forward to refining and sharing in the next volume in this book series.

Meanwhile, this chapter focuses on "Negotiation 2.0" because problem-focused negotiation cannot help with wicked problems if the process we bring into play "at the table" is incapable of focusing our attention on the two-level process of negotiating a particular problem and the social context that gave rise to the problem. Three features of this "two-level game" need to shape the way we think about, practice, and teach problem-focused negotiation. First, meaning-making plays a central role in wicked problems. Therefore, "Negotiation 2.0" must be imbued with a deep cultural awareness and a rich understanding of culture as a central feature of all negotiations. Second, ethical judgment is also critically important when dealing with wicked problems. Therefore, "Negotiation 2.0" must include a clear focus on the *social ethics* (general societal principles of right and wrong) as distinct from the *procedural ethics* (typically incorporated into professional codes of conduct) sometimes taught in "Negotiation 1.0." Third, as stated above, wicked problems can never be addressed only through problem-focused negotiations. Therefore, "Negotiation 2.0" should be taught in a manner that helps negotiators understand the difference between tame and wicked problems, so that they understand both the limitations of problem-focused negotiations and their potential power to play a significant role in addressing wicked problems.

In the rest of this chapter, I explain what I believe *must* be included in "Negotiation 2.0" if we are going to use it to address particular sub-sets of problems and thereby leverage desired changes in a larger wicked problem. Because I am talking about problem-focused negotiation, many of the issues I address are equally impor-

tant for dealing with tame problems today. Using a story from a negotiation I engaged in during the second Rethinking Negotiation
Teaching conference in Istanbul, I will make the case that many of
these requirements are also necessary for addressing standard transactional negotiations in a world that is, in the words of Thomas
Friedman (2009), becoming hotter, flatter and more crowded (and I
would add, more beset by wicked problems) every day.

Our Assumptions About Negotiation

First Assumption: Negotiation is a Culturally Specific Universal Practice

Every human group identifies issues that they choose to manage by
exchanging information, developing shared definitions of the problem, and creating responses to the problem that allocate the costs
and benefits of action among the members of the group. In other
words, the presence of problem-oriented negotiations appears to be
universal in human communities. However, every human community also engages in disagreements which appear to be universal
"concerning who properly should engage in negotiation and how
those individuals ought to act" as well as "the procedures and rules
to be followed in negotiation" (Stolte, Fine, and Cook 2001: 395).
The disagreements about how to negotiate problems are settled
through processes of shared meaning-making about power, authority, privilege, legitimacy, group membership, rights, and a host of
other socially constructed variables. Or put another way, any problem-focused form of negotiation is socially negotiated through the
creation of shared cultural meanings. To summarize: negotiation is a
universal human activity, but there is no universally applicable form
of negotiation.

Every cultural group *does* develop problem-focused negotiation
practices; many of those practices may look similar, while others
look radically different. However, we can never assume that surface
similarities implicate deep cultural similarities or that surface dis-
similarities indicate large cultural differences (see Figure Two). The
best we can do is to compare which problems different communities
are willing to negotiate, along with those they consider non-
negotiable, the processes they use for negotiating specific problems
and reaching agreement, and the social rules and norms that regulate the entire negotiation process.

Let us refer to the tennis skills metaphor first described earlier
by Howard Gadlin (see Honeyman and Coben, *Navigating Wickedness*,
Chapter 24). Let us describe the sometimes simple and sometimes
complex negotiations around transactions for the exchange of goods

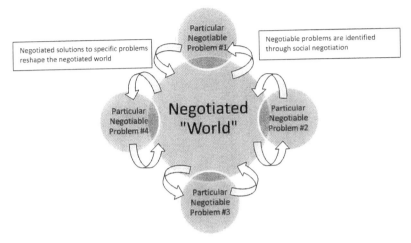

Figure 2: A Post-Modernist Explanation of Negotiation

and services – a relatively tame problem – as analogous to a sort of meta-game of sport played with a racquet. Let us further suggest that different cultures on Planet Earth have developed their own sets of rules for playing the game, as well as implicit understandings of a game well-played, both in terms of "sportsmanship" and of caliber of play. And let us further suggest that members of each culture have developed skills at handling complex problems and situations which arise in their version of "racquet sport," problems and situations more complex than those in which the players first learned the basic skills, and which have presented the players with opportunities to integrate those skills creatively into a much more sophisticated repertoire of responses.

Those carefully drilled skills *and* the more sophisticated expertise acquired through years of play will be invaluable for a player who engages with opponents (and partners) who share her understanding of the game that is being played. Those same skills will need to be "held loosely" and adapted if she finds that her opponent (or partner) has been schooled in another racquet sport – say squash or badminton – and even more loosely held if she discovers that her opponent (or partner) comes from a culture where they turn the racquet into a bat, and play a game called cricket.

From this perspective, any effort which takes a local negotiation practice and treats it as immutable over time, and universally applicable in other cultures or subcultures, is problematic from the outset. One of the central issues for the project that has given rise to this book is how we can correct for problems arising out of the fact that "Negotiation 1.0" is largely an "American export product." Or put differently, "Negotiation 2.0" is expected to correct the problems that grew out of the fact that the first generation enterprise seems to have forgotten that the negotiation practices being taught were socially negotiated by a particular community in a specific location in order to address a set of problems that are themselves socially negotiated. If we are serious about making a generational advance, then we need to "remystify" what is currently being taught, by approaching it with fresh eyes in order to remind ourselves of the worldview assumptions embedded in our particular way of playing the "racquet sport" of negotiation.

According to John Paul Lederach, Reina Neufeldt, and Hal Culbertson (2007: 3), the first step toward becoming a reflective practitioner is taking the time to remystify our practices and demystify our theories. We remystify our practices when we slow down enough to ponder, "Why am I doing this the way that I do it?" This is quite different from engaging in drills and training to refine our skills, which is also a useful activity. We demystify theory when we slow down long enough to ponder our tacit theories of change: "How do I think things are connected or related? How do I think things are related? What do I think will happen if I do X or if I do Y?"

We need to demystify theory and remystify practice because it is increasingly apparent that "Negotiation 1.0" not only does not transport across cultures, it may also not be transporting well over time even within its culture of origin. Current realities no longer resemble the background against which the first generation practices were developed. I illustrate this point not with my own experience in "exotic" locales, but with problems identified by Leonard Greenhalgh and Roy Lewicki (2003) when considering how to update or alter first-generation teaching practices to meet the rapidly changing demands of the organizational and business world that gave rise to "Negotiation 1.0."

According to Greenhalgh and Lewicki, the failure to account for the co-construction of a negotiated social order and problem-focused negotiation practices was reflected in the way the researchers and teachers involved in the enterprise approached knowledge creation and teaching. Knowledge about negotiation was frequently generated through artificially de-contextualized simulations or role plays that focused on isolated variables in the problem-focused negotiation process. Information gleaned from research was then translated into lessons for practitioners. Consequently, what is being taught frequently does not match the students' everyday experience of negotiation. Specifically, much of what is being taught fails to account for the fact that most students spend most of their time negotiating with "people with whom they have a past history and an anticipated future relationship" so that they cannot easily identify a best alternative to a negotiated agreement, they cannot separate the person from the problem, and "their commonwealth bond [makes] interests inseparable within the dyad" (Greenhalgh and Lewicki 2003: 25).

In addition, consider the gender, culture and class biases that were inculcated into first generation negotiation practices by the pioneers of the field, who were primarily "relatively affluent Western white males culturally situated in a free-enterprise context... [whose] world view emphasized individualism, self-interest, economic rationality, dominance-submission, rights and rules" (Greenhalgh and Lewicki 2003: 26). And apropos to our experience, first generation practices also tended to isolate out contextual factors and tended to assume relative stability in the milieu surrounding the parties at the table. Consequently, the model of first generation negotiation does not easily take into account the problem of rapid change, instability or contextual turbulence (Docherty 2005). But change occurs whether it is examined or not, and rapid changes have overtaken even the original contexts (business, law, and governance) in which first generation practices were developed. For example, globalization has led to larger power differentials among the parties at the table, greater diversity in the types of parties at the table, and competing rule systems for regulating negotiations and their outcomes (Greenhalgh and Lewicki 2003: 28-29). It should be noted here that when they talk about greater diversity at the table, Greenhalgh and Lewicki are not speaking only about the ethnic, cultural and gender diversity of individual negotiators. They are also noting that whereas first generation negotiation practices seemed to assume that the organizations involved in negotiation were similar in type, the new global context often brings together corporations of various sizes, governments, international regulatory bodies, and NGOs in a single negotiation.[8]

Second Assumption: Context Matters

We can say context matters because the type of problem-focused negotiation we are teaching in "Negotiation 1.0" programs needs to be tweaked for somewhat different contextual factors. In that case, we push negotiators to become a little more alert to features of the surrounding context that "intrude upon" the negotiation process or that might impact the implementation of an agreement. The underlying image of negotiation is that of a bounded time and space apart from the surrounding context; a location for interactions that are governed largely by tacit or explicit rules agreed to by the parties. This *is not* what I mean when I say context matters. I am arguing that the context of negotiation matters because problem-focused negotiations and social negotiations are interdependent and dynamic activities.

The very problems we negotiate and the way we negotiate them are *constituted by* the ongoing process of social negotiation. Even when the goal is only to solve a problem, we are either reinforcing or challenging the negotiated social order as we deal with that problem. In other words, every problem-focused negotiation has power in relation to the social order, and we should not overlook that power just because we or others *choose* to use that power to reinforce and sustain the existing order. This is the social ethics piece of our work.

We can see the influence of social negotiation on problem-focused negotiation if we look at the "moral orders" of the parties at the table. "The term *moral order*... denotes the patterns of one's compulsions and permissions to act in certain ways and one's prohibitions against acting in other ways" (Pearce and Littlejohn 1997: 54). The parties can only freely enter into a problem-focused negotiation if they all see themselves as permitted (or even required) to be there. And they will only come freely into the process if it does not force them to violate cultural prohibitions that they have internalized. Of course, parties can be forced into a negotiation if they are overpowered, but I do not hold out much hope that agreements reached in this manner will be sustainable.

The same internalized but culturally derived system of compulsions and prohibitions influences the *ways* the parties conduct their negotiations once they enter into the process. The influence can be as simple as engaging in prescribed social rituals, such as offering tea or hospitality or shaking hands. Or the influence can be as complicated as determining who sits where, who does and who does not speak, in what order they speak and to whom, how directly a participant may speak, and which issues may or may not be discussed. These cultural patterns are carried by the parties in the form of scripts or schema for action.[9] Referring back to our "racquet sport" metaphor: if a negotiator has negotiated only with others who play the game as tennis, he will just assume that "this is how negotiation is done," because he has never encountered someone who holds a different script or schema (perhaps squash or badminton) for negotiation.

When Dean Pruitt (1995) talks about collective scripts, he is trying to capture some of the ways that negotiators work together so that they can anticipate the reactions of others. Collective scripts "are enacted only if other people are also enacting them, and they involve interlocking roles and/or substitutability (i.e., if one person fails to perform an element of the script, others fill in)" (Pruitt 1995: 44). The interesting thing about Pruitt's work on collective scripts is that he grounds it in a fundamentally Western, individualist and modern view of the world by locating collective scripts as part of working (or as he notes, instrumental) relationships. This is in contrast to communal relationships. In several of the stories in *Negotiating Wicked Problems* (Chapter 25), however, we saw places where some of the parties were playing a different negotiation game – one shaped by collective scripts that are grounded in communal rather than instrumental relationships, or as is commonly the case, in a mix of communal and instrumental relationships, with the balance tipped toward communal rather than instrumental relationships. I certainly see this type of script significantly influencing patterns of negotiation in Myanmar/Burma.

We cannot assume in today's world that individuals arrive at a negotiation with the same script (individual or collective), or the same balance between individual and collective script elements. Let us return again to our metaphor of racquet sports. When playing a particular racquet sport (say tennis) we do not know for sure what actions our opponent will take in response to our play. However, their range of possible responses is not infinite, because they are shaped and delimited by the rules of the game, norms regarding sportsmanlike behavior, the equipment authorized for use in play, contextual variables such as type of surface or weather, and the limitations of human endurance and fitness. If, however, we were to try playing a racquet sport against someone who plays a different game (we play tennis and they play squash), many of these variables would be contested, as we each tried to tell the other how to play properly. If we just started to play without negotiating the rules, we would be mutually puzzled (perhaps even offended) by the "wrong play" of the other.

Problem-focused negotiations also require that the parties have some ability to anticipate how others will respond to their ideas and their proposals. In addition to scripts which direct our attention to the moves and countermoves of an interaction, negotiators need to develop an understanding of the "bounded decision-making" of the others involved in the process: How will they define the problem? How will they respond to an alternative definition of the problem? How will they evaluate the merits of a proposed solution to the problem?

I am using the concept of bounded decision-making as a form of shorthand for two different constraints on the negotiators' choices. First, there are the constraints and mandates on individual action created by *social norms*, which manifest in moral orders as compulsions and prohibitions. Second, there is the person's limited ability to gather information, process options, and evaluate the costs and benefits of action proposals. To deal with this cognitive limitation, negotiators use heuristic devices and reasoning short-cuts to reduce the number of options from which they select a course of action; this is known as *bounded rationality*.[10] Social norms and bounded rationality intersect when the negotiator uses social norms to limit (based on concepts of what is and is not permissible) the range of possible "rational" decisions[11] and simplified heuristic devices to identify a solution that is effective and logical, although not rational in the way that term has been used by economists. A really effective negotiator will understand the need to gather information about the social norms that shape the bounded rationality of her interlocutor. But even gathering that information does not locate both players in the same game, and leaves much uncertainty about how the other person will respond to our play.

In inter-cultural situations, the challenge of defining a range of "rational" solutions and "appropriate" responses to the moves of other negotiators is sometimes handled by establishing a "third culture" that bounds the negotiation. Wendi L. Adair, Catherine H. Tinsley, and Masako S. Taylor note that

> multicultural teams that come together for a common purpose may develop not only shared knowledge about their team and task and similar behaviors, but also a shared set of values and norms that underlie and guide those behaviors. Such a shared knowledge structure, consisting of team and task knowledge, as well as values and norms rooted in the traditional cultural belief system of one or more team members, is what we call a third culture (Adair, Tinsley, and Taylor 2006: 2).

Some researchers focus on the development of a third culture in close personal relationships between individuals from different cultures. Through their repeated interactions they create a new set of shared meanings that form the basis for a "third culture [that] is characterized by unique values and norms that may not have existed prior to the dyadic relationship" (Broome 1993: 104). Others have noted that third cultures or negotiation regimes that establish standard ways of framing and resolving disputes arise in business (Weiss 2006), international diplomacy (Bolewsky 2008), and other forms of regularized interaction among corporate actors.

However, the creation of a third culture as a process for handling cross-cultural negotiation encounters requires time and repetition, and therefore depends on contextual stability. Insofar as a negotiation is taking place in unstable environments, creating a third culture may not be achievable; in situations where solving a wicked problem requires shaking up entrenched systems (see *Negotiating Wicked Problems*, Chapter 25), the third culture may be part of the problem. A significant source of the presenting conflict is the competition to impose a set of "meta-rules" on society, and those include the rules for governing negotiation as a process as well as the frames for judging good or acceptable negotiated agreements.

Problem-focused negotiations are a powerful location for either supporting or challenging the surrounding (socially negotiated) context. Whether they understand it or not, negotiators are in a position of social leadership, because they enter into a space where existing social orders can be modified or reinforced. To operate effectively in these situations, negotiators need to understand their own goals and those of their interlocutors on two different levels: goals related to the specific problem, and goals related to the larger process of social negotiation. A failure to reach agreement on a particular issue – or even a failure to enter fully into a negotiation process – may say more about the parties' differences around (re)negotiating the social order than it does about the presenting problem under discussion.

To summarize our assumptions: Negotiation *per se* is a pervasive social practice, through which human beings create, sustain, and modify their relationships and institutions. What we currently teach in our trainings and basic courses is only one form of negotiation that was developed in a particular historical and cultural location for specific purposes. In other settings, different negotiation practices are used to accomplish similar goals, such as negotiating the sale of goods or services. If we want to develop a robust "Negotiation 2.0," we need to re-center our attention on the way negotiations manifest in different cultures and on the relationship between negotiating specific problems and negotiating our shared lives. To illustrate my points, I will share and then analyze a story of a seemingly simple transactional negotiation.

Buying a Red Leather Jacket in Istanbul

Based on our adventure learning outings to the Grand Bazaar and the Spice Market during our second conference in Istanbul, many participants were talking about how Turkish merchants "use" relationships to make sales. As with any cross-cultural observation, that statement says as much about the culture of the speakers as it does about the culture of those they are explaining. I did not see the local merchants as "using" relationship building; I saw it as an indicator of a relationally based social world. I surmised that if relationships are central to negotiating sales, then the marketplace itself might be a system of relationships of reciprocity. This thought was affirmed when merchants sent us to someone else for products they did not offer themselves. So, in theory, if an individual could gain entry into the network of relationships, she would experience greater negotiation success.

My theory about the local culture was put to the test the day after the conference. I made an offer on a jacket in the shop of seller Mr. A, but it was firmly rejected. Worse, Mr. A refused to bargain any further. The palpable sense of indignation in his rejection led me later to describe Mr. A. as grumpy – my "frame" but probably not his.

I had attempted to strike a deal by importing a technique which works well for me in the marketplace in Chiang Mai, Thailand: I bid a price less than the asking price, but a bit higher than what I believed Mr. A's "reservation price" might be. Thinking that Mr. A's reservation price might be the price "locals" might pay, plus 10 percent, I calculated my bid on the basis of a 15 percent markup. I hoped he might be pleased to negotiate with a "knowledgeable" and "culturally savvy" negotiator.

Walking out of Mr. A's shop without having even defined or entered a zone of possible agreement (ZOPA), I thought, "If I just had a Turkish person with me to negotiate on my behalf, I think I could have gotten that jacket for that price." Much later, while I was reflecting on what ensued, I remembered one of our Turkish colleagues talking about the issues of face and hospitality in Turkish culture. She said that if a Turkish person brought a foreigner into a shop, the foreigner was seen as the "guest" and the shopkeeper felt honor-bound to make the local person look good in front of his guest. In the moment, however, I was not so conscious of my logic.

In the shop of Sonny, another merchant, I was still pondering my disappointment about the jacket when he slid into his relationship-building patter. I learned all kinds of things about Sonny: he had worked at a U.S. Air Force base in Turkey; he loves Americans. My father was a career Air Force Officer, so we chatted about the Air Force. The chit-chat continued as Sonny tried to sell me earrings and a scarf. I told him that I loved the scarf. I would surely want to buy it, if I had been able to purchase the matching and beautiful red leather jacket for the price I could afford. But, alas, without the jacket, I did not need the scarf. Sonny asked me what I had offered for the jacket and I told him my offer as well as the original price. Sonny did not seem to think it was an unreasonable offer. He said, "You should have your jacket." And as he said that, he came out from behind the counter, took my elbow, guided me out of the shop and locked it up. Sonny walked me around the corner – chatting all the way – to see if his friend Mr. B. might sell the same jacket. Sadly, his friend's shop was closed. I figured it was a nice try, but I would leave Istanbul without my jacket.

Not so! Sonny walked me right back to Mr. A. As we entered the shop, Sonny greeted Mr. A. as he simultaneously urged me to try on the jacket. "Oh," he said, "you really should have that jacket. It looks like it was made just for you and it is so sexy." Another part of the relationship-building ritual in Turkey involves a great deal of flirtation with female customers – not a practice that would transfer well into many other cultures! As I was looking at the jacket in the mirror, Sonny started negotiating in Turkish with Mr. A. I departed Mr. A's shop with the jacket; I paid the exact amount I had originally offered.

Unpacking the Story

My working theory to explain this bargaining success is based on the meta-theory of two-level negotiation outlined above. I theorize that my "partners" in the negotiation process chose to accord me status within the culture-specific community of relationships within which a problem-focused negotiation could proceed. My participation in the process of social negotiation was matched by their generous re-framing of our mutual relationship. As someone "sponsored" by Sonny, I was at least temporarily transformed into someone other than an outsider tourist, but what was the nature of that transformation, and is this just an Istanbul phenomenon?

I reside for extended periods in Chiang Mai, Thailand. There, I have negotiated what I think of as "pseudo-insider" status with local merchants. I pay slightly more than locals do, but not what tourists are charged. Based on longevity of residence, loyalty to particular merchants, and my care not to take my special price in front of "those rich tourists," I pay close to the local price. In Istanbul, I think Sonny helped me get a good deal by sponsoring me as a "pseudo-guest of a local," so that rules of hospitality and face-saving came into play. Even though I was not Sonny's friend, he was playing the script of hosting a foreign friend and thereby invoking the norms for friendship. This might explain Mr. A.'s grimace as he conceded the price. He knew, as did Sonny and I, that I was not really a friend of Sonny's at all. I was just a customer that Sonny was treating as a friend. The rules for negotiating with "a foreign guest" should not have applied to me, but Mr. A. had no way out that would not damage his face and/or Sonny's face. He had to cooperate with Sonny's play-acting or he had to defy social norms he valued.

Taken together, my experiences in Thailand and Turkey indicate that relationships matter significantly when it comes to "getting into the game" of negotiation. Furthermore, socially negotiated identity (even pseudo-identity) affects the boundaries of the game and the range of possible agreements. This is just for buying a jacket! How much more complicated is the process for getting in the game and delimiting the rules of the game if we are talking about negotiations used as part of resolving a wicked problem?

From a "Negotiation 1.0" perspective, the questions about the jacket story might be more like: "How did Sonny 'use' relationship building as instrumental to making a sale? What did Mr. A. get out of this whole deal and, because we are talking about relationships of reciprocity, what did it 'cost' Sonny to negotiate with Mr. A. on my behalf?" Those very questions reflect a worldview rooted in less personal relationships, but they still have some validity. I bought the scarf and a pair of earrings from Sonny, both at discounted prices. He also got a great story to tell other customers as a way of building rapport. I know he did just that, because three of my colleagues sought me out to see my jacket and discuss the way the deal was done! They had all heard the story from Sonny. And, honestly, I think Sonny and I both had fun. Mr. A. was not thrilled about making the sale, but it was a very slow day and it did not hurt to add the money to his take for the day. His profit margin was low, but I do not think he lost money on the jacket. In addition, I am sure he reached a tacit agreement with Sonny that Sonny will send other customers to Mr. A. And some day, if Mr. A. shows up in Sonny's shop with a customer posing as a friend in tow, I am sure Sonny will need to return the favor.

Implications for "Negotiation 2.0"

What We Need to Teach

The social construction of negotiation
Buying a red leather jacket in Istanbul would appear to fall under the heading of a tame problem. It is a transactional negotiation made cross-cultural by the fact that I am not Turkish. How hard can it be? Viewed from this perspective, the red leather jacket story suggests the possibility that every culture, within its own particular brand of "racquet sport," employs its own version of certain key concepts (e.g., zone of possible agreement (ZOPA) or best alternative to a negotiated agreement (BATNA)) of problem-focused negotiations. We can choose to teach negotiation by focusing on these similarities; we can act as though ZOPA and BATNA are acultural or universal

concepts. Indeed, "Negotiation 1.0" trainings make just these assumptions. But in so doing, we miss much more important truths about negotiation.

If the way Sonny and Mr. A. do business is embedded in a culture, then we must assume that the way we negotiate – the tools we are teaching in our trainings and courses – are also culturally loaded. Our negotiation practices, like those of the Turkish merchants, were developed in a cultural and historical place (the "where") for use by individuals who are themselves products of larger social negotiation processes (the "who") in order to solve culturally negotiated and bounded problems (the "why"). If we want to offer our negotiation practices for consideration by others who work and live in different circumstances, then we need to teach them in a way that acknowledges *our* cultural assumptions *as well as* those of our students. Indeed, if we want our practices to continue to be relevant in our own lives as circumstances change, then we need to teach any negotiation tools we offer in a manner that is flexible, and adaptive, and we need to help our students develop self-awareness and cultural awareness.[12]

As my story illustrates, the *application* of concepts such as ZOPA and BATNA are culturally determined and are engaged through social negotiation. One way of looking at my negotiation is to say that Mr. A and I actually did share a ZOPA. However, we were unable to define or enter that zone until we had successfully completed the social negotiation, facilitated by Sonny, which gave me access to the problem-focused process as practiced in that Istanbul marketplace. That may or may not be completely accurate, since we do not know whether Mr. A. felt coerced by Sonny's ploy to bring me into the marketplace in the guise of a guest rather than a customer off the street.

There are many unanswered questions surrounding my purchase of the jacket. I do not know why Mr. A refused my initial offer so forcefully. He may have been offended by what he considered a "low-ball" bid; he may have been working from a foundational assumption that non-locals should pay a full price; he may have been constipated and having a bad day. Whatever his reason (and it may have been one I have not yet even considered), the fact is that I engaged in a process which was culturally informed without yet being fully informed of the cultural "givens" about the process.

I also do not know why Sonny decided to befriend me, or why Mr. A. cooperated with Sonny's actions. I do know, however, that the decisions they made were not just instrumentally rational cost-benefit decisions. They were making meaning and they were exercising judgment, as they negotiated my inclusion in the marketplace and decided on the rules that would apply to my purchase of the jacket. "Is she an insider or an outsider?" "Which set of negotiation rules apply to her?" "Is it appropriate for one merchant to sponsor a customer as a 'pseudo-insider' in the shop of another merchant?" "Do face-saving rules apply if one merchant is pretending that his customer is a friend?" These are all questions that evoke judgments loaded with meaning-making and ethical implications.

We have no way of knowing whether the fact that I could pass for Turkish (many merchants spoke to me first in Turkish) influenced their decisions to treat me as a pseudo-insider. Would I have been extended the same status if I were a member of a group being marginalized in Turkish society? Under those circumstances Sonny might have never extended the offer to help me. Or Sonny might have taken up my case only to have Mr. A. refuse to reach an agreement on the price – choosing to deny the relationships of reciprocity among merchants, because he disagreed with Sonny that I should be treated as a pseudo-insider or a foreign guest. The marketplace can and does serve as an indicator of social conflicts that need to be addressed in societies. This is true in societies experiencing large-scale social conflict and in societies undergoing significant but peaceful social changes, such as an influx of immigrants. It may be easier to see in societies where the marketplace is a bazaar, but it is equally – albeit differently – true in Westernized societies where the marketplace does not involve direct haggling between buyer and seller. For example, in the United States some communities have no access to a grocery store, but are populated with a plethora of fast food restaurants. The residents of those communities are so powerless in the *social negotiation* process that decides food distribution systems that others have decided for them that they will have nutritionally deficient and expensive diets and all of the attendant health issues.

Negotiation and social responsibility

The marketplace can also become a venue for renegotiating the wider social world, and merchants can become key allies for dealing with a significant social conflict.[13] If Sonny, Mr. A., and other merchants engage in enough modifications of their practices regarding inclusion and exclusion from the relationships of the marketplace, then the culture starts to shift in directions that are either positive or negative. Whether they like it or not, Mr. A. and Sonny are social leaders by virtue of the fact that they manage and apply a socially validated negotiation process.

The same is true for our students. Every negotiation encounter over an ordinary problem is an opportunity to reinforce, challenge, or transform our socially negotiated world. As such, every negotiation encounter involves *social ethics* (general societal principles of right and wrong) and not just *procedural ethics* (typically incorporated into professional codes of conduct). We need to acknowledge this power when we hand students tools for negotiating more effectively. They have stepped into the role of potentially influential social leaders; we have a responsibility to educate them to take that leadership role seriously. If we teach negotiation by only focusing on the questions of what and how and detach the process from questions of where, why, and by (and for) whom (see Lewicki and Schneider, *Instructors Heed the Who*, in this volume), then we risk creating negotiators who lack the critical capacity to recognize their own role in larger social issues of justice, power, and privilege. If we teach negotiators in a manner that allows them to disconnect their activities from larger social issues, we risk creating capable, efficient technocrats who can bring about social, economic, and political disasters.[14]

If we teach "that the negotiator's central challenge is learning how to develop and enact rational strategies to claim and/or create maximum value that satisfy the negotiator's (or her principal's) self-interest" (Fox 2009: 14), our students from cultures that construct the individual in more relational terms or cultures that rely on differently rational[15] decision-making processes are likely to be puzzled or even offended. I have had trainees tell me in no uncertain terms that this form of negotiation is just the latest in a long line of tools imported from the West for the purpose of imposing on others a hyper-commercialized, rabidly secular, and morally bankrupt worldview. From their perspective, negotiation as we teach it is just the latest means of colonizing and denigrating local cultures and turning local resources – including ancestral lands and water supplies as well as minerals and other portable materials – into monetized commodities. This is particularly true in situations where negotiation is taught to the privileged elites who have appropriated for themselves resources that belong to the collective. And U.S. trainers do not need to have a passport to get that reaction. Just take standard negotiation techniques to Native American communities, and if you really develop a relationship of trust and transparency with those you are teaching, you will hear this same discussion.

Negotiation and values

This is not to say that our model – or the worldview on which it rests – is wrong or deficient or defective. In fact, our practices carry several assumptions that I personally would like to uphold and promote. Our way of negotiating assumes that the participants in negotiation training experience themselves as (relatively) autonomous agents with the power to make (relatively) free choices about their goals and commitments. Or, put another way, negotiators are presumed to have developed a level of mental complexity beyond the "socialized mind" which makes the person "subject to the values and expectations of his 'surround' (be it his family of origin, his religious or political reference group, or the leaders of his work setting, who set terms in his professional and financial reality)" (Kegan and Lahey 2009: 52). We also assume that the participants understand what it means to live and work in places where decisions are made by groups of individuals who are – or who are willing to behave as if they are – more or less equal in status, authority and importance. Or, put another way, negotiators are presumed to have experienced – and embraced as valuable – relatively democratic decision-making systems in which value is attached to good ideas and creative problem-solving more than to the status of the participants and maintaining the status quo or preserving harmony.

These attitudes and assumptions are not universally held. My own experiences include conversations with younger individuals who believe that their cultural group's value of respect for elders prevents them from negotiating with anyone older or higher in status than they. For example, a very capable young leader recently lamented to me that he feels terrible that he is always unable to meet his obligations because he has double-booked appointments. Further exploration of why he booked double appointments revealed that, in fact, *he* had not done that at all. Rather, two different senior leaders in his organization were *telling him* that he needed to be attending different events at the same time. When I suggested that this was a situation where negotiation tools could be useful, he was horrified. "I could not possibly start that conversation with them. They are my elders and my leaders!" If this were just one person, I would attribute that response to a personal quirk, but the truth is that I have seen this pattern among young people in many organizations in more communally and hierarchically organized cultures. They have acquired negotiation skills in workshops, but they are unable to transfer them into their context when such a transfer requires that they challenge socially negotiated patterns of acceptable interactions. In similar fashion, their seniors have said similar things about moving negotiation skills from the "training" venue to their real-world problems. The context they are living in simply does not allow the creation of the space for negotiating the problems they want to address in the way I have been teaching them. There is a disconnect between their values and the values embedded in "Negotiation 1.0" practices; the result is internal dissonance and a sense of identity threat when they think about using their new "skills" to address the problems they know need to be handled.

So, "Negotiation 2.0" needs to be clear about the values behind the practices. I *value* both relative autonomy (tempered by interdependence, which is also part of our negotiation model) and democratic, non-hierarchical decision making. But I recognize that these are *values*; they are not value-neutral *tools*. As such, they are not universally held. I have exercised my autonomy and I have lived in a society that applauds me for doing that. I have also had personal experiences of democratic decision-making even in hierarchically organized institutions. But I know this is not a universally shared life experience. In a multi-cultural world, the individuals we are teaching may speak the language of autonomy and democracy in their workplace without fully embracing the values and behaviors associated with this language. This is not just an issue "out there" in some "underdeveloped" country, either. Many individuals we train live their personal lives in families and other organizations that value compliance to group-defined values over autonomy, while also relying on autocratic rather than democratic decision-making processes. This is as true for "mainstream Americans" (whatever that means) as it is for individuals from other cultures.

How We Need to Teach

Negotiation and "liberatory" education

The story of the young leader who cannot negotiate his appointment calendar with his superiors points to a pedagogical issue for "Negotiation 2.0." Kevin Avruch (2009) has argued that we need to think of our pedagogy as education rather than training, and I agree. But what type of education are we talking about? Our students come from diverse settings. They face different types of problems that can be negotiable *if* they so construct them. Contrary to the claim often made in "Negotiation 1.0," *not everything* is negotiable. We all operate in contexts that enable some negotiations and repress others, or that rule certain problems as non-negotiable. The definition of negotiable problems, the development of negotiation practices, and the rules for their application (what can be negotiated, who can negotiate, etc.) are intertwined processes of meaning-making and ethical judgment.

In a globalized context, everyone entering into a negotiation training or course arrives with culturally shaped ideas about negotiation and some life-experience negotiating in his or her own culture. I am suggesting that in a multicultural world, our pedagogy should not be using a "banking model" of education where we assume our students arrive as empty vessels and we fill them up with knowledge and coach them in skills. Rather, we should adopt a mutually reflective and liberatory educational approach (Freire 2009: 71-74) based on dialogue about the various ways that people and groups have learned to negotiate, what kind of problems they consider negotiable or non-negotiable, and the types of organizational or institutional systems they have developed to support the process of negotiation and the agreements reached through negotiation.

This approach to teaching negotiation weaves in a level of self-awareness and self-reflection that is not common in "Negotiation 1.0" courses, where self-awareness tends to focus on particular pre-defined skills. How well does the student listen? How well does she manage interactions with the other party? How well does he present proposals that create value? How well does she claim value? By contrast, "Negotiation 2.0" should work on helping students reflect on questions such as: Who am I in my society, and how does that shape the way I negotiate with others? Where am I able to negotiate and where am I not able to negotiate? How do I feel about those social rules? How can I use my negotiation skills *or other conflict transformation skills* to change social systems that I do not like or that I consider unfair or unjust? How can I help my group frame shared problems in a way that makes them amenable to negotiation (or other transformative activities)?

This type of self-awareness – or awareness of self in relation to a socially negotiated context – is a necessary step to prepare students to handle problems that are complex rather than technical (Kegan and Lahey 2009). Both technical and adaptive problems demand change, but not the same types of change. As noted by Kegan and Lahey (2009: 29):

> Technical changes are not necessarily easy, nor are their results necessarily unimportant or insignificant. Learning how to remove an inflamed appendix or how to land an airplane with a stuck nose wheel are examples of largely technical challenges, and their accomplishment is certainly important to the patient on the surgeon's table or the nervous passengers contemplating a crash landing.

We know how to teach technical skills: "the routines and processes by which we might help an intern or a novice pilot become an accomplished practitioner are well practiced and proven" (Kegan and Lahey 2009: 29).

It is not so easy to teach someone to handle adaptive problems, because by their very nature, they require that we name a new problem clearly and we make changes in *ourselves* in order to address the problem. We can teach technical skills by focusing on the physical and mental aptitudes of our students, but self-change requires a different model of teaching and learning. Part of the process of self-change involves identifying and learning to reflect on and modify our "theories-in-use," which "are means for getting what we want" (Argyris and Schön 1978: 15). Among other things, our theories-in-use "specify strategies for resolving conflicts, making a living, closing a deal, organizing a neighborhood – indeed for every kind of intended consequence [as well as for] maintaining certain kinds of constancy" (Argyris and Schön 1978: 15). Insofar as negotiators are embedded in and operating on behalf of organizations, dealing with adaptive problems also requires developing the ability to question and challenge the established theories-in-use that are embedded in organizations.

The process of uncovering theories-in-use, including those theories-in-use that guide our practice of negotiation, is referred to as double-loop learning (Argyris and Schön 1978, citing Ashby 1952). Interestingly, Chris Argyris and Donald Schön use the following example to illustrate the difference between single-loop and double-loop learning:

> In the context of theories-in-use, a person engages in single-loop learning, for example, when he learns new techniques for suppressing conflict. He engages in double-loop learning when he learns to be concerned with the surfacing and resolution of conflict rather than with its suppression (Argyris and Schön 1978: 19).

In our project, we might say that a person engages in single-loop learning when she learns how to employ "Negotiation 1.0" practices for problems similar to those she negotiates at home in unfamiliar cultural settings, but she engages in double-loop learning when she learns how to uncover the existing negotiation practices in an unfamiliar cultural setting and blend those with "Negotiation 1.0" practices to manage, resolve, or transform a conflict effectively.

This sounds complicated, but it is really not that difficult if we (the instructors) alter our own self-perception and adopt a more humble stance toward our subject matter. After all, we are only offering a set of practices that was developed in a particular context; we are not offering a set of universal truths or the magic bullet for handling all problems. Perhaps trainings should always start with an activity that uncovers the existing negotiation practices in a particular setting. I do this either before or at the start of any training. I start with a minimalist definition of negotiation: negotiation involves two or more people or parties who communicate with one another in order to promote shared understandings, overcome differences, reach compromises, or make mutually beneficial tradeoffs. After making sure that they understand all of the concepts – I ask them for examples of reaching a compromise, making tradeoffs, etc. – I ask the participants (or a pre-training consultation group) to identify situations where they have participated in or observed any of those activities. Then, I have them act out several cases they have identified, selecting the cases so as to get a variety of issues, venues, and parties.

Together, we identify the patterns of negotiation that are revealed in these cases, and we explore some of their assumptions about conflict, power, relationships, and norms for communication. Only after this grounding in their own situation and their own culture do I start to introduce "Negotiation 1.0" practices and ideas, with careful attention to identifying the similarities and differences between existing practices and what I am sharing, and between their context and the environment in which the "Negotiation 1.0" practices were developed. The participants are the ones who ultimately need to decide how much or how little they want to take from what I bring into the discussion and how they want to use it in their context.

If we start with a "Negotiation 2.0" educational program that incorporates the issues and uses the methodology described here, it is not difficult to direct students' attention to the differences between tame and wicked problems. Furthermore, they will be prepared for the following complex activities:

- Holding a "two-level vision" of the world that allows them to see both the immediate problem and the systems that create and sustain that problem.
- Recognizing the meaning-making and ethical judgment processes that are giving rise to wicked problems.
- Identifying their own power to act as change agents by the way they use negotiation, and reflecting on their own ethical obligations as leaders of their society.
- Engaging in – and modeling for others – the process of personal change necessary to address a wicked problem.

Conclusion

In this chapter, I have focused on what needs to be taught in "Negotiation 2.0" in order to prepare negotiators for the more complicated process of using negotiation as part of the solution to wicked problems. In the chapter to follow (*Design: The U.S. Army's Approach*), Leonard Lira provides a sobering tale of the limits of "Negotiation 1.0" training as it affected his summer 2007 U.S. Army mission in Iraq.

He goes on to detail the Army's current and ambitious effort to prepare troops to negotiate more effectively in such situations. This is only the start of our discussion. We look forward to continuing the conversation with our colleagues, and invite others to help us figure out ways to prepare negotiators for the kinds of situations we described in *Negotiating Wicked Problems* (Chapter 25).

Notes

[1] For purposes of this chapter, the term "wicked" describes problems that exhibit some combination of the following features:
- The problem is ill-defined and resists clear definition as a technical issue, because wicked problems are also social, political, and moral in nature. Each proposed definition of the problem implies a particular kind of solution which is loaded with contested values. Consequently, merely defining the problem can incite passionate conflict.
- Solutions to a wicked problem cannot be labeled good or bad; they can only be considered better or worse, good enough or not good enough. Whether a solution is good enough depends on the values and judgment of each of the parties, who will inevitably assess the problem and its potential solutions from their respective positions within the social context of the problem.
- Every wicked problem is unique and novel, because even if the technical elements appear similar from one situation to another, the social, political, and moral features are context-specific.
- A wicked problem contains an interconnected web of sub-problems; every proposed solution to part or the whole of the wicked problem will affect other problems in the web.

See generally Rittell and Webber (1973), Ritchey (2005-2008) and Conklin 2005). This stands in sharp contrast to the nature of problems that the planning profession has labeled "tame." As summarized by Ritchey (2005-2008: 1), a tame problem:
- Has a relatively well-defined and stable problem statement.
- Has a definite stopping point, i.e., we know when a solution is reached.
- Has a solution which can be objectively evaluated as being right or wrong.
- Belongs to a class of similar problems which can be solved in a similar manner.
- Has solutions that can be tried and abandoned.

[2] I am using Kevin Avruch's (1998) approach to culture by focusing on interpreted social action or practice that locates culture both outside the individual (in images or schemas or models) and inside the individual (in meaning-making processes that shape action).

[3] Adapted from Docherty (2001: 55).

[4] I am using agency in the social-psychological sense although I realize that might be confusing to some readers who are more accustomed to using the term "agent" to mean someone who represents a party in negotiations. An individual who claims and uses her agency is engaging in the exercise of power, by using her ability to bring about effects and to (re)constitute the world (Karp 1986: 137).

[5] The concept of "moral order" is taken from the work of W. Barnett Pearce and Stephen W. Littlejohn (1997). It focuses attention on the internalized patterns of "must do's" and "must not do's" that individuals bring into a conflict situation. Looking at the moral orders that negotiators bring to the table is a useful way to uncover the meaning-making processes that shape individual action. In this way, we begin to uncover the individually internalized dimensions of culture identified by Avruch (1998) as critically important in understanding conflict and efforts to resolve it.

[6] Worldviewing is another useful way to focus on the meaning-making processes of individuals (and groups) in conflict. It is also a good antidote to the tendency to think of worldviews as coherent packages of ideas, when they are more amorphous, less tidy and therefore more malleable than we often assume. Worldviewing is a universal human activity; we can obtain useful information by focusing on the socio-cognitive and emotional processes of worldviewing such as "categorization, boundary establishment, and the creation and use of scripts of schema" (Docherty 2001: 50).

[7] Examples of questions that we hope to have answered in a "guidance system" include: How do you recognize which specific problem-focused negotiations are most likely to generate opportunities for renegotiating the social order? When working in situations where multiple problem-focused negotiation processes are vying for legitimacy, how do you help the parties craft a shared negotiation process? How do you know when to use negotiation and when to use other processes such as dialogue? How do you move from other processes to negotiation and back again in the most effective way? How do you avoid "overselling" the efficacy of negotiation for dealing with a wicked problem?

[8] This is a common experience in public negotiations, and it is becoming more common in the business world. See Jayne Seminare Docherty and Marcia Caton Campbell (2006) for guidance on factors that need to be taken into account when dissimilar parties negotiate complex problems.

[9] Leigh Thompson, Erika Peterson and Laura Kray (1996), summarizing a wealth of literature, define a script as "an implicit theory of a situation that specifies a coherent sequence of social activities. Individuals may have several scripts relevant to negotiation. For example, a script about selling cars may evoke the familiar used-car lot scenario, or a script of a luxury automobile car dealership, or a script of a college student selling her car through the local classified ads. Each script calls for different behaviors from the actors in the negotiation" (p. 18). And that is just talking about selling a car! Wicked problems and conditions of instability usually call forth an even greater variety of competing social scripts.

[10] "[Herbert] Simon's vision of bounded rationality has two interlocking components: the limitations of the human mind, and the structure of the environments in which the mind operates" (Gigerenzer and Todd 1999: 12). Humans use heuristic devices to simplify their decision making and this reasoning works "if the structure of the heuristic is adapted to the environment" (Gigerenzer and Todd 1999: 13). This is why Gerd Gigerenzer and Peter Todd use the term "ecological rationality" to remind us that "a heuristic is ecologically rational to the degree that it is adapted to the structure of an environment" (Gigerenzer and Todd 1999: 13). When we are talking about a social ecology made up of human actors, heuristic devices may be more difficult to maintain at optimal adaptation, and it is constantly necessary to monitor and adjust the heuristics that guide our decision making.

[11] It is important to combine the social normative elements of decision making alongside the idea of bounded rationality. Otherwise we risk losing an important ethically critical perspective. Or, in the words of John Forester (1985: 77), "'Bounded rationality' in its standard political and administrative form had perversely socialized rationality by presuming existing relations of power to be fully legitimate (or, in what amounts practically, if not theoretically, to the same thing, by presuming them to be above challenge in any specific case). If policy analysts and planners, as satisficing rational actors, are ever to assess potentially illegitimate or coercive influences constraining their satisficing solutions, they must consider the political legitimacy of the relations of power at hand."

[12] Elsewhere I advocate for teaching negotiators to become adept at practicing a "symmetrical anthropology" that subjects their own culture to the same scrutiny they direct to the culture of the others (see Docherty 2004).

[13] For a good example of a group of individuals using the marketplace to deal with the problem of clan violence, see *The Wajir Story* (1998). This thirty-minute video captures the complexity of using a series of negotiations and other activities to deal with community violence.

[14] Carrie Menkel-Meadow and Michael Wheeler (2004: 367) note that "beyond the parties who participate in a negotiation, most negotiations have consequences for others outside the negotiation. Whether thought about as humans or economically based "externalities," there are a whole host of people (and things) who will be affected by what is accomplished (or not) in any given negotiation. How absent parties…are treated or accounted for in negotiations is a seldom discussed but often crucial issue in evaluating the effects and fairness of any negotiation process." These issues are rarely included in "Negotiation 1.0" training. If, however, we recognize negotiations as locations where socially negotiated patterns of power and resource allocation are addressed – either through reinforcement or through challenge – this is an issue that warrants greater attention in "Negotiation 2.0."

[15] "[Max] Weber classifies social action according to four ideal types: (1) goal-rational (*zweckrational*) action; (2) value-rational (*wertrational*) action; (3) affectual action, and (4) traditionally oriented action" (Docherty 2001: 167. See also Varshney 2003).

References

Adair, W. L., C. H. Tinsley, and M. S. Taylor. 2006. Managing the intercultural interface: Third cultures, antecedents and consequences. In *Research on managing groups and teams*, edited by E. Mannix, M. Neale and Y. Chen.

Argyris, C. and D. A. Schön. 1978. *Theory in practice: Increasing professional effectiveness*. San Francisco: Jossey-Bass.

Ashby, W. R. 1952. *Design for a brain*. New York: Wiley.

Avruch, K. 1998. *Culture and conflict resolution*. Washington, DC: United States Institute of Peace Press.

Avruch, K. 2009. What is training all about? *Negotiation Journal* 25(2): 161-169.

Bolewsky, W. 2008. Diplomatic processes and cultural variations: The relevance of culture in diplomacy. *Whitehead Journal of Diplomatic and Interantional Relations* 9(1): 145-160.

Broome, B. J. 1993. Managing differences in conflict resolution: The role of relational empathy. In *Conflict resolution theory and practice: Integration and application*, edited by D. J. D. Sandole and H. van der Merwe. Manchester: Manchester University Press.

Conklin, J. 2005. Wicked problems and social complexity. In *Dialogue mapping: Building shared understanding of wicked problems*, edited by J. Conklin. New York: Wiley.

Docherty, J. S. 2001. *Learning lessons from Waco: When the parties bring their gods to the negotiation table*. Syracuse, NY: Syracuse University Press.

Docherty, J. S. 2004. Culture and negotiation: Symmetrical anthropology for negotiators. *Marquette Law Review* 87(4): 711-722.

Docherty, J. S. 2005. *The little book of strategic negotiation: Negotiating during turbulent times*. Intercourse, PA: Good Books, Inc.

Docherty, J. S. and M. Caton Campbell. 2006. Consequences of principal and agent. In *The negotiator's fieldbook: The desk reference for the experienced negotiator*, edited by A. K. Schneider and C. Honeyman. Washington, DC: American Bar Association.

Forester, J. 1985. *Critical theory, public policy, and planning practice*. Cambridge, MA: MIT Press.

Forester, J. 2009. *Dealing with differences: Dramas of mediating public disputes*. New York: Oxford University Press.

Fox, K. H. 2009. Negotiation as a post-modern process. In *Rethinking negotiation teaching: Innovations for context and culture*, edited by C. Honeyman, J. Coben and G. De Palo. St. Paul, MN: DRI Press.

Freire, P. 2009. *Pedagogy of the oppressed*. 30th Anniversary edn. New York: Continuum.

Friedman, T. L. 2009. *Hot, flat, and crowded: Why we need a green revolution -- and how it can renew America*. 2nd edn. New York: Picador/Farrar, Straus and Giroux.

Gigerenzer, G. and P. M. Todd. 1999. Fast and frugal heuristics: The adaptive toolbox. In *Simple heuristics that make us smart*, edited by G. Gigerenzer and P. M. Todd. New York: Oxford Univesity Press.

Greenhalgh, L. and R. J. Lewicki. 2003. New directions in teaching negotiations: From Walton and McKersie to the new millennium. In *Negotiations and change: From the workplace to society*, edited by T. A. Kochan and D. B. Lipsky. Ithaca: ILR Press.

Karp, I. 1986. Agency and theory: A review of Anthony Giddens. *American Ethnology* 13 (1):131-137.

Kegan, R. and L. L. Lahey. 2009. *Immunity to change: How to overcome it and unlock potential in yourself and your organization*. Boston: Harvard Business School Press.

Lederach, J. P., R. Neufeldt, and H. Culbertson. 2007. Reflective peacebuilding: A planning, monitoring, and learning toolkit. The Joan B. Kroc Institute for International Peace Studies, University of Notre Dame and Catholic Relief Services/USIP. Available at http://kroc.nd. edu/sites/default/files/reflective_peacebuilding.pdf (last accessed July 30, 2010).

Menkel-Meadow, C. and M. Wheeler (eds.) 2004. *What's fair: Ethics for negotiators*. San Francisco: Jossey-Bass.

Pearce, W. B. and S. W. Littlejohn. 1997. *Moral conflict: When social worlds collide*. Thousand Oaks: Sage.

Pruitt, D. G. 1995. Networks and collective scripts: Paying attention to structure in bargaining theory. In *Negotiation as a social process*, edited by R. M. Kramer and D. M. Messick. Thousand Oaks, CA: Sage.

Ritchey, T. 2005-2008. *Wicked problems: Structuring social messes with morphological analysis*. Swedish Morphological Society. Available at www. swedmorph.org (last accessed June 28, 2010).

Rittell, H. W. J., and M. M. Webber. 1973. Dilemmas in a general theory of planning. *Policy Sciences* 4: 155-169.

Stolte, J. F., G. A. Fine, and K. S. Cook. 2001. Sociological miniaturism: Seeing the big through the small in social psychology. *Annual Review of Sociology* 27: 387-413.

Thompson, L., E. Peterson, and L. Kray. 1996. Social context in negotiation: An information-processing perspective. In *Negotiation as a social process*, edited by R. M. Kramer and D. M. Messick. Thousand Oaks, CA: Sage.

Varshney, A. 2003. Nationalism, ethnic conflict, and rationality. *Perspectives on Politics* 1(1):85-99.

Wajir Story, The. 1998. Streaming video, available from Responding to Conflict at http://www.respond.org/ (last accessed June 25, 2010).

Weiss, S. E. 2006. International business negotiation in a globalizing world: Reflections on the contributions and future of a (sub) field. *International Negotiation* 11(2): 287-316.

∝ 27 ∞

Design: The U.S. Army's Approach to Negotiating Wicked Problems[1]

Leonard Lira[*]

Editors' Note: Over twenty years of dealing with problems in post-conflict settings since the end of the Cold War, the U.S. Army has increasingly recognized that the character of the conflicts it is involved in now routinely includes pervasive, complex, and ill-structured problems – in other words, "wicked problems" – which the Army must deal with using non-violent means. The specific concept of "Design" is the foremost step yet taken by a U.S. military service toward setting forth ways of addressing wicked problems as a frequent, core need in the field. This radical departure in military doctrine is already finding its way into field manuals and training courses.

Introduction

In Rome at the 2008 initial conference of the Rethinking Negotiation Teaching project, the coordinators argued for an evolution of negotiation pedagogy (Honeyman, Coben, and De Palo 2009). The conference's theme implied that "Negotiation 1.0" instruction was mostly applicable to contexts that were two-sided, person-to-person, linear in structure, and focused on set conditions that are in dispute and well-definable. To me, attending this conference while on R&R during my second tour in Iraq, this also implied that standard approaches to negotiation pedagogy did not apply to the prevalence of negotiation practices employed by conflict professionals who deal with social problems in conflict settings. In my view, such settings include war or peacekeeping situations where violent conflict is prevalent, but also other non-violent social conflict contexts where

[*] **Leonard Lira** is a Lieutenant Colonel in the U.S. Army and an assistant professor in the Department of Joint, Interagency and Multinational Operations of the Command and General Staff College at Fort Leavenworth, Kansas. His email address is leonard.lira@us.army.mil.

conflict professionals employ negotiation skills as a main facet of their operations to resolve problems which are not as easily definable or structured as one might infer from negotiation pedagogy.[2]

I have observed, if only confirmed anecdotally in conversation with skilled negotiators well practiced in the delivery of negotiation education, that the majority of current negotiation pedagogy seems quite narrowly focused on preparing students for "tame," well-structured problems, as compared to the sorts of "wicked" problems that are prevalent in major conflict. For example, Michael Wheeler and Gillian Morris (2002) recognized the lack of accounting for or dealing with unknown settings in the negotiation literature. They emphatically state that

> Most popular negotiation books give little attention to strategy in fluid, uncertain situations. Instead, they typically posit a static world with clearly defined parties whose interests and non-agreement options are implicitly unchanging. Little is said about formulating and implementing strategy in ever-changing environments (Wheeler and Morris 2002: 1).

If the extant literature is void of this discussion, it follows that the pedagogy would be also.

One gap in current negotiation pedagogy appears to be its inability to prepare practitioners for negotiation scenarios in settings of complexity and uncertainty, or in the "formulation and implementation of strategy," which is a planning function. Although there is a rich history of negotiation practice related to managing multi-party public conflicts (see, e.g., Forester 1980; Bingham 1986; Forester 1985; Forester 1999; Susskind, McKearnan, and Thomas-Larmer 1999; and Carpenter and Kennedy 2001), the lessons learned in these venues have not made it into "Negotiation 1.0" pedagogy in other settings, in particular with regard to dealing with "wicked problems."

In company with my colleagues in this section of this volume I use the term "wicked problems" from the planning literature to describe what is missing in the current pedagogy (Rittel and Webber 1973). A detailed description of wicked problems as compared with tame problems is included in Chapters 24 and 25. The definitions themselves are reproduced for convenience of the reader here in endnote three.[3]) Here I will assert that we need to develop education and training skills for the strategic level planning process so that people dealing with wicked problems can better know when, where, and how to use negotiation to transform larger conflicts.

This chapter will illustrate how wicked problems are prevalent in the conflict settings the U.S. military deals with. Using a story from my own experiences in Iraq, I will illustrate what those challenges look like "on the ground," and examine how the U.S. Army has reformed its planning processes by developing and including in revised military doctrine a comprehensive cognitive methodology – a set of "thinking tools" – to address complex and dynamic operational environments, in order to allow Army personnel to better address the missions they are being asked to accomplish.[4] Under the rubric of "Design," this begins to account for the requirement to deal with problems of uncertainty in complex operations. Note, however, that the term Design here is used as a military term of art. Its civilian connotations can be somewhat misleading in the present context. The chapter finishes with some thoughts and questions about what the need for strategic level thinking and planning implies for "Negotiation 2.0" pedagogy.

The U.S. Army in the Post-Cold War Reality

With the end of the Soviet-U.S. standoff at the end of the Cold War, the primary risk of armed conflict or war between contending superpowers became less likely. In fact, the largest source of violent conflict now comes from *intranational* (within a single country) conflicts that tend to *internationalize* "to the degree that some conflictants, particularly opposition movements, inhabit neighboring countries; weapons and money for the conflict flow in from the surrounding region and from more distant locations; and displaced refugee populations cross immediate and distant borders" (Lederach 1997: 11).[5]

The states where these so-called new conflicts occur are often fragile or weak. Even if their governments had the will to handle such conflicts, they usually have neither the reach nor the resources to respond effectively to conflicts that are both intranational and internationalized regionally or – in the case of transnational terrorism – globally. Furthermore, many of the governments are themselves part of the problem. This is particularly true in conflicts where minority groups, or numerically superior groups that have nevertheless been pressed into positions of submission (e.g., South Africa), believe the state apparatus has been captured and used by a dominant group to cement its own position of privilege.

Countries from outside a region that are directly affected by violent conflict find it difficult to promote sustainable peace in wartorn areas. With the invasions of Afghanistan and Iraq as notable exceptions, governments are usually loath to use force in the sovereign territory of other states in order to handle internal violent conflicts. Consequently, debates have gone on for over two decades regarding the merits and risks of either U.S. unilateral actions and/or participation in multi-national activities that represent the array of U.S. government policy options implemented for responding to these conflicts.

However, while the debates have raged, the U.S. government has nonetheless initiated several policy initiatives that led to the use of U.S. Army resources for the purpose of promoting stability and peace in war-torn countries. The most recent challenges have, of course, been Afghanistan and Iraq, where U.S. military forces in co-operation with international coalitions have been juggling combat operations to root out terrorist organizations *and* the stabilization and reconstruction of societies damaged by years of misrule and violence. Doctrine follows experience and the military follows civilian policy. So it is no surprise that the U.S. military services have been evolving their doctrine, training, and resource allocation.[6]

Based on over twenty years of operations in post-conflict settings since the end of the Cold War, the U.S. Army has come to recognize the pervasiveness of mission assignments that involve complex and ill-structured problems that have to be dealt with using non-violent measures. The Army more recently has articulated this understanding of conflict complexity in one of its capstone doctrinal publications. The U.S. Army Field Manual *The Operations Process* states that in the era of globalization, conflict is invariably complex because it is fundamentally human in character, occurring more and more between and among diverse actors, both state and non-state, and in non-Western settings (FM 5-0 2008: 3-5). Furthermore, the Army has articulated its understanding of the paradox of accomplishing its missions without relying on its primary functional capability, the use of violent force, in its doctrinal manual on counterinsurgency operations. FM 3-24 specifically states:

> Sometimes, the more force is used, the less effective it is. Any use of force produces many effects, not all of which can be foreseen. The more force applied, the greater the chance of collateral damage and mistakes. Using substantial force also increases the opportunity for insurgent propaganda to portray lethal military activities as brutal. In contrast, using force precisely and discriminately strengthens the rule of law that needs to be established (FM 3-24: 1-27).

Given the size and complexity of these particular conflict settings, the U.S. Army had to develop strategies that relied on resourcing and sequencing non-violent activities, known in military jargon as non-lethal operations. Examples of such non-violent activities include peace operations conducted in Kosovo and Bosnia, such as the Croatian example provided by Calvin Chrustie (*Negotiating Wicked Problems*, Chapter 25), but also counter-insurgency operations conducted in Iraq and Afghanistan.[7]

Negotiating with local leaders to coordinate and implement nonlethal activities such as rebuilding the local infrastructure and establishing inclusive governance structures has become a regular part of operations for many Army units (Schultheis 2005). As various militia or insurgency units decide to use non-lethal means to achieve their political goals, Army personnel can find themselves in negotiation with individuals they were fighting against in the recent past. They might even be negotiating during the day with individuals they suspect are engaged in fighting at night. For example, in Iraq the move to non-lethal strategies meant employing negotiation in support of reconciliation efforts as an operational approach to solving *military* problems and to achieving security.

To begin formal "negotiations" in these settings seems almost impossible. Often, practitioners cannot completely define a negotiable problem, let alone one that they are certain will leverage the larger changes they are ultimately trying to achieve. They also find it difficult to build and sustain agreement about which parties should be involved, and the parties are prone to reconsidering the benefits of negotiating rather than using other options to achieve their goals. In all of these settings, negotiations have rarely (if ever) occurred in a person-to-person or linear fashion. In Iraq, they occurred in multiactor settings among local nationals, host governments, international government organizations, nongovernmental organizations, multinational armed forces, and multinational intergovernmental agencies. Furthermore, others not involved in the negotiation could and did take actions that distorted any initial problem set that the local negotiators identified. For example, if the national government, insurgency leaders, or coalition forces changed their strategies or allocation of resources, the local negotiators recalculated their best and worst alternatives to a negotiated agreement. This continuous evolution usually exceeded the time available for analyzing the situation prior to action.

The stories of negotiating in the context of wicked problems (see *Negotiating Wicked Problems*, Chapter 25) illustrate the difficulty of using negotiation as a tool for responding to these complex challenges. One problem is the need to implement planning on multiple operational programs, in which negotiations occur in multiple settings, with multiple actors, all of which have different goals but all of which require the practitioners to manage the actions needed to achieve those goals. Many times negotiations to address parts of a wicked problem take place in situations where no one is managing the overall "game plan" or coordinating the negotiations with other activities, including negotiations that are happening on other levels.[8]

It is interesting that the one story from Chapter 25 that seems to have been resolved successfully ("High Drama in a High City") involved a strong leader able to marshal multiple resources in an environment that was not beset by serious violence or insurmountable corruption. In the absence of a central organizing authority, the ground level personnel can only coordinate their actions in reference to a shared strategy and a shared assessment of the opportunities for action. This is why the military and civilian leaders now working on developing a "whole of government" response for unstable conflict situations are expending considerable time developing and testing conflict assessment tools such as the Interagency Conflict Assessment Framework (ICAF).[9] This type of organizational activity requires an interdisciplinary understanding of how to develop negotiation strategies at the organizational level, and how to oversee programs that require teams of practitioners to implement the negotiation strategies required for conflict management programs to succeed. This type of learning is not typically associated with "Negotiation 1.0" instruction, to put it gently.

But a number of authors and practitioners, especially those associated with public policy and environmental matters, *have* addressed these issues (see, e.g., Forester 1980; Bingham 1986; Carpenter and Kennedy 1991; Forester 1999; Susskind, McKearnan, and Thomas-Larmer 1999; and Carpenter and Kennedy 2001).

Negotiating Support for National Reconciliation

An example of a "wicked problem" faced by the U.S. Army was its attempt to facilitate reconciliation between members of the Tamimi tribe and Dulaimi/Jibouri tribes in the Taji Qada during the final days of the "Surge" operations during the Army's campaign in Iraq. In the summer of 2007 during the Iraq war, the Sunni Awakening had overturned Al Qaeda control, the Shia factions called for a cease fire, and former insurgents appeared willing to work with U.S. and Iraqi governments. At this ebb of the sectarian violence that swept Iraq, reconciliation was driving every security action by the coalition forces. When the Army unit I was assigned to on my second tour, 2-14 Cavalry, arrived and assumed responsibility for securing Taji, the sectarian fighting largely fell off across Baghdad. Consolidating gains made from the respite in violence became the order of business for 2-14 Cavalry, and facilitating the reconciliation process among the various local tribal members residing in the Taji area was top priority. Negotiation was one of our tools, but the reconciliation did not fall into place easily.

Taji is a rural region approximately twelve miles north of the city of Baghdad. It contains a predominantly Shia population, who are made up from the Al Tamimi tribe, but it is also intermixed with Sunnis, such as the Al Dulaimi in the western portion, and the Al Jabouri in the eastern portion. Several social issues laced with human dynamics caused fissures in the fragile peace that coalition forces won in this area, and threatened to reverse the move to reconciliation.

One such example was the creation of local tribal reconciliation councils to negotiate the implementation of the reconciliation process, which created conflict between members of the Al Tamimi Tribe and the Al Jabouri and Al Dulaimi tribes that resided in the Taji area. The Iraqi government had created the National Reconciliation Committee in the Iraqi National Council of Representatives, the Iraqi national legislative body; the National Reconciliation Committee in turn had devised explicit rules on how local committees were to be formed. This could be seen as evidence of a national movement toward reconciliation; but progress was not easy in Taji.[10] Even though one committee was authorized for Taji, each sectarian faction wanted to create their own committee.

My unit, 2-14 Cavalry, took on the task of negotiating the implementation of the national reconciliation process – or more accurately, the role of facilitating the negotiation among the parties to implement the process. In hindsight, it is clear that we were trying to negotiate a particular problem (establishing the reconciliation council) in order to negotiate changes in the social order (rebuilding trust among the tribes and creating mechanisms or organizations that could manage future conflicts). (See Docherty, *"Adaptive" Negotiation*, Chapter 26.) But at the time, we were working with "Negotiation 1.0" tools, and it appeared to us that the tribes would never reconcile no matter how many times U.S. forces brought them all to the table. At forums we sponsored, all of the tribes made public declarations of reconciliation, but away from the forum table they would return to their entrenched positions and try to exclude each other from the local committee. It turned out that this "seemingly irrational" behavior occurred for a number of complex reasons, and it was not until roughly nine months into the mission that 2-14 Cavalry started to uncover them.

We learned that a series of sectarian killings that had occurred two years earlier, and the mutual fear amongst the tribes of the cultural need for blood retribution was preventing the discussion of reconciliation. The killings took place in a village of Taji called Bassam. Bassam is located between Abu Ghraib and Taji, but lies predominantly in the western portion of Taji. This village was on a sharp dividing line between the rival Sunni and Shiite tribes, following the overthrow of the Saddam regime. Bassam was being torn apart by sectarian violence in 2006 and 2007. Many of the villagers of Bassam were Sunni who supported insurgents and Al-Qaeda in fighting Shiites. Control over Bassam was contested by Al-Qaeda on the one side and the Mahdi Army militia of Shiite cleric Moqtada al-Sadr on the other.

One particular issue that haunted the reconciliation process in this area occurred in July of 2006. Sunni insurgents besieged a small Shiite settlement in the area, preventing the 190 or so inhabitants from reaching food supplies or water. After three days, on July 19, the Shiite families surrendered and negotiated a settlement for safe passage, provided they left the area, never to return. The women, children and some men boarded a convoy of minibuses and trucks and began to leave. Not far along into their route, the convoy was stopped by gunmen. Five men were ordered out of the vehicles. The women and children were forced to continue in the convoy and the men were held. As the convoy headed off, shots were heard, and the men were never seen again.

The facts of the incident were not readily known by the U.S. military unit charged with managing the tenuous security of Taji shortly after the event. And in fact, this incident, and several others in the area, kept clouding the issues of stability and reconciliation for the entire time that unit was in Taji, up to when it passed control over to 2-14 Cavalry. So even though the fighting had largely stopped, sectarian suspicions still ran deep, and violence was always liable to surface. For example, one local Sunni leader, Sheikh Zeydan, who was trying to lead attempts at reconciliation with the village's Shiite neighbors, was assassinated for his attempts, presumably by Sunni relatives.

It was in this context that we were trying to facilitate the establishment of a joint reconciliation council. This is a clear case of socially negotiated rules of behavior intruding upon and complicating an attempt to negotiate a particular problem. The tribes had a shared fear that if the truth about this and other killings emerged in the process of reconciliation, the cultural norms about blood retribution would lead to more bloodshed. The outcome was that the Shia dominated the reconciliation council meetings, and would rarely let the Sunni tribal members into the meetings or let them voice their opinions at the meetings.

Adding to this was the fact that the government of Iraq, which was predominately Shia, appeared to not be servicing the Sunni areas in Taji. Sectarian bloodletting, in 2005 and 2006, had sharply redrawn local village boundaries around Taji: Sunnis in one area; Shia in another. And the Sunnis of Taji did not get the representation they thought they deserved from the government. For example, in the Sunni areas, schools lacked the simplest things, such as desks and doors; roads went unpaved, and Sunni farmers did not get enough irrigation water, fertilizer, or seeds.

In addition, Government of Iraq (GOI) official recognition of local tribal reconciliation councils, which were extensions of the national reconciliation council, gave legitimacy to the Taji Tribal reconciliation council's actions and decisions. But the reconciliation council had a mixed agenda. They were not just focused on reconciling the past, they were also authorized to make decisions about significant economic matters, including awarding contracts for recovery work. Due to the overwhelming need to reconstruct the cities, roads, and institutions of service, many contracts were issued by the U.S. military and the GOI. Sometimes the competitions over the contracts turned deadly, adding to the violence already caused by sectarian conflict, as disagreements sometimes led to Sunni on Sunni or Shia on Shia killings.

To handle all of these challenges, the leaders of 2-14 Cavalry received negotiation instruction in their one-year "train-up" for this deployment. This training was "Negotiation 1.0" and it included lessons for the staff on how to assess, and determine for their commander, zones of agreement, best alternatives to a negotiated agreement, and other well-known principles of negotiation. The commander and other leaders at all levels then were afforded opportunities to implement the training in role-playing exercises. Although the negotiation training was extensive, none of it adequately prepared the unit for what it encountered in Iraq. This was because most of the training, conducted by negotiation contractors at the Army's National Training Center, centered on singular problems, with singular root causes, to solve which the leaders would negotiate personally with an actor playing an Iraqi. In other words, these exercises were constructed in a linear, lock-step, checklist fashion: we were being taught negotiation as a process for dealing with "technical problems" when we were going to be confronting "adaptive problems" (Kegan and Lahey 2009).

In fact, what the leaders of 2-14 Cavalry encountered in Iraq was very much like Rory Stewart's description of his own Iraq negotiations there. As Stewart explained in his book *Prince of the Marshes*, "It is one thing to negotiate with a sheik in your office, quite another to predict what he might do, still less judge how 25 million others will collectively feel, plan, and act or how you ought to respond" (Stewart 2007: 397). This type of ill-structured problem and the complexity it created caused the commander and staff of 2-14 Cavalry many challenges in deciding what course of action would best facilitate reconciliation.

As a result, the members of 2-14 Cavalry were unprepared for facilitating multiple issues, with multiple actors, and had no formal training to develop a clear understanding of the true underlying reasons for the conflict, nor for implementing a process for deciding on courses of action to deal with the multiple variables involved in those issues. Eventually, the leaders of this unit came to understand that their goal in reconciliation was not to heal old wounds, but to facilitate the process in which all of the actors could continue to form their own consensus as to how to reconcile. The goals of the unit became, in effect, to keep the parties coming to the table, to keep them talking, and to learn how to deal with each issue as it cropped up.[11]

As the Operations Officer, and then the Executive Officer of 2-14 Cavalry, I had several more experiences similar to those described above and to those Stewart describes in his book. In addition to the tribes, we dealt with various military and police organizations, the Iraqi government, and each echelon in the ministries of that government. We also dealt with several insurgent groups, which all had varying associations with the other groups just listed. The preeminent lesson we took away from these engagements was that the variables that affected the environment we were operating in were almost infinite. We found it very difficult to apply the required conceptualization and implementation of non-lethal operations, even though we felt very well trained in negotiation and other non-combat functions. Based on this conclusion, we found ourselves looking for a process to help us deal with the uncertainty, while we developed courses of action to deal with the security problems we encountered.

With the Army's greater involvement in peace and post-conflict operations, this has been a vexing problem for military professionals elsewhere too, because they are used to managing such environments with the use or threat of the use of violent force. As evident in the current historical literature of both recent campaigns in Iraq and Afghanistan, this approach did not always lead to accomplishing the objectives that the military set out with at the beginning. This was not due to the military not understanding how to solve problems. In fact, the military has been using an operational planning process for years to develop courses of action to solve all sorts of problems, very successfully. However, due to the repeated involvement of U.S. military forces in conflict settings that present complex problems requiring other than violent military means for solutions, military staffs have adapted their decision-making processes for problem-framing and re-framing in adaptive and complex conflict settings. The way in which the military has attempted to deal with such situations is through *reforming the military problem solving methodology* to incorporate a critical and creative thinking skill. This is described by the Army as Design, "a methodology for applying critical and creative thinking to understand, visualize, describe, and assess complex, ill-structured problems and to develop approaches to solve them" (FM 5-0: 3-1). Brigadier General Edward C. Cardon, the Deputy Commandant of the U.S Army Command and General Staff College (CGSC), emphatically states that this reformation is "arguably the most significant change to our planning methodology in more than a generation" (Cardon 2010).

As Lieutenant General William Caldwell, the former Commandant of CGSC, describes in his Foreword remarks in the U.S. Army CGSC's publication *Design: Tools of the Trade*, by Jack Kem, "Design is not a process, but a set of 'thinking tools' that complement and reinforce our operations process with a rational, logical approach to an increasingly complex and dynamic operational environment" (Kem 2009: iii). Kem also indicates in the first chapter that the new way of thinking in Army plans and operations reflects the reasons that the Army updated its capstone field manual, *Operations* (FM 3-0):

The manual reflected six years of wartime experience, written in response to a changing environment characterized by:
- An era of persistent conflict
- Operations among the people
- A pervasive information environment
- Unpredictable, asymmetric threats
- Conflict resolution that requires a "whole of government" approach

(Kem 2009: 3).

From the Army's emerging doctrine, there are essentially five mental activities expressed from employing this critical and creative thinking skill called Design.[12] The first activity is to *understand the current context*, which entails understanding the environment, why it exists as it does, how it got to the state that it is in, and what that means for all the actors involved. The second activity is to *visualize a future context*, or desired state, based on the perspectives of all stakeholders involved in the environment. The third activity is to *develop a problem frame* that articulates the difference between the current environment and the potential future environment. It should clearly articulate the obstacles impeding the movement of the environment from the current setting to the envisioned one. The fourth activity is the development of a *"theory of action"* that will help change the environment to the desired state, one in which the correct problem is solved.[13]

The fifth activity is to develop a *continuous assessment system*, to gauge a) if the environment frame and problem frame are the correct frames, and b) that the approach is shifting the environment from one to the other. The goal is not to predict where reframing will need to occur, but merely to anticipate that it will, by humbly assuming that the hypotheses that form the three design frames (the environmental frame, the problem frame, and the solution frame) are faulty in some manner. This assessment system will eventually develop into identifiable measures of performance (MOPs) that indicate if the organization is implementing the approach correctly, and measurements of effectiveness (MOEs) that indicate that the approach is in fact shifting the current environment to the desired environment. Based on the prevalence of negative indicators in the MOPs or MOEs, military organizations may adjust how they are implementing the solution, or they may have to reframe either the environmental or the problem frame and then adjust the theory of action, or the approach, to solving the problem. This indicates not only that the development of the measures of performance and effectiveness should be developed holistically, with all stakeholders' perspectives taken into account, but that they need to be developed early in the preparation phase.

A final and very important note is needed about the "how" of Design, according to the way the Army has indoctrinated it and is teaching it at the CGSC. While the five mental activities described above are presented in an apparent lock-step and iterative manner, they are in fact conducted simultaneously in a holistic fashion, even though the Commander's and his staff's efforts may be emphasizing one activity more than another. And while there will be a tendency to want to rationalize them as just another planning or decision making process, they are in fact, more: they constitute a different form of sense-making, required for the problem solving of complex problems. A simple and successful example of a process that uses Design thinking as described above is Peter Checkland's and John Poulter's *Soft System Methodology* (Checkland and Poulter 2006).

These five Design mental activities represent a seismic change for how the U.S. Army conducts its planning. As an organization, the Army has long developed in its leaders the cognitive skills required for a strategic and logical rationale for its problem-solving methodologies.[14] The process for analysis was linear in its logic, lock-stepped, and driven by a single individual, the commander. However, these Design activities require a change in the cognitive processes needed, to see issues from the perspectives of others, even if those others are your real or potential enemies. Additionally, the cognitive skills used in Design are not just requisite individual skills, but require the collective skills of all members of a planning organization to identify and frame issues in a creative and holistic fashion based on a communicative rationale. This requires not only employing a creative cognitive skill, but also employing collaborative analytic activities that develop approaches to the identified problems in a manner that accounts for all stakeholders' perspectives.

This fundamental collaborative characteristic of Design is causing the Army to evolve even further in order to incorporate this concept fully. Internally, this means that commanders, while retaining overall authority and responsibility, have to share with their staffs the authority for sense-making of the environment. Previously, commanders would set the boundaries of analysis and the staff would work within those boundaries to solve the problem as the commander saw it. However, as FM 5-0 states, "today's operational environment presents situations so complex that understanding them – let alone attempting to change them – is beyond the ability of a single individual" (FM 5-0: 3-4). Now both commander and staff must jointly set the boundaries of the perceived problem. Externally, this means that Army units not only have to take into account other worldviews, like those of other U.S. Government agencies, international organizations, or the local population, but they may even have to collaborate with them to gain a full appreciation of the environment, its problems and how to move forward. This incorporation and working with others has even, sometimes, included the enemy. In Iraq, for example, strategists recognized that the best way to get rid of the extremists who were attacking U.S. soldiers was to "work with them" (Ricks 2009: 157).

So how does this apply to what conflict management professionals may normally associate with negotiation theory? I would argue that the preparations that all conflict management practitioners go through to manage conflict in complex adaptive settings are similar to those that the military professionals have to go through, when their practitioners determine that the use of violent military force is not feasible, acceptable, or appropriate to accomplish their goals. Therefore, Design as applied in military problem-identification and solving processes during the preparation for military operations in complex adaptive settings is applicable to the evolving "Negotiation 2.0" theory for general conflict management professionals, specifically in the negotiation preparation period that all conflict management professionals must undertake in the complex adaptive settings in which they too operate.

Conclusion

What this chapter has attempted to demonstrate through the presentation of a military example of a wicked problem is the need to develop cognitive skills that allow for creative and critical judgment, in deciding a course of action to pursue when solving such complex problems in conflict. This example also demonstrates the need to create a different training or education approach, one that instills in the professional conflict practitioner the ability to judge how, when, and in what degree to employ negotiation skills to solve complex problems, when the normal principles of negotiation are not easily applied in the manner prescribed in current negotiation pedagogy.

The application of Design doctrine to the Army's current professional education courses on problem solving is an arduous process, one not easily conveyed through the military's classical regimented drill and training methodologies. I anticipate that the task of conveying this information to other students of negotiation would be just as arduous, as it requires a level of appreciation of complexity that a classical "Negotiation 1.0" training regimen cannot convey. This issue raises the question of what is the best way of teaching this type of thinking for students of negotiation – in the military or in very different organizations – who will need to employ negotiation skills in complex adaptive settings. The next volume in the *Rethinking Negotiation Teaching* series will begin, but certainly not conclude, a discussion of this critical question.

Notes

[1] The views expressed are those of the author and not necessarily of the Department of the Army, the U.S. Command and General Staff College, or any other agency of the U.S. Government. I would also like to express immense gratitude to Christopher Honeyman, Jayne Docherty, James Coben, and Howard Gadlin, all of whom helped nurture this chapter into its present form through patient editing, without which many of my ideas would not be as well articulated. However much help they were, I humbly will admit that any and all mistakes are completely mine.

[2] By conflict professionals I mean those professionals in the government, private, and nonprofit sectors who deal with conflict, i.e., the military, lawyers, diplomats, NGO representatives, labor mediators, lobbyists, etc.

[3] For purposes of this chapter, the term "wicked" describes problems that exhibit some combination of the following features:

- The problem is ill-defined and resists clear definition as a technical issue, because wicked problems are also social, political, and moral in nature. Each proposed definition of the problem implies a particular kind of solution which is loaded with contested values. Consequently, merely defining the problem can incite passionate conflict.

- Solutions to a wicked problem cannot be labeled good or bad; they can only be considered better or worse, good enough or not good enough. Whether a solution is good enough depends on the values and judgment of each of the parties, who will inevitably assess the problem and its potential solutions from their respective positions within the social context of the problem.
- Every wicked problem is unique and novel, because even if the technical elements appear similar from one situation to another, the social, political, and moral features are context-specific.
- A wicked problem contains an interconnected web of sub-problems; every proposed solution to part or the whole of the wicked problem will affect other problems in the web.

See generally Rittell and Webber (1973), Ritchey (2005-2008) and Conklin 2005). This stands in sharp contrast to the nature of problems that the planning profession has labeled "tame." As summarized by Ritchey (2005-2008: 1), a tame problem:

- Has a relatively well-defined and stable problem statement.
- Has a definite stopping point, i.e., we know when a solution is reached.
- Has a solution which can be objectively evaluated as being right or wrong.
- Belongs to a class of similar problems which can be solved in a similar manner.
- Has solutions that can be tried and abandoned.

[4] Even the term "doctrine" differs in military and civilian settings. Military doctrine is a guide to action, not a set of rigid rules. It provides a common frame of reference across the military in an effort to standardize operations and facilitate readiness, by establishing common ways of accomplishing military tasks. Doctrine must change in the face of new ground realities, which is why military doctrine has undergone such rapid and significant revisions in the past ten years.

[5] Many of the so-called "new" conflicts are not new at all. They were simply being repressed and distorted by the superpower rivalry of the Cold War. Once that pressure was removed, the conflicts became more violent and more prone to expansion.

[6] There has been a parallel development of civilian activities to help societies torn by violent conflict. Jayne Seminare Docherty is writing a paper about civilian peacebuilding as an emergent profession responding to wicked problems. She is finding similar issues about the role of negotiation in these contexts.

[7] For examples of the complexities in Iraq, see Ricks (2009) and Robinson (2008).

[8] For a case study of lessons learned from Kosovo, see Covey, Dziedzic, and Hawley (2005). One take-away lesson is the importance of a "custodian" of the peace process (see Chapter 4 of Covey, Dziedzic, and Hawley 2005). The

custodian emerged late in the Kosovo process out of the chaos recounted by Calvin Chrustie (*Negotiating Wicked Problems*, Chapter 25 in this volume). It is not at all clear from subsequent experience that a clear custodian is readily established in situations such as Iraq, where coalition forces and local political leaders vie for credibility and legitimacy.

[9] The *Interagency Conflict Assessment Framework* (2010), developed by an interagency working group and now being used and refined by the Office of the Coordinator for Reconstruction and Stabilization, is one of several initiatives to promote "unity of effort" based on a shared understanding of the situation that is derived from an assessment of threats and opportunities.

[10] There are several problems with this "top down" initiative. First, reconciliation is a long-term process that requires opportunities for truth-telling and, if possible, restorative justice activities along with opportunities to rebuild trust. Second, the legitimacy of the Iraqi government was not universally acknowledged, so the mandate itself was suspect. And last but not least for 2-14 Cavalry, it was not clear whether the Iraqi national government seriously wanted reconciliation or whether they were acting at the behest of coalition forces and outside advisors. Insofar as the local people suspected that national reconciliation was either a ploy by some at the national level to enhance their own power or an effort by international actors to build an Iraq to their own liking, Cavalry 2-14 was working against the handicap of suspicion about their motives and integrity.

[11] As Jayne Docherty argues in a work-in-progress (tentatively titled *Wicked Problems in Peacebuilding*) being developed for the next book in this teaching series (copy on file with author):

"Reconciliation is *not* accomplished through the kinds of negotiations taught in "Negotiation 1.0" training programs. Reconciliation is a long-term process that requires opportunities for truth-telling and, if possible, restorative justice activities along with opportunities to rebuild trust. In this case, if the Army personnel had been trained to use collaborative learning instead of or in addition to standard negotiation techniques, they would probably have uncovered the truth about the killings more quickly, and then could have asked the parties to help them identify culturally appropriate ways to negotiate a durable reconciliation process.... In other words, they stumbled their way into using collaborative learning techniques. Thus did 2-14 Cavalry find its own way into peacebuilding practice. More appropriate and more sophisticated training, however, would probably have speeded up that process...."

[12] The FM 5-0 currently only articulates four activities, or components: framing the environment; framing the problem; developing the operational approach; and reframing. However, once these components are unpacked, the reader can extrapolate the five activities presented in this paper.

[13] Currently, Army practitioners are using the term "operational approach" as opposed to "theory of action."

[14] For a detailed explication of the four rationality paradigms underlying this approach (strategic, communicative, coordinating, and frame-setting), see Alexander 2000. The type of rationality paradigm required by the cognitive process discussed in this section is communicative, that is, a holistic

approach. This is in stark contrast to "Negotiation 1.0" pedagogy, which places a primary emphasis on the strategic.

References:

Alexander, E. R. 2000. Rationality revisited: Planning paradigms in a post-post modernist perspective. *Journal of Planning Education and Research* 19: 242-256.

Bingham, G. 1986. *Resolving environmental disputes: A decade of experience.* Washington, DC: Conservation Foundation

Cardon, E. C. and S. Leonard. 2010. Unleashing design: Planning and the art of battle command. *Military Review* XC (2): 2-11.

Carpenter, S. L. and W. J. D. Kennedy. 1991. *Managing public disputes: A practical guide to handling conflict and reaching agreement.* San Francisco: Jossey-Bass.

Carpenter, S. L. and W. J. D. Kennedy. 2001. *Managing public disputes: A practical guide for government, business and citizen's groups.* San Francisco: Jossey-Bass.

Checkland, P. and J. Poulter. 2006. *Learning for action: A short definitive account of soft systems methodology, and its use for practitioners, teachers and students.* West Sussex, England: Wiley and Sons.

Conklin, J. 2005. Wicked problems and social complexity. In *Dialogue mapping: Building shared understanding of wicked problems*, edited by J. Conklin. New York: Wiley.

Covey, J., M. J. Dziedzic, and L. R. Hawley. 2005. *The quest for a viable peace: International intervention and strategies for conflict transformation.* Washington, DC: United States Institute for Peace.

Docherty, J. 2006. The unstated models in our minds. In *The negotiator's fieldbook: The desk reference for the experienced negotiator*, edited by A. K. Schneider and C. Honeyman. Washington, DC: American Bar Association.

Forester, J. 1980. Critical theory and planning practice. *Journal of the American Planning Association* 46: 275-286.

Forester, J. 1985. *Critical theory, public policy, and planning practice.* Cambridge, MA: MIT Press.

Forester, J. 1999. *The deliberative practitioner: Encouraging participatory planning processes.* Cambridge, MA: MIT Press.

Honeyman, C., J. Coben and G. De Palo. 2009. Introduction: The second generation of negotiation teaching. In *Rethinking negotiation teaching: Innovations for context and culture*, edited by C. Honeyman, J. Coben and G. De Palo. St. Paul, MN: DRI Press.

Kegan, R. and L. L. Lahey. 2009. *Immunity to change: How to overcome it and unlock potential in yourself and your organization.* Boston: Harvard Business School Press.

Kem, J. 2009. *Design: Tools of the trade.* Fort Leavenworth, KS: US Army Command and Staff College. Available at usacac.army.mil/cac2 /repository/Materials/Design.pdf (last accessed June 25, 2010).

Lederach, J. P. 1997. *Building peace: Sustainable reconciliation in divided societies*. Washington, DC: United States Institute of Peace.

Ricks, T. 2009. *The gamble: General Petraeus and the American military adventure in Iraq, 2006 -2008*. New York, NY: Penguin Press.

Ritchey, T. 2005-2008. *Wicked problems: Structuring social messes with morphological analysis*. Swedish Morphological Society. Available at www. swedmorph.org (last accessed June 28, 2010).

Rittel, H. W. J. and M. M. Webber. 1973. Dilemmas in general planning theory. *Policy Sciences* 4: 159-163.

Robinson, L. 2008. *Tell me how this ends: General Petraeus and the search for a way out of Iraq*. New York, NY: Public Affairs.

Schultheis, R. 2005. *Waging peace: A special operations team's battle to rebuild Iraq*. New York: Gotham Books.

Stewart, R. 2007. *The prince of the marshes: And other occupational hazards of a year in Iraq*. New York: Harvest.

Susskind, L., S. McKearnan, and J. Thomas-Larmer (eds). 1999. *The consensus building handbook*. Thousand Oaks, CA: Sage

U.S. Army Field Manual (FM) 3-24. 2007. *Counter-insurgency operations*. Washington DC: U.S. Government Printing Office.

U.S. Army Field Manual (FM) 3-0. 2009. *Operations*. Washington DC: U.S. Government Printing Office.

U.S. Army Field Manual (FM) 5.0. 2010. *The operational process*. Washington DC: U.S. Government Printing Office. Available at http://www.fas.org/ irp/doddir/army/fm5-0.pdf (last accessed July 30, 2010).

Waldrop, M. M. 1992. *Complexity*. New York: Simon and Schuster.

Wheeler, M. and G. Morris. 2002. A note on maneuvering in war and negotiation. *Harvard Business School Note* 9-902-157.

༼ Epilogue ༽

Two to Tango?

Ranse Howell & Lynn P. Cohn[*]

Editors' Note: *Light of foot, light of heart? Not exactly: in an overture to a longer ballet next year, the authors contend that the appropriate way to use dance as an element in negotiation teaching starts with...fear!*

Negotiation has often been described as a dance, though for many people negotiating is more like fencing than dancing. But what if we took the metaphor seriously? Would that help more people learn to be graceful and observant in negotiating? Would they benefit from that?

Just as you cannot learn to paint by reading about it, learning the dance of negotiating should be experiential. Dance is unencumbered by words or the need to play an instrument. Because dance uses the body as an instrument and form of communication, dance can be used to understand how to actually "feel" something – perhaps, a negotiation. Dancers, like negotiators, often improvise and frequently display unconscious competence. In many, if not most, of the world's cultures, dance is an integral way for people to connect and share feelings and moods. Messages can be transmitted from subtle movements of the body and understood by both the participant and an observer. When negotiation teachers talk about the need to understand body language, they are already part of the way toward dance, and not just as metaphor.

In Istanbul, we began experimenting with taking negotiating-as-dance more seriously in our training. We have reached conclu-

---

[*] **Ranse Howell** is commercial manager and a trainer and mediator at the Centre for Effective Dispute Resolution (CEDR), London, UK. He is a former professional ballroom dancer and Latin American dance champion, coach and adjudicator in the UK and USA. His email address is rhowell@cedr.com. **Lynn P. Cohn** is the director of the Program on Negotiations and Mediation and a clinical associate professor of law at Northwestern University School of Law in Chicago, Illinois. Her email address is l-cohn@law.northwestern.edu.

sions about some basic elements; dance used as a teaching tool should:

- Not be overly complex;
- Not have too many rhythms;
- Appeal to a cross-section of potential participants, and
- Not require too much space.

Salsa is an ideal choice within these parameters, and readily fits within a negotiation exercise. Salsa is easy to learn (the basic structure consists of three movements which are then repeated); has a good rhythm; has wide appeal; and can be danced in a small area (with chairs and tables moved aside, most training rooms will probably provide sufficient space).

We would start such an exercise with no advance explanation, but by getting all the participants to stand, facing the same way (a large group can form several shorter lines). Only at this point would we reveal that they are going to learn a dance, the salsa. There will be an immediate reaction – we promise. The reaction itself is the beginning of the learning obtainable from dance.

Teacher's Notes/Questions

STEP ONE

How do trainees feel when they do not have key information, in the dance or in a negotiation? (e.g., uncomfortable, excited, curious, impatient?) What does this reveal? (e.g., importance of establishing authority and providing rules/framework). What do the different trainees' responses to learning salsa suggest? (some may find it fun, while others may think it stupid. It is important to note the individual level of discomfort, and refer back to this either in open session or in a side conversation).

We might begin the exercise with everyone marching in place, and then introduce the rhythm, asking the participants "dancing is like –

what ?" (We can hint, if necessary: "it's movement, it has a rhythm and you use one foot after the other....") – "Hey, it's like walking!"

Teacher's Notes/Questions

STEP TWO

Walking can be compared to negotiation, as something that is done every day, often without thinking about it. To reinforce the core concepts of negotiation, we already know – from various writers in this volume and elsewhere – that we need to increase awareness through reflection. Awareness provides individuals with the confidence to become more flexible and responsive negotiators.

And we might intentionally withhold information from the participants so that they will begin to feel the disorientation and discomfort of the unknown. The specific impact, however, depends entirely on the personality types among the trainees. This not only provides a time-efficient entry point into discussion of personality and its effects on different students' negotiating; the feeling of authentic discomfort in negotiation (probably varying among the students from almost-none to severe, and including both feelings related to the unknown, and to being left behind by others who are visibly more adept) is often very hard to replicate in role-play simulations. We think that even ignoring the other potential learning elements, the raw feelings that will be accessed as part of this exercise are hugely valuable, and will provide the trainee with a greater understanding of "self."

Teacher's Notes/Questions

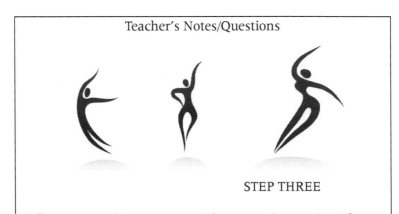

STEP THREE

Different personality types cope with stressors in a variety of ways, depending on the amount of information and the importance of the outcome. How do the trainees cope with this new requirement, and how do they cope with the stressors they encounter in a negotiation?

And perhaps that is enough for just now. Having 1) made the students thoroughly uncomfortable, 2) revealed people's different reactions to stress and 3) begun to analogize to something they are more comfortable with, how do we resolve the tensions and suggestions thus created? What does the use of dance look like on the second day, or the third? By the end of the course, can we really use this strategy to help trainees become more elegant negotiators (and perhaps, to fall over their feet less often on the dance floor, into the bargain)?

All will be revealed – but only after the next dance in Beijing. Stay tuned: our answers are for a longer article, now in preparation. We invite you back for another spin round this topic in the successor volume.

ABOUT THE EDITORS

Christopher Honeyman is managing partner of Convenor Conflict Management (www.convenor.com), a consulting firm based in Washington, DC and Madison, Wisconsin. He is co-editor of *The Negotiator's Fieldbook* (with Andrea Schneider; ABA 2006) and *Rethinking Negotiation Teaching* (with James Coben and Giuseppe De Palo; DRI Press 2009), and author or co-author of more than 70 published articles, book chapters and monographs on dispute resolution. Honeyman has directed a twenty-year series of major R&D projects in dispute resolution, and has served as a consultant to numerous academic and practical conflict resolution programs in the U.S. and elsewhere. He has also served as a mediator, arbitrator or in other neutral capacities in more than 2,000 disputes since the 1970s. He is currently vice-chair of the Independent Standards Commission, International Mediation Institute, The Hague.

James Coben is a professor of law at Hamline University School of Law in St. Paul, Minnesota and former director of Hamline's Dispute Resolution Institute, consistently ranked by *U.S. News & World Report* in the top five among U.S. law school dispute resolution programs. He teaches civil procedure and a variety of alternative dispute resolution (ADR) courses, and created three Hamline foreign programs – an international commercial arbitration program in London, an international business transactions negotiation program in Rome, and a program in democratic dialogue and mediation in Budapest. He has published numerous ADR-related articles, and is co-editor of *Rethinking Negotiation Teaching* (with Christopher Honeyman and Giuseppe De Palo; DRI Press 2009) and co-author of the third edition of *Mediation: Law, Policy & Practice* (West Group, forthcoming 2010).

Giuseppe De Palo is the international professor of ADR Law and Practice at Hamline University School of Law. De Palo is chairman of the Rome-based ADR Center, the largest neutral ADR firm in continental Europe (www.adrcenter.com) and now a member of JAMS International. He regularly mediates international business disputes, and is the director of numerous major projects – financed by the EU, the World Bank and other global organizations – to promote effective dispute resolution mechanisms. He is co-editor (with Mary Trevor) of *Arbitration and Mediation in the Southern Mediterranean Countries* (Kluwer 2007) and of the column *Worldly Perspectives* in CPR's *Alternatives*. He is also the author of several other books and articles published in Australia, France, Germany, Italy, the Netherlands, Turkey, and the United States.